THE
ROBERT
LUDLUM
COMPANION

THE
ROBERT
LUDLUM
COMPANION

Edited by
Martin H.
Greenberg

BANTAM BOOKS
NEW YORK · TORONTO · LONDON · SYDNEY · AUCKLAND

THE ROBERT LUDLUM COMPANION

A Bantam Book / June 1993

Photographs and captions provided by Robert Ludlum

Library of Congress Cataloging-in-Publication Data

The Robert Ludlum companion / edited by Martin H. Greenberg.
p.   cm.
ISBN 0-553-35196-6
1. Ludlum, Robert,   —Criticism and interpretation. 2. Spy
stories, American—History and criticism. I. Ludlum, Robert, 1927–
II. Greenberg, Martin Harry.
PS3562.U26Z84   1993
813'.54—dc20   93-9271
CIP

Published simultaneously in the United States and Canada

Bantam Books are published by Bantam Books, a division of Bantam Doubleday Dell
Publishing Group, Inc. Its trademark, consisting of the words "Bantam Books" and
the portrayal of a rooster, is Registered in U.S. Patent and Trademark Office and in
other countries. Marca Registrada. Bantam Books, 1540 Broadway, New York,
New York 10036.

PRINTED IN THE UNITED STATES OF AMERICA

FFG   0 9 8 7 6 5 4 3 2

Contents

Introduction   vii
Robin Cook

An Interview with Robert Ludlum   1
Martin H. Greenberg

Master of the Thriller   25
Roy S. Goodman

A Robert Ludlum Concordance   137
Elizabeth Gaines

Ludlum on the Screen   445
Roy S. Goodman

Ludlum on Ludlum   451

Introduction
by
Robin Cook

The most unfortunate side effect of that infectious malady, "Acute and Chronic Robert Ludlum Addiction," is that the vast majority of those so afflicted will never have the chance to meet Robert Ludlum the person. Not that Robert wouldn't want to meet them; he's that social and that friendly and, most surprising, that appreciative of his fans taking the time and energy to read one of his wildly exciting, engrossingly entertaining, yet hefty novels. The problem is that meeting the man is tactically and strategically impossible. There are too many fans. Besides, Robert is up at the uncivilized hour of 4:30 A.M. when the rest of us mortals are fast asleep, and he is already in bed when we are beginning to contemplate dinner and companionship.

I met Robert fifteen years ago at the Literary Guild fiftieth birthday bash. *Coma* had recently been released, and the gala affair was one of my first opportunities to connect faces with the books that I had been devouring in an attempt to overcome the handicap of having taken all the wrong courses in college. Robert and his wife Mary were sitting at a table across the expanse of the dance floor. With some of Robert's titles reverberating in my head, I set off to say hello, fully expecting a rejection similar to those experienced by Rodney Dangerfield in his beer commercials. As I passed the ice sculpture in the center of the dance floor, I thought seriously about veering off, pretending I'd been heading for the bar (just like the teenager passing the condom display to pick up yet another tube of toothpaste). Yet despite my reservations I was committed. I wanted to thank Robert for the hours of entertainment he'd provided me as well as the inadvertent instruction he'd imparted on how to construct a thriller.

As I got closer I became more nervous. My steps slowed. I thought about turning back and retreating to the safety of my own table. I didn't need another rejection. After all, I was an amateur, an upstart, with one "best seller" that probably was a quirk. I was a doctor, for goodness' sake. What was I doing there will all these writers? I should have been home doing something safe, like brain surgery.

Yet it was too late. I'd arrived, and I can remember the episode as if it were yesterday. Robert and Mary had the entire table in animated glee. I looked down at Robert and, to make matters worse, I saw that he was a physically formidable man, broad in the face with muscular arms and spadelike hands. From a barrel chest emerged a booming, commanding voice.

Mary saw me before Robert, and her eyes were like the twin cannons on a Spitfire guarding a bomber. I guessed that she'd had lots of experience with the likes of me. Of course it was my own paranoia. Mary's eyes were merely drinking in the excitement and glitter of the evening.

"Mr. Ludlum," I stammered, interrupting the table's revelry. "My name is Robin Cook and I wanted . . ."

I never got any further. Robert leaped to his feet and shook my hand and thumped my shoulder. He introduced me to Mary and the rest of the table. Now I'm not about to lie and say that he'd read my book and enjoyed it, but surprisingly enough Mary had. But what he did display was a sincere friendliness, ebullience, and forthrightness that was disarming. Prepared for rejection or at best a perfunctory greeting and a quick brush-off, I was surprised to be pushed into a chair that miraculously had appeared. I had been asked to join the table.

Soon I was to learn that Robert and I had lived for a number of years in the same, small, special town of Leonia, New Jersey, and that we had both graduated from the same, small, special college, Wesleyan University in Middletown, Connecticut, although, in his words, a century apart (that's evidence of the novelist's creative license; it was just over a decade).

Now I have the pleasure of living in the same condominium building as Robert and Mary in Naples, Florida (the list of residents in the lobby is the only list where I'll ever be higher than Robert Ludlum; it's alphabetical). To my continued delight I see Robert and Mary quite often, and we share meals together, at least those that can be eaten in the middle of the afternoon. Some of my most memorable Christmas dinners have been with these folks. Such dinner parties are always enormously entertaining events, especially with a touch of liquid lubricant. Robert favors amber scotch, while Mary leans toward ruby-red Pommard. But the results are the same. Both begin quoting passages from Shakespeare to Tennessee Williams, taking cues from each other. Of course, such episodes only remind me again of having taken all the wrong courses in college. No matter how much scotch and wine I offer I've never gotten the conversation around to plasma physics or protein chemistry.

As the following volume unfolds and you, the reader, become caught up in the labyrinthine web of conspiracy and violence that Robert

Ludlum can conjure on the printed page, it's astonishing to realize that the man behind this creativity is so different as to be almost a metaphorical oxymoron. He's certainly not violent; in fact he has an almost childlike glee for animated toys and gadgets. He's not overbearing; if fact he is self-deprecating. He loves to recount self-deprecating anecdotes like the time he boarded a plane to find the gentleman sitting next to him reading one of his novels. "Any good?" Robert asked. "Quite" was the answer. "I've heard his books are terrible," Robert said, "too serpentine, too complicated, too preposterous." "Careful," said the man. "I must warn you. I happen to be very dear friends with the author."

Robert Ludlum has never been a member of any terrorist organizations apart from some of his publishing companies. He's never been in intelligence or counterintelligence; in particular he's never been associated with the CIA other than in his nightmares. Instead, he'd been a successful actor and producer before turning to writing.

Although there are suggestions that Robert had been a rambunctious teenager with stories that include brawling, football, and running off to join the Marines during World War II, today Robert Ludlum is a cultured, immensely interesting, generous, gentle, friendly, fun-loving, and gregarious individual who loves to stop to chat with fans in the local supermarket. In short, he's the type of man we'd all like to have for a father, a teacher, or—best of all—a friend.

AN INTERVIEW WITH
ROBERT LUDLUM

Martin H. Greenberg

This interview was conducted over the phone in the late spring of 1992. Robert Ludlum was an "easy" interview—kind, patient, and enthusiastic. My agenda was simple—I wanted to know how he got started as a writer after a long career as an actor and theatrical producer; I wanted to know about the way he worked his travels into his novels; I wanted to know if any of the characters in his books were based on real people; and I wanted to know (among many other things) what writers he reads and which ones, if any, influenced him.

We started with the last question.

GREENBERG: What are your personal tastes in reading?

LUDLUM: Mainly history and political biography.

GREENBERG: And do you make use of that reading?

LUDLUM: Yes, I do. I don't read a great deal of fiction, I must be honest about that.

GREENBERG: Are there other espionage writers or other writers of the types of books you do that you read?

LUDLUM: My books *aren't* all espionage. Of course, I admire le Carré, Deighton, Follett, and a number of others but, as I say, I'm not a heavy fiction reader and there's a reason for that. I think it was Hemingway or Faulkner who said it, and I subscribe to the premise. If you write fiction constantly, there's always the fear that unconsciously you'll use something that you shouldn't if you *read* a great deal of fiction.

GREENBERG: Yes, I guess that's always a worry.

LUDLUM: Yes, it is, and it happened to me. Years ago, I was shooting the breeze one night with one of the most honorable men I've ever known, whose name I won't mention. I described an idea that I thought would make a good novel, you know, a fairly clear concept. A year later he called me. He said, "Listen, I want to send you a manuscript; I think it works." I received it and read it; it was my idea. I never mentioned it to him, never said anything. But it's something that I'm very aware of, so I stay clear of an unconscious repetition.

GREENBERG: That's interesting.

LUDLUM: Yes, it was kind of a shock.

GREENBERG: Well, in terms of your own books, are there some that in retrospect you like best?

LUDLUM: You know, I've been asked that question a lot and I think the only honest answer is that you always have a feeling for the first book. I mean, it's like the first child, I suppose, although I probably shouldn't say that for print about my own children. It wouldn't apply anyway, they're so wonderfully different. But you always think kindly about the first book that actually was published. Beyond that aspect, I think what excites me is the book I'm working on. In other words, you've got to psych yourself up for this kind of work, and I've found that I always feel that the book I'm working on is *the* book. When that's finished, I'm sure that when I start another, it will be *that* book.

GREENBERG: I think all serious writers and successful writers seem to feel that way.

LUDLUM: Yes, I think so. It's perfectly normal.

GREENBERG: Are there some techniques you use to fire yourself up?

LUDLUM: Well, I do an outline, and it can last anywhere from fifty to one hundred pages. The odd thing is that except for specific research and geographical locations, I never go back to it. It's like building signposts in my head. At least I know where I'm going and I know the statement I want to make. Now, as I've said many times before, whatever statement I have—whether everybody gets it is not necessarily important to me—but *I've* got to have it, otherwise I'd be writing in a kind of shallow manner, and I try to avoid that.

GREENBERG: What's your favorite book of history?

LUDLUM: Probably *A Distant Mirror* by Barbara Tuchman. I love that book. As a matter of fact, I constantly find myself just picking it up and rereading sections of it again.

GREENBERG: Yes, I think she was very good and underrated. It was very hard to do what she did.

LUDLUM: Oh, when she describes such things as the battles of Plassey and the manners, the intrigues, and the courts of the time, I just get all wrapped up in it. I think she's marvelous.

GREENBERG: She was the victim of a lot of envy by academic folks.

LUDLUM: Oh, yes, I know she was. That's so foolish. Also, the *Memoirs of Saint-Simon*. That's fantastic reading!

GREENBERG: I agree of course. Was there a book of yours that was the most difficult to write or to gather the material for?

LUDLUM: That first one; the first one always is. I wasn't sure whether I'd turned in three hundred pages of sheep dip or the start of a novel. I'll never forget when Henry Morrison and I met. We had lunch in a very expensive restaurant—the Chauveron in New York—and as a producer in the theater, I'd always pick up the tab. We talked for a while about the manuscript, and he said he wanted to represent me. Wow! At the end of the meal I simply, just automatically, said to the waiter, "Check, please," and Henry said, "No, talent doesn't pay." I looked around and said, "Where, where, where?" Then I asked him—I was so puffed up—"Well, I suppose you think there should be a little rewriting, fixes, something like that," and he replied, "Oh, yes, from page one!" That was the toughest book!

GREENBERG: Do you recall how you came to Henry's attention?

LUDLUM: I'll never forget it. I gave the manuscript to a friend of mine who was in advertising in New York. He was with BBD&O, and as I had done a number of voice-over commercials for the agency, I knew him very well, and I gave him what I'd written of the manuscript. I guess it was about three hundred pages, and he gave it to a fellow named Don Bensen. I don't know if you know Don Bensen.

GREENBERG: Well, I know him from his involvement in the science fiction field.

LUDLUM: He was with Pyramid Books at the time, and without my knowing it, Don gave it to Henry Morrison. Then one day, out of the blue, this fellow called me and he said his name was Morrison. I said, "That's nice," and he said, "Well, I'm a literary agent." And I said, "That's *very* nice." Henry said, "I'd like to meet you for lunch and talk." I said, "Really, what about?" He said, "Well, I like what you wrote." I didn't even know he had it!

GREENBERG: That's almost a story that could be made into a stage play.

LUDLUM: It certainly is. Then I called up my friend at BBD&O, another Don named Wilde—and his name fit the circumstances. "Don, what did you do with the manuscript?" He said, "Hey, listen, I think it's pretty good." I said, "Well, gee, thank you. Did you give it to a guy named Morrison?" He said, "No, I gave it to Don Bensen, you met him at our house." Then I said something as stupid as "Is he in the publishing field?" He said, "Yes, Robert." I said, "Well, a guy named Morrison called me." He said, "Oh, yes, Don told me that Morrison was going to start his own agency." So it was very fortuitous.

GREENBERG: I think Morrison had just left Scott Meredith at the time.

LUDLUM: I guess so. It was all kind of crazy.

GREENBERG: Have you ever tried your hand at short fiction?

LUDLUM: Short stories, you mean? Yes. Only when I was very, very young and not published.

GREENBERG: Do you have any unpublished works?

LUDLUM: No, but I *did* have one. When I was in the Marines I wrote a long, involved kind of novel that took in a lot of the South Pacific experience and all the insanities that went with it. But I lost it on the Oakland ferry. So when anybody asks me, I say, oh, sure, you never heard of *Tales of the South Pacific*? Jim Michener loved that story.

GREENBERG: Well, I would imagine; it's a good story.

LUDLUM: It was spontaneous. I've always loved Michener's books. You know, an eighteen-year-old Marine back from the Pacific, being discharged, you can imagine what we did at the Top of the Mark the night before. We had a few drinks, and the next day I woke up on the Oakland ferry . . . without shoes, without money, without the manuscript!

GREENBERG: And they say those things happen only in New York.

LUDLUM: No, this happened in San Francisco. Don't tell Tony Bennett.

GREENBERG: Have you ever thought about collaborating with another writer?

LUDLUM: No, and there's a reason for that too. For years in the theater, which is basically a collaborative process, I was always working with directors, actors, and, in several cases, playwrights. And I really felt that when I left the theater I wanted to work literally by myself. I have nothing but great affection for people I worked with, but I wanted to do something by myself, without participating with someone else, without collaborating.

GREENBERG: How about screenplays?

LUDLUM: I wouldn't touch them but I tried once. Years ago we were at Alan Alda's house in New Jersey, where he had a party after an early opening night at the theater. This was before *M*A*S*H*. And that night everybody left almost en masse at eleven-thirty sharp. It was one of those things where you couldn't understand why everyone was leaving. It turned out that everybody wanted to go watch a television airing of Errol Flynn in *Captain Blood*. So the next day I was talking with Henry and I said, "You know, isn't it time to really do a grand old pirate picture?" He mentioned it to Elliott Kastner, the fellow who produced *Hud* and a lot of fine pictures.

GREENBERG: Oh, yes, many good ones . . .

LUDLUM: So, lo and behold, Kastner's fancy limousine came down to our little New Jersey town with a screenplay—it was Bill Goldman's *Butch Cassidy and the Sundance Kid*—so I could take a look at it and learn something. All because Henry had said, "Bob thinks it's time to do a pirate movie." I took a month or so off and began doing a screenplay for a pirate film. My wife, Mary, read it and said, "You just put the movies back fifty years!" A friend of mine then was John Patrick, the fellow who wrote *Teahouse of the August Moon* and all those terrific screenplays like *Suzie Wong*, and I showed it to him and he roared with laughter because I had roughly 310 pages. Nobody told me that a screenplay should be limited to roughly no more than 125 pages, and I'm afraid I didn't count the pages in *Butch Cassidy*. So the joke going around town was—I think Don Westlake made it up—"Oh, yeah, Robert wrote a screenplay. It's 310 pages. The hero comes in on 295 and the heroine on 298!" So no, I've stayed away from screenplays.

GREENBERG: Are there writers whom you see regularly, in a social context?

LUDLUM: Mainly Henry's clients or previous clients: David Morrell, Eric Van Lustbader, Don Westlake, Larry Block, and also our close friend and frequently my personal physician after very late nights, Robin Cook, who lives here in Naples, actually twenty stories above us in the spectacular penthouse he designed himself. But outside of that I don't know too many writers. My friends are mainly the people Mary and I knew in the theater.

GREENBERG: You obviously read *some* mysteries. Are there certain mysteries and mystery writers that you admire?

LUDLUM: Yes, Don Westlake and Larry Block especially.

GREENBERG: They are very different.

LUDLUM: Yes, very.

GREENBERG: I still think that *When the Sacred Gin Mill Closes* is one of the best novels of the last decade.

LUDLUM: Oh, I agree with you.

GREENBERG: You make many references to literature, philosophers, musicians, artists, historical events, and so forth in your books. Do you have a formal background in some of these areas?

LUDLUM: I was the first Fine Arts major to graduate from Wesleyan University. And I had to take the whole spectrum of related courses. Whenever you have—and you would know this far better than I do—a new department being set up at a university, it means that other departments lose a little money. So I was put through the rigors of the damned by what I call the "fiends from academic hell." Included were the fine arts, scores of history courses, the humanities, literature, philosophy—the whole enchilada, as they say. I had to take all of it for the comprehensive exams, oral and written, which if they hadn't turned out all right, there probably would not have been the new department.

GREENBERG: You're taking me back now because I was the third Ph.D. to graduate from the University of Connecticut's political science department when they started the Ph.D. in political science. And we had such a rigorous array of courses that when I would talk to friends who were in the Yale Ph.D. program in political science, they would just laugh. They were doing about half the work that we were doing.

LUDLUM: Oh, yes. Of course we have a fond memory of the University of Connecticut because my wife did her very last job there. She's a superb actress, but she decided she wanted to leave the theater to spend more time with the children. Her next to last job was in the sixties, doing *Luv* with Robert and Alan Alda; and UConn's chairman of the theater department knew the director, the so-talented J. Robert Dietz, who had directed *Luv*. Dietz asked Mary to do

Edward Albee's version of *Everything in the Garden* at the university, and she said, "Okay, but this is my *very* last job," and so we've always remembered UConn.

GREENBERG: With this background, why did you start writing suspense and espionage?

LUDLUM: I think it's probably a hangover from, or hangup with, the theater, because the theater is all suspense. You know, if you don't involve an audience and they don't care to know what happens from Act One to Act Two, you're dead in the water. So it's probably my theatrical background.

GREENBERG: Let's talk about some of your books. *The Matlock Paper* is very different from many of your other books in that it takes place entirely in the United States. Was this a conscious decision?

LUDLUM: Yes, it was. Both my boys were in prep school in Connecticut. There was quite a stir about drugs at the time, and offspring of some pretty heavyweight families, you know, sons of important political and social figures supposedly were involved—nowhere near as seriously as the press made it out to be, I'm happy to say. And that started me thinking, so I thought I'd write a book about the spreading drug network that was *not* restricted to the ghettos and the neglected underprivileged. It was kind of a shock to a lot of well-heeled parents, and I think it opened a few eyes—and, I hope, minds.

GREENBERG: Was there a reaction either from your publisher or readers to this?

LUDLUM: Other than what I just said, no, not that I know of.

GREENBERG: I don't know why there should be. But sometimes when well-established writers do a different kind of book, they hear about it.

LUDLUM: Well, you see, that was only my third book. So I don't think anyone knew me from a chocolate Popsicle.

GREENBERG: From all of your books, do you have a favorite sort of a good guy character?

LUDLUM: Yes, outside of Jason Bourne—who was a character I enjoyed very much—there's another one I wanted to do something with but I haven't been able to figure it out. That's Scofield in *The Matarese Circle*.

GREENBERG: How about the nastiest villain? Do you have a favorite villain?

LUDLUM: I can't honestly say I do; I suppose Carlos the Jackal is the closest, but the book would not permit me to go into the real roots of his demented psychosis. I don't know, I'd have to think about that. Nothing comes to mind at the moment. However, I try to follow Shaw's dictum that says "give your antagonists the best arguments you can think of, otherwise they're shallow straw men and not credible," or something like that.

GREENBERG: Do you ever intend to do a book where a woman is the main character? Have you thought about that?

LUDLUM: I'm doing it now.

GREENBERG: Then the second part of this is, do you think men can successfully write this type of book?

LUDLUM: Well, I'm trying like hell, and this came out of another interview. When the Soviet Union collapsed and Moscow began buying novels for publication, I had an interview with a Russian journalist. He said, "Have you ever thought of having a female villain?" I thought for a while and began making notes, and decided it was a terrific idea. That's why I'm doing it.

GREENBERG: That's great.

LUDLUM: It's an exhilarating challenge because I think it's one of those characters where you've got to hate what she does but you've got to understand why she does it. And then, of course, there is vis-à-vis, I suppose you'd say, the co-protagonist. A fortyish retired naval intelligence officer who has been recruited to try to find her and stop her.

GREENBERG: You mentioned before that your wife read that screenplay. Does your wife read your manuscripts on a regular basis and does she let you know when she doesn't like something?

LUDLUM: I'll tell you the way it is. It always starts this way. "Hey, Robert, this is terrific!" Then I know the next word is "*but*"! And it's back to

Hong Kong with Mary (THE BOURNE SUPREMACY)

the drawing board. She's very good. As all genuinely fine actors, she can spot weaknesses because actresses and actors in general tend to put themselves into a narrative as they are reading, subconsciously thinking how something might be performed. If something is weak or doesn't, shall we say, really play, they're very quick to spot it. I've found the best critics of my work are people in the acting field. And, of course, directors.

GREENBERG: Are any of your fictional characters based on real people?

LUDLUM: No, not really. They're either totally imaginative or a combination of people I've known.

GREENBERG: A couple of people that I know think that Manny Weingrass sounds a little like George Burns.

LUDLUM: I can understand that, but no. As a matter of fact, a variation of Manny Weingrass was actually a dear old friend of ours who was a dentist. He was one of these guys who, up to his dying day, was always checking out the right colognes, wearing the right clothes, a bon vivant. He was a wonderfully colorful character. I used parts of him in Manny Weingrass.

GREENBERG: I know that you are an avid reader. Do you have a substantial reference library?

LUDLUM: Oh, yes. I have two Britannicas, I favor the older one; and I have all of Fodor, you know, the travel books. In fact, I'm looking at them right now. When I'm working on something, I'll go out and find foreign magazines and newspapers.

GREENBERG: I was going to ask if there are certain magazines you subscribe to on a regular basis or buy on a regular basis that you make use of?

LUDLUM: Well, no, I had to give that up. I had twenty or thirty coming into the house every month. It just got to be overwhelming. What I do is when I'm working on a project, I'll go out and find the material.

GREENBERG: This is a question that I've found to be a sensitive question to some writers. In terms of genres or in terms of that word, do you consider your books to be in one genre or in several genres or do you reject the whole notion?

LUDLUM: No, I don't reject it. I dislike labels, but I can understand them, too, because I do write in a genre. I write in the genre of suspense, with certain geopolitical and quite biased political and philosophical overtones. However, I also write comedy, which is the new book that's just out. As a matter of fact, it just came out a few days ago. It's a sequel to *The Road to Gandolfo*, which I wrote years ago. As comedy is the flip side of tragedy, I think that farce is the flip side of melodrama, and I admit that I write melodramatically. *Omaha* is really a thriller told in farcical terms.

GREENBERG: A lot of your readers and folks in general are interested in how writers work; for example, do you clip things from newspapers?

LUDLUM: Oh, yes, sure, I'll do that. As a matter of fact, I just did this morning. I was reading the *Times* and I saw something that I felt could be applicable to what I'm doing now. I simply circled it and tore out the page. And I think that page was close to if not part of that hideous crossword puzzle my wife is addicted to. She went out early this morning, and if I don't put that page back, I'll be in trouble.

GREENBERG: How long does it take you to write a book? Is there much variation in that?

LUDLUM: It's generally pretty much the same. I think, as I look back, that I do about four weeks of travel. Mary and I try to go to everyplace that I'm writing about. And then a couple of weeks of heavy reading and research, then after that it's between fifteen and seventeen months on the manuscript. Now, of course, that's as of the last ten years. Before that I was writing a book a year.

GREENBERG: That includes rewriting. Do you find yourself doing a lot of rewriting?

LUDLUM: Certainly. I believe in that phrase Moss Hart once wrote: "A play is never written, it's rewritten." I constantly rewrite. And having come from the theater, I don't really believe that I wrote the Old Testament because there's always those two phrases repeated constantly in rehearsals, and they stay in my mind. "Hey, that works, keep it in," or "That doesn't work, try something else," and I'm forever doing that. Even before an editor sees it.

GREENBERG: Have you ever wanted to go back to the theater?

LUDLUM: No, I'm very, very happy doing what I'm doing.

GREENBERG: We're very happy with what you're doing as well.

LUDLUM: Thank you. Oh, I've been offered parts in films and television movies, a lot of television, and I simply say no. I couldn't take a job from an actor for the life of me, because it's rough out there.

GREENBERG: How do you write? Do you use a typewriter? Word processor?

LUDLUM: No, I write longhand on legal pages. I'm looking at the pad right now. When we're in Florida, I fax it up to my secretary, Mary Ann Champagne, in Connecticut. She uses the computer and makes it legitimate. When we're up north, her office is right upstairs above my cell.

GREENBERG: Have you ever used a tape recorder?

LUDLUM: I carry a tape recorder when I walk, and I usually walk on the beach. I try to walk about six or seven miles a day, carrying a recorder with me, sometimes just to do dialogue or at other times to formulate ideas or clarify plot points.

GREENBERG: More like a notebook, then?

LUDLUM: Yes, like a notebook, exactly. Why didn't I think of that? Thanks.

GREENBERG: Do you have a specific time of day that is set aside for writing?

LUDLUM: Well, Marty, you're pretty young and I don't know if you want to hear this, but I'll shock you anyway. I get up at four-fifteen every morning. In the theater I used to go to bed at four-fifteen with a half bottle of Scotch. Now I get up at four-fifteen with a cup of coffee. At least it's healthier. I get up at four-fifteen—a little bit before actually—brew coffee, and go into my cell. *Time* magazine said I work "by the creative mists of dawn." Before he died, I called Ed Demerest, who wrote the article, and I said, "Ed, that's a lovely phrase, but I hate to tell you I get up and write then because the phone isn't ringing."

GREENBERG: When do you finish for the day?

LUDLUM: I'll take breaks, but I'll generally taper off around eleven o'clock. And, of course, in the afternoon I'll either do chores or whatever Mary's got scheduled for me. But then I go back, later in the afternoon, to reread and rework what I did in the morning.

GREENBERG: Given the references and all your travel and all the international locales in your books, and given the fact that you can probably live almost anywhere you want to live, what is so attractive about the west coast of Florida?

LUDLUM: Well, outside of the weather, which is great, as is the water, there's a wonderful sense of privacy here. In other words, you can join the social scene if you want to; but if you don't, nobody holds it against you. And there's a *respect* for privacy which I like very much. As there is also in Westport, Connecticut. There's that same kind of thing, and I enjoy that as well as the New England summer. I was once a big winter fan—skied, skated, hockey, the whole thing. But I developed a minor—and it is just minor—arthritic problem with my hands. And if it gets really cold, you know, those little joints stiffen up.

GREENBERG: Especially serious since you write in longhand.

LUDLUM: Yes, it is. That's why I sort of follow the sun.

GREENBERG: Are there plans to film any of your other books?

LUDLUM: Oh, yes. I'm told they're working on—how far along they are, I don't know—but they have the rights to the other two Bourne books; *The Matarese Circle* is still owned by a film company. Let's see, I think there's another one, I just can't remember right now. Then we've had offers on a number of books, but Henry is more knowledgeable about this sort of thing. He has said no several times because they weren't the right people, I guess, and I can't remember when Henry's been wrong.

GREENBERG: I've been reading about Tom Clancy's problems with Hollywood and it's a difficult situation.

LUDLUM: I think Clancy's public reaction was somewhat extreme. He's no more a proven "writer for the ages" than I am; only decades in the future will determine that status. We commercial authors can always say no to the lucrative offers from films or television, but we don't because we're afflicted with the normal human desire to fill our coffers, either for ourselves or our survivors. To protest in print so severely after the fact, knowing the difference of mediums, is going a little far. I think the thing to remember is that *nobody* starts out to make a bad movie. Yet, withal, I do understand Clancy's reaction. I had a similar one but kept my mouth shut. When they sent a work tape of *The Osterman Weekend*, Mary and I put it in the VCR, after calling both my sons to tell me how to use that damned machine. Twenty minutes into the film I picked up the phone and booked passage to Hong Kong so we wouldn't be here when it opened. I've got nothing against adult pornography, but I don't happen to write it. However, I felt it behooved me not to make public statements. Hemingway did it best when he sold a novel to movies. He tore up the manuscript and threw it into the Mississippi River.

GREENBERG: I hate questions to writers about where they get their ideas, but just one perhaps. In *The Cry of the Halidon* is, I think, a very unusual story line.

LUDLUM: I can tell you exactly how that happened. We were down in Jamaica, where I was working on that screenplay, that infamous screenplay, because it was about the two female pirates Bonnie Flagg and Maggie Flood, who "treasured" in that Caribbean port. We had rented a house for three weeks—just to absorb the ambiance for where the movie would take place, back in the seventeenth century. My daughter was very young then, very blond, and we were in Port Antonio. One morning we went down to the village to pick up frozen food—that's the only way you can eat what you normally eat, if you're not partial to the native fare. And once in the village I went into the store with the maid—a tall, statuesque lovely lady in her late sixties. My wife and daughter stayed in the car, when suddenly there was a whole crowd around it because this wasn't in the tourist area and the natives were all attracted by my daughter's very, very blond hair; they were staring through the windows. When I came out of the market, I was suddenly alarmed, as one lean, muscular fellow was being rather offensive. Well, the maid literally beat away a lot of the curious with her parasol, but this one mean fellow began saying things that alarmed me further. So I took him aside—I was wary and observant, and much younger, but having been trained as a Marine, I had no compunction doing so—and led him across the road and sat him down on a large rock. Right below us was a huge, deep cliff; he wouldn't have survived if he had tried even the most minor violence. By then I was furious because he kept making very nasty, actually obscene remarks about my eight-year-old daughter. And then he suddenly stopped—I think he was high on grass or something—and he said, "Give me, give me money, give me money for the church of the Haleedonne, the Haleedonne, the Halee-donne, give me money for the Haleedonne!" And I'm looking at this guy and I'm thinking he doesn't have both oars in the water. He's *crazy*! I gave him several Jamaican dollars, lifted him up, and sent him down the road. That night my wife and I were sitting out on the porch, watching the sun set, and I told her the story, eliminating the more threatening parts. I recounted how I asked the mentally disturbed man, "What is the church of the Haleedonne?" He had replied, "The church of the miracles, the miracles, the *miracles*, and you may never know of our holy *place*!" And that's how that whole book began, from the fragments of a true experi-ence. It was a scary situation, I'll tell you that, and one I doubt I would handle so well sixteen years later.

GREENBERG: Well, somewhat related to that, you've used many locations throughout the world in your stories. Are there any locations you'd avoid using for any particular reason?

LUDLUM: No, but right now I wouldn't be too happy about going to the Middle East, especially doing research in Beirut. Otherwise, I'm perfectly open to anything—whatever suits me in terms of the idea, the concept of the book.

GREENBERG: Which book of yours has been the most popular or sold the best in foreign countries?

LUDLUM: I don't know. I'm in, I think it's forty countries now. I couldn't answer that. Danny Baror could, that's Henry's marvelous foreign-rights director. He would be able to answer that.

GREENBERG: Sometimes you find interesting little twists to this question. Are you avoiding it?

LUDLUM: Hell, no, but I never discuss finances; in truth, I stay away from them. But I'd be interested myself. I know that in most places the books have done fairly well just by the royalty statements that Mary lets me see!

GREENBERG: I think you've been on a number of foreign best seller lists.

LUDLUM: Oh, yes, I think on most of them. I get reports that I've been number one in England, France, the Scandinavian countries, the Netherlands, and Italy.

GREENBERG: It doesn't always work that way, where best sellers here are not necessarily as popular overseas. It is also the reverse, where midlist authors here sometimes get on best seller lists in other languages.

LUDLUM: I've been enormously fortunate, as well as astonished, that the books have done that well.

GREENBERG: Well, one of the things you have working for you is that the locales are so international. I think that would help.

LUDLUM: I think you're right. Somebody mentioned that in the *International Herald-Tribune* a couple of years ago. I guess it's true, especially where Europe is concerned.

GREENBERG: One of the things that fascinates your readers the most is the very secret organizations, such as the Inver Brass, the Halidon, et cetera. Are these, I presume, strictly from your imagination? Are there some things that have inspired them in a sense?

LUDLUM: Only my abhorrence of the abuse of power. I think we've seen far too much of it. Someone once wrote, "Ludlum's paranoid about authority." Well, I've lived long enough to *become* paranoid from what I've observed. All of these things can't be happening all over the place without people getting together and colluding. When I wrote *The Icarus Agenda*, and I wrote it long before the Iran-Contra hearings, so there was no way I could have taken anything from them. Many suggested that I must have written that book overnight because so much of it was in the hearings, and then when—was it Senator Rudman? . . . yes, it was—got up on the steps of the Capitol and said, "If Robert Ludlum had written this, even his editors might have thought he was crazy!" I'm not, I've simply been around too long. Incidentally, I'm a committed liberal, but I'd cross over party lines and vote for Mr. Rudman any day of the week, and it would have nothing to do with *me*. At this writing, he's leaving the Senate on his own wishes. It's a terrible loss for the nation. We need men of his caliber.

GREENBERG: We'll make sure that Senator Rudman gets a copy of the *Companion*. The next question you've anticipated, because typically you portray governments and areas of governments containing a high number of corrupt folks.

LUDLUM: You know, we've got the best system in the world, but there's always the sleazy manipulators trying to louse it up. Usually for greed, or misplaced zealotry.

GREENBERG: So this is not from your point of view a literary device; it's something taken from the real world.

LUDLUM: Certainly. I mean, I employ it as a literary device, but I think there's enough evidence to give it credibility.

GREENBERG: How do you choose names for your characters and organizations?

LUDLUM: I've been asked this before and the only answer I can give you is that I'll play around with names when I'm working on a character or an organization because I want a name that somehow *fits* that character or that group of people. I know that probably sounds silly, but I try to find something a little off the beaten track but still has the ring of authenticity. And, oh, Lord, I've changed names dozens of times because I felt that the name I first chose would stand in the way of something—too weak or too strong.

GREENBERG: They're very fascinating, more so, I think, than many of your contemporaries—the choice in their names.

LUDLUM: If it is, it's only because I do a little bit more thinking about it than maybe is normal.

GREENBERG: Do you have a research assistant?

LUDLUM: No, not at all! That's part of the fun! I'd never do that because I love calling up people and getting information. On my new book about SAC headquarters, which is this comedy sequel, I called up a high-ranking Air Force officer here in Florida, and he sent me tons of material because he had been a command pilot with SAC. One of the funniest things happened about four or five weeks ago, long after the galleys had gone in. He called me up and said, "Hey, did I tell you something about the Cynpac computer that monitors the Looking Glass operations?" I said, "Yes, you did." He then said quietly, "Holy shit, I *think* it's still classified." So if you suddenly find me in Leavenworth because I wouldn't reveal my source, now you know. I hope I'm okay, because we're going to Omaha to get the key to the city next month. My wife said that after they read the book, they may want it back. I've checked with friends of mine who are in the Air Force and they said no, that Cynpac thing was declassified about a year ago. So we're clean . . . I *hope*!

GREENBERG: How do you handle reader mail?

LUDLUM: You can't answer it all, obviously. I try to answer the ones from the younger people. You know, the youngsters who are in high school and college—and especially if they're genuinely curious letters, kids trying to really learn something. Of course I get a lot of crank letters, and you don't answer those. Also, I get an awful lot of mail from guys in prison who simply want me to take on their cases and write a book about how they got shafted. And I get a great many from lawyers, strangely enough, generally quite favorable. I've never understood my appeal to homicidal killers and lawyers. I'm sure there's a professional linkage somewhere.

GREENBERG: Do you know offhand the percentage of women in your readership?

LUDLUM: I'm told it has been growing since about the third book. Because, as you can gather, I'm married to a girl who was independent long before it was fashionable, and I do believe in strong female characters. As a matter of fact, my first book had one of the strongest in Madame Scarlatti. I'm told that my readership is almost fifty-fifty now. I was delighted to hear that.

GREENBERG: Do you find yourself watching television?

LUDLUM: Oh, sure, but mainly to put myself to sleep. Oh, that's terrible to say, but I'll tell you what I do watch. I'll get a call from somebody saying, "Hey, I'm doing a pretty interesting part on so-and-so," and Mary and I will turn it on and watch that, of course. One doesn't deny old friends. But in terms of television per se, it's not a great factor in our lives. One thing I've got to admit, though, is I like those two game shows at night that our old friend Merv Griffin created. I like *Jeopardy!* best of all, I really do. Also, it doesn't hurt when they use me as one of the questions.

GREENBERG: Oh, yes, it's a very informative program and fun. Its game version is popular on college campuses.

LUDLUM: Oh, really. Is there a video game?

GREENBERG: There's a game equivalent, something like the Trivial Pursuit kind of game.

LUDLUM: I'll go out and get it this afternoon. Tell Merv the royalty's on the way!

GREENBERG: In terms of films, are there films that have impressed you over the years?

LUDLUM: Yes, of course, all of the standard classics; we constantly watch them. You know, the ones made in the forties and fifties, really. I revel in all those great costume movies with Ty Power, whom I knew in the Marine Corps; and Cesar Romero, a great friend and superb actor Mary and I cherish today; and, you know, the Errol Flynn spectaculars. (That huge crazy guy salvaged two very young enlisted Marines one night in the Brown Derby, circa forty-four. We were supposed to be judo trainers, but he had no trouble subduing both of us.) I love that kind of entertainment. And almost every one of the Dickens's novels—we knew Fred [Freddie] Bartholomew very well. The dear man passed away a little while ago. He was a neighbor of ours when we lived in New Jersey. He never watched them. We did.

GREENBERG: Have you ever played the game of trying to cast in your mind some of your characters and who might play them?

LUDLUM: Naturally, I do that all the time. And as a matter of fact, whenever anything is being done of mine, either on television, audios, or for the movies, I have a list of suggestions, many of which have worked out. "All the dear old darlings" as the multitalented, masculine Robert Lansing amusingly puts it. He, Darren McGavin, Joe and Frank Campanella, Robert Loggia, Franklin Cover, Henry Sutton, Wayne Tippit, Marty Balsam, Phil Bosco, oh, *God*, so many I've left out in a telephone interview—*forgive* me, fellas! And some newer talents I've never met, like Mr. Moriarty, Mr. Dukes— et cetera. What's really missing? I'll tell you. *Women. Actresses!* Let's do something about that!

GREENBERG: Do any of your children write?

LUDLUM: My older son is a composer and also performs classical and modern guitar, a total professional whose union affiliations guarantee him a living far beyond anything I dreamed of at his age. He has multiple degrees and was an associate professor at a well-known university until he decided that he didn't have the cowardice to surmount campus politics. My second son, a pilot, and a leader in the search and rescue teams in the Rocky Mountains, wrote three chapters of a novel which I would *kill* for to put under my name! He was offered two advances, but turned them down, saying he "wasn't ready." I think he's nuts, but he's a hell of a writer. My daughter, also a composer and a lyricist, has written what I think is far better than the junk I hear on the media. I think somebody ought to discover her, but she refuses to let me help, which I probably couldn't do anyway.

GREENBERG: Do you think that the James Bond books—which some people feel started this—do you think the acceptance of the kinds of books that you do and some of your colleagues do was accelerated because of that phenomenon?

LUDLUM: Oh, I'm sure it was. I think we all owe a debt to Ian Fleming. Some people quibble with his basic writing, but he really started this genre off in contemporary terms. I mean, Eric Ambler was, of course, the past master, but with the enormous promotion of the Bond phenomenon, I think anybody who tries to deny it is being very pretentious.

GREENBERG: This is probably irrelevant, but it is of interest to some people. How old were you when you sold your first book?

LUDLUM: Forty.

GREENBERG: I think that a lot of people find that wonderfully encouraging.

LUDLUM: I have a theory about that, if you want to hear it. I think that if, when people everywhere were reaching middle age, and a global bell went off signifying that they could change their jobs, there'd be mass traffic jams all over the world with people racing to change occupations. I got to the age of forty and was doing reasonably well, but I just simply said *no*, I've got to do something else! And as I say, fortunately I had a number of voice-overs going. Voice-overs, as you know, are morally one step below theft. And I had a number of them covering the larder.

GREENBERG: It has that wonderful word *residuals* attached to it.

LUDLUM: Oh, I did one with only three words and they wild-tracked it on to dozens of commercials. I sent one of my kids through two years of college on those three words.

GREENBERG: You're such a wonderful speaker, do you take many speaking engagements or appearances?

LUDLUM: That's very flattering, but I take far fewer than I did in the beginning; there simply isn't time. Having been an actor and having been in the theater, microphones and audiences and cameras don't frighten me. In other words, I'm comfortable and I'll "perform" on book tours, of course. I'm starting next week; I'll be doing the *Today* show, *Good Morning America*, the Regis and Kathy Lee hour, and a whole bunch of other things as well as a dozen luncheons. Other than these tours, however, I don't seek them out because they take so much time away from work. And I certainly would never charge for appearances. I just try to avoid them, especially where I'm living, because if you take one, you've got to take more, or you lose a lot of friends.

GREENBERG: Do you do some appearances outside of the United States?

LUDLUM: Oh, sure. Mary and I just got back from Australia and New Zealand. I was reading in the paper how Dean Koontz's book had replaced *Scarlett* as number one. I did it down in Australia a month ago, not that it's important—it's *not*—but it happened.

GREENBERG: I was talking to Dean just the other night. I've known him for many years, and he was one of those writers who was in the trenches for many years.

LUDLUM: I know that, and I'm so *happy* for him! If you talk to him, tell him I think he's terrific and so does my wife. When we saw he was number one in the *Times*, we both said to each other, "Hey, *right* on, Dean!"

GREENBERG: You are very generous. Not all writers are.

LUDLUM: Oh, good God, there's so many potatoes on the boardinghouse table. Come on, I hate it when writers get jealous in that way.

GREENBERG: It shouldn't happen, but it sometimes does.

LUDLUM: Well, again, I'm from the theater and we have an old saying. "God almighty, if they like *this* play, maybe they'll come to yours! Let's all of us *eat!*"

GREENBERG: A question about pen names. Why did you decide to do the two Jonathan Ryder books?

LUDLUM: *I* didn't decide. I was told by the publishers—I was not young in years, but I was young as a writer—that you can't do more than one book a year. I said, "How come?" They said, "Well, you see, then you get into the area of being a hack." "Well," I said, "you've never heard of Dickens or Thackeray or Trollope? They published more than one a year." They didn't reply. I think they thought I was talking about fast-food restaurants. Well, I was so young in the business, I said, "Okay, sure, fine. So put them under another name." And then, of course, later they have released them under my own name and they haven't gone belly-up.

GREENBERG: Are there other books out there that you've written under another name?

LUDLUM: No, it was just Jonathan Ryder and Michael Shepherd. And the total number was only three: *The Cry of the Halidon*, *Trevayne*, and *The Road to Gandolfo*.

GREENBERG: One other question about plotting. You mentioned *The Road to Gandolfo*. Did that idea spring out of the terrorism episodes?

LUDLUM: Oh, no, as a matter of fact, it came long before, from a screenwriter, a very famous one, John Patrick. He came to me and said that the producer, Ray Stark, would like me to do a novel about the kidnapping of the Pope. This was all *before* the Vatican crises. And I began to laugh, because I thought about an Italian melodrama of the sixteenth century, the author long forgotten, about the kidnapping of the Pope, the kidnappers being the papal princes who demanded absolution for their physical and carnal sins. It might have been a gas then—I suspect, frankly, a comedy, for everyone knew of the papal offspring, but to do it now as a serious contemporary thriller, you'd have to proselytize all over the map. But Patrick kept telling me, "You don't understand. We want a Ludlum thriller about this horrible thing, and how the world reacts to the magnitude of its terror!" I tried to stop laughing long enough to say, "You know, you're going right back to a biblical kind of thing, and in terms of modern technology, it's not credible." But then I began to think in comic terms. And the minute I did, I began to giggle, but I kept quiet and said, "Sure, go back and try it yourself." Well, he returned six months later and said, "Oh, hell, you're right! All I'm doing is giving sermons." I said, "That's the trap with something like this. If you want to do a comedy, that's different, it might be done that way." He said, "Well, go ahead and try it your way." I said, "No, I don't have time." At that point I had finished the book I was working on but began playing around with the idea, and again fantasizing. You have a Pope named Bombalini. He's got a look-alike cousin named Frescobaldi, who is a spear carrier at the La Scala opera, and this and that, and this and that, and your imagination goes a little nuts. I thought I could just have fun. And that's how the book happened.

GREENBERG: I've heard this asked of several writers in the technothriller, espionage, and suspense areas where there's a lot of international intrigue. With the Cold War officially declared over, do you see any effect on the kinds of books that you will write?

LUDLUM: No, because if you look back over my work, and I don't, frankly, but in very few cases have I ever subscribed to Reagan's evil-empire theory. God knows, communism, as far as I'm concerned, is not only self-defeating but self-destroying, both in theory and in practice. And I have certainly never approved of that form of government. But when a country loses twenty million human beings in a war we fought together, I can't call those people, regardless of their errant government, an "evil empire." The people who suffered deserve more than hollow, provocative "sound bites." In several

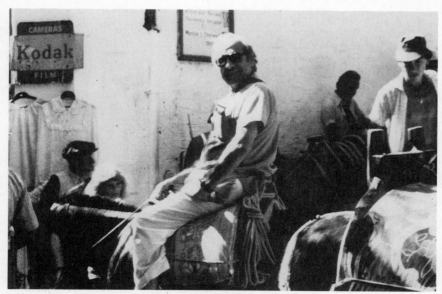

Lyndos, a Greek island (THE AQUITAINE PROGRESSION)

books of mine the Soviets have worked with Americans. And so it doesn't really affect me. I've rarely dealt in realistic extremist ideology. I prefer to think that rational thought ultimately overcomes irrationality. I've dealt mainly with *characters* in conflict, not political theories in conflagration.

GREENBERG: Also showing at the same time that there's millions of readers who don't need that element to find a book intriguing.

LUDLUM: I agree with you. I've sort of stayed away from that.

GREENBERG: Do you have any notion that you might do any more books with World War Two backgrounds?

LUDLUM: No, but I came close, though. A few years ago we were in England, and I heard a fantastic story about something that happened in World War Two, but no, I haven't really seriously pursued it.

GREENBERG: About your heroes—I don't know whether I could quote chapter and verse on this, but I seem to have noticed that your heroes want to ultimately settle down. The women, outside of the peripheral siren/manipulators, also search for a peace beyond the violence they're involved with, which is almost the opposite of what you find, well, certainly in James Bond. But is this conscious?

LUDLUM: Well, yes, I try to make them more normal, more like you and me and our wives or close friends. In other words, when a hero or heroine of mine is called upon to display outstanding traits, they're generally forced to do it. They're forced to find strengths within themselves that they might not have had, had they not been put under severe stress. But I try to make them more identifiable with the rest of us, God forbid we should be placed in like situations.

GREENBERG: Is there an official biography of you?

LUDLUM: Not that I know of. I know that there's a whole bunch of stuff that's put out by publishers. I look at it sometimes and I laugh like hell because they ascribe to me such successes in the acting field, as if I put Olivier on relief, and I've got news for you, it never happened. I get a kick out of those things. My friends get a bigger kick out of it.

GREENBERG: And finally, since this book is really for people who are very serious readers of yours, do you have any message for them that could reach hopefully several hundred thousand of them at the same time?

LUDLUM: I said something on a public broadcasting station recently that just came out quite instinctively. I remembered what Thurgood Marshall said upon his retirement. Someone asked, "What would you like to be remembered for?" And he said, "Well, I guess, 'He did the best he could with what he had.' " I've always liked that. I don't know if you saw that press conference. It was marvelous. It was really kind of inspiring. It really was. That old curmudgeon there; he was just wonderful.

MASTER OF THE THRILLER

AN ESSAY ON THE WORKS OF ROBERT LUDLUM

Roy S. Goodman

It was the mid to late 1960s. Camelot had died with John F. Kennedy, and Lyndon Johnson's Great Society was seen less and less as a panacea. A few years into Johnson's tenure, the long honeymoon between the press and the presidency was definitely over. By the late sixties it was becoming obvious, and the media were making it painfully obvious, that the administration was systematically lying to the public about the war in Vietnam. The military-industrial complex had existed for years—the term was originally coined by Dwight D. Eisenhower—but now it was a shadowy force manipulating events according to its own agenda. Other industries were quietly wrecking the environment, seemingly oblivious of the long-term concerns of mankind, seemingly unaccountable. Then, in 1968, Richard M. Nixon was elected President of the United States.

It was a wonderful time to be paranoid.

At the same time, a fortyish thespian was becoming bored with life in the theater and looking for a change. Not that he wasn't successful— within six years of finishing his hitch in the Marine Corps he was making a living as an actor. He went on to appear on Broadway, and by the time he was thirty he had moved into producing as well. He had won numerous awards for both aspects of his theatrical career. Brief voice-overs for commercials were providing him with a very respectable income. But for whatever reason, he wanted to do something else with his life. His name was Robert Ludlum.

THE SCARLATTI INHERITANCE opens in 1944. The mysterious Heinrich Kroeger wants to make contact with American intelligence, possibly even to defect and thereby to potentially shorten the war. Kroeger is known to be influential in the inner circles of the Third Reich, but his dossier in Washington is woefully incomplete. He has close connections with the most prominent American industrial firms, and before the war he probably used those connections to help build Germany into the power that brought so much bloodshed and misery to the world. He may even be an American. And he will talk to nobody except Matthew Canfield, an obscure, deskbound officer with a minor post in intelligence. Canfield is married to Janet Scarlett, the widow of Scarlatti Industries scion Ulster Stewart Scarlett. But here things become just a bit confusing. Ulster Stewart Scarlett may not, in fact, be dead—he may be Heinrich Kroeger.

We now flash back to the origins of Ulster Scarlett. Ludlum takes us rapidly through the meteoric rise of Giovanni Scarlatti and his industrial empire. By 1908 Giovanni is dead of natural causes, his wife, Elizabeth, has acquired near-royalty status, and their youngest son is becoming a brutally unpleasant problem. When the Great War breaks out, one of Ulster's older brothers is killed in action. Chancellor Drew Scarlett is kept a civilian to carry on the line, and Ulster Stewart Scarlett is sent overseas. In the war, he finds himself—rich, garrulous, handsome, sought after by high-ranking officers who are convinced they could profit after the war through his family's connections. It's as though an upper-class Flashman were serving in the trenches. Through a fluke, Ulster is forcibly converted to the vision of a Germany rebuilding itself after the war. He comes home believed to be a hero, but in his dark heart he is committed to the cause of national socialism. He is becoming Heinrich Kroeger.

Meanwhile, Matthew Canfield is undergoing his own evolution. Trained as an accountant, he spends the Great War working for Group Twenty, an obscure arm of the Department of the Interior investigating "conflicts of interest, misappropriations, et cetera." It's almost all paper-pushing, going through the books creatively to see what's been hidden by creative bookkeeping. Then one night in 1925 Canfield's work breaks out of the routine and into sudden violence. On the New York waterfront he crosses paths with Ulster Stewart Scarlett.

Scarlett's family connections protect him from the consequences of his own illegal activities, but the confrontation with Canfield and the ensuing revelations drive him out of his involvement with organized crime and into something more mysterious, something that will become just as dangerous. He develops a sudden interest in his family's financial empire and in his own enormous and complex trust fund (presumably the inheritance of the title). He courts and marries Janet Saxon, a Vassar alumna with the proper bloodlines—and the proper looks, although Ludlum does not dwell at any length on her appearance or their conjugal activities. But is Scarlett really preparing himself to take his rightful place in the world of business and finance? Of course not! The honeymoon takes Ulster and his bedazzled if somewhat bewildered wife on a wild and wildly spendthrift journey that crisscrosses Europe in a seemingly random pattern that must look like spiderwebs on a map.

Back in New York, Ulster and the pregnant Janet set up housekeeping in a dignified brownstone. With a surprising attention to detail, Ulster has already found in Europe the perfect housekeeper, and he sends her to New York ahead of the couple. She comes highly recommended, of course. And she is fluent in English and . . . German.

Soon—in fact, right before the end of Scarlatti Industries' fiscal year, right before the bank will have to make a full accounting to Elizabeth of Ulster's financial activities—a son is born. One day after the christening, Ulster disappears.

Not only is Ulster gone, so is his share of the family's capital. But a quarter of a billion dollars (this is 1926, so a quarter of a billion dollars is real money) can't be moved around without leaving a trail. The aging but still very formidable Elizabeth knows that she must pursue the missing funds. If news of their disappearance got out, it would devastate Scarlatti Industries. She'd like to get the money back, of course, and she probably wouldn't mind finding Ulster, although Janet, a few months into this period, is hoping that she's a widow—and is already acting like a merry one. But Elizabeth's main concern is that the financial world never learn that the stacks of bearer bonds no longer rest in the musty vaults of a very proper New York bank.

Group Twenty is also most interested in Ulster and his funds, in part because they've already had a brush with him, but also because shadily transferred securities are beginning to show up at one of the stops on Ulster's honeymoon. Naturally, the patrician head of the group assigns Matthew Canfield to the case. Canfield's first step as an investigator is to watch Janet's Manhattan residence. Soon they "meet cute"; it's not deliberate on his part, but he's quick to invite himself inside for a drink, followed in somewhat natural order by dinner and a roll in the hay. Well, Janet is his best lead to Ulster at this point, and he is supposed to stick with her closely.

From Janet, Canfield learns that Elizabeth is preparing to follow Ulster and his missing funds to Europe. The matriarch has already enlisted Janet's cooperation—blackmailed her into providing it, actually—and Canfield is quick to realize that the best way for him to remain close to the investigation is to talk his way into the expedition. Thus it is that Elizabeth finds herself with a charming but surprisingly young companion at the captain's table of the opulent liner *Calpurnia*. A good thing it is too, because Canfield is all that stands between Elizabeth and an attempt on her life. Canfield has no formal training in this sort of thing, but then, neither do the husband-and-wife team of assailants who appear to be volunteers, or else fanatical followers of a cause seemingly at odds with their on-the-surface identities. With the would-be assassin safely consigned to the waves, the indomitable old woman and the brash young accountant explain to each other their respective quests, and they become partners. Actually Canfield becomes her employee, at a salary that is princely for the day but still a fraction of the interest on the interest to Elizabeth, but their relationship is that of colleagues rather than employer and employee.

The ship's arrival in England hardly places Elizabeth in a safe harbor. With mysterious forces close behind her—there is another murder attempt within a few pages, this one heedless of the innocent lives it claims—she sends Canfield back to New York to recruit Janet into her mission of financial investigation and luxury travel. Meanwhile, Group Twenty has not been idle. Ulster Scarlett and his vanished millions are linked, loosely at first, to a group of fourteen industrialists who have recently bought adjoining estates outside Zurich. Three of the fourteen are German, but two are Swedish, two French, and three British—and the largest national contingent consists of four Americans, not counting Heinrich Kroeger.

Further attempts on Elizabeth's life are thwarted by the alert Canfield, and thanks to rather inept security procedures on the part of the villains, he begins to penetrate the mysterious circle of rich men who wear black and red cuff links. Meanwhile, Ulster sneaks into Elizabeth's hotel suite. He has figured out what she must know about his financial dealings, and what documentation she must have in hand. Making drastic and gory threats against his own family—the family that he has renounced to become Heinrich Kroeger—he compels her to give him the seemingly essential documents.

But Kroeger has underestimated the old woman's resolve and resourcefulness. While he has been meeting with National Socialist bigwigs—even Adolf Hitler puts in a cameo appearance—and plotting an unsavory future for Germany, she has been tracing his business partners. Finally at an oversize conference table she faces them down, turning them away from Kroeger's plans through economic blackmail. She may not have more money than they do, but she has the willingness to dismantle Scarlatti Industries, bringing herself down with her adversaries. One by one they capitulate, until Kroeger can stand their defections no longer and shoots one of his colleagues. Canfield has come prepared with a revolver in his pocket, and he shoots Kroeger.

That would seem to be the end of the story, but from the flash-forward that opens the book, we know that it isn't. There will be one final meeting between Matthew Canfield and Heinrich Kroeger, a meeting that could affect the course of the war. The actual outcome of the meeting, and the reasons behind it, provide the surprising but satisfying end of the novel.

THE SCARLATTI INHERITANCE reads like a fairly conventional thriller. Looking at it in retrospect, however, we can identify many of the elements that will serve Robert Ludlum well in his early conspiracy period. They figure much less prominently than they will in later works, and although the result is very entertaining, it's not nearly as distinctive.

The subterranean currents of secret finance, especially of dark international machinations that rebuilt Germany along nightmarish lines, are a favorite subject of Ludlum's. There aren't many details, as there will not be many details in some of the other books. Here Elizabeth's financial death-struggle with the cabal forms a major part of the plot, if not a major aspect of the book's length.

Matthew Canfield is very much a prototypical Ludlum hero. He's not James Bond or Quiller, not a professional adventurer. Canfield has had a minimum of on-the-job training in his brush with Ulster's waterfront hoodlums, but he's still primarily an accountant. Like the heroes and heroines created by Helen MacInnes—by 1968 she had fifteen thrillers in print—he is a citizen thrown into dark events that are well over his head. Like her protagonists, he adapts very well to his strange new surroundings; in fact, he adapts more rapidly than the average MacInnes character, who is often drawn gradually into dangerous affairs and who is usually much more of a babe in the woods at first.

Ludlum's choice of heroes also appears to shape his view of violence. The violence in his books, mostly involving firearms, does not receive the calm, almost clinical treatment that thriller readers generally expect. Instead, his scenes of violence are shrill, strident, practically hysterical in some cases. It's different and disconcerting, but it makes sense. Canfield isn't Matt Helm explaining that there's no practical difference between shooting someone in the back and shooting him face-to-face. He's a civilian who could reasonably have expected to go through his entire life without hearing a shot fired in anger, and the narrative style reflects his reactions.

Canfield is also, like so many of Ludlum's heroes, commitment-minded in a way that is not found in many thrillers. Janet has certainly been a very naughty girl—Ludlum alludes to many of her ill-advised exploits, but does not supply the explicit detail that most of his counterparts favor—but Canfield wants more than a one-night stand, and in fact goes on to marry her. (She's not really a widow, of course, because her husband is alive, but she and Canfield are unaware of this at the time.) Ludlum is not the only marriage-minded thriller writer; Alastair MacLean became positively grandmotherly in this regard as his writing career progressed. It's still unusual, and a refreshing change, although I for one would like to see adventurers and paramours showing a little more concern for safe sex and contraception.

Helen MacInnes's characters join the fight against evil through patriotism or common decency. Ludlum's would like to fight on the side of right, but they are often manipulated into their involvement. Canfield is no exception; his Group Twenty superiors concoct his assignment with the thought: "There was no question about it. The fastest way to solve the mystery behind the Scarlattis was for Matthew Canfield to become a pawn. A pawn who trapped himself." It's a subtle point, easy to miss if you aren't looking back with subsequent books in mind. There is no further manipulation of Canfield, and from that point on he becomes a very active participant in events. If he is trapped, it is only in the sense that he has been sent out untrained and largely uninformed to literally and figuratively draw the fire of Ulster's organization. A more fully realized group of superiors in a later Ludlum work would probably have a plan in mind whereby Canfield's death would be informative, even productive from their cynical point of view.

Finally, in THE SCARLATTI INHERITANCE we see glimmers of Ludlum's flair for plot twist and surprise. The climax lasts only eight pages, and even though it's a major part of the plot, it's virtually an anticlimax. In fact, the final eight pages contain an important revelation about Ulster/Kroeger's motivation, and it is there we learn that much of what has been happening—certainly much of what we have been anticipating after the long flash-forward that introduces the novel—is not at all what it seems.

———————

THE OSTERMAN WEEKEND is an almost complete change of pace for Ludlum. He had only one book behind him at this point, and was still developing his plotting style, but already he knew how to generate suspense, how to keep the reader in the dark.

The setting is the sleepy New Jersey suburb of Saddle Valley, which on the surface has much more in common with the location of Ludlum's theater than it does with the exotic European locales of SCARLATTI. When we meet protagonist John Tanner, a news producer for a major television network, he's engaged in the last thing that a typical secret agent would be found doing—he's cleaning out his garage with his wife while the kids play in the backyard pool.

Very soon we realize that Saddle Valley is not quite what it seems. A Saddle Valley police officer makes a long-distance call to New Hampshire and is covertly connected to an untraceable number at the CIA, where he gives a cryptic report to a superior with an ominous code name. The subject of his report is John Cardone, seemingly another solid suburban citizen. On the surface he's as normal as can be—wife, kids, suburban house, overpriced lawn service—but has he used his Italian background to bring Mafia clients into his brokerage?

And what's an Osterman weekend? We quickly learn from another respectable couple, Richard and Virginia Tremayne, that the fourth couple of the social circle is flying east for a visit in a few days. So far there's nothing more sinister about the coming weekend than the amount of alcohol that the characters expect to consume (although they can apparently perform impressively in this department even without out-of-town guests) and the hangovers they may wind up nursing.

As for the Ostermans, they're lounging around their own pool. The only difference is that they're in Southern California, so they're lounging in the nude. Unlike almost all other writers of escape fiction, Ludlum provides next to no description of their nudity except to point out that it doesn't stand up to close scrutiny in the bright sunlight. Bernie and Leila Osterman are just an ordinary Jewish couple from the Bronx, except that they have the ability to make words live on paper and they've "willingly, happily trained their talents for the exploding world of the television residual." Could they write the Great American Novel instead? A few quick laps in the pool is all it takes to banish that thought in favor of rewrites that will be more acceptable to their producer. At about the time he wrote this, Robert Ludlum was sending his daughter to college on the residuals from a three-word voice-over, so he could well identify with his characters.

As Bernie Osterman's aging-college-athlete body splashes through the invitingly chlorinated water, he contemplates bringing the Tanners in on a mysterious involvement with Zurich; he's already cleared their names with the appropriate gnomes.

The book is about ten percent finished before it gets beyond the level of vague hints. Tough, muscular CIA agent Laurence Fassett reviews some of the details of his plan with Alexander Danforth, a charming elder statesman with a nonspecific position but plenty of influence. Fassett's wife was killed in East Berlin by agents of the Soviet group called Omega. Now, by manipulating events in Saddle Valley, he has his chance to strike back.

Fassett brings Tanner to Washington under the pretext that he needs to sign a few pointless FCC forms. Once the producer is inside a borrowed office at the FCC, Fassett presents his real identification and informs Tanner that the CIA wants his cooperation. (Actually, according to a later Ludlum book, it would be illegal for the CIA to involve itself with matters inside the United States. Veteran thriller aficionados are convinced that the CIA engages in clandestine operations anywhere it feels like, so they can easily let that one pass.) Omega, he explains, is a long-standing Soviet operation aimed at creating economic chaos in the United States by blackmailing a few thousand key executives into making specific decisions. Each decision alone will appear to be only a minor mistake, and none by itself will be ruinous, but if all occur together at the proper time, they could wreck the country's economy. The CIA knows of this plan only because moderates in the USSR are horrified by it, horrified by their knowledge that the hard-liners have a timetable for activating Omega—and time is running out!

And that neatly concludes part one of Fassett's story. Tanner is perfectly free to walk away, and the government will trust his common sense and basic decency to keep him from revealing any of this information. Naturally he can barely wait to hear part two.

In part two Tanner learns that the agents of Omega are "the very same type of individual it will attack." If they weren't working in high positions at large corporations, they'd hardly come in contact with those who are.

Let's set the narrative aside for a moment to reflect on Omega. Deep-cover Soviet agents in the United States are hardly unusual in thriller fiction. The submarine captain in *Boomer* has lived a normal American life until the time comes for him to invent a fictitious mission for his attack submarine. Walter Wager's *Telefon* involves a deep-cover group whose cover is so deep that the agents themselves don't even know their missions of sabotage until activated by posthypnotic command. The test pilot in Dale Brown's *Day of the Cheetah* has been the prototypical American success story, living completely the part of the rising young air force officer until he can get behind the controls of the thought-controlled fighter Dreamstar and steal it for his masters.

On the other hand, when the Americans wanted to appropriate Firefox, in Craig Thomas's *Firefox Down*, they placed a pilot-agent into the cockpit through much more conventional means. There was one very clever novel—name regretfully forgotten by this writer—in which an ivory-tower research unit has been studying Soviet life so that they can advise American agents on how to function behind the Iron Curtain. They're all fluent in Russian, they've trained themselves in typical Russian habits, they even get all their dental work done by an expatriate Russian dentist who treats their cavities according to obsolete Russian methods. Eventually, of course, one or two of them become the only possible choice to carry out a real mission, and they are hurled from their safe study carrels into the gritty, dangerous streets of Moscow. The west has placed a few fictitious moles in the Kremlin, such as Tom Clancy's "Cardinal" (in *Cardinal of the Kremlin*). But aside from that, the American and British intelligence communities of fiction don't train deep-cover sleepers, don't let them sleep for decades before activating them. Perhaps it is too sneaky a tactic for the good guys, but it can make for an interesting novel.

There are many things that a thriller author can do with the concept of deep-cover Soviet agents integrating themselves into American lives, working their way up to positions of responsibility. One excellent novel even revolves around the necessary training facility, Nelson DeMille's *The Charm School*. Ludlum's version is, in its quiet way, probably the most logical of all, and it gets even better when he elaborates on it in THE PARSIFAL MOSAIC. How many deep-cover agents would the Soviets have to plant, at no small expense and with no assurance that the agents wouldn't grow up to consider themselves Americans, to have one of them reach the right place in the Air Force or Navy at just the right time? How much damage could a small band of saboteurs really do?

Omega's plan for economic sabotage makes a lot of sense, right down to the type of person developed to implement it. But having introduced the concept, Ludlum here makes no further use of it! In three or four pages he outlines the basic idea behind an entire book, potentially a very interesting one (Paul Erdman meets Walter Wager?) but he doesn't bother with it because he's got plot and narrative to spare. We will see Ludlum do this in the future; his flair for plotting is so fertile that he can afford to be profligate with plot lines.

As Fassett goes on, Tanner learns what the reader suspects: The nerve center for Omega, the menacing "Chasm of Leather," is actually Saddle Valley, New Jersey. And that's the end of part two! Now they're getting into serious national security matters, and before Tanner can hear anything more, he has to sign an affidavit. Up to this point he could walk away; once he passes this point, his secrecy is mandated by law. Of course

Time out in Istanbul (THE ICARUS AGENDA)

he could no more stop listening than the reader could close the book, so he scribbles his name on the form. He quickly learns that any or all of the Tremaynes, Cardones, and Ostermans may be involved in Omega. Before the Ostermans arrive for their visit, all the couples will be harassed, subjected to messages that suggest Tanner is somehow involved—perhaps as a double agent, perhaps working for the CIA. If they're innocent, they'll call the police or the FBI. If they're working for Omega, they'll learn from Moscow that Tanner is actually a sheep in sheep's clothing, and they'll come to suspect the other couples. The resulting confrontation should give them away. Confused? You'd better get used to it! Soon each of the couples receives a cryptic message. They've got no idea who wants them to suspect Tanner or why, but each has something to hide. Within a day they're all panicky, confused, and drinking heavily—and Tanner isn't handling the situation very well either. Meanwhile, the CIA has everyone under close observation and the situation under control.

If Tanner is tense on Tuesday, Wednesday draws him one notch closer to the breaking point. His wife and children disappear, and he finds them chloroformed in their station wagon on an isolated country road. Is it an ordinary robbery, as the missing televisions and silverware would indicate? Naturally he knows that it isn't. He confronts the CIA men in charge of watching his house and learns that this was the result of a minor glitch. Furious, he demands to get out of the plan, but Fassett assures him that this would only result in the death of his family. Omega killed Fassett's wife, not through operational necessity but just because she was married to him, and they wouldn't hesitate to do the same to Tanner.

In fact, that night a CIA man on patrol around Tanner's house is murdered and mutilated. There's no reason for Omega to kill him—his death is a message to Fassett. Fassett and his agents can discuss the implications of this calmly and professionally, even though Fassett's three children may be targeted for retaliatory killings. Tanner is sickened by the sight of the murdered body, and by what he is learning of the shadow existence around him. " 'What kind of world do you people live in?' " he asks a CIA agent. " 'The same one you do.' " It's a classic statement of the difference between professionals and amateurs, of the fact that the comfortable Saddle Valleys of the world can remain comfortable only through the continuing secret wars of the intelligence community.

The next day, while the Tanners are playing tennis at their club, bugs and metal detectors are being installed in their house, and the three suspect couples are all having extremely suspect meetings with various unsavory characters. The stage is well and truly set for the weekend.

The Ostermans finally arrive in Saddle Valley, and Tanner is amazed to find that just as Fassett had assured him, he is able to function quite normally. Yet every action could have two meanings, every conversation is tense. The old friends talk easily enough, but in spite of the free-flowing liquor, nobody can really open up about personal matters. One moment Tanner is convinced that Richard Tremayne is Omega; then the next statement out of Tremayne's mouth convinces him that his friend is innocent—and he expects that the tone and the words will be equally persuasive to the CIA technicians manning the output from the hidden microphones all over the house. By the end of the evening, everyone is tense and at least somewhat drunk. It doesn't help at all that while the husbands all have something to hide, the wives seem to have no idea what's going on or why everyone is behaving strangely—or could one or more of them be pretending not to know? Unformed accusations start to fly, and John Cardone roars the single word "Zurich" into the night. But his cry does not catalyze any relevations, and the first evening of the reunion breaks up peacefully.

In the quiet of their bedroom, Tanner and his wife discuss the odd events of the evening. He explains why his old friends are tense, why they're trying to persuade him to do something. Every word of the explanation is a lie. "Fassett had been right. He could manage them all. Even [his wife] Ali." In spite of his newfound confidence in himself as a liar and manipulator, Tanner can't sleep. Neither can Bernie Osterman, and the two men find themselves sharing a reflective conversation, but one that could lead to mysterious implications. Then the night is pierced by the screams of Tanner's young daughter. The family's Welsh terrier has been killed, its small body messily mutilated. And the only one who could have done it, the only one who could have eluded the electronic security system because she was already inside, was Leila Osterman!

The police are called, of course, and now Tanner must function at a higher level, because some of the police are CIA plants working on the case and some really are what they appear to be. The police point out that the dog was killed several hours before, so that any of the guests could be responsible. As the police try to reconstruct the events of the evening, they call the Tremaynes and the Cardones, only to discover that neither couple is at home!

A damp, cloudy dawn is breaking as the missing couples shake themselves out of a drugged sleep on the same little-used road where Tanner and his family found themselves only a few days before. What does this mean? The reader isn't the only one who wants to know; Tanner calls Fassett to demand answers, only to discover that the entire CIA presence is gone. Fassett has checked out of his motel headquarters. The emergency telephone number has been disconnected. And a few hours later Tanner gets through to the CIA and learns that they have never had a Laurence Fassett working for them!

Would the CIA really give out personnel information over the telephone? It's a mark of Ludlum's prowess as a storyteller that I didn't begin to question this assumption the first or the second time I read the book, only when I was preparing this summary. If you stop and look for such pieces of illogic or errors of fact in THE OSTERMAN WEEKEND or in any of Ludlum's other books, you can find them easily enough. What's significant is not the mistakes, but that he gets away with them so readily. Compare Robert Ludlum to two other well-known authors of escapist fiction. The classic precursor of modern detective fiction, and to a certain extent of modern adventure fiction, is Sir Arthur Conan Doyle. Yet a leisurely trip through the late William S. Baring-Gould's fascinating *The Annotated Sherlock Holmes* reveals that Conan Doyle was careless and cavalier with many of his facts, and that many of Holmes's apparently logical deductions don't stand up to close scrutiny. We easily miss some of Conan Doyle's errors because we're not steeped in the facts of the period involved, others because the author is skillful enough to make it all sound credible, even brilliant. In contrast, consider a thriller author who began his career at just about the same time as Ludlum, Frederick Forsyth. In his research for *The Day of the Jackal*, Forsyth spent time with an armorer, a passport forger, and a professional assassin. By the time he was ready to knock off the actual manuscript, he could equally well have knocked off Charles de Gaulle! His preparation for *The Dogs of War* was so thorough that he was rumored to have engineered the real-life overthrow of a small African nation, although his agent insists that Forsyth is too frugal to hire the necessary mercenaries. Forsyth's attention to detail is admirable, but Ludlum clearly manages to make his books work without such exhaustive detail.

Back in Saddle Valley, Omega is closing in, and Tanner must face it alone. The Ostermans have packed their bags; the tensions of the weekend have been too much for them. Tanner confronts his friends. Don't they have money in Zurich? Of course! So do the Cardones, the Tremaynes, and half of the people that the Ostermans know on the coast. Finally Tanner asks them directly about Omega, and he comes away convinced that they are innocent. With their help, he can begin the long climb back to sanity.

Meanwhile, the clouds of the morning have begun pouring rain, and the winds are building to gale force. Amid the fury of nature, the fury of man intrudes. Someone is shooting at the Tanners' house! The phone lines are cut, the cars in the garage immobilized. Now it's the Tanners and the Ostermans, armed with only a rusty ax and a garden pitchfork, against fanatics with automatic weapons. And there's an omega [Ω] messily spray-painted on the wall of the garage.

There is one final attack. Assault rifles on full automatic thunder into the basement, and choking clouds of cement dust fill the air. John Tanner and Bernie Osterman acquit themselves amazingly well, pushing at hot rifle barrels to deflect the worst of the fire and wounding at least two attackers with their primitive weapons. But are the attackers deliberately firing away from Leila Osterman, whose green brooch virtually glows in the dark basement? Much too late, the police arrive and the firing stops.

Finally everything seems to be under control. CIA men enter the house disguised as phone repairmen. Omega is falling apart, and Fassett is on top of the situation not two miles away. His alleged absence from CIA personnel files was only a ruse. But just when you think it's safe to go back to the suburbs, a single round of gunfire crashes through the window and wounds Tanner. It's messy and painful, but fortunately one of those superficial wounds often required in thriller plots.

All the suspect couples are now behaving suspiciously. The Tremaynes and the Cardones have been untraceable for hours. The Ostermans are packed and ready to rush back to California, the Cardones are setting out for Philadelphia, the Tremaynes have plane tickets but won't say to where. And Tanner, wounded and in pain and driving a hastily borrowed car, is moving toward a rendezvous on the same little-used road where the three families had been abandoned in a drugged stupor. There's one last exchange of gunfire, and as Tanner collapses, he stares at the face of the fallen enemy. He knows that he has finally killed Omega.

THE OSTERMAN WEEKEND is part psychological thriller and part espionage thriller, with strong overtones of a conventional mystery. By the end of the book all of the herrings are red and we are surprised to learn which characters are (Reds), but Ludlum has played scrupulously fair and dropped several clues, if only we could catch them with all the bizarre and suspicious behavior going on. As in any good mystery, all the misleading actions have rational explanations. OSTERMAN also continues the development of Ludlum's own brand of thriller; the hero is consistently manipulated, lied to, and placed in danger, and he can save himself and some small part of the world only by unraveling the fabric of lies and beating the cynical professionals at their own game.

In **THE MATLOCK PAPER,** this plot device will approach its full growth. As cunningly plotted as MATLOCK is, however, it has real problems. While any readers of thrillers must be able to willingly suspend disbelief, in many cases to just chuck disbelief and reality testing altogether, MATLOCK pushes this ability to its limits. I enjoyed MATLOCK when I read it in the seventies, but upon rereading it recently, I found it less than wholly satisfying.

OSTERMAN is set in the nonspecific present; the current breakup of the Soviet Union has created a real problem for thriller writers, but you could just as well fit the book into last week's headlines by stating that the events in the Soviet Union have galvanized the hard-liners into going ahead with their doomsday plot. SCARLATTI is centered around World War II, even though little of the action in the book takes place during the actual conflict. "The Good War" has been over for nearly five decades, but it's still possible to come up with new ideas about the conflict and its aftermath; in fact, no other war in history provides nearly as suitable a framework for thriller fiction. But THE MATLOCK PAPER is set in the late 1960s and early 1970s, and it feels dated.

But being dated is not MATLOCK's only problem. It's awkward—awkward because the protagonist has to infiltrate subcultures where he doesn't belong, awkward because all the subcultures are largely artificial. I'd like to think that Ludlum wrote MATLOCK or at least started it before SCARLATTI and OSTERMAN, but the real-world events don't support that hypothesis. The administration in MATLOCK is pretty clearly Nixon's, and Ludlum is rightly furious about Watergate. If you race through the book at the pace it demands, you can very easily ignore its shortcomings and enjoy it for what it is. If you must focus on the shortcomings, then view it as a precursor of THE CHANCELLOR MANUSCRIPT and appreciate it for its part in Robert Ludlum's development as a plotter of Byzantine conspiracies.

THE MATLOCK PAPER opens in Washington, D.C. Justice Department agent Ralph Loring is leaving a meeting where the plans for a clandestine operation have just been finalized. It's a complex and cynical operation based on sending a rank amateur, Professor James Matlock, up against vicious professionals. "The problems were far too complex, too filled with traps for an amateur. . . . The terrible irony was that if this Matlock made errors, fell into traps, he might accomplish far more far quicker than any professional." Matlock has been carefully chosen—partly because he's in the right place, partly because he's got a more adventurous background than your average specialist in Elizabethan English, partly because this is an antidrug operation and Matlock's younger brother died three years before from a heroin overdose. Loring, to his credit, has grave doubts about the morality of throwing an amateur into a morass of violence, but the nameless and seemingly emotionless planners on the committee prevail.

Taking elaborate and apparently needless precautions to conceal his movements, Loring journeys to the lovely Connecticut campus of Carlyle University. Carlyle is a prestigious institution graced by old trees, ivy-covered buildings, and ivy-covered professors. In fact, it's quite reminiscent—including its size, which is small for a university—of Ludlum's alma mater, Wesleyan. In the majestic mansion of President Adrian Sealfont, Loring meets with Matlock and the irascible Sam Kressel, dean of colleges. He explains that the fastest-growing concentration of drug trade in the United States is in New England. At the very center is Nimrod, a mysterious organization with tentacles reaching into every dark corner of human vice: prostitution, loan-sharking, gambling, and other postgraduate employment. Nimrod has no known ties to organized crime, in fact seems to go out of its way to avoid dealing with organized crime. But organized crime wants to deal with Nimrod, to avoid conflict and maximize ill-gotten gains for all. To this end there is a furtive meeting scheduled somewhere within fifty miles of Carlyle, and the meeting date is only three weeks away.

The Justice Department has even obtained an invitation to the meeting, a curious piece of silver-colored stationery covered with writing in an obscure Corsican dialect that can't really be translated. The paper has been cut irregularly from a larger sheet; if it matches the cut edge perfectly, it will establish the bearer's bona fides. The writing lists map coordinates, but not in enough detail to place the meeting precisely. And it ends, ominously, with the words "Venerare Omerta." " 'Roughly translated, respect the law of Omerta. Omerta is an oath of allegiance *and* silence. To betray either is asking to be killed.' "

Matlock is given every chance to back out of the mission, but he insists on accepting it. For several hours he and Loring review long lists of drug users and drug dealers, plus other information that Matlock will need but dare not commit to paper.

They leave the house through separate doors, ten minutes apart. Matlock is surprised when Loring jostles him on the street. It seems that his precautions against being followed were anything but needless, and that they weren't elaborate enough. Loring manages to make a quick conversation look like a chance encounter, but that is his last action. Minutes later he is killed by a bullet from a silencer-equipped rifle.

Matlock panics, behaving like the incredulous citizen that he is supposed to appear rather than the newly recruited operative that he is. It is this panic, and his normal reaction in yelling for help, that save the mission. Once again he is offered a chance to get out—Sam Kressel virtually demands it—but declines. Loring's replacement, a very human and likable FBI man named Jason Greenberg, decides that Matlock can safely continue—at least as safely as he could before.

To maintain its anonymity, Nimrod won't sell drugs to Carlyle students; they have to go off campus for their connection. But the shadowy organization does deal to faculty members, so Matlock's first undercover mission is to invite himself for dinner with known user Archie Beeson, a junior professor of amazing pompousness, pretentiousness, and affectation. After awkward hors d'oeuvres and an awkward dinner, Matlock maneuvers the conversation and the evening's festivities around to drugs. The Beesons and their guest ingest a seemingly lethal dose of Seconal and wine, and Matlock almost winds up under the covers with the simpering, pneumatic Mrs. Beeson. " 'Pinky groovy,' " she intones as her see-through blouse and her lingerie come adrift. Something in Matlock's performance rings false to Beeson (The reader will have found it unconvincing long before the stoned junior professor does.), who excuses himself to make a panicked phone call. He seems to be mentioning Lucas Herron, the revered elder statesman of the campus whose "concern . . . was a welcomed sedative in faculty crises."

Matlock realizes that he must not be acting suitably wasted, so he quickly overcompensates and appears to reassure the blithering, spaced-out Beeson. But perhaps his performance is not quite sufficient, because when he staggers back into his apartment, he finds that it has been messily torn apart. All his possessions have been searched, many destroyed. Like the naive citizen he is supposed to be, he calls the Carlyle police, who display some disturbing inconsistencies in their behavior. His girlfriend, Pat Ballantyne, drives over in panic, and Matlock promptly lies to her. The next day, when he is reporting to Jason Greenberg, he omits any mention of Lucas Herron's name. And who should be trying to eavesdrop on the meeting but the same local policeman who was at the apartment!

Matlock's next expedition is to Lumumba Hall, formerly Alpha Delta Phi. The one-time fraternity house has been extensively redecorated in Early African Village, with a substantial Black Power motif in many areas. Ludlum has some concise and caustic observations about both the previous occupants and the new ones. Tonight's entertainment is the re-creation of a Mau-Mau puberty rite carried out with potentially lethal enthusiasm under the direction of one Julian Dunois, a young lawyer originally from Haiti and obviously a gentleman of much influence. Dunois draws Matlock aside for a private conversation, and Matlock discovers that the cultured young black man knows a disturbing amount about him—his exact birth date, his biography, even his drink preferences. But Matlock's taste in whiskey doesn't extend to three tabs of LSD in his sour mash bourbon, and the professor is soon whirling through horrendous hallucinations while black faces demand to know where the paper is. Disoriented though he is, Matlock manages to deny any knowledge of a paper, then injures Dunois and breaks away. Jason Greenberg and Pat Ballantyne find him and nurse him back to health.

What are the blacks up to? How do they know about the paper? They accuse Matlock of racist behavior—a prescient piece of writing on Ludlum's part, because today such an accusation would immobilize our hero on any politically correct campus. In the book's era, Dean Sam Kressel can listen to Matlock's defense. The blacks will later withdraw their charge, but not before once more demanding the paper. A leader of the black students visits Matlock in his apartment. The place has been cleaned up considerably (through the simple if sexist subterfuge of Matlock's leaving Pat there, ostensibly for her own protection but really because he knows that she will tidy up), but the shattered casement window hasn't been repaired yet. The black denies that this is Dunois's style—there must be another group out to get the paper. But who?

Greenberg has ordered him to stay put, but Matlock drives off to confront Lucas Herron. World War II hero, scholar, alchemist of gourmet Tom Collinses, Herron is the grand old man of Carlyle. Matlock immediately spills his guts to Herron, divulging much of the top-secret information he has been entrusted with. At first Herron is skeptical; then he tries to talk Matlock out of pursuing matters. Finally he becomes terrified, and he dives into the thick woods around his manicured lawn. From among the trees Matlock can hear his despairing cry: "Nimrod!"

Back at his apartment, Matlock meets with Greenberg and learns that Julian Dunois is much more than a choreographer of Mau-Mau puberty rites. The young black lawyer has a half-dozen aliases and an alarming reputation as a rabble-rouser and agent provocateur. Matlock also learns that the Justice Department wants him off the case. Well, they don't really want him off the case, but they do want him to sign a weasely disclaimer so they can cover their own posteriors. Their "advice" that he pull out is an offer they know he'll refuse. They've picked a typical Ludlum hero to do their dirty work, so of course he insists on pressing ahead. However, the case is going to become a lot more intense very quickly. Matlock goes out to dinner with Pat. He is called to the telephone, and when he returns to their table she has disappeared.

Matlock returns to his apartment to wait. He passes a most uncomfortable hour, made much worse by the news that Lucas Herron is dead, an apparent suicide. Greenberg thinks it was actually murder, and he hopes an autopsy will tell; Sam Kressel is horrified at the idea of an autopsy. (In New York, a suicide would automatically by law become a medical examiner's case.) Now Greenberg decides that the case is getting too rough to be pursued by an amateur, and that Matlock really should take himself off the case. The professor is about to agree, when suddenly his house is rocked by two explosions. As they pick themselves up off the

floor, Matlock and Greenberg realize that the explosions were intended
to get their attention, not to harm them. Outside the apartment Pat
Ballantyne lies semiconscious and moaning, oozing blood into the sheet
that covers her lacerated body.

This brief scene says a lot about Ludlum's approach to violence. It's
certainly no gorier than scenes in many books, including others of his.
Pat Ballantyne will live and function normally; in fact, her cuts have
been planned and placed like surgical incisions, and after she heals you'd
have to look hard to find the scars. Yet when I was reviewing THE
MATLOCK PAPER, I tried to avoid going over this scene again. There
was none of the morbid fascination that readers experience with Flashman's descriptions of such inhuman devices as the knout and the wire
shirt. James Bond may be rackingly nauseated after a poisonous six-inch
centipede finally crawls off his body, but the reader isn't. Even the
indignity of James Bond's torture at the hands (and mundanely simple
but horribly effective instruments) of Le Chiffre in another book attracts
while it repels. Of all the material I can recall, only an impersonal
beating in *The Godfather* and the shooting of Jack Ryan's wife and
daughter in *Patriot Games* come close to being so repugnant.

Our reaction to the torture of Pat is purely intentional on Ludlum's
part. One of the author's favorite reviews stated that after you finish a
Robert Ludlum novel, the last thing you'd want to do is go out and beat
somebody up. Violence and death are routine instruments for the villains
in Ludlum's world, and an unavoidable response for the heroes thrust
into the same milieu. But as in the "judgment day" scene of *Termi-
nator 2* or the brutally clinical analysis of a thermonuclear attack in *The
Third World War*, violence and its effects are displayed for what they are,
not glorified as in so many movies and books.

The effect of the violence on Matlock is to galvanize his resolve. Now
he will pursue the case to the end, no matter what the advice from the
Justice Department. Before they found Pat, Greenberg was ready to have
Matlock held as a witness (remember, Matlock was nominally the last
one to see Lucas Herron alive) just to take him out of circulation. After,
Greenberg will still need a replacement because he's been in the area too
long, but he offers all the support he can. Matlock also gets financial
support—and some surprising, gratifying emotional support—from his
rich, aloof father. Armed with sufficient funds, he is prepared to plunge
into Nimrod's world of vice.

First Matlock covers his most exposed flank by hiring a distinguished
and expensive private investigating firm to protect Pat in her hospital bed.
He lies glibly to the head of the firm about the reasons Pat needs the
protection, and he talks the man into giving him a list of the illegal
gambling clubs that supposedly dot the Connecticut countryside. Liber-

ally dispensing bribes and falsehoods, he talks his way inside the elegant and expensive Avon Swim Club, which is actually anything but the harmless suburban institution it appears to be. From there he talks his way into fancier and fancier clubs, only to find that he has talked his way into a front-row seat for a massacre. With gunshots ringing in his ears, Matlock sees a distinctive black limousine drive away from the bullet-riddled suburban casino—the same black limousine he spotted on the streets of Carlyle when Ralph Loring was killed.

Undaunted, Matlock proceeds to the next casino on his list. By now the proprietor is convinced that he's some sort of traveling inspector for Nimrod, so the management extends every courtesy—including the services of an attractive young woman. Matlock recognizes her school ring and browbeats her into revealing that she is only one of many blackmailed into service. He concludes their session chastely, perhaps at the risk of blowing his cover, and convinces his host that he must rendezvous with at least one of the other invitees to the Nimrod-organized crime convention. He finally arranges a meeting, which turns out to be a trap. Through guts, ingenuity, and much luck, Matlock defeats two professional killers—one of whom was driving the now-familiar black limousine.

Now Matlock turns to an old lead, Lucas Herron. The dead profes-sor's house has been torn apart, perhaps by the same searchers who shredded Matlock's apartment. But Matlock remembers a clue from his last conversation with Herron, and he succeeds where professionals have failed. Soon he is able to unearth (literally as well as figuratively) Lucas Herron's dreadful secret, which is intimately interwoven with the history of Nimrod. Herron's diary reveals that Nimrod is not the name of an organization, but of the position held by a single man. The first two Nimrods were known to Herron; the third is the most ruthless master yet, both as leader of the organization and as the holder of dreadful power over Herron. In his last entries Herron has learned the identity of the new Nimrod, and this is the most terrible knowledge of all. He needs to confirm this identity for sure before he can commit even seemingly solid clues to paper, but then the diary ends abruptly with Herron's death.

While Matlock was looking through the diary, the amoral men in Washington have been busy. Through his communications with the private security firm, he learns that there are now warrants for his arrest on charges of murder and drug trafficking. The security firm wouldn't abandon Pat Ballantyne; they've turned her protection over to the Carlyle police department. This is small comfort for Matlock, for the diary has just confirmed that the Carlyle police are really Nimrod's private army.

There's only one place for Matlock to turn now. He telephones Carlyle University President Adrian Sealfont, and Sealfont arranges to meet with Matlock and Sam Kressel. Matlock drives by Kressel's house to offer him a ride to the meeting, but there is a Carlyle police cruiser parked outside. Kressel must be the newest and most vicious to hold the position of Nimrod!

On his way to Sealfont's house, Matlock is pursued by a heavy, powerful car. Looking out of a passenger window is the bandaged face of Julian Dunois. Matlock is run off the road, and he recovers consciousness in a windowless basement room of Lumumba Hall. Now he learns what Dunois is really about. The black lawyer heads a ruthless organization dedicated to stopping Nimrod and its criminal associates. Dunois is working outside the law—in fact, he's so far outside the law that he would murder Matlock and Pat without a second thought if he felt that it would help him—because the authorities have sold out. Matlock and Dunois forge an uneasy alliance, and together they prepare for the final confrontation with Nimrod. If they had any illusions that this confrontation would be peaceful, they are dispelled by the news that Sam Kressel and his wife are dead, a supposed murder-suicide.

Nimrod will be bringing his palace guard to the meeting, but Julian Dunois has his own palace guard—a group of highly trained, fanatically dedicated young black men. In the climactic final scene we learn the shocking truth of Nimrod's identity. Nimrod is Adrian Sealfont, and the entire drugs-and-prostitution ring was really the ultimate university fundraiser! Listening to Sealfont describe the financial plight of colleges and universities, we can understand how he and others were sucked into solving the problem by going outside the law. Dunois's private army overcomes Sealfont's, and the university president will simply disappear—to answer questions for Dunois, possibly under torture, until the black's organization can eliminate Nimrod. We learn in an epilogue that Dunois is dead, although he could simply be stage-managing his own disappearance.

In the end Matlock and Pat are resting and recuperating on a beach in the Caribbean. It's got all the trappings of a happy ending, except that Matlock thinks that he should blow the whistle on Nimrod, on Dunois's organization, and on the Justice Department—but he's stalemated because he knows that he'll be an ineffectual outcast if he does. Ludlum's world is a complex one, fraught with moral ambiguity, and here as in many of his other books he eschews the neat resolution.

Ludlum's next book was **TREVAYNE,** published under the nom de plume Jonathan Ryder and later released under the author's born identity. "Ryder" would also go on to write THE CRY OF THE HALIDON.

Both of these are excellent, two of my favorites among Ludlum's early work. TREVAYNE is by no means the most complicated or convoluted of Ludlum's early "conspiracy" novels, but it is in many ways the deepest and the most thought-provoking.

TREVAYNE was written in response to Watergate—and later reissued with new publicity and a new, more famous name on the cover when Robert Ludlum saw the same abuses of power taking place all over again. In the foreword to the 1989 edition he describes his outrage: "One of the most frightening statements to come out of the Watergate hearings was the following, delivered, in essence, by the nation's chief law enforcement officer. 'There's nothing I would not do to keep the presidency . . .' I don't have to complete the exact sentence; the meaning was clear—to keep it *ours*. The presidency and the country was *theirs*. Not yours, or mine, or even the neighbors' across the street with whom we frequently disagreed in things political. Only *theirs*." Yet in spite of the author's visceral fury, a reaction that still seethes within him, TREVAYNE presents a remarkably balanced picture. Here, power has its uses as well as its abuses.

The title character is Andrew Trevayne, a young, self-made multimillionaire industrialist and well-known iconoclast. As the book opens, a distinguished old friend is relaying an invitation to Washington; the President wants Trevayne to head a subcommittee investigating corruption in the military-industrial complex. But before Trevayne can go, before he can even make up his mind, surreal and suspicious events begin to swirl around his family. His daughter is at an innocent slumber party (maybe not so innocent—there is some marijuana in the house) when the police arrive in response to an anonymous tip and find a quarter of a million dollars worth of heroin in the milk box on the porch. And his son is or is not involved in a fatal accident, in which the son can be proved to have been drunk, although we know that he wasn't. Faithful readers of Ludlum can recognize all the symptoms: They are being set up for subsequent blackmail. It must be important, because even the "accident" must have required elaborate planning and expensive personnel. And we know that the perpetrators are ruthless, because they really did kill someone in the accident. But who is doing it, and why?

Although he has misgivings about heading the subcommittee anyway, and although he realizes that these bizarre events involving his family leave him wide open to blackmail, Trevayne travels to Washington. The very sympathetic and persuasive President induces him to stay with the subcommittee. Unfortunately for Trevayne and the reader, he next has to get through Senate hearings. His appointment is eventually confirmed, but not before the congressional question-and-answer period has produced some plodding prose. He selects a team made up mostly of old buddies and iconoclastic young experts, but one member is selected for him: Major Paul Bonner, his liaison with the Pentagon.

From this point the plot becomes surprisingly linear. We learn that there is a Mafia–industry connection. We learn early and easily that Bonner is assigned to spy on Trevayne's committee. We even learn too early the identity of the one company that's responsible for most of the corruption; Trevayne and his crew make up a list of corporate suspects, and the guilty party turns out to be Genessee Industries, the only one on the list that doesn't exist in the real world.

If the plot is simple, the issues aren't. Betrayal is a major theme in TREVAYNE. A highly placed White House aide is betraying the President. Bonner has been placed on the committee specifically to betray it, yet later he will turn against his covert employers in revulsion at their methods. Trevayne's lawyer is chronically betraying him. And at times the various factions of the military-industrial-Mafia complex betray each other.

What makes TREVAYNE especially interesting is that all the bad guys (except Mario de Spadante, the caricaturish mafioso) have fairly reasonable motives. Paul Bonner describes his opposition to the subcommittee's work in a peculiar but apt ecological metaphor. "Beavers, thought Bonner. Earnest, intense, chipping away at a thousand barks so the trees would fall and the streams be dammed. Natural progression thwarted? Trevayne would call it something like ecological balance. . . . It was far more important that the fields below be irrigated than a few earnest beavers survive. The beavers wanted to parch the land, to sacrifice the crops in the name of concerns only the beavers cared about. There were other concerns, frightening ones that the smaller animals would never understand. Only the lions understood; they had to, because they were the leaders. The leaders stalked all areas of the forests and jungles; they knew who the predators were. The beavers didn't." His metaphor may be strained, but he's got a point. So does the elegant lawyer who feels that his elitist group, in effect covertly running the country, is far more qualified to do so than the electorate.

The senator who justifies a pork-barrel project has a point. By manipulating a defense contract, he has brought new jobs to an area where they were desperately needed, where the unemployment level of twelve or thirteen percent was tearing families apart.

Even the corporate villain Genessee Industries is very progressive. It may be a world leader in bribery, blackmail, and cost overruns, but it's also a leader in convict-rehabilitation programs, cancer research, day care, and outreach to inner-city ghettos. Actually, Genessee is just an instrument for the benevolent behind-the-scenes despots. "Through its massive resources those privileged to execute Genessee's policies would be capable of rushing in where national problems were critical—before those problems disintegrated into chaos. . . . There were unemployment areas pulled out of the doldrums by Genessee; labor disputes settled reasonably [i.e., by Mario de Spadante's goons, but it sounds pretty sensible if you don't stop to think about the methods] in scores of strike-bound plants; companies saved from bankruptcy. . . . The Genessee laboratories were working on major socioscientific studies that would be invaluable in the areas of ecology and pollution. Inner-city disease crises had been averted with Genessee medical units. . . . The key to these successes was in the ability to move quickly and commit vast sums. Sums not hampered by political considerations. Sums allocated by the judgment of an elite corps of wise men, good men, men dedicated to the promise of America. An America for all, not a few. It was simply the method."

That sounds like a pretty good deal. And while Genessee's methods may not always be legal, Trevayne is reminded that if he obstinately exposes all the abuses, the result could be the dissolution of Genessee Industries and economic disaster for the entire country. As readers, we're all for Trevayne the reformer, but we have to admit that too many revelations from his subcommittee could cause far more harm than good.

Is the President involved? "Nixon knew," but there's no evidence that the character in this book did. Ludlum clearly has a lot of respect for the presidency, if not for the incumbent President at the time he wrote this. In TREVAYNE, the President is the most consistently balanced thinker. Where some of the bad guys have rationalizations, he has reasons. Ultimately he will very neatly sandbag the subcommittee's report, but even then his reasons are decent.

In the writing of John le Carré and Len Deighton, moral lines blur because the good guys are none too good. In Ludlum's world, the bad guys aren't all bad. To further complicate matters, Trevayne isn't above some very unsavory manipulation; on two different occasions he blackmails three people, all to advance his noble pursuits. Nineteen years after he wrote TREVAYNE, Ludlum can still quote George Bernard Shaw on the subject: "If you have a statement to make, make damned sure that your villains have the best arguments." In Ludlum's own words: "If your villain's a straw man, your heroes are straw." TREVAYNE, perhaps more than any of the other books, takes this concept to its thought-provoking extreme. At what point does cynical expedience (neatly summed up as a "trains run on time" policy) become admirable realism? It's a very good question, and TREVAYNE doesn't provide any easy answers. Of course TREVAYNE is still a Robert Ludlum novel, and there are four wild plot flip-flops in the last forty pages.

———————————————

By now Ludlum readers have come to know and love shady deals, especially shady deals involving Nazi Germany. **THE RHINEMANN EXCHANGE** is virtually a slow-motion close-up replay of one of those deals.

It opens with a brief flash-forward. David Spaulding is leaving the U.S. Army on his own terms. He has stripped his uniform of its insignia, even the national initials. What has he been through to make him so bitter?

When the story begins, David Spaulding is a typical Ludlum hero. Trained as a construction engineer, he has an unusual background in languages, thanks to his globe-hopping musician parents. In 1939 there isn't much call for construction engineers, so he has been supporting himself acting in radio dramas. His background attracts the attention of American military intelligence. Even though the United States is scrupulously staying out of the war, someone is looking ahead, and the United States needs an undercover presence in Lisbon. David Spaulding is recruited and sent to the brutally effective training camp in Fairfax, Virginia, under the direction of Colonel Ed Pace. In Lisbon he proves to be a very successful agent. His abilities grow with the challenges and dangers he faces, and by the time he is ready to join the plot, he is no longer an amateur.

Now it's 1943, and both sides are having their problems prosecuting the war. The new V weapons hold out great promise for Germany; they may not win the war, but perhaps they can force a settlement. But just as the V-2 is ready to go into mass production, the facility at Peenemünde runs into a critical shortage of industrial diamonds. Meanwhile, Allied bombing raids are losing effectiveness and taking unnecessary casualties because their high-altitude guidance systems are unreliable.

In Berlin they look to the maps; is there anywhere that the Reich could conveniently conquer a diamond mine? A military solution is eventually ruled out, and they realize that they must look for a nonmilitary solution.

In Washington, D.C., General Alan Swanson, Colonel Pace, and highly placed Undersecretary of State Frederic Vandamm meet with aircraft industry executives Howard Oliver and Jonathan Craft and their technical expert, Gian Spinelli. To these men, and in particular the obese Oliver, the "arsenal of democracy" is just a chance to make enormous profits. It's a very adversarial meeting in which the businessmen don't see why they shouldn't be paid for their aircraft just because the lack of a reliable guidance system renders those aircraft largely useless. To them the situation is urgent because they want their check; to Swanson and Vandamm the situation is urgent because accurate bombing is needed to pave the way for Overlord. The fat cats call in Walter

Kendall, schemer and cooker of books par excellence. He offers hugely lucrative subcontracts to virtually everyone with a research lab.

They're feeling the crunch in Germany too. Reich Official Wilhelm Zangen meets with von Schnitzler, Heinrich Krepps, and Johann Dietrich and learns that all efforts to synthesize diamonds have failed. Finally someone brings up another nonmilitary solution in a conversation that exemplifies Robert Ludlum's view of human nature (not all humans, but enough to change the course of events in some cases):

> "We are suggesting that shipments can be sidetracked, destinations altered in neutral territories. By the expedient of omitting normal security precautions. Acts of incompetence, if you will; human error, not betrayal."
>
> "Extraordinarily profitable mistakes," summed up von Schnitzler.
>
> "Precisely," said Wilhelm Zangen.
>
> "Where do you find such men?" asked Johann Dietricht in his high-pitched voice.
>
> "Everywhere," replied Heinrich Krepps.

General Swanson eventually learns that the sorely needed gyroscopic guidance system has been perfected—in Germany. In Germany they know that the Allies need the mechanism. They haven't been able to buy anyone with money; maybe they can buy someone with the gyros, which are a product of Peenemünde. The Germans offer a deal, and word reaches Swanson. Their mediator will be Erich Rhinemann, a Jew exiled to Argentina. Rhinemann is filthy rich, and although he knows what's happening in Germany, he still hasn't gotten the message; he supports the Nazis, and he's more conservative than they are. Everyone assumes that after the war, win or lose, the final solution will be rescinded, and then Rhinemann will return with his money and his expertise to rebuild Germany in victory or defeat.

The Germans arrange a meeting in Geneva. Swanson sends the devious, perverted, unsanitary Kendall; the Germans send the overweight, nervous, perverted, expendable Dietricht. They agree to make the exchange in Buenos Aires.

The American fat cats are far gone in their thinking by the time they get Kendall's report. " 'We've [the Germans and Americans] got a common enemy and it's not each other,' " says one. " 'Hitler's generals there, the War Department here,' " agrees another. They need a technical expert who won't talk, so Kendall finds one who can't. Eugene Lyons was once a promising young physicist, but he took to drink because of marital problems. Eventually he burned out his throat with raw alcohol, and he has spent four years in jail. He's still got it intellectually, but he's a recluse and it takes two husky male nurses to keep him from falling off the wagon.

Swanson has been keeping these devious arrangements at arm's length, but he knows of the plans for Rhinemann. He realizes that this transaction will make Rhinemann far too powerful in the postwar world, so Rhinemann has to go. So does Kendall, but the slovenly accountant sees ahead to this and protects himself with elaborate blackmail schemes. Swanson needs his own man in Buenos Aires. The agent will have to be fluent in Spanish and German, able to understand complex engineering, and a proven killer. There's only one natural choice, David Spaulding.

David is furious at being pulled out of Lisbon. He doesn't like what he has to do and he's still sickened by killing, but he knows that he is making a contribution to the war effort. While his plane refuels at Lajes Field in the Azores, he gets the first part of his assignment: travel to New York and learn all he can about aircraft blueprints. The plane explodes on takeoff, and David barely escapes. Was this an attempt on his life, or random sabotage? Sifting through the wreckage, investigators find the insignia of the Haganah welded to a strut.

A new plane is arranged, and David makes it to New York, where his cover story is that he has been discharged from the Army due to injury. He has barely arrived when he runs into Leslie Hawkwood, an old girlfriend who has since been married and divorced. She says she looked him up, but she's lying about details she can't possibly know. While he is out with her, getting an extremely thorough welcome to New York, his hotel suite is searched—and later Leslie is nowhere to be found! On New Year's Eve a mysterious stranger stops David at gunpoint and warns him not to deal with Altmuller. We know that Altmuller, a close associate of Albert Speer's, has been orchestrating the deal; David has never heard of him. And the man is not really a stranger, it's David's cryptographer from Lisbon. David calls Pace to ask what the man is doing in New York, only to learn that Pace has been killed within the supposedly secure compound at Fairfax. Another unknown man will threaten David in an elevator, warning him again not to deal with Altmuller and asking him where "Tortugas" is. Tortugas is the name for the gems-for-gyros deal, but David knows it only as a code word in his dossier at Fairfax. Later the same group will try to kill him.

David flies to Buenos Aires. He meets Ambassador Henderson Granville and Granville's daughter-in-law, the lovely widow Jean Cameron. He's barely getting settled when he notices two armed men watching him from the roof of his apartment building. They can't be trying to kill him, because they passed up an early chance. Jean and David hit it off extremely well. Their developing relationship is relatively believable, but they wind up in bed in practically record time.

Moving on to less pleasant pursuits, David realizes that he is being followed. He tries to overcome the surveillance team and winds up unconscious in an alley—but not before he learns that the watchers are from the Gestapo! Kendall has flown to Buenos Aires, and David confronts him with his knowledge of Gestapo involvement. According to Kendall, the gyro designs were stolen by the German underground and are merely being sold by Rhinemann, so the Gestapo's interest fits his story very well. Then Kendall remembers a plane he has to catch, and suddenly he's gone back to New York.

Kendall left without giving David a way to contact Rhinemann, but no need to worry; the contact man calls David. He's Heinrich Stolz, an undersecretary at the German embassy, and he's very aware of David's exploits in Lisbon. At a meeting he probes David's grasp of the deal and confirms that David knows nothing of the diamonds.

After meeting with Stolz, David is strolling through downtown Buenos Aires when he spots—Leslie Hawkwood. He accosts her and drives her out of town in a rented car so he can ask her some questions. She explains that she tried to save his life in New York, not set him up. She has a cause which she won't reveal; she's been following orders without knowing the reasons behind them. He's about to take her back to the embassy when armed men pull up in a Duesenberg and drive away with her.

Later David is dining with Jean. It would be a pleasant evening except that she's upset that he's keeping secrets from her and courting death. " 'The rules are different [for an agent]' " he explains. " 'That is, the rules don't have any meaning . . . there aren't any rules for these people.' " Then he is called away to a meeting with Rhinemann. The exiled financier is extremely security-conscious, and has David and Stolz switch cars. The precautions are justified, because someone really is following them.

The Rhinemann homestead is known ominously as Habichtsnest, roughly translated as "the Hawk's Lair." Experienced fans know that it must be a veritable fortress, but for now we see only that it is huge and obviously very expensive. As a result of the meeting, Rhinemann realizes that he isn't being told the full picture by Berlin.

As David is being driven back to Buenos Aires, the car is followed. Rhinemann's chauffeur tries to get away, but a pitched gun battle ensues; Rhinemann's Bentley just happens to have a convenient set of gun ports. Everyone dies except David. Examining the corpses, he finds that one of his attackers has a number tattooed on his arm—a number that would have been affixed only at a concentration camp.

" 'What kind of world do you live in?' Jean asked the question with concern, not humor. 'One that you'll help me leave.' " But David is still in his undercover world, and now he's off to investigate a couple of shady waterfront warehouses. They appear inactive but they're heavily guarded by Rhinemann's men, and nearby is a trawler whose destination is listed as Tortugas.

Lyons has arrived in Buenos Aires, so Rhinemann's minions bring David and the plans to Lyons's apartment, pausing only to terminate a hired killer who's after David. Who hired the killer? The Jews? The Gestapo? American aircraft manufacturers out to stop one of the competitors from gaining a major advantage? Lyons approves the first installment of the plans, and the plans remain in the apartment with heavily armed German guards. The physicist's minders are more than just nurses, and they don't like giving up their own guns.

David is walking down a street full of surveillance personnel when Leslie Hawkwood stops and gives him a lift. She's in Buenos Aires to stop him, and she blurts out the names of those who need to be stopped: Altmuller, Rhinemann, Tortugas, Peenemünde, and " 'those pigs in Washington,' " and she's not referring to the offensive line of the Washington Redskins. Her people will kill Lyons and his guards. David cold-cocks her and hurries to the apartment, where he finds a massacre. The guards outside are dead in their cars, the guards inside and the male nurses are dead on the floor. Lyons is fine, and he's hidden the plans very effectively. Three assailants in stocking masks are trying to make him give up the plans, but David gets the drop on them and has Lyons remove their personal arsenals.

The attackers are from the Haganah. Their leader, Asher Feld, explains the designs-for-diamonds deal and Altmuller's involvement. They didn't blow up his plane—that was done by a far-out and short-sighted splinter group—and they're glad David survived. The Haganah were the "Gestapo" in Buenos Aires and killed Ed Pace in Fairfax. They're especially concerned about the V-weapon program because it might force a settlement of the war, and that settlement could allow the Nazis to continue the Final Solution.

Lyons and David are on the move. They hog-tie two Marines from the embassy and take their car. The diamonds must be on the trawler, so now David is swimming half naked through the filthy harbor. He clambers onto the ship, where he finds the diamonds and the team of experts sent out to inspect them. He takes a few packets of diamonds for evidence and smashes every microscope optic he can find. The guards are alerted, but David gets away into the harbor with only a superficial wound.

Lyons is gaining confidence and ability and breaking out of his shell, and he pulls David out of the harbor. By this point the embassy wants to disown David and ship him back to the States, but Jean finds him a safe

Gentlest looking attack dog I ever saw, the Chamonix Alps (THE AQUITAINE PROGRESSION)

house. He gets himself patched up and arranges to meet Rhinemann; by claiming that he is in the deal for personal profit, he will try to dupe Rhinemann out of the designs and the names of the American conspirators.

Stolz calls; they have captured Jean and taken her to Habichtsnest. David's presence is requested. Now we see the estate "backstage" with its electrified fences, armed guards, and killer Dobermans. Altmuller has flown out to protect the deal, and after some tense bluffing and counterbluffing he believes that David will let it go through if the price is right. David is allowed to call Ballard, the cryptographer at the embassy, and manages to convey the situation during a supposedly innocuous phone call.

After Lyons verifies the plans, he and Jean are driven back to the embassy. She gets a message to Asher Feld. Now David sends the release code, allegedly to lift all air and sea activity and allow the trawler to rendezvous with a submarine. The real message is "Destroy Tortugas!"

Feld and his men attack the estate, and David has timed his escape to take advantage of the confusion. He kills Rhinemann and Altmuller, and the Haganah captures the designs. David will fly back to the States, but the men in Washington have ordered his execution!

As the sun sinks slowly in the west and the trawler full of diamonds presumably sinks rapidly in the Atlantic, we have something of a happy ending. Swanson kills himself when he sees what he has created. The Haganah agent at Fairfax vanishes with a pile of secret files on concentration camp officials. Ballard gets the execution order voided. Lyons has a lucrative new job, and he's scheduled for surgery to restore his voice. David confronts Kendall, Oliver, and Craft. He could kill them—but he'll let them go to work on postwar reconstruction at low government salaries. He himself has been wounded physically and mentally, but that should heal with time and Jean's love.

THE CRY OF THE HALIDON takes Robert Ludlum, or, rather, "Jonathan Ryder," into the realm of the conventional secret-agent saga. The Jamaican setting, the hidden city in the middle of the jungle, the innocuous-looking car loaded with weaponry, armor, and communications equipment—James Bond would feel right at home with any or all of these. The primary British agent, R. C. Holcroft, even shares Bond's rank of Commander. He's not licensed to kill, but he doesn't let that stand in his way.

Along with the trappings of more conventional espionage fiction, HALIDON abounds with the touches we have come to expect from Ludlum. The hero is manipulated and lied to. The apparent plot and the apparent allegiances shift rapidly and repeatedly. I probably couldn't keep track without taking notes, but I was able to identify no fewer than seven different factions, each with its own goals and agenda, all working at cross-purposes in a wild kaleidoscope of uneasy alliances and unclear relationships—and that's not counting the three other secret services with a vested interest in the proceedings!

Alex McAuliff is a young, highly regarded American surveyor with a slightly checkered past and rather peculiar banking habits. He's minding his own business in London when he receives a peculiar offer from a peculiar filthy-rich gentleman named Julian Warfield. Why does Warfield insist on clandestine meetings? Why does he offer an outrageous sum of money? It appears to be a routine surveying job in Jamaica, and if Warfield's conglomerate Dunstone, Ltd., is planning to build a city there, that's what Dunstone does for a living.

Within an hour of his meeting Warfield, McAuliff has a visitor in his hotel room. It's not room service, it's R. C. Holcroft of MI5. Holcroft helpfully informs McAuliff that his survey team won't be the first on this job. There was another team, but all of its members, including a British agent, have disappeared and are presumed dead!

There's more, of course. The multinational Dunstone, Ltd., isn't just planning to build a city, it's planning to set up its own government of the island or else coopt the existing government. The new government will establish international banks whose procedures for secrecy will make the Swiss seem positively loquacious by comparison. There's a good chance that Dunstone will have McAuliff killed if he declines the commission or talks. Holcroft basically blackmails the young surveyor into working with MI5 by convincing him that it's the only way for him to have protection.

McAuliff is put through extremely quick basic training. " 'You'll find it quite acceptable to operate on two different levels,' " Holcroft explains. At this point McAuliff is shuttling between clandestine meetings with Dunstone and clandestine meetings with MI5, so he's operating on two different levels already. Meanwhile, both Dunstone and MI5 are aware of the mysterious "Halidon," which has its own agents operating in London. Two of Halidon's men take cyanide rather than risk capture; these are fanatics who will protect their organization's secrecy with their lives.

Having accepted the surveying job, McAuliff puts together his team. They're all highly qualified, but we soon learn that they all have skeletons in their closet. The lovely Alison Booth will quickly become his romantic interest, but her ex-husband was a drug courier who married her just so he could use her professional travels as a cover. She's rid of him now, but she's done undercover work for Interpol, and the ex-husband's organization has a long memory. Now she'll never be safe from the organization and the sinister Marquis de Chatellerault.

The team's checkered past becomes even more apparent after they arrive in Jamaica. Sam Tucker, "a one-man Peace Corps with a vibrating crotch" and the only one who has worked with McAuliff before, disappears before McAuliff is reunited with his luggage. Young James Ferguson is feigning drunkenness and following McAuliff. He used to work for the plutocratic Craft Foundation until he was messily fired; now Craft offers him a lavish inducement to stay with McAuliff's party, and he is manipulated into detouring the missing luggage so that electronic bugs can be placed into it. Charles Whitehall has acquired a veneer of British culture over his Jamaican origins, but he still has covert political connections in Jamaica. " 'I'm a Fascist. Fascism is the only hope for my island.' " And why is he meeting with the Marquis de Chatellerault?

It seems as though the only innocent members of the team are the Jensens, husband and wife scientists. But soon they are decoding a secret cable. Their hidden loyalty is to Dunstone, which has an iron grip on them because of a dark chapter in their past. Soon everyone in McAuliff's party has secret alliances and secret agendas.

McAuliff gets the message that a Dr. Piersall has news of the missing Sam Tucker. Before McAuliff can reach him, Piersall is run over by a car and killed. Traveling through downtown Kingston, dodging pursuers with the enthusiastic and skillful aid of a taxi driver, McAuliff is now well and truly enmeshed in the world of espionage. He meets his emergency contact with MI5 in a luxury fish store and announces confidently that he has figured out the identity of Halidon. Now all British intelligence has to do is to mop up the secret organization, and McAuliff will be free to carry out his survey in peace. Experienced readers know, however, that with 256 pages to go, this is not the definitive solution. A few pages later McAuliff is back in the hotel, prying the bugs out of his suitcase and lying to Alison.

Soon he meets his link to Halidon, but they, too, are searching for the mysterious organization. Sam Tucker is with them, Charles Whitehall is with them, and it's good to learn that the murdered Professor Piersall was with them. It is not so reassuring to learn that Halidon had men planted inside MI5. Later we will learn that half of MI5's West Indies section consists of moles from Halidon and the other half consists of moles from Dunstone. Piersall may be dead, but he has left the results of his scholarship behind. Two opposing Jamaican political factions, both represented on McAuliff's team, put aside their differences long enough to kill a local policeman and unearth old documents from in and around Piersall's mansion. The papers tell a grim tale of events beginning two centuries before, and finally identify Halidon as a tribe—sort of.

The survey group does have to do some surveying, and they begin on a beach at the edge of the jungle. From out of the green depths come mysterious, terrifying sounds that none can explain. And if this isn't unnerving enough, we learn that McAuliff is marked for death if only so that his demise will shake up the various factions and make them reveal their identities.

Finally the survey group moves into the sprawling jungle known as the Cock Pit. A fifteen-minute flight from downtown Montego, the jungle teems with fiercely competitive life. "The sounds of screeching bat and parrot and tanager intruded on the forest's undertones; jungle rats and mongoose could be heard intermittently in their unseen games of death. Every now and then there was the scream of a wild pig, pursuing or in panic." Or as the coolly British Peter Jensen puts it, " 'Majestic place in its way, rather.' " There's more to the forest than animals and undergrowth; the survey team soon finds it to be a place of fertile soil and untapped mineral riches. They're still trying to find the

Halidon, and their best hope is to make contact with the Colonel of the Maroons. The holder of this hereditary post holds great sway over the inhabitants of the jungle.

McAuliff never meets the Colonel of the Maroons (an omission that I found very disappointing) because the Halidon finds McAuliff first. The surveying party is held at its camp while McAuliff and his captors trek into the heart of the jungle, where he finally beholds a secret village concealed within the mountains. There he learns that Halidon is many things: a plan for the development of a free Jamaica, a multinational Eden with representatives everywhere, a religious cult, and a dispense of anonymous charity worldwide. Halidon also has its no-more-Mr.-Nice-Guy side. McAuliff is returned to a hotel in Montego Bay and instructed to watch the news; soon Halidon will begin operations against the corrupt Dunstone. And sure enough, the television begins to flash reports of international killings. The victims are all distinguished businessmen and politicians, all of them deeply (but not demonstrably, not to a court of law) involved in cynical, dishonest deals.

Halidon is exposing "the tip of the Dunstone iceberg," but Dunstone is striking back, killing Halidon agents—and they're after McAuliff and Holcroft. These two are now in a very uneasy alliance: "'I don't trust liars. Or manipulators. And you're both, Holcroft.'" "'We all do what we can.'"

There is a violent chase through the city of Montego Bay. Holcroft may have seemed to be mainly an administrator, and a fatuous one at that, but he is now revealed to be a very competent professional—and McAuliff is learning fast. It's action all the way to the finale now as McAuliff calls on his rusty piloting skills and flies into the jungle to save Alison and Sam. The surveying team is now stalking the killers from Dunstone who are stalking them. Charles Whitehall's martial-arts skills finally come in handy.

The ending is short and remarkably neat. The bad guys mainly get what's coming to them, the good guys mainly are rewarded. You can finally tell most of the players without a program, and two or three rival factions will try to shape the emerging Jamaica according to their own visions, without the interference of greedy outside elements. Alex McAuliff and Alison Booth are free to live their own lives together, unthreatened by MI5 and Dunstone. Whew!

Robert Ludlum's next book was something completely different, so different that he didn't even use the Ryder pen name for it. **THE ROAD**

TO GANDOLFO was published under the name of Michael Shepherd in 1975 and didn't appear under Ludlum's name until 1982.

If some Ludlum thrillers seem at times to be teetering perilously close to inanity, GANDOLFO crosses the line early on and keeps on teetering gloriously. You could think of it as Ludlum meets Dortmunder, but actually it has more in common with Donald E. Westlake's hilarious early works such as *The Fugitive Pigeon, The Busy Body,* and *God Save the Mark.* Westlake's penny-ante criminals inhabit a milieu of dingy bars and cheap motels, while GANDOLFO features and parodies Ludlum's usual five-star settings and international scenarios. Messrs. Westlake and Ludlum happen to have the same accountant, but I doubt that this is how THE ROAD TO GANDOLFO was inspired.

What's funny about blackmail and kidnapping, about acts that could get a promising young lawyer disbarred or dismembered? If you can't imagine, read THE ROAD TO GANDOLFO—and read it before you read on!

General MacKenzie Hawkins is the prototypical warrior, a legend in his own time. Major Sam Devereaux is the reluctant soldier, a virtual prisoner in his own army through a string of ludicrous coincidences. When they meet, they will be an odd couple indeed.

Hawkins is in China on a diplomatic mission, which is no job for a straight-talking, straight-thinking general. He's also a straight-shooting old warhorse, and one night in Son Tai Square he defaces a ten-foot jade statue with a couple of deft pistol shots—actually, defaces isn't quite the correct word, he degenitalizes it. This puts delicate trade talks in jeopardy, and the government decides that the talks are more important than Hawkins. They assign an Army lawyer to dig up the dirt on him and placate the Chinese, and naturally their choice is Sam Devereaux.

Hawkins could save himself with a simple apology, but he insists that he was drugged when he shot the statue, and he stands his ground. " 'Americans don't crawl!' " Instead, he escapes from house arrest and breaks into the U.S. embassy compound. There they want no part of him: " 'No one's home, sir.' "

At about the time MacKenzie Hawkins is scaling the embassy and urinating off the roof, Sam is in California, meeting his four ex-wives. They usually get together on Thursdays, but they've called a special session. Fans of Ludlum know that he is rarely graphic about the details of sex: "I don't think it's necessary to pull out *Gray's Anatomy.*" But in THE ROAD TO GANDOLFO he has checked thoroughly under M for mammaries in describing Hawkins's Harem.

With photos of Hawkins on the roof, the government has all it needs—but Sam is dispatched to China just in case. Regina Sommerville

Hawkins Clark Madison Greenberg, leader of the Harem, shows up at his hotel to give him a rousing sendoff.

The two mismatched soldiers meet in Mac's prison cell, right after the General punches out Devereaux by way of greeting. Mac finally agrees to give the Chinese their face-saving apology and get out of the Army. All he wants is three days to do the final evaluation of his old G-2 files, which regulations state he is supposed to do anyway.

Sam will later learn to his horror that he has to escort Mac into the files—and Mac announces that he wants to hire Sam as his lawyer. Sam has grave doubts about both roles, but it's either go along or see old charges reopened by another general who's an old friend of Hawkins's. Soon he finds himself escorting a bulging briefcase *out* of the archives.

> "Oh, Christ! You removed raw files on subjects that weren't *yours?*"
> "No, Sam," replied the Hawk as he squared off some pages, "*you* did. It says so right at the security desk. Your signature."
> Devereaux sank back in the couch. "You devious son of a bitch."
> "That kind of says it," agreed Hawkins sadly.

Sam gets his discharge—and a retainer—from the Shepherd Company, Hawkins's new corporation. His first job is to check out a prospective investor who just happens to be Mafia bigwig Angel Dellacroce. Then he's supposed to make up an open-ended corporate filing. The next thing he knows, he's in bed with a luscious would-be actress, he's the secretary-treasurer of Shepherd, and Angel Dellacroce is on the phone. Hawkins will meet the mafioso at midnight on a deserted golf course.

Sam comes along very unwillingly and shivers in his shoes while Hawkins takes out a dozen or so dim-witted bodyguards. The G-2 files are not only enough to put Dellacroce in jail, they show that he stole from his own people. Faced with the threat of exposure, Dellacroce is only too happy to invest $10 million.

With part of his working capital in place, Mac reveals to Sam his company's plan: They will kidnap Pope Francesco I and extract a ransom of one dollar per Catholic, or four hundred million dollars.

It's off to Geneva for Sam, then on to London. Who should he meet at the Savoy but ex-wife Anne, whose suite just happens to be fifty feet down the hall from his. They rapidly wind up in bed, but then he's off to coerce another investment out of a morally repugnant Briton. Mac calls and reaches him in Anne's suite. His tickets to Berlin are ready.

Sam has just arrived at the plush Kempinsky Hotel when another ex walks into his suite and then into a *long* shower with him. He has to enjoy the cleanliness while he can, because he's whisked away in a foul-

Macao Temple, Sao Pedro, destroyed by fire and typhoon

smelling poultry truck to blackmail a German evil-doer. The chicken feathers and chicken feces have barely settled on his suit when he's off to Algiers via Paris.

Meanwhile, one ex-wife is interviewing the Pope about cuisine—it's a pleasant conversation, but she really wants to know if a special diet will be required once he is in captivity. Another ex-wife interviews the Pope's look-alike cousin, a would-be opera singer with more energy and persistence than talent.

Sam's flight to Algiers is hijacked by fanatics who insist on flying to —Algiers. The hijacking cancels the in-flight meal service, and by now Sam hasn't eaten in over a day. He arrives at his hotel to find the restaurant closed for a religious festival. There's another ex-wife waiting for him, but their impending carnal feast is interrupted by a phone call summoning Sam off to blackmail a sheik. The sheik's advisers pore over the contract interminably, then finally it's time for dinner. The main course will be the sheik's favorite: boiled testicle of camel braised with the stomach of desert rat. And Sam misses even that!

Sam eats his way from Algiers to Zurich. And who should enter his compartment on the Orient Express but the luscious Regina? Fortunately the door can be locked.

MacKenzie Hawkins has been busy recruiting seven soldiers of fortune with shady pasts. Sam wakes up at the Chateau Machenfeld, chosen because it offers secrecy and because the surrounding grounds can be sculpted into a replica of "ground zero." He'll thwart the plot—he'll tell the help about the kidnapping and they'll leave the chateau. Well, he won't get far without clothes! All he has is a pair of boxer shorts, and these won't stay up because the elastic is broken. On closer examination, he finds that it has been cut, and his current bedmate has a pair of scissors on her nightstand. An evil-looking domestic informs him that all his clothes have been taken to the laundry.

Things are looking even worse when Hawkins's henchmen arrive, a group of seven tough, paranoid professionals. Sam tries to explain that they were recruited for a crime that can't possibly come off. He's sure that they'll be grateful to escape with the Swiss bank account numbers he has graciously provided, but there is honor among thieves. They immediately hog-tie him, and only Mac saves him from an impromptu firing squad. The hapless lawyer is still plotting his escape, when who should show up but two more of the ex-wives.

The kidnapping proceeds toward its climax. Like all good comedy thrillers, THE ROAD TO GANDOLFO could perfectly well be played for serious, and the plan is definitely serious and ingenious. The Pope's look-alike but none-too-bright cousin has been relieved of his beard, which he grew to conceal the resemblance, and fitted out in imitation robes. In a relatively nonviolent assault on the motorcade, he is substituted for the Pope.

Sam finally makes good his escape and flies to Rome in a small plane. He arrives at the kidnap site just as the maneuvers are being completed. The Carabinieri are coming, but now the Pope cooperates in his own abduction and runs willingly to the waiting helicopter.

Three weeks later Francesco I is comfortably installed in a papal residence especially constructed at Machenfeld. He's becoming friendly with one of the exes, and Sam is settling down. Hawkins goes to his untraceable communications to send out his ransom demand—but the Vatican doesn't know what he's talking about, because the Pope is right there and doing fine!

In the end, they all live happily at Chateau Machenfeld. Mac brings in horses so that they can ride for exercise. The Pope virtually takes over the kitchen and begins a long and friendly chess rivalry with the General. And after his wild round-the-world series of sexual adventures, Sam finds true love at last.

———————

It's just an iron box, but its contents could rock the world. It is the Vault of Constantine, resting place for many centuries of documents that could shake Christianity to its foundations, setting nation against nation. For ages it has been safe at an obscure Greek monastery; scholars were aware of its existence, but none could say for sure what its potentially shattering contents really were. Now, with Nazi Germany growing stronger by the day and war spreading throughout Europe, the monks of the Order of Xenope know that they must hide their secret trust lest the Nazis find it and use its contents to spread discord that could favor their cause of conquest. Little do they know that they are setting in motion events that will sweep across oceans and across decades, literally pitting brother against brother.

Thus begins **THE GEMINI CONTENDERS**. The idea of the Nazis hunting religious relics for their own twisted purposes seems familiar now, but GEMINI appeared in 1976, five years before *Raiders of the Lost Ark*. We won't learn the contents of the vault until much later in the book, but suffice it to say that they are considerably more plausible than the supernatural powers which George Lucas ascribed to the Ark of the Covenant. Whether the documents would have had the effect that the monks fear is another question. The question is interesting but entirely peripheral to the story; the characters believe that the documents would stand the world of Christianity on its ear, and because they believe it, their search for the vault has an intensity that will fill 411 pages with excitement and leave a trail of corpses in its wake. In characteristic fashion, Robert Ludlum provides first one and then a different explanation of what the vault contains and why a sheaf of ancient parchments could be so explosive. Naturally we believe along with the characters that the documents could reshape the world; we accept the first explanation, then the second. Finally we are left sharing an archeologist's doubts . . . but this is getting ahead of our story.

The Order of Xenope, with its cross-and-thorns emblem, is "the harshest monastic brotherhood under the control of the Patriarchate of Constantine. Blind obedience coexisted with self-reliance; they were disciplined to the instant of death." The monks have renounced worldly things, and their contacts with the world are limited, but they understand enough of the mundane to transport their critical trust in absolute secrecy. With forged papers and deliberately confusing false routings, their train winds its leisurely way through an Italy that is being drawn closer and closer to war. Speed is secondary; concealment is everything. In a remote mountain pass the train's engineer and his brother, the monk, will meet the one man who knows the vault's destination. He is Savarone Fontini-Cristi, fabulously wealthy industrialist and head of a distinguished family.

With the box secreted in its Alpine fastness, the train rolls on, protecting the location of its vital cargo by leaving another meandering false trail. Then, in a crowded railway yard, the secret is given its final protection: the silence of the grave. The monk shoots the engineer—his brother—and then himself.

When we meet Vittorio Fontini-Cristi, the eldest son of Savarone and the heir apparent to the family's industrial empire, we are not impressed. Vittorio is supposedly running the Fontini-Cristi companies, but he has really devoted his energies to fast cars, fast horses, and fast women. While Savarone is meeting with partisans who tell him that a raiding party from Milan is heading toward the family mansion at Campo di Fiori, Vittorio is driving his Hispano-Suiza to an assignation with someone else's wife. He receives the message that he is urgently needed in Campo di Fiori to create the picture of a family gathering. (Naturally the message reaches him after he has completed much of his business with the restless and lovely contessa. He is an expert lover, of course, and unlike nearly all thriller characters, he displays at least a sketchy knowledge of reproductive physiology.)

Vittorio does return to Campo di Fiori, but he is too late. Only Savarone's instructions that he enter the grounds through the stable road will save him from the raiding party. He cannot complete the picture of a happy family gathering, although it is extremely doubtful that this would have made any difference to the implacable raiders in their matching black suits and black coats. The ruthless leader will always be recognizable, thanks to an unusual shock of white in his hair. A family retainer restrains Vittorio from rushing uselessly and suicidally to his family's aid as the raiders herd men, women, and children onto the front steps. Suddenly the night explodes with gunfire, and Vittorio can only watch helplessly as the raiders methodically, impersonally, annihilate his family. But above the roar of German-made automatic weapons, Vittorio can hear Savarone's voice raised in a cryptic message: " 'Champoluc . . . Zurich is Champoluc . . . Zurich is the river.' "

The partisans get Vittorio out of Campo di Fiori and rendezvous with undercover agents of British intelligence. Together they will smuggle Vittorio out of the country—out of harm's way for the duration of the war, if he so chooses. The wastrel playboy is quickly exposed to a world he never dreamed existed, a world where dark forces move beneath the still-peaceful surface of Italy, beneath even the surface of the war that is beginning to convulse all of Europe. It is a world of betrayal, but one in which men entrust their lives to their comrades and their superiors. It is a world in which causes are more important than individuals, in which men willingly sacrifice themselves if need be. And it is a world that Vittorio can fit into with surprising ease. Lying convincingly, fighting in ways he never knew he could, he receives "some very practical on-the-job training."

Although he is offered a chance to sit out the war safely, Vittorio volunteers his services to the Allied cause. He is extensively questioned by men in London who are convinced that he must know where his father hid the Vault of Constantine, but he cannot help them. After his debriefing and a romantic interlude in the blacked-out capital, he finds himself at a top-secret training facility in a remote portion of Scotland. Top-secret training camps in Scotland with chronic bad weather and sadistic drill instructors are a staple of World War II thriller fiction, but Vittorio is being prepared for a most unconventional mission. His team members will be managers and bureaucrats who have fled Nazi-occupied Europe. He will train them into teams of inefficiency experts and infiltrate them back onto the Continent, where they will proceed to foul up the Reich's paperwork. It's an interesting concept, and Ludlum makes it believable. Once again we see his gift for plot at work; Vittorio and his paper pushers from hell could be the premise of an entire novel, but Ludlum has so many ideas that he can dismiss this one in a few pages.

Although he is doing his best on the Allies' behalf, Vittorio—by now known as Victor Fontine—realizes that he is being used and lied to. " 'You're a terrible manipulator!' Fontine laughed [to his MI5 contact]. 'And so obvious.' " Meanwhile, two different British intelligence agencies are maneuvering each other and spying on each other. Their machinations aren't a major part of the plot, but Ludlum fans always enjoy Byzantine intrigue.

Part of the play involves the romantic interest, Jane Holcroft. She would be happy to play house indefinitely, but Victor insists on marrying her. Jane soon finds herself in the middle of a bombing raid that is accurate enough to raise real questions. Are the fanatical monks of Xenope in league with the Germans? Is the Vatican in league with the Germans? Jane survives to bear twin sons.

As the war winds down, Victor returns to Campo di Fiori. He now realizes that one of his coworkers from MI5 is a turncoat, and he kills the man. But Victor is seized by fanatical priests, led by the man with the distinctive shock of white hair, who turns out to be a prominent Cardinal. Under the Cardinal's direction, the priests torture Victor, using nothing but their bare hands to break most of his joints. It's a horrendous picture of zeal gone too far, of human decency sacrificed to fanaticism. Any man would confess under this torture, but Victor can't reveal the hiding place of the vault because he doesn't know it. The Cardinal and his minions leave Victor to die, pausing only to recite the appropriate benedictions.

Victor doesn't die, although he will never walk normally again or have full use of his hands and arms. He returns to England, Jane, and two energetic toddlers, and they decide to emigrate to America. The

Cardinal kills himself; three of the renegade priests are excommunicated and jailed, and two are exiled to South Africa on permanent missions of penance.

When we rejoin the plot, it is 1973 and the twins are grown men. They always fought as children, and now they really can't get along as adults. Andrew is a career soldier, a major in the U.S. Army. Adrian is a bleeding-heart-liberal lawyer. Andrew has a second, secret career. He is part of a select group called Eye Corps, a self-appointed conscience of the military. Strengthened by its own moral certainty, Eye Corps plans to blackmail its way to saving the Pentagon.

Adrian has uncovered the activities of Eye Corps, "eight self-deluded elitists who concealed evidence for their own purposes. . . . Just what the country needed; storm troopers out to save the nation." His Justice Department section, led by a lawyer named Nevins, is about to subpoena everyone involved with Eye Corps.

Also in 1973 Enrico Gaetamo, the most fanatical of the renegade priests, is released from prison. Soon it is old home week. Victor learns of Gaetamo's release and meets others from his past. He realizes that he must return to Campo di Fiori. There he is greeted by an aged Greek priest who tells him that the estate is now owned by the Order of Xenope. Thinking back to his father's dying words, Victor realizes where the clue to the vault must be. He finds the clue, only to look up and see a huge man in black standing over him. It is Enrico Gaetamo, older but still burning with a fanatical zeal, ready to break the rest of Victor's bones if need be. The old priest happens along just in time and shoots Gaetamo.

There is death in Washington too. Nevins is killed in a bizarre accident—or is it? His briefcase full of evidence is gone, and it looks like he took a load of buckshot before a truck tore away the side of his car.

Andrew flies to Vietnam, where he will verify that the Eye Corps files are safe. He has a fair idea who leaked the critical material, and he plans to kill the informer. But before he can carry out his mission, he gets a note recalling him because his father is very sick.

The twins are united briefly at Victor's bedside. "Theirs was now the responsibility of the Fontini-Cristis." Victor gives them his reasoning on where the vault must be, or at least a list of possibilities. The Goldoni family, guides for generations, may be able to help, and likewise the Capomonti family in whose inn the Fontini-Cristis always stayed. He gives them a list of good men in the Vatican who will know what to do with the vault once it's found. The brothers call a truce, but Andrew is lying; he wants the vault for Eye Corps. Although Adrian has delayed the subpoena, Eye Corps is still in deep trouble. The Inspector General's office has struck, and five men are now sitting in maximum-security cells in Saigon. Andrew convinces Adrian that Eye Corps didn't kill Nevins because it would have led the Inspector General straight to them. Actually, unbeknownst to Andrew, a member of Eye Corps *did* order the hit.

Where does Theodore Annaxas Dakakos fit in to all of this? He's a shipping magnate, and son of the original train engineer. Earlier, he called on Victor, and he's looking for Adrian now. Thirty years ago he arranged for the Filioque Denials, supposedly contained in the vault, to be burned—but we know that this was faked. More recently he assembled the information about Eye Corps and fed it to the Inspector General's office.

Andrew steals Adrian's passport and checkbook, and then he's gone, leaving Adrian behind. This delays Adrian somewhat, but he flies to London. He thinks the Inspector General's agents are trailing him to find Andrew, and flying to Paris, he learns that he's right. The amateur with money and imagination beats the professionals at their own game, and soon he's off to Rome unobserved.

Reaching Campo di Fiori in search of the last clue, Andrew is still well ahead of his brother. There's a Maserati in the driveway; Dakakos is there walking with the old priest. Andrew captures them and tries to learn what they are up to. Dakakos breaks away enough to start a struggle in which he is killed. Ever thorough, Andrew administers the coup de grâce to the old priest. We learn later—as Adrian learns by phone that his father has died—that Dakakos was a good guy and wanted to work with Adrian. Adrian arrives at Campo di Fiori to find the sickening stench of decomposing bodies there, and the painting with the last clue gone.

Andrew calls on Alfredo Goldoni. The guide is now an old cripple who lost both legs to exposure after an avalanche that wiped out most of the family. Goldoni seems helpful, but he is concealing his panic. He alerts the rest of the family, but Andrew is hidden in a field outside and sees Goldoni leaving with a huge ledger. He brutalizes and kills the old man's wife after first forcing her to show him the shelf of ledgers. Of course, the missing volume details the climbs made on the date in Victor's recollections.

Adrian flies into Champoluc in a small plane. When he reaches the Goldoni house, the old man almost blows his head off with a vicious sawed-off shotgun called a lupo. Adrian learns that Andrew has the ledger *and* maps *and* a young guide *and* a young woman hostage—but Adrian has the patience to talk to Goldoni, and soon he wins the old man's trust. Together they reconstruct his grandfather's last trip to the mountains, and he learns where the vault must be buried.

Andrew has spent much of his life with maps, and they soon give up their secrets to him. He finds the vault, then shoots his hostages as they try to escape. Adrian is close enough to hear the shots and the screams. He sneaks up as Andrew unearths the vault. In the final showdown, Adrian shoots Andrew, but the soldier fights on. Adrian inflicts a more serious wound, then is forced to finish his brother as Andrew attacks once more.

Fortunately the documents are in airtight containers, small and light enough for Adrian to hike out with them. The young guide is dead, but the girl survives and limps down the mountain with him.

The ending is happy but ambiguous. Eye Corps will be quietly dismantled but not exposed; exposure would cause too many problems for the military. Just in case Adrian wants to call a press conference, the Inspector General's office has plenty of material that would discredit him and ruin his career.

Adrian's girlfriend is an archeologist, so he gets a close view as she works on the ancient documents with one of her old professors and a sympathetic Vatican representative named Land. And in the end, the most terrible document of all is a confession like many others that have been found, more complete but not necessarily more true. Would the foundations of Christianity crumble before it? Land's faith is strong, and he explains that old as it is, the document would be a serious blow to the church. Men and women have died for it and killed for it, but ironically it will become only a footnote to history.

Similar questions of faith and archeology are raised in *The Body*, a quiet, cerebral thriller by Richard Ben Sapir. If you enjoyed the doctrinal aspects of THE GEMINI CONTENDERS, you should look for a copy.

On May 2, 1972, a sick old man passed away. In his prime he was the stuff of legends; in his declining years he was the subject of unsettling rumors. Five years later, Robert Ludlum turned the rumors and speculations into perhaps his finest "conspiracy" novel, **THE CHANCELLOR MANUSCRIPT.**

When we meet Peter Chancellor, he is a graduate student in history at Park Forest University. His thesis, "The Origins of a Global Conflict," is all but assured of prestigious publication, but then it is rejected. In tracing the complicity of the free world's industrial leaders in the rise of Nazi Germany, he has made up meetings and conversations, and he has failed to maintain rigorous standards of documentation. Distinguished elder statesman Munro St. Claire has been spending the semester at Park Forest, and he has some advice for the disheartened student: Why not turn the thesis into a novel?

It seems like a helpful hint, and it will certainly pay off handsomely for Peter. But soon St. Claire is making mysterious phone calls and speaking in code names—his own is Bravo. *"Inver Brass cannot permit you to go on,"* he muses silently, and we learn that he put in the time at Park Forest just so he could engineer the rejection of the thesis. Why? Because " 'he's [Chancellor] right and he knows it.' "

Peter takes the advice and turns the thesis into *Reichstag!* The novel achieves commercial success, if not unquestioned critical acclaim. Peter's rise as a novelist is briefly outlined with reviews of *Reichstag!*, *Sarajevo!*, and *Counterstrike!* (Like another well-known author, he tends to use the same format for his titles.) " 'Mr. Chancellor has a conspiracy complex of a high order,' " notes one reviewer. Scholars will later note that " 'he's hardly a writer of lasting distinction,' " and that " 'he bases his conclusions on intentionally misinterpreted facts and on exaggerated associations.' " Robert Ludlum staunchly denies that he's really Peter Chancellor, even though they both do their best work at an ungodly hour and they're both partial to Ticonderoga No. 2 pencils, but you can't help feeling that Chancellor's press notices are spoofs of Ludlum's. The two authors certainly share a central philosophy. In *Counterstrike!* Chancellor's protagonist must accept great risks to expose "the knowledge that the administration of justice and fairness no longer mattered to the country's leaders." And a major plot device of *Counterstrike!*—sending an amateur into the field to fail and die—is virtually the same as THE MATLOCK PAPER.

Life is good for Peter Chancellor. The royalties are rolling in, and he is engaged to a charming young woman. He's preparing to start work on a new novel about the Nuremberg trials, when an accident changes his life forever. His Lincoln Continental is run off the road by a truck; his fiancée is killed and he is seriously injured.

Now we meet Munro St. Claire's secret organization in more detail. In an obsessively secretive session they discuss highly sensitive files and the aging, paranoid owner of those files—J. Edgar Hoover. They feel that Hoover is getting crazier and crazier, feeding information to the White House which is using it to control the country through blackmail. They make the grim decision to kill Hoover and seize the files.

The accident and his fiancée's death have removed Peter's will to work, so instead he goes to Malibu to consult on the screenplay for *Counterstrike!* He's scarred and still in pain from his injuries, drinking too much and waking up with hangovers. The project is getting away from him, but at least he's getting the girl—in this case, the producer's vapid but buxom wife. As the movie diverges further and further from the book—from what Peter believes to be a true story of domestic meddling by the CIA—he decides that he wants out of the project. The studio is willing to pay him off if he'll just keep quiet; if he won't accept the hush money, they'll blackmail him or destroy his credibility. Why is the studio determined to avoid controversy, even though the most derogatory press conference from Chancellor would be valuable free publicity? The government must be pushing them.

The assassination of Hoover proceeds under the direction of Stefan Varak, an NSC agent who is Inver Brass's man of all undercover work. He stages an elaborate murder designed to look like death from natural causes, then he shows up at the FBI to carry away and destroy the files. But half of the material is missing! Some three thousand files, letters M through Z, are gone, and since the files often dealt in code names, almost anyone could be in the missing section.

The impact of the files begins to surface. General Bruce MacAndrew, noted Pentagon gadfly, and Paul Bromley, a whistle-blowing accountant with the GSA, resign unexpectedly. When Bromley is debriefed, we learn that he resigned because of blackmail threats whispered to him over the phone. And an eight-month chunk of MacAndrew's service record is missing.

Clearly Inver Brass must recover the files. Varak and St. Claire decide to "program" Peter Chancellor; they will send him after the story and use him for bait.

> "Chancellor cannot be allowed to recover. He can't be permitted to function at his previous rational level. He's got to draw attention to himself, to his research. If he remains volatile, he becomes a threat. If that threat is dangerous enough, whoever has those files will be compelled to eliminate it. When he does—or they do—we'll be there."
>
> Bravo [St. Claire] sat forward, his expression one of sudden concern. "I think that goes beyond the parameters we established."
>
> "I wasn't aware we'd established any."
>
> "They were intrinsic. There are limits to our use of Peter Chancellor. They don't include putting his life in jeopardy."
>
> "I submit it's a logical extension of the strategy. Quite plainly put, the strategy may be useless without that factor. I think we'd willingly exchange Chancellor's life for those files. Don't you?"
>
> St. Claire said nothing.

Presenting himself as retired FBI agent Alan Longworth—he matches the man's description down to a very impressive scar—Varak calls on Peter at Malibu. He gradually reveals that Hoover was murdered and that the files are missing. For confirmation, he refers Peter to General MacAndrew and Judge Daniel Sutherland.

The scene shifts to the Washington area. We discover two more blackmail victims: Congressman Walter Rawlins and influential columnist Phyllis Maxwell. Carroll Quinlan "Quinn" O'Brien, an FBI agent and former war hero who used to exchange information with Varak, is introduced. He has been searching to learn the fate of the missing files, but he has his own dark secrets, and a whispered voice on the phone dissuades him from pursuing his hunt.

Peter meets Sutherland, an outsize judge of legendary stature. Sutherland is a black man who rose from an Alabama hovel to the point where the Supreme Court would be a demotion. The jurist explains that he is part of a group that was monitoring Hoover, which is at least partly true. He knows of Longworth, an agent who helped assemble many of the dirty files and is now working to reduce the damage they could cause. Sutherland assures Peter that the files were destroyed, but he doesn't sound convincing.

Peter realizes that "Longworth" led him to MacAndrew as an example: " 'If those files were really missing, in the hands of a fanatic, and this fanatic wanted to use the information against another person—well, you're what that other person would be like.' " He finds the General frightened of something, his wife chronically and pitifully insane. The visit confirms only that blackmail is going on. Driving away, he is run off the road by a mysterious car—a silver Lincoln, the same make, model, and color he was driving when he had his shattering accident. But the Lincoln vanishes, and so does the damage to Peter's rental.

Back at his Washington hotel, Peter meets Phyllis Maxwell and grants her an interview. Later she tells him about Hoover's files and his abuse of them. Then they have desperate, unsatisfactory sex. Peter finally begins to outline his book.

Congressman Rawlins was also visited by "Longworth," so he knows about Peter and arranges a meeting for the early hours at the Cloisters in New York. Suddenly bullets whiz by, fired from silenced weapons. Rawlins is killed, but "Longworth" saves Peter, who will realize that Longworth precipitated the meeting to give Peter another example of a blackmail victim.

General MacAndrew's wife dies of natural causes, then MacAndrew washes up on a beach in Hawaii with two bullet wounds in him. "Longworth's" cover story is that he retired to Hawaii, which the real agent did; the General must have gone after him and gotten himself killed. Reading about the deaths in the newspaper, Peter learns that there is a daughter named Alison. He calls on her and learns of her father's career. He'd been an outspoken critic of Pentagon excesses and the war in Vietnam—exactly like a character that Peter created for his novel! He tells Alison the whole story to date and accompanies her to the airport, where she breaks down as MacAndrew's coffin is rolled off a military cargo plane. This is too much for Peter, and he decides to give up the book. " 'Say you're right,' " remonstrates Alison. " 'Isn't that all the more reason to go on?' "

They fly to Washington for the funeral, and Alison decides they should stay at her parents' house in Rockville, Maryland, because there may be clues there. But the house has been broken into and searched. There is a bloody nightgown on the floor, and the rooms reek of spilled perfume. Painted on the wall, the bloodred enamel still soft, is "MAC THE KNIFE. KILLER OF CHASONG."

Peter learns that Mrs. MacAndrew's insanity followed a near-drowning in 1950 or 1951. At that time Alison was about six, they were living in Tokyo, and the General was involved in leading the Korean War. A few more acts of terror occur, which Peter assumes are directed at Alison—but he's wrong. They're intended for him.

Peter and Alison wind up having sex for mutual comfort. Their physical relationship begins abruptly, but it will soon blossom into true romance. Like many Ludlum protagonists, Peter Chancellor wants a long-term commitment and marriage.

We learn that Chasong was the American forces' worst defeat in North Korea. It corresponds to the missing period in MacAndrew's service file. Varak comes to realize that the missing Hoover files must have been stolen by a renegade member of Inver Brass. We discover that Inver Brass was founded in the depths of the Depression to help alleviate the worst of that dreadful period, and that it has been working behind the scenes ever since to direct the course of history and American government. Its members may have a superior wisdom, which they feel allows them to make decisions for the populace, but they're not infallible. One of their feats of economic engineering had the unfortunate side effect of creating Nazi Germany. This is the connection that Peter stumbled upon in researching his thesis, and why Inver Brass became involved with him. They also did some unfortunate things at Nuremberg, and Peter's earlier "accident" was staged to keep him from pursuing these.

At Arlington, a dark-complexioned officer stares at General MacAndrew's coffin with burning hatred. He is Major Pablo Ramirez, once the token Hispanic at West Point and now a nonrising lightweight at the Pentagon.

Phyllis Maxwell hears that she will be a character in Peter's book; he thinks he disguised her, but it seems that wasn't enough. She calls Peter and insists on meeting him at the house of some friends who are out of town. Suddenly more silenced weapons begin to hurl slugs through the windows. Peter decides to deal with the situation just as one of his characters once did in a similar fix. Using fire as a distraction, he gets himself and Phyllis away as the house burns to the ground. Phyllis leaves town, but another visitor is on his way. Paul Bromley was told somehow that Peter's book would expose him and make good on the blackmailer's threat, so he leaves a phone message that he is planning to kill Peter.

Peter goes to the FBI, where he is fortuitously directed to Quinn O'Brien. O'Brien's career is on the decline, but he has been building up a group of like-minded agents who want Hoover's files destroyed. Peter tells Quinn about the attack on the house; a call to the Washington police confirms that there are shells on the lawn, and now Quinn believes Peter. Peter tells him the whole story, and Quinn agrees to find him protection. The FBI is out, since the pro-Hoover "maniacs" could find out about Peter, so Quinn calls his old working colleague Stefan Varak at NSC and gets a few CIA men on the case.

When Varak finally reaches Peter, it is clear from his voice that he is badly injured. He explains that he tried to stop the attack on the house, and he gives Peter a cryptic set of clues to follow. Pausing only to get shot at and ditch his pursuers, Peter follows the trail to a dying Varak, whose face bears the ugly marks of torture. Varak explains everything he can, including the fact that a traitor at Inver Brass must have the files. He identifies all the members of Inver Brass except Bravo, who he feels is above suspicion. The men who captured and tortured Varak spoke an unfamiliar language—unfamiliar even to the NSC agent, who speaks six or seven—but he recognized the word "Chasong." Chasong is the key; Mrs. MacAndrew, not the General, is the key. Varak dies.

Peter gets back to O'Brien, who tells him about the maniacs, five or six FBI men who want the old regime back. O'Brien thinks that the files are in their hands.

Peter goes off to confront Ramirez, who explains that he is really a general specializing in race relations. He uses the rank of major publicly to make himself more accessible to junior officers and other ranks. The conversation confirms that Chasong is important, but not why.

O'Brien has arranged for Peter and Alison to rendezvous at a secure motel in Quantico. En route, Peter is nearly killed by Bromley. Before the broken, crazed accountant leaps from a moving train, he lets slip information that tells Peter that Munro St. Claire is Bravo. Peter takes Alison through the story of her mother, and he learns the terrible secret that drove her into madness.

Munro St. Claire meets with Peter. The novelist knows that he was manipulated, but he doesn't realize that he's still being manipulated—or that it will probably get him killed along with the traitor. "Even in death Varak orchestrated events." St. Claire has the decency to be very uncomfortable with these manipulations and the callous disregard for Peter's life. " 'Four and a half years ago I steered you into the world of fiction. Go back to that world; leave this one to others.' "

It is the swirling blend of "fact" and "fiction" that makes THE

CHANCELLOR MANUSCRIPT so successful. Peter's book is looking more and more like the "real" events, and many "real" events are presaged in his outline. " 'I invented you before I met you,' " Peter tells a slightly nonplused Quinn O'Brien. Later "the amateur was leading the professional," because vicarious experience taught him what to do. " 'How can you be so sure?' " someone asks Peter about details of intrigue and deception. " 'Because . . . I've invented this sort of thing myself. In books.' " Later we will learn that THE CHANCELLOR MANUSCRIPT is really a novel within a novel within a novel, and we would be hard pressed to decide what is "real" and what is "fiction."

The hero of James Brady's *Six Days of the Condor* is entitled to act like a professional because he's always reading about cloaks and daggers; Peter Chancellor is entitled to act like one because of what he's been writing. But then there's an assault on a safe house. " 'They want us to panic; they're counting on it,' " says O'Brien. Chancellor is still really an amateur, and he has the logical response " 'Why shouldn't we panic?' "

Varak's body is dumped on the lawn and the safe house is destroyed—a safe house O'Brien obtained very illegally. Quinn and Peter are now disowned and discredited; their only hope is to find out who has the files. One by one Peter reaches the members of Inver Brass and blackmails them into meeting. The first is killed by O'Brien, who thinks he's going for a gun. Actually he was pulling out a letter that clears him, so at least they know he was innocent. The second and third also pass. But in talking to Daniel Sutherland, Peter realizes that the judge lied to him earlier. One slip of the tongue and Peter knows that he has found the traitor. Suddenly the dawn erupts in silenced gunfire. Sutherland is cut down by fanatics screaming "Chasong!" Peter and Alison flee. Were they betrayed by O'Brien?

Peter is now well outside the law, but Alison has her own resources and connections. They penetrate the secret of Chasong with the help of a sympathetic Army doctor, Major Philip Brown. The files are signed out to General Ramirez, but that doesn't stop Brown. We learn that all the troops at Chasong were black.

Brown gets them in to see Ramirez, but the General has Brown seized by MPs, and he holds a gun on Peter. He admits that Chasong was genocide, but says it was an accident—which Peter realizes is a lie. Peter overpowers Ramirez, who confesses that he ruined MacAndrew's wife. He pumped her full of drugs and used her to feed false information to the Chinese, who were holding her missionary parents hostage. Ramirez arranged the lethal failure of Chasong by giving correct information to the Chinese. Mrs. MacAndrew was raped at a seedy bar in the Ginza, where she was looking for drugs. Supposedly the rapists were black—actually they could have been any strung-out GI addicts—and the genocidal assault was made to look like MacAndrew's revenge. The whole bloody affair—the rape, the carnage, the supposed evidence of racism—was all created just to cover Ramirez's intelligence operation.

Peter forces Ramirez to call the MPs and have Brown released. Ramirez explains that he removed the eight-month section from Mac-Andrew's service record; this was apparently *routine* with promising officers. He somehow knows about Longworth and about Hoover's files, and he mentions almost casually that Hoover was killed.

This is Peter's first hint that Hoover did not die a natural death, and he is shocked as "life" parallels his book. This means that Inver Brass must have had Hoover killed. Therefore Varak was the killer, and Munro St. Claire must have the files.

Peter meets Munro St. Claire, who gives him the rationalizations of Inver Brass, which ring hollow. " 'Then, you're no better than he [Hoover] is,' " says a character in the manuscript. But when he has the full story, Peter admits, " 'You're better than he was.' " St. Claire convinces Peter that Varak didn't get the missing files, and he becomes Peter's ally. Together they figure out who the traitor must be.

But then there's a gunshot and in strides Sutherland, who had faked his own death. He's followed by five black commandos speaking that unfamiliar language, which turns out to be Ashanti. They gun down Munro St. Claire.

Sutherland explains that he has killed the remainder of Inver Brass as well. He has a large organization that reaches everywhere, even into the State Department. They used Peter Chancellor, and they used the pro-Hoover fanatics at the FBI. Now they will use the files for good—the ultimate civil rights program, achieved through blackmail.

Peter will have to die, of course, but Sutherland generously offers to let Alison and Major Brown live if Peter will lead him to O'Brien, who did not betray Peter and Alison. Peter calls O'Brien to arrange a meeting, and laces his conversation with cryptic messages. O'Brien comes through and wipes out the murder squad. Sutherland kills himself.

In the end the files rest with Sutherland's son, a radical lawyer. He says he burned the files, and Peter believes him. Now he can live peacefully with Alison—but what will he do for a sequel?

THE HOLCROFT COVENANT blends the usual ingredients of a Ludlum thriller with those of more conventional secret agent fare. Noel Holcroft is a typical Ludlum hero, an amateur in over his head. Over the course of the book he will be lied to and manipulated by professionals.

It's 1945, and the Third Reich is being consumed in a final conflagration. Every man, every piece of materiel, is needed in a last-ditch effort to salvage at least a more favorable peace treaty. Yet at a top-secret pier, a U-boat that can ill be spared from its military duties is taking on a cargo of—children? Yes, and this is one of many contingents being brought out of the dying regime. They're not all boys and they're not from Brazil, but they're the seeds of the Fourth Reich. Their intended future will be revealed to us gradually; even if you accept the pseudo-scientific premise behind Ira Levin's quintessential thriller (*The Boys From Brazil* preceded THE HOLCROFT COVENANT by about two years), Robert Ludlum's scheme for reestablishing German domination over the world is considerably more plausible.

We now jump ahead to the 1970s. Noel Holcroft is in Geneva, meeting with Herr Manfredi, the director of a Swiss bank. But rather out of keeping with staid Swiss financial practices, the meeting takes place on a train at the Geneva station. Noel should have known that sooner or later he would be involved in some sort of unusual affairs; although he has lived almost all of his life as an American, his father was Heinrich Clausen, one of the major financial architects of the Third Reich. His background is perfectly legitimate—his mother divorced Clausen in absentia and married an American, who adopted Noel—but it is shrouded in secrecy. His 1939 birth in Berlin is covered by a false death

Paris (THE BOURNE IDENTITY AND THE BOURNE ULTIMATUM)

certificate issued in London in 1942, and there is an equally false document that says he was born in New York.

Manfredi has a letter for Noel from Heinrich Clausen—and $780 million! The money was smuggled out of Germany when Clausen and his colleagues realized what they had created and were horrified by it. The funds will be released under a stringent set of conditions, with orders that they be used for charity to make amends to the victims of the Holocaust. Noel will be handsomely paid for his work as executor. But if the intentions are beneficent, why is there another letter, elaborately sealed, written by anonymous fanatics and threatening him from beyond the grave? Or are these good fanatics, part of the failed plot to kill Hitler at Wolfsschanze? And who is the man with the distinctive salt-and-pepper eyebrows watching Noel on the station platform, and who are the two others who are apparently after him? Soon bullets are flying, but Noel gets away with his instructions. To release the money he must locate the eldest children of Heinrich Clausen's two co-conspirators, Erich Kessler and Wilhelm von Tiebolt. If they are dead or unwilling, younger siblings will do, but all must be acceptable to the bank. One set of offspring is living openly in Germany, but the other family went to Brazil and then disappeared without a trace.

Noel has a lot to mull over as he flies home to New York. He's in the lounge of the 747 when a fellow passenger sips his scotch, then convulses and dies. Was the poisoned drink meant for Noel? Was it diverted by two shady passengers who later disappear, passengers whose passports have a dubious and disturbing provenance? Or were the other two passengers supposed to kill Noel?

Mercifully unaware of the gunplay at the airport, Noel returns to his apartment to find it subtly rearranged, presumably by someone searching it. He gets a phone call from an MI6 agent who wants to meet with him and warn him, but the call is suddenly cut off and the agent is killed. There is a yellowing note in the apartment, written in the same Germanic printing as the letter from the fanatics of Wolfsschanze. Who broke into the apartment? If Noel ever had a chance of learning, he loses it when the doorman of his building is killed. His banker dies as well, an apparent suicide. Clearly someone isn't fooling around here, but we have no idea who.

Noel discusses the situation with his rich, strong-willed mother. (She gets extra points in my books because she disapproves of Noel's smoking.) She doesn't trust anything to do with her late first husband, but she appears to go along with his plan of restitution. After Noel leaves, however, she makes a mysterious phone call to Geneva. Noel arranges to leave his business—he is an architect who has achieved critical acclaim if not financial success: "He was taking himself out of a garden he had cultivated to work in an unfamiliar forest."

Clearly the first item on the agenda is to locate the offspring of von Tiebolt. Living in New York, Noel is within walking distance of many consulates, so he goes to see a Brazilian attaché. The problem is difficult, the attaché explains, because many people arrived in Brazil under assumed names " ' "sometime in the forties" . . . such people as you speak of do not disappear without cause.' " Actually the problem is even more difficult than Noel could realize, because the attaché isn't who he appears to be. He knows who Noel is, he knows about the plane flight, and he infers correctly that Noel is looking for the von Tiebolts.

Since the consulate can't or won't help, Noel is soon on a plane to Rio de Janeiro. One of his fellow passengers is the man with the salt-and-pepper eyebrows, last glimpsed amid the chaos at the Geneva station. In Rio, Noel wades through the musty archives at the immigration office. Many of the papers are false, many have been altered according to an ingenious and deliberately frustrating pattern. The rules imposed on Noel as a researcher are specifically designed to make his reading as unproductive as possible, and he fails to turn up any leads.

Back in his hotel, he sees evidence that the room has been searched. He receives a mysterious phone call from a woman known only as Cararra; later he will meet with her and her brother, and they are able to provide him with some clues. He learns that she was once the fiancée of Johann von Tiebolt. They claim to be Portuguese Jews, yet they are given to saying "Mother of God" in moments of stress. Later Noel will learn that everything they have told him is a lie—at least according to another character, who also may be lying.

Noel's research leads him to Maurice Graff, an immensely rich leader of the German community in Brazil. Herr Graff—excuse me, now it's Senhor Graff—is allegedly from the Wolfsschanze group. They have a cordial meeting at the German expatriate's palatial estate, and Noel learns that Graff is very aware of his search—and mentions the Tinamou, although Noel has no idea what or who the Tinamou is. Then Noel mentions the von Tiebolt family, and the meeting suddenly turns very uncordial indeed. But is Graff's uncontrolled fury really carefully planned and orchestrated? Noel narrowly escapes from gunshots and attack dogs, learning some tradecraft—although not quickly enough to shake men from MI5 later on, and not capably enough to deceive the New York Police Department.

His next stop is London. This time members of British intelligence live long enough to meet with Noel. They inform him that Johann von Tiebolt is living as a British journalist named John Tennyson, and that von Tiebolt/Tennyson may well be the Tinamou. A tinamou is apparently a small and innocuous bird. *The* Tinamou is a well-known assassin. (" 'Have you ever heard of the Tinamou?' " Noel will ask another character in a later exchange. " 'The assassin? Certainly. Who hasn't?' " Well, Noel hasn't, but then, he's led the sheltered life of a typical Ludlum hero.) British intelligence thinks that Noel is a courier delivering a payment to the Tinamou for lethal services rendered.

Now that he has the new name of the von Tiebolts, Noel is able to locate Johann's sister, Gretchen von Tiebolt Tennyson Beaumont. She's not just attractive; she has an unnaturally perfect face and body, and she has a bizarre philosophy to go with her looks. She seduces Noel rather mechanically under standing orders from Johann. Later Noel will see and pocket a framed photograph that looks familiar. It is her husband, Commander Anthony Beaumont, R.N. [Royal Navy]—the man with the salt-and-pepper eyebrows! Leaving his adulterous playmate, Noel finds his car disabled. Chased down by unidentified figures and beaten unconscious, he wakes up someplace else, hours later, reeking of alcohol.

Having apparently extracted all the available information from Gretchen, Noel must next journey to Paris to locate the other von Tiebolt sister. Unfortunately his passport and possessions are in his London hotel room, and the hotel is under surveillance. "His unfamiliar forest was lined with traps; every protective instinct he possessed told him to turn back. Geneva needed a man infinitely more cunning and experienced than he. Yet he could not turn back." He enlists the help of an old friend, a flamboyant interior designer of dubious sexual orientation.

When he finally reaches Paris and gets in touch with Helden von Tiebolt, alias Helen Tennyson, she agrees to meet with him. However, the meeting will require elaborate security precautions, Helen briskly instructs Noel, and we suspect that she must have her own secret organization. Well she might be dubious about Noel's amateur status; in spite of his best efforts, there are two MI5 agents on his tail. Helen takes Noel to meet her mentor, the aged ex-general known only as Herr Oberst. Noel learns that there are two organizations hounding the children of Nazis: Odessa wants to recruit them for a Fourth Reich, and the Rache (fans of Sherlock Holmes will recall that this is German for "revenge") wants to kill them. As the offspring of a very prominent Nazi, the von Tiebolts have been intensely pursued by both groups.

Meanwhile, in spite of Helen's precautions, she and Noel have been followed to Herr Oberst's forest retreat by both Anthony Beaumont and John Tennyson. John allegedly detests the naval officer, but in reality the two are part of the same organization, an organization that despises and uses both Odessa and the Rache.

We learn that the Sonnenkinder, whom we have assumed are the children of the damned, are really the children of the sun. They are the children we saw leaving a disintegrating Third Reich in the opening scene, a group selected to be genetically pure and superior. Over the last three decades they have grown up into positions of authority in many countries—Beaumont, for example, who now has command of his own ship! The Sonnenkinder have already bought elections here and there, partly for the power and partly as experiments. It cost $27 million to purchase control of Chile, and Panama was a real bargain at $6 million. When they get their hands on Clausen's $780 million, they will be able to buy positions of leadership all over the world.

John Tennyson kills Beaumont because the Commander had carelessly allowed himself to be observed *and* because Noel has the photo. However, the photo has been stolen, and neither the characters nor the readers know by whom. John is not only violent and ruthless, he's having an incestuous relationship with Gretchen. (Carlos finds sexual release with his cousin in THE BOURNE IDENTITY, and with a sister in a non-Ludlum novel. The von Tiebolts' relationship may not be unique, but it still adds a nice unsavory touch.) The two of them are using Helen as a pawn in their deadly intrigues. Helen at least has good intentions, and she will go on to become Noel's romantic interest.

Still in Paris, Noel learns that his stepfather has died in a suspicious accident. Richard Holcroft has virtually nothing to do with the plot, and his death is just a device to push Noel closer to the breaking point.

Noel and Helen are followed to a colorful fair in a small French town, where they are inexplicably attacked by unidentified assailants. MI5 is following Noel, a shady character in a Fiat is following Helen, and an agent of the Tinamou is following everybody to see who follows who. An MI5 agent gets himself killed trying to save them; Helen is captured but Noel gets her back. Noel and Helen agree to ignore the dying agent's advice, which was that they reach MI5 in London and get a specific file opened.

The next stop is Berlin, where Noel finds the Kessler brothers easily enough. Noel is still under surveillance, but who is the watcher working for? Our hero spills his guts to Erich Kessler; it's a pleasant enough meeting until the man who was following him staggers through the restaurant and dies at their table. We learn that Kessler is meeting with John and undoubtedly conspiring with him, but now there is a fourth player. The Nachrichtendienst is a covert anti-Nazi intelligence unit formed in World War II and still actively trying to prevent the formation of the Fourth Reich. Nowadays it is led by old men, headed by Herr Oberst. Most of the manpower comes from a kibbutz in Israel founded by Jews who are not just concentration camp survivors; each one is the sole survivor of his family. Needless to say, their background has made them fervent believers and fanatical warriors.

Now it's back to Paris and Helen for Noel. While they are dining, John is meeting with Gretchen. He finishes the tryst by killing her to tie up some loose ends. We learn that Manfredi the banker has been part of the plot all along. So has Noel's mother, Althene Clausen Holcroft, who has fled New York and managed to shake surveillance. Or has she? Was she a willing part of the plot, or a puppet manipulated to advance the plot and made to look like a conspirator? Why has she maintained an escape route in readiness for all these years? Where did she acquire the fanatical assistant who met her in Mexico City and then killed himself to protect her secret? And was he helping her or tailing her?

We begin to learn more about John Tennyson as the Tinamou. He is planning to protect his cover by "capturing" the understudy Tinamou he has been grooming. He will claim that the assassin's masters are the Nachtrichtendienst, and he concocts a very plausible motive. Meanwhile he's holding on to a list of previous Tinamou customers so that he can blackmail them when it suits him. Ludlum's conspiracy complex is still working overtime; the Tinamou's greatest hits include both Kennedys, Martin Luther King, Jr., Lee Harvey Oswald, and Jack Ruby.

John kills Herr Oberst. Being impartial about distributing blame, he makes it look like the work of Odessa. But Herr Oberst has carefully hidden his last instructions to Helen.

Helen travels to Près-du-Lac, Switzerland, where she will meet with a Nachtrichtendienst contact, an old man who has the entire village convinced that he is senile. The reader is convinced that this will be the turning point, this will be the ally who tips the balance, but Ludlum's writing isn't so simple or obvious. John finds out and orders Helen and her contact killed; the old man dies, but not before Helen learns the truth. Thousands of miles away the kibbutz is bombed and practically wiped out.

Althene travels to Lisbon, where she activates an old escape route and meets an old courier.

" 'You bring up names so long in the past, there are no faces. Requests that have not been made in years.'

" 'I can't believe times have changed that much.'

" 'Oh, but they have, senhora. Men and women still travel secretly, but not with such simple devices as doctored passports. It's the age of the computer. False papers are not what they once were.' "

Nostalgia aside, the courier has apparently kept himself up-to-date, because he will be able to get Althene to Geneva in secret.

Noel is also on his way to Geneva in the company of John. He is alive only because he is needed to sign papers for the release of the money. Helen and Althene, resourceful ladies in their own right, meet and rendezvous with a surviving Nachtrichtendienst operative.

In the final rush of plot, the bad guys win. The money is released to them, to *their* Wolfsschanze organization which orignially wanted to kill Hitler—not to end the war but to pursue it more efficiently! Noel and Helen succeed only in surviving, which is a significant triumph in view of John's efforts to the contrary. In a few pages we wade through enough material to make a sequel: The original plot is working, the world is changing along ominous lines. As the book ends, Noel has completed his training at the hands of the wounded Nachtrichtendienst survivor. Now he is prepared to strike back. Now he has become a second Tinamou.

With **THE MATARESE CIRCLE**, Ludlum becomes more firmly entrenched in the secret agent mode. The two heroes are in effect Ludlum's full-time professional secret agents. (David Spaulding of THE RHINE-MANN EXCHANGE becomes an undercover operative, but only through chance and necessity.) Still, the book is full of manipulations and lies, secret deals, and layer upon layer of puzzles.

MATARESE has two heroes, and the book follows a parallel construction perhaps a little too closely in introducing them. The Chairman of the Joint Chiefs of Staff is gorily assassinated during a kinky menage à trois. Evidence points very clearly to a Soviet-made weapon, and the CIA narrows the modus operandi down to three top KGB assassins. The Premier of the USSR knows who the leading suspects are, but he is sure they couldn't have done it. The President may not be convinced, but the reader is.

Back in the USSR, respected scientist and bomb designer Dimitri Yurievich is spending a jolly weekend at his dacha with his son and some friends, when their hunting party is cut short by a series of slugs from an American-made rifle. Not only is the weapon clearly made in the USA, it's the favorite of one particular CIA operative. Once again the hot line is ringing off the hook, and this time it's the President, who must insist that the usual suspects are otherwise occupied.

The leading suspect is Brandon "Bray" Scofield of Consular Operations. When we finally meet him, he is running a dirty operation in Amsterdam against a Soviet double agent. Scofield is disillusioned, almost burned out; he is ready to let the Soviet mole live, but a younger and more zealous colleague rectifies that situation. Scofield walks away into the cold, damp Amsterdam night. At his debriefing it becomes clear that the mole was not what he seemed.

Vasili Taleniekov is the prime suspect on the Soviet side. Was Scofield connected with the brutal rape and murder of Taleniekov's East German girlfriend in Berlin years ago? Did Scofield murder Taleniekov's brother for revenge after the revenge killing of Scofield's wife? The book is a little unclear, but the result is the opposite: Scofield and Taleniekov hate each other's guts and each plans to kill the other as soon as the situation permits.

Is Taleniekov walking into an ambush at his apartment? No, it's just a terrified teenager with a message summoning the KGB agent to the bedside of his wounded and dying mentor. The old KGB general has been shot by Corsicans. As his life oozes away, he rants about the Matarese, which to hear him tell it killed Stalin, Trotsky, and Franklin Delano Roosevelt. The Matarese is uniting terrorist organizations so that it can throw the superpowers into chaos and take them over. Already it has infiltrated the highest circles of the Soviet and U.S. governments. Only Taleniekov can stop it, and only with the help of the American agent Beowulf Agate—Brandon Scofield!

In Washington, D.C., Robert Winthrop, the crumpled, elegant elder statesman who originated Consular Operations, is advising current director Daniel Congdon about Scofield. We learn some of Scofield's background as they decide to retire the agent—actually they will have to buy him off—and retain him as a consultant. Later Consular Operations will decide on a more permanent form of retirement for Scofield, the kind that includes a 9mm slug instead of a gold watch.

Taleniekov begins his investigations into the Matarese, and suddenly he finds that he is persona non grata within the KGB and the USSR. He begins his escape from the country with the unwilling help of a CIA stringer, but soon the entire Soviet intelligence apparatus is on his tail. He gets away, leaving behind him the corpses of the CIA man and a sympathetic Soviet cryptographer.

Now both agents are on the run from their own agencies. Taleniekov is looking for Scofield, and their paths finally cross at a hotel in Washington, D.C. Taleniekov saves Scofield from an attack that practically levels the hotel, and Scofield saves Taleniekov from a demonstrably Soviet assassin. They finally come to rest and manage not to kill each other, although at this point both are sorely tempted. Taleniekov tells Scofield about the Matarese. The shadowy organization has a timetable to take over the governments of the U.S. and the USSR—and the deadline is only two months away!

Scofield calls Robert Winthrop for information about the Matarese. They meet secretly in the woods of Rock Creek Park, but Taleniekov detects terminal surveillance. The would-be killer appears to be a CIA man. But is he a KGB plant? Or is he working for the Matarese? Looking for the answers, our heroes travel secretly and separately to Corsica.

Taleniekov finds himself being followed by dozens of infuriated armed peasants, and someone has already tried to blow him away in response to his inquiries. Taleniekov finally isolates and captures a single Corsican in order to torture the man for information. Another Corsican, this one armed with a vicious sawed-off shotgun, has been tracking Taleniekov and the intended victim. But Scofield has been tracking the tracker and shoots him before he can do any damage.

A mysterious armed woman—soon identified as Antonia Gravet, daughter of a Corsican woman and a Frenchman—finds the two agents and leads them into the hills to meet her grandmother. The blind old woman is "the whore of Villa Matarese," at one time the girlfriend of Guillaume de Matarese, founder of the organization devoted to his insane theories. Guillaume was seventy at the time, but still vigorous enough to keep a beautiful young woman busy when he was not pursuing his intrigues. She bore him two sons, who would grow up and go into business, only to be ruined and killed by cynical government manipulations—mostly the British and French. Still energetic enough to bend others to his will, still rich enough to have an impact in international finance, Guillaume de Matarese formed his infamous council for revenge. He brought a small group of powerful men to his villa, where they were wined and dined and where the Spaniard who declined to go along with the plan was shot. The remaining conspirators inherited Matarese's hidden fortune and a diabolical plan. Then, just to make sure that the meeting remained a secret once the men left, Matarese had all the servants, cooks, and hookers in the villa killed, then the killers killed, then himself killed by a shepherd boy. As the villa burned, "the whore of Villa Matarese" escaped more by accident than by intent. The lands around the smoldering ruin were turned over to the local peasantry, giving them an incentive to protect the secret.

The old woman has retained a list with the names of the original guests. They come from Italy, Britain, Russia (the meeting was in 1911), and the United States, and the current Matarese are their heirs. Scofield and Taleniekov recognize two of the names, but the old woman reveals that the leader is not on the list—he is the shepherd boy who was hired to kill Guillaume de Matarese.

The two agents escape from Corsica to Rome with Antonia in tow. We learn that she is a fugitive from the Red Brigades (who may well be a puppet of the Matarese) under the terrorists' sentence of death for desertion. Suddenly Scofield is knocked unconscious and Antonia is captured. Scofield recovers in time to save her while she is being beaten and tortured. With his old connections he finds a highly specialized doctor to treat her, an MI5 asset. The doctor informs Scofield that Antonia's recent ordeal was by no means her first, and that she has suffered similar trauma in the recent past. Scofield chivalrously offers to send her someplace safe and set her up with plenty of cash, but Antonia refuses. She's had enough of terrorists and fanatics in any form, and she wants to help in the campaign against the Matarese. Soon she is also Scofield's romantic interest, while Taleniekov will have to struggle along without a paramour of his own.

The most accessible name on the list is the Scozzi family. Scofield wangles an invitation to a charity ball at Villa d'Este, where he can meet the current leader of the family, Count Guillamo Scozzi. He pretends to be looking for the services of an assassin, which shakes up Scozzi. Scofield follows the Count in time to see him shot by his true boss, Paravacini, leader of the rich but lower-class family allied by marriage to the Scozzis.

Meanwhile Taleniekov is in Leningrad, looking for information about the family of Prince Andrei Voroshin. He is greeted by three Matarese killers but gets the better of them until they kill themselves to avoid capture. Each one has a circle—"per nostro circolo"—tattooed on his chest! Soon Taleniekov is poring over moldering papers in a locked section of the library, where he learns that the Voroshins bought a new identity in Germany, then faked their own fiery end at the hands of the revolution. This information takes him to Essen, leaving behind a continent littered with the bodies of Matarese operatives, dead friends killed by the Matarese, and a KGB turncoat with false information. In another musty archive he identifies Prince Voroshin as Ansel Verachten, whose firm has grown up to rival Krupp.

Taleniekov confronts the elderly Verachten heir, who admits that his family is the Voroshins but says he has never heard of the Matarese. That connection now rests with his beautiful, sexually rapacious daughter Odile, who has her father and his Russian Orthodox priest killed. Taleniekov captures the perfidious Odile, but then her men capture him and demand he agree to join the Matarese. But Odile's soldiers are more loyal to the parent organization than to their direct employer; they gun her down, and Taleniekov escapes in the ensuing confusion. Now he's on his way to Paris to link up with Antonia.

Scofield has found his way to London, where he meets an old buddy from British intelligence. He very quickly discovers that all his old contacts are being followed. British intelligence has been thoroughly penetrated by the Matarese, and so has Soviet intelligence. Scofield, Taleniekov, and a forcibly drugged Antonia meet in London. They set up a meeting to capture David Waverly, part of Matarese and now high up in the British government. The plan will probably result in the death of Scofield's old friend Symonds, who has been helping them; Scofield doesn't like it, but he knows what he has to do. Then everything falls through with a phone call from Symonds: Waverly has been massacred along with his entire family! Scofield meets with Symonds, who agrees to give him a few weeks to work on the case unofficially.

Suddenly Taleniekov and Antonia are captured by the Matarese, and Symonds is killed. Scofield is ordered to a meeting in Boston with Joshua Appleton IV. Appleton is a senator, seemingly a shoo-in to win the next presidential election if he doesn't drive off a bridge or something. He's also enormously rich; his family owns a big piece of Trans-Communications, which owns more than half of Verachten. Scofield journeys to Boston in his own roundabout way. En route he visits a professor he knows and gets more information about Trans-Communications. The founder is Nicholas Guiderone, eighty years old now but still vigorous. Guiderone is the shepherd boy!

Scofield talks his way into the house of Appleton's aging, alcoholic mother. The full-time nurse is also a full-time Matarese operative who must be overcome before Scofield can learn that Appleton has a dreadful secret from the Korean War. Was it that he was tortured by the North Koreans? Or something more complicated? In about 1954, Joshua Appleton IV was in a terrible automobile accident. He was hospitalized for months, never expected to survive. Yet he made a miraculous recovery, and most of those who treated him either vanished or died mysteriously. Tracking down old X rays, Scofield finally discovers the truth: "Joshua Appleton IV," sure to be the next President of the United States, is really Julian Guiderone, son of the shepherd boy.

Scofield makes copies of the proof and sends one to Winthrop. Now he is ready to visit Appleton Hall, which has been purchased by the Guiderone family and converted into a private fortress patrolled by armed guards. Taleniekov and Antonia are being held there. Scofield finally gets his audience with Nicholas Guiderone, as well as Guiderone's promise to release Antonia and the wounded, dying Taleniekov. We learn that Matarese is by now a corporation, actually Trans-Communications. Where does it find its fanatical operatives? They're just very advancement-oriented junior executives!

Scofield has his escape all figured out, but Winthrop's longtime faithful retainer is actually a Matarese plant and neutralizes the packet of information. Winthrop, probably the last honest man in Washington, helps Scofield to overcome the guards, but it is his last act. It is also Guiderone's last moment, as Scofield kills him too.

Naturally Scofield has another string to his bow. He draws the police to Appleton Hall with a phony bomb threat—so that's why he's been constructing showy but harmless little time bombs! Scofield personally massacres a few dozen Matarese bigshots, most holding high positions in the U.S. and Soviet governments, who are conveniently gathered for a meeting. The grievously wounded Taleniekov makes the final sacrifice to ensure Scofield and Antonia's escape.

THE MATARESE CIRCLE ends on a seemingly happy note, with Scofield and Antonia living anonymously and idyllically on a boat in the Caribbean. But then they happen upon a week-old newspaper. There's a series of seemingly business-as-usual corporate mergers going on. Trans-Communications and Matarese are preparing to rise from the ashes!

THE BOURNE IDENTITY is also the story of a professional secret agent. But if the hero's profession is straightforward, his adventures here are certainly not; Robert Ludlum has found a new and intriguing way to complicate the plot and confuse his readers!

The book begins with a brief overview of Carlos's recent activities. Carlos occurs as a villain in the writings of many thriller authors, but he is based on a real-life individual. Usually he is described as a leader of international terrorists; Ludlum's version of Carlos casts him as a free-lance assassin much along the lines of the Tinamou.

The book's action starts in earnest as an unnamed man, riddled with bullets, hurls himself clear of a trawler on the storm-tossed Mediterranean. Moments later the trawler explodes and sinks. The man drifts all night, more dead than alive, until he is pulled out of the sea by fishermen. Acting out of a resentful sense of obligation rather than kindness, they bring him back to their island of Ile de Port Noir and leave him in the questionable care of Dr. Geoffrey Washburn.

Washburn is an alcoholic expatriate thrown out of a cushy job in London after one besotted mistake too many. In his work with the islanders he has his good days and his bad days, days when he can function like the professor he was and days when the islanders know that the sutures will be shaky and uneven. He knows himself very well, and he knows his tolerance for alcohol to the nearest ounce. Faced with his new patient, he dries himself out and performs major surgery, then manages to stay mildly inebriated but never incoherent or incapable. Dr. Washburn's brief appearance is a concise and compassionate portrait of a flawed man who finds inner resources when he has to.

At last the mysterious patient wakes up, muttering in three languages. Who is he? He has no idea—the physical and psychological trauma of his shooting and near-drowning have combined to give him amnesia. " 'Drunk or not, I *am* a doctor,' " Washburn informs his patient. " 'I was once a very good one.' " He still maintains his curiosity, and he is determined to help the patient learn his identity.

What does Washburn and the man himself know about the unidentified amnesiac? He is trilingual in English, French, and an Oriental language. He has an extensive knowledge of geography, and he is no stranger to violence. He has had extensive plastic surgery, his hair has been dyed, and there is evidence that he has worn contact lenses despite his normal vision. Implanted under his skin is a microfiche with information about a Swiss bank account. Later it's revealed—and the rough fishermen of the island will find out the hard way—that the man has a dangerous command of the martial arts.

After he severely injures several islanders, the man becomes persona non grata on Ile de Port Noir. He is sufficiently recuperated to go on his way, and he finds a ride to Marseilles. He is beginning to remember what readers will identify as secret agent tradecraft, but almost immediately he is located by the men who tried to kill him on the trawler. His martial arts skills barely save him.

Naturally he must journey to Zurich in the hope that the bank account will provide the information he needs. Once in Zurich, he finds that things are coming back to him slowly. "It was a street filled with the sights and sounds of forgotten memories, thought the man who had no memory to forget." He knows his favorite hotel, and fortunately the desk staff knows him. It's just a little awkward checking in without knowing his own name, but the assistant manager helpfully supplies it: J. Bourne of New York City. Now we finally know what to call the character, after he has spent almost ten percent of the book without a name! Bourne learns that only one party is entitled to make contact with him directly, Treadstone Seventy-one Corporation. What is Treadstone? It's not listed in any telephone directory. We'll find out later, but now Bourne has business in the bank. He turns out to be the proud owner of a three-zero account with a balance of about $5 million. He promptly transfers most of the funds to an account in Paris, and as a token of his gratitude he wires a million dollars to Washburn's account in Marseilles. (Unfortunately Blue Cross is never so generous in real life.) At the bank Bourne also acquires a first name, Jason.

It's a good thing Bourne gets his banking business out of the way, because he hasn't left the building before there's another attempt on his life. A sweating, terrified fat man in a restaurant implies that Bourne is a highly paid assassin—where did the $5 million dollars come from, after all?—but now he's just a confused amnesiac on the run. His flight takes him through the hotel, where he acquires a hostage in Marie St. Jacques, a lovely Canadian economist who finds that her boring international conference has suddenly become a bit too exciting.

The men chasing Bourne appear to be the police—but would the real police be planning to kill his hostage? No, they're actually Carlos's men, and Carlos will pay handsomely for Bourne's corpse. Bourne manages to break away and saves Marie from a fate worse than death. She realizes that he didn't have to come back, that he has risked his life to save her, and she turns very quickly from indignant bystander to enthusiastic helper. She is highly placed in the Canadian government and enlists Ottawa's resources to track down Treadstone.

Jason and Marie make it out of Zurich alive and romantically entangled, and wend their way to Paris. Here as in Zurich Bourne's banker is working for Carlos, but this time Bourne is ready and safely manages to get his hands on his funds. Meanwhile, Marie's friend who has been making inquiries turns up with a bullet hole in his throat—Carlos's trademark technique for dealing with unsatisfactory employees. Could Bourne be a defector from Carlos's organization? The murder in Ottawa doesn't make any newspapers; there's definitely something strange going on here. Marie is ordered home by her government but ducks the order.

Jason Bourne is a hot topic at a secret committee meeting back in Washington. We learn that he is called Cain, both by Carlos and by the Pentagon, which may or may not know his real name. He's a free-lance assassin trying to outdo and underbid Carlos. He'll botch an occasional contract because he's rushing too much, then make up for it with a spectacular freebie just to demonstrate his abilities. The Pentagon wants him and the CIA wants him; the plan is to play Cain against Carlos and ideally take them both. A deceptively slow-talking congressman with the committee does know Cain's real name and origins: Bourne is a veteran of Medusa, a covert team working in Vietnam, "a modern-day pirate in the purest sense." The identity is also known to Carlos's well-disguised message center.

Still in Paris, Jason is preparing to ditch Marie for her own protection. Then they see a newspaper with Marie's picture prominently displayed—she is wanted for murder in Zurich! The victim is one of the many left strewn in the streets during Bourne's earlier escapades. Now Marie's protection demands that Jason stay with her. Fortunately this task shouldn't be too onerous because Jason's relationship with Marie's body by now extends beyond guarding it.

Meanwhile, a major in the U.S. Army is heading for a top-secret meeting at the Manhattan headquarters of Treadstone Seventy-one. He is the same major that Cain and the Medusa organization rescued from the Viet Cong, and Treadstone Seventy-one is a hush-hush intelligence agency housed in an elegant brownstone which is actually a high-tech fortress. Is Treadstone working with Carlos by promulgating the story of Marie St. Jacques as a murderer? No; Bourne's entire pretense of being Cain the assassin was designed to trap Carlos while actually saving some potential victims on Carlos's hit list.

Paris—(THE BOURNE IDENTITY, THE BOURNE SUPREMACY, THE BOURNE ULTIMATUM) had to know it!

With this revelation, the mind-boggling complexity of THE BOURNE IDENTITY becomes clear. It's taken Jason Bourne much of the book to learn who he is—and now that he's beginning to know, he's wrong!

Carlos has a mole within the U.S. government. Watching the secret comings and goings on Seventy-first Street, the mole realizes that Cain is a fake. He confronts one of the top-secret planners as the man is leaving, and his deductions are confirmed. One of Carlos's European agents is in the car with the mole and his victim, and he proceeds to shoot and kill . . . the mole! Then he shoots the Treadstone planner, but not before the man has explained that the real Jason Bourne was executed by Medusa years before in Vietnam. The European breaks into the brownstone and massacres the remaining staff and guests. In his pocket is a special tape bearing "Jason Bourne's" fingerprints, lifted from a glass at the bank in Zurich and brought across the ocean to be transferred to a fragment of another glass. The survivors of Treadstone will later meet in Washington and swallow this frame-up whole. They declare "Bourne"/ "Cain"/whoever (for the sake of simplicity and sanity I will henceforth refer to the character as Jason Bourne, even though he's really a wolverine in fisher's clothing with a marten disguise and this isn't his real name) to be "beyond salvage." The meaning of this euphemism is clear: terminate on sight.

Jason and Marie make their way out of Paris, changing hotels in an attempt to avoid leaving a trail. She thinks that someone is trying to reach them in order to help. Fortunately Jason and experienced readers realize that she is hopelessly naive and that to answer the messages would bring them only one kind of help—the 9mm kind!

Bourne has identified Carlos's message center, an overpriced couturier known as Les Classiques. He is able to trace calls from Les Classiques to the residence of the retired General Villiers. Villiers sneaks off to a clandestine meeting; Bourne follows and finds him addressing a group of old but still vigorous retired officers. For what reason? Bourne confronts the General and is convinced that he is not working for Carlos. Someone at his town house must be answering the calls from Les Classiques. Is it the General's chauffeur? His longtime aide? His much younger and extremely sexy second wife? The wife is seen talking to a known Carlos contact, and the General realizes that she must be the traitor in his house.

Bourne shows up at Les Classiques, nominally playing the part of a rich customer but quickly shaking things up and scaring the hell out of two employees, each with unrelated sins to hide. Soon Mme. Villiers's phone is ringing off the hook and she is summoned to a hasty meeting, where Bourne spots a disguised Carlos. Carlos gets away, of course. Another employee at Les Classiques recognizes Bourne from their days in Medusa. There is an attempt on the employee's life by Carlos and his minions, and this scares the employee into spilling his guts to Bourne. Jason learns that Mme. Villiers is Carlos's cousin (she's not just fashionably suntanned, she's Venezuelan) and incestuous lover, that his own "Cain" role is really a decoy, and that he killed the real Jason Bourne.

Bourne makes contact with the American embassy and announces that he wants to come in from the cold. His call is relayed to Alexander Conklin, a survivor of Medusa and Treadstone who is convinced that Bourne has to be killed. Conklin activates his own outside-of-channels network and soon he is on an SST bound for Paris and an unlogged meeting with Bourne at a deserted cemetery. Bourne spots Conklin's car, which has also been "made" by Carlos. Conklin's backups are a trifling inconvenience; Bourne captures two punk observers and steals their car, then sneaks up on the man who is covering the rendezvous with a short, powerful rifle. Now Bourne can disarm Conklin, and Conklin has to talk. He tells Bourne about the massacre on Seventy-first Street. One of the victims, Major Webb, was "Bourne's" brother! (After all, his code name *is* Cain.) Suddenly someone else is shooting at Bourne and

Conklin, but Bourne shoots back and kills him. He probably should kill Conklin too, but he refrains.

Jason realizes that Mme. Villiers is the key—but before he can reach her, the General can stand her domestic treachery no longer and kills her. Villiers is a broken man, but Jason whips him into shape. He—Jason/Cain—will claim credit for the kill, at least as far as Carlos will know. General Villiers uses his army connections to spirit Jason out of the country.

Like many Ludlum thrillers, THE BOURNE IDENTITY ends in a rush. Bourne is flying into New York. Alexander Conklin goes undercover to kill Bourne. Marie is flying in under U.S. diplomatic immunity—the government will get her cleared of the murder charges in Zurich. And Carlos is coming to New York too.

The final confrontation takes place in the brownstone. Before Bourne and Carlos are through, the elegant rooms will once again reek of cordite and spilled blood, and the recently repaired walls will be pocked with fresh bullet holes. Both Bourne and Carlos are wounded, but both survive. To be continued . . .

The ending of THE BOURNE IDENTITY cries out for at least one more confrontation between Bourne and Carlos, but before Robert Ludlum produced the further adventures of David Webb alias Jason Bourne, he turned out two more books. The first provided one of his most complex plots ever.

THE PARSIFAL MOSAIC is a typically cryptic title, but thoroughly apropos. Like a mosaic, the book is assembled from innumerable tiny details. And like a mosaic, the overall pattern isn't at all identifiable from close up. It's only when you step back—in this case when you finish the book—that you will be able to discern the full picture.

On a moonlit beach on the Costa Brava, Michael Havelock watches his paramour, Jenna Karras, running through the surf, shouting in a foreign language. Suddenly she is transfixed by the beams of powerful spotlights and riddled with bullets. Is she really Michael's partner in the U.S. intelligence apparatus? Is she KGB, or, worse yet, part of a fanatical splinter group called the VKR? Did Michael arrange her death?

Whatever the circumstances, they are so disillusioning that Michael gives up a sixteen-year career with the State Department. He's touring Europe, revisiting by daylight the places he has seen only in the shadows, when an old friend cables and offers him a university teaching position. But before he can reply, he runs into the local CIA station chief, who offers him a job of quite a different kind.

Michael is not interested, but the undercover world is still interested in him. In Paris he speaks to Monsieur Gravet, an elegant older gentleman who deals in objets d'art and secret information. Gravet informs him that both the CIA and the KGB think he has not really retired. He still hasn't digested this information when in Athens he is reintroduced at gunpoint to Pyotr Rostov, the KGB's Director of External Strategies. Rostov's intent appears to be peaceful—he could sedate Havelock and drag him back to Lubyanka if he were not in a charitable mood. Finally somebody believes that Michael is really retired. He informs Michael that Jenna wasn't working for the KGB, but he has no way to prove this.

Relieved, Michael accepts the university teaching position. But the old friend who found him the job is now making a coded call to Washington, D.C.!

Suddenly a random encounter turns Michael's new life upside down. At a crowded railway station in Rome he sees Jenna Karras. Her face appears long enough for him to be sure. Then she is gone, and even the trained agent cannot catch her. He can, however, trace her. She's on her way to Civitavecchia, a seaport where she will be shipping out in a few hours. Michael drives furiously to the deteriorating seaside town and beats her whereabouts out of an old wharf rat. She is due to sail on the rusting tramp steamer *Miguel Cristovao*. Michael intercepts her before she can board—but it isn't Jenna! Moments after he realizes it is just a decoy, Michael is beaten senseless as Jenna watches from a warehouse. Her insistence on avoiding Michael is understandable—she thinks he is trying to kill her. The *Miguel Cristovao* was just a decoy; Jenna gets away on a different boat. Michael is only yards away when it sails, but he must watch helplessly as the boat pulls out of the harbor. Then he extracts its destination from a frightened second-rate hoodlum.

Michael has found an old contact in Rome, Lieutenant Colonel Lawrence Baylor alias Lieutenant Colonel Lawrence Brown. He announces that he's back in the game and explains why. He's furious at the anonymous decision-makers in Washington. " 'What kind of world do you people live in?' " asks Brown. " 'The same one you do,' " Michael replies, " 'only we've been in it a little longer, a little deeper.' " Attentive readers will recognize this exchange from THE OSTERMAN WEEKEND. The words are almost the same, but the point is still valid; even in times of peace, secret wars rage beneath the veneer of tranquility, and perhaps the peace exists only because shadowy forces fight to keep the balance of power. Michael deduces that he knows something that forced Washington to push him out of spying—but he doesn't know what!

They're discussing Michael back at the State Department, and we learn more about him. He was born Mikhail Havlicek in Czechoslovakia, where his father was a professor until World War II. Then his father joined the Resistance and killed Reinhard Heydrich, setting off a massive series of reprisals. Michael spent his boyhood in the brutal existence of a partisan, surviving like an animal, risking his life regularly, killing without a qualm. His mother did not survive the war, and his father was shipped off to a Gulag by the Soviet "liberators." Michael Havelock hates and fears weapons but mastered them out of a brutal necessity. After the war he was adopted by an American couple. He did very well in his new country, going on to Princeton for his higher education. There he met Anton Matthias, a Czech who was also to succeed in America. In the present of THE PARSIFAL MOSAIC, Matthias is Secretary of State, a sort of souped-up Henry Kissinger solving the world's problems with informal negotiations.

In Washington they're sure that Jenna is really dead, that Havelock is hallucinating, and that Havelock never met with Rostov—after all, if Rostov really could have taken him, why isn't he tied up, tranquilized, and crated in the cargo hold of some Aeroflot jumbo jet on his way to Moscow? Havelock may have left "insurance" behind, devastating information to be released in the event of his death. John Phillip "Red" Ogilvie, the field agent who has risen too high to be risked in the field, volunteers to go back into the cold and bring back Havelock. He's got a terminal illness anyway, so he's perfect for a final high-risk mission. His code name for this mission is Apache—the same code name he used when he rescued Michael Havelock years before.

Ogilvie flies to Rome, where he is briefed by "Brown." Ogilvie meets Havelock, who thinks (with pretty fair justification) that Ogilvie plans to kill him. Havelock takes out the two Italian stringers who are following for Ogilvie's protection; now they can have a real conversation. Ogilvie explains that he came to talk Michael back to Washington—or to take him by force if necessary. State has information confirming Jenna's death, but where did they get it? Was it planted by a mole? The man who brought back the information died three weeks later . . . of natural causes?

Suddenly shots ring out. Ogilvie has inadvertently placed himself in the line of fire, and the bullets that were meant for Michael end his pain-racked existence. The gunman is LTC Brown!

Jenna appears to be on her way to Paris via Col des Moulinets, and Michael will follow. First he pauses to make a couple of phone calls, thereby blowing Brown's cover and effectively ending the man's career.

Meanwhile, back in Washington they're starting to think that Michael may just be sane. The death order is rescinded. Could he be right about there being a mole in the White House? Their good intentions will go for nought—two are killed when their car is run off the road and crushed by a giant earthmover, and another is shot dead. Undersecretary of State

Arthur Pierce is still alive, and now we learn that he is a very-deep-cover Soviet mole whose primary allegiance is to the VKR. He calls the Rome station and gives the coded order to terminate Michael Havelock, declaring the agent "beyond salvage." Appropriately enough for a Ludlum book, Pierce's authorization is the code name Ambiguity.

Michael reaches Col des Moulinets before Jenna, so he has time to identify a notorious Corsican assassin and a termination unit. He takes out the bulk of the unit and gets away, but he can't reach Jenna and now she is on her way to a small airport. Michael breaks into the airport, but once again he just misses her. This time he is close enough to see her face, and it is set in a glare of purest hatred. Suddenly he is clobbered from behind by an unidentified assailant. We never do learn that man's identity, or his allegiance, or why he didn't kill Michael when he had the chance.

It didn't go all Michael's way at Col des Moulinets; he was wounded, and he's been losing blood. Fortunately he knows a doctor who's familiar with the undercover world. The doctor has been alerted to look out for the renegade agent, but he owes Michael a very large debt of gratitude. He's a small fish in the world of espionage, but he is able to call a KGB contact and get the latest: The KGB doesn't want Havelock and wouldn't touch him if it could. Now Michael borrows the doctor's dictaphone and tapes testimony that would be devastating to the American intelligence community if it ever became public. He calls Matthias on the Secretary's ultra-private line, but a bureaucrat answers—on a telephone that is supposed to be touched only by the great man—and won't connect him. He does reach Matthias's neighbor and fellow emigré, Leon Zeliensky, who informs him that Matthias is being systematically kept out of touch.

The next stop is Paris, where Gravet confirms that the KGB isn't interested in Michael—but the VKR wants him very much dead! Gravet reveals the hotel room of the VKR agent in Paris, who has mobilized a small army of lowlifes and informers. Michael confronts the VKR representative, who suggests that Michael defect. Why does the VKR man divulge information he can't have? How did he know that Michael was headed for Paris? Even with aggressive persuasion he can't tell Michael what happened on the Costa Brava, but it appears not to have involved the Soviets.

Back in Washington, top advisers are meeting secretly with President Charles Berquist. Curiously, this President is the first in Ludlum's writings to have a name, or, for that matter, an appearance. Like other presidents in Ludlum novels, Berquist is a sympathetic character. He's got a larger role than the president in any of the other books except perhaps for TREVAYNE, but the office and the fair-mindedness it requires (but doesn't always receive) are more important than the politician who fills the office. The meeting is about Parsifal, which we now learn is a "who" rather than a "what." Parsifal has some connection to Consular Operations and to the Costa Brava. There is information floating around which if released could easily start the third world war. At a later meeting we learn that Parsifal has blackmailed the United States out of $800 million—but not for the sake of the money, just to show that he could. We learn that Matthias set up the events on the Costa Brava, based on information that only he provided. The President and his top advisers are positive that Jenna was with the KGB—but we know that their conclusive proof is false, and one of the advisers has checked and has good evidence that she wasn't.

" 'In history's most advanced age of communications we're doing our damnedest to louse it up, to misuse it, really,' " the President says. Someone has shut down one line of communication permanently, by killing the man in Rome who took the call from Ambiguity and accepted the order to kill Havelock.

The United States is looking for Parsifal, and so is someone else. Someone in Moscow knows about Parsifal, but if the Soviets found out officially, they would launch first and ask questions later.

In Paris there's a bureaucrat and old Resistance heroine named Régine Broussac, who may have a lead to Jenna. She is sure that Michael is a turncoat, and plans to capture him at a deserted rendezvous. He convinces her that everyone has been lied to, and she explains that she sent Jenna to the United States. After all, nobody will look for her there! She agrees to send Michael via the same covert methods.

Back at the White House, they've finally accepted the existence of a deep-cover Soviet mole. They realize that he's going outside usual Soviet channels. Normal records won't help to trace the mole; people at this level are so used to secrecy that they obscure their whereabouts out of habit. Has Matthias been used by Parsifal? The President realizes that Michael Havelock is innocent . . . but orders him killed anyway because failure in this department would reveal the government's knowledge of Parsifal. And what's happening on Poole's Island, presumably a secret project that reports directly to 1600 Pennsylvania Avenue?

Michael arrives in New York and gets Jenna's forwarding address from a "halfway man" who specializes in hiding extremely illegal immigrants. She's in Mason Falls, Pennsylvania, on a farm run by an Eastern European named Kohoutek. Michael begins to suspect that it's more than just a farm when he encounters an extremely sophisticated alarm system. On closer examination, the complex proves to be a miniature concentration camp. Michael is captured and brought to Kohoutek, who turns out to be a very dishonest trafficker in smuggled humans. Finally the lovers are reunited, and Jenna proceeds to stab Michael with a fork.

After this inauspicious beginning she quickly comes to understand the situation, and now they're a team again! Kohoutek and his thugs are no match for the two working together, and they escape.

Michael looks up Raymond Alexander, an influential journalist and an old friend. Naturally, he lies to Alexander, and he learns that someone—probably Matthias—is being treated at a secret facility, probably Poole's Island, off the coast of Georgia. Alexander can't get through to Matthias on the ultra-private line either; when he called, the phone was answered by Undersecretary of State Emory Bradford. Bradford is the one who convinced Jenna that Michael had sold out to the Soviets. But what if the deception operations against Jenna and Michael are completely separate, or what if one group intercepted another's plan and changed it?

The next stop is Poole's Island. Security is tight, so Michael plans to walk in and be caught. For protection, he leaves Jenna with a packet of information that would devastate American intelligence operations. Michael does manage to bypass the electronic alarms and gets into the secret compound within the secret island. He is stunned to find a surrealistic movie-set version of Washington, D.C. Matthias's Georgetown house is there. It has its own alarm system, but this one is inside out; it's designed to keep the occupant inside. The occupant is Matthias, clearly gone insane!

While he is staring in shock, Michael is captured. The order for his death is still in effect, but the information he left with Jenna proves an effective bargaining lever. Soon the President is flying out by helicopter to meet him.

The President explains that Matthias was driven mad by his own enormous powers. He graciously rescinds the "beyond salvage order," reassuring Michael " 'There are many lies and there will continue to be lies, but that's not one of them.' " Now Michael and the reader are due for a guided tour of Poole's Island and Matthias's brain. The entire complex, with its sophisticated telemetry and its eerily realistic models of Washington landmarks, exists to take Matthias through past conversations, past negotiations. As his thinking became more and more unstable, the Secretary of State sought out more unstable negotiating partners. In the wake of his descent to madness is a string of absurd deals and impossible promises, all of them in writing and most of them unknown to the government. The most destructive of all is a pair of documents known as Parsifal. There's a plan for the United States and China to launch a surprise nuclear attack and obliterate the USSR, and a corresponding attack plan for the United States and the USSR against China. What makes the agreements believable is not just Matthias's signature, but complete details of the American, Soviet, and Chinese arsenals, not to mention targeting and civil defense plans. There's a deadline on both agreements, and it's approaching fast. The blackmailer has copies, and if he makes them public, it will start World War III. Who negotiated the memoranda with Matthias? Who gave him the details of Soviet and Chinese armaments? Why did Matthias arrange events at the Costa Brava to push Michael out of intelligence work? Did Parsifal (the individual, not the documents) rearrange the Costa Brava? Why didn't Parsifal have Michael killed?

Now that the entire American intelligence apparatus isn't trying to kill Michael anymore, the President enlists him to find the mole known as Ambiguity.

At a safe house known as Sterile Five, Michael, Jenna, and Emory Bradford are trying to piece together the few clues that they have. Parsifal used, then abandoned Ambiguity. Parsifal must be a Russian, Ambiguity a Russian mole. Michael has information in his head that could provide the answer—if only he knew which information it was! Even his own debriefing, enhanced by psychopharmaceuticals, can't help him.

Armed with new suggestions from Michael and Jenna, Bradford returns to the State Department and pores over the recorded activities of the most likely suspects. He calls and leaves a message that he has found the mole, and in fact he has correctly deduced that it is Pierce. Experienced thriller readers will know that the phone call giving the triumphant result but not the name is a definite death sentence, and sure enough Pierce confronts Bradford. Bradford has documentation of Pierce's unexplained absences at the time of Costa Brava; Pierce explains that his undercover work and Parsifal are all in the interests of a better world. Then he throws Bradford out of a window. Michael and Jenna are in real trouble now because Pierce knows all of the sterile houses, and there aren't that many.

Michael is checking into the death of the CIA man who authenticated Jenna's "death" at the Costa Brava. In a roundabout way he finally finds a lead to Ambiguity and Parsifal. This portion of the book is an impressive example of Robert Ludlum's powers of logical construction. It's basically a digression; most of the characters are irrelevant to the plot, and essentially all of the medical details are pulled out of thin air, yet Michael winds his way through fifteen or sixteen pages of elaborately connected circumstances and cryptic linkages until finally he has identified one of the deep-cover Soviet agents. Then the agent breaks out of surveillance and disappears.

With Bradford's death, the President brings on a man to replace him—Pierce! Naturally the Undersecretary of State has been fully briefed.

A team that Michael trusts has been busy, and finally they capture a deep-cover agent . . . of Ambiguity? Of Parsifal? He's only a low-level operative, working as a policeman, but he gives them a lead to the next level. Meanwhile, Michael finds out where Matthias got most of his technical information, from a Lieutenant Commander Decker. Is he a deep-cover agent too? No, just a patriot who feels that the cause of freedom would be improved by blowing up half the planet. Michael brings Decker around to reality.

Michael doesn't know yet that Pierce is the Soviet mole, so he tells the undersecretary about the captured policeman, who is promptly killed. But by ordering the killing, Pierce has given himself away. Michael wants to confirm the mole's identity with Rostov, but half a world away his KGB buddy is killed by the VKR. If there was any doubt in Michael's mind before, this removes it; he had mentioned Rostov to Pierce.

Now that Michael knows Pierce is the mole, we learn more about his origins. The Soviet paminyatchik or "travelers" figured in THE OSTER-MAN WEEKEND and in other authors' work as well. THE PARSIFAL MOSAIC omits the nuts and bolts of the paminyatchiks' training, but it provides the best overview of how they are groomed, put into place, and motivated. After all, how do you maintain the Soviet ideology in someone who spends his entire life living as—in fact being—an American? Do you keep your moles in place by showing them Polaroids of other moles who have been caught trying to defect? Ludlum's answer is far more logical.

By the time Michael convinces the President who the mole is, Pierce is off and running. He has to get away before he can obtain copies of the Parsifal documents, but he's got something almost as damaging: the psychiatric files on Matthias. If he releases these, ten years of American foreign policy will be out the window and nobody will ever trust the United States again.

Michael finally figures out who Parsifal is—it's Raymond Alexander! But when he confronts Alexander, he learns that the columnist was only a pawn of Parsifal's . . . as was Matthias, who was deliberately driven insane! The real Parsifal is a Soviet defector who has been given a new identity courtesy of the State Department . . . but his "real" identity was false. He's Leon Zeliensky, Matthias's supposed friend. If there's a weak spot in the book, it's Parsifal's identity, shocking to the characters but not to the readers. (The situation is similar in THE OSTERMAN WEEK-END, THE MATLOCK PAPER, and THE CHANCELLOR MANU-SCRIPT, but in each of these books the cryptic villain has been better established as a good guy.) Parsifal agrees to burn the nuclear agreements, but then Pierce seizes them and escapes. Michael and Jenna, working as a team, kill Pierce and his henchmen. Finally the false agreements and the psychiatric reports go up in flames, and the world doesn't. Michael and Jenna are able to settle down to a quiet life on a university campus. And Anthony Matthias, unaware of the fury created in his name, dies quietly, released at last from his world of madness.

When **THE AQUITAINE PROGRESSION** begins, attorney Joel Converse is in Geneva working on a complicated merger. He meets one of the opposing attorneys and is surprised to find the man an old friend under the new name of Preston Halliday. Halliday goes through Joel's life story, confirming to himself and to us that Joel is unentangled—divorced, no children, and without Joel's knowledge, Halliday's principals have negotiated a well-paid leave of absence from his law firm.

Halliday explains that he represents a client who can't be involved openly. The client wants to hire Joel to put out of business a company that is really a government in exile, an international consortium of influence buyers. "The generals . . . they're coming back," led by General George Marcus "Mad Marcus" Delavane, the man who gave the orders for the suicidal air strike on which Converse was shot down over North Vietnam and captured.

Joel is still deciding whether to take on the mission, when Halliday staggers into a routine business meeting bleeding from multiple gunshot wounds. "Aquitaine," he breathes, then dies.

Fortunately Joel already has his first contact, a banker named Kostas Laskaris on the island of Mykonos. Laskaris introduces him to Dr. Edward Beale. Beale was once a fast-rising young general, "the Red Fox of Inchon." Now he's sick of war; when they tried to sign him up as part of Aquitaine, he killed the recruiter. His old military connections still

The blinding white sun of Mykonos, Greece (THE AQUITAINE PROGRESSION)

provide him with access to information, including a list of five principals in Aquitaine. Four have been located and identified, one has not. The four known members are from France, Israel, Germany, and South Africa.

Dr. Beale explains that "Aquitaine" is apparently a reference to Aquitania, an almost legendary kingdom in southwestern France that came close to taking over all of Europe. Had it done so, it would presumably now control most of the world. The modern-day Aquitaine's plan is to foment increased terrorist activity, then have the military take control when the public begs for stability and law and order. In fact, the increased violence now going on in Northern Ireland is a test shot using cluster bomb units to devastating effect.

The idea of fomenting disorder to create the "need" for repressive order makes a lot of sense, so much so that Ludlum has already used it in THE HOLCROFT COVENANT. In the simplified movie version of HOLCROFT, it forms the entire of the villains' scheme. There's nothing new under the sun, especially in Robert Ludlum's world of conspiracy and cabal, but this plot element doesn't seem stale even though it's repeated. In both HOLCROFT and AQUITAINE, an amateur hero, manipulated by forces beyond his grasp, must take on a reactionary organization that seeks to achieve power by promoting chaos. Yet the heroes, the villains, and the manipulations are so different that the plots have little in common.

While Joel Converse is on the coast of Mykonos, his ex-wife, Valerie Charpentier, is looking at the waters off Cape Ann, Massachusetts, and noting nervously that the same boat—registered to an American army officer—has been moored off her beach for the past few days.

Joel flies to Paris to meet General Bertholdier. Born in 1924, Bertholdier made his name with the Resistance. In spite of a rapid rise within the military he retired early; now he makes an excellent living in the world of business. He is a notorious womanizer known in some circles as "La Grand Machine."

Joel visits René Mattilon, a Parisian lawyer and an old friend. Mattilon doesn't travel in the same circles as Bertholdier, but one of his clients belongs to the same club. Joel wangles an invitation to lunch and an introduction to the General. He lets slip that his future itinerary includes Bonn, Tel Aviv, and Johannesburg.

That evening Bertholdier drops by Joel's hotel, alarmed about something. Joel implies that he represents a client hoping to peddle arms on a large scale, then confronts Bertholdier about a diverted shipment of weapons. He's using a false name at this point and wants to get out of France quickly and covertly so as not to give it away, but Bertholdier has men covering all the exits of the hotel. Joel recognizes the man by the service entrance—the General's "chauffeur." His old war-trained reflexes take over, and he flattens the man, probably injuring him seriously. This gets the Sureté involved; the Sureté obtains Joel's real name from Mattilon, and Bertholdier obtains it from a plant in the Sureté. Then, just to make sure Joel is in real trouble, he orders the chauffeur killed in his hospital bed.

Joel gets out of Paris before there is a warrant for his arrest. He hopes that by taking a roundabout route to Bonn he can shake off any surveillance, but someone is following him. He gets off at the Köln airport, and now he's following the followers—all the way to Bonn, where their limousine stops at the American embassy! Someone at the embassy is very interested in Joel, but very upset at the idea of the ambassador being notified.

Soon Joel learns that a central player in the anti-Aquitaine group has been killed back in the United States. Is Joel being cut loose? He learns that Field Marshall Erich Leifhelm and General Bertholdier are in contact through one Ilse Fishbein—Göring's illegitimate daughter! Eventually someone from the embassy reaches Joel; it's Lieutenant Commander Connal Fitzpatrick, a Navy lawyer and the late Preston Halliday's brother-in-law. Connal isn't really with the embassy, in fact he's with the anti-Aquitaine forces and helped Halliday select Joel. After all the deception and deceit, Joel doesn't believe him and doesn't accept his help, although this will change later.

Interpol is now after Joel for the death of the French chauffeur. But Aquitaine has changed its collective mind; having set Interpol after Joel, they don't want him found. They'd rather negotiate with him until they can learn who is behind him. Leifhelm drops in on Joel and Connal at their hotel and invites·Joel to dinner. No need for him to travel all over the map, meeting the principals of Aquitaine—they'll all be there! "Was he an inept gladiator marching into a Roman arena facing far stronger, better-armed, and superior talent?" The answer to the author's question is an emphatic yes, and Joel knows it. " 'I'm the most amateurish fox you've ever heard of in a chicken coop—only in this case it's a vultures' nest.' "

In Tel Aviv, Aquitaine bigwig Chaim Abrahms is meeting with a favorite Mossad agent, who feels that Joel is a soulmate of Aquitaine and wants to join. In Washington, military men who are part of Aquitaine know about Connal Fitzpatrick. Soon their phone is ringing with a call from Mykonos. In Bonn, the U.S. ambassador finds out about Connal. Now American forces are after both Joel and Connal. And back in San Diego, Joel's service records are sealed under an order from Connal— but the order is effective for only seventy-two hours, and an admiral with apparent Aquitaine sympathies is trying to get the seal order removed.

Connal and Joel try to figure out who Joel's "employer" is. The dossiers on the Aquitaine leaders and their Pentagon contacts have all the earmarks of military research. Joel is on a need-to-know basis, and he knows that he's being manipulated. They call Beale in Mykonos, but he has disappeared! Now "he [Joel] was a puppet on the loose, his strings gone haywire, leading only to shadows."

The seal order on Joel's records is voided because Connal lied about his whereabouts. What's so important about the records? Is it Joel's justifiably hating General Delavane's guts? Whatever it is, it's important enough to get Connal's second-in-command killed in a transparently faked accident.

In Bonn, Joel comes to dinner at Leifhelm's estate. It's a cordial meeting once he gets past the metal detectors and the oversize, blood-thirsty Dobermans. Leifhelm and Bertholdier he knows; now he's intro-duced to Chaim Abrahms and General Jan van Headmer, "the Slayer of Soweto." It's a jolly dinner party until Leifhelm confronts Joel over the lamb à citron. Suddenly Joel is shot—but it's only a tranquilizer dart! Under further drugs, he tells everything he knows. Fortunately for the anti-Aquitaine forces, that isn't much.

Connal is back in the hotel, waiting to alert the authorities if Joel doesn't return. He's easily put off by a phone call about an overnight meeting, and when he wakes up the next morning he finds that Joel's room of the suite is spotless. Joel has checked out, he's told, and the hotel needs the room by afternoon, *auf Wiedersehen*. Connal calls Leifhelm and is told that Joel left the estate after the meeting. Now the JAG lawyer is on his own. Is Joel being held? Connal calls Ilse Fishbein and feeds her a cock-and-bull story about an inheritance from a forgotten relative in the United States. He needs a statement about her late father, and who better to give it than Leifhelm? Connal buys a gun, and at the meeting he captures the Field Marshal and his armed chauffeur. He orders Leifhelm to call the estate and have Joel brought to the airport, where there are reservations to the United States awaiting. But Leifhelm has more men in place, these disguised as beer-sodden Bavarians. They burst in, inflict a painful gunshot wound on Connal, and subdue him easily.

The scene shifts back to Joel, who wakes up groggy—and no wonder, he's been drugged into submission for some thirty-six hours! He finds himself still at the estate, in a room conveniently outfitted as a prison cell. Giant Dobermans pad by outside, but in spite of the dogs and the armed guards, Joel manages to get out of the cell and off the grounds. Crawling through the underbrush brings back unpleasant memories of his escape from a North Vietnamese prison camp, but the skills that he learned the hard way serve him well now. Soon he is on the run in Bonn, and he'd be in great shape except that everyone is after him and he doesn't speak the language. Fortunately he is able to get his hands on some of the money entrusted to him on Mykonos, and he is a resourceful liar.

Aquitaine has many resources of its own. The U.S. ambassador has been murdered, and Joel is the prime suspect. His picture is plastered all over the papers, which allege that he became psychopathic after Vietnam. New clothes and clear glasses form an effective disguise.

Once again Joel has to wonder who started the mission and supplied his half-million-dollar stake. At least some questions about this are answered for the reader; in an anonymous room in the United States, two junior officers are discussing the situation with a burned-out, washed-up ex-CIA agent named Peter Stone. They may be able to find Connal Fitzpatrick; they know that the military attaché at the Bonn embassy is working for Aquitaine.

Joel calls his friend Mattilon, who fortunately doesn't believe everything he reads in the newspapers. He has the connections to supply false documentation . . . in Holland. Joel is to identify himself as a friend of "the Tatiana family," a reference to a near-mythic survivor of Imperial Russia. Connal has had the presence of mind to leave clues so that Joel can track down his attaché case. He recovers the case and mails the sensitive files to his ex-wife. Joel doesn't know it, but she still has faith in him; his senior law partner definitely does not. Meanwhile, Mattilon has performed his last favor for Joel. His temporary secretary was planted on him by Aquitaine, and she shoots him to death.

Joel is on a train to Essen and then out of Germany when he learns that he is being blamed for another murder, that of the Supreme Commander of NATO. Now there's an all-points bulletin for an American with a wounded left arm—supposedly wounded by the Commander's bodyguards, actually by Aquitaine. Joel decides to leave the train at Wesel, but he's cornered by a gun-toting colonel of the Luftwaffe. He's really getting into the swing of things now, so he kills the colonel and jumps off the moving train . . . only to be pursued by police and by a Leifhelm trooper who has a score to settle after Joel humiliated him by escaping. Joel manages to kill these pursuers as well.

Peter Stone is trying to trace Connal through Thomas Thayer, a shady operative in Europe who owes him some big favors. Stone invokes the authority of "the Tatiana family." Needless to say, he doesn't give Thayer the true picture of what's going on, but Thayer manages to capture the military attaché from the Bonn embassy. Under drugs, the attaché reveals where Connal is being held.

When Joel was flying into Köln, he met a charming character actor named Caleb Downing—perhaps the Robert Ludlum character? Downing realizes that Joel didn't kill the ambassador, and that the attaché and others are lying. He begins to make his own arrangements.

The border still stands between Joel and the false papers he needs. He bribes his way onto a run-down barge and across the river. A train should carry him to Amsterdam and relative safety, but there's a killer with a silenced gun in the next seat. Joel turns the tables and turns the gun on the would-be captor, but there are Aquitaine agents at the station. Now they know he's in Amsterdam.

Meanwhile, Valerie flies to Germany. Joel sees her being interviewed on television. She's lying about inconsequential details, and Joel realizes that this is her way of alerting him to reach her. He gets her on the phone and manages a cryptic conversation, and soon they are reunited in Amsterdam in a shot-up stolen car. Both of her parents were Resistance heroes in World War II, so she still has connections with their compatriots. Soon there is a small troop of superannuated former Resistance fighters protecting Valerie and Joel. They love it—nothing in the last forty years has made them feel quite as vital and needed as risking their lives in the war.

Val left Joel's father house-sitting at her house—a bad decision for him, as he's killed and the mailed information stolen. Joel tells Valerie everything at her insistence, although they both know that she could be killed for what she knows. She suggests exposing Aquitaine's scheme, and who better to go public than General Sam Abbott, Joel's fellow captive in Vietnam? First they've got to reach General Abbott. Valerie has some of Joel's travel plans figured out, including disguising him as a priest. Will Valerie become the love interest? They haven't done anything more romantic than annihilate an operative of Aquitaine, but Joel is really starting to regret their divorce. Val, however, is firmly over him.

We haven't heard from Connal Fitzpatrick for a while, but things are looking grim for him. He's manacled with other prisoners at an old U-boat base (he doesn't know it, but it's got an interesting history from the beginning of THE HOLCROFT COVENANT), now an Aquitaine training camp. The trainees are building their expertise in assassination; the prisoners are forty-three officers of various armies, all unattached bachelors and all on leave from their units. Connal learns that there are thirteen days to Ground Zero—then eleven, then eight. He overcomes a rather dim-witted guard but doesn't get away.

Joel is leaving Amsterdam in clerical garb, but two Aquitaine agents recognize him at the station. They're on to Val in New York City too, but she's learned from her parents' cronies and knows how to hide and leave a false trail; if only she knew that one of the officers she escapes is working with Stone! Finally she reaches Sam Abbott. Joel makes his own escape with the help of aging Resistance workers, who then proceed to deliver him to agents of Leifhelm.

Abbott listens to Val and is convinced, convinced enough that he will accompany her to Washington and have her meet with someone he trusts. But on a routine training flight, his F-18 crashes and burns! Abbott had confided in Colonel Alan Metcalf, who called people in Washington. With the crash of Abbott's jet, Metcalf realizes that he has trusted the wrong set and he resolves to carry on in Abbot's place.

Joel makes another hairbreadth escape, this time killing three and punching out Val's elderly aunt. They connect for another cryptic phone call and agree to meet in Chamonix. Val's passport sets off alarms at de Gaulle Airport, but fortunately the man who responds to them is a sympathetic Parisian policeman named Prudhomme. He was one of the two policemen who investigated the beating of Bertholdier's "chauffeur"; his partner is on the take to Bertholdier, and Prudhomme realizes that Joel didn't kill the man. He knows that Joel wasn't in a position to commit at least some of the other murders attributed to him: " '. . . if your former husband did not cause the man in Paris to die and could not have shot your old friend Monsieur Mattilon, how many others did he *not* kill . . . ?' " Now firmly on her side, Prudhomme gives Val his private number and the Tatiana family identification.

Valerie and Joel finally rendezvous in Chamonix. Old passions are rekindled and they fall into bed, Joel's priest disguise notwithstanding. Val remembers Metcalf's name from conversations with Abbott, and they decide to call Metcalf. Stone and his boys are also looking for Metcalf—who, like Joel and Abbott, was a POW in Vietnam—but he has left the Air Force base and disappeared. Stone finally reaches Colonel Metcalf and brings him to New York. He also figures out that Aquitaine's secret base has to be the island of Scharhorn.

Now the amateurs are starting to strike back. Joel is a lawyer, don't forget, so he's building a legal case against Aquitaine. He starts by taking depositions from Stone and the junior officers, and we finally get some background on their group. One of Stone's idiosyncratic semi-retired cronies photographs business-suited assassins leaving Scharhorn. Leifhelm, Abrahms, and Bertholdier are all captured by sympathetic ex-military and security types working for Joel and brought to a chateau in France.

Joel's boss, Nathan Simon, brings Joel's own deposition to a Supreme Court justice. From there it would be a short step to involving the President, and Stone could probably mount an undercover operation in eight or ten days—but Simon realizes that the plot will begin with massive antinuclear demonstrations that are scheduled three days hence.

Meanwhile, Joel has a captive audience, so he feeds them lies and plays them one against another. Soon he's got enough material on videotape to prove the conspiracy. He learns that the Scharhorn base houses the master computer with coded instructions, elaborately booby-trapped of course.

The photos from Scharhorn reach Washington, where international intelligence leaders attempt to identify as many of the assassins as possible. Stone realizes that the unidentified fifth boss of Aquitaine is his old friend Derek Bellamy, head of MI6. Bellamy has played a very minor role in the novel and is not especially established as a sympathetic character, so this revelation is a shock to Stone but not to the reader. Bellamy believes in the mission of Aquitaine, and he believes that once control has passed into the hands of the military, the extremists can be displaced; presumably he will then become a benevolent despot.

This is not to be, of course, because there's still time for an assault on Scharhorn. Joel's old skills as a pilot came in handy, and he lands on the island with the burned-out intelligence type, a small force of freelance commandos (don't ask where they came from), and a computer maven. They manage to deprogram most of Aquitaine's instructions; enough are released, and enough assassins uncaptured, to create a fair amount of chaos and a none-too-neat conclusion for the book. But in the end, world stability is restored, and Valerie and Joel are remarried. This typical Ludlum amateur hero finishes by billing various world governments handsomely for his services!

Devoted readers of Robert Ludlum appreciate his swaggering plots, where often nothing less than world domination is at stake. Not all critics

In Mykonos the only color structures are windows, doors and a few roofs. (THE AQUITAINE PROGRESSION)

share this appreciation. Thomas R. Edwards refers to the books as "a distinct genre, 'ludlums' . . . Any reader of ludlums knows that no sensible reference to geopolitical reality is intended." The clever but uncalled-for derision aside, Robert Ludlum has in fact created a genre of which he is the only practicioner. Many authors have written thrillers about military hardware since Tom Clancy showed the way; nobody plots like Robert Ludlum because nobody else can. Alastair MacLean at his most complex matched Ludlum for plot twists, and an occasional thriller will come close. My favorite recent example, especially suitable for those who enjoy technology with their treachery, is *Endgame Enigma* by James P. Hogan. This extremely clever novel owes more to MacLean than to Ludlum; I tend to think of it as "Space Station Zebra."

The complaint about "geopolitical reality" is correct to a certain extent, but it could easily be leveled against nearly all other thrillers as well. The Japanese are systematically bankrupting American companies and buying this country; does it ignore "geopolitical reality" to wonder what would happen if they stepped up their economic assault, a possibility that Thomas Hoover explores to excellent effect in *The Samurai Strategy*? (The format of the title is an example of Ludlum's influence, although he was not the first to use it.)

If we insisted that all thriller writers remain within the confines of "geopolitical reality," there would be practically no suitable large-scale thriller topics outside of World War II. Factions within the French government may well have wanted to assassinate Charles de Gaulle—as I understand it, much of the American government wouldn't have objected—but this more-or-less correct historical connection makes *Day of the Jackal* highly unusual. Dealing with current events is always risky. Adam Hall's *Quiller KGB* climaxes with the destruction of the Berlin Wall; it made sense at the time, but not after the real Wall was broken up for souvenirs. Harold Coyle's *Bright Star* is set in a postwar Middle East, but the war it's post is his own Sword Point, not Desert Storm.

Robert Ludlum's distinctive thrillers ignore "geopolitical reality" only in that his vision is more all-encompassing than most, his villains' ambitions wider-reaching. Some of James Bond's adversaries have designs that will affect the world, but even when they scheme globally they act locally. Grandoise they may be, but Ludlum's plots make as much sense as any other thriller. Couldn't the Nazis have looked beyond the death throes of the Third Reich to planning the fourth? Could a multinational corporation take over a small country? What would happen if Henry Kissinger went nuts? I find these concepts easier to accept than the notion that a single airplane, helicopter, or submarine could change the balance of power in the world. Ludlum's plots also gain credibility because most of his villains have themselves genuinely convinced that their motives are benevolent.

"Geopolitical reality" in the form of current events is the basis of **THE BOURNE SUPREMACY.** There are going to be enormous changes in the Far East when Hong Kong becomes part of the People's Republic of China, and with these upheavals come enormous opportunities for evildoers. For Robert Ludlum, there is an opportunity to create conspiracy, complexity, and confusion.

At a nightclub in Hong Kong, a westerner disguised as a Chinese priest blows away a roomful of shady Oriental business types, including the Vice Premier of China. The killer obviously has a well-organized and well-funded support group, and he has no interest in hiding his identity—he leaves behind a bandanna with the name Jason Bourne!

Bourne is back in lethal action . . . but since we've read THE BOURNE IDENTITY we know that Jason Bourne is a myth, a decoy. Now Edward McAllister, Undersecretary of State and Far East expert, learns it from Ambassador Raymond Havilland.

While "Bourne" is engineering a string of assassinations, the "real" "Jason Bourne" is living quietly under his really real name, David Webb. He still gets tortured flashbacks to a past that he can't completely remember, but he's married Marie St. Jacques and taken a teaching post in Oriental Studies at a small university in Maine. Actually, all of these false and falsely false identities are convoluted, but not nearly as confusing as the quotation marks make them sound. The U.S. government needs Bourne/Webb in China to "neutralize" Sheng Chou Yang, Minister of State in the People's Republic of China. Sheng is a Nationalist plant, a deep, deep-cover agent whose career has been carefully planned and orchestrated. He is actually the son of a corrupt Nationalist, and he has spent his entire life under a false name. Now he is ready to carry out the economic takeover of Hong Kong within one to two months. The plan is a serious enough problem for world stability, but what's worse is that it won't work and the Chinese will blame the United States! Since the false Bourne is Sheng's creation, the plan is for the "real" Bourne to replace him and thereby reach Sheng.

It's not easy to recruit David Webb for this kind of work because he still doesn't trust the government. A pile of federal money is being spent to protect him, but he thinks it's just a trap for Carlos and that he's still being used as bait. McAllister tells Webb about the false Bourne, but Webb isn't interested. " 'Jason Bourne—*that* Jason Bourne—doesn't exist anymore. He never *did!*' " But, like it or not, Webb is going to become involved because "Bourne" has killed the wife of drug lord Yao Ming and now Yao Ming seeks his revenge through Marie St. Jacques.

McAllister has extra guards laid on, but then one day they vanish and McAllister is unavailable. David rushes home to find the place a shambles and Marie gone. There's a note, obviously from Yao Ming; perhaps they can trade, it insinuates. Is there really a Yao Ming? Or did U.S. intelligence plan this to motivate David in the same way that the random strafing death of his wife and children in Southeast Asia turned him into Delta/Jason Bourne/Cain originally? David just happens to have a supply of guns, garottes, and false papers ready to go. A few minutes in the secret closet and he's back in business as Jason Bourne.

David starts calling old contacts in the intelligence community. They all think he's crazy, or at least they say so, and they refuse to help him. He's got a well-documented psychiatric history, and even if he tries to rake up the toxic ashes of Medusa, nobody will believe him. And perhaps he murdered Marie himself and faked her abduction—after all, there's no Yao Ming, and the note was typed on his own typewriter!

At least one old contact is willing to listen; it's Alex Conklin, who in THE BOURNE IDENTITY practically made a career of trying to kill Webb. Lately he's crawled into a whiskey bottle. "Black coffee had a sobering effect on Conklin, but nowhere near the effect of David's confidence in him." They brainstorm strategies and Conklin visits CIA headquarters to spread lies and disinformation. He learns that Marie was taken by "blind" workers. Not only can't the government be incriminated, it can't reach them to call off the kidnapping! Conklin realizes that the operation has been taken over by someone else, someone who wants Bourne even more than the U.S. government does.

David Webb is now having a Bourne identity crisis. " 'They needed you,' " Conklin explains. " 'Not you—Webb, they needed Bourne.' " David replies, " 'Because they say Bourne's already there.' " Later he acknowledges, " 'I'm back, Alex. Back into so much I can't remember.' " He also engages in the following remarkable exchange: " 'You are not listening, Delta.' " " 'I'm not Delta.' " " 'Very well. Bourne.' " " 'I'm not—go on, perhaps I am.' "

David knows that Marie's abduction was intended to lure him to Hong Kong, but as long as she's in Hong Kong he must take the bait. A hotel suite has been reserved for him—by whom? He announces his presence in Hong Kong by giving his name as Jason Bourne and blowing up an illegal arms dealership, then returns to the hotel and shakes down the assistant manager, who seems to know something about what's going on. The man does know something, but it's just a blind phone contact. Jason/David traces this back to the people who are holding Marie. She is allowed to talk to him and tries to relay information. He arranges to meet the taipan in the Walled City, which is the worst slum in Hong Kong if not the entire Orient.

At this point it's worth noting that THE BOURNE SUPREMACY gives a better feel for the locations than any of the books before it. Perhaps the European and American locales in the previous books weren't exotic enough to let Ludlum exercise his descriptive powers. There's enough in a Ludlum thriller that you don't need the scenery, but this book really takes us to the Far East. [In fact, as photos in *The Robert Ludlum Companion* will attest, Ludlum traveled extensively through the area doing on-site research.—Ed.]

Jason approaches the rendezvous cautiously, taking out hidden guards as he goes. But there are more guards where those came from, and they get the drop on him. Jason insists that he didn't kill Yao Ming's wife—and Yao Ming readily states that he already knows it! The taipan is being hounded by the false Jason Bourne, who has been killing his clientele and disrupting his business. He hands the "real" Jason Bourne a list of leads and encourages him to go after the impostor . . . just stay out of Macao, or Marie will be killed instantly.

And speaking of impostors, we learn very shortly that "Yao Ming" is really Major Lin Wenzu of Hong Kong intelligence, and that he is working with McAllister. The Undersecretary is now in Hong Kong, staying in a hastily arranged safe house.

Meanwhile, Marie is wasting away in captivity, and the doctor tending her is becoming very concerned. He needn't have worried; she was only faking and the deception allows her to knock out a guard and escape.

Jason makes contact with a captain of crime, who tells him that the false Jason Bourne is in Macao. He learns some of "Jason Bourne's" procedures, and he is nonplussed to find that they include code phrases known only to the "real" Jason Bourne and his handlers. Impersonating the false Jason Bourne, he discovers that there is an assassination scheduled in Shenzen.

There's nothing to do but to enter the People's Republic of China. He's one of only fifteen Caucasian males on the train, and none of the others fits his description or that of the false Jason Bourne—which is eerily close to his own. He finally spots the false Jason Bourne—getting into an official government car! The car pulls up to a plane that is headed for Guangdong on the Macao border.

On the run in Hong Kong, Marie proves as resourceful as her husband. She's also learned a lot from him and managed to disguise herself subtly but effectively. She tracks down old friend Catherine Staples at the Canadian embassy. Catherine's boyfriend is Ian Ballantyne, retired from Scotland Yard and now chief of Crown Colonial Affairs for Hong Kong. He confirms that there is no Yao Ming, and furthermore that Yao Ming's wife wasn't murdered! Marie realizes that the State Department's reasons for tracking down the false Jason Bourne are illogical lies, and that someone has reasons that go beyond the false Jason Bourne.

The "real" Jason Bourne travels to Macao, where there's a watcher checking each face off the ferry. Jason gets by him and heads for the casino, where there's an essential link in the false Jason Bourne's chain of communications. He spots and follows a series of relays, finally catching one who knows where in China the false Bourne will be the next night and who agrees to take him there.

Crouching in the high grass in China, David sees a figure approach the campfire at the rendezvous—it's himself! Suddenly the countryside erupts in machine-gun fire and grenade explosions. Someone is trying to ambush the false Jason Bourne. David jumps the fleeing figure, but he's got the wrong man. It's just as well, because the man he has is Philippe d'Anjou, another veteran of Medusa and the creator of the false Jason Bourne. We learn that the new "Bourne" is a psychotic British commando; with a little extra training and a little plastic surgery he was perfect for the part. His only secret from d'Anjou is his real name, but now he's working on his own. D'Anjou now wants to stop his protégé, who has accepted a contract that could have disastrous political repercussions. He agrees to work with his old cohort David.

Back in Hong Kong, Catherine learns of the sterile house, and she learns that Ambassador Havilland is there. The inquiries are traced back to her, and now she and Marie are on the run. Catherine is finally captured and brought to the sterile house, where Havilland explains Sheng's scheme to her. It takes a phone call from the President, but he convinces her that State is doing the right thing and he enlists her cooperation. Later Marie will see Catherine with McAllister, draw the wrong conclusions, and escape. Her only hope is to call Alex Conklin. Alex rounds up David's sympathetic psychiatrist, Mo Panov, and the two of them catch the next flight to Hong Kong.

D'Anjou learns that the false Bourne plans to assassinate the Crown Governor at a meeting at Kai-Tak Airport. Soon he and David are on their way disguised as Hong Kong police. At the airport David runs through the killer's options—the ones that he would consider as Bourne! He actually gets face-to-face with the impostor—also disguised as a policeman—who flattens him and gets away. David does manage to thwart the assassination, which was ordered by Sheng Chou Yang.

David and d'Anjou insert themselves back into China and manage to fly to Peking. They spot the false Bourne at the airport, follow him easily to his hotel, and learn his room number. But when they break down the door, they find another man! The impostor has bested his own tutor and the original, and he's given them the slip. When they pick up his trail again, he's disguised as a priest (a favorite trick of Carlos's). He appears to be meeting his employer, who must have Tiananmen Square staked out. David follows the killer into the Chairman Mao Memorial Hall, but then the doors close behind him! Is it a trap for the false Jason Bourne? No, the false Jason Bourne has trapped the real one! David escapes from the mausoleum, putting a couple of slugs into Chairman Mao's corpse as a diversion, but d'Anjou disappears.

On his own in Peking, David finds that every move is a major undertaking. He makes his way to the bird sanctuary, which must be the headquarters of the plot to destabilize Hong Kong. At the gates, he finds that the guards have been replaced by Nationalist conspirators. He watches six limousines pull up, one of them carrying the false Bourne. Next to arrive is a truckload of bound and gagged prisoners, among them Philippe d'Anjou.

In Hong Kong, Conklin and Dr. Panov shake surveillance at the airport and learn that Havilland is in town at the safe house. They drive to Catherine's apartment and arrive just in time to see her gunned down.

David breaks into the bird sanctuary. D'Anjou remembers his old tricks from Medusa, and he's left a trail of gravel pebbles as the prisoners were led away. David catches up in time to watch a prisoner messily executed with a ceremonial sword. His "crime" is very unclear—perhaps thought crimes against "the true China," but the leader's mental status is perfectly clear. Not only is he a fanatic and a lunatic, we learn from his exchanges with a woman prisoner that he's a male chauvinist pig. He's Sheng Chou Yang!

D'Anjou knows that he's doomed no matter what he does. His last words contain a cryptic message for David, then he hurls himself at Sheng. The false Bourne watches with detachment as Sheng's sword cleaves the Medusa veteran's skull. David captures the impostor but fails to kill Sheng.

Meanwhile, Alex Conklin has secured the reluctant cooperation of a State Department functionary. He casually drops in at the safe house. McAllister and Havilland realize that Conklin is too furious and too well-informed to simply dismiss, so they bring him on board. They're speaking in euphemisms, which Conklin angrily dismisses. But even while despising their manipulations and the way they try to distance themselves from the human cost of their dispassionate decisions, he has to give them some credit. " 'I'm in the presence of a master bastard,' " he says with grudging admiration. Lin Wenzu, ever a font of ancient Oriental wisdom, is not altogether fond of McAllister: " 'May the eagle's beak be caught in its elimination canal.' "

Catherine's death indicates that the operation has been penetrated, and that means one of Lin Wenzu's nine handpicked aides is a traitor. To catch the traitor, Lin will have to play traitor himself. The ruse works with comparative simplicity and brevity; Lin is grievously wounded but manages to kill the double agent and his contact.

David is now in a sticky predicament, fleeing through China with an unwilling and potentially lethal companion whom he must deliver alive. He hijacks an airplane, blows up a few fuel trucks as a diversion, and parachutes back into Hong Kong. Holed up in a cheap hotel, the false Bourne reveals his real name. Not that it matters to the plot, but he's the disavowed son of a famous general. His motivation is much clearer; he's always known that he was sadistic and sick, and he's in the assassination game for the kicks.

David calls the number he was given to report the capture of the false Bourne—and it isn't working! Actually the "operator" is working for McAllister and stalling David. He eventually catches on because a real Hong Kong operator would never be polite or helpful, but by then several American or Hong Kong agents have arrived at the hotel. David subdues them and gets away with the false Bourne.

Now there's nothing to do but break into the safe house with the "real" Jason Bourne and the false one working together. David has to hand his double a gun and some plastique.

Conklin, Panov, and Marie are all heading to the safe house to intercept David when they hear the first explosion. They're too late to prevent a near-massacre of the Marine guard detachment. David is on the verge of leveling the house and killing everyone inside when Conklin limps into view—but David still thinks that Conklin is trying to kill him! Now Marie makes an appeal for sanity. She's forgotten that she's still disguised, and it might not matter; David is lost within the mentality of Delta. The false Jason Bourne makes his break and is cut down by the Marines. As the echoes of gunfire subside, Jason Bourne gradually returns to himself as David Webb.

Havilland explains all to David, Marie, and Mo Panov. Sheng's plot to take over Hong Kong is also backed by the Triads. Experienced readers can guess what's coming now—David will have to impersonate the Jason Bourne impersonator. The corpse will be identified as the real Jason Bourne.

That's what David is told, and in Havilland's thinking it would be best if he can reach and kill Sheng. But the real plan is for David to be captured and reveal everything to Sheng. This will let Sheng know that the United States knows about the conspiracy, and he'll have to call off his plot. Everything is duplicity; when David and McAllister helicopter to Macao, even their covert journey is a miniature masterpiece of blackmail and counterblackmail.

Havilland has a secret plan, but McAllister has his own. He will pretend to be disgruntled with his career at State; he is tired of seeing others with less intellect but more charm pass him by, and now he wants a piece of the pie. He will arrange a meeting with Sheng on the pretense of asking for a massive bribe, then he will kill Sheng. He has left behind records of past illicit transactions and a long-standing blood feud with Sheng, so that if McAllister is captured or killed, the U.S. government will not be held responsible. And even if he and Bourne fail to kill Sheng, the details of McAllister's confession would destroy Sheng's credibility or even get him killed.

David feels that the best way to take out Sheng would be to subcontract some of the work to other killers, but McAllister insists that these could be traced to the U.S. government. They'll do it his way, especially since Marie is a virtual prisoner in the safe house.

At the final meeting, McAllister has Sheng along. Why doesn't he shoot? Sheng's elite troops, all armed to the teeth with automatic weapons, are creeping up on the meeting ground. McAllister finally steels himself to shoot, but Sheng shoots him first. Jason tries to shoot Sheng, but his gun jams. Finally he gets the job done and leaves an incriminating document on the body. How are Jason and the wounded McAllister going to get out of this one? Fortunately Sheng's helicopter is parked nearby with the motor running, and the pilot is only too happy to defect to Hong Kong.

In Hong Kong (THE BOURNE SUPREMACY)

After the climactic resolution, the ending is brief, unambiguous, and positively cheerful. Lin Wenzu will recover, although he will lose the use of his left arm. His future with MI6 looks extremely bright. McAllister will become the chairman of the National Security Council. He's concerned because he isn't telegenic enough, but Havilland assures him that the government needs thinkers too. David and Marie are finally back together, and as the sun sets over the beaches of Hawaii, they can bid a not-so-fond farewell to David's identity as Jason Bourne. Of course they don't know that we already have a copy of THE BOURNE ULTIMATUM on our bookshelves. . . .

———————

Hong Kong, destabilized by its impending connection to China, is a trouble spot ripe for the kind of political machinations favored by Robert Ludlum and his readers. In **THE ICARUS AGENDA** he takes us to another one, the Middle East.

Under the sweltering sun of Oman, the terrorist takeover of the American embassy grinds into its twenty-second day. Eleven of the two hundred forty-seven hostages have already been murdered. This isn't Iran—the fanatics have no connection with the government. In fact, the entire event has been externally programmed and only one terrorist in ten is actually from Oman.

Back in Washington, D.C., an obscure Congressman from Colorado drops into a Consular Operations headquarters and offers his help—in Arabic. He's Evan Kendrick, and he's done a lot of work in the Middle East in general and Oman in particular; in fact, his construction company built about half of it. He's been on his annual whitewater camping pilgrimage and out of touch for weeks, but he flew back to Washington as soon as he heard the news.

He sees the embassy takeover as a move to destabilize the region and force legitimate companies out so that illegitimate companies can move in and reap massive profits. His own Kendrick Group was targeted for harassment by this cartel led by "the Mahdi." In his case the pressure worked; after an "accident" killed off most of his personnel plus their families at a company outing, he sold the company for a rock-bottom $25 million and got out of the Middle East. Kendrick's motives are clear; he feels he owes the region something, and he'd like to return there and work again someday. But is he being manipulated by the unseen genius recording his strategies on a heavily shielded computer? Or is the man in front of the CRT manipulating the Mahdi?

Frank Swann of Consular Operations explains that U.S. intelligence can't acknowledge Evan's help. That's fine with him—he wants anonymity to protect his old friends from reprisals. Cons Ops can fly Evan to the Middle East in secrecy, and there he is met by "believers" who supply him with Arab clothes and dye for his skin. Encountering an old friend, he learns that the forces of reason are silent in Masqat, Oman, for fear of reprisal.

In spite of efforts to keep his arrival secret, a beautiful woman named Khalehla has been following and photographing Kendrick!

Evan is spirited to a military encampment in the desert, where he meets with his friend Ahmat, the young American-educated sultan who has only recently ascended to the throne. Evan explains that the original Mahdi (the word means "successor" in Arabic and refers to the prophet who will follow Mohammed) set the Sudan ablaze with war against the British a century ago. The new Mahdi is a financier whose goals are purely commercial. Ahmat doesn't believe him until a prominent citizen of Masqat is gunned down just for being an old friend of Kendrick's.

The next step takes Evan into Masqat's worst slum. Khalehla has traded her camera for a pistol. She misses her chance to kill Evan, and he goes on to meet with El-Baz, a well-known forger of documents and identities. We will learn later that Khalehla is working for the Sultan— in fact she was the roommate of his American wife back at Radcliffe. She wasn't trying to kill Evan, just to protect herself from local thugs.

Evan arranges to have himself arrested as a terrorist and thrown into a reeking jail packed with real terrorists. The inmates brutalize the new arrival, but soon they come to accept him as Amal Bahrudi, a notorious Eastern European terrorist. The real Bahrudi has just met his violent end elsewhere, and that news is being suppressed. Evan meets the leader of the incarcerated contingent, Azra ("blue" in Arabic), whose sister Zaya Yateem is one of the leaders at the embassy. To ensure his acceptance, Evan leads several of his fellow inmates in an escape that has, of course, been carefully staged with the cooperation of the authorities.

Meanwhile, a fumbling, besotted, overweight Briton named Tony McDonald changes into dark clothing and slinks into the night. Khalehla will realize that his cheerfully idiotic image is a cover, and that he must have a wide intelligence network in the region. Whom is he working for? Soon it is clear that it is the Mahdi.

As Evan and his newfound terrorist friends make their way down the road, Khalehla is following them and McDonald is following her. In a blacked-out aircraft overhead, five commandos from Israel's Masada Brigade are about to parachute into Masqat. One of the hostages is a leader of Mossad, trapped while in a deep-cover identity, and the commandos are coming to rescue him. If they can't get him out, they'll kill him to protect the information in his head. The leader of the raid, Yaakov, is actually the man's son, but he probably wouldn't have too much trouble with the last part of the plan; Masada is the historical site where hundreds of Jewish zealots killed themselves and their families rather than submit to their Roman besiegers.

The commandos learn of Kendrick's mission. They think he's nuts and that the U.S. government is nuts, but the government has cut him off completely, and he may be able to help them, so they'll try to help him—if they can find him. The best man for the job of locating Kendrick has to be Emmanuel Weingrass, self-appointed and unofficial but not unpaid "consultant" to Mossad. He is now living out his idiosyncratic retirement in Paris, but before that he was the keystone of the Kendrick Group.

Evan finally gets into the embassy, where he claims that he is supposed to be flown to Bahrain to meet with the Mahdi. Again his transport is actually set up through the Sultan. McDonald also enters the embassy, in his case disguised as a journalist—and he recognizes Evan! Evan bluffs his way out of this one and onto a plane to Bahrain, with Khalehla locked in the cockpit.

Evan explains to McDonald that he really is the disguised Kendrick, but that he is working for the Mahdi. McDonald obviously doesn't believe this; his response is to throw Evan in front of a moving car. Confusing? Now not even the hidden puppet master with the computer is sure what's going on. Khalehla and a sympathetic doctor patch Evan up in the luxurious dwelling of a royal family relative. She explains to Evan that she is working for a benevolent Arab organization and with the Sultan. Then she gives Evan a bit of the more personalized therapy that experienced readers have been expecting. Soon she's phoning Frank Swann of Cons Ops. Kendrick gets his own phone call; they're on to him, and he'll be killed if he leaves the building. Taking this advice with a grain of salt, he creates a new disguise and leaves.

The Israeli commandos capture McDonald, but he is cut down by three Arab assassins. The commandos kill them in turn, but McDonald's secrets have died with him. Soon they will kill Azra too, a rather inopportune bit of timing, as Evan is on his way to meet the terrorist who will lead him to the Mahdi. Evan and the commandos meet over a blood-soaked corpse in Azra's hotel room. By this point he is thoroughly sick of extremists and fanatics, no matter what side they're on. " 'Shoot up the [expletive deleted] world. I don't give a damn.' "

Finally Evan gets to meet the Mahdi, whom he recognizes as a black fraud from Chicago masquerading as an Arab. The Mahdi explains his business philosophy: " 'We set people against people with forces they cannot control; we divide and conquer completely without ourselves firing a shot.' " He plans to use Evan as evidence of American meddling in the internal affairs of Middle Eastern countries. Weingrass and the commandos are poring over contracts and deeds and manage to identify the Mahdi's business as Zareeba Limited, headquartered in Khartoum. (To complete the parallel with his namesake, the Mahdi should have an address in Omdurman.) Weingrass, too, is able to identify the Mahdi. The commandos rescue Kendrick, and the Mahdi is forced to end the siege at the embassy. Weingrass and Kendrick are reunited; the Congressman will bring the wily old architect to Colorado to remodel his property.

Well, that's plenty of action for one book, right? Wrong! THE ICARUS AGENDA is slightly less than one-third over. We're not finished with Evan Kendrick, and neither is the manipulator at the computer screen.

A year later, limousines roll up to a mansion in Cynwid Hollow, Maryland, and five power brokers assemble in a distinguished study where the Franklin stove provides warmth, rustic charm, and a convenient way to dispose of their top-secret notes. If this sounds familiar, it's because the group is a resurrected Inver Brass. They've even got an agent-of-all-trades named Varak; this one is Milos, nephew of the famous Anton. The new Inver Brass knows of Kendrick, even his adventures in Oman which were supposed to be kept tightly under wraps. Evan is a very reluctant politician who ran for his seat in the House only because he couldn't stand his corrupt predecessor; Inver Brass wants him on the national ticket. President Langford Jennings is virtually assured of victory, and if Kendrick is elected Vice President, he will be President within eleven months. Does Inver Brass know something we don't know about Jennings's health—or are they prepared to do something about it?

Using blackmail for benevolent purposes, Inver Brass engineers for Evan a series of prestigious committee appointments which he grudgingly accepts. He is beginning to make a name for himself when his exploits in Oman are revealed on network news. The media descend on him like locusts, but Evan escapes rather than exploit the publicity. The reporting has a very anti-Arab slant, which serves to alienate Sultan Ahmat from Evan. The congressman reaches Frank Swann, who has also gotten his share of flak over the exposed secret. Trying to identify the source of the leak, he reviews those who knew. It's a very tight circle, and we learn that it includes one Adrienne Rashad, a.k.a. Khalehla, an agent of U.S. intelligence. Swann also had a visit from the disturbingly well-informed Eastern European, undoubtedly Varak. The Cons Ops pro explains things to Evan in convoluted jargon. " 'Will you please speak English, or Arabic if you like.' "

Evan's newfound fame garners him an invitation to meet President Langford Jennings and Herb Dennison, the President's obnoxious but effective chief of staff. He's due for a medal which he doesn't want; until the ceremony, which he also doesn't want, he'll stay at a safe house in Cynwid Hollow. It's not the Inver Brass house—it's next door!

While Manny Weingrass is being followed in Colorado, Khalehla is flown back to the United States. She meets Evan at the safe house. The meeting starts on an uncomfortable note because he thinks she leaked the story of his adventures, but she convinces him otherwise. She is quick to point out that he's very much an amateur; his travels after leaving Cons Ops may have been concealed, but he left a wide trail on his way there. Khalehla realizes that Evan's travels were reconstructed by Varak—they know of him, but not his name or his affiliation. Khalehla will stay in the United States and work with "Uncle" Mitchell Payton to find the leak. Payton is a college classmate of Khalehla's mother's, her old control after she joined the CIA, and currently very big at the Agency.

There's another leak, this one at Inver Brass, and Varak is now in Colorado, trying to trace it. He, too, learns that someone is following Weingrass. The follower is with the FBI!

After the medal ceremony, Evan's house in Fairfax, Virginia, is transformed into a veritable fortress to protect him from terrorist reprisals. It will also serve as Khalehla's headquarters. She moves into the house, but she makes it clear that she is not moving in with Evan.

Varak traces the FBI man to a special unit investigating threats on the Vice President's life. We learn, from an unsavory Secret Service agent blackmailed into providing the information, about Mrs. Ardis Vanvlanderen, the Vice President's tough-as-nails chief of staff. She's a recent appointment and exercises a great deal of control over the VP—perhaps on behalf of the industrial fat cats who plan to run the country. Even without Ardis, the moneyed interests have the VP in their pocket, which is why Inver Brass wants to replace him. Could Ardis have been the boss of a sleazy international financing scam that once tried to bilk the Kendrick Group? Of course she was, *and* she had a brief affair with Kendrick. She has located Weingrass and plots against Evan through the elderly architect. She is actually working for her current husband and thus for the fat cats, thereby against Inver Brass, of which the fat cats are at least somewhat aware.

Back in Washington, Evan is nowhere to be found. His loyal and resourceful secretary sends her husband (a policeman of Irish extraction, highly regarded in Washington) out to Fairfax, where he finds the gates open and the guards and faithful retainers all dead. He calls Payton, who sends for the "shroud squad" to clean up. Evan is safely in the Bahamas; he should have told his secretary, but she was out of the office so he told Phillip Tobias, the head of his staff. Tobias soon turns up dead in the boiler room of the Capitol building.

When the phone lines to the Fairfax home were cut, so were the lines to the house in Colorado. Weingrass is heading for the tiny nearby town to make a call, when he spots shadowy figures sneaking up on the house. In spite of his age, he manages to take out two, then two more whom we recognize from Masqat. He tries to take them alive, but the only survivor is a fanatical but not-too-bright teenager. Evan and Khalehla are flown to the scene in a military jet. He identifies the bodies; he can't really blame them for being just a little upset after he pretended to be part of their group and then betrayed them. " 'Yes, I know each one. . . . They wanted their revenge, and if I were them, I'm not sure I'd feel so differently.' " " 'You're not a terrorist, Congressman.' " " 'What separates a terrorist from a "freedom fighter"?' "

This question has been raised before in one form or another, and it's usually used to justify the unconscionable. Ludlum has an answer for it, though, spoken by a CIA man: " 'For starters, *sir*, terrorists make it a point to kill innocent people. Ordinary men and women who just happened to be there. . . .' " All concerned fail to note that even before Kendrick was betraying the terrorists, the terrorists' own sponsors were manipulating and betraying them. And speaking of these sponsors, it now appears from the logistics of operations in the United States that there must be two different groups out to get Kendrick.

It's been a long day in Colorado, and everyone turns in. Weingrass isn't feeling well. . . . Could his new doctor—the replacement for the one who just conveniently died of a heart attack—have injected something unpleasant while taking a blood sample? Evan and Khalehla finally turn in together.

The reader is pleasantly surprised to find that Weingrass wakes up the next morning. But more terrorists are flying into Denver; that isn't pleasant, and it's not really a surprise. We learn that Andy Vanvlanderen (husband of Ardis) supplied their funds and their lead to Kendrick. Khalehla has to fly off somewhere just when they could really use her help in Colorado. All of this has happened within a day of the massacre in Fairfax. The President and Payton manage to completely suppress the news of this last event. Their ploy may not catch the terrorists, but it provokes Vanvlanderen into a fatal stroke.

The teenaged hit man finally spills the beans. The next team will be disguised as priests—and they're visiting Kendrick's house right now! A bloody assault leaves the house and grounds littered with dead guards, dead nurses, and dead Arab assassins.

Khalehla was on her way to San Diego, where she confronts Ardis Vanvlanderen and supplies information that will panic the conniving widow. Varak is also there, watching the hotel. The traitor within Inver Brass shows up, thus giving himself away. Actually, he's a traitor to a group that thinks it knows best on the country's behalf—working for another group that also wants to run the country and considers Inver Brass a "benevolent society of misfits." The difference between the two is that the second group has its own interests very much at heart and its noble motives are hollow-sounding rationalizations, but then, Inver Brass's paternalistic machinations aren't necessarily much better.

The two agents naturally run into each other. Khalehla is suspicious of Varak but comes to accept him as an ally. She infers the existence of a group promoting Kendrick, and Varak confirms her theory. Varak sneaks into Ardis's suite to remove electronic listening devices; he spots a photo of Ardis with a man whose face rings a bell. He's a shady Saudi financier of some sort, and his association with the Vice President's chief of staff is a bad sign. Varak will later kill the traitor, but he is mortally wounded in the assault. Before he dies he passes his information along to Khalehla.

Evan joins Khalehla in San Diego, where they go over the transcripts from the bugs in Ardis's suite. Evan plans to ingratiate himself with the Vice President and his fat-cat buddies by pretending that he, too, can be bought. They seem to accept this completely, but then he is drugged and captured. First, however, he sees the VP with the false doctor who injected a slowly lethal virus into Manny Weingrass. He wakes up imprisoned on an unnamed island with Mafia-connected guards. He's drugged again and wakes up in a mansion on the island, where he meets the fat cats' lawyer, Crayton Grinnell. Kendrick's execution is ordered, but he breaks away. He sabotages or blows up most of the equipment on the island—after all, he is a construction engineer, so he's just doing his job in reverse—and gets away in a stolen boat with the help of a sympathetic gardener who will take a few slugs for his trouble. He makes a call on the boat's radio and gets the President to send in the Marines, but Grinnell has already had himself picked up by a seaplane.

Payton confronts the head of Inver Brass. He very much approves of the organization's high-handed methods and threatens to expose it. The man kills himself.

Payton has also gotten his hands on Grinnell's secret ledger, and the CIA is able to decode it. With this information, the President confronts the Vice President and other malefactors high in government. He fires the VP but tells the rest that they have to stay on and clean up the mess they've created.

Evan survives yet another murder attempt, this one by an infiltrator disguised as a nurse. Not having had enough adventures, he decides that he will return to the Middle East and take on Abdel Hamendi, the dealer who sells eighty percent of the armaments in the region. Meanwhile, the son of the Mahdi has all the old contacts and is ready to resurrect his father's business empire. Sultan Ahmat finally gets the whole story and is friends again with Kendrick.

Rather than assault Hamendi directly, Evan will sabotage a shipload of weapons and thereby ruin the dealer's reputation. He assembles a balanced if potentially disputatious commando force: six Omani royal guard troops, six Palestinians, and six Israelis. The Congressman, the Sultan, and the glamorous Khalehla go along with them. As the weapons are unloaded at Nishtun, South Yemen, Hamendi watches—with Grinnell by his side. Evan encourages the waiting mob of customers to try out some of their lethal new goodies, and of course the resulting misfires, malfunctions, and explosions infuriate the mob. Grinnell and Hamendi talk their way out of trouble, but Kendrick can't stand to see them go free. Still disguised as an Arab, he cuts them both down.

We finally learn who the man behind the computer is: Varak's successor, whose talents lean more to data processing than skullduggery. He is working for a benevolent and powerful Inver Brass that will carry on despite the loss of its leader. Evan finally decides to accept the nomination for Vice President. It wouldn't do to have the candidate living in sin, so at the urging of the President and Manny Weingrass, he will marry Khalehla.

THE ICARUS AGENDA has a lot going for it: a believable amateur hero, some of Ludlum's best locales, a wonderful comic-relief character in Manny Weingrass, explosive geopolitics that make a great basis for a story, conspiracies within conspiracies, and our old friends Inver Brass. If the book has a failing, it's that it tries to do too much. The Abdel Hamendi subplot is a largely irrelevant addition to a book that is definitely long enough. Son of Mahdi deserves an entire sequel, although it's difficult to see how even Robert Ludlum could make it plausible for the Vice President of the United States to go undercover in the Middle East; if the resurrection of Zareeba Limited can't be followed and foiled in depth, then it's just a distraction.

THE BOURNE ULTIMATUM suffers from no such surplus of story lines. It's just Jason Bourne against Carlos for the final time; the involvement of a worldwide conspiracy is just a side issue. The story opens with a flash-forward. Creeping up on General Norman Swayne's fortified estate in Virginia, David Webb is Bourne again. There's a new and evil Medusa destroying whole segments of national economies for its own profit, but Bourne's only interest is whether it can lead him to Carlos. Webb/Bourne is now fifty years old; he's getting too old for this sort of thing, and he's got two children at home.

At a surrealistic carnival outside Baltimore, Alex Conklin and Mo Panov push their separate ways through the milling crowd. Each is there in response to a summons from their old friend David Webb. Just as they meet, a sniper's bullet shatters an innocent bystander's throat. Is it a trap for them? For David? It must be Carlos on his trail. They alert David, and very quickly he is on the run with Marie and the kids.

Alex confronts CIA director Peter Holland. How did Carlos learn of his and Panov's involvement with Jason Bourne? How did any of the Bourne file get released, especially since he's supposed to be notified if it's accessed? The director brings in Steven DeSole, a sympathetic analyst now tied to a desk. (" 'I haven't had a briefcase chained to my wrist since I can't remember when.' ") DeSole assures him that Bourne's records have not been touched. Conklin then brings the director and his aides up-to-date—the file is so secret that even the head of the CIA doesn't know the full story of David Webb's masquerade as Jason Bourne.

The plan is that Alex and Mo will be followed to see who is after them. Their next pursuers are a group of geriatric Orientals, who tell them that a great Tai Pan from Hong Kong wants to meet them. But before the messengers can be captured, they are shot dead and therefore unavailable for further information. Their wounds are in the throat, Carlos-style; David Webb has to remind Alex that legions of oldsters are another Carlos trick. Things are getting serious, and Marie and the kids are on their way to the Caribbean.

Alex and David/Jason realize that many Medusa alumni have gone on to careers in business and government, in some cases far bigger careers than their abilities and backgrounds would seem to indicate. Why not shake them up by having Bourne threaten to expose them? If they hire Carlos to assassinate Bourne, this will lure Carlos into the open.

In Boston, Harvard Law professor Randolph Gates, legal champion of plutocratic causes and defender of the rich, has traced Marie and the children at least to the Caribbean. He telephones the news to Paris, and we know that he is somehow working for Carlos. Carlos dispatches an elderly assassin to Montserrat, but help is on the way in a most unlikely form. Brendan Prefontaine is the washed-up, alcoholic, disbarred former judge who did Gates's dirty work for him. He extorts a generous fee from his dishonest employer, then decides to take a vacation . . . in Montserrat.

Prefontaine happens to choose the resort on Tranquility Isle run by John St. Jacques, brother of Marie. The superannuated killer is traveling under the name of Fontaine, so naturally the two meet. "Fontaine" thinks that Prefontaine is an observer sent by Carlos to verify the hit and kill Fontaine's dying wife; actually he's close—this task is planned for the "nurse" who accompanies the old couple. When Carlos and company learn of Prefontaine's presence on the island, they think he's Gates, who has secrets of his own beyond his involvement with Carlos.

Now we're caught up to the flash-forward. Sneaking up on a fortified estate isn't so easy at age fifty, but Jason Bourne makes his way into the house. There he meets Master Sergeant Flannagan, actually General Swayne's boss and the General's wife's unconcealed lover. Flannagan is working for Medusa; he was recruited by a limping CIA man.

Swayne kills himself. Alex sends a CIA-stringer physician to investigate, and we learn that the General was really murdered. His wife is the obvious suspect, but actually it was done by an outside hit man from Medusa.

Swayne's notes reveal the name of Randolph Gates. Conklin calls the Boston lawyer and bluffs him into admitting that he knows that Marie and the kids are in the Caribbean. Alex calls John St. Jacques, who is off Tranquility Isle and on the "big island" of Montserrat. A storm cuts off phone service and boat access to the island, but John races over in a borrowed drug boat (which he proceeds to total) to save his sister, nephew, and niece. But the real saving is done by "Fontaine." He realizes that the "nurse" was to kill both him and his wife; then his last shreds of decency come to the fore and he cannot kill the children. They fake the murder, knowing that Carlos will be there the next day to finish off David Webb/ Jason Bourne. Jason flies in, Marie and the kids fly out. On arrival, Jason stages a scene over three coffins, which are, of course, empty. Soon three guards are found dead with gunshot wounds to the throat, a sure sign that Carlos is there. Eventually Jason traps Carlos in the resort's chapel, but as the building burns, it is Carlos who has the drop on him. Jason is shot in the neck, but it's another of the lucky wounds so essential in thrillers, painful but not serious.

" 'What kind of world do you live in?' " asks John, who now has no doubts that his brother-in-law is seriously involved.

" 'One I'm sorry you ever became a part of. But now you are, and you'll play by its rules, my rules.' "

The "final" showdown leaves innocent bystanders and corrupt henchmen bleeding and dying all over the resort. Carlos escapes in a boat before the last corpuscle has oozed into the rich tropical earth.

Back in the United States, we learn that the mole at Langley was Steven DeSole. The modern Medusa is a very competitive conglomerate whose methods go far beyond the free market. We later learn that it is working with the Mafia and also with the Soviets, for whom it is a prime source of restricted technology. (In reality, the Soviets would have no need to deal with criminals when some corporations are happy to sell them restricted technology at list price.) DeSole meets with a Mafia capo and Albert Armbruster, the head of the FTC. They later order him killed, then Armbruster orders a Mafia hit on Jason Bourne. DeSole is an easy one and a relative bargain; to take care of Bourne will cost $5 million. Armbruster will shortly be shot dead by an unidentified hit man.

Jason is still after Carlos, so he arranges hush-hush transportation to Paris. On arrival he is recalled so that the CIA can debrief him about the new incarnation of Medusa, but he dodges the order. Marie decides that she, too, will go to Paris; since she knows Jason's old haunts, she should be able to find him. In nearby Belgium, the Supreme Commander of NATO is assassinated and the hit attributed to Jason Bourne. We know that the General was with Medusa, and that a top CIA executive was flying out to question him.

Back in the United States, Morris Panov is kidnapped—and just after Alex Conklin had dinner with him and revealed Jason Bourne's plans. The Mafia plans to wring him dry under chemical interrogation, and not only about Bourne. Don't forget he's a psychiatrist; he must know something they can use to blackmail his patients in government positions. Fortunately the resourceful psychiatrist escapes, leaving behind a dazed thug and a demolished car. Later Dr. Panov will insist on being debriefed under chemicals, unpleasant though he knows the experience will be, so that he can find out what he revealed. Little of his session is useful, but it does hint strongly at the Medusa-Mafia connection.

Although Jason Bourne is Robert Ludlum's perennial professional secret agent, THE BOURNE ULTIMATUM blends his tradecraft with the amateur heroics that Ludlum writes so well. Besides Panov's adventures and Marie's insistence on entering the lion's den, we have Brendan Prefontaine developing another lead to Carlos.

Jason's next stop is Argenteuil, and a seedy bar popular with disreputable Foreign Legion veterans. The bar is a known message center for Carlos. Just as Jason is getting a promising lead, he is clubbed unconscious and captured. Fortunately his captor is Santos, the bartender, not Carlos, and Jason talks his way out of trouble and into the next lead.

Prefontaine's phone number for Carlos is different from the one Jason got from Santos, and Jason smells a trap. He blows up a van full of Carlos's henchmen, but Carlos escapes from his headquarters which is disguised in part as a nunnery; in fact it is a working convent filled with innocents who have no idea what else goes on in their building. Jason tracks down a fleeing "nun" who turns out to be none other than Jacqueline Lavier, an executive at Les Classiques. But, no, it's not really Jacqueline, it's her sister, Dominique, who has been living the part unwillingly for years. She knows that Carlos will kill her as he just killed Santos, so she has no choice but to help Jason. Actually she betrays him, but he is one step ahead and sets her up. His trap is set for the Hotel

Meurice. It's a place dimly remembered by Jason, well remembered by Marie—and she's staying there! Fortunately she is able to decipher a cryptic message in a newspaper and reach Bernardine, an aging Deuxième Bureau retiree and elegant boulevardier type who warns her to leave the hotel. Carlos pulls up with a limousine full of false priests. Naturally there is a gun battle, and Bernardine is killed.

Back in Washington, the CIA is still more interested in Medusa than in the Webb family's personal problems, and properly so. However, director Peter Holland agrees to fly Conklin and Panov to Paris. Later he will put Conklin in touch with Dimitri Krupkin, the head of KGB at the Soviet embassy in Paris. The KGB has long wanted Carlos dead. He is a former trainee from their ultra-secret deep-cover training facility at Novgorod; they realized that he was too crazy and uncontrollable to be of service, and he escaped just before they could flunk him out 9mm-style. Conklin reaches Jason through a cryptic message on his answering machine. In spite of the CIA's precautions, Alex and Mo are spotted at the airport by a Mafia stringer and their arrival is signaled to Carlos.

Jason, Mo, Alex, and Carlos's troops all come together with Krupkin—a humorous, worldly, westernized fellow and an old buddy of Conklin's, usually known as "Kruppie"—at an inn outside Paris. There's another massacre, but again Carlos gets away. The sight of more innocent victims, plus a note from Carlos indicating that he knows where the kids are hidden, drives Jason into screaming incoherence. He makes a quick recovery and soon he is plotting with Alex and Kruppie to lure Carlos to Moscow, where the support systems will be on their side. En route to Moscow, they pause only to thwart an attempted hit at the airport. The

Grenada during a rough time (THE BOURNE ULTIMATUM)

Mafia's best assassin isn't in Bourne's league and comes off a definite second in the shootout, but Mo Panov is gravely wounded.

The new Medusa is also on its way to Moscow in the person of Bryce Ogilvie, Esq., senior partner of a prestigious Manhattan law firm. Things are getting too hot for his illegal operations. The Soviets could turn him in—or they could protect him and continue to reap the benefits of Medusa's trade connections.

In Moscow, Kruppie is able to identify Carlos's mole: it's General Rodchenko, the number-two man at the KGB. Soon Carlos is meeting with Ogilvie. The treacherous lawyer has an old connection to Jason Bourne; back in Vietnam, Jason actually caught and had brought to trial murderers in the U.S. Army, and Ogilvie helped them beat the rap.

Once Carlos confirms that the KGB is on to Rodchenko, he shoots the General in the throat. He then learns that Jason Bourne is in Moscow.

At this point the pace of the plot is becoming faster and faster. Carlos's cadre of Soviet middle-management types rebels and refuses to take further orders from him, and he is quickly losing control of himself. There's a shootout at a Moscow hotel, and Carlos is wounded. Jason stalks him through the corridors and stairways and wounds him again, but even though the KGB has the hotel surrounded, he escapes. Carlos is unarmed at this point, but that's no problem for the Soviet-trained assassin—he just breaks into an armory. He leaves with hostages, but Jason realizes this is just a decoy and he must take on Carlos alone. Carlos sets a trap which fails to get Jason but wounds both Alex and Kruppie.

Carlos appears to be headed for the secret training complex at Novgorod. Jason has the Soviets release the news that he, Jason, has been killed. Marie will eventually see the news item, but he loads it with enough false details to let her know it's a fake. With the cooperation of the KGB, Jason becomes the first American to enter the "American" compound at Novgorod. Ludlum paints a fascinating picture of the facility; although brief, it is more plausible, more complete, and more fraught with possibilities than any other thriller author's. His Novgorod includes microcosms of many different countries, and of course "international boundaries." We'd like to see more of it, much more, but Carlos has snuck in with revenge on his mind and soon much of the place is in flames.

The resulting panic plays right into Carlos's hands. Jason attempts to control the situation with the reluctant help of a trainer named Benjamin who doesn't understand the necessity for his brutal methods. Finally he catches Carlos, but Carlos fools him again and Jason pays for his mistake with two bullet wounds. Carlos finally is killed, but not by Jason;

Benjamin brings about his grotesque end by activating some of the complex's intricate security devices.

The ending is as neat and happy as Ludlum's endings ever get. Prefontaine dries out, and he will have a handsome annual income provided by Randolph Gates through a combination of gratitude and blackmail. He is still disbarred, but he will live in the Caribbean and have a chance to use his legal skills and savvy. Randolph Gates will be working for the public, using against the conglomerates what he learned working for them. Mo Panov survives his wounds. He will have a disability, but he will come to live with it through his own fortitude and the help of the crippled Alex Conklin. Medusa won't be exposed, as that would cause economic chaos. Instead, it will be gradually dismantled with Ogilvie's help. Even Benjamin's mother, doing time in the United States for espionage, is released and repatriated to Russia. However, Dimitri Krupkin is as good as dead; the KGB will pursue him to the ends of the earth because he disobeyed a direct order to let Jason escape from Russia. But wait! He's somehow managed to escape, and he shows up to join the party on Tranquility Isle.

What kind of world is this? That's a question Robert Ludlum's characters often pose to each other, and although the answers are different, the world is consistent. It's a world where some men (and they are almost all men—Ludlum is not an equal-opportunity creator of villains) are greedy enough to step far outside the law and all logical morals. It's a world where power corrupts, so that powerful men begin to believe they know what's best for the Army, the country, or the planet. In Ludlum's world, they will go to any extreme to implement their ideas and ideals. It's a world in which the constant secret war rages just beneath the thin veneer of civilization and peace. Usually the public knows nothing of this, but woe to the innocent bystanders who find themselves in the crossfire.

It's a world where these bystanders, these ordinary citizens, can often be made to do dishonest, immoral things, things that they know are wrong. Some are motivated by greed; some have terrible secrets that they will do anything to keep hidden. But the picture of ordinary people is not all bleak; sometimes they become involved by chance or necessity and find unsuspected reserves of courage and cunning within themselves.

It's a world in which even a professional secret agent can be a decent individual, and this is one of the things that sets Robert Ludlum apart from his fellow thriller writers. David Spaulding, Michael Havelock, David Webb—all are inured to violence but all still hate it. All are loathe to involve civilians, and all want to settle down to a normal life. Can you imagine James Bond or Quiller teaching at a university, or even questioning the desirability of his job? Ludlum's heroes are heroes—Jason Bourne isn't Carlos—defending the normal life because they want to live the normal life. For Robert Ludlum it's not America versus Russia or Britain versus China, it's the forces of decency versus the manipulators, the users, the amoral rationalizers who will do anything to advance their cause.

" 'What kind of world do you people live in?' " asked Swanson [in THE RHINEMANN EXCHANGE] softly.

" 'It's complicated,' " said Pace.

Nobody complicates it better than Robert Ludlum.

In 1992, Robert Ludlum was on the road again with **THE ROAD TO OMAHA.** Surprisingly, for an author who has found plenty to keep himself occupied and his readers happy with variations on the thriller theme, OMAHA is a complete departure from all of his previous work. Even though it shares its main characters and the format of its title with THE ROAD TO GANDOLFO, the new book is quite different. GANDOLFO was a comic thriller that managed to poke a little fun at organized religion and a few other ripe targets. In OMAHA, the master of plot gives us a novel in which the story line is largely incidental to broad parodies of government, law, theater, and many other suitable subjects.

"The Forbidden City," Kowloon (The People's Republic of China) which even Mao refused to clean up (THE BOURNE SUPREMACY)

The plot is certainly there if you decide to follow it, but in this novel following the plot is strictly optional. After a portentous introduction—surely a parody of itself and of introductions in general—we find General MacKenzie Hawkins (Ret.) in a ramshackle office of the Bureau of Indian Affairs. His old buddy, General Helestine Brokemichael (Ret.), was unjustly forced out of the Army, as was Hawkins. Now that he is the Director of the Bureau, he becomes a sympathetic accomplice to Hawkins as they search through musty archives for evidence of forgotten land rights once ceded to the obscure Wopotami tribe in a now-forgotten document.

In the next scene we learn that a none-too-brief legal brief from Chief Thunder Head of the Wopotamis has reached the Supreme Court, petitioning for the return of their lands. What was once pasture and forest now includes some very valuable real estate. In the basement of the White House, this brief has the full attention of a crisis management team that includes Vincent Mangecavallo, the mafioso who is now director of the CIA, an ineffectual Vice President who is a minimally disguised caricature of Dan Quayle, Secretary of State Warren Pease, and a slightly disoriented President.

Meanwhile, distinguished Boston attorney Aaron Pinkus is calling on Sam Deveraux's widowed mother. Both characters are mystified by Sam's erratic behavior and his unexplained supply of funds, which we know to derive from his activities in THE ROAD TO GANDOLFO. They discuss the prodigal over copious amounts of brandy, and soon they are making their unsteady way into Sam's "lair" in the east wing of the mansion, where they finally get a hint of the events in GANDOLFO.

Who is Chief Thunder Head of the Wopotamis? The question has official Washington in a stew. Mangecavallo sends Hyman Goldfarb's high-priced thugs to find out, and they fail miserably. Their best lead is a half-naked savage, whom we later see pleading frantically with the chief—none other than MacKenzie Hawkins—to return his clothes, his housing, his indoor plumbing, and his Chevy. He's actually the lawyer on Hawkins's brief to the Supreme Court, but there's a small problem with that: He hasn't gotten his bar exam results yet. Now there's only one lawyer who will suit Hawkins's purposes—Sam Deveraux.

After a lunatic chase across half of Boston, Hawkins finally catches up with the reluctant advocate, but Aaron Pinkus beats him to it and begins a peaceful if slightly off center conference. Naturally the result is that once again Sam is an unwilling member of the Hawk's team.

Another lawyer is soon to be involved as well. When we first meet Sunrise Jennifer Redwing, she is working for a prestigious law firm in San Francisco and learning that her brother was the original dupe attorney on Hawkins's brief. In proper thriller fashion, Jennifer is a full-blooded Wopotami, a full-fledged Harvard Law graduate, and a full-breasted beauty. She realizes that Hawkins has laid claim, on the tribe's behalf, to land that includes Strategic Air Command headquarters, and she fears that after the brief is thrown out of court, new laws will disperse and effectively destroy the tribe. She journeys to Boston to stop Hawkins, and of course she runs into Sam on an elevator. He is smitten; she is less than impressed, as Sam is somewhat the worse for wear from lack of sleep and coffee stains on his trousers. Together Sam and Jennifer discover that Hawkins really does have a case. The old records were destroyed in a very suspicious bank fire in 1912, but he has recovered official copies.

Now Sam and Aaron are after justice for the Wopotamis, Jennifer is after Sam's body (which is fine with him), and Hawkins calls to inform them that a hired killer is now after Sam. Fortunately help is on the way in the form of Aaron's burly chauffeur, Paddy Lafferty. Paddy is a former gunnery sergeant who venerates General Hawkins from his World War II days, and he quickly rounds up a group of his inebriated Irish buddies. The ethnic stereotypes are Ludlum's, as are the two broadly drawn Latino cutpurses who prove to be amazingly resourceful once Hawkins recruits them to be his aides.

Hawkins and company handle the first threat easily, but can they handle a collection of stiff-upper-lip old-school-tie Wasps? These captains of government and industry form a classic Ludlum conspiracy, except that they're all incongruous and incompetent. They'll stop at nothing to thwart Hawkins, even when it comes to unleashing the notorious SFIs. These are the Special Forces Incorrigibles, the worst of the worst. Hawkins ought to know—he trained them!

Not only must the aristocratic connivers stop Hawkins, they decide to eliminate CIA Director Mangecavallo because they can't afford to have any links with him. So now instead of trying to eliminate Hawkins and company, Mangecavallo finds himself trying to keep them alive and meet with them.

Of course our heroes can handle the SFIs, even the Filthy Four who are sent after them next. Mangecavallo fakes his own death with the help of one of the bluebloods and sends an ill-assorted team of mercenaries to protect Hawkins and company. The three mercs are quickly reduced to two when the dignified black Cyrus M takes exception to working with a racist neo-Nazi.

If the Filthy Four have failed, there's still the Suicidal Six, a supersecret elite Army unit of . . . actors? Yes, actors who have failed to garner leading roles in spite of their histrionic and fistic talents, commanded by General Ethelred Brokemichael. In THE ROAD TO GANDOLFO this officer developed an abiding hatred of Sam Deveraux, thanks to a serious bit of confusion involving his brother (after all, how many General Brokemichaels could Sam have expected to find in the Army?) and he still nurses a grudge.

The Suicidal Six fly into Boston disguised as the Nobel Prize committee, there to give MacKenzie Hawkins an award as Soldier of the Century. The Hawk is naturally inclined to believe this implicitly, but he gives in to the suspicions of his accomplices and recruits his own actor to impersonate him and check out the "committee."

This actor is very full of himself, as are the Army's actors. Their dialogue and behavior display an intimate knowledge of the thespian's craft plus a full catalogue of the foibles involved in Ludlum's original profession. Of course the Suicidal Six see right through "Sir" Henry Irving Sutton, and suddenly it's a reunion—a reunion that helps neither Hawkins's cause nor the government's. Hawkins does manage to trace the Suicidal Six back to Brokemichael, whom he tricks into revealing that Secretary of State Warren Pease is behind this dubious operation.

With about two days left before the Supreme Court hearing, matters go into high gear—but since MacKenzie Hawkins is orchestrating them, they're a mystery to Sam, Jennifer, and the reader. Among other machinations, Hawkins gets a couple of his ex-wives involved in creating a blockbuster movie version of the Suicidal Six.

At about the time that Hawkins is meeting with a befuddled Brokemichael, Pease, and Mangecavallo, Sam is escaping from their beachfront hideaway. "It's Switzerland all *over* again," booms the Hawk when he learns of this. Sam may be trying to stop Hawkins, but this time he's also incensed over the government's corruption and double-dealing. He doesn't get far, but there's every indication that he'll finally get far with Jennifer, who is smitten by his idealism. Hawkins is less impressed. He's seen Sam like this before and refers to this as the attorney's "righteous rabbit" phase.

Is Hawkins being paranoid when he worries about attempts to stop him and his merry band from presenting the tribe's case before the Supreme Court? Of course not; as the big day approaches, twelve professional hit men station themselves at the Supreme Court with orders to take out Mac, Sam, and company. And eight FBI agents station themselves at the Supreme Court with orders to arrest Mac, Sam, and company. *And* seven Ranger Commandos station themselves at the Supreme Court with orders to capture Mac, Sam, and company. To make matters worse, the Chief Justice has rigged the hearing.

In the end, Hawkins's genius for maximum chaos gets the protagonists in and their case heard. The inevitable happy ending is a virtual anticlimax. The tribe doesn't get what Hawkins originally asked for—that would have been too much for the government to tolerate, and the results would have been disastrous—but it does get enough to lift it into the twenty-first century. The various lawyers get a return to sanity, and Sam, of course, gets Jennifer.

THE ROAD TO OMAHA stands outside of everything else that Robert Ludlum ever wrote. GANDOLFO could have worked as a serious thriller, but it was funny because of the interplay among MacKenzie Hawkins, Sam Devereaux, and Hawkins's four ex-wives. The characters were mostly outlandish and exaggerated, but they and the plot were grounded in plausibility. In OMAHA, virtually all the characters and plot details fall into the realm of caricature. For example, the President's Chief of Staff, Arnold Subagaloo, exists mainly to put in a brief cameo appearance late in the book.

GANDOLFO was somewhat reminiscent of Donald E. Westlake's *God Save the Mark* or *Help I Am Being Held Prisoner*, in that a naive character (Devereaux) is thrown into an adventure that is well beyond him, and the comedy comes from the character's reactions. OMAHA is much more akin to Westlake's Dortmunder series (or Ed McBain/Evan Hunter's *Every Little Crook and Nanny*) in which Westlake spoofed his own tough crime fiction by creating a cast of criminals who were half-baked instead of hard-boiled. Similarly, OMAHA features a prototypical Ludlum conspiracy (there's even a character named Smythington-Fontini) but one perpetrated by absurd blunderers.

Waxing eloquent about his long and distinguished career as he is extremely wont to do, Henry Sutton reveals, "My voice-over commercials . . . sent one of my children through college." Fans of Robert Ludlum should catch the reference and understand what it means: In THE ROAD TO OMAHA, Robert Ludlum took nothing seriously—not even himself.

A
ROBERT
LUDLUM
CONCORDANCE

Elizabeth
Gaines

ABBREVIATIONS USED FOR BOOK TITLES

AP	The Aquitaine Progression
BI	The Bourne Identity
BS	The Bourne Supremacy
BU	The Bourne Ultimatum
CM	The Chancellor Manuscript
CH	The Cry of the Halidon
GC	The Gemini Contenders
HC	The Holcroft Covenant
IA	The Icarus Agenda
MC	The Matarese Circle
MP	The Matlock Paper
OW	The Osterman Weekend
PM	The Parsifal Mosaic
RE	The Rhinemann Exchange
RG	The Road to Gandolfo
RO	The Road to Omaha
SI	The Scarlatti Inheritance
T	Trevayne

ABBOTT, DAVID (BI)

Also known as "The Monk," "The Silent Monk of Covert Operations," and "The Jesuit." "Former Olympic swimmer whose intellect had matched his physical prowess." In his late sixties now, he had an erect bearing, sharp mind, lined face, and silver hair. He was a pipe-smoker. He was currently a member of the Forty Committee and in charge of the Treadstone Seventy-one Corporation. He had been with the CIA since its origins in the OSS and had been active in Berlin and Vienna. He was the creator of Operation Medusa, where he met David Webb. He was the main inventor of the Cain character to catch Carlos. He trusted very few people—he operated on the theory that his circles were infiltrated, yet Gillette managed to lead Carlos's men to the Treadstone house, resulting in Abbott and Gillette's deaths.

ABBOTT, BRIGADIER GENERAL SAMUEL "SAM THE MAN" (AP)

Chief of tactical operations; one of the finest pilots in the United States Air Force as well as a superb aerial tactician. He had brown hair with a tinge of gray around the temples, gray eyes, and a strong, relaxed face.

Colonel in the Air Force during the Vietnam War, he was shot down over the coast of the Tonkin Gulf three days after Joel Converse was shot down. Joel said without Sam he would have died twenty feet down in the earth; Sam crept out at night and threw a crude metal wedge into his "punishment hole," which enabled him to crawl out and escape. After the war Joel and Sam stayed in close contact. Sam stayed in the Air Force, married, and had two daughters.

Sam worked hard to get into the NASA program, but they turned him down because he was too valuable where he was. They sent him to Washington to evaluate the new Soviet and Chinese equipment; he worked over at Langley at the safe houses, questioning defectors and appraising photographs brought by agents. Valerie tells Sam about Aquitaine, and Sam dies in an airplane crash very shortly after that.

———, ABDUL (IA)

Fictitious name of an Arab whose son's throat was cut because his father actively opposed the fanatic faction of the Mahdi.

ABRAHMS, CHAIM YAKOV (AP)

One of the main Aquitaine leaders. "Chaim Abrahms and his followers make the Begin regime seem like reticent, self-effacing pacifists. He's a Sabra tolerated by the European Jews because he's a brilliant soldier . . ." He has a stocky frame and usually wears a safari jacket, boots beneath his khaki trousers, and occasionally a beret. He is of medium size, with a fringe of close-cropped hair on a balding head. He's a whiskey drinker. He can act like a court jester or be deadly serious.

When he was a young terrorist for the Irgun he had been condemned to death by the British for the slaughter of a Palestinian village. In 1948 the British commuted his sentence and gave him a large settlement to govern.

His wife was bitter over the loss of their son. She is accidentally killed with Chaim's service revolver. He claims she committed suicide; other people don't think so. He is captured and interrogated by Joel and then released. When the rioting starts and the Israelis call for him to establish order, he is nowhere to be found.

ABRAHMS, MRS. CHAIM (AP)

Wife of Chaim Abrahms for thirty-eight years and mother of three daughters followed finally by a son. She was a frail woman who dressed in black; she had soft white hair, gentle features, and dark brown eyes. She had been with Chaim in the Negev Desert when Israel was fighting to establish itself as a nation.

After listening to Chaim's many telephone conversations with Aquitaine, she decided to kill him with his own service revolver. She and Chaim struggle, the revolver goes off, accidentally killing her; Chaim is distraught, but shoots her again in the chest to make it look as if she has committed suicide and to gain more popular support for himself.

ABRAMS, ——— (PM)

FBI field agent, a paminyatchik.

ACQUABA (CH)

Original leader of the Halidons. His corpse was preserved, dressed in robes of reddish-black, and laid on a slab of gold. He had huge hands, feet, and head; he must have been near seven feet tall. He "was something of a mystic, but essentially a simple man . . . his ethics were sound."

———, ADELE (BS)

Worked at the Scully Agency with Jack. Jim Crowther was to contact them for David Webb.

AGNELLI (BI)

Firm in Italy that might pay a delegate to an economic conference to get information for making a deal with another country. Used as an illustration by Marie St. Jacques.

AHBYAHD (IA)

Arab terrorist with premature gray streaks in his hair. His code name was Ahbyahd, White. One of the leaders of the terrorist council in Masqat. He led the terrorist group that attacked Kendrick's home in Mesa Verde; he was killed by a CIA man during the attack.

AHRENS, LIEUTENANT TOM (SI)

Stationed in the CIC, Boston. Canfield asked him to cover Andrew's phone calls while he was in Switzerland for the weekend.

AIELLO, ROCCO (MP)

Rocco owned the Hartford Hunt Club, an after-hours gambling casino. It had two floors of private gambling rooms; the waiters were mostly college boys, war veterans who specialized in peddling drugs. Rocco was murdered inside Sharpe's club.

AL FALFA (IA)

Kendrick called al Farrah al Falfa, which was meant to be insulting.

AL FARRAH, ——— (IA)

Black con man in Chicago who later became the Mahdi. Manny had met him in Basra, where he was using the name Sahibe al Farrahkhaliffe.

AL FARRAHKHALIFFE, SAHIBE (IA)

The Mahdi; his American name was al Farrah.

———, ALAN (BI)

First Assistant Director of the Canadian Treasury Board. He was a friend of Peter and Marie's. He had to tell Marie about Peter's death and ask her to return to Canada.

ALBANESE, ANGIE (AP)

Wife of Joey Albanese. She didn't know the details of her husband's business, but didn't like his business hours. "Angie would be pissed off at him, maybe shout a little because he didn't come home last night . . . he would never go into . . . details with his wife."

ALBANESE, JOSEPH "JOEY THE NICE" (AP)

One of the killers of Judge Anstett. He drives a Pontiac, lives on a quiet tree-lined street in Syosset, Long Island, and is well liked by his neighbors. He thinks he is a sweet guy, some kind of saint.

The night after he killed Judge Anstett, he was shot and killed in front of his own house. He was found with the gun he used to kill Anstett in his hand.

ALCOTT, MRS. ——— (CM)

The "stern-faced but cheerful housekeeper he [Peter Chancellor] had inherited with the house" he bought in Bucks County, Pennsylvania. She approved of Alison and felt the "home needed that lady."

ALDERSHOT, BINGHAMTON "BINKY" (RO)

Banker nephew of Bricky's, a very handsome young man with shining dark hair, a womanizer. He used his sexual attractiveness to find out from Pinkus's secretary where the Hawk and his group were hiding.

ALDOBRINI, GUIDE (GC)

One of the priests of Xenope. He was in Donatti's group when they severely injured Victor Fontine and left him for dead. For his part in this crime, the church of Rome sent him to the Transvaal for twenty-five years, where he caught a number of tropical diseases. When he retired, he traveled to the United States and gave a letter to Victor Fontine warning him that Enrici Gaetomo, another member of Donatti's group, who had been defrocked and sent to prison, had been released and would try to reach Victor; Gaetomo was still after the vault of Salonika.

ALDRIDGE, ROBERTA "BOBBIE" (IA)

Daughter of well-to-do New England parents, friend and roommate of Adrienne Rashad at Radcliffe. Adrienne introduced her to Ahmat, whom she married. Mother of Khalehla Yamenni.

ALEXANDER, RAYMOND (PM)

Well-known journalist, "Alexander the Great," mutual friend of Havelock, Matthias, and Zelienski. He was an analyst, not a muckraker; he did in-depth interviews of people in his home at Fox Hollow and wrote articles for *The Potomac Review*. Alexander was sixty-five years old, portly, with a cherubic face, full arched eyebrows, clear green eyes, and disheveled dark hair; he spoke in a clipped, high-pitched voice. He had quit writing and drank too much; people thought this was because of his wife's death. Alexander had cooperated with Matthias and Zelienski in their schemes because he was afraid he would be revealed as a traitor to his country; he was unable to stop Matthias and Zelienski.

ALIANDRO, JOAO (PM)
Captain of the *Miguel Cristovao* for the past twelve years. He knew every island and shoal in the western Mediterranean.

ALIZONGO, MONSIGNOR HECTOR (RO)
Desi Two was disguised as a Catholic priest to get into the Supreme Court building. He was to help Aaron get inside.

ALLCOTT-PRICE, ——— (BS)
The Bourne impostor created by the Frenchman. Allcott-Price, a former English Royal Commando, a captain at twenty-two and a major at twenty-four, he had gotten drunk and killed seven people with his bare hands in London. The English sent him to a psychiatric hospital in Kent, from which he escaped and made his way to Singapore. He was careful never to let anyone know his real name. None of his men would complain about him because he always brought them out of combat situations. Unlike Bourne, he had no conscience. He knew he was psychotic; as a child he tortured animals. At eleven he raped the vicar's daughter, then walked her to school. During a hazing in college, he'd drowned another student. His father, General Allcott-Price, kept him out of Sandhurst because he didn't want him near the Army, but he managed to get in anyway. He preferred a bullet in the head to being hanged. He was killed during Webb's assault on the safe house on Victoria Peak.

ALLCOTT-PRICE, GENERAL ——— (BS)
Father of Allcott-Price, the Bourne impostor. The impostor was the son of his third or fourth wife—the General was a womanizer. The General was also known as "Slaughter Allcott," and "England's Patton." He had been Montgomery's boy genius in World War II, the man who led the flank attack on Tobruk and later barreled through Italy and Germany. He was extremely upset when his son, who he knew was psychotic and wanted dead, joined the army. His son wanted the world to know all the horrible things he had done and that he was the General's son; he figured the General would be so embarrassed and hurt that he would blow his own brains out.

ALLCOTTS, ——— (RE)
Old friends of Leslie Jenner's who kept a suite at the Montgomery Hotel in New York; she wanted to avoid them.

ALLEN, ——— (T)

Allen worked for Genessee and thought they had made a big mistake by getting involved with de Spadante. Allen, Goddard, and de Spadante all wanted to get access to the subcommittee's files. Allen was Webster's contact with Genessee. He was short, in his sixties, and wore stylishly tailored clothes.

ALLISON, SENATOR ——— (IA)

Milos Varak made contact with Frank Swann by posing as one of Allison's top aides.

ALTMULLER, FRANZ (RE)

Trusted friend and adviser of Albert Speer; his expertise was in production administration. Altmuller was a forty-two-year-old cynic, tall, blond, and aristocratic; he didn't subscribe to the racial nonsense of the Third Reich. He would, however, agree with anyone who might do him some good, and he had no patience with tact. Altmuller was one of the Nachrichtendienst. They decided to engineer a swap of blueprints of the guidance system for industrial diamonds because they were unable to buy diamonds anywhere. Altmuller planned the German side of the exchange. Spaulding was unaware of Altmuller's existence until confronted by a man from the Haganah. Rhinemann didn't trust Altmuller because of rumors about the Gestapo being in Buenos Aires; he insisted Altmuller come to Buenos Aires or there would be no exchange. When the Haganah attacked the Rhinemann estate, Altmuller personally tried to kill Spaulding; he knew he would not be able to return to Berlin alive if Spaulding escaped. Spaulding killed Altmuller at the estate.

———, AMAN (IA)

Young Arab terrorist with a harelip. His mother and father had been killed when his home on the West Bank was blown up. He accompanied Yosef to kill Kendrick in Mesa Verde and survived to be interrogated by Mitch Payton.

AMANDAREZ, PABLO (AP)

Madrid's specialist in KGB Mediterranean penetrations; attended secret meeting at the White House set up by Peter Stone to identify members of Aquitaine from photographs.

AMBIGUITY (PM)

Code name originally established by Daniel Stern to investigate the Costa Brava affair and bring in Havelock. Someone else used the code to order the termination of Havelock with "extreme prejudice." Ambiguity was then used to indicate the mole in the State Department.

AMSTERDAM (MC)

Congdon wired Amsterdam that Scofield was beyond salvage; they sent a man, code name Amsterdam, to kill Scofield, and if Taleniekov was there he was to kill him also. Taleniekov killed Amsterdam in a hotel elevator before he could reach Scofield.

ANDERSON, ——— (HC)

Worked at the American embassy in Rio de Janeiro. He didn't believe the story Noel told him about seeing Graff, having his car destroyed, and nearly being killed by Graff's men. The Americans protected Graff because they thought Graff had been one of the men who tried to kill Hitler at Wolfsschanze.

ANDERSON, ALEX (MP)

Local banker in Carlyle, he graduated from Carlyle University in the forties. He was a cautious man, easily frightened. Matlock called him when he needed to deposit his check and withdraw some funds during the weekend before he left to visit the local gambling clubs.

ANDREWS, ——— (OW)

CIA agent at Langley who was coordinating the operation to trap Omega.

ANDREWS, ELIZABETH "LIZ" (PM)

Emory Bradford's longtime secretary.

ANDROS, MISS ——— (MC)

Specialist in overseas communication, Consular Operations.

ANGELINA "ANGIE" (RO)

Angie and Meat had seven children. She had a problem with her sweat glands.

ANGELINA, AUNT (RO)

Little Joey the Shroud swore on his aunt's grave; she died after eating clams at Umberto's.

———, ANGIE (BU)

Wife of Mario. She and Mario had five children, the oldest of which was Anthony.

ANGLETON, JAMES JESUS (AP) [REAL PERSON]

Peter Stone twice identifies himself as being associated with Angleton, a legendary figure in the CIA, saying he was "a once disciple of Angleton" and that he had spent "a decade with Angleton" in the tunnels. One of Angleton's big discoveries was that Donald Maclean, while in position as First Secretary of the British embassy in Washington, D.C., had been passing information on our nuclear technology and intelligence secrets to the Soviets. He discovered this because of the suspiciously high volume of traffic out of the Soviet consulate in New York following visits from Maclean twice a week. A Soviet cipher clerk mistakenly used a simpler code for lower-grade material while transmitting, and the Americans caught it. Maclean was associated with Kim Philby, the notorious spy for the Soviets, Burgess, and Blunt.

ANGLETON, JAMES JESUS (IA) [REAL PERSON]

Mitch Payton succeeded him as Director of Special Projects.

ANGRY YOUNG COMMANDERS OF SAINT-CYR (BI)

Group of retired French military commanders, graduates of Saint-Cyr military academy, led by General Villiers. They had not approved of the military decisions made preceding the fall of France; they became leaders of the French Resistance.

———, ANN (CH)

Former fiancée of McAuliff. While he was forced to attend a hastily called research meeting, she was murdered at night on the streets of New York.

———, ANNE (AP)

Intermediary between Peter Stone and "Gentleman Johnny Reb"; operated out of Charlotte, North Carolina, and had had contact with Johnny before. Peter Stone had been in love with her, but she retired from the service, said she hadn't fitted in with Peter's life. Johnny Reb said he hadn't had a chance with her with Peter around but would like to renew the acquaintance now.

———, LADY ANNE (RO)

Name Sam used when thinking about his lost love, Anne. Sam had photographs and news clippings of Anne all over the wall of his lair.

———, SISTER ANNE (RO)

Anne left the chateau with the Pope and became a nun. She served the poor, like Mother Teresa, and was being considered for sainthood.

ANSTETT, JUDGE LUCAS (AP)

Sat on the bench of the Second Circuit Court; an exceptional judge whom Anstett had strongly recommended to the Talbot firm.

Judge Anstett's murder by the Mafia followed two phone calls from René Mattilon to Larry Talbot and a visit by Larry to see the judge because Larry was concerned for Joel's welfare. Evidently René's phone had been tapped and Talbot had been followed. The Mafia had been hired by Aquitaine, of course.

Delavane figured the judge was still after him even though it had been forty years earlier, in October 1944, that Anstett had been a legal officer in Bradley's First Army. Delavane had wanted to make an example of a man who had cracked under fire. Anstett put Delavane himself on trial, calling into question his fitness for command. This did not end Delavane's career, however. Anstett's murder by the Mafia could be connected to Delavane through Mario Parelli, his former aide and U.S. Senator.

ANTELOPE FEET, COUSIN (RO)

Wopotami who took over the controlling interest in a distillery in Saudi Arabia. He was over eighty.

——, ANTHONY (BU)

Fifteen-year-old son of Mario and cousin to Louis De Fazio. Mario expected Louis to send gifts to Mario for special occasions.

——, ANTONIO (RE)

Guard at the Rhinemann estate knocked out by Spaulding.

ANVIL (HC)

An agency formed in Zurich by the false Wolfsschanze group to consolidate their control over the general population of the world.

APACHE (PM)

(1) Red Ogilvie's code name.

(2) Code name for the agents guarding Dr. Randolph; they were killed by Ambiguity's men.

APFEL, WALTHER (BI)

Official at the Gemeinschaft Bank in Zurich, Switzerland. He was "a tall, slender man with aquiline features and meticulously groomed gray hair. His face was patrician . . . his English refined." He handled the Treadstone account, releasing funds to David Webb (as Jason Bourne);

Gordon Webb used him as a drone to send a message to his brother to come in.

APIS (CM)

Character in Chancellor's Book *Sarajevo!* Code name of the leader of the organization called the Unity of Death, founded in 1911 in Serbia; his real name was Dragutin.

APPLE (GC)

Code name for Geoffrey Stone. He was slender and intense, a member of MI6. His orders were not to come back to London unless he brought Vittorio back safely; he had no idea at that time why Vittorio was so important. Because of Vittorio's error in releasing the young soldier, Stone's right hand was badly shot up, causing him to lose the use of it. He hated Vittorio and anything Italian after that.

APPLETON, JOSHUA (MC)

Wealthy Episcopalian Bostonian, member of the original council of the Matarese. He enjoyed harpsichord music.

APPLETON, JOSHUA, II (MC)

Guiderone's father worked for him; Joshua sent Guiderone to school during a time when the Appletons had very little money. Guiderone put Appleton's companies back on top.

APPLETON, MRS. JOSHUA, III (MC)

Elderly alcoholic mother of Senator Joshua Appleton IV. Guiderone bought the Appleton estate when her husband died; she lived in a brownstone on Louisburg Square with her nurse. She knew her son was not the same as before the auto accident.

APPLETON, JOSHUA IV (MC)

Senator from Massachusetts, protector of the workingman, possibly next President of the United States. Captain Josh Appleton had been a marine combat officer in Korea who wouldn't ask his men to do anything he wouldn't do himself; he had been decorated for bravery on five separate occasions. He had been critically injured in an auto accident after the war but appeared to make a miraculous recovery and then be elected to the Senate.

APRIL RED (SI)

Code name for Andrew Roland Scarlett.

AQUITAINE (AP)

Secret organization established by General George Marcus Delavane, who is the primary leader. General Bertholdier, General Leifhelm, General Abrahms, Derek Belamy, and Jan van Headmer are the other established leaders. Under the cover of international corporations they have recruited members from all governments, many of them military and intelligence people. They also use these corporations to furnish weapons and explosives to terrorist organizations. Their common aim is to cause a great general civil disturbance, then rush in to establish order and take over the governments and divide the world among them, each governing by a Fascist dictatorship, with one main leader.

ARCHIE (BU)

Code name used by David Webb while in the Russian spy-training complex at Novgorod.

ARDISSON, JEAN-LOUIS (BS)

French textile salesman Bourne met in a tour group in Peking [Beijing] outside Mao's tomb. He was slightly taller than Bourne, dressed well, and he spoke very little Chinese; he was gullible and easily frightened by Bourne. Bourne persuaded him to give him his tour identification badge, allowing Bourne to safely leave the area; Ardisson, however, was detained and questioned. At their second meeting Bourne managed to get his billfold and identification papers from him. The hotel desk clerk said he was very disagreeable and Minister Wang Zu called him "an idiot—we'd send him back to Paris on the next plane if the fools he represents weren't paying so much for such third-rate materials."

ARGONAUT ROCK (GC)

Special rock in a stream not far from Campo di Fiori; Adrian carved a record of each trip into the mountains on the rock. Savarone left a message carved into the rock for Adrian.

————, ARMAND (IA)

Worked at the Casino de Paris in Monte Carlo; Manny was one of his regular customers.

ARMBRUSTER, ALBERT (BU)

Chairman of the Federal Trade Commission. He was a wealthy man; he had close to $100 million in Zurich. He was married, but couldn't stand the thought of living alone with his wife. He had ulcers as well as high blood pressure and was under a doctor's care. He was a member of the old Medusa and the new Medusa. He had the traditional tattoo on his underarm. He learned from Bourne that the Teagarten fax line had been uncovered. He met with DeSole to get the information about Bourne and Panov, then had DeSole killed by De Fazio; De Fazio's men then killed Armbruster.

ARMBRUSTER, MAMIE (BU)

Wife of Albert Armbruster for thirty years. Described by him as yapping all the time, wanting to know everything about everybody, then blabbing it all over town, exaggerating everything.

ARMBRUSTER, SENATOR MITCHELL (T)

Sixty-seven-year-old California senator; he had two years remaining in his term and didn't plan to run again. The senator was a small, compact man whose wit was as much a part of his reputation as his judgment; he wasn't afraid to clash with important people and was a policy setter. During the last election he was faced with a tough challenger; he was able to tell his supporters that he was in the process of getting $150 million in defense money for California industry. Armbruster was willing to discuss Genessee with Trevayne. Trevayne was surprised when Armbruster approached him about running for President.

——, ARNOLD (AP)

Artillery officer in the IDF who had been transferred recently to the Security Branch, Jerusalem. He was identified as a member of the Aquitaine by Josef Behrens at the secret White House meeting set up by Peter Stone.

——, ARTHUR (SI)

Gentleman with Basil, waiting for an audience with Bertholde; he left when it was announced the Marquis would not see anyone else.

ASHCROFT, LADY (RE)

Main character in a radio show in which Spaulding played a part.

ASHTON, RALPH (OW)

Undersecretary of State. Ashton was a "witless, prosaic businessman whose main asset was his ability to raise money." It was a mistake to let him appear on the Woodward program.

ATHENS (RG)

Other code name Rouge. Paranoid secret agent pulled out of forced retirement by Hawkins for the kidnapping of the Pope. He liked to wear a red scarf and tell jokes.

ATKINSON, PHILLIP, II (BU)

Wealthy father of Phillip Atkinson III. When the younger Atkinson finished school, his father bought him a seat on the New York Stock Exchange; this lasted thirty months, and Phillip III over three million dollars. Through his valuable political contributions, Phillip II next managed to secure a post for his son in the Foreign Service.

ATKINSON, PHILLIP, III (BU)

American Ambassador to the Court of St. James's, member of both the old and new Medusas. Had the Medusa tattoo on his forearm. Ogilvie described him as "a rich dilettante—does what he's told, but he doesn't know why or by whom." He'd do anything to hang on to the ambassadorship. When he was younger, he attended Andover and Yale, then served in Vietnam. He was twenty-nine when he returned to the States and took a seat on the New York Stock Exchange, followed by a foreign service post thirty months later. When his connection to Medusa was uncovered, he resigned from his post "for health reasons."

———, AUGIE (BU)

Name on one of the five drivers' licenses of Nicholas Dellacroce.

———, AUGIE (RG)

One of Dellacroce's bodyguards; he was heavyset and walked like a gorilla. Hawkins knocked him unconscious on the golf green.

AURIOLE, MADAME (SI)

Madame Auriole's chateau, the Silhouette, was known for its weekend narcotics orgies.

AUSTIN, PENELOPE (BS)

Name under which Marie Webb was registered into the Empress Hotel in Kowloon by the banker Jitai. When Panov called her later, he asked for Mrs. Austin.

———, AXEL (PM)

One of Kahoutek's guards; he handled the schedules.

AXELROD, DR. (IA)

Kendrick's name when he traveled incognito.

AZAZ-VARAK, SHEIK (RG)

Sheik in Kuwait. During World War II he sold oil to both the Allies and the Axis for cash. Between 1946 and 1948 he bought land in Tel

Aviv, then sold oil to the Israelis during the Mideast crisis to protect his property. He was a spindly, ugly little man with an outsized narrow hooked nose and a black mustache plastered up against it. Hawkins blackmailed him into contributing $10 million to the Shepherd Company.

———, AZIZ (IA)

Member of extremist Arab faction, questioned by covert-operations officers to find out who was holding the hostages in the American embassy in Masqat.

AZRA (IA)

Young Arab on the terrorist council in Masqat. Azra, Blue, was his code name. He was slender, in his early twenties, with high cheekbones; dark, intelligent eyes; and a sharp, straight nose. He spoke English fluently. He and his sister, Zaya, had seen their parents shot to death by the Israelis. He fought not for religious reasons, but to survive and live like a human being. Azra was killed by Yaakov before he could lead Kendrick to the Mahdi.

BABCOCK, HARRY (BS)

One of the experts in clandestine operations who interviewed David Webb at the safe house in Virginia after the killings at the Treadstone house. He was an easygoing man, a southerner with a slow drawl. He refused to discuss anything with David, as David was out of sanction.

BABCOCK, MRS. HARRY (BS)

Wife of Harry Babcock. She answered the phone when David Webb called.

BADOGLIO AND GRANDI (GC)

Italians who were negotiating the Italian collaboration with the Allies in Lisbon prior to D-Day.

BAHRUDI, AMAL (IA)

When Kendrick went undercover to reach the people who could reach the Mahdi, he assumed the identity of Amal Bahrudi, well-known terrorist in Eastern Europe. The real Bahrudi was a Saudi from Riyadh, a construction engineer. One of his grandfathers was European; Amal had blue eyes and was taller than the average Arab. Everyone thought Amal had a large scar across his neck; people who knew him well knew this was not true. He died in East Berlin.

BALBO, COLONEL (GC)

Italian commanding officer of the Genoa garrison at the time Vittorio escaped from Italy.

BALDEZ, GERALDO (RE)

Owner of an apartment building in Buenos Aires where Jean obtained an apartment for Spaulding. Geraldo was a partisan; he had no use for the Germans.

BALDWIN, FRANKLYN (T)

One of the original giants of New York banking, an elderly man. Trevayne respected him and consulted him many times for guidance on international finance during the ten years he had known him. Baldwin was delegated to offer Trevayne the chairmanship of the Defense Allocation Subcommittee; he was willing to give Trevayne whatever he needed to get the job done. Hill and Baldwin had been close friends for years; Hill felt that Trevayne's thought processes were very much like Baldwin's. The day Baldwin buried Hill, President Trevayne attended the funeral and brought him back to Barnegat with him.

BALDWIN, PETER, ESQ. (HC)

His business card said Wellington Security Systems, Ltd., London, but he was really a courier specialist for MI6, had been for twenty years. He operated out of Prague and sold information to the highest bidder; the British thought he was a double agent and fired him. He maintained he was innocent. He heard the rumor about Clausen and the funds in Geneva, traced it to Manfredi and then to Holcroft and his mother. He passed on his information to MI5. He told Noel to cancel Geneva because Noel had no idea what he was doing. Manfredi contacted the false Wolfsschanze group, and they killed Baldwin before he could give his information to Noel.

BALLANTYNE, ——— (RE)

Middle-aged undercover agent with Azores-American. He drove Spaulding to his briefing with Hollander.

BALLANTYNE, INSPECTOR IAN (BS)

Friend and lover of Catherine Staples. He was a late middle-aged English widower who had opted for retirement from Scotland Yard to become chief of Crown Colonial Affairs in Hong Kong. He "shook up the Intelligence division of the colony's police, and . . . shaped an aggressively efficient organization that knew more about Hong Kong's shadow world than did any of the other agencies in the territory,"

A floating restaurant in Hong Kong

including MI6, Special Branch. He had met Catherine at a bureaucratic dinner; they enjoyed each other's company, no strings attached. He concealed how much he knew by answering questions with other questions. He and Catherine both thought John Nelson was very good.

BALLANTYNE, PATRICIA (MP)

Matlock's current girlfriend was completing her doctoral studies in archaeology at Carlyle. She had soft brown hair and lived in an efficiency apartment. Pat and Ballantyne had intended to spend spring break together on St. Thomas, but Matlock's activities for the Narcotics Bureau prevented this. She was unhappy about Jamie's involvement with the government; in the fifties her father had lost his job as a translator with the State Department because of McCarthy. Her family had no money, so she worked her way through college on scholarships. Nimrod's men tortured Pat on two different occasions to force Matlock to give up the silver paper with the information about the conference for the drug dealers; huring her just made Matlock all the more determined to stop Nimrod. After Nimrod was killed, Pat and Jamie took a vacation in the Caribbean.

BALLARD, ROBERT "BOBBY" (RE)

Head cryptographer at the American embassy in Buenos Aires, a casual cynic and a font of information. He spoke seven or eight languages and was "an absolute whiz at parlor games." Bobby "was a linguist with a mathematical mind and a shock of red hair on top of a medium-size muscular body; a pleasant man." He lived at the embassy because messages came in at all hours. Bobby had dated Jean Cameron, but she wasn't interested in developing a relationship; they remained good friends. He refused to authenticate an order from the War Department for the execution of Spaulding; the State Department congratulated him for recognizing and refusing to act on a serious error on the scrambler.

BAMBOLINI, GIOVANNI (RG)

Giovanni had been born north of Padua in the early 1900s to poor parents, their second child. He never shirked his work in the fields, but he loved to read. The village priest recommended him to the holy fathers in Rome; by the age of twenty-two Giovanni was an ordained priest. He didn't look like a priest—he was short, stocky, and wide of girth—but more like a farmhand. He also didn't have a stern visage and proper attitudes of certainty with regard to Church teachings, so he was sent to posts in remote areas of the world. Through an error he was sent to Monte Carlo; before long he was a guest at many of the finer homes, and substantial contributions were made to the Church in his name. During the war he served in various Allied capitals and with various Allied armies because he could not remain neutral about Hitler; his friends from Monte Carlo were also officers and wanted him with them. After the war he became a Cardinal and developed a close friendship with Roncalli and followed him as Pope Francesco I.

BAMBOLINI, ROSA (RG)

Sister of Giovanni Bambolini, wife of Guido Frescobaldi and mother of their six children. Guido was forced to come home from his musical studies in Milan and marry her; she weighed three hundred pounds and was self-indulgent and hysterical. On their seventh anniversary Guido decided he was going to go back to Milan and devote himself to his music. Rosa went back to her village and died several years later from overeating.

BANNER (CM)

Inver Brass code name for Frederick Wells, youngest member of Inver Brass.

———, BARBIE JO (BU)

She was "sort of" Willie's wife.

BARDEN, COLONEL IRA (RE)

Agent at Fairfax who took command after Pace was killed. "Barden was a thick, short man with the build of a football tackle and close-cropped black hair"; he spoke five languages, including Hebrew. He spent two years at the American University in Beirut, transferred to Harvard, then to a small college in New York, where he majored in Near East studies; he went into the family textile business until the war. Barden was responsible for Pace's murder. When Spaulding broke up the Rhinemann exchange, Barden disappeared from Fairfax, taking personal dossiers of ranking Nazis involved with the concentration camps with him.

BARICOURS, PÈRE ET FILS (GC)

Victor Fontine thought he had sold Campo di Fioro to this Franco-Swiss company in Grenoble; there was no such company.

BARRISH, COLONEL ROBERT (IA)

Barrish saw himself as a modern-day Davy Crockett holding the Alamo; Kendrick saw him as an accountant who was trying to justify the theft of millions of the taxpayers' money. He felt Kendrick insulted him during the televised hearing, so they met for a debate on a talk show program. Barrish couldn't defend his position; the Pentagon was very unhappy with him, so they promoted him to brigadier general and shipped him out to oversee the base on Guam.

BARSTOW, DR. (SI)

Barstow, a highly regarded surgeon, was supposed to sit next to Elizabeth Scarlatti at the captain's table on the *Calpurnia*; Canfield took his place.

BARSTOW, CAPTAIN JEROME (GC)

Professional soldier, member of Eye Corps in Saigon. Andrew thought he was a good man in the field; Greene thought he was a smart-ass with too many decorations. He betrayed Eye Corps to Tarkington; Barstow's death was made to look whore- and booze-oriented.

BARTOLUZZI, JACOPO "JOCK-O" (MP)

Very short, obese Italian who owned the private Avon Swim Club. Part of it really was a swim club; the spa, however, was a gambling casino. Bartoluzzi directed Matlock to Rocco's place when he asked where he could get some pot. He was killed the same night as Rocco at Sharpe's club.

BARTON, JESSE (RG)

Senior partner and son of the founder of the Barton, Barton, and Whistlewhite law firm and old friend of Sam Devereaux's. Sam went to him to find out what was known about Angelo Dellacroce.

BARZINI, GUIDO (GC)

Gnarled, huge, aging servant of the Fontini-Cristis at Campo di Fiori. He had spent his life in service there as a groundskeeper and stable master. He was a partigiano and close to the family. When Vittorio's family was murdered by the Germans, Barzini held Vittorio down to prevent him from also being discovered and shot. Barzini didn't understand the significance of *Champoluc*, the last word Savarone screamed. Guido smuggled Vittorio across Italy to Alba, where MI6 took him to the coast and then to England. When Vittorio went back into Italy after the war, he contacted Guido, who had aged perceptibly. Guido had been allowed to live at Campo di Fiori by the Germans because they thought he was mentally deficient. For two years he had watched groups of priests search the house and grounds. Vittorio asked Guido to spread the word around that he was back, to flush out Stone. Vittorio wanted Barzini to return to America with him when this was over, but unfortunately Guido was killed by Stone.

———, BASIL (RO)

Lady Cavendish's adenoidal English butler.

BATTELAS (OW)

Mafia friends of Joe Cardone's, in the construction business. They called Tanner a vulture. Joe Cardone was their investment counselor.

BAYLOR, LAWRENCE (PM)

Real name of Lieutenant Colonel Lawrence Baylor Brown.

BAYOU, BILLY-BOB (RO)

Real name of Wolfgang Hitluh. He was a southern redneck who trained with the neo-Nazis in Germany.

BEALE, DR. EDWARD (AP)

Retired history professor from the University of California, Berkeley. Born to a wealthy family, he had inherited both money and a conscience. He is a slender, white-haired man of medium height, his face deeply lined. He is a man whose character and reputation are of the highest order; he insists on anonymity.

One day one of the field commanders he had known in Korea visited him on Mykonos. He went out on a boat with Beale and tried to recruit him for Aquitaine. Beale quickly killed him and dropped him "over a cluster of sharks beyond the shoals of the Stephanos." He gave Joel a thick manila envelope with all the information in it they had about the leaders of Aquitaine.

Later, when Beale is the only contact Joel has left because all the others have been killed, he tries to telephone Beale. Laskaris has the unpleasant task of telling Joel that Beale and another man had gone out in his boat that morning, the boat was found crashed on the rocks beyond the Stephanos, and there was no one aboard.

BEANTOWN BERNIE (BS)

Worked for the Boston office of Honeywell-Porter, an advertising agency. When Bourne met him on the hydrofoil from Kowloon to Macao, Bernie was slumped in a corner, drunk, wearing a Red Sox baseball cap. Bourne borrowed his cap and joined his group to get safely ashore in Macao.

BEAUMONT, COMMANDER ANTHONY (HC)

A "career officer of no mean standing" in the British Navy; he commanded the patrol ship *Argo* and was extremely close to his second-in-command, Morgan Llewellyn. His most distinguishing feature was his thick, coiled and matted, salt-and-pepper eyebrows; he had blunt facial features. Beaumont's Scottish parents had been quite poor, owners of a greengrocery or florist shop in Dunheath, yet he had been able to attend the university as a regular student without scholarship; his parents disappeared a few years after the war. Beaumont's real father was a Reichsoberführer. His second marriage was to Gretchen von Tiebolt; they had no children. Johann disliked him but worked with him closely for the Fourth Reich. When Noel discovered who Beaumont was, Gretchen ordered his death. Beaumont's death and Gretchen's were reported as occurring when their boat capsized during a weekend pleasure trip in the Mediterranean.

BEAUMONT, GRETCHEN VON TIEBOLT TENNYSON (HC)

Noel thought Gretchen was one of the most beautiful women he'd ever seen. "She was of medium height with long blond hair that framed a face of finely boned, perfectly proportioned features." She had large, wide light-blue eyes and a curvaceous body with large breasts. She did not smoke or drink, and said she loathed her husband; she manipulated Beaumont. "She knew the horror of Berlin after the war. At the age of thirteen she slept with soldiers for food." She learned to use sex to get what she wanted. She worked with Johann for the coming of the Fourth Reich and met his sexual needs, but she knew too much to stay alive.

BEESON, ARCHER "ARCHIE" (MP)

Young history instructor at Carlyle. He and his wife enjoyed LSD and amphetamines; when their supply dried up in Bridgeport, it was assumed they obtained their drugs at Carlyle. Archie was flattered when Matlock approached him about teaching a course together and invited Matlock to dinner. Matlock had to pretend he was making love to Ginny to prevent Archie from knowing he'd overheard his phone call to Herron's contact.

BEESON, VIRGINIA "GINNY" (MP)

Ginny was petite, large-breasted, and wore short skirts and translucent blouses. Her aristocratic accent sounded as though it had been acquired at a finishing school. She had a distinctive giggle and said everything was "marvy" or "groovy." She loved parties and Seconal and worked at the Carmount Country Club.

BEHRENS, YOSEF (AP)

The Mossad's leading authority on terrorism. Attended the meeting set up by Peter Stone at the White House to identify members of the Aquitaine.

BEIRUT (RG)

Other code name Brun. Out-of-work intelligence agent hired by Hawkins to help him kidnap the Pope. He'd had several run-ins with the Zurich police, so he hired an ambulance instead of coming in by train. Rudolph drove his car into the ambulance and didn't recognize him. He was dark-skinned with distinctly northern features and he spoke with an accent like people at the Savoy.

BELAMY, DEREK (AP)

Chief of Clandestine Operations for Britain's MI6. He is brilliant, perceptive, and has a quiet, pleasant, even prosaic exterior. He is at the meeting with Joel at Leifhelm's country house, disguised probably as a servant; he calls Fitzpatrick with the story that he is Philip Dunstone, aide to General Berkeley-Greene, that Joel will be unavailable to contact him until the next morning.

He was one of the only real friends Peter Stone had in his years with the CIA. Peter Stone has no idea Belamy is one of the key people in Aquitaine; he wants his help in setting up a network to catch the members of Aquitaine. Belamy attends the meeting set up by Peter Stone at the White House to identify members of Aquitaine from their photographs; Stone realizes Belamy is one of them when he doesn't identify his personal aide's photo. Stone attempts to call Joel on a scrambled line at the White House, Belamy attacks Stone in the throat and escapes through the East Gate. Stone recovers and gives the signal to start the operation at Scharhorn. Belamy disappears, perhaps never to be found again.

Santorini (THE AQUITAINE PROGRESSION)

BELFORD, DR. TOMMY (MC)
Highly skilled plastic surgeon who reconstructed Appleton's face after his accident.

BEN-AMI, ——— (IA)
Mossad agent from Masqat who met the Masada Brigade to tell them their orders had been changed and to take charge of the group. Khalehla called him Benny: "He's a good guy and one of the best control agents Israel's ever had. We worked together in Damascus; he's small and a little cynical, but a good man to have on your side. Tough as nails, actually."

BEN-GADIZ, YAKOV (HC)
Yakov survived the slaughter at Har Sha'alav because he had left there to get the list of the Sonnenkinder. He was a slender man with dark skin and very dark eyes, trimmed dark hair; he was neither tall nor short, had enormous shoulders, and "emanated raw physical power." His family, Sephardic Jews, immigrated to Krakow in the early 1900s. He had been a violinist with the Tel Aviv Symphony. First he worked with Helden and Althene, then later with Noel. He was seriously injured while protecting Noel; he lived but was crippled, so he trained Noel to take his place.

———, BENJAMIN (BU)
Young, sandy-haired trainer in his mid-twenties at the spy-training compound at Novgorod; he was Bourne's guide. His parents had been

assigned to the Russian consulate in Los Angeles for nearly twenty years. He was educated in America and attended UCLA, completing a minor in English literature and a major in American history. His mother was caught in an FBI sting operation at the San Diego naval base, and he and his father were recalled to Moscow. His mother was serving time in prison in the U.S.; Bourne promised to help his mother if Benjamin would help him. Benjamin trapped Carlos in the tunnel, then helped Bourne get away in a helicopter.

BENNETT, SAM (OW)
Joe Cardone's partner. He had no knowledge of the Zurich manipulation until Joe offered to resign.

————, BENNY (IA)
Private security guard at the hangar containing Grinell's plane. He was "quite large and very full in the waist and shoulders." Milos "borrowed" his clothes, to get close enough to Sundstrom to kill him.

BENSONS (CH)
Family from Kent, England. They were mutual acquaintances of McAuliff and the middle-aged couple with Holcroft at the Owl of Saint George in Soho.

BEOWULF AGATE (MC)
One of Scofield's code names.

BERGERON, ———— (RE)
Agent, Frenchman, who worked for Spaulding in Spain. The Germans caught him, tortured him, broke him, finally killed him. He gave them the information that led them to the two scientists who were trying to escape. Spaulding had trained Bergeron; he was the closest friend Spaulding had in the north country.

BERGERON, PAUL (MC)
Attorney friend of Robert Winthrop's. He handed the envelope containing the evidence about Senator Appleton and the Matarese to Stanley, Winthrop's aide.

BERGERON, RENÉ (BI)
Famous clothing designer under exclusive contract to Les Classiques, an employee of Carlos's. He was "a tanned, muscular man of indeterminate age . . . his face was taut, his lips thin, his close-cropped hair thick, dark brown, and disciplined." For a while David Webb thought Bergeron

was Carlos. He was very close to Carlos, and Carlos told him to go to Athens for a while, as he was too important to lose.

BERGSTROM, EDWARD (MC)

CIA field agent who had penetrated Russia, spoke the language fluently, and was a known killer. Bergstrom was currently assigned to a desk in Washington.

BERKELEY-GREENE, GENERAL (AP)

English general invented by Derek Belamy to prevent Connal Fitzpatrick from discovering the location of Joel Converse. He told Fitzpatrick the General had been a guest of Leifhelm's and had instructed him to relay a message to him from Joel.

BERNARD THE BRAIN (BS)

Also known as "Beantown Bernie." Known as "the Brain" because of the type of presentations he made.

BERNARDINE, FRANÇOIS (BU)

An old Deuxième Bureau acquaintance of Alex Conklin's. He was a stoutish, well-tailored Frenchman, seventy years old with a close-cropped white chin beard. He was unmarried, had no family, no really close friends, and only sporadic lovers because of his profession. He smokes cigarettes, drinks Tanqueray, and drives a Peugeot. He has a phone that cannot be tapped without breaking the connection. He felt they had retired him too soon and thought about buying real estate in Beirut. He was shot to death by Carlos's men outside the Hotel Meurice, defending Marie Webb.

BERQUIST, PRESIDENT CHARLES (PM)

Highly respected president from Mountain Iron, Minnesota. He was a stocky, tough individual with a heavy, Scandinavian face, and he didn't care whether certain people liked him or not—he just wanted to do the best job for his country. Berquist was afraid that Havelock's exposure of the Costa Brava affair would panic Parsifal more quickly than anything else, so he reluctantly reinstated the order for Havelock's execution. If Havelock connected with Jenna, he would find out that Bradford had set up the Costa Brava operation, so Berquist ordered around-the-clock protection for Bradford. When Havelock was captured on Poole's Island, Berquist showed him proof of Matthias's insanity, explained all the other problems to him, and asked him to help find Parsifal.

BERTHOLDE, MARQUIS JACQUES LOUIS AUMONT (SI)

The Fourth Marquis of Chatellerault, owner of Bertholde et Fils, London. Since the company had most of its properties within British territory, the main office was in London; he also had extensive holdings in the Ruhr Valley. Bertholde was somewhat short, well-groomed, relatively handsome, with a resonant voice and immensely likable. His hobbies were automobiles, dogs, and horse breeding; he participated in polo and sailing and was a member of the Matterhorn Club. When Strasser could no longer communicate with Ulster, he sent him to Bertholde; Ulster used Bertholde as a cover while trying to kill his mother. Bertholde was supposed to have had the Rawlinses killed in Switzerland; he disobeyed the party by having them killed in the Poconos. Bertholde was garroted by Labishe.

BERTHOLDIER, ALPHONSE (AP)

Father of Jacques-Louis Bertholdier. Career officer in the French army, reputedly autocratic and a harsh disciplinarian. Sometime around 1924 or so he was stationed at Dakar, where Jacques was born. In 1938 he was a member of general staff and was back in Paris. He knew the Maginot Line could not hold and was outspoken about it, so he was transferred to the field, in the Fourth Army. He was killed in the fifth week of the war.

BERTHOLDIER, GENERAL JACQUES-LOUIS (AP)

Retired French Army general, "the arm of Aquitaine in Paris." Fifty-nine years old, he is the only son of Alphonse and Marie-Thérèse Bertholdier, born in the military hospital in Dakar. He moved from post to post with his parents. When France fell in 1940 he joined the Resistance.

Disliking de Gaulle's accords with the Algerians, he fled to North Africa and joined the OAS; he was involved in the assassination attempt on de Gaulle in 1962 but was pardoned by de Gaulle, who said he would not hold one error against him and reinstated him as an officer. After de Gaulle resigned in 1969, Bertholdier's assignments were far from the centers of power and remained so until his retirement four years ago. He became a director in the insurance firm Compagnie Solidaire and is the director of Juneau et Cie., a firm on the Paris stock exchange. He likes to travel in his dark blue Lincoln Continental. He frequents L'Etalon Blanc, a private club in Paris with restricted membership, mainly military. He always sits at table eleven by the window.

He is an extremely popular man. He is of medium height, but his haughty, regal bearing makes him appear taller. His command of English is excellent. He is married, not for love, but for reasons that are "socially,

professionally, and financially beneficial to both parties." He is a known
womanizer and has as many as three mistresses at once; he enjoys young
males as well as females. When Converse has him brought in for
questioning, Prudhomme's people take Bertholdier's picture while he is
in the middle of a sexual act with a young woman; they threaten to
retouch the picture to make the woman look like a young boy, then
publish it. Bertholdier decides to go along quietly but demands the
negatives. After Joel finishes questioning Bertholdier, Joel gives him a
gun; Bertholdier realizes Aquitaine has lost, walks out of the chalet, and
kills himself.

BERTHOLDIER, MARIE-THÉRÈSE (AP)

Mother of Jacques-Louis Bertholdier. Jacques never spoke about his
mother, so nothing is known about her.

BERTINELLI, DR. EUGENIO (BI)

Economist from the University of Milan, Italy. He was giving a talk
and slide presentation at the Sixth World Economic Conference in
Zurich at the Carillon du Lac Hotel. His lecture was interrupted by
Carlos's men chasing David and Marie across the stage.

BERYZFICKOOSH, BRIGADIER GENERAL (RG)

One of Hawkins's cronies in the file room of army intelligence. He
presented himself to Devereaux as the brigadier general and attached a
heavy briefcase to Devereaux's arm with a chain. He was barrel-chested
with twelve rows of ribbons, an eye patch, and a fright wig on his head.

———, BEULAH (RO)

Sharp-eyed maid at the Four Seasons who talked to Little Joey the
Shroud.

———, BIG TOM (IA)

Six foot five, suntanned yachtsman, one of the contributors who
controlled Bollinger.

———, BINKY (BU)

In the Metropole Hotel, the elderly Englishman who had stolen a
white robe from the Beau-Rivage in Lausanne. He received numerous
knife wounds when Carlos removed the robe from him.

BIRCH, COLONEL AUBREY (GC)

Officer of the vaults at Loch Torridon. Stone forced him to get the
file on Victor Fontine, then killed him. Birch was found locked in

Stone's office clad only in undershorts and shoes, a "single, clean gunshot wound in the upper center of the naked chest."

BIRCHTREE (PM)
Code name used by Dr. Harry Lewis.

BIRNBAUM, JOSHUA (RO)
Only child of Sarah and Sidney Birnbaum. His godmother was Erin Lafferty.

BIRNBAUM, SARAH (RO)
Sidney's wife and Joshua's mother.

BIRNBAUM, SIDNEY (RO)
Aaron Pinkus's brother-in-law. He had a summer house in Swampscott on the beach that the Hawk and his group could use while the Birnbaums were in Europe.

BISCAY (RG)
Other code name Bleu. An unemployed intelligence agent hired by Hawkins to help kidnap the Pope. He was extremely secretive. His coded identification when meeting Rudolph was a pair of white gloves with black roses stitched on the backs. He was French and worked around boats.

BLACK (IA)
A member of the Masada Brigade, he went with Yaakov to the Hotel Aradous in Masqat.

BLACKBIRD (BU)
Code name used on the telephone for Carlos and the four people who had direct access to Carlos.

BLACKBIRD (IA)
Lanky, red-haired FBI man who followed the orders of Bollinger's crowd. From him Milos found out where Grinnell, Ardis, and Sundstrom had gone following the death of Andy.

BLACKBURN, GENERAL "MAD ANTHONY" (MC)
Chairman of the Joint Chiefs of Staff. He was highly respected by the Russians, who felt that Blackburn would go to any length to avoid pointless slaughter. He was the kind of officer that men would follow to hell and back. His way of relaxing after a particularly strenuous day at

the Pentagon was to secretly visit a brothel. His assassination in the brothel was made to look like the work of the Russians.

BLACKBURNE, ——— (BU)

Brendan Prefontaine told Edith to tell Randy that he was a man named Blackburne from the island of Montserrat; he knew Randy wouldn't talk to him if he used his real name. Blackburne was the name of the airport on Montserrat.

BLACKSTONE (OW)

Cover that Fassett used to contact Tremayne and panic him.

BLACKSTONE, MICHAEL (MP)

Owner of Blackstone Security, Inc., Hartford. Michael was a short, compact man in his early fifties, obviously very physical and tough. Aetna regarded his company as expensive but the best. Matlock hired them primarily to guard Pat Ballantyne; they also were willing to give Matlock a list of the private gambling club owners. When two of the men on the list were murdered, Blackstone told Matlock he didn't want to work for him if Matlock was involved in their murders; he warned Matlock that the service would be terminated if there was a warrant filed for his arrest.

BLANCHARD, ——— (MC)

Taleniekov presented himself to the switchboard operator at the hotel in Washington as Blanchard, a Swiss financier; he persuaded her to let him see the telephone logs.

BLEU (RG)

Other code name Biscay. He was a master of camouflage and escape cartography. He was to disable some of the Pope's police escorts and priests.

BLOCK, IRVING (MP)

The agent in New York who handled Matlock's book *Interpolations in Richard II;* Matlock mentioned he might be able to show his agent some of Archie Beeson's work.

BLUE (IA)

Code name Blue was used by both the Arab Azra and the Israeli Yaakov. They met in a hotel room in Masqat and fought to the death.

BLYNN, ROGER (AP)

Caleb Dowling's director on the movie he's making in Bonn.

BOCCEGALLUPO, CAESAR (RO)

A capo primitivo in the Borgia family in Brooklyn, New York. He was told to assassinate Hawkins, but Hawkins captured him, injured his back, and left him in the lobby of the Four Seasons Hotel for the police.

BOCK, GENERAL (GC)

German commander whose headquarters was Pripet, Poland. Someone from Loch Torridon intercepted a courier dispatched to him from General Guderian, whose troops were close to Minsk.

BOLASLAWSKI, KASIMIR (IA)

Kasimir was a "strange-looking, disheveled man with wide, popping eyes and long, wild hair that fell over his ears and his forehead." He knew all the latest news because he had seven television sets in his house. When he was interviewed on television, he said he'd seen Kendrick and snatched his hat.

"The Forbidden City"—woman cutting out entrails of cobras which are used for aphrodisiacs (A SCENE IN THE BOURNE ULTIMATUM)

BOLLINGER, V. PRESIDENT ORSON (IA)

Also known as Viper. Bollinger was "a man of medium height, medium build, medium middle-age, and . . . medium high voice." He was a "party glad-hander with an insider's grasp of every . . . thing that goes on. . . ." He was a "pawn of the President's unseen contributors— men who intended to run the country." He knew that Jennings didn't particularly want him to be his running mate again. Milos collected information through Bollinger's telephone calls, to persuade him to withdraw from the ticket. When it was learned that Bollinger had Kendrick kidnapped, Jennings forced Bollinger to withdraw and said if he ever did anything else wrong, he'd make sure Bollinger went to Leavenworth.

BONELLI, ALICE (MC)

One of the three nurses who died in the boating accident the night of March 26, 1954, after tending Senator Appleton.

BONNER, CINDY TOTTLE (RE)

Bitter widow of Paul Bonner. "She was petite, with reddish hair and very light, almost pale skin. Her posture was *Vogue*, her body slender. . . ." Leslie swore that Cindy had seen Spaulding while she was exchanging a Christmas present for Paul and had called Leslie. Cindy told Spaulding her husband had died four months earlier, and she hadn't been in touch with Leslie. Cindy and Paul had been "an item," a long-standing one, and Cindy was accused of forcing Leslie to move to California.

BONNER, PAUL (RE)

Bonner was killed on a scout patrol covering an ambush evacuation during the Sicily invasion; he received a posthumous Silver Star. He and Cindy had mutually sued for divorce because of Leslie.

BONNER, MAJOR PAUL (T)

Special Forces, Intelligence Section, assigned by the Department of Defense to assist Trevayne. Bonner was in his late thirties or early forties, with close-cropped hair and the complexion of an outdoorsman. He resented his assignment because he'd been told that Trevayne was out to cripple the defense industries. Bonner was unaware of Cooper's tie-in with Genessee. Cooper told him he was to be an informer; if any impropriety was charged, Bonner was expendable—however, the Army would take care of him. Bonner was to get copies of any subcommittee files related to Genessee Industries; Cooper gave him the key to Trevayne's file cabinet. Bonner paid L.R. for information about what questions

Trevayne was asking about Genessee; he discovered that Sam had also used L.R. for information. He knew Trevayne was lying when he told him he had to return to Washington because Phyllis was being admitted to the hospital. He'd also discovered that Trevayne was being followed by de Spadante's men and requested a fighter jet to take him to Washington. When Bonner arrived at the hospital, he noticed the 1600 Patrol had been dismissed, and he set up new guards. He then followed Trevayne to Barnegat and found a gunman waiting outside for de Spadante; he immobilized the gunman, then warned Trevayne. Augie attacked Bonner and he killed Augie. Bonner tried to talk to de Spadante, de Spadante attacked him and slashed him, and Bonner shot him in the stomach. Trevayne and Lillian kept Bonner alive until he could be taken to a hospital. Gallabretto had Bonner arrested for murder; it was proven he acted in self-defense and was acquitted. Then the Army decided to court-martial him for disobedience; Bonner brought in his own lawyers to defend him. Bonner found out that Trevayne had been the Pentagon's candidate all along and that once in the White House, Trevayne wouldn't be able to expose Genessee without revealing his connection to it. When Trevayne took this information back to the President, the President had the court-martial charges dropped and elevated Bonner to the permanent rank of full colonel. He was to enter the War College for highest level strategic training after which he was to be assigned as liaison officer to the Joint Chiefs of Staff.

BOOKBINDER, CONGRESSMAN (IA)

Bookbinder's home in Silver Springs was the scene of a wild party thrown by young congressional aides.

———, BOOMER (RO)

Wrestling champ of New England and prelaw student at Tufts, a handsome, crew-cut young man whose muscular arms were inordinately long. He was delighted to be asked to help Sam Devereaux, his hero.

BOOTH, ALISON GERRARD (CH)

Ralston didn't tell McAuliff that the British geologist he was going to interview, A. Gerrard Booth, was female. She had studied sheet strata in Iran, Corsica, and southern Spain and had several articles published in *National Geologist*. This professional lady was in her late twenties or early thirties, outgoing, had a nice smile, a firm handshake, long wavy brown hair, and light blue eyes. She wanted to go to Jamaica to get away from David Booth and Chatellerault; Interpol had informed her of the opportunity. They had also taught her how to use bugging devices, and had furnished her with weapons with which to defend herself. Holcroft knew about her and asked McAuliff to watch her. Warfield knew all about her. She became McAuliff's lover and confidante.

BOOTH, DAVID (CH)

Ex-husband of Alison Booth. He came from a socially prominent family and was a partner in an export-import firm that specialized in art objects on the decorator level. Neither the family nor the firm had much money, yet he had several homes, drove expensive cars, and belonged to the better social clubs. He was a womanizer, had heavy gambling debts, and drank, which is why he became a courier for the narcotics trade under Chatellerault. He decided it was advantageous to have a wife whose work forced her to travel, and he used this as a cover; they had been married for a year when she discovered what he was doing. He was a very sick, very vicious man, an extraordinary coward, yet he loved Alison enough to make Chatellerault believe she had no knowledge of his activities.

BOOTHROYD, CECILY RAWLINS (SI)

Dark-haired daughter of Thomas Rawlins, wife of Charles Boothroyd. She assisted her husband when he tried to kill Elizabeth Scarlatti. Cecily didn't expect to become a widow so soon; she left the pier in a Rolls-Royce registered to Bertholde.

BOOTHROYD, CHARLES "CHUCK" CONAWAY (SI)

Husband of Cecily Rawlins; his father-in-law owned Godwin and Rawlins. He was a huge, broad-shouldered fullback type with very blond hair. Canfield noticed Boothroyd's tie and cuff links—both deep red and black—when Boothroyd was talking to him on the *Calpurnia*. Boothroyd pretended to be drunk and pass out, requiring someone to carry him to his cabin. He then went to Elizabeth Scarlatti's cabin to kill her; he didn't figure on finding Canfield there. Canfield killed Boothroyd and threw him overboard.

BORIN, ILITCH (PM)

Visiting professor, doctor of philosophy, at the University of Belgrade; he, Matthias, and Havelock had dinner together.

——, BORIS (PM)

One of the "state troopers" who entered Randolph's hospital room and killed Randolph and several other people. Although wounded himself, Loring caught the paminyatchik killer and strapped him to a bed in a motel, keeping him alive until a doctor could get there. Taylor drugged him, and Havelock obtained the code for his source control and the telephone number of the mole. After "Boris" was transferred to a hospital, someone killed him before Havelock could get any more information from him.

BOURNE, JASON CHARLES (BI)

Name used by David Webb for the bank account in Zurich that was controlled by Treadstone Seventy-one. He was also registered at the Carillon du Lac Hotel in Zurich as J. Bourne. The real Jason Bourne was a Medusan from Sydney, Australia, a runner of guns, narcotics, and slaves throughout Southeast Asia. He was "an expert in communications who could assemble . . . a high-frequency radio in the dark." He went into Tam Quan with Webb's group and used the radio to tell the Viet Cong their position. Webb discovered this and executed Bourne on the spot. Later, when Webb joined Treadstone, he took the name Jason Bourne because it fit the requirements of authenticity and traceability for the origin of his Cain character.

BOURNE, JASON CHARLES (BS)

Webb thought the names Cain and Jason Bourne were buried in his file in the vaults of the CIA. When Jason Bourne was observed killing in the Far East, the State Department knew it wasn't Webb and set up Webb to eliminate the impostor.

BOURNE, JASON CHARLES (BU)

The original Jason Bourne was a paranoid drifter from Tasmania.

BOUTIER, HORACE (SI)

President of the Waterman Trust Company. He made Cartwright responsible for assisting Ulster Scarlett.

BRADFORD, EMORY (PM)

Controversial Undersecretary of State. Bradford was a slender middle-aged man with straight dark hair; he had been married at least three times. He had two sons and two daughters by his first wife. He had been an impassioned hawk until one day during the Vietnam War, when he decided he and his advisers had been wrong and the hawk became a dove. He was nicknamed "the Boomerang." Havelock trusted him because he had a conscience and had paid for it. Bradford carried out the main part of the investigation within the State Department after it was discovered that Matthias had concocted the Costa Brava incident to force Havelock out of Cons Ops; Bradford had set up the operation with no intention of harming Jenna. He discovered by viewing videotapes of the meetings that Pierce had not been at the Security Council meetings during the Costa Brava incident. Pierce drugged him and threw him out a seventh-floor window of the State Department before Bradford could reveal that Pierce was the mole.

BRAVO (CM)

Inver Brass code name for Munro St. Claire. He became acting head of Inver Brass after Genesis died.

BRAYDUCK, UNDERSECRETARY OF STATE (SI)

Hull requested his presence at the meeting with General Ellis about Kroeger's request to contact Canfield. He was a university man who favored gray flannels and herringbone jackets and smoked a pipe. Brayduck didn't want anything negative about the administration four weeks before the national election.

BRAZUK, ———— (MC)

KGB man who defected in 1972; Scofield gave him to MI6 because he wouldn't have anything to do with the Americans. His name was changed to Grimes; he was a chronic alcoholic, linked to a leak in security at MI6.

BR'ER RABBIT (BU)

Cactus's nickname for Jason Bourne.

BREVOURT, AMBASSADOR ANTHONY (GC)

"For a number of years (he) was the crown's ambassador of the Greek court of George the Second in Athens." During that time he had known Savarone, who was an emissary to Athens from Rome. Brevourt was responsible for having Vittorio rescued and brought to England, because he thought Vittorio had the information about the train from Salonika. He was extremely upset when he found out Vittorio had no knowledge of it; Vittorio didn't trust him, so he didn't tell him everything he knew. Vittorio was sent to Loch Torridon and trained for intelligence work; Brevourt had a close watch on him through Geoffrey Stone. He gave Stone permission to draw up contingency plans in case Teague was killed; instead, Stone had a document drawn up giving him license to kill Vittorio. Teague was ordered to stop Stone. Brevourt came to Vittorio's hospital room after the attack by Donatti; Vittorio demanded and received a complete explanation from Brevourt. Brevourt, however, didn't know the entire story. He refused to tell what he knew to Land and died a few months later.

BREWSTER, ROGER (T)

Roger Brewster was Roderick Bruce's real name; he was born in Erie, Pennsylvania. The only one who called him Roger was Coffey.

————, BRICKY (RO)

Owner of New England's largest lending institution and fraternity brother of Warren Pease. He was forced to help Warren get rid of Mangecavallo and Hawkins because he was taped by Subagloo.

BRIELLE, MADEMOISELLE (BU)

Name used by Dominique Lavier when she registered at the Meurice Hotel; Brielle is the name of a lovely seaside town in France.

BRIELLE, MONIQUE (BI)

Salesgirl at Les Classiques, Lavier's number-one girl. She lived in a small hotel. She had a sinewy physique and exuded confidence. David Webb planted the rumor with her that someone high up had turned, for her to contact Lavier; she was part of his plan to disrupt Carlos's setup at Les Classiques.

BRIGGS, CHARLES (BI)

One of the false identities assumed by David Webb. He used it twice. The first time he was supposed to be a rich banker from the Bahamas buying designer clothes for his young third wife in Cap-Ferrat. The second time he used it to reserve a room down the hall from him and Marie at the Auberge du Coin.

BRIGGS, MRS. CHARLES (BI)

Fictitious-wife character invented by David Webb (as Charles Briggs). The first time she was a very young, spoiled third wife of a rich banker from the Bahamas; he had been away for quite a while, so was buying designer clothes to pacify her. He had sent her to Cap-Ferrat. The second time she and Charles were to join Webb and Marie at the Auberge du Coin, one of Marie's dresses was shot to pieces by Carlos's men.

BROKEMICHAEL, MAJOR GENERAL ETHELRED "BROKEY THE DEUCE" (RG)

Cousin of Heseltine Brokemichael's. West Point '43. He was stationed in Vientiane; Sam Devereaux found piles of evidence that he was a big narcotics dealer. The trouble was that Sam built his case against the other Brokemichael and Ethelred got away.

BROKEMICHAEL, BRIGADIER GENERAL ETHELRED "BROKEY THE DEUCE" (RO)

Heseltine's cousin. Ethelred and Heseltine never reconciled their differences after Sam's investigation; Ethelred dropped from a brigadier general to colonel but remained in the Army. He was duped by the drug dealers in the Far East; he accepted money for the facilitation of shipments of medical supplies, then used most of the money for the local orphanages and refugee camps. The Army put him in G-2, where he trained a special covert-operations group known as the Suicidal Six; they were a team of "trained professional actors capable of altering appearance and attitude commensurate with whatever targets they were to penetrate." They'd been extremely successful, not killing anyone or suffering any casualties themselves; Ethelred was returned to his former rank. He was quite willing to send his group to Washington to capture Hawkins and Devereaux and transport them to the far north. Hawkins flew to Benning to warn Brokemichael that he and his group were being set up by Warren Pease.

BROKEMICHAEL, MAJOR GENERAL HESELTINE "BROKEY ONE" (RG)

Cousin of Ethelred Brokemichael's. He was stationed in Bangkok and believed he was gathering evidence on a corrupt IG investigator. Supposedly he was always in the shadow of his corrupt cousin; according to Hawkins, Heseltine wanted to reopen the investigation and clear his record.

BROKEMICHAEL, MAJOR GENERAL HESELTINE "BROKEY ONE" (RO)

Director of the Bureau of Indian Affairs. When the Pentagon refused to give him his third star because of the case Sam built against the Brokemichaels, Heseltine quit; the government gave him a job that supplemented his retirement pay. He gave Hawkins access to the archives in the hope that he could get back into uniform at his correct rank.

BROMLEY, PAUL (CM)

Ill sixty-five-year-old accountant at GSA, code name Viper. He had testified before a Senate hearing on cost overruns concerning the Pentagon; in return, the GSA filed an unsatisfactory service report that prevented a grade raise for him; Bromley sued the GSA. He retired after an anonymous telephone caller threatened to reveal his daughter's past history if he didn't drop the lawsuit and resign from the GSA. He attempted to kill Chancellor after another anonymous caller told him his daughter's story was being printed in Chancellor's next book. Bromley leapt to his death from the door of a moving train after failing to kill Chancellor.

"THE BRONK" AND HIS WIFE (BU)

The wife was a platinum blonde in her mid-thirties; she had large breasts and wore too much makeup. She loved driving her flashy red sports car. "The Bronk" was a tough truck driver who thought it was all right for him to have multiple sex partners but it wasn't right for his wife. She was running away from him when she picked up Mo Panov; she tried to hang on to him because she found out he was a doctor—she needed an abortion done. Another truck driver helped Mo escape from her.

BRONSONS (OW)

The Bronsons were friends of the Ostermans from years before; they were also on the Attorney General's subversive list.

BROOKS, AMBASSADOR ADDISON (PM)

Addison had been a "lawyer, an international banker, a consultant to statesmen, an ambassador, and finally an elder statesman himself and adviser to presidents." He was of the eastern establishment aristocracy; Brooks was a tall, slender man with silver hair, aquiline features, and a perfectly groomed gray mustache. He was one of the four men in government who knew about Costa Brava, Parsifal, and the mole; the President considered him the equal of Matthias. Brooks cared deeply about his country and was "held in awe by the power brokers on the Hill."

BROOKS, JOHN (AP)

The overseas man, the brilliant international negotiator with Talbot, Brooks, and Simon; Joel Converse is his replacement. Brooks had said he was tired of adjusting to all of those time zones. When Brooks decided he would rather go to a reunion than an international conference, Joel was sent to represent them in Geneva; Valerie had accompanied him. On another trip in place of Brooks he was sent to Strasbourg, France, where he had the opportunity to become familiar with the countryside; this was a factor in his choosing Strasbourg as the border crossing point when he was attempting to get to Champonix to meet Valerie.

BROUSSAC, RÉGINE (PM)

First Assistant Deputy, Section Four, Ministre des Affaires Étrangères. An older woman, years ago a heroine of the Resistance, her husband was taken by the Gestapo and murdered; she had carried on, a tough lady. Régine set up a diplomatic cover so Jenna could go to the United States. Havelock had a difficult time convincing Régine that he was not trying to reach Jenna to kill her; Régine gave Havelock Handelman's name and address and helped him with passage to the United States. She admitted to the Americans that she'd had an appointment to meet Havelock; the President convinced her that the American government was not trying to kill Jenna and Havelock. Régine told him where Jenna and Havelock were going.

BROWN, CAROL (OW)

Friend of Peggy Tremayne's. She liked the Choate boy.

BROWN, LIEUTENANT COLONEL LAWRENCE BAYLOR (PM)

Havelock's D.C. conduit in Rome, an experienced field agent. Baylor was a qualified expert in weapons, a Rhodes scholar, Special Forces, and tactical guerrilla warfare. He was "posing as the only first-level black attaché at the embassy." Baylor was his real name, Brown was a cover. Havelock convinced him that Jenna was alive and that she wasn't a KGB agent; he threatened to reveal various undercover operations, including Baylor's, unless the government cooperated with him. When it appeared that Ogilvie could not persuade Havelock to come back with him, Baylor shot at Havelock but hit Ogilvie instead. Havelock shot Baylor in the hand and exposed his network. Baylor's injury was severe enough to discharge him from the army.

BROWN, MAJOR PHIL (CM)

Forty-three-year-old doctor at Walter Reed and close friend and protector of Alison MacAndrew's. When General MacAndrew met him, he was a medic in Korea, flying to the front to treat wounded soldiers. He came from a poor family, and MacAndrew helped him get into medical school via the Army. He had read and enjoyed Chancellor's books. He located the six of the survivors of the battle of Chasong in the VA hospital near Richmond. He made the telephone contact with Ramirez and fought alongside Chancellor. Ramirez had him picked up for violating national security and then was forced by Chancellor to release him. Daniel Sutherland wanted him dead.

BROWNLEE, SENATOR (SI)

The senator set up an appointment between Reynolds and Elizabeth Scarlatti; he thought Reynolds represented the Land Acquisition Agency.

BRUCE, RODERICK (T)

Aggressive Washington newsman, syndicated in 891 papers across the country. Bruce's lecture fees were donated to charities and he was very much liked by his peers. He guarded his sources of information zealously and was relentless in exercising his curiosity. He was a very short man, five three, with sharp features, deepset eyes, and longish hair. Roderick Bruce was his by-line; his real name was Roger Brewster. Trevayne's first contact with him was in connection with a story he was writing about inoperable atomic submarines. In exchange for suppressing the story, he wanted information from Trevayne about Paul Bonner. He hated Bonner because his lover, Alexander Coffey, had been in Bonner's intelligence group in Cambodia when he was captured and killed. When Bonner was arrested for killing Augie de Spadante, Bruce tried to convict him in his news articles before Bonner came to trial. Webster gave Bruce photographs of Tremayne and de Spadante together and wanted articles written linking the two in order to discredit Tremayne and convict Bonner. Tremayne forced Bruce to quit writing the articles by threatening to reveal his homosexual affair with Coffey.

BRUN (RG)

Other code name Beirut. He was an Englishman who had darkened his skin for life in Beirut. His special interest was sedative medicines. One of his jobs was to destroy all the communications equipment in the vehicles with the Pope.

BRUNOV, ——— (MC)

High-ranking party functionary, Military-Industrial Planning in Russia. His task was to contact Dimitri Yurievich for the Americans. Brunov's assassination was made to look like the work of the Americans.

BRYCE, GERALD (IA)

Director of Global Computer Operations, Department of State, working under Frank Swann. He was the foremost technologist of computer science in the country. "The kid's twenty-six and better-looking than he has a right to be. He's also unmarried . . ." and completely dedicated to the service of his country. Without him Milos could never have done what he did; Gerald became the new coordinator for Inver Brass after Milos died and also the White House communications expert.

BUFF (PM)

One of Ambiguity's observers outside Sterile Five; she was disguised as a horsewoman who had hurt her leg.

BUONAVENTURA, SAM (HC)

One of the best construction engineers in the business, and close friend of Noel Holcroft. He was a "fifty-year-old professional drifter, a City College graduate from . . . the Bronx." After a brief tour of duty in the Army Corps of Engineers, he decided to spend his life working on construction jobs in Latin America and the Caribbean. He'd worked with Noel on two jobs outside the country; in Costa Rica Sam had taught Noel how to handle a handgun. Noel asked Sam to cover for him professionally and take messages for him while he was working on a special project; he regularly checked in with Sam. The last time he called, a man told him Sam had been garroted by a native and they were trying to catch the murderer.

BURGER, WARREN (CM) [REAL PERSON]

U.S. Supreme Court justice. He delivered the eulogy at John Edgar Hoover's funeral.

BURGESS, GUY (RO)

Name Hawkins used when he called Ginny from the Waldorf-Astoria.

BURLAP BILLY (BI)

An old Dallas tramp frequently seen panhandling in the area where President John Kennedy was killed. He was called "Burlap Billy" because he wrapped his shoes in coarse cloth to play on people's sympathy. Supposedly Carlos was dressed as "Burlap Billy" and killed Kennedy from the grassy knoll. Billy's body was found several days later. Although he was a drunkard and could not afford drugs, it appeared that Billy had died from an overdose of drugs.

BURROWS, ——— (CM)

Taciturn groundskeeper at Chancellor's house in Bucks County; he liked Alison.

Warnings in Grenada　(THE BOURNE ULTIMATUM)

BURTON, ADMIRAL JONATHAN "JACK" (BU)

Also called "Joltin' Jack" Burton; former admiral of the Sixth Fleet, current Chairman of the Joint Chiefs of Staff. Member of both the old and new Medusas, he was considered an errand boy for Medusa. He was forced to retire "for health reasons" when his link to Medusa was uncovered. He knew very little about the financial operations—he thought Medusa was "essentially an ultraconservative veterans' lobbying effort that grew out of the Vietnam disgrace." He had very strong patriotic feelings.

BUSH, ——— (SI)

Messenger who delivered a cable from London to Poole in person.

———, BUZZ (BS)

Young American male, dressed in blue jeans, an art history major. His college had an arrangement with the Chinese University of Hong Kong for sleeping space. He helped Marie get a bed there for the night.

———, CACTUS (BS)

Elderly black man whose specialty was photography and false identification papers. He had worked with Treadstone and the CIA in the past, but the CIA didn't want to be associated with him anymore because of his other illegal activities. He liked David and made three passports for him, all different. He didn't worry about being paid by David, and he made sure David was taken safely out of the area by his grandson.

———, CACTUS (BU)

He lived in a run-down neighborhood in northeast Washington, where taxis would not stay and wait for a customer. He wore a green eyeshade above his warm black eyes. He still worked at his trade for certain people like Jason Bourne, for whom he provided two more aliases with passports, drivers' licenses, and voter registration cards; he agreed to help Bourne only because the Jackal was threatening Bourne's family. He had been one of the only people allowed to see Bourne after the Treadstone killings, because Panov realized the two of them were good friends. Ivan Jax, M.D., was indebted to Cactus for helping his family, and he didn't want Cactus involved with the situation at the Swayne estate; he was more than upset when Cactus was nearly killed.

CAESAR, ——— (OW)

Caesar had been dead for several years; he had been a friend of Amos Needham and had lived in Maryland. He'd made a dozen fortunes out of the rackets; his oldest son was with the Attorney General's office and hated the Mafia.

CAFFERTY, LIEUTENANT (RO)

Cafferty of the Boston Police Department traced Sam's call to Geoffrey Frazier for Aaron.

CAIN (BI)

Since "Charlie" became synonymous with the Viet Cong, "Cain" replaced "Charlie" for the letter C in the military alphabet. Cain was the name David Webb used for his identity as the assassin who would replace Carlos (the Spanish for Charles).

CAIN (BS)

The underworld of Europe knew in reality Cain was Asia's Jason Bourne. Cain was the identity Webb used while pursuing Carlos.

CALFNOSE, JOHNNY (RO)

Mac's special adjutant for security matters for the Wopotamis; he still owed Jennifer Redwing bail money from his last escapade. Johnny lived comfortably in the Wopotami Welcome Wagon Wigwam, selling souvenirs made in Taiwan. He supervised the movement of the Wopotamis from Omaha to the Supreme Court building in Washington for Hawk; inside the building he had the Wopotamis selling yaw-yaw juice to the tourists and guards.

CALLAHAN, ——— (T)

Guard from the 1600 Patrol who was supposed to be guarding Mrs. Trevayne at the hospital in Darien; someone who knew the secret code gave him the night off. Callahan was forty-six; he'd been in the Secret Service for twenty years and had protected four presidents. He was relieved he was nowhere near the White House the day the President was assassinated.

CAMELLIA (BU)

Santos's code name that signaled that everything was all right.

CAMERON, ANDREW (RE)

Jean Cameron's former husband, Henderson Granville's stepson; both had loved Andrew deeply. Andrew left his law books and entered the war as an aircraft carrier pilot; he had been flying since his teens and hoped to get a stateside instructor's job. He had a fear of taking other people's lives and would have sought conscientious objector status if it had not been for embarrassing his family. He was killed in the Leyte Gulf.

CAMERON, JEAN (RE)

Andrew Cameron's widow. Jean lived at the embassy in Buenos Aires and accompanied Granville to diplomatic social functions. She was a moderately tall, slender woman with light brown shoulder-length hair, wide blue eyes, a thin nose, full lips, and a clear skin bronzed by the sun; she was also comfortably over thirty and sometimes wore glasses. She hated the war and what it had taken away from her. She'd been widowed for a year when she met Spaulding; neither she nor Spaulding had been looking for a commitment. She was extremely upset when she realized Spaulding was an intelligence agent; she found out about "Tortugas" when she looked at his file. Stoltz lured Jean out of the embassy and took her to the Rhinemann estate as a hostage; she and Lyons were returned safely to the embassy because of the agreement Spaulding made with Rhinemann. Granville made sure she received a letter of commendation from the State Department for her work in Buenos Aires; she planned to spend the rest of her life with Spaulding.

CAMERONS (OW)

Tremayne had represented the Cameron family in a legal dispute over the ownership of the Cameron clothing label; the Camerons lost, closed their factories, and the town went bankrupt. Tremayne thought the daughter might be trying to get even with him.

CANBRICK, CONGRESSMAN OWEN (IA)

Member of the Partridge Commission who made a statement on television about cost overruns of the military.

CANFIELD, JANET SAXON SCARLETT (SI)

Matthew Canfield was Janet's second husband. She met him while he was investigating the sudden appearance of American stocks on the Swedish exchange and their connection to Ulster Scarlett. Janet had slightly graying hair, an upturned nose above a delicate, sensitive mouth and wide brown eyes. She knew nothing about Matthew and Andrew going to Germany to meet Kroeger; she thought Kroeger was dead.

CANFIELD, MAJOR MATTHEW (SI)

Competent, experienced intelligence officer, second husband of Janet Saxon. He entered government service in March 1917 as junior accountant, government frauds section of the Department of the Interior. In 1918 he was promoted to field accountant attached to Group Twenty. He met Janet while he was investigating the missing Scarlatti securities for Group Twenty. In 1927 he resigned to enter the executive offices of Scarlatti Industries; he married Janet six months after Scarlett's reported death in Zurich.

In August 1940 Canfield returned to government service, in Army Intelligence. In 1944 Kroeger approached the U.S. government about defecting; one of the conditions he set was to have Andrew at the meeting in Germany. Cordell Hull didn't want Kroeger's name associated with American industry and realized that Kroeger's disappearance might contribute to the demise of the Nazis. Matthew and Andrew are sent to meet Kroeger; Matthew kills Kroeger, this time for certain.

CANNON, MITCH (SI)
Name that Canfield used while working as a customs inspector on the docks of New York. He saw Ulster Scarlett order the death of the captain of the *Genoa-Stella*; one of Ulster's men tried to kill him but was killed by Canfield and thrown into the river.

CANTOR, ALAN (MP)
Owner of the West Carlyle Sail and Ski Resort.

CAPALBO, ——— (MP)
Nimrod's messenger; he died of an overdose, not self-administered.

CAPOMANTI, ——— (GC)
(1) Family who ran an inn north of the village of Champoluc; Savarone's family always stayed there whenever they traveled to that area. The Capomantis were the people closest to Savarone.

(2) The nephew of Alfredo Goldoni and son of Francesca Capomanti farmed Alfredo's land and drove his car for him. The nephew was "a short, stocky Italian Swiss, ruffled brown hair above dark eyebrows, and the rugged, sharp features of a northern Mediterranean," and he was "at least ten years older than [Andrew] Fontine."

CAPOMANTI, FRANCESCA GOLDONI (GC)
Elder sister of Alfredo Goldoni. She lived with her son in Champoluc on the Via Sestina. When Alfredo's elder brothers died, Francesca was given the envelope containing Savarone's instructions.

CARALLO, EMILIO (IA)
The Mexican on the *Passage to China Island* who helped Kendrick escape. His usual occupation was fisherman, but there was no decent pay on the boats, so he worked on the island and took his pay home to his

family in El Descanso; he was not part of the Bollinger group. He was fluent in English, and his knowledge of the island and the routine was immensely helpful. He lost one lung and had a shattered hip from gunfire; Kendrick gave him a "fishing boat, along with its ownership papers, a prepaid course for his captain's license, a bankbook, and a guarantee that no one from the *Passage to China* would ever bother him in El Descanso."

CARDIONE, GUISEPPE AMBRUZZIO (OW)

Joe Cardone's real name.

CARDONE, ELIZABETH "BETTY" (OW)

Wife of Joe Cardone. She was a rich debutante from Chestnut Hill, and she couldn't cook like Joe's Italian mother; she was prim, stoutish, and Anglican. Betty and Joe slept in separate double beds because he was an early riser and she was a late riser. She had a special private telephone line into Joe's office; Joe was really panicked when Da Vinci called him on this private line. When Joe had too much to drink at the Tanners', it was quiet Betty who took charge of the situation.

CARDONE, JOSEPH (OW)

Specialist in the commodities market; he and Sam Bennett were partners. He was a private man who never asked for more from the company than his fair business share. He was a large man and loved his mother's cooking. He had his own private gymnasium in his home, and he would get up early to work out.

His real name was Guiseppe Ambruzzio Cardione, but he changed it somewhat to deemphasize his Italian background. He chose a scholarship to Princeton and was an All-American football player, the first from Princeton to be so honored in years. Grateful alumni brought him to Wall Street, where Italians flocked to him for help with their investments.

He figured the note from Da Vinci was from the Cosa Nostra; he was nervous about his "Mediterranean" customers, who were lucrative but dangerous investors. He was thoroughly panicked by the time the Osterman weekend began; he admitted being drunk and nervous. Fassett played off the Cardones against the Tremaynes and the Ostermans. When the Zurich deal was exposed, Joe told his partner about it and offered to resign; he offered to turn State's evidence in return for immunity from prosecution.

CAREW, "SCREW" (IA)

Representative for Sonar Electronics. The Kendrick Group bought sounding devices from them—the devices "didn't work, and they still wanted payment after we sent them back."

————, CARLO (RG)

One of Dellacroce's men that Hawkins knocked unconscious on the golf green.

CARLOS (AP) [REAL PERSON]

Also known as Carlos the Jackal. His real name was Ilich Ramirez Sanchez. Joel Converse was compared to him on two different occasions by the press, at the instigation of Aquitaine. First it was said he might join Carlos in a killing spree, then that he was "the most talented assassin since that maniac they call Carlos." Carlos was the notorious international terrorist responsible for the kidnapping of eleven oil ministers in Vienna in 1975. He was involved both with Palestinian extremists and European terrorists for at least twenty years. When he was driven out of Beirut in 1982 with the Palestinian guerrillas, he went underground again, the next year reportedly living in either South Yemen or Libya.

CARLOS (BI) [REAL PERSON]

Carlos was tall, tanned, narrow-waisted, broad-shouldered, and dressed most frequently as a priest. David Webb spent three years of his life pursuing Carlos, daring him to come out into the open by competing with him in the number of kills he made. He caught up with Carlos inside the Treadstone house; because of Conklin's misjudgment, Carlos escaped and Webb was nearly killed.

CARLOS (BS) [REAL PERSON]

Webb scoffed at the guards the government provided him; he figured he was the bait in the trap for the government to catch Carlos. Carlos, however, didn't know where he was. He would have heard of Jason Bourne's killing spree in Asia, however.

CARLOS (BU) [REAL PERSON]

Supposedly as a young man Carlos studied for the priesthood and was rejected; he could never let got of his lost faith and consistently used it as a viable cover. He was a real revolutionary. His "solution for all things disagreeable was to eliminate them violently," which was too much for the KGB—they expelled him. "There was a standing order in all branches of Russian intelligence that if Carlos was tracked, he was to be shot."

He was a master of the turnaround tactic; he could change a trap into an escape. In *The Bourne Ultimatum* the Jackal was deathly ill; he felt he had to kill Bourne to get the worldwide recognition he deserved, especially from Russia.

CARPENTER, FRANKLYN (PM)

Attaché to the American delegation at the Security Council's meetings the last week in December; he worked in Pierce's place. His wife and children were killed the week before Christmas, and Carpenter attended the meetings at the request of Pierce. One day Carpenter did not show up for work, sent in his resignation, and disappeared.

CARRARA, MANUEL (HC)

A man calling himself Manuel Carrara worked for Graff. This man was in his early thirties with dark skin, hair, and eyes. He said Johann was his closest friend. Johann said he didn't know him. The real Manuel Carrara, according to Johann, was a leader in the Brazilian Chamber of Deputies; however, his real allegiance was to the Odessa. Johann killed him, which was why he had to leave Brazil in such a hurry.

CARRARA, SENHORA (HC)

She and her brother were employed by Graff. "Her English was passable, but not good." She was in her late twenties with dark skin, hair, and eyes, and resembled her brother. They contacted Noel with information about the von Tiebolts. They said they were Portuguese Jews and friends of the von Tiebolts. She said she was to be married to Johann. When Noel described them to Johann, Johann said they were the Montealegres, and that they used the name Carrara because they knew he would recognize it.

CARTWRIGHT, JEFFERSON (SI)

Second vice president of Waterman Trust. Boutier made him responsible for assisting Ulster with his inquiries about the family's wealth. Cartwright was a "blondish, large, aging man . . . a product of the playing fields of the University of Virginia." He had an easy, outgoing, southern charm; he was a prime social stud and brought large accounts to Waterman because of his sexual activities. Cartwright became alarmed and sent notes to Chancellor when Ulster started moving his money to foreign banks during his honeymoon. Ulster did his research in the Scarlatti vaults, removing negotiable bearer bonds worth millions. If Cartwright revealed this, it would cause the destruction of Scarlatti Industries. He blackmailed Elizabeth into helping him get a better position at the bank and making him an advisory consultant to her foundations at fifty thousand dollars per year. His agreement with Elizabeth was stolen, and Cartwright was poisoned because of his knowledge of the missing securities.

CASSETT, CHARLES (BU)

Deputy Director of the CIA; he had been an analyst, not a field man. He covered up the fact that Conklin was an alcoholic. He was physically lean. He and Valentino were the only men Conklin trusted at Langley until he met Holland; Cassett wasn't someone you could con. When Cassett made the deal with Krupkin to assist Bourne and Conklin, he had no idea that Conklin and Krupkin knew each other.

CASTELANOS (OW)

Mafia friends of Joe Cardone's, in the construction business. They went to Joe for financial advice.

CAVENDISH, LORD CHAUNCEY (RO)

Ginny's fifth husband, a very wealthy Englishman, former Grenadier. He was a great admirer of Hawkins.

CAVENDISH, LADY GINNY (RO)

Ginny had gotten a divorce from Manny Greenberg and married Lord Chauncey Cavendish. She still had enough clout with Manny and the Hollywood crowd to help Hawkins find a producer for the Suicidal Six movie. Ginny wanted Manny to produce the film so she could keep an eye on him and the Suicidal Six.

CAWLEY (IA)

At first Evan thought Khalehla's name was Cawley.

CHAMELEON (BU)

Name used to describe Jason Bourne, because he could change his appearance so quickly and easily, even without makeup.

CHAMFORD, MARQUIS DE (BI)

Marcel, the butcher, calls him the "Marquis of the Dungheap." He was a drunkard and frequently visited prostitutes. Supposedly he had a difficult marriage and many problems. He was quite tall, about the size of David Webb. Webb took his clothing, his watch, his billfold and money and car keys, and also the prostitute's clothing, then pulled the telephone out of the wall, leaving them both naked. Later he used de Chamford's telephone card to call Langley from New York City.

CHANCELLOR, ———— (CM)

Peter Chancellor's father was a newspaperman near retirement. "In the early fifties he was a Washington correspondent for Scripps-Howard"; he provided Peter with the names of men who had financial dealings in prewar Germany, which started Peter on his research for his doctorate. Peter's mother was also a writer. His parents lived in Pennsylvania.

CHANCELLOR, PAUL (CM)

A blond-haired female columnist at an art exhibit at the Corcoran Gallery mistakenly identified Peter Chancellor as Paul Chancellor.

CHANCELLOR, PETER (CM)

Young doctoral candidate turned writer as a result of the manipulations of Inver Brass. Peter was almost thirty years old, dark-haired, with an angular face, sharp features, and deep-set, very light blue eyes. He had obtained a master's degree on scholarship, served in Vietnam, then used the G.I. Bill and tutoring money to attend Park Forest University to complete his doctorate in history, "The Origins of a Global Conflict." His thesis was rejected because Munro St. Claire put pressure on the honors college committee; St. Claire suggested he write a book on the origins of World War II, never thinking Peter would be successful.

Peter had an apartment in a brownstone on East Seventy-first Street in New York. He enjoyed playing tennis and skiing and he was a good cook. He liked to rise early and write; his method was to write on yellow pads, photocopy the pages, and send them to a typing service. His first book, *Reichstag!*, came out in early May 1969; *Sarajevo!* came out in April 1970; and *Counterstrike!* was released in April 1971. His next book was to be *Nuremburg!* All his books had sold well; he had been able to buy a silver Mark IV Continental and a home in Bucks County, Pennsylvania. He and his fiancée, Catherine Lowell, planned to live in that home after their wedding. Catherine was killed and he was seriously injured in a car crash on the way to visit his parents.

He recovered physically, but was extremely depressed, drank too much, and did no writing for months. His agent, Joshua Harris, sold the screenplay for *Counterstrike!* and persuaded Peter to go to Hollywood for a while, hoping the change would help him. Inver Brass decided to con Peter into writing a book about Hoover's death and the missing files (M-Z) in order to draw out the thief, so Inver Brass could obtain and destroy the files. The mystery of the missing files had the effect of bringing Peter out of his depression. Inver Brass passed on to him the information about General MacAndrew; after MacAndrew died, Peter decided to contact his daughter, Alison. Alison was interested in what had happened to her parents and decided to join him in his project. They came together because of their loneliness and fell in love.

After Bromley (Viper) threatened to kill him, Peter went to the FBI, where he just happened to meet O'Brien, who was on night duty. O'Brien wanted those files destroyed because he was in them, so he joined Peter and Alison. Varak, using Longworth's identity, tried to keep Peter from getting hurt, but things didn't occur the way Inver Brass thought they would, and Varak was killed. O'Brien, Alison, and Peter, along with some help from Phil Brown, Alison's ex-boyfriend, solved the mystery of who had the files.

CHANCELLOR, PETER (IA)

Samuel Winters told Mitch Payton that Chancellor was a writer whose manuscript "caused the demise of Inver Brass but couldn't prevent its resurrection."

CHANG, ——— (BS)

Friend and client of the banker Mr. Jitai's. He owned a fabric shop in Tuen Mun. When Marie was attacked by two young men, members of the Young People's Auxiliary Police, Jitai's friends rescued her and took her to a room in the back of Mr. Chang's shop.

———, CHARLES (SI)

Dossier custodian at the Home Office in London. Derek took out the file on Bertholde for Canfield to use.

CHARLES, R. (PM)

Superintendent of the building in which Jacob Handelman had an apartment. He was a huge, muscular young man, perhaps one of Columbia's larger linebackers. He knew that Handelman had visitors at odd hours.

CHARLIE BROWN (CM)

Alison's pet name for Phil Brown—Alison was a *Peanuts* fan. They had lived together for more than a year; Alison decided not to marry a military man.

CHARPENTIER, ——— (AP)

Valerie Converse's father met Valerie's mother when he was the Free French liaison between the Allies and the German underground in Berlin during World War II. He had been assigned to the cell in Charlottenburg because he could speak German. They emigrated to St. Louis, Missouri, where her mother had distant relations.

Valerie had just settled in New York after the two years in Paris when her father told her her mother was dying of cancer. Six days after that her mother died; one day six months later, after smoking a Gauloise while sitting in his chair on the front porch, he fell asleep and died.

CHARPENTIER, MRS. ——— (AP)

Valerie Converse's mother, born in Germany, sister of Hermione Geyner. Valerie's father described her fondly as "the crazy Berlinerin"; she was part of the German underground during World War II. Valerie thought her mother to be "slightly mad, always loving, always supportive in anything and everything"; she would take photographs of Val's paintings and send them to her family in Germany, lying outrageously about museums, galleries, and commissions. She died of cancer shortly after Valerie returned to the United States after her schooling in Paris.

CHARPENTIER, J. (AP)

Name used by Joel Converse to receive a message by wire at American Express travel offices in Paris, London, Bonn, and New York. Charpentier was his ex-wife's maiden name, and the message contained sets of numbers to the accounts holding the money from Dr. Beale.

CHARPENTIER, VALERIE (AP)

Maiden name of Valerie Converse. Name she used for the flight from Los Angeles to Champonix. (See also Converse, Valerie.)

CHASM OF LEATHER (OW)

CIA code name for the center of operations of Omega, specifically, Saddle Valley, New Jersey.

CHATELLERAULT, MARQUIS DE (CH)

Henri Salanne was the Marquis and David Booth's boss. He passed himself off as a financier, but he was really the head of a narcotics organization. Alison was persuaded to report on his activities for Interpol while she was married to David. The Marquis tried to hire Charles Whitehall to spy on McAuliff's expedition for him; he thought he could hold Whitehall's past political activity over him. His appearance in Jamaica confirmed his association with Dunstone, Ltd.; he did not trust his associates. Chatellerault was one of the first of the Dunstone, Ltd., group killed by the Halidon.

CHAUNCEY (BU)

Name Conklin threatened to use if Dellacroce didn't tell Conklin his correct name.

CHERNAK, M. (BI)

He was tied into the Zurich-Munich criminal underworld; David Webb (as Cain) used him as a drop or intermediary. He was a legless man with gray hair, confined to a wheelchair; he lived in an upstairs flat at 37 Lowenstrasse in Zurich. During World War II he was a Czechoslovakian translator and interrogator at Dachau. He was brutal, sadistic, and went to any length to curry favor with his superiors. While he was there, he recorded other officers' crimes. After the war he escaped, got his legs blown off by a land mine, and then lived nicely on his Dachau extortion payments.

———, CHET (CM)
FBI agent on telephone duty covering Surveillance, Washington, D.C., area, when O'Brien called.

CHILDREN OF THE DAMNED (HC)
Also known as "Children of Hell" and "Die Verwunschte Kinder." They were children of Nazi parents, hunted by many groups who wished to kill them or force them to join those groups. Many of the children fled from Germany, rejecting everything German, seeking new identities and life-styles. They formed a cultural subgroup and tried to support and protect one another.

CHIVIER, ——— (RE)
Agent, Frenchman, who worked for Spaulding in the north country of Spain. He and Bergeron led the Germans into an ambush.

CHOATE, ——— (OW)
Carol Brown's boyfriend.

CHRISTOPHER (CM)
Inver Brass code name for Jacob Dreyfus, oldest member of Inver Brass.

CHURCHILL, WINSTON (GC) [REAL PERSON]
Brevourt reported directly to Churchill about progress on the Salonika papers. Churchill wanted them for England.

———, CLAUDE (BI)
Economist friend of Marie St. Jacques's who tried to stop Marie and David Webb when they were being chased by Carlos's men at the Carillon du Lac. He tried to reach the police, then was hurt in the crowd and taken to the infirmary.

———, CLAUDE (BU)
Brother of the old French lady known as Régine Fontaine. He was one of the old men of Paris who worked for Carlos. He told his sister that

Michel accepted too much from Carlos and one day he would pay for it. He was sent to Montserrat by Carlos, where he assisted in the killing of Michel, and then was killed by Rickman.

CLAUSEN, ALTHENE (HC)

Althene's first marriage was to Heinrich Clausen; they had one child, Noel. Althene was manipulated just as Noel was, as part of Heinrich's scheme for the Fourth Reich. She thought she was protecting the funds so they could be used to make amends to the Jewish people for the crimes committed by the Third Reich.

CLAUSEN, HEINRICH (HC)

Master strategist of the Third Reich, financial magician who put together the resources to support Hitler. He was one of the false Wolfsschanze who wanted Hitler killed because Hitler wasn't radical enough. When they saw that Germany would lose the war, Clausen diverted funds into a secret account handled by Manfredi; together they planned the strategy for the emergence of the Fourth Reich. Once the plans were in place, the group killed him.

CLAUSEN, NOEL (HC)

Son and only child of Heinrich and Althene Clausen, born in summer 1939 in Berlin. Althene was persuaded to leave Heinrich and take Noel to the U.S. There was a death certificate made out for him in London; when Althene married Richard Holcroft, a new birth certificate was issued for him as Noel Holcroft. Noel was to be the key to releasing the millions stolen by the false Wolfsschanze to create the Fourth Reich.

———, CLIFF (MP)

Cliff worked for Blackstone Security, Inc., in Hartford. He retrieved the triangular paper from Matlock's apartment for him, relayed messages, and guarded Pat Ballantyne. He was an enormous man with a lean, intelligent face.

COBRA (BU)

Using the code name Cobra, Bourne contacted Armbruster to get information and panic him. Later he told Jim-Bob and Willie to tell people that Cobra was responsible for what happened at the Swayne estate.

COFFEY, ALEXANDER (T)

Roderick Bruce's lover. He was young enough to be Bruce's son and was his first love. Coffey was a genius with an expertise in Far Eastern languages and cultures, with a doctorate from the University of Chicago. He'd been sent to Washington to evaluate Oriental artifacts willed to the Smithsonian. When his deferment ended he went into the army, in the Asian Affairs Bureau in Washington. One day he was suddenly flown out to act as an interpreter for an intelligence team in Vietnam. His commander was Paul Bonner, who respected Coffey's abilities but tried to toughen him up so he'd survive. Coffey was taken prisoner in Chung Kal and executed.

COLE, ——— (OW)

CIA field agent who worked with Fassett.

COLONEL OF THE MAROONS (CH)

The treaty of 1739 between the British and the Maroons guaranteed the Maroons ownership of the Cock Pit territories in perpetuity. Formal permission was still sought from the Colonel of the Maroons for entry into their lands. Whitehall was convinced they could reach the Halidon through the Colonel; however, Whitehall's message never reached him.

COMMANDER Y (RO)

Code name Hawkins used for Vinnie.

COMMAND SAIGON (BI)

In *The Bourne Identity* Command Saigon is not identified as a particular person; although General Crawford spent a lot of time there, he did not agree with all the decisions made by the group.

COMPAGNIE SOLIDAIRE INSURANCE CO., PARIS, FRANCE (AP)

Director is Jacques-Louis Bertholdier. The company lost money when a shipment of munitions was supposedly lost on its way from Beloit, Wisconsin, to Northern Ireland via Tel Aviv and Marseilles. There was no record of it after Marseilles.

CONGDON, DANIEL (MC)

Undersecretary of State, director of Consular Operations; his last position was with the NSA. He was required by the Secretary of State to report to his field people that Scofield was "beyond salvage."

CONKLIN, ALEXANDER (BI)

Forty-six-year-old veteran of the CIA, originator of Operation Medusa and Treadstone. He was commonly referred to as a "shark killer; he directed individual strategies throughout the world when defection and treason were suspected." He was slender and walked with a cane; his foot had been blown off when he was a deep-cover agent with Medusa in Southeast Asia. He had a drinking problem and had been treated by Dr. Panov for the last five years for his own mental problems related to his work. He had worked with David Webb in a half-dozen sectors and was stationed with him in Phnom Penh before Medusa. He had been a close friend of David and his family before David's family was killed. He understood why David went into Medusa and felt sure he had turned on Treadstone; he was the control on the CIA's operation to kill Webb.

CONKLIN, ALEXANDER (BS)

He had been a close friend of David Webb and his first wife's in Cambodia. Conklin had been in the CIA at the time and had found a place for Webb in Medusa after the death of his family. While Conklin was working for Medusa, his foot was shattered by a land mine, which ended his career as a field strategist. Two years later the Monk requested him to monitor the Bourne operation. When Bourne disappeared and then resurfaced, he decided Bourne had turned and twice tried to kill him. When he discovered he'd been wrong, Conklin became an alcoholic; Panov couldn't help him. When Webb's wife was kidnapped, Webb turned to Conklin to help him. Conklin and Panov traveled to Hong Kong to find Marie and David and get them out safely if they could; Conklin felt he had to do this to make up for his past behavior toward David. After David returns from killing Sheng, Conklin leaves David and Marie in Hawaii to fly to Washington to demand accountability from the U.S. government intelligence services.

Wo Lu border to People's Republic of China—Ghurka guards patrol "Defector's Point" (THE BOURNE SUPREMACY)

CONKLIN, ALEXANDER (BU)

"Saint Alex," saint of the black operations. He has a black belt in karate. Covert-operations officer in the CIA, retired for past four and a half years. He is a slender middle-aged man who dresses neatly; his face has premature lines and deep shadows under his eyes. He takes stress and blood pressure tablets. When he gets upset, he sticks his head under the cold water faucet. He has no wife or family, no really close friends other than the Webbs and Panov, only sporadic lovers, and he uses the normal world as a cover. He does his job because he's trained to do it. He's not much into high-tech gadgets—admits he can't even program his VCR.

He had been the youngest valedictorian in his high school's history, and the youngest freshman ever accepted at Georgetown. He was recruited by the CIA and had served all over the world, mastered many languages, and become master of covert operations. In Vietnam he had made it back through one hundred forty miles of enemy territory and came into camp casually asking for a bottle of bourbon. It was in Vietnam that he had his foot blown off by a land mine. He was extremely unhappy when he had to take a desk job with the CIA. He felt great remorse because he had tried to kill Bourne; he was "about to go under" when Bourne came back into his life at the time of Marie's kidnapping. He felt he owed it to Bourne to help him in Hong Kong and again in France and Russia.

He'd known Krupkin for years—they were "friendly enemies"—but he wouldn't hesitate to kill him if necessary for his country. When Carlos tried to kill him and Krupkin at the armory, he was lucky—the bullets passed through him—but he was still wounded seriously enough to have to use a wheelchair.

CONLEY, ——— (CM)

Conley was an M.N. subgroup specialist. Phil Brown told Chancellor to assume this identity while they were at the VA hospital near Richmond.

CONNALLY, KATHERINE (MC)

One of the three nurses who died in the boating accident on March 26, 1954, after tending Senator Appleton.

CONSULAR OPERATIONS (CONS OPS) (MC)

There were frequent conflicts between the CIA and Consular Operations. Consular Operations was originally founded to "facilitate the defection of thousands from a political system they found intolerable." The objective was finally narrowed down to assist a handful of scientists, soldiers, and intelligence agents, people who had specialized information.

Conte and Contessa (bu)

Also known as Paolo and Davinia. They operated out of Rome from government circles, and had direct contact with the dons in Sicily. De Fazio tried to hire them to kill Bourne, Conklin, and Panov, because they could go places the regular hit men couldn't.

The conte was a "distinguished-looking olive-skinned man with wavy dark hair"; the contessa was a "fashionably dressed, well-coifed middle-aged woman." When they discovered they would be in conflict with the Jackal, they refused to take the contract. They did manage to get over a million dollars out of De Fazio for the location of the three men and for furnishing weapons and a car and driver for him.

Converse, Joel (ap)

Attorney who is recruited by an unidentified group of patriotic Americans legally to defeat Aquitaine. He's the son of Roger Converse, and he's forty to forty-nine years old. He is five foot ten or eleven with pale blue eyes, and regular facial features. His father was a pilot, and both he and his sister, Virginia, learned to fly before they were old enough to get a driver's license. He attended Taft High School in Watertown, Connecticut, in the early sixties, where he became friends with Avery Preston Fowler.

He was a lieutenant in the Navy, one and a half stripes, carrier-based off the coast of Vietnam. He had been ordered by Delavane to fly in unfit weather to support the ground troops. He was flying low over Vietnam when his left engine exploded; unable to stabilize, he bailed out and was taken prisoner.

He led two escapes, but both groups were recaptured—he lost eight men, which still disturbs him. He escaped from solitary confinement and went back through the jungle for over a hundred miles until he reached the American lines. He was discharged in June 1968. At his discharge hearing he said that men like Delavane can't be allowed anymore.

He found a job with the law firm of Talbot, Brooks and Simon; he expected that if he proved satisfactory, he would replace Brooks as their international representative. He had made at least two trips to Europe in Beale's place—one to Strasbourg and another to Geneva. He had also met René Mattilon, the French lawyer who sometimes represented them, and he and René had become good friends.

He had been with the firm for five years when he and Valerie were divorced, because of his obsession with his job. He respected Talbot and

Brooks; he not only respected Nathan Simon, but he liked and trusted him. He had learned more about law from Nathan than anyone else he had ever met. He knew Nathan would use the law to help him defeat Aquitaine.

He had not remarried, although he admitted to Halliday that he did have a few good women friends.

He used some of the things he learned from Valerie during the marriage to help him while he was being pursued. When Valerie was at the agency, the secretary there was very nosy and a real gossip, so Joel would call pretending to be a client; he used the same ruse when calling Valerie in Berlin.

Joel is a smoker; he drinks black coffee, scotch, whiskey, bourbon, or, if he can get it, Armagnac brandy. He is able to swim but doesn't jog. He was embarrassed by the public display of sexuality in Amsterdam; he enjoys sexual encounters but prefers privacy. He enjoys flying; while he was continuing his education after Vietnam, he flew single-engine airplanes to relieve the stress of studying.

He is unable to learn foreign languages. When he was in Europe he liked to carry a transistor radio to listen to the BBC. He was quite creative in figuring out how to get information in Europe while speaking only English. He likes to read the *International Herald-Tribune.*

He is a very cautious man and he hates violence. He admits to having fears but uses anger to overcome the fear. He is not a good shot. The last man he killed he emptied the gun at without hitting him once, and finally tackled him and hit his head against the ground. Killing people makes him physically ill. For someone who hates violence, he left at least nine bodies behind him in Europe; they were all killed, however, in self-defense or so he could survive. He hates Aquitaine and all it stands for; he hates fanatics. He decides, though, that the only way to defeat Aquitaine is to infiltrate it and get the evidence.

CONVERSE, ROGER (AP)

Father of Joel Converse; he was an airline pilot, later an executive for Pan Am. Joel had ambivalent feelings about his father.

Nathan Simon liked Roger because Roger brought his business where his son was. Roger also liked Nathan and was teaching him to fly; he was now flying multi-engine props.

Roger was the closest friend Valerie had, even after her divorce from Joel. He also loved Joel very much, and could not believe the news reports that said he was an insane killer.

Roger was staying at Valerie's seaside cottage when the package came from Joel. He undoubtedly opened it, read it, called Nathan, and described the contents. Joel had said he wouldn't have had sense enough not to blurt out everything on the phone. Unknown to Valerie and Roger,

Valerie's phone line had been bugged by Aquitaine; Roger was murdered and the package went into the hands of Aquitaine.

CONVERSE, VALERIE (AP)

Ex-wife of Joel Converse, she lives in Cape Ann, Massachusetts. She is fairly tall; has long, dark hair; wide eyes; long, graceful legs; and walks like a dancer. She paints seascapes for a living. She can live only where she does because of Joel's alimony checks.

At first she and Joel were good for each other—they were both ambitious. Then he became mesmerized with his own progress to the exclusion of everything else. She told him one day that he was emotionally burnt-out—he agreed and left.

Valerie would not believe the things they were saying about Joel in the news. It made her angry that Larry Talbot seemed to believe them. Joel abhorred violence. She admitted she was frightened by what Larry and René had said.

She was very fond of Roger Converse and he was equally fond of her. Roger stayed at her place while she was in Europe hunting for Joel. Joel sent the package with instructions in it to her to take to Nathan. He knew she would know how to handle it.

CONVERSE, VIRGINIA "GINNY" (AP)

Only sibling and sister of Joel Converse. Two years younger, she soloed in an airplane before Joel did and never let him forget it. While Joel was in Vietnam she was a war protester. She maintained a close relationship with Valerie even after Joel's divorce. When her father called Valerie, Valerie told him Ginny was frantic. She felt it was her fault that Joel was being hunted. Her father said she was paranoic. Valerie told Joel that his sister and brother-in-law were confused, angry, and bewildered, that they spoke through their attorneys supporting him, and that they loved him very much.

COOPER, MRS. (BU)

Elderly black maid on Montserrat who took care of David and Marie Webb's two children. She had seven children of her own.

COOPER, BRIGADIER GENERAL LESTER (T)

Bonner's commanding officer, an ex-commandant of West Point whose father had held the same position. Cooper had "acquitted himself superbly in three wars"; he'd been a tank commander in World War II under Patton. He was a white-haired, tough, facile-tongued exponent of the Pentagon's requirements. Cooper didn't like Bruce attacking Bonner; he didn't like to feel that Bonner was expendable. Cooper reported to

Allen about Trevayne's activities, using information supplied by Bonner. He provided the jet plane for Bonner, then later accused him of disregarding his orders; physical violence was the last thing he wanted. He admitted to Bonner they had been using de Spadante. When Allen gave the order, Cooper set up the logistics for the military to support Trevayne for president. Trevayne learned of the plan from Bonner and forced Cooper to retire immediately.

Cora, Cousin (RO)
Devereaux's maid, family cousin. She was plump, middle-aged, rude, and drank too much. She was also a good cook and felt that guarding the house and its inhabitants was her duty.

Corbellier, Dennis (BI)
Attaché in the Canadian embassy in Paris that Peter trusted; he and Peter had been classmates at the University of Toronto. Marie asked him to trace a car license and a telephone number for her. The last time she called him, Marie spoke to one of Carlos's men; Dennis had been shot in the throat in front of the embassy in the early morning hours.

Corescu, Arvidas (PM)
Handelman gave Jenna papers identifying her to Kahoutek as Arvidas Corescu.

———, Corky (RO)
Chairman of the Joint Chiefs of Staff. He couldn't understand why the EC-135's had to be kept in the air over the SAC base in Omaha for an extended period of time.

Corsican (PM)
Mediterranean specialist hired to kill Jenna and Havelock crossing the border at Col des Moulinets.

Cotter, Floyd (CH)
Floyd worked for Piersall and was also Barak Moore's second-in-command. It was decided that he would be hired by McAuliff and provide protection for the survey group. One of his jobs around camp included helping Alison take deep bore samples. Floyd was shot to death by the Trelawney Parish police outside Piersall's house, giving his life so McAuliff and the others could escape safely with Piersall's research papers.

CRAFT FOUNDATION (CH)

Organization in Jamaica that was headed by Arthur Craft, Jr., and Arthur Craft, Sr. (semi-retired). They wanted only what they could get out of Jamaica and didn't care about the people living there.

CRAFT, MAJOR ——— (BU)

An entry in Swayne's diary referred to a Major Craft, Croft, or Christopher. Randolph Gates refused to have this man on his staff; Medusa was willing to blackmail Gates to get the man appointed.

CRAFT, ARTHUR, JR. (CH)

Head of the Craft Foundation. He fired James Ferguson, then met him at the airport in Kingston a year later, apologizing profusely and complimenting him on his work. While he was talking with Ferguson, Craft had McAuliff's bags picked up, bugged, then transported to the hotel. He wanted Ferguson to keep a log on everyone McAuliff dealt with, then he would hire Ferguson back. He didn't count on Ferguson telling McAuliff about it, or on having his bugging devices discovered and moved, or on having Ferguson request money for his services. After McAuliff beat up Craft's men, who were monitoring the bugging devices, Craft decided to have Ferguson videotaped receiving money, so that he could quit paying Ferguson and prevent him from revealing anything. His father discovered what happened and sent his son to the South of France.

CRAFT, ARTHUR, SR. (CH)

According to Tallon, "Arthur Craft, *père et fils*, have been raping this island for half a century. They subscribe to the belief that theirs is a mandate from God." Craft sent Ferguson a letter of apology for his son's behavior and asked him to return so he could finish his research on baracoa fibers. He provided a way for Ferguson to leave the expedition.

CRAFT, JONATHAN (RE)

Representative for Packard, major subcontractor for Meridian Aircraft. Pace described him as "a social-register flunky." Craft had a soft, high voice, delicate hands, and manicured fingernails; his family was old money and he'd attended the "right" schools. He was living in Ann Arbor but intended to be back on the New York Stock Exchange as soon as the war was over. Swanson told him that the company's failure to produce the guidance system under contract was treasonable; Craft sent this message on to Oliver, who contacted Kendall. Craft despised Kendall because he was afraid of him, but Kendall was their only hope of getting the guidance system. Craft had to sell all his holdings and go to work as a government clerk the rest of his life because of his participation in the exchange.

CRANE, DEAN (PM)

Jenna was supposed to attend a student foreign-exchange committee meeting at Dean Crane's home. Dean Crane was associated with the small university in New Hampshire where Havelock accepted a teaching position.

CRANSTON, ——— (MP)

Cranston was a field agent for the Narcotics Bureau, an overseas route specialist. He had done the research that led to a suspected drug center at Carlyle.

CRANSTON, ——— (OW)

Cranston worked for the FCC. Two pages concerning service features had been missing from the folder from Washington to Tanner; Cranston had agreed to leave these blank for another month, pending network decisions. Fassett used this as an excuse to get Tanner to Washington, where he could interrogate him and enlist his help to catch Omega.

CRAWFORD, GENERAL IRWIN ALLEN "IRON ASS" (BI)

Current ranking officer in charge of American intelligence data banks. He had been in Medusa and had observed David Webb in the field; he had also been a commander in Saigon attached to covert operations, but would not defend the "gross stupidities often rampant in Saigon." He had a well-known antipathy to the CIA. Webb was not his choice to go after Carlos; he admitted Webb was qualified, but he wanted a more balanced man. He had told Webb to come in and he didn't, so he figured Webb had turned. When he found out Webb had amnesia and had brought Carlos to Treadstone, he stood in front of the Treadstone house in plain view, risking his life to contact Conklin to stop the operation to kill Webb.

CRAWFORD, GENERAL IRWIN ALLEN "IRON ASS" (BS)

He now headed State's Internal Security. He was unaware that Marie Webb had been kidnapped until Conklin informed him. He also didn't know Webb had been cleared by the government doctors. Conklin pressured him to get some answers.

CRAWFORD, JAMES (CM) [REAL PERSON]

John Edgar Hoover's private chauffeur. The dent in the chrome bumper of the limousine was left there to remind Crawford of his carelessness.

CRAWFORD, LESTER (IA)

The CIA's analyst for covert activities in the Middle East. He was an old-line professional and extremely angry when asked if he'd leaked information on Kendrick's Mideast activities.

CRAWFORD, DR. NATHANIEL (MC)

Surgeon who initially treated Senator Appleton after the accident. Crawford was retired, living in Quincy. He had been head of surgery for nearly twelve years and had made very few mistakes in his career. He knew that Appleton had a massive cerebral hemorrhage; when Appleton lived, Crawford thought he must have made a mistake in his prognosis.

CRETE (RG)

Other code name Noir. Intelligence agent hired by Hawkins to help kidnap the Pope. Crete was the first to show up; Rudolph refused to let him into his taxi because no one had told him that Crete was black. He was a brilliant aeronautical engineer and a Soviet sympathizer as long as the Russians would pay him; he spoke an English refined in university lecture rooms.

CRISPI, ——— (MC)

The oldest Crispi brother ran an expensive restaurant on the Via Frascati; he was known for his discretion. Scofield had used him before as a drone; he asked Crispi to send telegrams to him from Antonia and received information from him about the Scozzi-Paravacinis.

CROSS, MRS. (PM)

Havelock introduced Jenna to Decker as Mrs. Cross.

CROSS, ROBERT (PM)

Robert Cross was listed as an assistant to the President, researching old agendas; he had his own private office in a high-security area, complete with an assistant who was a secret service agent waiting to capture anyone who came around looking for Mr. Cross. This was Havelock's cover while he was looking for the mole in the White House.

CROWN GOVERNOR ON MONTSERRAT (BU)

Fontaine obtained his first instructions from the Jackal through the Crown Governor. He was a member of a family of landed gentry and his brother was high up in the foreign office. Since he was not a young man, there was a question as to why he'd been sent to such an outpost. Henry Sykes considered him to be a pompous idiot. The CG went out alone on his boat while Carlos was trying to kill Bourne; his boat was found smashed on a reef with no sign of survivors.

CROWTHER, JAMES (BS)

One of David Webb's graduate students. He made arrangements with him to cover his classes while he was gone and take care of the newspaper, mail, and the house.

CRUETT, HOWARD (BS)

Name on one of the passports that Cactus made for Bourne, the one that made him look like he had blue eyes. When Bourne met the Honeywell-Porter group on the boat to Macao, he introduced himself as Howard Cruett.

CUPID (IA)

Andy Vanvlanderen referred to Sundstrom as Cupid because of his appearance.

DAKAKOS, ANNAXAS "THE STRONG" (GC)

Gentle, strong older brother of Petride, the monk. He had a large face, lined from exposure to the sun and wind, and wide-set eyes; he was a bull of a man, nearer fifty than forty. He and his wife had five children and were expecting their sixth soon. Petride said he'd trust Annaxas with his life, that he was the finest man he knew. When their father died, thirteen-year-old Annaxas went to the railyards to work; the money he made kept his family together and made it possible for his younger sisters and brothers to get schooling. There was a chasm between the brothers because Petride had become well educated and Annaxas had not; Petride thought Annaxas's skill driving the train was remarkable. Annaxas told his family he was taking a freight to Corinth; he told his wife he was going to help his brother and the church. He had no idea this would be his last trip.

DAKAKOS, MRS. ANNAXAS (GC)

Annaxas's wife went crazy because the Order of Xenope would not give her any information about her husband's death. She knew about the train because Annaxas had told her about it. She was left alone with six children to raise. A month after the priests took her and her family in, she was dead, killed by the order because of what she knew. They raised and educated her six children.

DAKAKOS, PETRIDE (GC)

A bearded young priest of the Order of Xenope, the harshest monastic brotherhood under the control of the Patriarchate of Constantine. After

With Mary in the Gardens of Topkapi, Istanbul (THE GEMINI CONTENDERS)

transporting the sacred documents to Savarone, who was to hide them in the mountains, Petride was to kill his brother and then himself. He deeply loved his brother Annaxas, but followed his orders; their bodies were found with no identification on them on a Greek train in the freight yards of Milan.

DAKAKOS, THEODORE ANNAXAS (GC)

A well-liked young Greek shipping tycoon. He was the son of Annaxas the Strong, raised by the priests of the Order of Xenope. He was a big man; his shoulders were wide and heavy. His "face was large, the eyes set wide apart, beneath light brows and a tanned forehead." He was in his middle forties, and he spoke precise English. He had a reputation for integrity and an acute business sense. Dakakos knew about the train from Salonika from his mother; he researched the records and worked with Land. It was Dakakos who took over the care of Campo di Fiori under the name Baricours, Père et Fils. Greene found out Dakakos was behind the investigation of Eye Corps. Dakakos was trying to prevent Andrew from getting the sacred documents and trying to help Adrian, who thought Dakakos was trying to stop him. At Campo di Fiori Andrew found Dakakos alone with an elderly priest; he bound them both, then pistol-whipped and interrogated Dakakos, who had been waiting for Adrian. Dakakos broke away and attacked Andrew, but he was no match for the professional soldier. Andrew shot Dakakos and the old priest to death.

DALE, SERGEANT (OW)
Desk sergeant on duty when Tanner called for MacAuliff.

D'ALMEIDA, LOUIS FRANÇOIS (SI)
One of the group of merchants supporting the Nazis. True owner of the Franco-Italian rail system; he had purchased the majority shares from the Italian government through bribery.

D'AMACOURT, ANTOINE R. (BI)
Vice President and senior executive officer of La Banque de Valois, Paris; his office was on the main floor at the rear. He was a "middle-aged man with a face older than his age," thinning dark hair combed to hide the bald spots, and cold, darting eyes surrounded by small rolls of flesh. He smokes, drinks whiskey, and wears conservative clothing. He followed directions on the account as part of his job (which included a call to Carlos's men), but would also accept pay for special favors. He traded information for money with Webb (as Bourne) so Webb could get access to the money in his account. He was paid again by Webb and Marie when the money was transferred.

DAMBERT, JESUS (MP)
An alias of Julian Dunois's.

D'AMBOIS, MARQUIS (BI)
David Webb asked Marcel if he is speaking about "that jackass d'Ambois . . . someone told me he lived around here." This was a fictional character Webb invented in order to get information about Marquis de Chamford.

D'AMBROSIA, SALVATORE "MEAT" (RO)
Mangecavallo's street gorilla; not too bright but he got the job done. Meat was married and had seven children. Meat delivered the messages to the Wall Street brokers that caused the ruin of Pease's old school-chum group.

DAME BOUNTIFUL (IA)
The security staff for the Vice President listed Ardis in the logs as Dame Bountiful, which she liked.

DANFORTH, ALEXANDER (OW)

Seventy-year-old aide to the President of the United States, the liaison between the White House and the CIA. He lived in Georgetown and collected Degas watercolors. Danforth had every confidence in Fassett, although he'd met him only once.

DANFORTH, LORD SIDNEY (RG)

One of the wealthiest men in England, seventy-two-year-old paragon of British industry. Danforth had made a huge sum of money brokering hardware and ammunition to the North Vietnamese. He used Chilean vessels to transport the goods and had payment made to the Chilean companies. He had also supplied war goods to the Axis, using the same scheme during World War II. Hawkins blackmailed him into donating $10 million to the Shepherd Company.

————, DANIEL (CH)

Minister of the Council, elected for life by the council of the tribe of Acquaba. "He was black Jamaican (in his early forties) with sharp Afro-European features, slightly more than medium height, and quite slender." He had broad shoulders and a body tapered like that of a long distance runner. His symbol of office was a white silk kerchief held together by a gold ring, worn around his throat. He wanted Holcroft and his group out of Jamaica so Jamaicans could determine their own destiny; in exchange he was willing to give Holcroft the list of the members of Dunstone, Ltd.

DANIELS, PETER (MP)

Matlock knew Peter Daniels, who worked in Yale's admission office. Daniels helped him identify Alan Pace by looking through senior class photographs.

DANILOVICH, ANDREEV (MC)

He was a teenage boy, tall for his age, who lived in Cheremushki. He was to take Taleniekov to the home of Aleksie Krupskaya.

D'ANJOU, PHILIPPE (BI)

"An oddly out-of-place middle-aged man dressed in a conservative business suit" who operated the telephone switchboard at Les Classiques in Paris. He had thinning gray hair that fell slightly over one ear. He had owned companies in Saigon and a vast plantation in the Mekong delta. France abandoned their people in Vietnam when they pulled out, so d'Anjou became part of Medusa. He knew David Webb as Delta, and had accompanied him on the mission into Tam Quan to rescue Gordon

Webb. D'Anjou stole from Medusa and set up his own activities to survive. He was hired by Carlos to identify Webb (as Cain). He made the mistake of going to Parc Monceau and Carlos marked him to be killed. Webb warned him, d'Anjou gave him as much information as he had about Carlos, then d'Anjou left for Asia.

D'ANJOU, PHILIPPE (BS)

Jiang Yu referred to him as "the Frenchman," the contact to Jason Bourne. D'Anjou realized the real Bourne would disappear, that the Bourne legend was still alive in Asia, and people would pay well for Bourne's services, so he created another Jason Bourne. Unfortunately, the impostor decides to do business without the assistance of d'Anjou, making contracts that would imperil the safety of the Far East, and d'Anjou decides to find him and kill him. He and the real Bourne join forces, and Sheng's forces capture and torture d'Anjou. Bourne finds him but is unable to prevent Sheng from killing d'Anjou; as he is dying, d'Anjou makes it possible for Bourne to capture the impostor and get away from Sheng.

———, DAPHNE (RO)

(1) Slender, attractive British woman in her mid-forties who worked for Hyman Goldfarb. She and her companion pretended to be British anthropologists trying to find the descendants of a long-lost tribe who was owed money by the British government to lure Chief Thunder Head from his hiding place. She was captured and tied to a tree by the Wopotamis.

(2) Froggie's wife. They lived in Fairfax.

D'ARTAGNAN (RG)

Real estate broker from the highly secretive Les Chateaux Suisse des Grands Siècles. He made the arrangements for Hawkins to occupy Chateau Machenfeld.

DAUDET, CLAUDE PIERRE (SI)

One of the group of merchants supporting the Nazis. Frenchman whose ships safely carried supplies to France's enemies during the war under the Paraguayan flag.

DAUMIER, HEYSOU (MP)

An alias of Julian Dunois's.

D'AVENZO, COUNTESS (GC)

Young, blond-haired, Italian lover of Vittorio Fontini-Cristi. She was married to a count, a dreadful businessman who was very envious of Vittorio.

DA VINCI (OW)

Cardone received a telegram from Zurich signed by Da Vinci, warning him against Tanner; he thought it was from the Cosa Nostra. It was from Fassett.

———, DAVID (IA)

One of the young children of a member of the Kendrick Group; he was killed when the building the Kendrick Group was in exploded because of sabotage by the Mahdi's people.

DAVIS, BILL (MP)

A black student of Matlock's. When he was told he would flunk the course, he decided to go to work and passed with high marks.

DAWSON, VICTOR ALAN (PM)

Strategist for Consular Operations, an attorney and specialist in international law, brilliant in international treaty negotiations. Dawson and Stern were personal friends as well as fellow strategists; they occasionally enjoyed a couple of hours of quiet talk together by themselves. While they were driving home together, their car was destroyed by a large bulldozer; their security guards had been involved in a freeway accident and had been too late to help them. The President put a news blackout on their deaths and immediately moved their families to a security compound in Colorado Springs.

DE FAZIO, LOUIS (BU)

A middle-level, ambitious capo supremo in the Giancavallo family from Brooklyn Heights, in N.Y., he lived in an opulent apartment near the East River. He was short and stocky, with dark eyes, eyebrows, and hair. He wanted everyone to know it was his group that was responsible for the killing of Bourne. He thought the Jackal was fictional until the conte and contessa refused the contract. He was homosexual and had a male lover, Frankie. He was responsible for numerous murders. His front was the Atlas Coin Vending Machines, Long Island City. He was wounded in the fight with Bourne at the airfield near Paris and was taken into custody by the Americans.

DE MATARESE, GUILLAUME (MC)

Original founder of the Matarese. He was widowed and had two sons; when he was seventy he married a seventeen-year-old girl from a convent. His two sons, directors of his businesses, had been tricked into losing the business by bankers cooperating with their governments; the sons were then murdered. Guillaume decided to take revenge on these governments by forming the council of the Matarese; he had several secret accounts that he gave to the council to get them started toward establishing an organization that would control the governments through financial means and violence when necessary. Everyone at the house the night the council was held was murdered to keep the plan secret, except for the four men who were to carry out the plan, the shepherd boy, and the young wife. The land owned by Guillaume was distributed to the villagers with the understanding they would bury the dead, set fire to the house, and never tell anyone about what happened there that night; if they failed to carry this out, they would lose their land and/or be murdered.

DE SPADANTE, AUGUST "AUGIE" (T)

Forty-two-year-old younger brother of Mario de Spadante. Augie accompanied Mario to Barnegat to kill Trevayne. Bonner knifed him in the back.

DE SPADANTE, MARIO "MARIO THE SPADE" (T)

Mafia boss who worked for Genessee. Mario was a large man with an enormous head and a deeply tanned complexion; he was in his early fifties and wore horn-rimmed glasses. He had attended New Haven High School and was married with one daughter. Trevayne had known Mario for about nine years; Mario owned a construction company that bid on some buildings Trevayne wanted built. He still hated Trevayne because his bid had been rejected. Mario terrorized Trevayne's family before the confirmation hearing. After the hearing his men trailed Trevayne for Genessee. Finally he decided Trevayne had to be removed; he called Webster to have the 1600 Patrol removed, then followed Trevayne to his home to kill him. Bonner interfered with Mario's plans, shooting him in the stomach. Mario was flown to a Greenwich hospital, where his own men stood guard. He was recuperating at home when Gallabretto's men killed him. His death was reported as a gangland slaying.

DECKER, LIEUTENANT COMMANDER THOMAS (PM)

Annapolis '61, former skipper of the submarine *Starfire*, and member of the Pentagon's Nuclear Contingency Committees. He was an excellent officer, a fair and decent man with deep Judeo-Christian beliefs, respected by his men; he loved his country. Decker, however, went to great lengths to please and support his fellow officers and superiors and made sure to justify everything he did. He was flattered to be asked to work with Matthias and provided him with documents showing the strategies and nuclear-strike capabilities of the United States. He was devastated when he learned that what he did could have started a nuclear war. Decker preferred dying with some honor to living in disgrace; he walked directly into gunfire from Pierce's men, giving U.S. agents the opportunity to kill them.

DEERFOOT, COLONEL TOM (RO)

Air Force officer in line for the chairmanship of the Joint Chiefs of Staff; he was a full-blooded Mohawk. When he heard the Indian music in front of the Supreme Court building, he was curious. He almost collapsed in hysterical laughter when he saw the Wopotamis protesting to the "Celebration of the Wedding Night." The Wopotamis never got anything right.

DELAVANE, GENERAL GEORGE MARCUS (AP)

The organizer and generally acknowledged leader of Aquitaine. Delavane's father had named his first son in honor of Marcus Aurelius. Marcus saw himself as "a student of history—in the tradition of Caesar, Napoleon, Clausewitz . . . even Patton."

Hong Kong

When Joel first met him he was a young Navy pilot flying from an aircraft carrier off the coast of Vietnam. Delavane personally came aboard and ordered the commander to send his men up because he wanted coverage for troop movements on the ground. He was extremely nasty about it; Joel was standing there and dared to tell him he hoped he'd meet him later under other circumstances. The commander had no choice but to send Joel and his men up. They had to fly at low altitudes because of the weather and took heavy losses (although not as bad as the losses on the ground); Joel was shot down and taken prisoner.

Although leader of Aquitaine, Delavane is confined to a wheelchair in his home in Palo Alto, California; he lost both his legs due to diabetes. He spends his time behind a large desk with a fragmented map of the world behind him. He has a large head with a lined, square-jawed face, an aquiline nose, thin lips, and skin like parchment; his hair is close-cropped, the color of salt and pepper, and his voice, when raised, sounds like "a tomcat screeching across a frozen lake." He is the only one not present at the meeting of Joel and the Aquitaine leaders in Bonn.

He praised Paul for being the best adjutant he ever had; however, he didn't trust him. After the riots started, Paul takes a revolver from the desk drawer to kill Delavane. Delavane pulls a gun out of a secret place in his wheelchair. While shooting Paul he says he hadn't trusted anyone, including the other leaders of Aquitaine. Although mortally wounded, Paul kills Delavane with his only shot.

DELLACROCE, ANGELO (CH)

Reputed Mafia figure, member of Dunstone, Ltd., killed when his car exploded in Scarsdale.

DELLACROCE, ANGELO (RG)

Untouchable Cosa Nostra boss. He insisted on meeting Hawkins alone at the sixth hole of the North Hampton Golf Club between midnight and one in the morning. Of course Dellacroce brought his whole group with him. Hawkins disabled all of them and then proved to Dellacroce that he had enough evidence to send him to prison. Dellacroce agreed to give Hawkins $10 million for the Shepherd Company.

DELLACROCE, MRS. ANGELO (RG)

Dellacroce donated $10 million to the Shepherd Company via the North Hampton Corporation, Mrs. Angelo Dellacroce, President.

DELLACROCE, NICHOLAS (BU)

Mafia man who was Panov's caretaker. He was short, heavyset, with a rasping voice, a large head, and bad teeth. He wore a mask to conceal his identity from Panov. He gave his sister's son the money he needed to go through medical school. While they were in the car, Panov convinced him that he might have oral cancer; Nick became so upset that he let Panov take off his blindfold so Panov could check his mouth. Panov grabbed the wheel and steered them into a tree. Nick was seriously hurt, but survived to give evidence to the CIA about the Mafia connection to Medusa.

DELTA (BI) (BS)

Code name used by David Webb while he was working for Operation Medusa in Vietnam. Members of Medusa used Greek-letter code names instead of their real names.

DELVECCHIO (AP)

Mafia crime family in New York associated with the murder of Judge Anstett. Joey the Nice, an executioner for the family, had accompanied a major from the Aquitaine to kill the judge; he described the man as a crazy gumba, a sadist who questioned and tortured the judge before killing him. Delvecchio had a grudge against Anstett because the judge had put the oldest Delvecchio son in jail for twelve years with no appeals left; however, Anstett's execution was ordered by Delavane.

DEMARTIN, LIEUTENANT COMMANDER JOHN (IA)

A U.S. Navy fighter pilot, DeMartin picked up the mortally wounded Milos Varak near the airport in San Diego. He discovered a written message Milos had left in the car and called the base's chief of intelligence.

DEMOPOLIS, FATHER (IA)

Ahbyahd traveled across the U.S. as a Greek priest named Father Demopolis.

DEMPSEY, MISS (RG)

Secretary who worked for Jesse Barton.

DEMPSEY, MISS (SI)

Theatrical artist who was supposed to have had an early lunch at the Venezia Restaurant with Ulster Scarlett the week he disappeared.

———, DENISE (BU)

Maid at the home of Randolph and Edith Gates.

DENNING, R. B. (PM)

Network executive of Trans American News Division who supplied library footage of the Security Council meetings to Emory Bradford. Pierce had the tapes destroyed.

DENNISON, HERBERT (IA)

The White House Chief of Staff. He had stomach problems from stress and kept the Maalox handy. He was sixty-three, with a rigid posture, outthrust jaw, jowls, thinning gray hair, and gray-green eyes. He'd served in Korea and been married three times. He'd worked his way up on Wall Street to president of a corporation, making millions in profits; he was tough and ruthless. He had left Wall Street to support a senator from Idaho who espoused the values Herb believed in. He had worked for three years to get the man into the White House and become his Chief of Staff. Kendrick persuaded Dennison to help him find out who leaked the Oman file. Herb prevented the director of the National Security Agency from reaching the President with information about unorthodox developments they had found, and the President persuaded him to take a personal leave. He left the position when one of the old firms on Wall Street asked him to come back.

DePINNA, R. (AP)

Name Valerie used in New York City when she registered at the St. Regis Hotel. Her fake street address and name came from her childhood days in St. Louis; the R was perhaps from Roger, Joel's father's name. She gave her city and state as Tulsa, Oklahoma. Peter Stone's group found her by calling all the hotels in New York City and mentioning the flight from Amsterdam. When she called Peter at the Algonquin Hotel, he addressed her as Mrs. DePinna, so she knew he had been the caller at the St. Regis.

DEREK, JAMES (SI)

Counterpart of Canfield in London. Derek was a pleasant-looking man in his early fifties, somewhat rotund, terribly polite, but essentially cool. He escorted Elizabeth to the Carmelite nunnery in Cardiff. Canfield and Elizabeth persuaded Derek to bring them Bertholde's dossier. Derek knew Canfield was lying to him about the connection to the embassy, but helped them anyway.

DESI ARNAZ ONE (RO)

(D1, Desi One, Desi Romero) One of two Puerto Rican holdup men that Hawkins met in the airport rest room; they showed promise, so Hawkins hired them to be his adjutants. Desi One had bad teeth; both of the Desis had been in jail. Hawkins paid for shaves, haircuts, suits, and ties and gave the Desis on-the-job training along with increases in rank and pay. Pinkus thought the Desis were wonderful and fired Stosh and Knute. Desi One had worked in New York and spotted Boccegallupo in the Four Seasons and warned Hawk. Desi One was disguised as Reverend Pristin when they entered the Supreme Court building. The Desis were impressed when they found out Hawkins was a famous general and decided they wanted to go into the Army too. After the court case was over, Hawkins sent the two Desis to Brokemichael at Benning.

DESI ARNAZ TWO (RO)

(D2, Desi Two, Desi Gonzalez) Desi Two was good at mechanics and cooking; he could open or jam doors, jump-start cars, or lace food with sedatives. He'd worked as a waiter in Miami, room service. The Desis liked Hawkins because he made them feel better, just like his ex-wives. He was Catholic and enjoyed being disguised as Monsignor Alizongo when they entered the Supreme Court building.

DESOLE, STEVEN (BU)

"DeSole the Mute Mole"—thought to be honest, able to keep his mouth shut, and a thorough professional in the CIA. He was of medium height, slightly overweight, and had wide eyes that appeared to be magnified behind his steel-rimmed glasses. He rarely went out after dark because of severe night blindness. He was married and had children and grandchildren. He felt he wasn't paid enough for what he did and was bought by Medusa. He lost his life when Medusa found out his secret direct fax line with Teagarten had been uncovered.

DEVEREAUX, ——— (T)

Trevayne and de Spadante were both to be at the Devereaux in Arlington the same evening; de Spadante decided not to attend because Trevayne was on the subcommittee.

DEVEREAUX, ELEANOR (RO)

Sam's mother and widow of Lansing Devereaux III. She was an erect, fine-boned woman with an aging face once beautiful, and large blue eyes. After Lansing's death she refused to give up the appearance of wealth; she felt obligated to take care of Cora. Eleanor enjoyed her afternoon tea, especially the pot with the brandy in it. She was puzzled over Sam's odd behavior and the missing five months; she fainted when she learned that Sam helped kidnap the Pope. When Hawkins told Sam to take her to Nanny's, Eleanor had drunk too much "tea" and Jennifer had to take care of her; fortunately, she liked Jennifer. Eleanor recovered her composure briefly at the Four Seasons. At the Birnbaum estate she was befriended by Erin Lafferty and Roman Z.

DEVEREAUX, JACQUES (MP)

An alias of Julian Dunois's.

DEVEREAUX, LANSING, III (RO)

Sam's father and Eleanor's husband. He had been the son of a wealthy Boston family, a bold risk-taker in the world of high finance. "While watching a stock market report on television, he had died of a stroke when Sam was a boy of nine, leaving his widow and his son a fine name, a grand residence, and insufficient insurance to maintain the lifestyle to which they were accustomed."

DEVEREAUX, MAJOR SAMUEL LANSING (RG)

Field investigator for the office of the Inspector General for four years. His home was in Quincy, Massachusetts, and his specialty was criminal law. He had been able to go through Harvard Law School, two years of postgraduate specialization and clerking, and fourteen months of practice with the prestigious Boston law firm of Aaron Pinkus Associates because of Selective Service deferments. Then one day the government decided it had a scarcity of lawyers for courts-martial and brought him into the Legal Investigation Division. Sam was sent to the Golden Triangle area, where he made charges of drug dealing against 133 individuals, only three of whom were indicted, the rest were "pending." Sam decided to concentrate on one of the big dealers, a Major General Brokemichael. Unfortunately there were two Brokemichaels, and Sam tried to trap the wrong one. The Army gave Sam the choice between reenlisting for two more years or serving time in Leavenworth; Sam reenlisted. One month before his final discharge Sam was told to build a case against General Hawkins. Sam flew to China and bargained with the Chinese to get Hawkins out of China. Hawkins was discharged from the service and insisted on Sam for his legal escort and to correct his file in the vaults. Sam did get his discharge but was blackmailed into doing legal work for Hawkins, who planned to kidnap the Pope. Sam became a wealthy man and met the love of his life, Anne, whom he hoped to marry and take back to Boston with him.

DEVEREAUX, SAMUEL LANSING (RO)

Sam was a tall, slender, handsome, brilliant attorney and he had settled back into his job with Pinkus. He had returned home after an unexplained absence of five months following discharge from the Army. Sam took part of his money and fixed up his mother's home, and added a wing he called his "lair," which was his private area; the lair held photographs and news clippings of Anne and the kidnapping of the Pope. Five years after the affair he was still hurt and angry because Anne chose not to marry him. Aaron was concerned about his recent erratic behavior because Aaron had chosen him to be his successor; Aaron and Eleanor entered Sam's lair and discovered his secrets. After Hawkins called Sam, Aaron hired bodyguards for him; the Desis overpowered them and Aaron met Hawkins. Aaron and Sam were conned into helping Hawkins help the Wopotamis; Sam was a totally honest man and hated Hawkins's deviousness. Sam had forced four judges to leave the bench because of their illegal practices; he was known as "Sam the Avenger." Sam met Jennifer Redwing when she came to Boston to stop Hawkins; they decided to spend the rest of their lives together in Boston.

DEVEREAUX, SEYMOUR (RO)

Sam Devereaux's uncle Seymour married a Cuban and was forced to move to Miami.

DEWHURSTS (RE)

Family who knew Leslie Hawkwood; they had a suite at the Montgomery and Leslie didn't want to be seen by them.

DIETRICH, JOHANN (RE)

Middle-aged, effeminate son of the Dietrich Fabriken empire. His family were heavy contributors to the Nazis. When his father and uncle died, Johann became manager, more in name than fact. He was fat from excess alcohol, plucked his eyebrows, had a high-pitched voice, and was homosexual. He was fluent in English and knew how to negotiate business deals. Altmuller chose him to be the messenger for the exchange because his name was unlikely to be connected to the High Command. Johann was expendable; he was found dead in a "blood-soaked bed, the stories of the evening's debauchery so demeaning, it was decided to bury them and the body without delay."

DIMPLES (IA)

A descriptive name Andy Vanvlanderen used for Sundstrom.

———, DINO (RG)

One of Dellacroce's men who was knocked out by Hawkins on the golf green.

DOBBINS, CECIL "CYRIL" (AP)

Identified as a member of Aquitaine by Peter Stone. He was in the British Army, transferred to British intelligence, and then made a personal aide to Derek Belamy.

DOENITZ (SI) [REAL PERSON]

Doenitz, German commander, allowed Kroeger to take the complete plans of the Berlin fortifications to Switzerland because he knew the Allies already had a copy of them and he expected Kroeger to be killed by the Allies as a traitor.

DOE NOSE, AUNT (RO)

She invested, in the name of the Wopotami women, in an oil rig on Forty-first Street and Lexington Avenue in New York City. She was over eighty.

DOLBERT, JANINE (BI)

Lavier's number-two salesgirl at Les Classiques. She was tall and very thin with short bobbed hair and wide eyes. She smoked and lived in an apartment house on rue Lasserand in Paris. She had smuggled designs to the House of Azur and expected to take a job with them in Los Angeles, California. She believed Webb's story about Carlos being a customer of Les Classiques and carried the tale back to Lavier.

———, DON (RG)

Second husband of Anne Hawkins. He had another woman and wanted to divorce Anne and take over all the restaurants she had worked so hard to make successful. He went to Detroit and dug up her police file.

DONATTI, CARDINAL GUILLAMO (GC)

One of the most powerful cardinals in the Curia and one of the most corrupt. As a child Vittorio had seen him arguing with his father at Campo di Fiori; he could be recognized by a distinctive white streak of hair shooting up from his forehead through his close-cropped gray hair. He found out about the train from Salonika from the Germans; Savarone wanted to expose him by showing the church his connections with the Germans. Donatti sat in his car and watched the German soldiers murder Vittorio's family; he and his group spent the next two years tearing apart Campo di Fiori, looking for the sacred documents. Stone discovered his identity and agreed to work with Donatti, but double-crossed him at Campo di Fiori; as Vittorio was leaving the house after killing Stone, he was stopped by Donatti and his group. Donatti tortured him to find out about the documents and left Vittorio to die when he discovered Vittorio had no information about it. When the Church was told about his behavior, they excommunicated him and refused his remains the sanctity of Catholic burial.

DONAVON, ———— (BI)

CIA man who operated in Yugoslavia; he used "The Yachtsman" on the Adriatic runs.

DONAVON, ANNIE (BI)

Matronly professional head nurse in charge of the psychiatric ward on the third floor at Bethesda's Naval Annex. She worried that Morris Panov was getting too old to stay up all night with his patients.

DONNELLY, OFFICER (CM)

Police officer from Rockville, Maryland, who arrived on the scene soon after Chancellor had been run off the road by the mysterious dark-haired woman in the silver Mark IV Continental. When Chancellor tried to reach him later by telephone, the duty officer in Rockville said there was no officer by that name at that station.

————, DOOZIE (RO)

Head of Petrotoxic Amalgamated, a snob who wore his family crest on his blazer jacket. He went to college with Warren Pease.

DOWLING, CALEB "CALVIN" (AP)

Joel met Dowling on the airplane trip to Bonn to meet Leifhelm. He had a craggy, lined face, deep ridges creasing a sun-tanned face, intense blue-gray eyes surrounded by crow's-feet under thick, wild brows; his brown hair was streaked with white. When he spoke his accent was distinctively Texas. When a stewardess brings Dowling his bourbon over ice she comments on how much she enjoys his role of Pa Rachet in the very popular series *Santa Fe*. Joel discovers he hates horses.

His wife, Frieda, still had nightmares about surviving the concentration camp. When Cal was working in Bonn, she would not enter Germany again and stayed with the companion in Denmark.

Dowling knows he can trust Walter Peregrine and that Joel's problem concerns the government. He sets up a meeting for Joel, himself, and Peregrine; Joel, however, sends Connal in his place. Connal will not give Peregrine any information and, as he starts to leave, Peregrine orders Washburn to hold him. Instead, Washburn shoots at him and Dowling tackles Washburn and disarms him, saying maybe Washburn's behavior should be questioned. Peregrine agrees, makes a call to the Undersecretary of State on the scrambler; then he is killed and Joel is blamed for it.

Dowling tells the studio he is leaving *Santa Fe*, saying he wants to spend more time with his wife.

DOWLING, FRIEDA "FREDDIE" OPPENFELD (AP)

Wife of Calvin Dowling for twenty-six years. Caleb says his wife is Jewish. She was separated from her parents and her three younger brothers in Auschwitz.

Caleb met her when he was teaching. He describes her as "a whiz of a secretary; when [he] was teaching, she'd always be this or that dean's gal Friday." They were both in their forties when they married, and they had no children. For a long time she had had nightmares and physical and emotional reactions to things that reminded her of the concentration camp. And for a long time, when psychiatry might have helped her, they didn't have the money for her to see a psychiatrist. By the time Cal was making good money as Pa Rachet, the problem had become much worse; she even tried to drown herself at one point. She and Caleb decide that she can't be alone anymore, so Caleb finds a former actress to be her companion when he can't be with her.

DRAGON BITCH (IA)

The security staff around the Vice President referred to Ardis in private as the Dragon Bitch.

DRAGONFLY (BS)

Special unit under the command of Lin Wenzu.

DRAGUTIN (CM)

Character in Chancellor's book *Sarajevo!* Director of Serbia's military intelligence and leader of the Unity of Death organization.

DREYFUS, JACOB (CM)

Oldest member of Inver Brass, he had been with them since the beginning. This patriotic eighty-year-old banker was Jewish and wore "a yarmulke on his hairless, gaunt skull." Jacob shunned public attention, but his "influence often formed the basis of national monetary policies. . . . His charity was known throughout the world. . . ." When Jacob reached inside his coat to take out a letter he had written to Paris requesting the dissolution of Inver Brass, O'Brien shot him to death. Chancellor and O'Brien buried him on the sandy beach north of Ocean City in Maryland.

DRIGORIN, COLONEL JANEK (MC)

Commander in the Soviet Army who was sent to a minor post because he had "spoken out against the corruption that was rife in the Select Officer Corps." He was Nikolai Yurievich's commanding officer and had been invited to Nikolai's father's home to hunt. His assassination at the Yurievich home appeared to have been carried out by an American agent.

DRUMMOND, JANET (MC)

Nurse who died in a freak boating accident on March 26, 1954. Her patient had been Senator Appleton.

DUFFY, BOBBY (RO)

Bobby and Petey were brothers married to sisters. They were the last ones to arrive at the Four Seasons Hotel because they'd had a fight with their wives and had been at the Legion Hall's bar since early morning.

DUFFY, PETEY (RO)

Bobby Duffy's brother. Petey had gray hair and Bobby was bald and fat; they were both middle-aged.

DUGAN, ———— (BI)

This large, red-faced man was the on-the-job supervisor from Belkins Moving and Storage Company. He sat in his chair while his crew removed the furnishings from 139 East Seventy-first Street, the Treadstone house in New York City. Dugan sent David Webb, disguised as a mover, to the top floor, where Carlos was waiting for him.

THE DUKE (RO)

Member of the Suicidal Six whose primary persona was John Wayne. He called everybody "Pilgrim."

DUNLOP, RICHARD (HC)

A news reporter from one of the local radio stations in New York. He was reporting the murder of Peter Baldwin.

DUNOIS, JULIAN (MP)

Also known as Jacques Devereaux, Jesus Dambert, and Heysou Daumier. He was a tall, thin black man who wore glasses and had close-cropped hair; he looked about twenty although he was thirty-four. Julian was a militant lawyer who had come from Haiti and obtained a law degree from Harvard; his undergraduate major was English literature and he admired Matlock's work. His goal was to get rid of Nimrod and the

Mafia, because these groups preyed on young blacks. He wanted the Corsican paper and Herron's diary. When he finally obtained them from Matlock, he helped Matlock get Pat back and he and his men killed Nimrod. Twenty-three men, including Julian, were killed at the drug conference in Carlyle.

DUNSTONE, LTD. (CH)

When McAuliff agreed to work for the Dunstone company, one of the largest corporations in the international market, he didn't realize it was "an organization of international financiers dedicated to building global cartels beyond the . . . controls of the European Common Market and its trade alliances." It wanted to set up its own government in Jamaica based solely on economic trade factors—in the process, it would take over the Jamaican government. Its members were kept secret.

DUNSTONE, PHILIP (AP)

Name used by Derek Belamy when he called Connal Fitzpatrick in Bonn about the whereabouts of Joel Converse; said he was an aide to General Berkeley-Greene.

DURRELL, TIMOTHY (CH)

Young English manager of Trident Villas, a graduate of London's College of Hotel Management, he had more knowledge and experience than would be expected for someone his age. He was unaware that all the guests converging on his hotel the same week were members of Dunstone, Ltd.

DUSTIN (RO)

Member of the Suicidal Six whose primary character was Dustin Hoffman; Dustin stuttered a lot.

———, DWIGHT (OW)

Dwight was Agent Andrews's superior, but he hadn't been cleared for Omega. He checked with the director of Clandestine Services and was told there was no alternative but to deny Fassett's existence.

E (IA)

Elderly Speaker of the House of Representatives. When he was a young, unhappily married politician, he had an affair with an Irish nurse. She returned to Ireland to have their baby; he sent money and visited as often as he could, as an American uncle. When they exchanged letters he always signed his with just an "E."

EAGLE (BS)
Code name used by Alexander Conklin when he called Lin Wenzu from Havilland's office.

EAGLE EYES, UNCLE (RO)
Redwing's uncle, a chief, over eighty. He bought a communal estate in the Arizona desert for the tribe's elderly; there was no plumbing. Uncle Eagle Eyes liked to drink.

THE EAGLES (HC)
Graff used an "eagle code" to contact the Tinamou. The Jewish man in the black leather jacket referred to his group as the eagles who would stop the pact at Geneva. The men of Wolfsschanze who attempted to assassinate Hitler were referred to as "the true Eagles of Germany" by Rommel.

ECHO (BS)
Code name used by d'Anjou during the time he was involved in Operation Medusa.

———, ED (HC)
The doorman who worked from four A.M. to noon at the apartment building where Noel lived.

EDINBURGH (CH)
Fictitious character used as a code name by Joseph Myers to warn Holcroft that something had gone wrong at the Owl of Saint George.

EDMONTON, ——— (MC)
Scofield registered as Mr. Edmonton at the Connaught Hotel and when he flew from Paris to Montreal.

EISENHOWER, DWIGHT D. (GC) [REAL PERSON]
Loch Torridon conceived a strategy that would remove German predawn coastal patrols from the Normandy zones during the first eleven days in June. Eisenhower was amazed; this was a great help during Operation Overlord.

EISENSTATS (HC)
The Eisenstats were Jewish residents of Rio de Janeiro; they had a fine estate in northwestern Rio.

EISZAPFEN, FRAULEIN (HC)

Also Mademoiselle Icicle. Herr Oberst's people thought Helden was cold and unfeeling; her coworkers thought she was a lesbian.

EL-BAZ, ———— (IA)

Aged Arab who created new passports and other documents for Evan Kendrick. Evan studied his cover details from El-Baz's computer. Much of El-Baz's wealth was tied up in expensive Persian rugs.

ELLIS, BRIGADIER GENERAL ———— (SI)

Presented the file showing that Kroeger wanted to defect to America to Cordell Hull.

ELLIS, ———— (T)

Secret Service agent on duty with Callahan at the hospital in Darien.

ELLIS, BILL (RE)

Attaché at the American embassy in Buenos Aires. Spaulding caught him listening outside his door at 7:30 in the morning; he told Spaulding he was there for an early morning meeting. The logs revealed that none was scheduled. Granville wanted to replace him, but Spaulding convinced him to let Ellis stay and use him as a reverse conduit.

ELLIS, WILLIE (HC)

A designer Noel had worked with several times and a good friend. Willie was an English stage designer who'd had a brief stint as an interior decorator on both sides of the Atlantic. He had an outrageous personality but was really an intelligent, talented man of the theater, an expert in the history of design. Oddly enough, he had powerful, muscular arms that could break a man in half. After he was doused with whiskey and left in a field, Noel called Willie and asked for his help. Willie got his belongings for him and took him to the airport. When Noel was in Paris, he called to ask Willie to take his mother safely out of Switzerland. Willie was murdered in Geneva, but managed to severely wound his attacker, Hans, before he died.

ELSON, EDWARD (CM) [REAL PERSON]

U.S. Senate chaplain and minister of the Presbyterian Church. He delivered the opening prayer at John Edgar Hoover's funeral.

————, EMMA (AP)

Prostitute in Amsterdam whom Joel visited in order to disappear from the view of the hunters of Aquitaine. She had spangled dark hair and heavily rouged cheeks. Her philosophy was that she did her job and called it what it was and used the money she earned to raise her children. She didn't consider herself a good person.

She was amazed that all Joel wanted to do was sleep, but it was his money. She awakened Joel and told him people were hunting for him, giving out his description, and offering to pay for information about him. Unlike Theodoor, Emma accepted Joel's money and helped him escape by renting a car and delivering it to the door for him. She told Joel she would stay out of trouble by telling the police the car had been stolen.

ENGLEHART, CHARLES "CHARLIE" (MC)

"Old Crimson Charlie," "from Planning and Development, a strategist for covert operations." He taped Scofield's interrogation in Amsterdam. He didn't like Scofield.

——, ENID (PM)

Maid who answered the door at Alexander's.

——, ENRIQUE (AP)

From Madrid, Spain. A major at the garrison at Zaragoza, his job was to make reports on the Basque provincials; his hobby was reading, because this was such a lonely outpost. Connal Fitzpatrick met him while they were both being held prisoner by the Aquitaine in the fortifications on Scharhorn.

——, ENRIQUE (BU)

A heavyset man in his early sixties, he was a trainer in the spy compound at Novgorod. He had known Carlos since their early days in Cuba, when he and Carlos were thrown out by Castro. They went to Novgorod together; he saved Carlos's life the day Carlos left Novgorod. Carlos rewarded him by sending money to Enrique's family in Baracoa. He had a Russian wife, who had died, and three children in Moscow University. He helped Carlos get into the compound at Novgorod, but was not willing to help Carlos destroy it, so Carlos killed him.

EVANS, SERGEANT (SI)

One of Major Canfield's chauffeurs. He enjoyed driving him out to Oyster Bay because the food and liquor there were the best. He was delighted when Canfield told him he could stay in the boathouse apartment for the night.

EYE CORPS (GC)

A small, select group of professional military men headed by Andrew Fontine. They were tired of the corruption in the armed services, so they compiled records of the corruption to use for blackmail to enable them to take over the Pentagon. Theodore Dakakos brought them to the attention of the Justice Department, who charged them with obstructing justice and withholding evidence.

FAIRFAX, MR. (RE)
Name used by Ed Pace to call Spaulding at the Montgomery Hotel.

FAISAL, DR. AMAL (IA)
Faisal had been the sultan's physician since Ahmat was eight years old. He was Kendrick's only contact to Ahmat in case Kendrick couldn't reach the sultan himself. The sultan's father had found Faisal as a Bedouin child and paid his way through Johns Hopkins Medical School. Faisal was intensely loyal to the sultan's family and was fully informed about Evan's activities.

FALKENHEIM, GENERAL KLAUS (HC)
He was one of the last survivors of the true Wolfsschanze group; Herr Oberst was the name he used as head of the Nachrichtendienst. He lived in a small, isolated house outside Paris. Klaus was an emaciated man in a wheelchair; his hair was white and thin, combed carefully over his head. He was well into his seventies, yet he had a strong face, and the eyes behind the steel-rimmed spectacles were alert. When he stood up, he was "extremely tall, over six feet two or three." He spoke English with an obvious German accent. He had been a general in the Wehrmacht, at one time fourth-in-command of all Germany. As a member of the High Command he saw the horrors and did not object because it was futile; he used his rank to countermand many orders, saving many lives. The Allies convicted him because of his high position in the military, and he served eighteen years in prison. He was considered a traitor by what was left of the Officer Corps and by many of the German people. He was one of the original Nachrichtendienst. Falkenheim realized Helden was not part of Johann's group and kept her close; the letter he left her after his death sent her to Switzerland to find Werner Gerhardt.

FAROUK, T. (IA)
Azra was registered at the Aradous Hotel in Masqat under the name T. Farouk.

FASSETT, LAURENCE "LARRY" C. (OW)
CIA agent. Fassett was forty-seven years old, with broad shoulders, a muscular neck, unwrinkled skin, and short-cropped blond hair; his very broad eyes were set far apart beneath bushy, light brown eyebrows. He

was five feet ten or eleven. His German wife, an artist, had been killed by the NKVD in East Berlin; he had three children. For ten years Fassett had been one of the best operatives in the Agency, then he became a double agent. The Agency trapped him by assigning him to defeat Omega while the NKVD required him to keep Omega intact. Fassett discovered the Swiss bank accounts of the three couples and used that to panic them to violence; then he could kill several of them and claim he had caught Omega. When that didn't work, he announced that Tanner was Omega, withdrew his men, and he and MacAuliff went in to kill Tanner. Tanner survived the attack and killed Fassett and MacAuliff at the old deserted depot.

FELD, ASHER (RE)

Commander of the Provisional Wing of the Haganah operating within the United States. The Haganah was trying to abort the Rhinemann exchange. Feld filled in the details of "Tortugas" for Spaulding and admitted they had killed Pace, to neutralize Fairfax. He didn't know who in the United States was manipulating Spaulding. When Spaulding needed help at the Rhinemann estate, he sent word to Feld via Jean Cameron.

———, FELIX (RO)

Secretary of Defense. He was a tiny man with a pinched face and a toupee. He wanted the EC-135's in the air at Omaha so the Indians wouldn't attack and destroy the planes.

FERGUSON, ——— (OW)

(1) Old-moneyed family in Rochester that was preyed on by corporate raider Tremayne.

(2) CIA agent who was killed and mutilated near Tanner's home as a warning to Fassett from Omega.

FERGUSON, ——— (SI)

Assigned by Derek's office to stay with Mrs. Janet Scarlett and guard her until Canfield returned from Bertholde's.

FERGUSON, JAMES (CH)

A specialist in botany with a background in geophysics. Ralston recommended him to McAuliff; he was twenty-six, outspoken and opinionated, and one of the best vegetation specialists around. He very much wanted to return to Jamaica to continue his research on baracoa fibers and readily admitted to McAuliff that Craft had thrown him out. When McAuliff's bags didn't arrive at the hotel, Ferguson panicked and pretended to be drunk to prevent McAuliff from being too hard on him. He admitted to McAuliff that he had been following him around and told him about the Craft Foundation. He was happy to receive the letter from Arthur Craft, Sr., as Craft offered him a percentage of the profits.

FERGUSONS (T)
Old Washington cronies of Trevayne's from his days in the State Department.

——, FERN (RO)
Secretary in the North Mall, a legend; she wouldn't allow any of her bosses to fall apart over government problems.

FERNALD, —— (SI)
Fernald was killed when Ulster Scarlett fired on his own troops.

FIELDS, ANNIE (CM) [REAL PERSON]
J. Edgar Hoover's housekeeper and cook. For her long years of faithful service, Hoover left three thousand dollars to her in his will.

——, FINGERS (RG)
One of Dellacroce's men, knocked unconscious by Hawkins on the golf green.

——, FINGERS, (RO)
Short, obese man who worked for Mangecavallo. He hired Hymie Goldfarb to find blackmail material Mangecavallo could use to force the Supreme Court judges to drop the Wopotami case.

FISHBEIN, ILSE (AP)
Born in 1942 in Germany, youngest illegitimate daughter of Hermann Göring. She married Jakov Fishbein, a Jew, probably mostly as a way to disguise her identity; he emigrated to Israel years ago without her.

She was tall and heavy but not obese—more statuesque—a full face with high cheekbones, dark shoulder-length hair with streaks of gray. She made her living as a translator and was the conduit between Bertholdier and Leifhelm. Connal Fitzpatrick conned her into thinking she had inherited two million American dollars—all she had to do was have Leifhelm verify her bloodlines, which he had to do in person. Connal was hoping to capture Leifhelm and exchange him for Joel Converse.

FISHBEIN, YAKOV (AP)
Jewish husband of Ilse Fishbein who left her and emigrated to Israel. The marriage had been one of convenience and cover for Ilse.

FITZPATRICK, LIEUTENANT COMMANDER CONNAL (AP)

Chief Legal Officer, SAND PAC, brother-in-law of Avery Preston Halliday. He was thirty-four years old, a man with sandy hair, a boyish face, five feet ten or eleven in height, a nonsmoker, and unmarried. When he drank, he drank bourbon. He spoke French, Italian, and Spanish fluently and also spoke many dialects of German, also fluently. Having this skill enabled Connal to obtain necessary services for Joel— such things as making telephone calls, hotel reservations, and drawing money out of a bank. Because he's a "news freak," he carries a small shortwave radio with him when he travels.

He reminded Joel of himself before Vietnam. Connal told Joel he was "very good on direct [examination]," that he would have known if Joel was lying to him. He said he'd been a Navy legal officer for eight years, both as defense counsel and judge advocate and had been to most of the countries where Washington had reciprocal legal agreements.

FITZPEDDLER, MAURICE (RO)

White House Press Secretary.

FLANAGAN, EDDIE (BU)

A very large, obese man with a large head, the lover of Rachel Swayne. He was a sergeant in Vietnam when Bourne met him; when he didn't bring the needed supplies from Saigon to Medusa, Bourne held a gun against his head. He was shocked to discover Bourne was still alive— he thought he'd been killed in Hong Kong. He'd been assigned to take care of General Swayne by Medusa; he knew Medusa didn't like him and would get rid of him as soon as his services were no longer needed. He and Rachel had been planning their getaway for a long time, and readily accepted Bourne's help in exchange for information. When they left, even the CIA didn't know where they went.

FLANAGAN, PEG (MC)

"The portly female clerk in the [Massachusetts General] hospital's Department of Records and Billing." When she gave Scofield information about the personnel working there during Senator Appleton's care, she thought Scofield was obtaining it for Senator Appleton.

FLEISHMAN, MORRIS (BU)

"Morris the Marine," a marine corporal who helped Mo Panov off the plane in Paris. Panov mentioned he was from Tremont Avenue in the Bronx and discovered he knew Fleishman's parents, as they lived on Garden Street across from the Bronx Zoo.

Teenage militia in People's Republic of China. Their faces were stern—hiding a lot of derisive laughter. Sudden parades are mounted twice daily in Beijing. The custom is to follow them amid much laughter. All of the rifles are wooden.

FONTAINE, JEAN-PIERRE (BU)

Alias given to Michel by Carlos. He was one of Carlos's old men of Paris. His primary occupation was thief and killer. During the German occupation he had blown up an Oberführer's headquarters on the rue St. Lazare. When he became old and ill, he was befriended by Carlos, who provided him with money in exchange for his services and, if necessary, his life. He was deeply in love with his wife. He had no children of his own, and he could not bring himself to kill the Webbs' children. He thought Prefontaine had been sent by the Jackal to kill him and his wife, and that angered him, as he had been promised they could stay at the inn until his wife died. His wife's suicide freed him from any responsibility to Carlos; he joined forces with Bourne and died after warning Bourne not to enter the chapel, which was booby-trapped.

FONTAINE, RÉGINE (BU)

Not her true name. She had been married to Michel for over forty years. She knew about his connection to Carlos and accompanied him on some of his trips. She had only a month or two to live when Carlos sent them to Montserrat, and she knew Michel did not want to complete Carlos's assignment. She committed suicide to set Michel free. She and Michel were buried on Montserrat.

FONTINE, ADRIAN (GC)

Younger of the twin sons of Victor and Jane Fontine. He was tall like his parents, but slouched, giving him an appearance of nonchalance. He had sharp features, dark auburn hair, and his mother's penetrating blue eyes and slightly mad English sense of humor. "Adrian had gone from prep school to Princeton to Harvard Law, with a year taken off to wander and grow a beard and play a guitar and sleep with available girls from San Francisco to Bleecker Street." It was during this time that he had the head-on conflict with Andrew over army deserters and returned to school with a sense of purpose. Adrian was a very dedicated, outspoken lawyer who believed there was no excuse for armed confrontation; he was a shark in the courtroom, but a very ethical man. He had worked for the prosecutor's office in Boston and then gone to Washington at the request of James Nevins, who was investigating Eye Corps. Adrian had been living in Boston with "a slightly mad, brilliant girl he adored," Barbara Pierson. Adrian told Andrew about Nevins's investigation and Nevins was killed. Adrian assumed he and Andrew would work together to find the sacred documents, but Andrew fought him each step of the way.

FONTINE, MAJOR ANDREW (GC)

Older of the twin sons of Victor and Jane Fontine. He was tall like his parents with a military bearing; his hair was very light, almost blond; he had sharp features and light blue penetrating eyes. He never questioned his own abilities and he thought Adrian was a fool. Andrew was a dedicated military professional and was well thought of by the Pentagon. After attending West Point, where he excelled, he made two tours of Vietnam; he wanted the military to "win or get out" of there. Andrew believed the military was America's strength—to be used wisely—and hated the corruption therein. He and a few others started Eye Corps to gather information on the corruption and use it to control the corrupters. His group came to believe they were the inheritors of the Pentagon. When Eye Corps was discovered, Andrew had learned about the sacred documents and realized the power that their possession would give him. He stopped at nothing to get the documents. He died in the Alps.

FONTINE, CAPTAIN VICTOR (GC)

The British changed Vittorio Fontini-Cristi's name to Victor Fontine and gave him the rank of captain when he went to work at Loch Torridon.

FONTINI-CRISTI, ANTONIO (GC)

Second oldest son of Savarone. He was a serious man, married with children. He and his family were killed in the massacre by the Germans at Campo di Fiori.

FONTINI-CRISTI, SAVARONE (GC)

Owner of Fontini-Cristi Industries, head of the most powerful family in Italy north of Venice and possibly the richest north of Rome. He had four sons, several daughters, and a host of grandchildren; Vittorio and Antonio were the two eldest sons. He was "an extraordinary man, of unparalleled integrity and utter commitment to free men" but not a member of any church. His voice was deep, aristocratic, and very used to authority. He was tall and slender; his face had large, penetrating eyes, and aquiline features.

Vittorio infuriated Savarone because he neither used his talents nor assumed his responsibilities. Savarone was a partigiano; he knew he was being watched by the state. He had originally endorsed Mussolini, but Mussolini "was letting Italy die," and Savarone had vowed to stop him. The partigianos met at Campo di Fiori and practiced their martial arts. The Italians and the Germans both wanted Savarone stopped and the Vatican wanted the sacred documents. Savarone and his entire family, except Vittorio, were killed at Campo di Fiori; he was killed before he could pass on the information about the documents to Vittorio.

FONTINI-CRISTI, VITTORIO (GC)

Eldest son of Savarone Fontini-Cristi. He had three younger brothers, several sisters, and numerous nephews and nieces. Vittorio was a tall man, over six feet, with straight dark brown hair that fell over this forehead, and sharp, aquiline features. He was chief executive officer of Fontini-Cristi Industries and he was brilliant—it angered Savarone that he didn't accept more responsibility. Vittorio's first marriage merged two wealthy families; he had been married four years when his wife was killed in a car accident; they had no children. Because Savarone hid the sacred documents and Donatti wanted them, Savarone's entire family was killed; only Vittorio escaped. MI6 brought Vittorio out of Italy to England because the British wanted the sacred documents and they thought Vittorio knew where they were. Vittorio volunteered to work for England against Hitler and Mussolini and was sent to Loch Torridon to learn some military skills; he was a very capable administrator, so they put him in charge of teaching mismanagement skills. During this time they changed his name to Victor Fontine, he married Jane Holcroft, and the twins were born. After the war he moved his family to the United States and established a very successful consulting business, Fontine, Ltd. His property was restored to him by the Court of Reparations and he sold it. Fanatic priests from the Order of Xenope pursued him during and after the war, resorting to torture to obtain information about the documents. Shortly before his death at home on Long Island, he gave the twins photocopies of all the information he had.

FONTINI-CRISTI, MRS. VITTORIO (GC)

Vittorio's first wife. His marriage was an alliance between two immensely wealthy families; it was an unhappy marriage for four years. She was self-indulgent and guided by possessions. She had an affair with Jane Spane's husband and died in an automobile accident in Monte Carlo after the casinos closed. She and Vittorio had no children.

FOWLER, —— (AP)

Biological father of Avery Preston Halliday. His suicide is covered up, and Avery and his mother return to San Francisco.

FOWLER, DETECTIVE (T)

Police detective in Greenwich, Connecticut. Fowler didn't believe there was a connection between the heroin found on the guest house porch and the girls having a party at the Swansens. Fowler accepted a thousand dollars to erase de Spadante's tracks at Barnegat the night Augie was killed.

FOWLER, AVERY PRESTON (AP)

(*See* Halliday, Avery Preston.)

FOWLER, FRANKLYN (SI)

Longtime friend of Elizabeth Scarlatti's family, associated with Fowler Paper Products. He didn't care how rich the Scarlattis were, they couldn't join the country club because they were Italian.

FOWLER, GORDON, ESQ. (CH)

Patriarch of the Fowlers, who owned their own brokerage house on the London exchange. He was the great-great-grandson of Jeremy Fowler and gave Walter Piersall access to all the documents relating to him.

FOWLER, JEREMY (CH)

Official Crown Recorder in the Foreign Service in Jamaica in 1883 who stole the Middlejohn papers after a trip into the Cock Pit country. He believed he was destroying the records of a tribal treaty so thousands of acres could be cleared for plantations. He was paid well by the Halidon, returned to England, and started his own brokerage house.

FOXLEY, ERNEST (IA)

Commentator on the Foxley program; he gave Kendrick "his first decent television exposure."

FRANCESCO, POPE, I (RG)

(*See also* Bambolini, Giovanni.) Francesco was an intellectual but also compassionate; his personal secretary was a young black priest from New York. Francesco was in his seventies and his doctors didn't expect him to live more than a few months; he had been selected as Pope as a compromise between two factions and because of his short life expectancy. Francesco was determined not to let Quartze become the next Pope. He had two hobbies he enjoyed—playing chess and cooking. When he discovered he was being replaced by his cousin Guido and that his escorts were unharmed, Francesco helped Hawkins and his group escape from the Italian police. When he saw that Hawkins could not obtain his ransom from Quartze, he joined forces with Hawkins and manipulated matters in the Vatican himself. His health improved and he continued to live at the chateau with Hawkins, Sam, and Anne, frequently preparing the meals for all of them.

FRANCESCO, POPE, I (RO)

Francesco had to return to the papacy and set affairs to normal after Guido broke the shortwave radio.

FRANCESCO, ZIO (RG)

When the Pope settled into his quarters at the chateau, it was easier for everyone to refer to him as Zio (Uncle) Francesco.

FRANÇOIS (BU)

Alias used by Bourne when dealing with "Maurice" and "Ralph" at Le Coeur du Soldat in Paris. "François" had supposedly been a member of the French Foreign Legion.

FRANGIANI, JOSEPH "FINGERS" (IA)

Cousin of the capo supremo who was the Secret Service guard. He was the second underboss of the Ricci family in Brooklyn. Milos traced the telephone calls between the guard and "Fingers."

———, FRANK (BU)

A retired gray-haired interpreter for the CIA; he also acted as house steward at Sterile Five. He knew Holland and Conklin by sight.

———, FRANK (IA)

Boyfriend of one of the nurses at Kendrick's home in Mesa Verde.

———, FRANK, (MP)

A cigar-smoking crony of Sharpe's who was killed the night Matlock was playing cards with them in the back room of Sharpe's club.

————, FRANKIE (BU)

Homosexual lover of Lou De Fazio, he didn't understand half of what De Fazio told him. De Fazio, however, believed Ogilvie when Ogilvie said Frankie talked too much about his associations and threw too much money around. De Fazio killed him.

FRAZIER, GARY (AP)

Responsible for meeting and protecting Peter Stone in Manchester, New Hampshire. He did a very thorough search of Stone before taking him to Wellfleet's home; this was evidently his regular job, as in his former job he had been "a cop in Cleveland."

FRAZIER, GEOFFREY (RO)

Functioning alcoholic grandson of R. Cookson Frazier, the last of the male Fraziers. He was known as "Crazy Frazie" and "Spaced Cadet." Actually he was extremely likable and generous with his friends. His parents had died in a seaplane crash in Monte Carlo. Geoff was a classmate of Sam's at Andover; Sam was not fond of him because Geoff abused and wasted his privileges. Sam called him when he wanted to stop Hawkins all by himself; Geoff picked him up with his speedboat. Due to his drinking, Geoff had no license to drive anything on land, sea, or snow; he enjoyed drinking while he was driving. His grandfather wanted to catch him and have him rehabilitated because he felt there was a good person inside. Geoff dropped Sam off, then was caught by the Coast Guard and taken into custody; they had to release him, however, because Geoff was an undercover agent working for the Drug Enforcement Agency.

FRAZIER, JAMES (BI)

The Honorable James Frazier, M.P., United Kingdom, was one of the scheduled speakers at the Sixth World Economic Conference held in the Carillon du Lac Hotel in Zurich. His talk followed Bertinelli's.

FRAZIER, R. COOKSON (RO)

Cookson's family had old money and lived in Louisburg Square in Boston. Cookson was one of the few people who paid his debts to the Devereaux family after Lansing died. The elderly Cookson exercised on a small basketball court on the top floor of his home. Aaron called him to tell him about Geoff picking up Sam in the speedboat; Cookson called the Coast Guard and asked them to hold Geoffrey and Sam. He was flabbergasted when he was told Geoff was an undercover drug agent. Cookson had homes in many parts of the world and hired Cyrus to take over the security; he also bought a chemical plant.

FRAZIER-PYKE, EMORY (IA)

London banker once married to Ardis; he lost a considerable sum of money with Off Shore Investments. He was a stickler for the straight and narrow, and the marriage didn't last very long.

FRENCH, ARTHUR (AP)

Name used by Valerie Converse when making a room reservation at the Croix Blanche Hotel in Chamonix for Inspector Prudhomme.

FRESCA, N. (HC)

Alias used on several occasions by Noel; he took it from a soft-drink sign.

FRESCOBALDI, GUIDO (RG)

Look-alike cousin of Giovanni Bambolini, born two days after him. He badgered his parents to send him to the academy in Rome to study opera. He studied for eight years but made no noticeable progess. His father ordered him home to marry Rosa; seven years later he rebelled, leaving Padua forever to return to his beloved opera in Milan. He was willing to work at any job just to be near the opera. In forty years he had worked his way up from sweeping to reciting parts. He was deeply hurt by the article in the Communist paper that compared his job and the pontiff's and thrilled when asked to visit the Pope. Hawkins's people drugged him and switched him for the Pope.

FRESCOBALDI, GUIDO (RO)

When Guido fell on the private shortwave radio, he had no more help from Francesco. He spent the Church's money on all kinds of strange projects, and Francesco had to relieve him of his job.

———, FROGGIE (RO)

Blond-haired owner and CEO of Zenith Ball Bearings Worldwide, married to Daphne. He stated that his group would have to get rid of Mangecavallo, since they were responsible for his becoming head of the CIA. He also wanted to get rid of the Wopotami's Supreme Court case.

FROST, CAROL (BU)

Very attractive wife of Hardleigh Frost. She and Hardleigh lived on Cape Cod, down the Shore Road in Dennis, Massachusetts. They were friends with both Ogilvie and Rodchenko.

FROST, HARDLEIGH (BU)

An attorney specializing in maritime law. He was not a member of Medusa. His firm, Frost, Goldfarb, and O'Shaunessy, covered the waterfront in Massachusetts.

Seahorses in Rhodes

G (IA)

Code name for Gray of the Masada Brigade.

GABRIEL (PM)

Secret intelligence organization allied with the French government. They wanted to interrogate Havelock.

GAETOMO, ENRICI (GC)

This huge man was a priest who worked for Donatti. Lubok was asked to find out what Victor knew about the documents; he decided Victor didn't know anything and gave his pay to Gaetomo to give back to Donatti. Gaetomo threatened to get Lubok. With Donatti's group he administered the beating to Victor; he was defrocked and put into prison for it. He was obsessed with the documents. When he was released from prison, he put on his collar and went after the documents again. He lived in a small hunting lodge near Campo di Fiori. When he heard Victor was back in Italy, he tracked him to the Argonaut Rock and tried to beat the information out of him again. The monk of Xenope who had been living in Campo di Fiori found them and shot Gaetomo to death.

GALLABRETTO, WILLIAM "WILLIE" (T)

West Coast lawyer, a member of the Mafia and Mario's nephew. Willie told de Spadante what to tell the news media. He didn't approve of Mario's violent methods; he had Bonner arrested for murder. Bobby Webster and de Spadante were both murdered, however, by Gallabretto's men.

GAMMA (BS)

An Oriental who spoke fluent English and wore the Chinese uniform. He was d'Anjou's contact on mainland China when they were pursuing the impostor. Gamma had attended the University of Southern California, then pursued graduate studies at Berkeley during the 1960s; he said he was a "staunch conservative," a member of the John Birch Society. D'Anjou describes him as a perfect intermediary—totally amoral, a double, triple, or even quadruple agent. He came back to China to make money. He was also an exceptional sailor and wanted to return to San Francisco someday. He had information about Soo Jiang and the impostor for d'Anjou.

GANDY, HELEN (CM) [REAL PERSON]

Personal secretary to J. Edgar Hoover for many years. She was left five thousand dollars by Hoover in his will. Inver Brass hired an actress to impersonate her.

GARCIA, JOSÉ (IA)

Waiter who worked for Gonzalez-Gonzalez; he and Gee-Gee knew how to spot and avoid federal officers.

GARVEY, ——— (CH)

MI5 contact from Port Maria who was sent out to meet McAuliff. He was a portly black liquor distributor with bloodshot eyes and overpowering body odor—even his briefcase was filthy. Garvey "sold anything he could get his hands on, including women, especially young girls." McAuliff realized Garvey was pumping him for information and was not offering him any reassurances for his safety except for the miniaturized radio-signal transmitter. Garvey died in a car accident on the road back to Port Maria; he was shot by a distraught father of one of the girls.

GATES, EDITH (BU)

Wife of Randolph Gates for thirty-three years. They lived in an elegant town house on Louisburg Square. When they married, she was young, passably attractive, and of average wealth. After he became a lawyer she bought the correct clothes and hired a voice coach for him, urged him to pursue an academic life, and then go into a private law firm. Things went well until six years earlier, after Randy's trip to Paris. Since then they didn't sleep together and Edith knew something had happened in Paris to change him. One evening she saw him injesting drugs into his veins. When Medusa was uncovered, she stayed with Randy and helped him rebuild his life.

GATES, DR. RANDOLPH (BU)

He taught at Harvard, an expert in antitrust law. He was six feet five inches tall, and his bald head was fringed with gray hair above his temples. He had been a student of Brendan Prefontaine. His wife, Edith, guided him into an academic career, where he developed such a high degree of expertise that prominent firms sought him. He became a champion of financial manipulators. He neither smoked nor drank, but when Carlos was done with him in Marseilles, he had become a drug addict and a frightened man, willing to do Carlos's bidding—yet he maintained the cleanest record for propriety of anyone in the Bar Association. He agreed to do anything to be free of Carlos again; when he was free, he went to a rehabilitation center in the Midwest. He then decided to fight legally for the people instead of the conglomerates and to go after a judgeship.

GENESIS (CM)

Code name of the leader of Inver Brass. The first Genesis had been a Scotsman, an investment banker. The second Genesis had previously been known as Paris; meetings of Inver Brass were held at Genesis's home. His regular job required him to spend time in London, at the U.S. embassy there. He died of cancer and Bravo took over his duties until either Paris or Banner could be selected as the new leader of Inver Brass.

GENOVESE, DON VITONE (SI)

Vitone was Mafia and worked for Ulster Scarlett, his padrone. Ulster ordered Vitone's men to kill the captain of the *Genoa-Stella* because he wouldn't cooperate with them on the unloading of his ship. When Ulster decided he'd made enough money from these operations, he gave Vitone the organization in exchange for the guarantee that Vitone would always swear he didn't know Scarlett.

GEORGE (AP)

Fictional name used by the station chief for the CIA in Bonn while talking to Caleb Dowling.

———, George (BI)

One of the four surviving members of Treadstone Seventy-one after the slaughter on Seventy-first Street. He was the middle-aged naval officer attached to Information Control, Fifth Naval District. He fed thirty-seven names to a Bureau print team and they identified the fingerprints on the broken brandy glass as Bourne's. The room had been swept clean except for that one set of fingerprints.

———, George (PM)

CIA station chief in Amsterdam who had worked with Havelock in the past. He offered to hire Havelock as a consultant; he couldn't believe that Havelock had retired.

George the Fifth (GC)

Code name by which Pear and Apple were identified by the fishermen on the coast of Italy; the fishermen were paid to transport the three men to a British submarine.

———, Geraldo (HC)

The consul general in Brazil. He pretended he was an attaché and took Noel's information, then called the Brazilian ambassador in New York and reported that Noel was looking for the von Tiebolts.

———, Geraldo (RE)

Geraldo was guarding the front of Rhinemann's warehouse in Ocho Calle.

Gerard, Commander (RO)

Commander of the 10th District Massachusetts Coast Guard station. He told Mikulski about the alert for Frazier and Devereaux.

Gerhardt, Werner (HC)

Eighty-three years old, a former diplomat, he lived quietly outside Près-du-Lac on Lake Neuchâtel. He was Nachrichtendienst; his cover was that he was a feeble-minded old man who sang songs and mumbled to himself and fed pigeons in the square. Supposedly his mind had snapped after months of torture by the Odessa. He was shorter and much puffier than Herr Oberst, with pallid, drawn skin marred by spider veins. He wore thick steel-rimmed glasses and tattered, frayed clothes soiled with pigeon droppings. His house was a miniature stone fortress with built-in sensors and extra-thick walls. He had come to Près-du-Lac from München five years before, where he had established his cover. Dr.

Litvak at the clinic was the only one who knew he was sane. Gerhardt was shot to death by one of Johann's people.

GEYNER, HERMIONE (AP)

Valerie's elderly German aunt, her mother's sister. When she was with the German Untergrund, she was wilder than Valerie's mother.

She made arrangements for people to guard Valerie and Joel while they were in Berlin, and found places for him to stay overnight. She said she would hide Joel. She did these things because she knew she and her group could do them—they had done these things in World War II.

GIANNI, ——— (PM)

Heavyset proprietor of the inn near Col des Moulinets; he furnished prostitutes as well as food.

GIBSON, COLONEL BRADLEY "HOOT" (RO)

Pilot of one of the EC-135's being kept in the air over Omaha. Hoot was married and wanted to get home to his wife's roast beef hash. He'd been in the air for fifty-two hours and his wife thought he'd been shot down over Mongolia; he told Richards to leave messages with his daughter.

GIBSON, LOUIS (SI)

Rich Texas oilman; one of the group of merchants supporting the Nazis. Gibson and Landor owned more wells than fifty of their competitors combined. He and Landor had gone into a joint venture in Canada, violating U.S.–Canadian treaties.

GILLETTE, SENATOR (T)

Elderly senior senator from Nebraska, chairman of the Senate panel on the confirmation of Trevayne as chairman of the Defense Allocation Subcommittee. Gillette wanted to know what had happened before the hearing to Trevayne to make him so demanding at the hearing; he was angry that someone would try to manipulate a Senate panel. When Trevayne wouldn't tell him the details, he told him that he was going to reconvene the panel and have Trevayne's confirmation withdrawn. Gillette was killed in an auto accident on his way home from the meeting with Trevayne.

GILLETTE, ALFRED (BI)

He was a member of the National Security Council and bitterly unhappy with his government position; he was employed by Carlos, and passed on the information in the Medusa files to Carlos. He was a balding, birdlike academic who wore rimless glasses over his owlish eyes; he was the director of Personnel Screening and Evaluation and was considered to be bright and vindictive and have friends in high places. He hated David Abbott and led Carlos to the Treadstone house, where Carlos's men killed him as well as all the people inside.

GILLIGAN, BILL (RO)

Guard-cum-bouncer at Nanny's Naughty Follies et Cetera in Boston. He was a "huge, heavyset middle-aged man, more apelike than human" with a coarse voice and straight gray hair. He'd been dismissed from the police force because his son had used "the wrong money" to buy Nanny's; Jennifer Redwing fought City Hall and got him a larger retirement pension. He served with Paddy Lafferty under Hawkins during World War II in France.

———, GINNY (T)

Steve Trevayne's girlfriend. When they left the Cos Cob Tavern, someone had damaged their car by emptying the ashtrays, ripping the seat cushions, and pouring whiskey all over the inside.

———, GINO (T)

Gino's brother owned Torrington Metals; someone from Torrington was trying to locate de Spadante for Pace.

GLOVER, ——— (SI)

Reynolds's subordinate in Group Twenty. Glover was fifty-three years old, married, with a son and grandchildren. Glover liked Canfield; he thought he had too much ability for government service. Glover didn't care much anymore about his job; he did connect the deal on the Swedish stock exchange with Ulster Scarlett's arrival time in Europe, reinforcing the notion that Scarlett was still alive.

GODDARD, JAMES (T)

President of Genessee's San Francisco division. Goddard was "middle-aged, middle-fat, and middle-brow, the essence of the pressurized corporate executive." He had a cherubic face and sweated excessively on his chin when agitated. He'd worked for Genessee for twelve years. He and his wife lived in an expensive home in Los Altos. He accepted a ten-year company pass on Trans Pacific Airways in exchange for furnishing certain labor statistics and advice to Armbruster.

Goddard was afraid of de Spadante and of what Trevayne had found out. He didn't intend to be sacrificed to preserve Genessee, so he obtained only the most damaging figures from the year-end report to give to

Trevayne in exchange for immunity from prosecution. Trevayne's report had been submitted before he received Goddard's information and the President refused to let him change the report and make the information public, mainly because he needed the support of Genessee. Goddard was now in a hopeless situation, out of a job and with little prospect of finding another one. He decided to kill the person who betrayed him, the President, then take his own life.

GODDARD, MRS. JAMES (T)

Goddard's wife had sagging breasts and fat legs, spoke with a nasal twang, and complained; he didn't care if he lost her.

GOEBBELS, JOSEPH (SI) [REAL PERSON]

"He was a tiny, ugly man with birdlike features, even to the hawk nose. He walked with a limp. . . . His knowledge of English was poor." Goebbels believed Hitler was the way to restore Germany. Goebbels loved theatrics and Hitler's ability to capitalize on an opponent's fundamental weakness. He didn't like Kroeger but was willing to use his resources. He knew Kroeger was really Ulster Scarlett.

GOLDFARB, HYMAN "HYMIE" (RO)

CIA consultant recruited by Hawkins when he was assigned to the Pentagon; Hymie's government agency clients read like the who's who of the Potomac. He was near fifty but still had an awesome, muscular athlete's body. He had studied to be a rabbi and was a Rhodes Scholar. Hymie was remembered for his athletic prowess; he had been the greatest linebacker in the NFL, playing for the Redskins. "Hymie the Hurricane," "the Hebrew Hercules," "the Golden Goldfarb"—he didn't need any defense, just broke through and nailed the quarterbacks. Hymie's people were sent out to capture and silence Chief Thunder Head; they were unsuccessful.

GOLDMAN, AARON (MC)

Son of Theodore and Anne Goldman. He was a young pilot in the U.S. Air Force who had gotten drunk in the Hague with men known to be KGB infiltrators of NATO. Scofield pulled him out of the area, sobered him up, and told him to go back to his base.

GOLDMAN, ANNE (MC)

Aaron's mother was grateful to Scofield for extricating Aaron in the Hague. She was a slender, pleasant, middle-aged woman.

GOLDMAN, DR. THEODORE (MC)

Well-known Jewish "dean of the Harvard School of Business and a thorn in the side of the Justice Department . . . he was an outspoken critic of the Anti-Trust Division." Scofield approached him to find out about Trans-Communications, the main headquarters of the Matarese.

GOLDONI, ALFREDO (GC)

Last living male member of a family of guides in the Italian Alps; his brothers had been buried in the same avalanche that caused him to lose his legs. Goldoni and his wife lived outside the village of Champoluc, and his nephew did the farming for him. Savarone had employed the family frequently; the Goldonis were also partigianos. The Goldonis kept maps and written records of each trip they made into the mountains; Alfredo inherited the record books from his father. Savarone's trip was recorded in those books, and the Goldonis were waiting for someone from Savarone's family to come back. Alfredo did not trust Andrew, so he took the book containing the record of Savarone's trip to a meeting at the inn with the Capomantis. Andrew took the book from him and also took Lefrac's grandchildren with him to lead him into the mountains. Alfredo was powerless to stop Andrew, but he was able to help Adrian, who went into the mountains after Andrew.

GOLDONI, MRS. ALFREDO (GC)

Gaunt, sullen, elderly, ascetic-looking lady with a wrinkled neck and straight gray hair pulled back into a taut bun. She and Goldoni were farmers, not as well off as when Alfredo also worked as a guide. It was fortunate for Andrew that Alfredo left her home alone; when Andrew found out what he wanted to know, he killed her and carried her body into the woods. He told Alfredo she had run away and he had caught her; Alfredo knew he was lying because she had swollen veins in her legs and could hardly walk.

GOLDSMITH, HEROLD (RE)

Leslie's very rich aunt was married to a banker named Goldsmith in California. Goldsmith had done more to get Jews out of the concentration camps than any man in America. When Washington turned their backs on him, he came to the Haganah; Leslie joined them in their struggle.

GONZALEZ, DESI (RO)

(D2, Desi Two, Desi Arnaz Two) Desi was made a second lieutenant and was trained for espionage work by Ethelred Brokemichael.

GONZALEZ-GONZALEZ "GEE-GEE" (IA)

"Stocky, mustached owner of the Mesa Verde café." He could easily spot federal agents as he engaged in illegal traffic of aliens. Gee-Gee assisted Kendrick in taking care of Manny; he alerted Manny that he was being followed and helped Manny capture Aman, then carried the bodies of the three dead terrorists into the garage and drove back to his café.

——, GRACE (GC)

Maid at the Fontine house on the north shore of Long Island.

GRAFF, MAURICE (HC)

This "old, heavyset man with thick jowls and steel-gray hair, cut short in the fashion of a Junker" was the contact in Brazil for Johann. He gave his profession as importer and lived well in a mansion in northwest Rio de Janeiro with his guards, guard dogs, and staff. For years Graff had kept and updated the Sonnenkinder lists, then presented them to Johann on his twenty-fifth birthday. Johann decided to kill off Graff because he was getting senile and careless. Graff was shot to death "by a man who left a note claiming vengeance from Portuguese Jews."

GRAHAM, —— (PM)

Special agent with extensive experience in military police and counterintelligence assigned to protect Dawson and Stern. While he and his partner were involved in a trafffic accident, someone killed Dawson and Stern.

GRANVILLE, AMBASSADOR HENDERSON (RE)

American ambassador in Buenos Aires. Granville was over fifty, a tall man with delicate hands and an aristocratic face; he was a decent man, professorial by nature. He'd been divorced for ten or fifteen years; he'd had three wives and twice as many mistresses. Granville wasn't happy to have an intelligence agent in the embassy but was smart enough to use the information Spaulding gave him.

GRAVET, —— (BI)

An old man who could hardly read; he lived in the apartment below Pierre Trignon and his wife in Paris.

GRAVET, —— (PM)

The most knowledgeable critic of classical art in Paris and on the Continent. A tall man, the essence of Parisian wealth and elegance, he traveled all over Europe. He was a broker with a wide range of information which he sold to various clients. He had known Havelock a long time; the Russians knew he was fond of Havelock. Gravet discovered the KGB had no interest in Havelock but the VKR did. Havelock paid him to find out about Jenna and Costa Brava and to find Régine Broussac and Jenna.

GRAVET, ANTONIA (MC)

Great-granddaughter of Guillaume de Matarese and Sophia Pastorine. She had naively joined the Red Brigades because of her political beliefs and had been used as a drug courier's whore; the men she worked with didn't hesitate to torture and abuse her. She escaped to her grandmother's cabin in the mountains and was found there by Scofield and Taleniekov, who took her with them to prevent her from being killed by the Matarese. She worked with the two of them to stop the Matarese and became Scofield's lover. She had an older brother and older sister, both of whom had families; they had not had as much education as Antonia, who had graduated from the University of Bologna. She had studied French and English because she wanted to enter a government program. She had long dark hair, clear wide brown eyes, high cheekbones, a chiseled nose, and full lips; she was slim and beautiful and younger than Scofield by several years.

GRAY (IA)

Tall, muscular member of the Masada Brigade; he hated parachute jumps. He was with the group that captured Tony McDonald; he was distraught when he had to kill the three terrorists because this prevented him from getting information about the Mahdi. When Yaakov was severely injured, Gray took over as their leader. He helped capture the Mahdi and forced him to tell them where they had taken Kendrick.

GRAYSON, JAMES "JIMMY" (IA)

Lester Crawford's station chief in Bahrain. He wouldn't risk throwing away his life's work by revealing information from Kendrick's files. He wanted a directorship so badly, he could taste it.

GREEN, AARON (T)

Owner of the Green Agency in New York. Aaron was a Jewish philanthropist, patron of the arts, and publisher of poetry and books at his own expense. His advertising agency, the most sought after in New York, funneled Genessee money into the aircraft lobby and many other groups. "Nothing was paid out that couldn't legally, logically, or emotionally be justified."

Aaron had been married in Germany and had a daughter; his wife and daughter were killed in a concentration camp. He came to New York in 1939, remarried, and had two sons and a daughter. His home was a fine mansion on Long Island. He had hired primarily Jewish immigrants and other minorities and was brought into court by the ACLU because he refused to hire anyone of German extraction. He paid the fines and continued the practice. He wanted to keep his country as strong as it could possibly be in all ways; never again did he want to be threatened by a group like the Nazis. Green wanted de Spadante removed from any association with Genessee. He and Hamilton wanted Trevayne to be President because he understood what they had done and why.

GREENBERG, EMMANUEL "MANNY" (RG)

Fourth husband of Regina Hawkins; he was a movie producer. They lived in a mansion in Tarzana.

GREENBERG, EMMANUEL "MANNY" (RO)

Ginny's fourth ex-husband. "He got bored with an older woman so [she] set him free for a large hunk of change." Manny liked sixteen-year-old girls. Hawkins's ex-wives were afraid he'd punch Manny when he saw him; Hawkins felt he was giving Manny a break just by letting him compete for the movie. The Suicidal Six liked his crying routine.

GREENBERG, JASON (MP)

FBI field agent, a Jewish lawyer who was Loring's contact. He disliked Kressel but agreed to work with him. Loring had been Jason's close friend for years, and Jason had the unpleasant task of telling Loring's wife about his death. Greenberg took Matlock to Pat's apartment and brought in a doctor after Matlock had been drugged by Dunois; Greenberg urged Matlock to withdraw after Dunios showed up. After Pat was left injured on Matlock's doorstep and Matlock's house was bombed, Greenberg had both of them hospitalized. Before Greenberg left for reassignment, he and Matlock agreed on a code and a telephone number where messages could be left. Fred Houston, Greenberg's replacement, had great respect for Greenberg.

GREENBERG, REGINA SOMMERVILLE HAWKINS CLARK MADISON (RG)

Hawkins's first wife. In her forties, Regina was dark-haired, tanned, with a lovely figure and huge breasts; she still talked like a southern belle. Regina was Virginia hunt country, spoiled rich. In 1947, when the young war hero Hawkins impressed the nation with his prowess on the football field, Regina decided to marry him. With Daddy's money and connections and Hawkins's talents, Regina expected to be a general's wife within a year, enjoying life in exotic places with house servants, and other luxuries. Hawkins, however, wanted to be with the troops and

Regina didn't like the army camps. Daddy had Hawkins transferred to West Germany and the marriage annulled. She was currently living with her movie-producer husband in a mansion in Tarzana; she and the other ex-wives usually met at her house every Thursday. She was the spokeswoman for the group because of her seniority. When Sam asked the wives about Hawkins, none of them would say anything negative about him; they said they couldn't live with him but owed him a lot for what he had done for them. Ginny agreed to interview Guido Frescobaldi and get him to the point of exchange with the Pope. She also took her turn guarding and entertaining Sam for Hawkins; Ginny was the most manipulative of the ex-wives. Sam couldn't get any information out of any of them; Hawkins was paying them well and they were loyal.

GREENE, CAPTAIN MARTIN (GC)

He was "stationed at the Pentagon after four years under heavy fire in the worst sections of the Delta." He was tough, a great soldier; "His people had come from Irgun; the toughest fighters in Jew history." The most recent member of Eye Corps, he was stocky, muscular, with broad, thick shoulders, thick legs, a shock of bright red hair shaped in a bristling crew cut.

He figured it was Barstow who'd been broken by Tarkington; he suggested Andrew think about hiring someone to kill Barstow. He had hired someone to kill Nevins. When the other five men from Saigon were put into jail, Greene took Nevins's briefcase and flew to Tel Aviv; he offered to take Andrew with him.

GREPSCHEDIT, COLONEL (GC)

The Colonel in Verdun-Meuse was having difficulties with occupation because the legal office was issuing regulations counter to those he was trying to enforce.

———, GRETCHEN (PM)

Gretchen worked as Alexander's maid for four years before Enid went to work there.

GRIMES, ——— (MC)

Name under which Brazuk lived after he defected to the British.

GRINELL, CRAYTON (IA)

He was no part of Bollinger's staff and remained in the background but was acting chairman of the political contributors group. He was a "slender man of medium height and a perpetually gray face," a forty-eight-year-old attorney who specialized in international law; he was the

Vanvlanderens' attorney. Grinell ordered the murder of the Secretary of State's group on Cyprus because they were going to sign an agreement that would hurt the defense industry; he had Ardis killed because she inadvertently exposed their group, and Dr. Lyons because they couldn't afford to have their names associated with his. He escaped from Milos at the San Diego airport and went to the *Passage to China Island*, where he held Kendrick in isolation then ordered him killed when the federal officers closed in on Bollinger's residence. He managed to escape from the island before the federal officers could reach it and fly to the mainland; he wanted the records being held by Ardis's lawyer. He got the records and the attorney was found dead. However, the attorney's secretary had made a copy, which Gingerbread managed to obtain. Kendrick managed to catch up with him and kill him as Hamendi was distributing the arms in Nishtun, South Yemen.

GRIS (RG)

Other code name Stockholm. He was a master of camouflage and escape cartography. One of his jobs was to disable the police escorts and others around the Pope.

GROVER, GEORGE (OW)

CIA's Deputy Administrator. He went into the field to direct the Omega operation.

GUARDINO, CAPTAIN (AP)

Army G-2. Removed Senator Mario Parelli from the cloak room, as Parelli had been deeply involved with Aquitaine.

GUDERIAN, GENERAL (GC)

His courier dispatch to General Bock about the Russian front was intercepted by Loch Torridon.

GUIDERONE, JULIAN (MC)

Julian was raised with Joshua Appleton IV. Supposedly he died in a skiing accident in Switzerland. Dental X-rays showed he had replaced Joshua after his auto accident.

GUIDERONE, NICHOLAS (MC)

The "shepherd boy," father of Julian, head of the Matarese and Trans-Communications. He was over eighty; he had come to the United States from southern Italy in the hold of a ship, with no mother and a barely literate father. His father worked for the Appletons, and Joshua Appleton sent Nicholas to the best schools; Nicholas made Appleton's companies successful. Guiderone may not have been his real name; *guiderone* means "shepherd" or "guide." He had a high-pitched, breathless voice, quite penetrating and cold.

GUIDO, UNCLE (RO)
Little Joey's uncle was a shoe repairman.

GUILIANI (IA) [REAL PERSON]
Federal prosecutor in New York who had been putting away Mafia members by the truckload.

GUNSLINGER (PM)
Nickname given to Red Ogilvie by his own people.

———, GUS (RO)
Fictitious bartender at the Pogo Lounge in Los Angeles.

HABERNICHT, FRIEDRICH (PM)
Handelman said he knew a man named Habernicht in Berlin in the old days.

HACKETT, VICE ADMIRAL (GC)
Royal Navy, rather formal and pompous. He, Teague, and Neyland questioned Vittorio about the Salonika papers. Hackett was irritated because they jeopardized a vital area of their operations to rescue Vittorio, and then Vittorio couldn't give them any information.

HAFAIYABEAKA, SHEIK MUSTACHA (RO)
The twelfth son of Tizi Ouzou by his twenty-second wife. He wanted to produce the Suicidal Six movie.

HAGATE, B. (MC)
Cockney waitress in a restaurant in Knightsbridge said there was a telephone call for B. Hagate.

HAJAZZI, ——— (IA)
One of Khalehla's contacts in Oman; he was a merchant.

———, HAL (RE)
Lyons's male nurse. Hal was pleasant but mentally somewhat dense. He and Johnny were paid by the research center of Meridian Aircraft; Hal's job was to keep Lyons away from alcohol and in good working shape. He was killed by the Haganah at Terrazza Verde.

HALIDON (CH)

Each tribe had a single sound applicable to it only. The sound for the Tribe of Acquaba was "Halidon," which was in reality three words from the African Ashanti meaning "a wailing instrument whose cry was carried by the wind to the gods." Through much research Piersall discovered the meaning of Halidon; this allowed him and others to reach the tribe.

HALLIDAY, AVERY PRESTON (AP)

Also known as Avery Preston Fowler, A. Preston Halliday, and Press Halliday. His hair was straight, dark, and neat, his nose sharp. He tells Joel Converse, "I think we're the best in the business under fifty." He loves having a home and family.

He met Joel while they were both in high school in Watertown, Connecticut. He was "Joel's American adversary in the . . . finalizing of last-minute details for a Swiss-American merger that had brought both men to Geneva." "Halliday's reputation . . . was as a troubleshooter, a legal mechanic from San Francisco. . . ." In order to make contact with Joel, it was necessary to use this as a cover, to hire Joel to put the Aquitaine out of business. He describes the Aquitaine as "a global Third Reich. All they need is a Hitler."

Halliday had learned about the Aquitaine plot while he was legally representing General George Marcus Delavane. He cannot go after Delavane himself because it would violate the lawyer-client relationship; however, Joel doesn't have that restriction. Someone from the Aquitaine kills Halliday to prevent him from passing on information about the organization. This is a major factor in Joel's decision to stop the Aquitaine.

HALLIDAY, JOHN "JACK" (AP)

Stepfather of A. Preston Halliday. Although Press was not his biological son, they were quite close. Larry Talbot says about Press's death: "The story now is violent robbery; he resisted and the packets were stuffed under his shirt after they shot him. I think Jack Halliday must have burned the wires from San Francisco, threatened to beat the crap out of the whole Swiss government. . . . He played for Stanford, you know."

HALLIDAY, MRS. JOHN (AP)

Mother of A. Preston Fowler. Originally from San Francisco, she went back there and married John Halliday after her first husband committed suicide. Had the suicide hushed up.

HALLIDAY, MEAGAN FITZPATRICK "MEG" (AP)

Sister of Connal Fitzpatrick, wife of Avery Preston Halliday, and mother of Halliday's five children. Meg knew something was tearing Press apart and she couldn't get him to share it with her. Connal says of them, "I know it's not fashionable these days to have two people with a passel of kids who really like each other, who can't wait to be with each other when they're apart, but that's the way they were." Connal had made a promise to Meg to "blow this whole thing apart." He asked Meg to relay telephone messages between himself and SAND PAC. Meg relayed the message that Remington had called and someone had attempted to get the flag released on Joel's service records and that Remington had stopped it.

HALYARD, LIEUTENANT GENERAL MALCOLM "TIGHTROPE" (PM)

A brilliant tactician, the General had been in Europe in World War II, in Korea, and in Vietnam. He never held a press conference or allowed pictures to be taken of him. He was one of only four men who knew about Costa Brava.

HAMENDI, ABDEL (IA)

"The most powerful arms merchant in the world with the lowest profile"; he was tied in with Grinell's group. Kendrick "knew him years ago in Riyadh. He was a minister for the Saudis until the family caught him . . . making millions with false leases and ersatz contracts. He was to be publicly executed, but he got out of the country." Kendrick believed Hamendi was destroying the Arab countries and went back over to expose him as an Arab who betrays other Arabs for money. Kendrick killed Hamendi at Nishtun, South Yemen.

HAMILTON, IAN (T)

Well-known, respected attorney, presidential adviser for many years. Hamilton was fifty-eight years old, tall, slender, and elegant. Hamilton came from very old Upstate New York money and had graduated near the top of his class at Harvard. He did a postlaw year at Cambridge in England and then spent the war years in London as a Navy legal officer attached to Eisenhower's general staff. He'd married an English girl, and their only child, a son, was born in Surrey. After the war he became a partner in one of New York's most prestigious firms. His specialty was corporate law with heavy diversification in municipal bonds. His wartime associations frequently brought him to Washington, where he became a presidential adviser. He had served on the President's Steel Import Commission; in February their report was given to the President. In March Genessee had imported shiploads of ingot from Japan just before the results of the report were revealed. In August Genessee floated a $100 million bond issue; the job was given to a Chicago firm that Hamilton had just joined. Hamilton was willing to show that the deal had been made before he joined the firm and that he received no money from it. He had moved to Chicago to become the midwest power for Genessee. His son had become a successful folk singer who had his own group; he concluded that "the old man 'did his thing' with more intelligence than imagination, but did it well because he was dedicated to the proposition that the elite had to show the way for the unenlightened."

HAMMER-ZERO-TWO (PM)

Code name used by Arthur Pierce, signifying the second in the delegation.

HAMMERLOCKER, "JAWS" (RO)

Professional wrestler. He was jogging in Boston when a nude man attacked him and tried to rip his sweat suit off him.

HAN CHOW (CM)

Prison camp where O'Brien was interred during the Vietnam War. O'Brien disobeyed his commanding officer and escaped; the eight men remaining were shot and killed by the Viet Cong. These facts were in one of the missing Hoover files.

HAND, JUDGE LEARNED (OW) [REAL PERSON]

After graduating from law school Tremayne was a law clerk for Judge Hand. Judge Hand felt the merger market was insane with fake purchases.

HANDELMAN, JACOB (PM)

Jarmaine Professor of Philosophy at Columbia University; "the Rabbi" lectured frequently at the Jewish Theological Seminary. Handelman was slightly overweight with a paunch, had long, white hair, and a short gray beard; he wore steel-rimmed glasses and walked slowly. His speech was Jewish-rooted German, delivered in a high-pitched singsong manner. Régine believed he had been rescued from the Bergen-Belsen camp in April 1945. He was the "[h]alfway man, broker of sanctuary for the pursued and the dispossessed. The man who . . . [concealed] Jenna Karas." Havelock recognized him as the former Nazi officer who had killed his father in Lidice; he forced Handelman to give him the information about Jenna's cover and destination. Havelock had intended to let Handelman live, worrying every day when Havelock would expose him, but Handelman attacked Havelock with a knife and Havelock killed him.

HANLEY, CAPTAIN ROBERT (CH)

Independent owner and pilot of a small plane in Jamaica. He sometimes worked for Tim Durrell. He didn't look much over forty-five—his close-cropped reddish-blond hair had no gray in it. He was a man who could be trusted, a tough man, a professional with a high degree of expertise; he flew covert missions. Sam and McAuliff were good friends of his; he was so upset with Sam for disappearing that he hit him in the mouth with his fist when he finally reappeared; he then picked Sam up off the ground, explaining that for the past few weeks Sam had caused him undue anxiety. The two of them then drank the night away in the bar of the Trident Villas. The next day they flew to Montego Bay to see an attorney, as they were going into partnership.

———, HANNAH (SI)

German housekeeper Ulster Scarlett brought to his home on Fifty-fourth Street; she spoke English fluently and supposedly had run a hunting lodge in southern Germany. One of the homeliest women Canfield had ever seen, she was obese, had huge hands, a jowled face, and pulled-back gray hair. Canfield caught her listening at doors. She tried to kill Elizabeth Scarlatti by pushing a luggage dolly into her at the Geneva rail station.

———, HANS (AP)

The nickname Johnny Reb called the German watchman at Scharhorn. Hans removed Johnny from the action by slapping him on the neck in a friendly way with a chemically treated needle.

HARDING, RICHARD "DICKIE" (IA)

English ferrous-metals salesman who helped a drunken Tony McDonald to his hotel room. He and Jack delayed their departure one day to enable them to visit the British embassy and report McDonald's peculiar behavior.

———, HAROLD (BS)

The female impersonator who met Panov at the train station in Kowloon, "she" called Panov Harold.

HARRIS, JOSHUA (CM)

Chancellor's literary agent. Josh was in his early forties, a large man of generous girth who moved gracefully; he had a black chin beard that lent a sinister quality to his face. After Chancellor was injured, Joshua sweated out the physical injuries, then the depression; he thought at times that Chancellor would never write again. He engineered the movie deal to get Chancellor away from Pennsylvania for a while, hoping this would help. He did research on Longworth for Peter. As an agent he was not universally loved, because he indulged in "uncomfortable confrontations based frequently on unfounded charges of abuse." Josh and Tony Morgan were well acquainted. Chancellor thought Josh and Tony were the best, because they cared about him and he could trust them.

HARRISON, ALEXANDER "LEX" (RO)

Hawkins disguised himself as Lex Harrison, a very influential journalist. Supposedly he wished to interview Ethelred Brokemichael about the effect of the cutback in defense spending.

HARRISON, ANDY (OW)

Head lawyer for Standard Mutual. He confirmed that two pages missing from the FCC documents were suspicious. Since Tanner produced investigative-reporting news programs, there was a necessary link with the government; Tanner called Andy for the telephone number for the CIA.

———, HARRY (AP)

Chief of Consular Operations (also known as Cons Ops), the State Department's branch of foreign clandestine activities. He could not understand why the Navy was interested in the embassy at Bonn since Bonn was not a seaport; he told Tolland he'd check at Langley and Arlington to see if they had an operation going on that they hadn't told him about and that he would also check the Navy's chief legal officers and the ABA to find out who Joel Converse was.

———, HARRY (IA)

Night maintenance man in the congressional office building who found Phil Tobias's body.

———, HARRY (MC)

Young double agent assigned to work for Scofield in Amsterdam as a CIA agent; he was a VKR agent trained since the age of nine at the American compound in Novgorod. Against Scofield's orders he killed the defector on the bridge. "Harry" also worked for the Matarese and was killed while trying to shoot Scofield and Taleniekov.

———, HARRY (MP)

The manager of the Cheshire Cat, a small country inn Matlock liked to visit.

——, HARRY (PM)

Proprietor of Harry's Bar in Mason Falls. The bar was a copy of Harry's in Paris. He helped Havelock get directions to Kahoutek's place.

HASSAN, —— (IA)

Bahrainian official Manny had known since the Kendrick Group built a country club on the archipelago years before. His home was a meeting place for officials from Bahrain, Oman, France, the United Kingdom, West Germany, Israel, the Palestine Liberation Organization, and Manny Weingrass after the Mahdi was captured.

HASSAN, KASHI (IA)

Wife of Dr. Sabri Hassan. She and Sabri lived with Kendrick and had a variety of duties. She could speak Hebrew and English as well as Arabic and was impressed with the American courts of justice and Congress. Kashi and Khalehla were instant friends and the Hassans were very fond of Manny. Paddy O'Reilly found the Hassans naked, with their throats slit, in the house in Virginia.

HASSAN, DR. SABRI (IA)

Married to Kashi. The Hassans had been old friends of Kendrick's in Dubai before coming to live with him in the U.S. He was afraid of the Arab backlash after news was leaked that Kendrick had been at Masqat. Sabri was usually calm, middle-aged, and very protective of Kendrick. He hoped to have a post at either Georgetown or Princeton in the spring; he had great respect for Khalehla's father, whom he had met in Cairo. Evan wasn't aware that Sabri knew how to operate a computer. After their bodies were found, Manny made arrangements for them to be flown back to Dubai for burial. Kendrick and Manny were extremely angry over their death.

HAVALATCH, —— (PM)

Charles thought Havelock's name was Havalatch.

HAVELLACHT, —— (PM)

Handelman thought Havelock's name was Havellacht.

HAVELOCK, MICHAEL (PM)

In the United States Havelock attended a prep school and then Princeton University; his adoptive parents, the Websters, died while he was in college. He met Matthias during graduate school, and Matthias took an interest in him because their families had been friends in Prague. Michael graduated from Princeton with a Ph.D. in European history and a minor in Slavic languages. He didn't need much urging to go to work for the State Department. He'd been an undercover field man for Consular Operations for sixteen years. He retired after he thought Jenna was killed at Costa Brava and accepted a teaching position at Concord University in New Hampshire. He was traveling in Rome when he saw Jenna alive. He decided they'd both been manipulated by the government and threatened to expose clandestine operations unless he received some help finding Jenna. He traced Jenna to Kahoutek's via Broussac and rescued her, then traced Matthias to Poole's Island, where he was captured and asked by the government to help them find Parsifal. He found Parsifal and the documents and decided to burn both the psychiatric file on Matthias and the documents; then he and Jenna moved to New Hampshire.

HAVILITCH, ———— (PM)

Charles said a man named Havilitch from the State Department had been in Handelman's apartment the night Handelman died.

HAVILLAND, RAYMOND OLIVER (BS)

U.S. Ambassador-at-large. He had been with the American government for years. As a young man he had attended an expensive prep school, and he had done his postgraduate work at several prestigious

The Ginza, Tokyo (DISCARDED CHAPTER FROM THE PARSIFAL MOSAIC)

universities in the British Isles. He had been married, but his wife had died. He was seventy-plus years old with gray hair, dark eyebrows, and a lined, elongated face; he dressed impeccably. He didn't know Webb as well as Conklin did, and he was the one who devised the plot to force Webb to become Bourne again. McAllister told him he was the most immoral man he'd ever met. He replied he'd go to any length to keep this planet from blowing itself up. He told Catherine Staples that had he been as moral as McAllister, he would never have accomplished what he had. He felt it was a dirty job, but someone had to do it. He hadn't asked for the job.

HAVLICEK, MIKHAIL (PM)

Real name of Michael Havelock. Mikhail was born in Prague in the middle thirties. In 1942, when the Gestapo rounded up the children of Lidice, Mikhail was chasing rabbits in the woods. He survived alone for a month before his father found him. For three years he was a courier for the underground. In 1948 his father disappeared and Mikhail was smuggled out of the country to England. The Websters heard about him, adopted him (changing his name to Havelock), and took him to Greenwich, Connecticut, to live.

HAVLICEK, VACLAV (PM)

Michael Havelock's real father; he and his wife and son lived in Lidice. He was a professor at Karlova University in Prague; after the German occupation he was dismissed from his job and worked with British intelligence. On May 27, 1942, he led the group of Czech partisans who killed Reinhard Heydrich and then went into hiding; one of the partisans from Lidice was recognized by the Germans. On June 10 the Gestapo took their revenge on Lidice; all adult males were killed, the younger women were taken to whore camps, and the children who were trainable were taken for other jobs, all others were killed. Vaclav was warned by the partisans not to return; his wife killed a Wehrmacht officer and herself at the whore camp. Vaclav found Mikhail, who had escaped into the forest, and they joined with others to resume their fight against the Germans. After the Germans were beaten, Vaclav and the others had to stand against the Russians; after Masaryk's assassination, Vaclav disappeared—either to a gulag or a local grave.

HAWKINS, ABE (IA)

Owned a grocery store with a telephone in a small town not far from Mesa Verde.

HAWKINS, ANNE (RG)

Hawkins's fourth wife, from Detroit, Michigan. She had sloping breasts, long, light brown hair, wide bright blue eyes, and tapered legs; she enjoyed bubble baths and was an avid reader. Anne had a rough childhood; her whole family had spent more time in jail than out of it. Anne, the only girl, survived by becoming a hooker. She wanted to improve her life; Hawkins recognized she was a fine person and married her. He had her dossier changed so that she appeared to be the only daughter of two deceased schoolteachers. After their divorce she built up a restaurant business and married Don. Don wanted to divorce her and take the restaurants. Hawkins paid Anne to take care of Sam in London for him, and he asked Sam to help her with her divorce. Sam intended to hire detectives to investigate Don. Anne came back to the chateau with Lillian, and Anne and Sam spent much of their time together, doing the housecleaning and taking care of Francesco. She and Francesco became good friends. Sam felt she was the most genuine, guileless person he had ever met and intended to marry her.

HAWKINS, LILLIAN (RG)

(*See also* von Schnabe, Lillian Hawkins.) Lillian was Hawkins's third wife, from Palo Alto, California. She was the blond Aphrodite with narrow, pointed breasts. Lillian kept an eye on Sam in Berlin for Hawkins, where she was supposedly taking a gourmet cooking course. She was very involved with nutrition and exercise. One of her jobs was to prepare the apartments in the chateau for the Pope; Sam escaped from the chateau in the trunk of the limousine that Lillian was driving to the airfield for Hawkins.

HAWKINS, GENERAL MACKENZIE "MADMAN" LOCHINVAR (RG)

Also called Mac or Hawk, Hawkins was accused of being drunk and shooting the balls off a ten-foot jade statue in Son Tai Square; he was at General Lu Sin's home at the time and had been drugged. The Chinese framed him to get concessions on a trade agreement with the Americans. Hawkins had been a youthful hero at the Battle of the Bulge, then a football hero at the Point; he was a career officer and had served in Korea and Vietnam and received two Congressional Medals of Honor. He was physically and morally tough, highly intelligent, and devious. He'd been a very successful intelligence officer in the Far East. Hawkins was a national hero, and there were books and movies about his career. He'd been married four times to beautiful, intelligent women who thought he was wonderful but couldn't stand living with him. His behavior was frequently outrageous but he always had a good reason for it. When he was discharged from the army with a reduced pension, he decided to use his background to provide him with a comfortable income. He had read the article in the Communist newspaper about the Pope and his look-alike cousin; he had also read all the background information he could get on the finances of the Church. Hawkins realized Sam was a good lawyer when Sam got him out of China, and he hired Sam to set up a corporation and bank accounts for him and contact investors. He also hired his four ex-wives and out-of-work secret agents to help him kidnap the Pope; he hadn't figured on the Pope's cooperation in his venture.

HAWKINS, GENERAL MACKENZIE "MADMAN" LOCHINVAR (RO)
Hawkins researched the Omaha problem for twenty-one months before approaching the Wopotamis and Brokemichael. With the assistance of Charlie Redwing he wrote the brief to be presented to the Supreme Court. Underneath Hawk's scams were fundamental truths, which is why Aaron and Sam supported him; one of his ex-wives described him as a windmill tilter. Hawkins led troops in most of the famous battles of all the wars fought since World War I and brought all the special forces into existence; most of the men he met had been in the Army and/or served with him. He had been in Intelligence and wore ridiculous disguises that worked. He disabled but didn't kill people, including the SFIs; he helped everyone else he met, especially the disenfranchised. Ginny persuaded him to come to Hollywood as co-producer of Greenberg's movie to keep an eye on Manny's financial dealings.

HAWKINS, MADGE "MIDGEY" (RG)
Hawkins's second wife, from Tuckahoe, New York. Midgey had a good figure with full, round breasts; she had auburn hair and was over thirty. Madge took care of Sam on his trip into the desert to meet Sheik Azaz-Varak; she was knowledgeable about Arab culture, the geography and customs of Arab lands, and she flew Sam out in the helicopter. Sam would not have survived without her.

HAWKINS, MADGE "MIDGEY" (RO)
Madge had always wanted to be a writer and had become one of the hottest screenwriters in Hollywood. Her most recent screenplay, *Mutant Homicidal Lesbian Worms*, had been highly successful. She was so successful she could live and write in Greenwich, Connecticut, instead of in Hollywood. She wrote a ten-page proposal for Hawk based on the audiotapes from the Suicidal Six.

HAWKINS, MCKENZIE "MAC" (BI)
Retired Canadian secret agent that David Abbott worked with in Burma. When Peter was killed, Abbott managed to reach him, and

Hawkins persuaded the Canadians to work with American intelligence. Mac contacted Alan, who instructed Marie to return to Canada immediately, which she refused to do.

HAWKINS, REGINA "GINNY" SOMMERVILLE (RG)
Mac Hawkins's first wife. (*See also* Greenberg, Regina Sommerville Hawkins Clark Madison.)

HAWKWOOD, BASIL (SI)
Basil was impatiently waiting for an audience with Bertholde the afternoon Bertholde was killed. Canfield noticed him glancing impatiently at his distinctive red and black cuff links. Canfield stopped him; Basil assumed he was one of their group and told him about the shipments of "damaged" leather goods he had been sending to Munich, to the Nazis.

HAWKWOOD, LESLIE JENNER (RE)
An old girlfriend Spaulding hadn't seen for the past five years; she called him when he arrived in New York, although he'd traveled incognito. He'd originally met her in 1936 at the Yale Bowl; they had a discreet affair for two months before her marriage to Richard. She had light brown hair, wide brown eyes, a sculptured face, and a lithe, full-breasted body. Spaulding spent an entertaining evening with her, then couldn't locate her the next day; his room was searched while he was occupied with Leslie. When he called her family he was told she'd moved to California and lived with the Goldsmiths. Through her uncle, Leslie became involved in the activities of the Haganah; she flew to Buenos Aires to warn Spaulding not to participate in the Rhinemann exchange.

HAWKWOOD, RICHARD (RE)
Husband of Leslie Jenner. His family had money and he had graduated from Yale. He was in England, a pilot with the Tenth Bomber Command down in Surrey. There was no record of a divorce from Leslie.

HEATHLEY, ENID (AP)
Private secretary to Walter Peregrine for nearly twenty years; said that Peregrine considered them a team. She was a middle-aged, "pleasant-faced woman with signs of gray in her hair and very intelligent eyes." Caleb Dowling contacted her after Walter's murder because he could not get in contact with the new acting ambassador; he had wanted to warn him about the people inside the embassy and the people pursuing Joel Converse. He convinces her that Norman Washburn is not to be trusted and may have been involved in Peregrine's murder. She passes him on to

"George," the station chief for the CIA in Bonn, a man Walter Peregrine didn't like but trusted completely.

———, HECTOR (BU)

One of the CIA guards at the safe house on Chesapeake Bay. He was a "muscular, medium-size man with clean-cut Hispanic features" who dressed as casually as a weekend guest, in white slacks and a white linen jacket. Hector, of course, was not his real name.

HEDRICK, JUSTICE (CH)

The real Justice Hedrick was a British agent sent to McAuliff's group as a carrier; Latham described Justice and his brother as Maroon, two of the best runners in Jamaica, knowledgeable about the Cock Pit country, and trustworthy. He was intercepted and replaced by a Halidonite before reaching camp. The man taking his place was described as "younger than his brother Marcus, perhaps in his late twenties, and stockily muscular." Ruth Jensen chose him to be her guide.

HEDRICK, MARCUS (CH)

A British agent sent to McAuliff's group to work as a runner. He was replaced by a Halidonite who told McAuliff that Marcus and Justice were dead—actually they had been released unharmed. Marcus took McAuliff to meet Malcolm; he had to restrain Malcolm when Malcolm attacked McAuliff after McAuliff called him "Mr. Bones." He returned with McAuliff to help him defend the survey party—it was his choice.

HEFFERNANS (PM)

An elderly, apparently wealthy, retired couple who supposedly owned Sterile Five. They had spent their entire lives in the foreign service and were two of the most efficient cryptanalysts in U.S. Intelligence. Their cover was that Mr. Heffernan had been an investment banker living in Europe for several decades.

HEFFLEFINGER, FRANK "FINGER FRANK" (RO)

Consultant to the State Department on Far Eastern military affairs, wined and dined by government contractors. Frank was a retired admiral who owed Mac a favor for covering up his error of blowing up beach radio stations in Wonsan, Korea; he was known as "Finger Frank" because he had his fingers on the wrong buttons. Hawkins asked him to make the call to the secretary of state for the clandestine meeting and to call the President about Warren Pease's state of mind.

HEFFLEFINGER, UNDERSECRETARY JASPAR (IA)

In charge of Strategic Deterrence. He was hauled out to defend the Pentagon whenever anyone attacked it. He was a jowled but handsome man with a strong face and a shock of silver hair; his voice would make a radio announcer envious.

———, HEINRICH (AP)

Erich Leifhelm's chauffeur and an Aquitaine soldier. He was Joel's guard at Leifhelm's country house. He spoke reasonably good English but didn't understand American jokes and would not give Joel straight answers to his questions. Joel estimated Heinrich was about ten years younger than he was.

Heinrich had been with Leifhelm since Brussels, when he was a sergeant in the Federal Republic's border patrol. He had been charged with strangling a man; the man was the father of a girl Heinrich had "taken advantage of" and he had been trying to kill Heinrich with a knife. Leifhelm took interest in his case and had him transferred to the Brabant garrison, where Leifhelm made him his chauffeur.

———, HEINRICH (RE)

Nazi soldier on board the trawler where the Germans were examining the diamonds for Peenemünde. Spaulding shot him.

———, HELGA (MC)

Maid at the Verachten estate. Taleniekov persuaded her to take him to Walther Verachten.

———, HENRI (AP)

Concierge of the Hotel Richemond in Geneva, Switzerland. He and Joel "had known each other nearly five years. Their friendship went beyond that of hotel executive and guest; they had gambled together frequently at Divonne-les-Bains, across the French border." He had heard about Halliday's murder, and worried about Joel's welfare. He sent Armagnac brandy to Joel's room after seeing him drenched from rain; he knew something was very wrong when Joel so quickly denied the drug story connected with Halliday's death. He told Joel that he was there if he needed him.

———, HENRI (BI)

One of Carlos's men who attempted to kill David Webb in the elevator in the Gemeinschaft Bank in Zurich. He was killed by Carlos's men when David Webb used him as a shield while Webb was leaving the bank.

——, HENRI (HC)

Henri was told to drive Althene and Helden away from the marina at Atterrisage Medoc.

HENRYK, CONGRESSMAN (IA)

Kendrick of Colorado was wrongly identified by a Cable News reporter as Henryk of Wyoming.

HEREFORD, —— (PM)

Havelock registered as Hereford at the King's Arms near the Columbia campus.

HERR OBERST (HC)

Herr Oberst ("the Colonel") was General Klaus Falkenheim.

HERRON, LUCAS (MP)

White-haired, elderly chairman of the romance languages department at Carlyle; he was as well known for his compassion as his brilliant scholarship. Lucas was over seventy and never married; he lived in a comfortable, isolated old carriage house eight miles from campus. He had been a middle-aged Marine Corps major in the Solomon Islands during World War II, an authentic hero. Lucas panicked when Matlock told him about the federal drug investigation at Carlyle. Shortly after that Lucas was found dead, apparently a suicide; forensics showed murder. Lucas had kept a secret diary of his activities for Nimrod. Lucas had been a drug addict for a quarter of a century and had become a courier for Nimrod; drugs made it possible for him to live with the pain from his war injuries and not be confined to a VA hospital for the rest of his life.

——, HERVÉ (BI)

White-haired bell captain in a small hotel off the boulevard Montparnasse in Paris. He became very solicitous of the needs of David Webb and Marie when David gave him a twenty-franc note.

HESS, RUDOLPH (SI) [REAL PERSON]

Hess was not a Junker but very much wanted to be included by Rheinhart and his officers. He was a tall man with thick, wavy black hair and prominent, dark eyebrows; his face was darkly cherubic with wide eyes. He was fluent in English.

HICKMAN, REAR ADMIRAL BRIAN (AP)

Commanding officer of SAND PAC. He called Remington into his office at the end of the day to find out what Remington knew. Hickman didn't know all the details of what Fitzpatrick was doing but he trusted his judgment, telling Remington that "Fitzpatrick must have a good reason."

Fitzpatrick had been with him in New London and Galveston and he had requested him as his CLO in San Diego. Fitzpatrick was sure Hickman wouldn't release the files without consulting him first. If Hickman had been part of Aquitaine, he wouldn't have talked to Remington. Hickman didn't like outside pressures, especially from the Navy. He was angry with Fitzpatrick when he discovered that he was in Europe instead of in California; he decided to have Remington release the file and wanted to see a copy of it "the minute it gets here."

When Scanlon called him Hickman mentioned that the only offensive material found in Joel's file by his legal exec, David Remington, was Joel's comments about Delavane. Scanlon said it had all been the mistake of an overzealous JG and Hickman didn't believe him. Shortly after that Remington was killed in an auto accident in the Sonoma hills.

HILL, AMBASSADOR WILLIAM "BIG BILLY" (T)

Ambassador-at-large. Hill was in his seventies, articulate, and soft-spoken. He was a "wealthy industrialist, friend to presidents, roving diplomat, war hero." Hill was a cynic who believed there was no solution to the world's problems, that any solution was in the search for the solution. Baldwin and Hill chose Trevayne for chairman of the subcommittee; it frightened them when they realized they had also chosen the next President. When Trevayne told him that Senator Knapp had announced the President would not run for a second term, Hill guaranteed the President that Knapp would resign within the month. Hamilton thought Hill would take his own life if he ever realized how great a part he'd unknowingly played in the development of Genessee Industries. Hill and Baldwin were lifelong friends; Baldwin took care of Hill's burial.

HITLER, ADOLF (SI) [REAL PERSON]

Hitler actively sought Junker approval; he was looking forward to Rheinhart's support of the Nazis at the rally in Oldenburg. Ludendorff thought Hitler was capable of poor judgment but had great vision. Hitler would not accept debate on his decisions, but he valued Ludendorff's opinions above all others.

HITLUH, WOLFGANG (RO)

An American Nazi who worked for Manpower Plus Plus. Wolfgang's real name was Billy-Bob Bayou and he was from Louisiana. He was hired by Vinnie to guard Hawkins. Wolfgang was a certified lunatic who burnt swastikas on the grounds of the United Nations and threw himself in front of a police van carrying a Nazi friend of his to jail. He needed the employment because he was drawing benefits on a stolen social security card he took from some loan shark he threw into the East River. Cyrus and Roman decided they didn't want to work with him and left him tied up and naked, with a copy of *Mein Kampf* on his belly, on the front steps of the Cambridge Street police headquarters.

Hobo Pete (ro)

Man who used to clean urinals in the Brooklyn subways. Mangeca-vallo wanted the group around Warren Pease so badly ruined that they would have the credit line of Hobo Pete.

Hogan (ro)

Bouncer at O'Toole's bar. He held back the crowd so that O'Toole could get Sam out of the bar after he told the story about Sister Anne and the Pope.

Holcroft, Althene (hc)

Noel's mother. A woman of intellect and perception, she was more friend than mother. She was approaching seventy and was a tall, graceful woman with gray hair. She had chiseled, angular features—high cheekbones, aquiline nose, wide-set eyes, and thin, aristocratic lips. She'd lived in Europe during the thirties, where she'd met and married Heinrich Clausen. She hated the Nazis; she thought Heinrich Clausen wanted to make amends for Germany, so she agreed to go along with his scheme and raise Noel as an American. She and Richard didn't tell Noel about Clausen until his twenty-fifth birthday. After Yakov told her about Heinrich's scheme, she flew to Geneva to stop Noel, using routes and contacts she'd known from World War II. She met Helden in Atterrisage Medoc and traveled to Yakov's apartment; to give Yakov time to get the master list of the Sonnenkinder, Althene agreed to meet Johann. Johann shot her to death. Noel received a letter from her that she'd left with Yakov for him.

Holcroft, Jane (gc)

The former Mrs. Spane and second wife of Victor Fontine (Vittorio Fontini-Cristi). The first time she met Victor, her husband, Spane, had been having an affair with Victor's wife. She'd been extremely angry and divorced Spane. When Victor met her the second time, she was a flying officer at the Air Ministry, sitting in the lobby of the Savoy in London. "Beneath the officer's visor cap her dark brunette hair fell in waves to her shoulders." She was tall and in her middle thirties; she had high cheekbones, a nose that was sharp and slightly upturned, full lips, and eyes of a very intense blue. Victor apologized for his past behavior and invited Jane and her husband to dinner, at which point she told him of her divorce. Five days later the article about his family showed up in the *Times*, and she came to his room and asked him about it. Their deep friendship and love developed from there. She was asked by MI6 to keep an eye on him—she did—she married him. When the area they were living in was bombed by the Luftwaffe, she was nine months pregnant. She was not killed, but gave birth to their twin sons, Andrew and Adrian, with her husband's assistance. She was unable to have any more children. Victor moved them to a more secure area, then after the war to the United States, to a house on Long Island. She was in her sixties when Victor died.

HOLCROFT, NOEL (HC)

Only son of Heinrich and Althene Clausen. The birth certificate for Noel Holcroft said born February 17, 1942; he was actually Noel Clausen, born in the summer of 1939 in Berlin. He had no idea what his father Heinrich looked like, because Althene had destroyed all his photographs; he didn't find out about Heinrich until his twenty-fifth birthday. Noel was tall with a sharp, angular face and light brown hair that fell over his forehead, and he was large and relatively well-coordinated. He avoided fights, so Richard insisted that he take a course in self-defense. Sam taught him how to use a handgun. He did not speak or understand much French and did not understand German; he had been educated in the United States. He was an architect who owned his own small company; he had "no partners, no wife, and no heavy debts." He had become a fair mechanic because he had to survive on his jobs in Mexico and the Caribbean. Noel was necessary to the plans of the false Wolfsschanze because there was no obvious link between Noel and the Third Reich. He decided to accept the terms of the covenant because his company could use the $2 million; he found he really had no choice when Manfredi and Johann started manipulating him. They didn't want to kill him—just force him to do what they wanted. The Nachrichtendienst wanted to stop him if it meant killing him. It was fortunate he met Helden, as she tried to teach him as much as she could about staying alive; he fell in love with her and wanted a home where they didn't need to worry about such things. When he discovered Kessler was lying to him and Sam had been killed, Noel decided to do things his way. He went to Johann's hotel room and found Yakov there instead; Yakov and Noel joined forces to try to get control of the funds at Geneva. Noel signed the documents, then he and Yakov were nearly killed. After months of recovery and training by Yakov, Noel was able to assassinate Johann.

HOLCROFT, COMMANDER R. C. (CH)

Fifty-year-old commander of the MI5 special unit, and he was the best; his cover was financial analyst assigned to the Foreign Office and Inland Revenue. From among the various international intelligence groups, his was chosen to make contact with the group in Jamaica who opposed Dunstone, Ltd.; his group was supposed to keep the others informed, but they fed them false information because the other groups had leaks. He didn't realize seven of his own group were on the payroll of Dunstone, Ltd., until they followed him and tried to kill him. He received a knife wound when McAuliff panicked the Halidons at the Owl of Saint George, and later risked his own life to save McAuliff.

HOLCROFT, MRS. R. C. (CH)

Middle-aged woman married to R. C. Holcroft. She was afraid for her husband's life, and in sending McAuliff after him, she nearly got him killed. R.C. loved her and wanted to spend more time with her, said she was a fine woman.

HOLCROFT, RICHARD (HC)

Stepfather of Noel Clausen and second husband of Althene Clausen. He was a highly respected retired banker with an ability to laugh at himself. Both Noel and Althene loved him dearly. Richard had obliterated all traces of Althene's first marriage, and he had a new birth certificate issued for Noel under the name Holcroft. Every Monday afternoon Richard went to the New York Athletic Club to play squash and talk with old friends. Noel's call to Richard at the club was traced by Johann's people. Richard was crushed against a wall by a car that jumped the curb; he died an hour later at the hospital. Althene found out from Yakov that it was no accident.

HOLDEN, JOHN (MP)

Associate professor of mathematics at Madison University in Webster. He was British and had been in the United States less than two years; he was a small-boned man of forty and had a hearty laugh. He and Matlock were both sailing enthusiasts and had met at a boat show in Saybrook. John knew the gambling games and agreed to accompany Matlock to Windsor Shoals; both he and Matlock were fortunate not to be killed that night.

HOLLAND, PETER (BU)

Director of the CIA for the past three and a half years, he considered himself a hard-nose. He was gray-haired, smoked cigarettes, knew and liked music, liked Oriental spareribs and lemon chicken, and didn't like killing and violence. His parents were agnostics, and they exposed him and his sisters to all the various religions; he remained an agnostic. His family had money and influence; he went to an expensive prep school, then to Annapolis. He was in the SEALS for a few years and made runs off subs into Kaesong and Haiphong harbors during the Korean War. He later became an admiral and ran U.S. Naval Intelligence. Conklin was relieved to deal with him because he had been a field man; he was understandably upset when he thought Holland might be part of Medusa.

HOLLANDER, PAUL (RE)

Agent with Azores-American. He was middle-aged, nearly bald, and wore steel-rimmed glasses. He was well informed about the man in Lisbon. He had orders for Spaulding but did not know about Tortugas. He and the British discovered that the Haganah had been responsible for blowing up Spaulding's plane.

HOOKER, DAVEY (PM)

Postman who delivered the mail on Fourforks Pike to Kahoutek's place.

HOOVER GROUP (CM)

A pack of extremists, very close to Hoover, in the main office of the FBI. "When Hoover died, they thought they'd take over. . . . Some are as paranoid as Hoover." (*See* the "maniacs.")

HOOVER, JOHN EDGAR (CM) [REAL PERSON]

Longtime director of the FBI. He had organized the original Bureau into an extraordinary, efficient organization. His face had sagging jowls, a drawn-out mouth, partially thyroid eyes overlapped by creased, blemished flesh, and touched-up dark hair. He had a "ferocious ego." He wore glasses, but was rarely seen with them on in public. He lived in a faded redbrick house, 4936 Thirtieth Street Place in northwest Washington; it was patrolled by an unmarked van checking for electronic surveillance from a foreign government. There was an agent on twenty-four-hour surveillance outside the house. He did not trust the CIA or the President. He had an enormous vicious bull mastiff whose face was said to resemble his master's; it was let out every evening around eleven P.M. to roam the grounds until morning.

In his office, "Flags," Hoover kept his secret files in a vault protected by a series of electronic releases, the first of which had to be triggered from his residence. He used the information in these files for blackmail; he was obsessed with getting sexual information into the files. Supposedly a number of people were coerced into making large campaign contributions for the President, and two presidential contenders for the opposition were forced to withdraw.

In the book Hoover told Sutherland if he continued to be an obstruction that he would use the files against all the prominent black leaders in the country. It was rumored he had hit teams and death squads. Hoover was operating outside the law, and people felt he had to be stopped. Toward the end of his life his mental processes deteriorated; psychiatrically he progressed from manic-depressive to acute paranoia. Varak told Chancellor that Hoover died a natural death, but a young doctor whose life Hoover had ruined gave him a lethal untraceable injection of a digitalis derivative, and released the electronic signal for opening the vault.

Hoover's body lay in state for twenty-four hours in the Capitol rotunda; no civil servant had been so honored before. When he was buried, a flag covered his coffin, and eight servicemen were pallbearers.

HOOVER, JOHN EDGAR (IA) [REAL PERSON]

Samuel Winters told Mitch Payton that Inver Brass had Hoover eliminated before he could bring the government to its knees.

HOPNER, ——— (HC) [REAL PERSON]

German army officer, one of the would-be assassins at Wolfsschanze. He was shot as a traitor.

———, HORST (AP)

One of the German guards employed by the Aquitaine on Scharhorn; he was on guard duty the night Johnny Reb led his forces in, and died of a knife wound.

HOUSTON, FRED (MP)

The real Houston, from the Narcotics Bureau, was in his mid-thirties, was married, and admired Greenberg. Fred knew the code words from Greenberg and delivered Washington's instructions to Matlock to cut back on his inquiries. Fred knew he'd been spotted and would have to leave Carlyle when Matlock told him about the phone call he'd received from someone pretending to be Houston.

HOWELL, MRS. (PM)

Counsel to White House internal affairs, ordered by the President to call the Secret Service if anyone inquired about Mr. Cross.

HULL, CORDELL (SI) [REAL PERSON]

Secretary of State during World War II. He had very light skin, thinning white hair, blue-green eyes, and wore a steel-rimmed pince-nez. He allowed General Ellis to give the file to Canfield because Kroeger's actions could cause an internal collapse in Berlin. Hull and his wife had been friends with Elizabeth Scarlatti for years; he despised Ulster Scarlett.

HYACINTH (GC)
Code that Teague used for entering the vaults of Loch Torridon, where the files were stored.

ICARUS (IA)
Code name of the operation of Inver Brass to make Kendrick the next Vice President of the United States.

ICARUS (PM)
Matthias was elevated to greatness, was blinded by his achievements and the praise of the people, and went insane.

INNES-BOWEN, DAVID (SI)
Owner of the largest single textile industry throughout Scotland and the Hebrides, one of the merchants supporting the Nazis. He loaded neutral ships off piers in India with textile cargoes bound for Bremerhaven and Cuxhaven.

INVER BRASS (CM)
A group formed in the last months of 1929 to act for the good of society, not themselves. The Scotsman who started the group gave the group its name, after a small lake in Scotland that was not on any map. This was related to the fact that the group had to act in secrecy, outside government bureaucracy. The leader of the group was known as Genesis; the Scotsman was the first Genesis. All the members were known by code names as well. There were never more than six members, and each of these was influential, well-respected, patriotic, and rich. They were ethical men. In the past they had sent massive sums of money to distressed areas to slow down the outbreak of violence born of need. They legally protected people from the information in Hoover's files, and they destroyed files A–L. They used Peter Chancellor to flush out the person who took the files M–Z, so they could destroy those also.

INVER BRASS (IA)
Third Inver Brass group: Gideon Logan, Margaret Lowell, Samuel Winters, Eric Sundstrom, and Jacob Mandel. Milos Varak was the coordinator; when he was killed, Gerald Bryce became the new coordinator. They were selected by the previous group of Inver Brass and their

On the *Stella Solaris* in the Aegean Sea. One marine who lost his "expert" status at skeet (THE ICARUS AGENDA)

attorneys. They decided that Evan Kendrick should become the next Vice President of the United States regardless of how he felt about it, and they launched Operation Icarus. One of their group was a traitor; his behavior caused the death of many people and exposed the existence of Inver Brass. Gerald Bryce would be responsible for the birth of the next Inver Brass group.

———, ISABEL (BS)

A distraught, obese American woman from Short Hills. She and her husband were staying at the inexpensive hotel in Kowloon where Bourne thought the impostor was staying. Her husband was embarrassed because she was in her curlers and bathrobe, going down the hallway screaming for the manager to fix the toilet and the phone.

ISHAAD (IA)

Last name of Azra and Zaya's mother.

———, ISHMAEL (BU)

Young black man who was a first head steward at Tranquility Inn. He was a fairly good fighter, taught by his father, the island champion; he wanted to attend the university in Barbados. Bourne enlisted him to help capture Carlos. He found Ishmael, badly beaten and bloody, on the altar in the chapel; he thought he'd been responsible for killing Ishmael. John St. Jacques had Ishmael flown to the hospital in Martinique, and Bourne promised to provide the money for his college education.

ISLES, ISRAEL (MC)

West Indian MI6 agent who worked for Roger Symonds; he was a young married man who had never killed anyone. During training he had studied some of Scofield's work.

IVY THE TERRIBLE (IA)

Frank Swann's secretary. She mistakenly arranged an appointment for a staffer doing confidential work for Allison. She was married and didn't want her husband to know about her old boyfriend in Allison's office.

———, JACK (BS)

Friend and/or neighbor of David Webb. He had the key to Webb's house and Webb intended to ask him to periodically check on the house while he was gone. May be the same Jack at the Scully Agency.

———, JACK (CH)

Doorman at the Savoy Hotel in London; he knew McAuliff.

———, JACK (HC)

Doorman who worked from eight P.M. to four A.M. at Noel's apartment building in Manhattan. Jack discovered the identity of one of the men who had rearranged Noel's apartment. He was killed as he was attempting to give the information to Noel.

———, JACK (PM)

Chauffeur who drove the limousines for the White House. He was constantly submitted to the most stringent security checks, had no wife or children, and was a combat veteran with extensive experience in guerrilla warfare and diversionary tactics; his job was to guard his passengers with his life. He frequently chauffeured General Halyard and Ambassador Brooks; he was flattered that Brooks always remembered his name. When Parsifal was mentioned, he remembered the music appreciation course he had taken in college while attending on an athletic scholarship.

JACKSON, ——— (PM)

One of the guards on Poole's Island. He had a habit of showing up late. He was captured by Havelock and left tied up in the woods.

JACKSON, BEN (PM)
Friend of Dr. Randolph's. Ben worked for Talbot Insurance and had set up MacKenzie's insurance policy.

JACKSON, LEVI (OW)
Black who had played against Joe Cardone at the Yale Bowl. He said they could always shake up Cardone by yelling "tomato sauce."

———, JACQUES (CM)
The captain of the Lafayette Room in the Hay-Adams Hotel in Washington, D.C. He knew Phyllis Maxwell by sight.

———, JACQUES (HC)
One of the hotel employees at the d'Accord in Paris.

———, JAKE (IA)
Local cab driver who took Manny from the Mesa Verde house to Gee-Gee's.

JAMES, ADMIRAL (PM)
Commander Decker was supposed to meet Admiral James at the Fifth Naval District. Admiral James was told by Havelock that Decker was needed for more pressing naval business.

JAMISON, RALPH (T)
Design unit head of Genessee in Houston, a genius in metallurgy. Michael Ryan knew Jamison quite well; they'd both been called in on the SST mockup at Lockheed as consulting specialists. Jamison falsified designs to get Genessee $105 million of Defense funds; in return Genessee gave him a private bank account in Zurich. Jamison needed the money to take care of his three ex-wives and four children. Jamison did not do well in close personal relationships and loved good times and good liquor.

———, JANE (AP)
Lawrence Talbot's secretary. There may have been two different women working for Talbot, one named Jane and one named Janet, but in reality there may have been only one named Janet, the "t" being dropped off somewhere in the process of printing the book.

———, JANET (AP)
A shorthand expert who worked for Lawrence Talbot. (*See also* Jane.)

————, JANINE (AP)

Bertholdier's most extravagant and desirable mistress, his "Egyptian," so called because of her raven hair and brown eyes; he had installed her in an expensive flat along a clean, tree-lined boulevard in Paris. She was a highly sexual twenty-five-year-old who loved money and fast cars and having her body penetrated sexually. She acted as though she had been smoking marijuana, but may have been drugged by the men who kidnapped Bertholdier; she was found unharmed later, bound naked on the bed with the word "whore" in lipstick across her breasts. All she could tell the police was that the men mentioned an airplane trip.

JANSENS (T)

Old Washington cronies of Trevayne's from his State Department days.

JAX, M.D., IVAN (BU)

Black doctor in Falls Church used by the CIA, introduced to Conklin by Cactus. He and Conklin were museum aficionados. He had trained at the Yale Medical School, Massachusetts General, and had a College of Surgeons appointment. He was Jamaican by birth. He had been married for twelve years and had several children. He was indebted to Cactus for making out the papers necessary to get his brother and sister out of Jamaica, and took good care of Cactus after Cactus was shot at Swayne's country estate.

————, JEAN-PIERRE (BI)

Common French male name, used by David Webb while he had severe amnesia and until he discovered the name Jason Bourne at the Gemeinschaft Bank. It is also the name of the young man who lived above the kitchen in the café; the young man rented out his room to the Marquis de Chamford at various times.

JEAN-PIERRE SANGSUE (BI)

"Jean-Pierre the Leech," name given to David Webb by the fishermen who worked for Claude Lamouche because he had replaced the brother of one of the men for a week, taking the man's wages.

————, JEANINE (CH)

Daniel's secretary, a black girl in her late twenties. Although the office was in a very isolated area, she had a typewriter and a pushbutton telephone.

———, JEANNIE (MP)

Prostitute in her late teens or early twenties who worked at Carmount Country Club; Stockton sent her to Matlock's room for entertainment, for which she would collect fifty dollars. She was slim and attractive and had pale blue eyes; at one time she had been a drug addict. Nimrod forced her to continue working for them by threatening to ruin her life or that of her friends. She was going to graduate from Madison University in two months and leave the country.

———, JEBEDIAH (RO)

Tourist in front of the Supreme Court building, trying to move around the Wopotami dance group.

JENKINS, OFFICER (OW)

CIA agent who had been undercover as a local policeman in Saddle Valley for more than a year before the main part of Operation Omega began. He was a bachelor. One of his jobs was to protect Tanner's family; this was complicated by his job with MacAuliff. The weekend Tanner's house was shot up, Jenkins and McDermott were not on duty with the local police. Jenkins found Tanner at the old deserted depot after Tanner had shot Fassett and MacAuliff. Jenkins was the senior officer at "Leather" and the only person there who knew about Fassett's defection.

JENKINS, CAPTAIN (SI)

Captain in B Company, Fourteenth Battalion, Twenty-seventh Division, Third Corps. He did not like Second Lieutenant Ulster Scarlett because he was very good at issuing orders but not executing them himself; he also had been pursued by officers wanting to have their pictures taken with him. Jenkins was amazed when Scarlett offered to go out on patrol by himself instead of leading four men; he hoped Scarlett wouldn't return. Scarlett faked an attack on the Germans (they were already dead), carried their helmets back to the lieutenant, and then went out to attack them again—by himself. Scarlett didn't come back, but met Strasser and the two of them left the area. He stayed away from his company until the cease-fire had been declared, then returned to watch Jenkins leading a memorial service for him.

JENNER, JAMES (RE)

Father of Leslie Jenner. He loved his racing horses.

JENNER, LESLIE (RE)

Leslie Hawkwood's maiden name.

JENNER, MADGE (RE)

Wife of James Jenner and mother of Leslie. Leslie had sent them a Christmas card but had not come home for a visit. Madge did not approve of her stepsister marrying a Jew.

——, JENNIE (CM)

Chancellor interrupted a telephone call between Jennie and another teenage girl in order to reach Longworth.

JENNINGS, LANGFORD (IA)

U.S. President. "The man from Idaho was tall and attractive, with a smile that had not been seen since Eisenhower or Shirley Temple, full of anecdotes and homilies that espoused the old values of strength, courage, self-reliance and . . . freedom of choice." His family had money; his father had been an Iowa farmer who bought "forty-eight thousand acres in the mountains that developers sold their souls for." When he found out that Bollinger had been used by the campaign contributors, he told Bollinger that he absolutely would not be his running mate in November. He told Mitch to let Kendrick go after Hamendi but not to let him get hurt, because he wanted Kendrick back for Vice President. Kendrick found out Jennings was more intelligent and moral than he thought, especially after he saw Jennings's reaction to the information about Inver Brass.

JENSEN, PETER (CH)

British expert in ore minerals. He and his wife worked as a team; they were childless. They were in their early fifties, financially secure, and genuinely interested in each other and their work. Warfield described them as "quite active in leftish political circles." Jensen smoked a pipe and was confident and good-natured. Warfield wanted the Jensens to keep McAuliff under close observation and report back to him; he wanted to know who his enemy was in the Cock Pit. When Warfield found the Jensens, they had been caught turning over information from covert geological operations to the Soviets. They agreed to work for him, as he persuaded the Crown to drop all charges against them. They were to continue their professional work and do certain assignments for him, for which they were well paid. It was Jensen who recommended McAuliff to Warfield as director of the survey party. When it was evident that McAuliff might be working with British Intelligence, Warfield asked Jensen to kill him, as soon as he found out who McAuliff's contacts were; Jensen had never killed anyone before and didn't want to kill McAuliff. He and his wife disappeared from camp just before it was attacked by Warfield's men, then turned up at Peale Court, shot Warfield to death, and left on a flight to the Mediterranean.

JENSEN, PHIL (RG)

Second-in-command at the Federal Prosecutor's Office. He joined the prosecutor's office with an eye to one day becoming a state senator. He had been working unsuccessfully for three years to catch Dellacroce.

JENSEN, RUTH L. WELLS (CH)

British paleontologist in her early fifties, married to Peter Jensen. She used R. L. Wells as her professional name. She and Peter enjoyed money and security beyond the reach of most academic couples. Warfield suggested they might be interested in Peale Court—she was. They both loved Jamaica. She also thought Charles Whitehall was impressive and Peter a bit envious of him. She didn't want Peter to shoot McAuliff; she was afraid for him. When Peter didn't return to camp, she quietly disappeared, probably meeting Peter before traveling to Peale Court and their meeting with Warfield.

———, JEREMY (BI)

Fictional nephew of Margaret and the Yachtsman at the Treadstone house in New York City.

———, JESSE (SI)

Customs inspection guard. Jesse ordered Canfield to sign the search papers for the load of liquor that was being unloaded illegally on the pier at New York.

JESUIT (BI)

Nickname given to David Abbott by Margaret. They had known each other a very long time.

THE JEWS OF HAR SHA'ALAV (HC)

"Har Sha'alav. The kibbutz in Israel with but one requirement for residency: The applicant has to be the sole survivor of a family destroyed in the camps." The kibbutz had more than two hundred men who could be called by Falkenheim to fight the false Wolfsschanze. These men were "potential suicide squads committed to the destruction of anything related to the swastika." The elder of Har Sha'alav had decided to get the Sonnenkinder lists and control the money in Geneva themselves. Johann had their houses bombed and their people massacred, particularly the elders and the men; he had it blamed on the Rache.

JIANG YU (BS)

Manager of a restaurant in Causeway Bay in Kowloon that specialized in French food and waiters who were as adept with guns as with food trays. He was slender with dark skin and his eyes were sloped as if he might be part Malaysian. He had been sent and paid well by a third party to reach the impostor through d'Anjou. Bourne learned of the contact in the Kam Pek casino in Macao from Yu.

———, JIM (IA)

Chief of intelligence at the San Diego air base; DeMartin called him about the message he found in his car.

———, JIM (MC)

Director of the CIA. He was on the current council of the Matarese; Scofield killed him when he tried to escape from Appleton Hall. The media reported that he had died in an airplane crash in Colorado.

———, JIM (MP)

One of the men who worked for Blackstone, Inc., and relayed messages to Matlock.

———, JIM (OW)

CIA agent, massive, over six feet tall. Disguised as a chauffeur, he followed Cardone and delivered a message to him from Da Vinci. He dropped off the Rolls because Cardone got the license plate number, then headed for Washington. He also delivered a message to Bernie Osterman about John Tanner.

———, JIM-BOB (BU)

A young, uneducated country man who worked as a guard at General Swayne's estate. He was content to accept Bourne's three hundred dollars, but was still concerned about the welfare of the guard dogs.

JIMBO-MON (CH)

Whitehall's name for James Ferguson. McAuliff and Lawrence also used it at different times.

———, JIMMY (MC)

Jimmy had been working at Massachusetts General when the three nurses died in the freak boating accident.

JITAI, ——— (BS)

Banker with the Tuen Mun branch of the Hang Chow Bank. Mr. Chang called him when Marie was attacked by the young men. Jitai and the other Chinese were embarrassed by their behavior and did all they could to help Marie, guarding her hotel room and forming barriers between her and the people who were chasing her. Jitai even led a funeral parade; he explained the people were always ready for this kind of action to protect Chinese coming across the border from the north to join their families.

———, Joe (IA)

1. Gerald Bryce told Kendrick he was Joe, a State Department aide, on the flight from Washington to Sicily.

2. Intelligence officer in the Bahamas who protected Evan and Khalehla with his own body when he thought they were in danger.

3. CIA man who went from Mesa Verde to the airport to meet Evan and Khalehla.

———, Joey (BI)

White moving-man who worked for Belkins Moving and Storage. He was killed by Carlos or one of his men inside the Treadstone house.

———, Joey (T)

Worked for Augie de Spadante. He drove Augie and Mario out to Barnegat to kill Trevayne. Bonner captured him and took him inside to wait for the police.

———, Johann (AP)

Dark-haired English-speaking young German who was studying to be a lawyer. Johann secured Joel a room at his boardinghouse in Bonn and helped get the wire from Laskaris at the American Express office. Johann also sets up an appointment for him at the Bank aus der Bonner Sparkasse so he can get the funds deposited there for him. When Joel and Johann leave the bank, there is a great commotion outside; the newspaper headline tells of the murder of Walter Peregrine, and there is a photo of Joel on the front page. Johann is very frightened, but reads the article to Joel; Joel tells him what he can, gives him the money he promised him for helping him, and tells him to tell the truth, as it is his best defense. Johann believes Joel has been telling him the truth and does not interfere with him as Joel leaves the area.

———, Johann (BI)

When David Webb (as Cain) was looking for M. Chernak in the apartment house on Lowenstrasse, someone called down and asked if he was Johann. A man named Johann was one of Carlos's men; he was left behind to tend a wounded man at the Stepdeckstrasse. He appeared in

Paris at the Valois Bank, looking for Webb, and again inside the back of the armored van from the bank. When he tried to shoot Webb from the back of the van, Webb shot and killed him.

————, **JOHN (HC)**

Anchorman of local New York radio station. He was interviewing Richard Dunlop, who was at the scene of Peter Baldwin's murder.

————, **JOHNNY (BS)**

One of the CIA men guarding David Webb at his home and university campus in Maine.

————, **JOHNNY (MP)**

One of the black students at Lumumba Hall that Matlock knew. He answered the door the night Matlock was invited to the initiation ceremony.

————, **JOHNNY (RE)**

Lyons's bodyguard and male nurse, an ex-Marine paid by Meridian Aircraft. If Lyons's life was threatened, Johnny intended to take him out of Buenos Aires. He was angry when he and Hal had to take off their weapons at Terrazza Verde and trust the Germans to guard them. He was killed by the Haganah with Hal.

JOHNNY REB (AP)

Former CIA operative, expatriate living in Bern, Switzerland, on money deposited in Swiss bank accounts by the U. S. government. He has a heavy southern accent, and is fluent in German and perhaps knew French. He says that Stone saved him three different times. Stone says he was too valuable to lose over a minor indiscretion.

Stone tells him as much as he feels he can about the Aquitaine situation. He mentions Washburn, and Johnny gives him additional information about him. Stone wants to hire Johnny to grab Washburn and drug him so they can find out where Connal is. However, he doesn't want Washburn to remember he had been questioned. Johnny plays the part of Thomas Thayer, an old friend of Washburn's mother's, to enable him to get close enough to administer drugs, then takes Washburn out to the waiting taxi and doctor. They question Washburn in the taxi.

Johnny was obviously a master of his craft. He was not a young man anymore. (Ludlum calls him elderly.) There were times when he let his team, all younger men, take over the action as they were taking over Scharhorn. He is described as having a flowing white mane and bushy white eyebrows when he was playing the part of Thomas Thayer, southern gentleman, but that may have been partly disguise. He is still young enough to be interested in Anne in North Carolina. He loves using southern dialogue and tacking names on people (for example, catfish). Even though he is an expatriate, he is still very much an American.

JOHNSON, ——— (BI)
Name used by David Webb when he called Belkins Moving and Storage to get information so he could get into the Treadstone house.

JOHNSON, ——— (BS)
Teaching associate of David Webb's. He'd been out for nearly a month with pneumonia.

JOHNSONS (MP)
The Johnsons from Canton, Ohio, liked to gamble; they frequented the Hartford Hunt Club.

JONES, MR. (BU)
Name given to John St. Jacques by the CIA at Sterile Five.

———, JUAN (HC)
Attaché with the office of the Brazilian consul general. The consul general used Juan's office while meeting with Noel.

———, JULES (BI)
One of the men in Paris who was hired indirectly by Carlos to follow David Webb out of the garage in Montmartre. He was a short, stocky man and inexperienced; Webb spotted him, captured him and his companion, and forced Jules to drive him to the meeting point with Alexander Conklin. Webb obtained the contact's telephone number from him and left the two of them stranded in an isolated area.

———, JULIA (T)
Large black Haitian maid who worked for Roderick Bruce.

JUNEAU ET CIE. (AP)
Jacques-Louis Bertholdier was the director of this conservative firm on the Bourse des Valeurs, Paris's stock exchange.

KABEL, ——— (AP)
Kabel was the code name of the old man left in Valerie's apartment by Hermione Geyner's group. Supposedly someone from the Aquitaine

showed up, looking for Valerie or Joel, and Kabel killed him by garroting him, then dragged his corpse down the fire escape, into the alley, and then into a basement behind an unused furnace. Geyner's group thought they were still fighting for the German underground; actually their group was being manipulated by Aquitaine and the man was elderly, so there is some reason to wonder if this killing ever really occurred.

KAHOUTEK, JANOS (PM)

Kahoutek had a farm in Mason Falls, Pennsylvania, with high fences, electric alarm systems, and barbed wire. He provided papers and jobs for the people he was sent by Handelman; for these services the people would pay a high price for the rest of their lives. Kahoutek was not tall, a bull of a man, with heavy shoulders, jowls, deep-set eyes, close to seventy— "Czech by birth, Moravian by conviction." Havelock convinced Kahoutek that he'd paid Handelman a large sum for Jenna and that Kahoutek would also collect money for transporting them to New York. Havelock and Jenna overcame Kahoutek and his driver inside their van and left them tied up inside their van along a country road. Later the federal authorities captured Kahoutek and made a case-by-case determination for each of the people found hidden at the farm.

KALIG, SHEIKH MUSTAFA (BI)

The unpopular sheikh of Oman was killed during an alleged aborted coup; the coup story was the cover for his assassination, probably by his own men, as he was heavily guarded at all times. Webb (as Cain) was given credit for the kill; however, neither the Americans nor Carlos believed he was responsible for it.

KALYAZIN, ALEXEI (PM)

(See also Zelienski, Leon.) Clinical psychotherapist who wrote definitive studies evaluating the effects of prolonged periods of stress on humans. His job with the KGB was to look for deviations by people in the field that might indicate they were double agents or no longer capable of functioning in their jobs. He convinced Alexander and Matthias that he was defecting and asked for their help. They assisted him and he spent the next six years spying on the U.S. for the Soviets. When the Soviets wanted to set up another Bay of Pigs incident and blame Matthias for it, Kalyazin decided to sever his ties with Russia and disappear. If Matthias and Alexander refused to help him again, he would reveal how they had betrayed their country by helping a Soviet agent.

KARAS, JENNA (PM)

Love of Havelock's life. She had long blond hair, clear brown eyes, and a slender body; she was about five feet five. In 1968 her parents were dead and she was living with her two older brothers in Ostrava. The younger one was crushed beneath a Soviet tank; the older one, an engineer, was interrogated and tortured by the Soviets, leaving him a total cripple. He shot himself in the head and his wife disappeared. Jenna left Prague and went underground to fight the Soviets. She had been an agent for ten years when Havelock met her. She was warned by Bradford to follow instructions, that Havelock had sold out to the Soviets; she didn't trust him and ran. She hid in various areas of Europe; when she saw Havelock in Rome, she ran again, thinking he was still trying to find her and kill her. She ran to Régine Broussac for help; Régine sent her to Handelman in America. Handelman sent her on to Kahoutek, who was holding her prisoner when Havelock arrived. When Havelock came into the cell after her, she attacked him with a fork. He was able to convince her they were both being hunted and that he'd come to help her get away so they could find out why. After they escaped from Kahoutek and Havelock made contact with the President on Poole's Island, Jenna and Havelock worked together to find Parsifal and the documents. When it was over, she and Havelock moved to New Hampshire, where she worked on the student foreign exchange committee at Concord University.

KARASOVA, JENNA (PM)
Russian version of Jenna Karas's name.

———, KARINE (MC)
Scofield's wife for twenty-seven months. Taleniekov's group had lured her across a checkpoint into East Berlin and killed her; Scofield had killed Taleniekov's brother.

KASSEL, HEINRICH (MC)
Patent attorney, a "partner in a firm that did legal work for many of Essen's prominent companies." Taleniekov had tried to enlist him for Moscow; they had gotten drunk together and Taleniekov altered the KGB file on him to state that he was working with the Americans. It had been twelve years since Taleniekov had seen him, but Kassel helped Taleniekov with his search for the descendants of Voroshin. Kassel was killed by the Matarese.

KAYANAKA, HIRU (GC)
Attaché, Japanese Embassy, Berlin. He complained to Reichsoffiziel Probst that the Japanese scientists were being sent everywhere in Germany except where they were supposed to be.

KEARNS, ——— (IA)
Policeman in Arlington that Paddy O'Reilly knew well.

KEMPSON, ALICE (GC)

Wife of Paul Kempson. She indulged in inane small talk with Victor Fontine at the birthday party on Long Island.

KEMPSON, PAUL (GC)

President of Centaur Electronics, well thought of by the Pentagon, a guest at Andrew and Adrian's birthday party on Long Island. He told Andrew that Andrew had a place with Centaur if he ever decided to leave the military.

KENDALL, WALTER (RE)

CPA, an antisocial individualist who was a brilliant statistician. His whole purpose in life was to outmaneuver other human beings. He owned a New York auditing firm and made a great deal of money, which he hoarded; he was unmarried and had few friends. Kendall was forty-six, of medium size, severely asthmatic, with ferretlike eyes, thinning, unwashed hair, a rasping voice, dirty fingernails, bad teeth, and heavy body odor which he tried to conceal with bay rum. His suits were ill-fitting and soiled and bagged at the knees and buttocks. He was good at manipulating projections and statistics and deception; he was the American negotiator for the exchange because he was also good at spotting other people's deceptions. Kendall and Swanson planned the details of the exchange, although Kendall didn't know why the Germans wanted the diamonds and was afraid of Swanson; Swanson intended to have Kendall killed after the exchange. Kendall flew to Buenos Aires but left quickly after Spaulding told him he thought the Gestapo was trying to stop the exchange. For his part in the exchange, Kendall had to sell his assets and spend the rest of his life as a highly skilled government clerk.

KENDRICK, CONGRESSMAN EVAN (IA)

First-year member of the House of Representatives, representing the Ninth District in Colorado. The only reason he ran for office was to get rid of the corrupt incumbents. He was financially very well off; he was an architect and had owned his own business, the Kendrick Group, which built all varieties of structures in the Middle East. He was fluent in many Arabic dialects. Manny was his chief architect, best friend, and the only father he had ever known. Evan's real father had died building a bridge in Nepal when Evan was eight. Evan was a tall, slender, blue-eyed, rather muscular man in his early forties. He had not gone to Vietnam because he had a graduate school deferment, but he did know how to shoot a gun. His annual vacation was spent white-water rafting in Colorado. Evan had returned to the United States four years earlier, after the Mahdi's people sabotaged a building containing the Kendrick Group

Somewhere in Turkey (I EDITED OUT THIS CHAPTER FROM THE ICARUS AGENDA)

employees and their families. When the terrorists captured the American embassy in Oman, Kendrick volunteered to go into Oman and capture the Mahdi, who was controlling the terrorists. Frank Swann let him go in under deep cover but disavowed any connection between Kendrick and the government; Kendrick himself insisted on anonymity. Kendrick was captured by the Mahdi, and Manny and the Masada Brigade team rescued Kendrick and captured the Mahdi. A year later Kendrick was asked to join prestigious congressional committees although he was an unknown; then news leaked out about his activities in Oman. He was awarded the Medal of Freedom by Jennings and Bollinger's people tried to get rid of him. It was discovered that Inver Brass knew Bollinger's group was corrupt and worked to get Bollinger out and Kendrick in as Vice President. After Bollinger's group was ousted, Jennings wanted Kendrick on his ticket and very reluctantly agreed to let Kendrick go back to Oman undercover to get rid of Hamendi. Kendrick killed Hamendi and returned to accept the nomination and marry Khalehla Rashad.

KENDRICK GROUP (IA)

Architectural company owned and operated by Evan Kendrick in the Middle East. They built everything from water systems to bridges. Manny was one of the chief architects.

KEPPLER, ———— (CH)

Member of Dunstone, Ltd., who had reservations at the Trident Villas. When he discovered Lufthansa would be late getting into Montego Bay, he radioed Durrell to get a charter flight for him.

KESSLER, ERICH (HC)

One of Heinrich Clausen's two associates in the scheme to establish the Fourth Reich. His two sons, Erich and Hans, were Sonnenkinder. The elder Kessler was killed by the Wolfsschanze.

KESSLER, PROFESSOR ERICH (HC)

Elder son of Erich Kessler. Erich was a professor of history at the Free University of Berlin; he was a recognized scholar, not a physical or violent man. He spoke fluent English in a deep, soft voice and appeared gentle and good-natured. He was in his mid-forties with a large girth and a full face framed by a short beard and thick brown hair combed straight back over his head; he wore glasses over his deep-set eyes. His father was shot to death by the false Wolfsschanze, and his mother died in July 1945 after a prolonged stay in the hospital. He and his brother Hans moved in with their mother's brother, an older man who had no liking for the Nazis. He said he had been married once, but his wife left him to marry an acrobat. Noel caught Kessler lying to him, yet he went to the bank with him to sign the release for the funds.

KESSLER, HANS (HC)

Younger son of Erich Kessler; his brother was Erich. Hans was a highly respected specialist in internal medicine in Munich. "Hans was a medium-size bull with enormous charm. A superb soccer player . . ." He was nearly Johann's equal. Willie Ellis ripped Hans's stomach apart with his bare hands; the first deputy's personal physician stitched him up. Although he had internal bleeding, he accompanied Johann to the meeting with Althene. Johann killed Hans to prevent him from killing Althene's driver and to dispose of Hans, since he couldn't be taken to a hospital for treatment.

KHAKI, ABDUL (RO)

Abdul was not a U.S. citizen but had never lived in the Middle East. He had numerous holding companies offshore and was as devious as Ivan Salamander, plus he had immunity from prosecution. Abdul agreed to consolidate many of Vinnie's 4,212 bank accounts into a blind trust for him and invest the rest in holding companies. Vinnie checked with him to see how the market was being affected by the purchase of stocks in the defense industry.

KHOURI, ——— (IA)

Old Khouri killed Jews, blew up kibbutzim and a hotel in Haifa. Aman was upset because the Jews hanged him.

KINDORF, ERICH (SI)

Merchant who supported the Nazis, supplying coal from the Ruhr Valley. Kindorf and von Schnitzler had secret conferences with Krupp, trying to draw him onto their side.

KING, ARTIE (MP)

Artie's job was to mow the lawns of the Carmount Country Club. When he dropped dead from a heart attack, the owner gave the family a large sum of money and set up a charge account at the local grocery for them.

KIRCHER, ——— (SI)

Kroeger's driver from Lisieux to Montbeliard for his meeting with the Nazi leaders.

———, KLAUS (AP)

Name given by Johnny Reb to the driver of the limousine he used while kidnapping and drugging Norman Washburn; it probably was not the man's real name. Johnny was known for using nicknames.

KLUGE, ——— (HC) [REAL PERSON]

One of the German army officers implicated in the assassination attempt on Hitler. He was shot as a traitor.

KNAPP, SENATOR ALAN (T)

Member of the Senate confirmation panel for the chairmanship of the Defense Allocation Subcommittee. He'd been in the Senate for seven years and had a reputation for uncompromising investigation and rudeness; he was known as the "unpredictable skeptic of the Senate." Knapp was in his mid-forties, with straight black hair combed carefully back from a wide forehead. He was allied with de Spadante and Genessee and worked with Cooper, Norton, Madison, Webster, Green, and Hamilton; he wanted to kill Trevayne. Knapp's job was to spread the rumor that the President would not seek a second term because of a severe illness.

KNOWLTON, PETER (BI)

An Associate Director of the CIA. He was in his mid-fifties but dressed like an Ivy Leaguer of thirty years earlier. His information placed David Webb (as Cain) in Brussels killing a covert dealer in diamonds at the same time he was killing Chernak in Switzerland.

——, KNUTE (RO)

One of the guards Aaron hired to prevent Hawkins from reaching Sam. He liked the porterhouse steaks that Cora char-broiled. He was overcome by the two Desis and left tied up, in his shorts, in an Oldsmobile in front of Nanny's. Aaron paid and fired him.

KOENIG, —— (BI)

Receptionist in charge of signature verifications on accounts at the Gemeinschaft Bank in Zurich. He was a middle-aged man with close-cropped hair and tortoiseshell glasses. He was employed by Carlos. He was responsible for changing the telephone number on the fiche for the transfer of funds to the Valois Bank, and he deactivated the scanning equipment in the elevator so Carlos's men could get through. He was killed in an auto accident set up by Carlos, and he was tied into a massive theft of money from the bank along with Marie St. Jacques.

KOENIG, HEINRICH (RG)

Heinrich lived like a country squire in a little village twenty miles from Berlin. Heinrich had gained his wealth from being a "double agent-cum-blackmailer." He used the money thus gained to build his business empire. Hawkins had a file of the several hundred people Heinrich had blackmailed, and threatened to furnish them simultaneously with enough information to bankrupt and jail Heinrich. Heinrich agreed to donate $10 million to the Shepherd Company.

KOENING, —— (RE)

Owner of the diamond mines in South Africa. He didn't want to deal with the Nazis.

KONIG, —— (AP)

One of the Aquitaine soldiers who attempted to kill Joel Converse outside Frau Geyner's house near Osnabruck; Joel shot and killed him instead.

KONSOLIKOV, —— (BU)

Father of Alexander Conklin. He and his wife were Russian immigrants and they settled in a Russian-speaking neighborhood. Late in his life he became a highly successful merchant, owning seven supermarkets in upscale malls—called them "Conklin's Corners." He had seen the name Conklin on a billboard and adopted it in place of Konsolikov. When Alex was a young man, his father was in his eighties. He was an ardent supporter of Joseph McCarthy, and he was very bigoted—he hated the Jews. He made an unrealistic bid to expand his stores, overextended himself, and lost six of his stores. He then had a massive stroke and died just as Alex's adult life was beginning.

KONSOLIKOV, ALEKSEI NIKOLAS (BU)

Alexander Conklin's name at birth. Krupkin knew about Conklin's Russian background. Conklin's parents were immigrants and he grew up in a Russian neighborhood and attended a Russian-speaking church school in the U.S.

KRAMER, JEFF (MP)

Old Carlyle graduate friend of Matlock's. He had a degree in psychology and worked for an impressive public relations firm. He also had an expensive wife and expensive kids in private schools; he agreed to loan Matlock his car for a week for four hundred dollars.

KREPPS, ——— (CM)

"Krepps" was a floating cover, a name with a biography "used by various agents at various times for clandestine operations." One of the men accompanying Varak into the Flags section of the FBI the night of Hoover's death used the name Krepps. Varak later felt it was necessary to kill this person to prevent a leak.

KREPPS, HEINRICH (RE)

Director of Schreibwaren, the largest printing complex in Germany. Schreibwaren had processed all the blueprints for Peenemünde.

KRESSEL, SAMUEL (MP)

Dean of colleges at Carlyle. He had a sardonic, slightly offensive sense of humor and was obnoxious and antagonistic. Sam could not believe that Nimrod was centered at Carlyle. Sam was asked to act as liaison between Matlock and the Narcotics Bureau. After Loring was killed, Sam notified Washington and went down to the police station to meet Matlock. Sam was afraid Matlock might be killed because he was in a position for which he was not trained; he was also afraid that Matlock's inquiries would tear the campus apart. Sam and his wife were killed by Nimrod's people but their death was reported as a murder and a suicide.

KROEGER, HEINRICH (SI)

The original Heinrich Kroeger was a young German corporal shot in the head by Ulster Scarlett in France. Ulster then shot back at his own troops to make them think they were being attacked. Gregor Strasser watched Scarlett, then joined him to desert until the war was over. When Ulster returned to the States, he and Strasser corresponded, Ulster using the name Kroeger. After Andrew was born, Ulster disappeared into Germany and assumed a more active role with the Nazis. The Germans knew him as Heinrich Kroeger but also knew he was a rich American with rich friends who supported their cause. With the exception of Goebbels, Ulster killed the few people who knew his true identity. When it was evident that Germany would lose the war, Kroeger tried to defect to the Americans; Canfield shot him as a traitor to both sides.

KRONESCHA, LODZIA (MC)

"Lodzia was a ranking mathematician, a doctoral graduate from Moscow University, and trained in the Lenin Institute. She was among the most knowledgeable computer programmers in the field." She had been blackmailed into cooperating with the Americans because of pictures showing her brother in sexual acts. Vasili followed her and confronted her, then sent word to Washington that he would expose Blackburn's indiscretions. She was not bothered anymore, and she and Vasili became lovers. Lodzia had long light brown hair, an aquiline face, and hazel-green eyes. Vasili killed a soldier of the Matarese in her apartment and hid him in another part of the building. He made the mistake of telling her about the Matarese; the Matarese tortured her before killing her.

KRUPKIN, DMITRI "KRUPPIE" (BU)

KGB officer who was asked by Cassett to assist Conklin and Bourne because the U.S. couldn't. He had been in the KGB for twenty-five or twenty-six years and was stationed in Paris; he spoke English (with a heavy accent) and fluent French. He was in his sixties, and appeared taller and fuller of figure than he actually was. He had a pleasant, somewhat fleshy face, full eyebrows, salt-and-pepper hair, chin beard, and blue eyes.

He worked hard for Moscow and was better than eighty percent of the people in the business; he really wanted to be appointed to the Presidium or even the Central Committee. He was obsessed with money—could be bought—had been bought, but not by Carlos. Conklin was paying him with some of David Webb's money. He warned Conklin and Bourne not to talk about his profitable connections with the West while they were in Russia.

He and his two commissars had a secret private apartment in Dzerzhinsky Square that they used as headquarters. He had Rodchenko under surveillance, and Rodchenko was monitoring all of Krupkin's calls. Krupkin wanted to see the Jackal killed. At the armory Krupkin's right shoulder is half blown away by the Jackal. Krupkin makes a deal with Bourne to get him into the compound at Novgorod, and then makes arrangements for Bourne to get out of Russia. Because he let Bourne live, he had to flee for his life. He knew how to get out, but it was dirty and expensive. He had to construct another identity so he could start a new life in the West.

KRUPP, GUSTAVE (SI)

The only man in Germany who lived in complete political isolation, the most feared and revered man in all Europe. He was fighting desperately to remain neutral for fear of a Weimar takeover. If the conferences with Kindorf and von Schnitzler were made known, Krupp had sworn to expose them.

KRUPSKAYA, ALEKSIE (MC)

Once "the greatest teacher in the KGB, a man of infinite talent for killing and survival . . . the last of the notorious Istrebiteli . . ." He had hidden documents that guaranteed him a personal old age; Aleksie had used those documents to get his son promoted to Premier of the Soviet Union. Aleksie was Taleniekov's teacher; he was dying when he sent for Taleniekov and told him about the Matarese and convinced him to work with Scofield.

KRYLOVICH, NIKOLAI (MC)

VKR agent who could not have killed Blackburn because he had been stationed at the Manchurian border for eleven months.

KWAN SOO (BU)

A sixteen- or seventeen-year-old Cambodian boy who acted as Bourne's point in Medusa. He ran drugs and something went wrong with the deal, so someone from Saigon decided to kill him as an example to others. Kwan had been sending the drug money back to three different villages so they wouldn't starve to death.

LA FONTAINE, ——— (BU)

Last name of the immigration official at Marseilles; he offered to be Marie Webb's guide.

LA TONA, ——— (SI)

Mafia member, a sneak killer who worked for Don Vitone Genovese; he tried to kill Canfield at the docks in New York. Canfield killed him, dropped him into the river, and escaped.

LABISHE, ——— (SI)

Labishe had worked for Bertholde for fifteen years as his chauffeur, but Labishe also worked for the Nazis. Bertholde disobeyed Munich by having the Rawlinses killed in the U.S.; Kroeger ordered Labishe to kill him. Labishe killed Bertholde in his office, then was flown out of the country.

LACATA, JIMMY (MP)

Jimmy owned a gambling casino in Middletown.

LACHMANN, ——— (AP)

Obese bank executive at the Bank aus der Bonner Sparkasse in Bonn. He was willing to conduct Joel's transaction within thirty minutes instead of several hours when presented with a twelve thousand deutsche mark bribe by Joel. Joel was dressed in a conservative business suit when Lachmann saw him, which is the description Lachmann probably gave to the police after the murder of Walter Peregrine.

LACKLAND, ——— (AP)

Nathan Simon registered Peter Stone under the name Lackland for his flight from New Jersey to Manchester, New Hampshire, to see Supreme Court Justice Andrew Wellfleet about legal and other procedures to use against Aquitaine.

———, LACY (BS)

Young American lady shopping with Buzz in Hong Kong. She was a business major in college.

LAFFERTY, BRIDGET (RO)

Youngest child of Erin and Paddy Lafferty. She was baby-sitting Dennis's children while their parents were on a cruise. She couldn't find the refrigerator.

LAFFERTY, DENNIS (RO)

Second oldest son of Erin and Paddy Lafferty. Dennis was a big accountant who did their taxes for them. He was married and his kids were staying with Bridget while he and his wife were on a cruise.

LAFFERTY, ERIN (RO)

Wife of Paddy Lafferty. She was plumpish with an Irish brogue, a fussy grandmother. She liked working with the Jewish people because they knew where to get the best meat and freshest vegetables. She hoped that Joshua Birnbaum and her daughter, Bridget, would get married one day. She was quite willing to help Aaron and his group and looked after Sam's mother.

LAFFERTY, PADDY (RO)

Aaron's chauffeur. Paddy was sixty-three and his red hair was now partially gray. Paddy had been a gunnery sergeant at Omaha Beach in World War II. Hawkins had led his division for ten days in France and made Patton look like a ballet dancer. Paddy was very fond of Sam and devoted to his protection, especially since Sam knew Hawkins. Paddy and the members of the Pat O'Brien Commemorative Post were delighted to be asked to help Hawkins at the Four Seasons Hotel.

LAFOLLET, AMOS (MC)

Black-bearded MIT graduate student who was assisting Peg Flanagan's girlfriend in the personnel record section of Massachusetts General. He helped Scofield locate the names of the nurses and doctors who attended Senator Joshua Appleton after his accident; he also procured Appleton's dental X-rays and flew a second set to Scofield from Washington.

LAMOUCHE, CLAUDE (BI)

Fisherman who had an infected leg and was treated by Dr. Geoffrey Washburn. Washburn made a deal with him to take David Webb (as Jean-Pierre) onto his boat for a week. The boat was filthy and oil-soaked, the captain, Lamouche, was a foul-mouthed tyrant, and both he and the other fishermen resented David on the boat. He ordered Webb off his boat after three of his men were seriously injured by Webb in a fight that they started.

LAND, MONSIGNOR (GC)

American priest from the archdiocese of New York. "Land was no more than fifty, of medium height, broad in the chest and shoulders. His features were sharp, Anglican; his eyes hazel, beneath generous eyebrows that were darker than his short, graying hair. It was a pleasant face with intelligent eyes." He had been in Rome for many years and then returned to the U.S. to visit Victor because of information he found in the Vatican archives—he was a student of political and social history. He had found little in the Vatican files, much more in the records of the Court of Reparations. From there he went through the sealed papers of

Donatti, which led him to Teague in London; Teague told him of the train to Salonika. He finally reached the elderly priest of Xenope, who told him about the Filioque denials. He met Theodore Dakakos in Istanbul and decided to work with him. Land's name was on Savarone's list of men to whom the vault of Constantine was to be delivered. Land decided not to accept the responsibility for the contents of the vault—he wanted to retain his faith.

LANDIS, LIEUTENANT (JG) WILLIAM MICHAEL (AP)

From his own testimony "U.S. Navy, a bachelor, twenty-eight; current address: Somerset Garden apartments, Vienna, Virginia . . . a computer programmer for the Department of the Navy, Sea-Armaments Procurements Division, stationed at the Pentagon, Arlington, Virginia . . . in command of most programming for Pentagon-Navy." He received a doctorate in advanced computer technology from the University of Michigan, College of Engineering. When given data on nine transfers concerning weapons and high-tech equipment, he was able to confirm six of these were initially related to Palo Alto International, owned by retired Army general Delavane; later he found ninety-seven more such illegal transfers, most involving Palo Alto. Honored in a private ceremony at the White House, but refused to accept the honor in deference to Joel Converse, the real hero.

LANDOR, AVERY (SI)

Texas oilman who supported the Nazis. Gibson and Landor between them accounted for nearly twenty percent of the oil interests in the American Southwest, to say nothing of their joint expansion in the Canadian Northwest Territories.

LANIER, WILLIAM (BS)

One of the CIA agents who had guarded and interrogated David Webb at the safe house in Langley after David was nearly killed by Carlos at the Treadstone house.

LAO SING (BS)

The Chinese delegation at the Kai-Tek airport was headed by Lao Sing, a ranking member of the Central Committee. Sheng hired the Bourne impostor to kill him because Sing objected to Sheng's policies openly on the Central Committee.

LARCH, JOHN (T)

Specialist in construction engineering picked by Trevayne to work on the subcommittee. "Larch was contemplative, sullen in appearance, thin-featured, and always seemingly tired. But there was nothing tired about Larch's mind." Larch was approached about the subcommittee's inquiries into Genessee and was offered a Caribbean holiday.

LAROUSSE, JEAN-PIERRE (BI)

A male name in France as common as John Smith in the U.S. The name was given by one of Carlos's men who rented a car at the de Gaulle airport; this man picked up three men who were trying to kill Webb (as Bourne) at the Valois Bank.

LARSON, DR. GEOFFREY (AP)

British computer expert brought in to get the list of Aquitaine members and agents at Scharhorn. He was a slender blond man in his mid-forties who wore tortoiseshell glasses. He went in with the assault team led by Johnny Reb, dressed as they were in "dark wool knit caps pulled down above their eyes and black turtleneck sweaters pulled up around their throats." Larson was the only one of the team who did not carry a gun and was not expected to climb or risk injury. When he did get onto the computer he realized the reels could not be released without an access code, which meant he needed Aquitaine's computer technician to get the codes. The technician is found, Joel forces the code from him, and Larson is able to transmit the needed information by satellite.

LASKARIS, KOSTAS (AP)

Chief manager of bank in Mykonos, Greece, who "greeted (Joel) cautiously over the phone, making it clear that he expected not only a passport that would clear a spectrograph but the original letter from Avery Preston Halliday with his signature, said signature to be subjected to a scanner, matching the signature the bank had been provided by the deceased Mr. Avery Preston Halliday."

"He was a balding, pleasant-faced man in his late fifties, with warm dark eyes, and relatively fluent in English but certainly not comfortable with the language." He represented Dr. Edward Beale on Mykonos—chosen as an intermediary, as he was a close friend of Beale's. He considers himself to be a good judge of character. He tells Joel about Dr. Beale, sets up the cash disbursement and the other bank accounts, and gives him Beale's telephone number.

Later, after all his other contacts have been killed, Joel tries to call Beale; a Greek police officer answers the phone. Joel calls Laskaris, who has the unpleasant duty of telling him about Dr. Beale's murder, which was made to look like a boating accident.

LATHAM, GERALD (CH)

He worked for the Jamaican ministry; he was Jamaican. He also worked with British intelligence, cooperated with Dunstone, Ltd. to get equipment for McAuliff, and belonged to Barak Moore's group of revolutionaries. He believed in Jamaica for Jamaicans. He lived in the Barbican district of Jamaica; Alison reached him easily by telephone at home.

LATHAM, HAROLD (GC)

Code name Pear, he worked with Apple to rescue Vittorio from Italy. He retired three days before the formal surrender of Germany in World War II. He had served the three years before that in the Burma theater, where he'd taken shrapnel in his back and stomach. He came to Loch Torridon to find Apple and celebrate the end of the war.

LATONA, ARTHUR (MP)

Latona was Nimrod from 1970 to 1971; he ordered Lucas Herron to make trips abroad, carrying money and drugs. Herron found it unbelievable that Latona was also the man who built the middle-income housing projects in Mount Holly. Herron told him he would give him his records if Latona kept him alive and comfortable for as long as possible. Latona died of a coronary before Herron died. Latona's wife was murdered in an "automobile accident" by the new Nimrod.

LATRONAS (OW)

Mafia friends of Joe Cardone's, in the construction business. Joe was their financial advisor.

LAVIER, DOMINIQUE (BU)

Younger sister of Jacqueline Lavier; they were very close in age and Dominique closely resembled Jacqueline. She was tall, slim, middle-aged, with green eyes. For years she had been a high-priced call girl, then had to live on the charity of her former lovers when her body gave out. When she took her sister's place at Les Classiques, she did not know her sister had been killed by Carlos. Her main job was courier for Carlos. She knew when Bourne captured her that Carlos would kill her if he could; she was interested in being free of him.

LAVIER, JACQUELINE (BI)

Managing partner of Les Classiques in Paris. She was a tall, imperious woman with a face that looked like a mask, streaked dark hair, but perfectly groomed. She was not a young woman, yet she wore much face powder and bright red lipstick and nail polish. She had a habit of patting her hair while she talked. She appeared to be a well-disciplined, efficient executive. She was an indirect relay to Carlos via Parc Monceau. She made the mistake of going to the Villiers home; she was killed in a confessional booth at the Church of the Blessed Sacrament by Carlos disguised as Father Manuel.

LAVIER, JACQUELINE (BU)

Bourne mistakenly identified Dominique as her sister Jacqueline.

LE CHAT ROUGE (HC)

("The Red Cat") Althene's French pilot and driver was known for his red beard and hair. He was stocky with thinning hair, smoked cigars, and spoke English with a heavy Alsace-Lorraine accent. He was used to dealing with secret cargoes and deliveries and knew how to negotiate, escape detection, and limit his risks. He protected Althene as well as he could. Althene waited for his call at the marina at Atterrisage Medoc; Johann left him there dead, his hands tied behind his back. He had been tortured and then shot.

LEACOCK, HAROLD (SI)

Englishman who was a big power on the British Stock Exchange and one of Bertholde's partners in a corporation; he supported the Nazis. Leacock owned one of the fourteen pieces of land in Switzerland where the Nazis intended to train their soldiers. Leacock also funneled money to the Irish rebellion, costing the lives of thousands of British soldiers.

LEATHER (OW)

Code name used by McDermott to contact Andrews at the CIA and the shortened code name for Saddle Valley.

LECONTE, ———— (BU)

Well-known Russian furniture designer. His furniture had no handles, but opened when you pressed certain spots. Confused with the *conte* from Italy.

LEE TENG (BS)

Hotel manager in Hong Kong, middle-aged with a balding head. He was in love with Catherine Staples, who was unaware of this until Marie pointed out how he had been protecting her in many ways at considerable risk to himself.

LEEB, ERNST (RE)

Nazi chief of the Army Ordnance Office. Ernst was a man of medium height, but excessively muscular well into his sixties. He smoked his cigarette through an ivory holder and had an imperious military bearing; Hitler liked him. The Ordnance Office was responsible for evaluating the mineral resources of occupied territories. He suggested an expeditionary force of four battalions to capture the diamond mines of South Africa. His suggestion was rejected as impractical.

LEFEVRE, ———— (HC)
Johann's backup man for the Tinamou registered at a hotel in Paris under the name LeFevre and hid some of his guns in that room.

LEFEVRE, SERGEANT MAJOR (AP)
A "short, middle-aged heavyset man with a gun" who worked for Prudhomme of the Sureté. Bertholdier court-martialed him in Algiers, sending him to the stockade for thirty-six months because he struck an officer who had brutally abused his men with excessive penalties for minor offenses. He was sent to arrest Bertholdier, who he knew would not want to accompany him peacefully; he persuaded him to do so by showing him a gun that would fire chemically treated darts that he intended to shoot into Bertholdier, causing his heart to burst; then he would take the photos they had taken of Bertholdier in the middle of a sexual act, and show the world what Bertholdier was really like. Bertholdier accompanied him on the condition he get the photos. Later Lefevre accompanies Joel and Valerie to Scharhorn; he is left by Joel to guard Valerie while she is transmitting information for Joel and to make sure that no one gets onto the pier at Cuxhaven.

LEFRAC, ———— (GC)
Naton's eighteen-year-old grandson, taken by Andrew to be his guide. He and his sister tried to get away from Andrew in the mountains; Andrew shot both of them. The boy died and his sister was severely wounded; they were found by Adrian.

LEFRAC, NATON (GC)
Naton was the current manager of the inn of the Capomantis; he was a descendent by marriage, son of a merchant who dealt with the Capomantis. When Capomanti died, he gave his instructions to Lefrac, his son-in-law; Lefrac knew only the word Leinkraus. Naton was one or two years younger than Victor, and his name was in the photocopied papers Victor gave to his sons. Naton was unable to prevent Andrew from taking his grandson for a guide and his granddaughter as hostage; Lefrac and his son had to remain at the inn to guarantee their safety.

LEIFHELM, ERICH (AP)

One of the key leaders of Aquitaine.

March 15, 1912: Born in Munich to Dr. Heinrich Leifhelm and his mistress, Marta Stoessel.

1912–1929: Lived with his mother in Eichstatt, north of Munich, where he was supported by his father, who visited occasionally. He had half brothers and a half sister in Munich he was not allowed to visit. His father's income decreased and so did their support. He felt he was denied what was rightfully his and set out to get as much as he could for himself.

1929: Completed studies at the Eichstatt II Gymnasium; excelled academically and on the playing field. He wanted his father to put him through college. He went to Munich and found his father had become a drunkard and was thrown out of his house by his father's wife, a Jew.

1930: He whipped his father into shape, physically and financially. He broke into the house in Munich where his father had previously lived, stripped it of everything of value, and took it to a fence. He also raped and beat the daughter so severely, she was emotionally handicapped the rest of her life.

1931: Erich was the Jungführer of the Hitler Youth Movement and was sent to the University of Munich. His father's marriage to the Jewess was declared invalid and their children denied all rights. A civil ceremony was performed between Heinrich and Marta and Erich became the only legitimate son. His name was changed to Leifhelm. Heinrich's first family tries to leave Europe—they are watched and cannot withdraw any large sums of money from the bank.

1934: Police report of the robbery at his father's house in 1930 disappears from the files. Heinrich dies. Erich completes three years at the University of Munich with honors and is sent to Officers Training School in Magdeburg.

1935: Erich is promoted to Oberstleutnant under von Runstedt.

1936: Heinrich's original family disappears. At the end of the war it was found they had perished at Dachau.

1937–1945: His reputation grew during World War II; he was a brilliant strategist and daring officer. At some time during the war he was married; his wife died in an air raid in Berlin in 1943 and he never remarried. He was the youngest general ever commissioned by Adolf Hitler. He foresaw the defeat of Germany and he did a sudden about-face. He joined the elite German general corps; he was rumored to have been part of the plot to assassinate Hitler at Wolfsschanze; and he was a member of Donitz's surrender team. He provided information for the trials at Nuremberg and was absolved of all guilt of war crimes.

1945–1950: The Allies ask him to join the Wehrmacht Officer Corps.

He becomes a privileged military consultant with full security clearance. It was during this time that he met and became friendly with Bertholdier.

1950s: He is put in command of the new German divisions under NATO. He receives valuable real estate and other items through legal settlements from the war.

Early 1970s: The job with NATO had lasted seventeen years, during which he'd been elevated to military spokesman for Bonn's interests at SHAPE headquarters near Brussels.

Early 1980s: The chancellor of the Federal Republic of Germany orders him home and gives him an innocuous post. He begins public speaking, pushing the old Nazi line. The chancellor knew there would be chaos if he let him continue; he called Leifhelm into his office, forced him to resign, and literally removed his voice from all government affairs. He continued to speak, but not openly.

Present day: Leifhelm is on the board of directors of a number of corporations. He is a "slender, elderly man in a dark suit with erect posture and very broad shoulders." He speaks excellent English. He has straight hair, still more blond than white, pale blue eyes, and pinkish skin that is lined and waxen. He drinks only light wine and very sparingly. He is known for his dinner parties and excellent cuisine. He owns a Cessna airplane and a deep-red Mercedes limousine. He lives near Bonn on a luxurious estate built like a fortress and patrolled by Doberman dogs. He doesn't have a boat because he gets seasick very easily. He was proud that it was his organization that made Joel a pariah. He bragged that he provided weapons and tons of explosives to the terrorists in Europe and the Mediterranean. He also set up the Scharhorn facility. After his interrogation by Joel, Joel hands him a gun; he walks out the door of the chalet and shoots himself to death.

LEIFHELM, DR. HEINRICH (AP)

Father of Erich Stoessel-Leifhelm. After Erich was born, Heinrich was torn between maintaining a successful practice—with no social stigma in Munich and a disinclination to abandon his mistress and child. After World War I the taxes increased greatly and Heinrich was unable to contribute as much support to Marta and Erich as before. Erich resented not being able to share his father's house and property because he was illegitimate. Heinrich's marriage was an unhappy one; he drank heavily with increased frequency. He started making errors in his medical judgment and he was charged with incompetency and barred from the Karlstor Hospital. His practice was in ruins. His Jewish wife and her father, who was also a doctor and a member of the hospital's board of directors, ordered him out of the house. Erich found Heinrich living in a cheap apartment house in the poorer section of the city earning a little money by dispensing drugs and doing abortions. Heinrich told Erich about his problems.

His son took over Heinrich's life. In the next few weeks he removed all alcohol and smoking materials from the apartment and never let his father out of his sight. He made him follow a harsh regimen of exercise and diet. Money was very scarce in Munich in 1930; Erich obtained money for his father's new wardrobe by stealing everything of value from his father's former home and taking it to one of the many fences that existed in Munich at the time. He received about $8,000, a fortune in those times.

With the money he bought Heinrich tailored clothes and the best bootwear. He had Heinrich's hair trimmed and made more blond and cut off his beard, leaving only a well-trimmed mustache. He read the Nazi doctrines to Heinrich every night until his father knew them by heart. He kept telling Heinrich that this was the way to get back everything that had been taken from him. One day he learned that Goebbels and Hess would be in Munich; he requested an audience for Heinrich and himself. Heinrich told the two men that he was a "physician of impeccable credentials, formerly head surgeon at the Karlstor Hospital and for years I enjoyed one of the most successful practices in Munich. That was in the past. I was destroyed by Jews, who stole everything from me. I am back, I am well, and I am at your service." Hitler made Heinrich his personal physician until Heinrich died in 1934.

LEINKRAUS, PAUL (GC)

Jewish man in his late forties, a merchant and grandson of a merchant. He owned the alpine equipment shop in Champoluc and had branches in Gstaad and Lake Lucerne. He didn't remember much about his grandfather Reuven. There was a precisely drawn map in the back of the family Torah, showing the way to the grave of his uncle, which Adrian copied. Before entering the mountains, Adrian left messages for Tarkington with Leinkraus, in case he didn't come back.

LEINKRAUS, REUVEN (GC)

Jewish man who started an alpine equipment store in Champoluc in 1913. Because they were Jewish, his family was threatened, and his oldest son was beaten to death by four boys from the village. Since there was no Jewish burial ground and because he didn't want his grave disturbed, the boy was buried in the mountains. Reuven died suddenly, unexpectedly, in a fire in his store, which many thought was not an accident.

LELAND, HOWARD R. (BI)

American Amassador to France. He had thick brows, a wide forehead, blunt nose, high cheekbones, thin lips, and a perfectly groomed gray mustache. He was formerly an admiral in the U.S. Navy, then an interim appointee as director of Naval Intelligence, followed by the ambassadorship. His primary purpose in Paris was to discourage massive arms sales by the French to Africa and the Middle East. He was assassinated on August 26 in Marseilles and the killing was blamed on David Webb (as Cain). It was confirmed later that he was killed by Carlos and Webb had tried to stop it.

LEMUEL, JONATHAN (BU)

A Cambridge-educated black attorney who had made his money in London and retired to the island of Montserrat. He was originally from the islands. Sykes asked him to represent the Pritchards. Later he and Brendan Prefontaine decided to open a consulting firm together in the islands, specializing in import and export law.

LEVY, JONATHON (IA)

Air crewman aboard the plan carrying the Masada Brigade to Oman. He was responsible for supervising the parachute jump.

LEWIS, OFFICER (PM)

Lewis was on patrol duty the evening Havelock and Jenna visited Alexander; Havelock made a point of talking to him so he would not be considered a stranger in town. He followed Lewis to Alexander's home.

LEWIS, HARRY (PM)

Havelock and Lewis had been classmates in graduate school at Princeton. Lewis was now chairman of the political science department at Concord University in New Hampshire and periodically traveled to Washington for consulting jobs. Harry was responsible for Havelock getting a job there when he retired from Consular Operations.

LEWIS, JONATHON (BS)

American consul general in Hong Kong. Nelson called him and gave him a story about Marie Webb, to get information for Catherine Staples. His story sounded wrong to Lewis, who then called Havilland. Havilland believed Lewis, because he had known him for a long time, said he was "something of a bon vivant, but he's no fool."

LIANG (BS)

Middle-aged Oriental assistant manager of the Regent Hotel in Hong Kong. He is married with a wife, two sons, and three daughters. He was second in his class at Fudan University. He had owned his own hotel in Shanghai and had been with Chiang with the Kuomintang. When the

Communists took over, he had fled to Hong Kong. When he called Yao
Ming's people as directed, someone tried to shoot him. Bourne saved his
life so he could get the phone number to reach Marie's captors.

Later, when Bourne attempts to leave the area of Mao's tomb, he
tells the guards he has a meeting with General Liang, the military
procurements chief of the Trade Commission.

LIEBOWITZ, ——— (AP)

Prospective client of Talbot, Brooks, and Simon. Nathan Simon gave
Joel a detailed lecture on why the firm should not take on this client—it
would "put too great a burden on the obligation to respect a client's
confidence."

———, LILLIAN (T)

Housekeeper, cook, and aide-for-all-seasons at High Barnegat. Lillian
didn't mind staying alone when the Trevaynes were gone; she was a
widow. Her husband had been a New York policeman. Lillian was upset
about the peculiar electrical outage and the way the gardeners kept
changing crews. When Bonner was slashed by de Spadante, Lillian held
ice compresses to his neck for nearly forty-five minutes until help arrived.

LIN SHOO (RG)

Second vice prefect for the Ministry of Education. He placed Hawkins
under house arrest for defacing a public statue; Hawkins was not in
United States territory. Lin admitted they chose Hawkins because he was
famous; they wanted him to make a public apology, reading from a script
they provided. He refused, knocked Lin unconscious, and escaped to the
American embassy, which refused to let him enter. Hawkins was recaptured by the Chinese and confined in more secure quarters. The Chinese
wanted to take Hawkins to trial, but Lin was willing to compromise with
Devereaux just to get Hawkins out of China.

LIN WENZU, MAJOR (BS)

With British Intelligence, MI6, Special Branch, Hong Kong. He mas-
queraded as Yao Ming. He was a large man, built like a wrestler. He was
ordered by London to work with Edward McAllister of the U.S. to
convince David Webb to capture the Bourne impostor. He had attended
Chinese schools and also Cambridge College in England and had studied
Oriental history. He spoke English well and was always polite to Marie;
he accepted the responsibility for her escape from the hospital. Conklin
considered him the best intelligence officer in the territory; he was said
to be brilliant and to hate failure in any form. When Catherine Staples
was murdered, he realized one of his men in his specially picked group

must be a traitor. He tested his men himself, and found and shot the traitor and his contact; bleeding from his wounds, he deposited the men at the feet of Havilland before collapsing. He was in critical condition for a long time, but recovered, although he lost the use of his left arm.

———, LISA (BI)

Secretary at the Canadian Treasury Board who knew Marie St. Jacques. Peter had told Lisa he was going to the airport in Ottawa to meet someone.

LISBON (RE)

David Spaulding was the station chief in Spain, which operated out of Lisbon. His code name was Lisbon.

LITTLE JOEY THE SHROUD (RO)

A little nondescript character who was excellent at tailing people because no one ever noticed him; he talked like a chicken and was very proud of his tailing skills. Vinnie forgave more than twelve thousand dollars in markers in Las Vegas for Joey and put him on the CIA payroll. Joey followed Hawkins from Omaha to the Boston airport, where Hawkins picked up the Puerto Ricans and the Vice President's Oldsmobile. He then connected Hawkins to Pinkus and Devereaux. Hawkins found him spying on him in the Four Seasons and interrogated him. Joey was about the same age as Hawkins and had served in the Fifth Army in Italy; he'd been made a lieutenant and sent north to radio back information on installations. The Army found him living high in Rome and busted him back to a private; he had no use for the military. When Vinnie disappeared, Joey maintained contact with Hawkins; Joey warned Hawkins to move his group out of the Ritz-Carlton because of the impending attack by the SFIs.

LITVAK, DR. WALTHER (HC)

A doctor at the clinic in Neuchâtel who had all of Gerhardt's medical records; he helped Gerhardt maintain his cover. He was in his late forties, with a balding head and clear eyes, slender, and highly intelligent. As a child he'd been hidden by Dutch Catholics and brought up by Lutherans and he had no tolerance for intolerance. His parents, two sisters, and a brother had been gassed at Auschwitz. He had spent five years at the clinic in Neuchâtel; he'd been recruited by a member of the Nachrichtendienst. Among other things, Litvak maintained the radio communications between Gerhardt and Har Sha'alav; his house was two kilometers north of the clinic on a very steep hill.

304 THE ROBERT LUDLUM COMPANION

LLEWELLYN, ——— (GC)

Adrian bought first-class tickets at the Air Afrique office in Orly airport under the name Llewellyn.

LLEWELLYN, IAN (HC)

Welshman who worked closely with Johann. Ian's brother, Morgan, was on Beaumont's ship. Ian was to send out the cables with code Wolfsschanze on them and to update the Sonnenkinder files for Johann. After he delivered the list, he was to be killed so his knowledge would die with him.

LLEWELLYN, LIEUTENANT MORGAN (HC)

Brother of Ian Llewellyn and second-in-command on Beaumont's ship. He had come from an obscure mining town in Wales; his parents were undistinguished and not well off, yet he attended a major university without financial aid and had become a military officer. He engineered Beaumont's death and reported the death of Beaumont and his wife Gretchen.

LOCH TORRIDON (GC)

Loch Torridon was a training camp in Scotland for refugees from the Germans; these people would be sent back to the occupied areas to cause problems through "mismanagement-at-all-costs"—misrouting supplies, intercepting dispatches, changing orders, and causing equipment failures. When Geoffrey Stone called Brevourt about Salonika and Fontine, he used the code name Loch Torridon.

LOCH TORRIDON (HC)

An "espionage and sabotage operation mounted by the British from 'forty-one to 'forty-four." Johann wanted access to their files in exchange for giving the Tinamou to the British.

LODESTONE, LIEUTENANT (RG)

A young lieutenant assigned to PR at the White House; he gave his name as Lodestone. Lodestone was to make sure that Sam Devereaux went to China to get Hawkins to admit that he defaced a Chinese statue; it was an obstacle to international trade negotiations.

LOGAN, GIDEON "GID" (IA)

Only black member of Inver Brass. He was middle-aged, with broad shoulders, dark eyes, and a large head. He'd been happily married for twelve years, and he'd made several fortunes in real estate. "It was said that he quietly did more for civil rights than any single corporation in the country." He'd refused a variety of cabinet posts, believing he could achieve more in the private sector. He'd disappeared for three years to be the "silent, unseen ombudsman of Rhodesia during its transition to Zimbabwe."

LONDON (GC)

Code name for Brevourt when called by Geoffrey Stone.

LONGWORTH, ALAN (CM) [REAL PERSON]

Longworth was a special agent for the FBI for twenty years. He had an exceptional record and was singled out by Hoover for high-echelon advancement. Hoover made him his personal liaison with La Jolla and put him in charge of all communications. He was also in charge of the files and was responsible for coordinating data on individuals with antipathy to the bureau or to Hoover. For several months before Hoover's death he sent information from the files to the Justice Department. He retired on March 2, 1971. "His reward was to spend the rest of his life in the Hawaiian Islands, his wants supplied, beyond the reach of those who might try to kill him. Hoover was told he died of natural causes . . . a memorial service was held for Longworth. Hoover himself gave the eulogy." The fake surgeon's report on his death was sent to Hoover. Varak used Longworth's identity as a cover; he looked like Longworth, even to the long scar across his stomach.

LOO MI (BS)

A beggar without legs who transported himself around Kowloon on a wheeled board. He was a lookout for the whore that David Webb was to contact to take him to Yao Ming.

LOOMIS, JIM (OW)

Tanner's neighbor. Tanner told his wife that Jim wanted to get him involved in a financial deal and he didn't want Janet going over there for a few days.

LOOMIS, JOAN (OW)

Jim and Nancy Loomis's daughter. She and Janet Tanner were good friends.

LOOMIS, NANCY (OW)

Jim Loomis's wife, friend of Alice Tanner's.

LORING, CHARLIE (PM)

Special detachment officer from Cons Ops. Havelock had worked with Charlie in Beirut. When he met him again on Poole's Island, he was angry at Charlie because Charlie knew Havelock's record but didn't question the orders to terminate him. Havelock respected Charlie's thoroughness; he requested that Charlie be put in charge of investigations for him. Charlie didn't like Havelock much, but was willing to work with him because of the Matthias affair. He was angry with himself when Shippers pulled a switch and escaped, and he couldn't find anything unusual about Decker's service record. Havelock called Charlie in to help the Apache team at Randolph's hospital; Charlie caught one of the paminyatchik killers but was seriously wounded. He managed to take the killer to a motel and tie him to a bed, then call Havelock. He refused to be removed to a hospital until he could brief Havelock. Charlie recovered but could not return to the field; he became a strategist.

LORING, RALPH (MP)

Narcotics agent. He was not in favor of using Matlock because Matlock was not a trained agent; the agency, however, felt that drastic measures were called for because of the three-week time period until the drug conference. Ralph was married and had a seven-year-old daughter. Shortly after briefing Matlock about Nimrod, Ralph was shot to death. Ralph's field cover had been the best at Justice for fifteen years; he had been a partner in one of the most disreputable law firms in Washington. His death was reported as an underworld killing.

———, LOU (MP)

Lou was impersonating a police officer during the investigation of the destruction and robbery of Matlock's apartment.

———, LOUIE (HC)

Doorman who worked from noon until eight P.M. at Noel's apartment building. He knew two different groups of locksmiths had worked on the fifth floor.

———, LOUISE (OW)

Cardone's maid and cook; she cooked much better than Betty did.

LOWELL, CATHERINE (CM)

Chancellor's former fiancée. She was tall with long brown hair and a delicate but strong face. Peter was deeply in love with her. They were driving to Pennsylvania so Catherine could meet Peter's parents; during a storm on the Pennsylvania Turnpike a large truck smashed into the side of the car, forcing them over an embankment. Catherine did not survive the crash.

LOWELL, MARGARET "PEG" (IA)

Only female member of Inver Brass, an elderly woman with silver hair and a cultured voice. She was a brilliant attorney who worked "on behalf of the oppressed, the dispossessed, and the disenfranchised. Both theorist and practitioner, she was rumored to be the next woman on the Supreme Court."

LOWELL, WALTER (IA)

Margaret Lowell's "alleycat" ex-husband. He was seeing Ardis when Margaret thought he was in London on business.

LU SIN, GENERAL (RG)

Hawkins told Lin Shoo that he was at the house of Lu Sin with his women and that he was drugged; he did not deface their statue.

LUBOK, ANTON (GC)

Code name Peacock. "Lubok was a Jew and a homosexual. He was a blond-haired, blue-eyed, middle-aged ballet master whose Czechoslovakian parents had emigrated to Berlin thirty years before. Fluent in the Slovak language as well as German, he held papers identifying him as a translator for the Wehrmacht." The Germans thought he was loyal to them, but he wasn't. "He operated as an underground courier across the Czechoslovakian and Polish borders." He was the best. Lubok volunteered to take Fontine to meetings with the various European underground groups. When the priests of Xenope captured Victor in Casimir, Lubok rescued him. Lubok worked for the Church of Rome and was convinced Victor didn't know anything. He reported that Victor was captured and executed in Casimir so the church groups would leave him alone for a while. Lubok made sure Donatti was exposed and discredited by the church. When Gaetomo was released from jail, he found Lubok and tortured him to find out about Victor and the documents.

LUBOQUE, SERGE ANTOINE (AP)

Friend and very wealthy client of René Mattilon, member of the club L'Etalon Blanc, and former pilot. René and Joel used him to get into L'Etalon Blanc and manage an introduction to General Bertholdier. René's firm was representing Luboque in a "futile case against an airplane manufacturer. He had his own private jet, and lost his left foot in [a] . . . crash landing. . . . He's a dreadful bore and . . . speaks very little English . . . he flew the first Mirages, brilliantly . . . and never lets anyone forget it." René tells Joel to laugh when Serge tells jokes—they're dreadful, but he likes it. "He thinks all government personnel work for Moscow."

He was a short, slender man—his physique reminded you of jet pilots of the early period when compactness was required. He had a short, waxed mustache attached to a miniaturized face with an expression of hostile dismissal on it. He loved to tell about his war experiences; all that was left was memories and anger.

LUDENDORFF, GENERAL ERICH (SI) [REAL PERSON]

German military leader, a Junker, who was defeated at the Meuse-Argonne. He was the sole member of the National Socialist Party in the Reichstag; the New Order was the brainchild of Ludendorff and Rosenberg. Ludendorff did not trust Kroeger and thought he was stupid, dangerous, and a bigot.

———, LUIGI (IA)

(1) Worked at one of the gambling casinos in Paris; he didn't want to interrupt Manny for a telephone call while he was winning.

(2) Kendrick called the Secret Service guard who was a mafioso Luigi.

———, LUIS (RE)

Guard in front of Rhinemann's warehouse in Ocho Calle.

LYONS, DR. EUGENE (IA)

He told Kendrick he was the local doctor assigned to Manny; when he took a blood sample, he injected Manny with an African virus that caused blood clotting and slow death. He'd been hired by Andy Vanvlanderen, and when Andy couldn't pay him, he went directly to the Vice President's home in California, where he unexpectedly met Kendrick. Bollinger couldn't afford to have him around, so he was quietly eliminated.

LYONS, EUGENE (RE)

Aerophysicist, a genius, chosen by Kendall and Swanson to evaluate the guidance system blueprints. He was an extremely thin man with blue veins that showed through his worn-out skin; he had deep-set, penetrating eyes and straight gray hair thinned out before its time. Lyons had been the youngest full professor at MIT. His marriage went sour and he went deeply into debt. He got drunk and woke up in a hotel room bed next to a whore he'd beaten to death. Lyons spent four years in the penitentiary and couldn't get a job when he got out; he joined the skid row bums and burned out his throat with raw alcohol. The doctor who treated him shipped him off to the CCC; Lyons was reasonably rehabilitated and went into defense work. Lockheed provided him with an apartment and male nurses to take care of him. He didn't like to be around people very much because he couldn't talk; he spent most of his time reading and working in the laboratory. He refused to leave Spaulding after his male nurses were killed and he heard Asher Feld's information; he wanted America to win the war and he wanted the last part of the blueprints. Lyons drove the car and pulled Spaulding out of the bay at Ocho Calle and treated his wounds. He went to Rhinemann's estate for the blueprints and was taken back to the embassy safely. He then took a lucrative job with Sperry Rand, had throat surgery, and built a Mediterranean-style house in the San Fernando Valley.

M, CYRUS (RO)

Mercenary hired through Manpower Plus Plus by Vinnie to guard Hawkins's group. Cyrus was a large, muscular black man who put himself through two universities in seven years, financing it through hiring himself out as a mercenary. When he received his doctorate in chemistry, he couldn't afford a suit, so his relatives went together and bought him one. He'd worked for the government and was loaned out to Bonn to help them in a fertilizer plant. He discovered they were making gas to be used against people in the Middle East; three men attacked him and he threw them into the chemical vats. He drew five years in jail in the U.S. and plea-bargained for one, serving it in Attica; he and Roman escaped and took the job guarding Hawkins. Cyrus was uneasy because he hadn't received the usual in-depth rundowns on his assignment; he wouldn't work for a cause he didn't believe in. He stayed to protect Hawkins's group because he'd also been the victim of government corruption. After the Supreme Court made their decision, R. Cookson Frazier hired him to take charge of the security of his various houses and bought a chemical plant where he could work.

MAC THE KNIFE, KILLER OF CHASONG (CM)

Epithet given to General MacAndrew, who lost nearly all his men at the battle of Chasong during the Korean War.

MACANDREW, ALISON (CM)

Only child of Bruce and Mal MacAndrew and lover of Peter Chancellor. She was thirty-one years old, tall, with a delicate bone structure; she had large brown eyes and light brown hair. She was employed as an artist for the Wilton Green Agency, and she lived alone in an apartment on East Fifty-fourth Street.

She lived in Tokyo with her mother during the Korean War; her mother had been mentally ill since Alison was nine. Alison's father sent her to private boarding schools when they lived in Germany and England. She and her father were very close; he had taught her how to shoot pistols and rifles. Her father had introduced her to Peter's books.

She didn't attend her mother's funeral because her father didn't call her until it was all over.

Before meeting Peter, she had lived with a writer for three years and then for one year with Phil Brown. She was a private person with a quality of quiet humor within her. She was afraid to have children because she thought her mother's insanity might be hereditary. She helped Peter by using her contacts with the military.

MacANDREW, GENERAL BRUCE (CM)

One of the people in the missing Hoover files. A career soldier, he was often at odds with the people at the Pentagon. "He loved the army; he wanted it to be the best it could be." At the top of his career, he unexpectedly resigned. Part of his service record, a period of eight months in 1950, was missing. He had opposed U.S. policy in Southeast Asia, considering it a terrible waste of life. While he was fighting in Korea, his wife and daughter lived in Japan. Intelligence did not want him to know his wife had been drugged and used as a reverse conduit to the North Koreans or that she had been raped by blacks, rather than nearly drowned. They put him in charge of an all-black unit at the battle of Chasong; U.S. troop movements had been given to the North Koreans, and nearly everyone in MacAndrew's group was killed.

As a result of the drugs, his wife became mentally ill; he loved her dearly and took care of her at home. Their daughter Alison was sent away

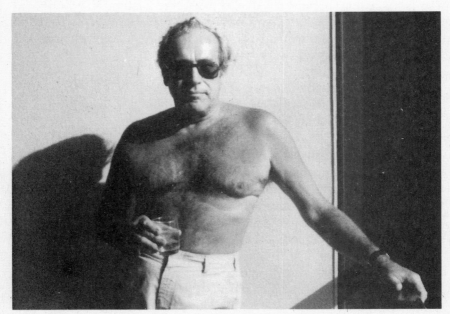

Athens—the Greek dramatists were right! *Nothing* like the Athenian Sun!

to private boarding schools; she and her father were quite close. When Chancellor found him, he and his wife were living near Rockville, Maryland, in an old house out in the country. MacAndrew was middle-aged, of medium height with broad shoulders and a stocky build; the skin on his face was taut with deeply etched wrinkles. He became extremely upset with Chancellor when he heard that Longworth threatened to expose his past. After his wife died, he went to Hawaii to find Longworth and kill him. MacAndrew was found shot to death on the beach at Waikiki. He was buried in a military ceremony at Arlington.

MacANDREW, Mrs. Mal (CM)

Wife of General Bruce MacAndrew and mother of Alison MacAndrew. She was born in Tulsa, Oklahoma, the daughter of Baptist missionaries. She traveled all over the Far East when she was young and was educated in missionary schools. She was happiest when they returned to Tulsa between trips; she hated the Far East and hated traveling. Both her father and her husband were strong, decisive men. She met her husband in Washington during World War II at an Army reception; she was working as a translator for the Army. She could read and write several Far Eastern languages, including basic Mandarin.

Mal and Alison lived in Tokyo while Bruce was fighting in Korea. She was forced to be a reverse conduit, under the influence of drugs, by the U.S. Intelligence Service; she was trying to gain the release of her parents, who were being held by the Chinese. She tried to break their hold on her by going to local drug dealers, where she was raped and nearly killed by a bunch of blacks. She did not pass on the information about Chasong because she was already hospitalized for mental illness at the time. Her husband was told she'd had a swimming accident, and he took care of her at home until she died.

MacAULIFF, Captain Albert (OW)

Chief of police in Saddle Valley. MacAuliff was a tall, obese man with a thick neck and big, thick hands. He'd been recruited from the New York police to keep Saddle Valley clear of "undesirable elements." He was a bigot—he hated blacks, Jews, and Puerto Ricans. No one knew MacAuliff had been working with Fassett until Tanner killed MacAuliff; the CIA had become suspicious when MacAuliff complained of suffering from a stomach ulcer but had no previous histsory of such an illness. Bernie had slashed MacAuliff's stomach with a garden tool during the attack on Tanner's house. MacAuliff had also been responsible for killing Ferguson, one of the CIA men guarding Tanner's house.

MACHEK, ——— (GC)

Refugee from Yugoslavia at the camp at Loch Torridon. He wanted to go back and take over the country.

MACINTOSH, ——— (CH)
Julian Warfield asked a business associate to send accrual statistics on to Macintosh even though he probably wouldn't agree with them.

MACKENZIE, MIDGE (PM)
Wife of Steve MacKenzie. When Steve went to work, Midge never knew when or if he would come back alive. He didn't tell her many details of his work. When Steve died, Randolph doctored the autopsy report so that Midge and the children would be able to collect Steve's life insurance.

MACKENZIE, STEVE (PM)
Foreign service officer, the most experienced black-operations officer in the CIA. Steve had been one of the best sailors on the eastern shore before becoming a naval officer in Vietnam. First he transported intelligence officers, then he became one of them. Steve and Midge were married after he came home, and he attended law school. A year later he went back to Washington and into the field again. Randolph recognized that Steve needed psychiatric care because of the stress and tried to get him out of the service. Steve had set up the Costa Brava operation that did not include harming Jenna; someone else took over his operation and killed a woman Steve thought was Jenna. Three weeks later Steve died of a heart seizure while sailing in Chesapeake Bay. Randolph thought Steve committed suicide and changed the medical report so Steve's family would get his insurance; Havelock convinced Randolph that someone murdered Steve.

MACKENZIE, STEVE (PM)
Son of Steve MacKenzie. Dr. Randolph had delivered both his parents, and him and his siblings.

MAD COLONELS OF ALGIERS (BI)
Refers to officers of the French Army who were disenchanted with de Gaulle's overtures of freedom for Algeria; many of them participated in terrorist activities. The OAS, led by Salan, tried to assassinate de Gaulle; Salan was arrested with a number of these officers. In *The Aquitaine Progression* Bertholdier had been a member of the OAS, and in *The Bourne Identity* Villiers had been associated with the "mad colonels."

MADISON, ELLEN (T)
Walter Madison's wife, an alcoholic.

MADISON, WALTER (T)

Trevayne's attorney. When his wife was raped, Trevayne called him; Walter made sure no police report was filed. Genessee was paying Walter $75,000 per year for four years into a Swiss bank account for relaying to them any extraordinary information related to Andrew and the subcommittee. Walter was horrified when he thought there might be some relationship between Genessee and what happened to Phyllis. He accompanied Trevayne to the subcommittee hearing; he was afraid of what Trevayne would tell the media if he was not confirmed as chairman. Walter thought that all Trevayne would find when investigating Genessee was some minor corruption and a little stealing. When Trevayne asked him to defend Bonner, Walter hesitated, saying he didn't think Trevayne's name should be linked with Bonner's and de Spadante's.

MAGDALEN SISTERS OF CHARITY (BU)

Legitimate religious society in Paris. Dominique Lavier and Carlos used them as a cover; she was a frequent visiting superior from the Convent of Saint-Malo.

———, MAGDALENE (RO)

Wife of the Vice President of the United States. She thought their Oldsmobile had been towed into a garage back home because it wouldn't run; it was stolen and left at the scene of a crime in Boston.

MAGINOT (GC)

Brevourt could be reached "through the Foreign Office channel, Code Maginot."

MAHDI (IA)

Also known as al Farrah and Sahibe al Farrahkhaliffe. An "unknown, obsessed financier . . . whose purpose was to drive out the Westerner from the Middle East . . . keeping the immense wealth of industrial expansion in Arab hands—specifically *his* hands . . . this same man who had spread his gospel of Islamic purity throughout the fanatic fringes had formed a network . . . of scores . . . of hidden companies and corporations. . . ." He intended to control the various governments through terrorism and financial pressures. The Mahdi was responsible for the murder of the employees of the Kendrick Group and the takeover of the American embassy in Masqat. When Kendrick reached him, he discovered the Mahdi was al Farrah from Chicago, who had stolen millions from his constituents and fled to the Middle East. Manny and the Masada Brigade located the Mahdi and forced him to release Kendrick before Kendrick could be dropped into the shark-infested shoals of Qatar. The sultan of Oman had the Mahdi executed without trial or sentence because of his crimes against humanity.

MAHMET, ———— (IA)

One of the CIA's contacts in the Middle East, he was pulled in by covert-operations officers for questioning concerning the hostage situation in Masqat.

MAHMOUD, ———— (IA)

Fictitious name of an Arab businessman whose daughter was raped and her face slashed because her father dared to offer opposition to the fanatics of the Mahdi.

MALETKIN, COLONEL PIETRE (MC)

Maletkin was a sound if uninspired professional KGB agent assigned to the border post of Vyborg; he also worked for the Americans. Taleniekov persuaded Maletkin to work with him in exchange for "the name of a high-ranking KGB intelligence officer from his own station, a traitor like himself, who could be manipulated unmercifully." Taleniekov told him the other traitor was his commanding officer; when Maletkin approached his CO with this information, he would be executed.

MALYEKOV, NIKOLAI PETROVICH (PM)

Arthur Pierce's real name. He'd been born in Ramenskoye, southeast of Moscow, then raised in Iowa. He was a paminyatchik.

MAN MOUNTAIN DEAN (BP) [REAL PERSON]

An American wrestler during the 1950s. Major Lin Wenzu was told by a lance corporal that he resembled Dean.

THE MAN WHO NEVER WAS (BI)

The creation of Cain was a variation on "the man who never was." During World War II the British loaded up a dead sailor with false information on the invasion of Europe and floated him off the coast of Europe. The information was found and taken back to the German High Command, who checked the story, believed it, and shifted a large part of their defenses.

MANDEL, AARON (RE)

Russian Jew, the Spauldings' concert manager, a very successful artists' representative. Aaron had lived in tsarist Kiev and had been expecting someone from the government to inquire about David; he loved and treated David like a son. His attempts to discourage the government from enlisting David into the State Department failed. Aaron felt America should have attacked the Germans a long time ago. David used Aaron to find the parties where Leslie and Cindy might be.

MANDEL, HANNAH (IA)

Wife of Jacob Mandel. She'd suffered greatly in Germany, and Jacob hoped she'd precede him in death so she wouldn't have to face losing another loved one.

MANDEL, JACOB (IA)

Jewish member of Inver Brass, "a slender, balding seventy-odd-year-old with sunken cheeks and wide, gentle eyes." He'd worked his way up from Lower East Side Yiddish poverty to being a venerated financial genius who had reformed the SEC. No decent man could call him an enemy. He and Hannah were happily married, and Samuel Winters was a longtime good friend. He was afraid Kendrick would run in disgust when he found out about Inver Brass; he knew Kendrick must have "a fire in his belly" for their plan to succeed.

MANERO, ——— (CM)

Desk sergeant in the police station at Rockville, Maryland. He told Chancellor there was no record of an accident between a Chevrolet and a Lincoln Continental the week of the tenth, no Lincoln-Mercury dealer in Pikesville, and no Officer Donnelly on the Rockville police force.

MANFREDI, ERNST (HC)

Director of La Grande Banque de Génève. He was "a short, rotund man in his middle to late sixties. He was completely bald, with a pleasant, gentle face; but the wide blue eyes, magnified beyond the metal-framed glasses, were cold." He received the funds from Clausen and set up the account for the Fourth Reich. Althene thought he was a friend because he had helped her and Noel get out of Germany. He allowed Gerhardt's group to read the documents at the bank for five hundred thousand Swiss francs; he wanted them to believe the money was to make amends for the Nazis. Manfredi gave Peter Baldwin just enough information to guarantee he'd be killed by the false Wolfs-schanze. Noel was told Manfredi was ill and had committed suicide, but he didn't believe it. The false Wolfsschanze killed him because Manfredi had wanted to control the funds in the account.

MANGECAVALLO, PEEWEE (IA)

"He had a little Italian place, a bar with good Sicilian food, about four blocks from the hospital." Although he was ninety, he remembered clearly many things about E and the Irish nurse.

MANGECAVALLO, ROSA (RO)

Mangecavallo's wife. She sat around knitting and talking to her maid all day except when they went to the market together to buy foods Vinnie wouldn't feed the cats.

MANGECAVALLO, VINCENT FRANCIS ASSISI "VINNIE THE BAM-BAM" (RO)

Code name Ragu. Director of the CIA and Mafia boss. His appointment was approved because most of the members of Congress had been threatened with blackmail. Vinnie was well educated but used street language for image. His only military experience was on boats in the Caribbean. Vinnie put pressure on the Supreme Court to dismiss the Wopotami case. When that didn't work, he tried to prevent the litigants from reaching the Supreme Court building. Warren Pease was assigned to work closely with Vinnie; when he discovered that Vinnie had called in hit men from New York to kill Hawkins and Sam, he was forced to call a meeting of his old wealthy school chums and find a way to get rid of Vinnie before he exposed them all. Pease also decided to send the SFIs in after Hawkins and Sam. One of the old school chums warned Vinnie and he disappeared, supposedly dead from a boat accident. Vinnie warned Hawkins about the SFI and hired three men from Manpower Plus Plus to protect Hawkins's group; he also engineered a financial collapse on Wall Street for all but one of the old-school-chum group. Vinnie stayed in hiding until the case was won, then was "rescued" from an island in the Dry Tortugas and returned to his CIA job.

THE "MANIACS" (CM)

Five or six agents who worked secretly with Hoover; they wanted the old regime back and wanted to control the Bureau. O'Brien knew they had tapped his office line. Chancellor nearly killed one of them at the Corcoran Gallery. At the hospital the agent was told to name the others in a deposition and resign or go to jail; he and the other "maniacs" resigned. (*See* Hoover Group.)

MANNING, COLONEL JOHN "JACK" (BI)

Colonel in the U.S. Army, assigned to the Pentagon. He had a high respect for David Abbott. He connected Bourne (as Cain) to the death of Chernak. He was at the meeting with Gillette, Knowlton, Congressman Walters, and Abbott.

———, MANNY (RG)

One of Dellacroce's men, knocked out by Hawkins on the golf course.

———, MANNY (RO)

Worked for Hyman Goldfarb. He was to accompany "the Shovel" and the English couple to the Wopotami village. He tried to make a deal with Chief Thunder Head while removing a short-barreled automatic from his belt and received several cracked ribs, then was tied up to a tree.

MANOLO, ERNEST "FAST ERNIE" (T)

President of the Lathe Operators Brotherhood and AFL-CIO negotiator who obtained a generous labor settlement with Genessee in Pasadena. Manolo had graduated with a degree in economics from the University of New Mexico. He was a crusader type, like Chavez. Manolo was twenty-six years old and looked like a twelve-year-old bullfighter; he had to jump over a lot of seasoned union stewards to get his job. Genessee had furnished the money and Manolo brought in a bunch of young, college-educated managers.

MANUEL, FATHER (BI)

Fictitious identity assumed by Carlos at the Church of the Blessed Sacrament in Paris. He was supposedly a visiting priest from the archdiocese of Barcelona. During his meeting with Jacqueline Lavier in a confessional booth, he murdered her.

MARBLE (BS)

Code name used by the elite group of soldiers employed by Sheng.

———, MARCEL (BI)

Owner of the butcher shop in La Ciotat, one of many stores in that area that catered to wealthy clients. In this shop Webb found out about the Marquis de Chamford.

MARCHETTI, LIEUTENANT (GC)

Italian soldier on duty at a checkpoint just outside Montenotte Sud; he stopped Apple, Pear, and Fontini-Cristi's car and was killed by Apple.

MARCUM, ED (OW)

Bernie Osterman's accountant in California.

MARCUS AURELIUS (AP)

The words Marcus, Aurelius, and Marcus Aurelius were used as code words by Peter Stone's group. Stone was registered in the Algonquin Hotel under the name Peter Marcus. He left the message "Marcus Aurelius ascending" on Metcalf's answering machine because Metcalf would have been aware that Valerie discussed Delavane with Sam Abbott.

Marcus Aurelius was the name of a Roman emperor and Delavane was the "emperor" of Aquitaine. When Metcalf called Peter Stone, he asked for Aurelius. Marcus was the name Chaim Abrahms used to address Delavane.

MARCUS, PETER (AP)

Name Peter Stone used to register into the Algonquin Hotel in New York City. The words "Marcus" and "Algonquin" could be deciphered from the cryptic message that Stone left on Metcalf's answering machine, left in the hope that Valerie or Joel would understand and would try to reach him.

————, MARGARET (BI)

Called "Sister Meg" by David Abbott, who had known her for a very long time. She had been "one of Intrepid's girls, a piranha with very sharp teeth." She was a "petite, elegant-looking, gray-haired woman with soft, aristocratic features." Her American dialect was refined mid-Atlantic. She was married to the Yachtsman and they lived in the Treadstone house in New York City. When Carlos's men attacked them, she blew off half of one man's shoulder with a shotgun before he killed her.

————, MARGARET (PM)

Havelock didn't know the maid's name at Alexander's, so he called her Margaret.

————, MARGE (T)

Secretary who worked for Trevayne's subcommittee.

————, MARIO (BU)

De Fazio's main executioner. He was Lou's cousin. He was married, with five children, and lived in Larchmont, N.Y. He liked to have a month off between out-of-town assignments so he could spend time with his family. He enjoyed gardening. He posed as the gardener for six weeks at the Swayne estate before killing Swayne. He tried to kill Cactus and killed one of Cactus's men. He also killed Steven DeSole. He and Lou attacked Bourne at the private airport in Pontcarré; he decided he could not kill Marie. He was captured by Bourne.

————, MARIO (MP)

Large Italian-looking man with dark eyes who was Stockton's bodyguard at the Carmount Country Club.

———, MARIO (RO)

Waiter in a restaurant in San Francisco where Charlie and Jennifer Redwing met to discuss his relationship with Hawkins.

MARLON (RO)

Member of the Suicidal Six whose primary impersonation was Marlon Brando.

MARSEILLES (MC)

Agent from Marseilles who was called out by Congdon to execute Scofield. Taleniekov killed him before he could reach Scofield.

MARSEILLES (RG)

Other code name Vert. He was making his living as a tugboat pilot when Hawkins called him to help kidnap the Pope. Marseilles and Stockholm had worked together during World War II, making money from both the Allies and the Axis.

MARSHALL, ——— (RE)

Cryptographer assigned to the American embassy in Lisbon. He met Spaulding at the airstrip and told him he was wanted for some big project because they were taking him out of strategy in Lisbon; he had worked with Spaulding in the most classified operations out of Portugal and Spain. Spaulding could not figure out what Marshall was doing in the back of a car in New York with people who told Spaulding to heed the warning of Fairfax. Supposedly Marshall was killed in an ambush in Valdero; later it was reported he was just wounded and cared for by the partisans. He was confined to the embassy and returned to duty. Marshall was a member of the Haganah.

MARSHALL, CYRUS (RO)

Hawkins's aide-de-camp for the meeting with the Nobel committee in the Ritz-Carlton was Cyrus M. He was supposed to be a retired Army colonel.

MARTIN, ——— (RO)

Top man at the William Morris Agency. Hired by the Hawk to manage the Suicidal Six's movie contract.

MARTIN, ALAN (T)

Member of Trevayne's subcommittee. His last job was comptroller of Pace-Trevayne's New Haven plants. "Martin was a thoughtful, middle-aged former stats analyst; a cautious man, excellent with details and firm in his convictions . . . He was Jewish." One of Alan's jobs was to contact Manolo and find out how he got a union settlement with Genessee so quickly and quietly.

THE MASADA BRIGADE (IA)
A little-known elite strike force of the Israelis' that specialized in interdiction, rescue, sabotage, and assassination. One of their jobs was to rescue Yaakov's father, a Mossad agent being held captive in Masqat. This operation was aborted in order to rescue Kendrick.

MASCOLO, ——— (PM)
Italian train conductor that Havelock saw talking to Jenna Karas. He received ten thousand lire from Havelock for telling him Jenna's destination.

MASCOLO, ——— (SI)
Headwaiter at the Venezia Restaurant. He said he saw Ulster Scarlett and Miss Dempsey having an early lunch the week Ulster disappeared.

MASON, CONGRESSMAN (IA)
A colleague of Kendrick's on the House Intelligence Subcommittee. He had a big profile in Tulsa or Phoenix, but there was a quiet movement to get him off the committee. When he was interviewed on television he reported that Kendrick was "the brilliant one whom everyone looked up to and listened to."

MASTERSON, SYDNEY (SI)
One of the merchants supporting the Nazis; he was a partner in an importing firm with Bertholde and Leacock, controlling half of the India imports. He also had illegal trade agreements with Ceylon.

MASTIFF (PM)
Roommate of R. Charles. They were studying together for a midterm exam the next day. He was on the wrestling team. Mastiff had noticed Jenna visiting Handelman the previous evening.

MATHER, TED (BS)
Representative of Honeywell-Porter advertising agency in Los Angeles. He had been in Hong Kong for a conference and was going to Macao to gamble when he met David Webb on the ferry.

MATTHIAS, ANTHONY "ANTON" (PM)
Secretary of State for the past six years, "a man for all seasons, for all people." "The Soviets treat him as a valuable go-between. . . . The

Chinese . . . call him a visionary." Anton's face was familiar all over the world: He had high cheekbones, an aquiline nose, generous lips, and wore horn-rimmed glasses. His family had known Havelock's family in Prague. Matthias had come to America forty years before, the son of a prominent doctor who had taken his family out of Czechoslovakia before the German occupation. Matthias was a scholar and Havelock met him at a lecture in Berkeley. Havelock trusted Matthias; Matthias loved him like the son he had never had. Matthias was slowly going insane; Zelienski was manipulating him and helping him write documents that, if released, could cause a nuclear war. Anton knew that Havelock would not approve of what he was doing and wanted him out of the State Department so that he could not interfere. Zelienski helped him set up Costa Brava. After the Costa Brava orders were changed, it appeared that Jenna really had been killed and Matthias was told that Havelock disappeared; Matthias thought he had killed Havelock too, and this was the pressure that triggered the final insanity. The President had Matthias transferred to a private medical facility on Poole's Island, where he couldn't cause any more international problems; his illness was a well-kept secret. Havelock had just destroyed the documents when the President told him that Matthias had died.

MATLOCK, DAVID (MP)

Deceased younger brother of James Matlock. Jim remembered him as a good-natured blond-haired boy of nineteen, a good but troubled kid. He had shot thirty mg. of heroin into his veins while out in a catboat in a Cape Cod inlet. They found him dead when his boat floated into shore.

MATLOCK, JAMES BARBOUR, II (MP)

Associate professor at Carlyle, a leading authority on Elizabethan literature. He was thirty-three years old, a tall man, modestly good-looking with sharp features and fairly long blond hair. He was described by security as "flawed but mobile in the extreme." His family was wealthy; he was educated at Andover and Amherst and was expected to take over the family business. He married a socially prominent girl from Greenwich. He went into the Army, served in Vietnam, and survived two summary courts-martial. When he returned to civilian life, he couldn't get along with his parents, and his wife of three months divorced him. During the next few years he completed a master's degree and a Ph.D. and took a position with the English department at Carlyle. He built a reputation for scholarship, reconciled with his parents, and found a steady girlfriend. His only sibling, David, ten years younger than himself, had died three years earlier of a heroin overdose. The Narcotics Bureau wanted Matlock to find out where the conference between Nimrod and the Mafia would be held; time was short and they thought he might be able to reach people they couldn't. They knew it was dangerous and that he could lose his life. Matlock was willing to try because of David. The more he and Pat were attacked, the more determined he became to find and destroy Nimrod. He had some unexpected help from Dunois's group, who decided to take care of Nimrod and the Mafia their own way.

MATLOCK, MRS. JAMES (MP)

She and Matlock were married for only three months. She didn't think he should want anything more than the security of working for his father and enjoying the good life. When he decided to chuck the job and enter the Army, she divorced him.

MATLOCK, JONATHAN MUNRO (MP)

Father of James Matlock. He and his wife were elderly, very healthy, and rich; they were retired in Scarsdale, N.Y. James was their only living child; their only other child, David, had died three years before. They wanted James with them more than he wanted to be there. It had been inconceivable to Jonathan that his son would not want to take over the family business; for a while there had been a definite rift in their relationship. James was able to ask his father for a $15,000 loan without telling him about Nimrod; when James opened the envelope from his father there was an affectionate note in it and a check for $50,000.

MATTILON, RENÉ (AP)

French lawyer in the firm Saint-Pierre, Nelli, et Mattilon, frequently called upon by Joel's firm when they need representation in the French courts, but also a good friend of Joel Converse. When Mattilon was a young attorney in his twenties he was conscripted by his government and sent to French Indochina as a legal officer. He felt as Joel did about the involvement of France and the United States in Vietnam. It was standard for them to find time for dinner and drinks whenever they were in the same city together. René was also amazingly tolerant of Converse's linguistic limitations.

René had been married twice; his first wife had died. His present wife is an excellent cook. He thinks he is a lucky man. He had also known Valerie and asks Joel about her paintings; he comments on her preparation of a duck dish he particularly liked.

He is described as having rugged, weather-beaten features. He "was in his mid to late fifties, but his stride, like his outlook, was that of a younger man. There was about him that aura peculiar to successful trial attorneys; his confidence . . . was born of diligence, not merely ego and performance . . . the secure actor comfortable in his role, his graying hair and blunt masculine features all part of a calculated effect . . . was a thoroughly decent man . . . they were both decent men; perhaps that was why they [he and Joel] enjoyed each other's company."

Joel asks him to get him into the L'Etalon Blanc to see General Bertholdier, as his firm wants to know about his associates. René agrees to help—he has a friend who can get them in and introduce them to the general. Later when he hears Joel has killed a man at the George V he doesn't believe it becuase he knows how Joel abhors any kind of violence. Bertholdier, however, realizes René asked Luboque to introduce Joel; he doesn't want to take the chance that René knows anything.

One day when both of René's partners are out of town and his usual secretary is in the hospital because of an auto accident (probably courtesy of Aquitaine), he is alone in the office. The temporary secretary, Suzanne, walks into the office and shoots him to death.

———, MAURICE (BU)
False name used by a former corporal of the French Foreign Legion. Bourne met him in Le Coeur du Soldat. He had been out of the legion for nine years, thrown out because he was overweight. He was originally from Belgium. His real name may or may not have been René, which was the name by which Santos knew him. Bourne paid "Maurice" to assist him in contacting Santos.

———, MAURICE (RO)
Elegant manager of the Fawning Hills Country Club in Maryland.

MAXWELL, PHYLLIS (CM)
Phyllis Maxwell was her by-line; Paula Mingus was on her passport. She had been a newswoman for twenty-five years, and did investigative news reporting; she had been in Washington for sixteen years. "She would not print what she could not document." She was forty-seven years old, elegant in appearance—"slender, the legs tapered, the breasts firm, the neck long," with a good face; her eyes were speckled, striking. Phyllis was a lesbian and flew to St. Vincent in the Grenadines once a year to vacation with other lesbians—and she was in Hoover's missing files. Twice she received anonymous threatening telephone calls. She was extremely angry when she found out she was the basis for a character in Chancellor's book. Chancellor and she were nearly killed at her friend's house on Thirty-fifth Street, and Phyllis left rather than face the police. She realized Chancellor had saved her life. Phyllis was terrorized because she had discovered evidence of criminal activity leading to the Oval Office. She took an extended leave for "health reasons" because her work

had been compromised. Her last column, edged in black in the center of the editorial page, revealed that Chancellor was writing a book based on fact about the FBI and Hoover's files, and saying the FBI's tactics had to be stopped.

McAllister, Edward Newington (BS)

U.S. Undersecretary of State in the Far East. He had received his doctorate in Far Eastern studies at Harvard and then been with the State Department for over twenty years. He was a slender, middle-aged man of medium height, carefully groomed; he had the habit of rubbing his temples when he was upset. He was considered a brilliant analyst but not a charismatic speaker. He was chosen for the Bourne-impostor problem because he had spent seven years in Hong Kong, had worked successfully with British Intelligence and with Sheng. He considered himself a very moral man, attended church, and felt physically ill after making the initial contact with Webb. Lin Wenzu describes him as one of the most thorough men he's ever met. McAllister was used to figure out the strategies while someone else did the work; he was shocked at how Havilland and Conklin talked about killings. Havilland told him he protested too much, that he could have walked out if he had really wanted to. He felt his career was going nowhere and he felt guilty about what he had done to Webb; he knew he could get close to Sheng and kill him, so he chose to accompany Webb back into China. He did it without Havilland's permission or knowledge and was wounded. When he re-

China border—photos are verboten (so I took this one from my hip).

turned, however, he was promoted to chairman of the National Security Council, as he was too valuable and knowledgeable to let go.

MCALLISTER, EDWARD NEWINGTON (BU)

He had his name added to the clearance procedures for Bourne's file because he wanted to be sure it could not be accessed without his knowledge and approval.

MCALLISTER, MRS. (BS)

When David Webb called the McAllister home, Mrs. McAllister answered. She had been married to Edward for eighteen years and had a son who wanted to attend college where David taught. She told David she would have to call the State Department to reach Edward, as he was in the Far East.

MCAULIFF, DR. ALEXANDER TARQUIN (CH)

Thirty-eight-year-old American geologist who was director of the survey party in the Cock Pit area of Jamaica. He was tall, with light brown hair, and his clear gray eyes were set deeply beneath wide eyebrows. His face was tan, and there were lines around his eyes. He had high cheekbones, a full mouth, and a casually slack jaw. He was from a close-knit family; his father was a highly regarded agroscientist, his mother was deceased. His older brother, a pilot, had been killed in the last days of World War II. Alex had served as an infantry officer in Panmunjon during the Korean War; he disliked being a soldier, but he had performed because it was the only way to survive. Academically he had received a B.S., M.S., and Ph.D. When his fiancée, Ann, was murdered while he was at a research meeting, he decided to leave academia. He hired out to several established geological-survey firms, then left them and underbid them on upcoming contracts. He had accumulated over three hundred thousand dollars in his bank accounts and was content to be his own boss. He was known in the field as an expensive director. Peter Jensen knew Alex despised all government interference, which was why he recommended him to Warfield. Alex was not happy to be caught between Dunstone, Ltd. and British Intelligence. Holcroft had promised him one million dollars if he would help them get Dunstone, Ltd.; Alex collected his money and made sure that neither he nor Alison would be bothered by the intelligence community again.

MCCALL, JASON (OW)

Alice Tanner's father had been a contemporary John Brown. He was unarmed when the Los Angeles police shot him down outside his canyon home; they denied they had actually murdered him. Alice had been with an aunt in Pasadena at the time.

McClaren, Paul (BI)

Colonel in the U.S. Army, probably with Army Intelligence. He was ordered by Brigadier General Crawford to go to the Treadstone house after the massacre and do absolutely nothing until Crawford arrived.

McDermott, ——— (OW)

CIA agent who was undercover as a policeman with Jenkins in Saddle Valley. McDermott took Alice and the children to the hospital after they had been gassed.

McDermott, Lillian (OW)

Wife of the CIA agent working with Jenkins; she liked the houses in the Saddle Valley neighborhood.

McDonald, Anthony "Tony" (IA)

Bald-headed, obese Englishman who worked for the Mahdi. His cover was an "overweight, overindulged, underbrained fop in sartorial plumage that could not hide his excesses." He hired the man who raped Mahmoud's daughter and killed Abdul's son; he paid the same man to get him inside the embassy. When Azra and Kendrick left the embassy, they took McDonald with them; McDonald escaped from Kendrick at the airport and went to a hotel room, under the name Strickland. Ben-Ami, Gray, and Manny captured McDonald at the hotel, but he was killed by the Mahdi's men before he could give them any information.

McDonald, Cecilia (IA)

Wife of Tony McDonald; she had a drinking problem. Her father owned the auto parts company McDonald worked for.

McGivern, ——— (BI)

The top man in Agency Controls who had retired two weeks before the order was signed with his name to remove the furnishings from the Treadstone house.

McLeod, ——— (IA)

Director of operations at the Cable Beach Hotel in Nassau. He mapped out an exit route that was secure for Evan and Khalehla.

McLeod, Captain (RE)

Base psychiatrist at Fairfax. "McLeod was stooped, slender, bespectacled—the essence of the thoughtful academician." His job was to examine the psychiatric profile of the twelve men who had been at the New Year's Eve party where Ed Pace was killed.

McLeod, Angus MacPherson (BU)

Canadian friend of John St. Jacques who vacationed at Tranquility Inn. He also spent a lot of time fishing with David Webb when he was there. He had been a corporal in the infantry in Korea during the war. Currently he was the owner of Canada's largest industrial engineering company. He helped St. Jacques keep the other guests at the inn occupied during Bourne's attempt to stop the Jackal.

———, Meat (RG)

Heavyset bodyguard of Dellacroce's; he walked like a gorilla. Hawkins knocked him out on the golf course.

———, Meat (RO)

Mangecavallo's street gorilla. (*See also* D'Ambrosia, Salvatore "Meat.")

Meehan, Colonel Daniel (RE)

Fleet Marine Force, Naval Intelligence. He was ordered to Terrazza Verde to assist Spaulding. He wanted to know what was going on because of a prospective radio-radar blackout and a four-zero order to intercept Spaulding; then he received a call from Marshall to assist Spaulding. Meehan thought Spaulding was a double agent when he left Meehan and his driver tied up along the road and took the FMF car; they were extremely angry because they also got stripped and rolled by some wandering vagos.

———, Melvyn (IA)

British MI6 agent who gave Khalehla the recipe for a brandy and vodka drink that was very potent.

Memom (or Meemom) (BU)

A nickname David Webb gave to his wife when his son called her "meemom" for a while instead of "mommy." He sent her a message on the financial pages of the *Herald-Tribune* by using this nickname to catch her attention.

The men of Wolfsschanze (HC)

The men of Wolfsschanze refers to two different groups of men: one group, "the true eagles of Germany" was trying to kill Hitler because of the horrible crimes he'd committed; the other group, the "false Wolfsschanze," wanted to kill Hitler because he was such a poor military leader. Only two or three of the "true eagles" escaped after the assassination attempt failed; the "false Wolfsschanze" group helped Hitler kill off the members of the eagles group.

MEREDITH, ALEXANDER (CM)

Hero of Chancellor's book about the murder of J. Edgar Hoover and the disappearance of the Hoover files.

METCALF, ALAN BRUCE (AP)

Chief Intelligence Officer, Nellis Air Force Base, forty-eight years old; close friend of Sam Abbott's. He has been "in the business" for twenty years. Both Sam and Alan had been prisoners of war in Vietnam.

Metcalf maintained a sophisticated telephone answering machine. He is a slender, muscular, middle-aged man dressed in summer slacks and a white jacket; he has a thin face, the tanned skin about the same color as his short, thinning brown hair. He has clear, authoritative eyes that have dark circles under them.

At the photo identification session in Washington Metcalf was the one who found Stone and gave first aid to him soon after he had been attacked by Belamy. He also called security and ordered them to detain Belamy, who unfortunately escaped. He sent down the orders to restrict to quarters all officers returning from summer leave, to try to keep some of the hitmen off the streets. He also had the pleasure of ordering the Chief Operations Officer at Nellis Air Force Base to throw into maximum security the major in charge of all aircraft maintenance.

METCALF, DORIS (AP)

Wife of Alan Metcalf, mother of his three children. Metcalf put them on a flight from Los Angeles to Cleveland, where they would stay with her parents "until he said otherwise." He figured if the Aquitaine could get to Sam Abbott, they could get him and maybe also his family, so he sent them where he hoped they would be safe.

MEYERS, LOIS (MP)

Lois lived across the hall from Pat Ballantyne in the graduate housing building; she came to visit Pat at the hospital.

MEZZANO, SIGNOR (IA)

A dark-featured, well-spoken, Secret Service guard who was a "well-compensated procurer for various high-ranking members of the government." His Mafia family had sent him to the finest parochial schools and a major university and had trained him for his avocation. Milos obtained information from him about Bollinger's staff. Kendrick killed him on the *Passage to China Island*.

———, MICHEL (BU)

Real first name of Jean-Pierre Fontaine, used by his wife.

MIDDLEJOHN, MAJOR ROBERT (CH)

Member of West Indian Regiment 641, in the year 1739. His information that the tribe of Acquaba would not be party to the Cudjoe treaty with the British was part of the official records of Jamaica.

———, MIKE (BU)

Black telephone repairman sent out by the Reco-Metropolitan Company to repair the answering machine that relayed messages between Ogilvie and the Mafia. The CIA had jammed it externally.

MIKHAILOVIC, PETRIDE (GC)

A Serbo-Croat in his mid-twenties, the youngest trainee at Loch Torridon when Victor was taking his training there. Petride was not his true name; he was really a priest of Xenope. "He was a stocky, powerfully built man, with a bull neck and large shoulders." He was an excessive talker, always questioning; he spoke very good English. He and Victor worked together so well that they were paired off for many projects. He told Victor he was "very, very religious," and had "many brothers." He attempted to force the information about the train from Salonika from Victor; when he realized Victor didn't know anything, Petride put the barrel of his automatic pistol to his temple and took his own life.

MIKHAILOVITCH, ——— (BI)

Russian secret agent who greatly admired the Yachtsman's sailing ability—"said he sailed on sheer nerve, bending the weather to his will."

MIKOVSKY, YANOV (MC)

Curator of archives at the Saltykov-Shchedrin Library in Moscow and former teacher of Taleniekov. He was an old man now, with gray hair and thick glasses. He helped Taleniekov trace Voroshin and was killed by the Matarese.

MIKULSKI, TADEUSZ "TEDDY" (RO)

Special Agent, FBI, due to retire in nine months. He didn't believe Sam Devereaux's wild story about the government conspiracy against the Wopotamis. He released Sam before hearing about the alert to hold him.

MILES, LIEUTENANT DAVID (HC)

New York Port Authority policeman. He investigated Thornton's murder on board the British Airways 747 to New York. He was convinced the victim was supposed to have been Noel Holcroft, and he was extremely angry when Noel left the country without telling him. Noel didn't want Miles interfering with his search for von Tiebolt and Kessler because he was afraid Miles would be killed. Noel learned from Miles that Richard Holcroft had been killed and that he was being pursued by Nazis; Miles wanted to know why. Miles also told Noel that his mother had left the country through Mexico. He wanted Noel back if he had to file extradition papers to do it.

MILLER, LAURENCE (T)

Senator Gillette's chauffeur. Miller had been driving the senator home when another car collided with them on a narrow bridge; Miller was hospitalized. He was loyal to the senator and would not repeat private conversations he overheard; Gillette left him a bequest in his will.

MILLER, DR. PAUL (PM)

A psychiatrist, one of the strategists of Consular Operations. He was an authority on diagnosing and treating stress. Miller concluded Havelock might be having a mental breakdown when he reported seeing Jenna Karas alive; he wanted Havelock brought in so he could be treated and any damaging depositions located. When Cons Ops received the report from Baylor, Miller decided that Havelock could be telling the truth. Because the strategists could not decide whether Havelock should be terminated or enlisted to help them find out about Costa Brava, Stern decided to confer with Matthias's office. A short time later Miller was found shot in the head while working with a patient at Bethesda Naval Hospital. It was impossible to prevent news of Miller's death from reaching the media.

MILLIGAN, HARRY (RO)

When Gilligan was injured in an auto accident, Milligan was put in charge of the Irish group assisting Hawkins at the Four Seasons Hotel.

MINGUS, PAULA (CM)

A plain, overweight girl from Chillicothe, Ohio, who was given the by-line Phyllis Maxwell by her first editor.

MONTEALEGRES (HC)

According to Johann, the Montealegres were Portuguese Jews when his group had to get out of Rio. "Their parents helped the Israelis; they were killed for it. The two children were hunted; they would have been shot too. They had to be taken south."

MONTEFIORI, SILVIO (MC)

The State Department contact in Murato, owner of fishing boats in Bastia; he wrote reports on Soviet naval maneuvers for the Americans. Silvio felt it was better to help Scofield find transportation and be alive to collect ten thousand dollars from him than it was to try to capture Scofield or be betrayed by Scofield to the Russians.

MONTELLAN, CARLOS (CM)

One of two candidates for Genesis of Inver Brass; he had been with them four years and was suspected by Varak and Bravo of having the missing files. He had Hispanic features, dark eyes, graying wavy hair; he was married with children. His family was originally wealthy, from Castile, but they had fled to the U.S. to escape the Falangists. His family fought both the Church and Franco. He was a naturalized American, "an archenemy of oppression in any form." He occupied the Maynard Chair of International Relations at Harvard and was one of the foremost analysts of geopolitical thought. For the past dozen years succeeding administrations had tried to persuade him to join the State Department. He was devoted to the U.S. and alarmed about the current government corruption. His wife was told he had been sent to the Far East by the State Department; he was reported as killed by terrorists to cover his murder in the U.S.

MONTREAUX, ARDIS (IA)

Kendrick met Ardis when she worked for Off Shore Investments, Ltd. She tried to con the Kendrick Group out of a large amount of money; Kendrick had been romantically involved with her for a while.

MOORE, BARAK "BRAMWELL" (CH)

Head of the Jamaican revolutionary group; he wants Jamaica for all the people, not just a selected few. Bramwell was his real name; he changed it to Barak. He wore a baseball cap over his shaven head. Charles had been a childhood friend. Charles regarded him as "black garbage"—too crude, too loud, too unwashed. Barak said he'd just as soon kill Charles; however, he realized he'd have to work with Charles to achieve his goals. He considered Charles to be a political criminal, but he respected his knowledge of Jamaica. He led the group going to Piersall's to retrieve Piersall's research papers about the Halidon. As he and McAuliff were escaping on the raft, he received a serious gunshot wound. A private doctor treated him, but he died; Lawrence buried him at sea. Daniel planned to replace him with a Halidonite.

———, MOOSE (RO)

Owner of Monarch-McDowell Aircraft, close associate of Warren Pease's. He agreed they had to get rid of Mangecavallo.

MORAY (BU)

Krupkin contacted the KGB car following him with the special Moray code, which involved switching from one ultra high frequency to another. The Russians had stolen it from the British.

MORGAN, ANTHONY "TONY" (CM)

Chancellor's editor and personal friend. He was the "physical embodiment of the Ivy League postgraduate turned New York publisher. He was slender and tall with shoulders slightly stooped," a thin face, brown eyes, and a mercurial temperament. He was forty-one years old, married to Marie. Chancellor thought he was the best, because he cared.

MORGAN, MARIE (CM)

Tony Morgan's wife. She told Tony he should protect his authors.

MORRIS, SENATOR JOHN (T)

Senator from Illinois. He was in his mid-thirties, a brilliant attorney, a black who had swiftly worked his way up within the system. He was on the confirmation hearing panel examining Trevayne for chairmanship of the subcommittee investigating defense spending by the Pentagon.

MORRIS, PHILLIP (BU)

Name Conklin told Morris Panov to use when he registered at the Brookshire Hotel in Baltimore, Md.

MOSSAD, SIGNOR (IA)

Name used by one of the Mossad when trying to contact Weingrass in Paris by telephone.

MOTHER (PM)

Code name for the VKR (Mother Russia); they were to kill Rostov.

MOTHER GODDAM (HC)

Althene was the object of an official surveillance for a very long time; her file was kept at the FBI under the code name "Mother Goddam."

MOTOBOTO, YAKATAKI "CRUISER" (RO)

"Cruiser" represented Toyhondahai Enterprises, U.S.A., Motion Picture Operations. He wanted the Suicidal Six movie.

MR. BONES (CH)

"Mr. Bones" was a name used by black-face players in comedy skits in minstrel shows. McAuliff called the black priest figure "Mr. Bones" to let him know he had made the association between him and the British intelligence service in the Owl of Saint George.

MULLER, ———— (RE)

Jean Cameron knew of a man named Muller at the German embassy in Buenos Aires, but not of anyone named Altmuller.

MULLER, ERNST (AP)

Oberleutnant in the German Luftwaffe, a highly skilled pilot who flew ministers of state to conferences both inside and outside West Germany. Identified as a member of the Aquitaine by the man from Bonn at the secret meeting set up at the White House by Peter Stone.

MURDOCK, ELLIOTT (MP)

Elliott was a biology teacher at Carlyle who closely resembled Matlock; he couldn't understand the message that was meant for Matlock.

MUSSOLINI, BENITO (GC) [REAL PERSON]

Fascist dictator of Italy before and during World War II. In the beginning Savarone had endorsed Mussolini; Mussolini had come to Campo di Fiori seeking alliance. He had been committed and filled with promise for all Italy. He betrayed the Italians by plunging them into a useless African war and joined with the Germans to enter an unpopular war. Savarone and others, partigianos, resisted. Mussolini joined with the Germans and Donatti to get rid of his opposition.

MUSTAPHA, "MUSTY" (IA)

The only minister of the sultan's cabinet and businessman friend of Kendrick's. He made arrangements for Kendrick to meet the sultan. Mustapha was gunned down in his car and killed.

MYERS, JOSEPH (CH)

Holcroft knew "Malcolm" by the name Joseph Myers, one of his agents.

MYRDAL, INGMAR (SI)

Myrdal had controlling interest in Donnenfeld, the most impressive firm on the Stockholm exchange. His own company had covertly absorbed Donnenfeld, a move made possible by the illegal transaction with Ulster Scarlett's securities. Myrdal also supported the Nazis.

NACHRICHTENDIENST (HC)

The Nachrichtendienst, enemy of the false Wolfsschanze, was originally an intelligence unit that developed as a result of Operation Barbarossa. It was "exclusively Junker, a corps of aristocrats . . . It loathed Hitler; it scorned the Schutstaffel . . . it hated the commanders of the Luftwaffe. . . . It was only for Germany. *Their* Germany." It survived under the leadership of General Falkenheim and attempted to stop the release of the funds in Geneva. The soldiers of the Nachrichtendienst were the Jews of Har Sha'alav.

NACHRICHTENDIENST (RE)

Select unit of the espionage service known to only a few of the upper-echelon ministers. A Gehlen specialty. The Nachrichtendienst suggested the trade of the blueprints for the diamonds.

NASSIR, ABU (IA)

One of the terrorist council leaders inside the American embassy where the hostages were being held. He was a better theoretician than fighter. "A marine guard jumped him, took his weapon, and shot him."

NAVAJO (PM)

Code name Havelock used when he and Ogilvie were undercover in Istanbul trying to prevent a KGB assassination.

NEEDHAM, AMOS (OW)

A vice president of Manufacturers Hanover Trust and the chairman of the special events committee at the country club. He told Cardone about Caesar. The same night Omega attacked Tanner's house, Needham's house was being robbed. Needham and his wife were both elderly.

NELSON, —— (RE)

Navigator who was killed on a bombing run over Bremerhaven.

NELSON, JOHN (BS)

Thirty-two-year-old American attaché. He was dark-haired and liked vodka martinis. He was indebted to Catherine Staples because she suppressed photos taken of him in a compromising sexual situation; he had been heavily drugged and the pictures were taken for blackmail purposes. He had a good job because he had learned Chinese; he'd attended Upper Iowa College in Fayette, Iowa. He knew that Catherine Staples and Ian Ballantyne were partly responsible for his success. Catherine found out from him that Havilland was staying at a safe house on Victoria Peak. She asked him to find out if there was a connection between Havilland and the Webbs. He risked his job finding out.

NESBIT, MISS (SI)

Chancellor Scarlett's secretary.

NEUMANN, CAPTAIN HANS (GC)

Victor was to meet Neumann in Block Seven of Casimir. He was "a devoted officer of the Reich with a cousin in the Gestapo."

NEVINS, CAROL (GC)

Jim Nevins's wife; she called Adrian to tell him Jim had been killed.

NEVINS, JAMES (GC)

A black attorney who worked for the Justice Department in Washington. He was the spokesman for a small group of government lawyers who were being manipulated by the Justice Department. They wanted Adrian to help them because he could not be harassed; they were outraged by so much illegality in the city where laws were made. Nevins was especially outraged by the discovery of Eye Corps; he asked Adrian to remove himself when his brother's name showed up. Afraid of conspiracy, he carried all his files in his briefcase and didn't leave copies at the office. Supposedly he had been killed when a truck smashed into his car. However, it was apparent that half his head had been blown away by a shotgun blast, and his briefcase was missing. The authorities denied he had been murdered.

NEWLAND, CHRIS (SI)

Man who supposedly introduced Matthew Canfield to Janet Scarlett at an Oyster Bay club.

NEYLAND, COMMANDER (GC)

A commander in the British Admiralty—"middle-aged, properly military, and quite impressed with himself." Although Vittorio spoke perfect English, Neyland didn't listen to him; he introduced him as Savarone Fontini-Cristi. He escorted Vittorio to his meeting with Brevourt, Hackett, and Teague; then he stood guard outside and signed him out after the meeting was over.

Nichols, Chris (ro)

News reporter on the scene at the Four Seasons Hotel in Boston; his wife thought he was at the Marblehead Yacht Club regatta.

Nimrod (mp)

An independent group that controlled the drug traffic in the New England area; they were also involved with gambling and prostitution. The head man was also referred to as Nimrod and periodically changed. Nimrod used organized crime in some of their activities but was in competition with them, which was why there was a conference scheduled in May between the groups. The Nimrod group operated through the faculty and staffs of colleges and universities; Matlock was asked to help the Narcotics Bureau find out where the conference would be held, so they could make their arrests.

No Name (rg)

One of Sam's guards at the chateau, perhaps a psychopath.

Noir (rg)

Other code name Crete. His specialty was aircraft technology; his exploits in Houston and Moscow were legend. One of his jobs was to rip the communications equipment out of the Pope's vehicles; another was to pilot the Learjet for Hawkins and the Pope.

Norcross, —— (gc)

Vittorio's tailor on Savile Row in London; he managed to provide clothes for him within a matter of hours after Vittorio's escape from Italy.

——, Norma (ow)

Tanner's secretary at Standard Mutual.

Norton, Senator James (t)

Senator from Vermont, member of the panel to confirm the chairman of the Defense Allocation Subcommittee. Norton was in his early sixties, with close-cropped gray hair. He told Trevayne he felt he was the best man for the job but wanted to make sure he was thoroughly investigated so there would be no repercussions later if something went wrong. Norton was allied to Genessee and was thoroughly alarmed by the visits made by Trevayne and his men to various Genessee plants.

The Nucleus (cm)

Group that paralleled Inver Brass in Chancellor's book about Hoover's death.

O'BRIEN, CARROLL QUINLAN (CM)

Senior FBI agent who worked with Chancellor to find the missing Hoover files. He was forty-nine years old, a stocky man with reddish-brown hair. He was married with children. He'd met Varak two years before, when he delivered profile data on eastern bloc UN personnel to Varak, which could have cost him his career. He and Varak often had dinner together.

He'd been an assistant prosecutor in Sacramento, a reserve officer who was called up for the Vietnam War, put into G-2 as an investigator for Army Intelligence. He ran into unexpected combat in the northern sectors, was captured, and spent two years in Han Chow before escaping. He returned a hero and was decorated by the President. Hoover noticed him and offered him a job with the Bureau. He'd been there four and a half years.

After Hoover's death there were no inquiries about the files, so he began asking questions as to where they were. He discovered Longworth's entry the night before Hoover's death and intended to go to the attorney general. He received an anonymous telephone call threatening to expose what happened at Han Chow if he continued his probe. After this he was removed from several committees, no longer received certain classified reports, and drew continuous night duty. He just happened to be on duty the night Chancellor came in looking for help. He tried to protect Chancellor and Alison MacAndrew and was hurt in the process, but he stuck with them until the end.

O'BRIEN, MR. AND MRS. CHANCELLOR (CM)

After "the maniacs" destroyed Saint Michaels One, a sterile house, they put an article in the newspaper, listing the owners of the property as the O'Briens, to let Peter, Alison, and O'Brien know they had proof their group had been there.

THE ODESSA (HC)

The Odessa wanted to revive the Nazi party. They pursued the children of Nazis to either get them to join their group or to kill them if they refused. The Odessa existed only outside of Germany, because the Germans wouldn't tolerate them. They were the sworn enemy of the Rache.

O'GILLIGAN, MONSIGNOR PATRICK DENNIS (RG)

Priest from Washington who played chess by telephone with the Pope.

OGILVIE, ANDREW (RO)

Friend of Lord Cavendish's; he had also been with the Grenadiers. He wanted to do the movie about the Suicidal Six.

OGILVIE, BRYCE (BU)

"Ice-cold Ogilvie," Manhattan lawyer in one of Wall Street's most prestigious firms, second only to Randy Gates in corporate and antitrust law. He was chairman of the new Medusa. He had been a young lawyer in Saigon when he met Delta, and had been part of the original Medusa. He hired De Fazio to kill Armbruster, Teagarten, Swayne, Marie Webb, DeSole, Conklin, and Bourne. The Russians warned him that the CIA was about to pick him up. They offered to help him—for a price. He was flown to Russia and his family to Marrakesh.

OGILVIE, MRS. BRYCE (BU)

She was married to Bryce Ogilvie and had two teenage children. They took a flight to Marrakesh via Morocco when Bryce left for Russia. In the early seventies Mrs. Ogilvie had been roommates at Bennington with a woman designer who was now associated with the Jackal.

OGILVIE, JOHN PHILIP (PM)

Also known as Red, the Gunslinger, Apache, and Jack. One of four major strategists of Consular Operations, field agent for twenty years, a killer. He was a red-haired, stocky man, unkempt, inrascible. Red had been married and had three children, but his wife divorced him and he hadn't seen the children for five years. He felt that whatever Consular Operations did was justified; he had seen the rehabilitation camps. He knew Havelock would believe only Matthias or himself, so he went into the field to reach Havelock and bring him back; Red intended to get close enough to Havelock to use nerve gas on him. If he was captured, he could use his hidden cyanide capsules; he had only five or six weeks to live anyway because of a terminal disease. The nerve gas didn't work and Havelock drew his gun; when Red couldn't persuade him to put it away, he shoved Havelock out of the line of fire and took the bullets meant for Havelock.

OGILVIE, THOMAS (SI)

Owner of Ogilvie and Storm, Ltd., Publishers, in London. Elizabeth Scarlatti called Thomas Ogilvie to get whatever information he had available on the Schutzstaffel, the National Socialists.

OHIO-FOUR-ZERO (IA)

"Translated, it meant 'Oman, maximum alert.'" It was a "designated situation room in the underground complex at the Department of State." Gerald Bryce ran the computers there.

———, OLAF (RO)

Tourist who couldn't get past the Wopotami dancers in front of the Supreme Court building.

OLAFER, SIR LARS "LAURENCE" (RO)

Leader of the Suicidal Six; he used his real name when portraying the head of the Nobel Committee arriving in Boston.

OLAFFSEN, CHRISTIAN (SI)

Olaffsen's many companies controlled the export of Swedish iron and steel. The Swedish government paid him thousands for hundreds of tons of low-carbon ingot from his factories; he gave them low-quality ingots from Japan. He was one of the merchants who supported the Nazis.

OLBRICHT (HC) [REAL PERSON]

A German Army officer, one of the Führer's would-be assassins. He was shot as a traitor to Hitler.

THE OLD MEN OF PARIS (BU)

"Carlos scoured Paris looking for old men who were either dying or knew they hadn't long to live because of their age, all with police records . . . these old men have loved ones. . . . The Jackal would . . . swear to provide for the people his about-to-die couriers left behind if they swore the rest of their lives to him."

OLDSMOBILE, JUDGE CORNELIUS (RO)

Cyrus M was disguised as Oldsmobile, a visiting *amicus curiae*, to accompany Hawkins into the Supreme Court hearing.

———, OLIVER (RO)

Head of the Pentagon.

OLIVER, HOWARD (RE)

Executive from Meridian Aircraft. Oliver was a glutton and a manipulator, making a huge sum of money from the war. He was obese and balding, with a rough voice and thick lips. Meridian's aircraft was operational but lacked the guidance system Meridian had agreed to provide in their government contract. Oliver was forced to go to Kendall for help in obtaining the guidance system from the Germans. Oliver was responsible for bargaining with Koening for the industrial diamonds; he offered them money up front and a few million profit. Spaulding threatened to expose Oliver's part in the exchange if he didn't sell his assets and become a government clerk the rest of his life.

OLSEN, JAMES (IA)

Gardener for Kendrick at his Virginia home.

———, OLYMPIA (RO)

Stavros's companion, a tourist in front of the Supreme Court building trying to get past the dancers.

OMEGA (OW)

A Soviet NKVD operation. The Soviets had a list of individuals in decision-making positions who were vulnerable to blackmail. They intended to use this information to create a major financial panic in the U.S. Tanner was asked by Fassett to help him expose Omega's operation.

O'NEILL, ——— (AP)

"O'Neill down at the commissioner's office" was keeping Lawrence Talbot posted about Judge Anstett's murder, partly out of courtesy, partly because Lawrence Talbot was nervous about being the last person other than the killer to see the judge alive.

OPEN TERRITORY (CM)

To the senior agents at the FBI this code meant the director was seriously, perhaps fatally ill.

OPERATION AZRA (IA)

Operation in which Yosef and his men hoped to kill Kendrick at Mesa Verde.

OPERATION BARBAROSSA (HC)

" 'Barbarossa' was Hitler's first invasion north. . . . He called it a victory. The Prussians called it a disaster." They lost many men and took only worthless, scorched earth.

OPERATION MEDUSA (BI)

The members of Medusa were known as "les mercenaires du diable." Medusa was a "clandestine outgrowth of the search-and-destroy concept, designed to function behind enemy lines during the Vietnam War." The priorities of the teams of volunteers were the disruption of enemy communications and supply lines, the pinpointing of prison camps, and the assassination of village leaders cooperating with the Communists and enemy commanders whenever possible. Some of the volunteers were smugglers and criminals who knew about night landing spots and jungle routes. They sustained over ninety percent casualties; their real names were not used, and of the ten percent surviving, many simply disappeared without a trace. Due to its nature, Operation Medusa was always classified material.

OPERATION MEDUSA (BS)
Most of the volunteers were criminals; "most wouldn't be allowed in any civilized army, Webb among them."

OPERATION SONNENKINDER (HC)
"Die Sonnenkinder" or "Children of the Sun." In 1945 thousands of young German children, selected genetically, were sent out to all parts of the world by the Third Reich to be trained as the leaders of the Fourth Reich. If they failed to live up to their birthright, they were never told about the Fourth Reich and they were quietly weeded out. The survivors waited for the funds to be released from Geneva; their names were on a list kept by Johann.

ORANGE (IA)
Member of the Masada Brigade. He was upset when the operation to free Yaakov's father was aborted and replaced by the operation to rescue Kendrick. He was killed by Azra in the Aradous Hotel.

ORANGE (RG)
Other code name Rome. Orange was in charge of native orientation. Part of his job was to provide clothing that would blend in with the locals and provide transportation to the site of Ground Zero for each assault captain. He was also to disable the people around the Pope.

ORDER OF XENOPE (GC)
The order was "the harshest monastic brotherhood under the control of the Patriarchate of Constantine. Blind obedience coexisted with self-reliance; they were disciplined to the instant of death." When it was obvious the sacred documents were in jeopardy from the Germans, the order took them into the mountains and hid them. Only Savarone, the priest Petride, and his brother Annaxas, the engineer, knew where they were. Petride killed Annaxas and himself; the order took in Annaxas's wife and children, killed the wife and raised the children. Donatti and his group wanted the documents for themselves and committed many crimes to get them; they were punished by the Church of Rome, and the order became almost extinct.

ORÉALE, CLAUDE GISELLE (BI)
Worked as a salesclerk for Les Classiques; he considered himself "a couturier, an artist." He lived on rue Racine in Paris, where he shared a

fifth-floor flat with two other men. He was an awkwardly moving thin man with long, dark hair that flowed like a mane; he wore Pierre Cardin suits. He was easily upset by Webb—he bit his knuckles until they bled and ran screaming to Lavier.

O'REILLY, ANN MULCAHY (IA)

Congressman Kendrick's secretary, a middle-aged veteran of Washington. Annie was married to Paddy O'Reilly. She was thrilled when Kendrick was put on the Partridge Committee. When Kendrick was gone he always kept in touch with her; when she couldn't reach him for two days she became alarmed and sent Paddy over to Fairfax to investigate.

O'REILLY, LIEUTENANT PATRICK XAVIER "PADDY" (IA)

He was a detective first-grade on the D.C. police force and was married to Ann Mulcahy, who described him as a "two-toilet Irish detective." The D.C. police department virtually bribed him to leave Boston for Washington; he'd been there twelve years. Paddy was a large, broad-shouldered, somewhat paunchy red-haired man with green eyes. He became acquainted with Manny when he accompanied Annie on the hospital visits; Manny persuaded Paddy to smuggle Scotch to him in Listerine bottles. Paddy contacted Mitch Payton after he found the bodies at the house in Fairfax.

OREJO, ——— (AP)

Identified as a member of Aquitaine at the White House meeting. Formerly a paratrooper, then a dealer in drugs, and a suspect in many killings, operating out of Ibiza, Spain.

ORLOV, ——— (BU)

One of Krupkin's trusted men. He was in the other car outside the Kubinka Armory and couldn't believe what he had been asked to do.

O'ROURKE, PADDY (PM)

Name Taylor used to refer to his conscience. Also the name of a pub in New York.

ORPHAN-9-6 (PM)

Telephone number for Voyagers Emporium, a KGB proprietary.

ORTEGA, MANUEL ORTIZ (MC)

Ortega was called by de Matarese to be a member of the first council of the Matarese; he called de Matarese a madman and de Matarese killed him.

ORTON, MATTHEW (MP)

Insignificant aide to the governor in Hartford. Orton was Nimrod from 1965 to 1970.

O'SHANTER, TAM (IA)

Provisional "wing commander" of the Irish Republican Amry, son of E and an Irish nurse. Tam O'Shanter was not his actual name.

OSTERMAN, BERNIE (OW)

Successful television writer. John and Ali had met Bernie and Leila in Los Angeles when John was first working in the newspaper business. Bernie had a wife and two children. He was thin but physically tough, and he was sensitive to bigotry. He graduated from CCNY in 1946 and had been a swimming instructor in the Army at Fort Dix. Bernie originally lived on Tremont Avenue in the Bronx and preferred the sanity of East Coast living to that of California. He wanted to bring Tanner into the Zurich deal but Leila wasn't sure this was a good idea. Tanner realized the Ostermans probably were not connected to Omega when they wanted to call the police after Tanner's dog was killed. Bernie and Leila didn't know anything about Omega, and they stayed with the Tanners and helped them fight off Fassett and MacAuliff. The Ostermans couldn't afford to have their reputation tarnished by the Zurich deal, so they had a syndicate in Paris assume their investments, and went back to California.

OSTERMAN, LEILA (OW)

Wife of Bernie Osterman. Leila and Bernie were Jewish; the other three couples made it a point to take them to the local country club when they visited because none of them liked bigotry. Leila had not come from an affluent background; she had once thought $30,000 was all the money in the world. She and Bernie were professional television writers and lived in Los Angeles; they enjoyed sunbathing in the nude when their children weren't around. The Ostermans were financially well off, even owned a couple of racing horses; part of their money came from their investments in Zurich. Leila and Bernie were very close, yet they risked their lives protecting the Tanners; Tanner wasn't sure he could trust Leila because none of the bullets came near her, yet she was wearing a shiny green brooch.

OSTERMAN, MARIE (OW)

Bernie and Leila's daughter; she was to call them before she came home from the beach.

OSTERMAN, MERWYN (OW)

Bernie and Leila's son; he'd been at the beach with his sister. He and his sister didn't go to the Tanners' for the weekend with their parents. He'd picked out a remote-control airplane for Raymond's birthday present.

———, OTIS (SI)

Otis was one of the two men Scarlett killed when he turned the German guns on his own men.

O'TOOLE, GAVIN (RO)

Owner of Sam Devereaux's favorite bar. His Catholic clients considered Anne to be a saint; O'Toole prevented them from bashing in Sam's head after his remarks about Anne and the Pope.

PACE, ALAN (MP)

Tall young man with light brown hair who was a waiter at Rocco's Hunt Club. He was a senior in government studies at Yale, an honors student with a fellowship to the Maxwell School of Political Science at Syracuse. Alan lived in an old apartment house on the outskirts of Hamden. He had spent twenty-eight months in the Army in Vietnam as an officer attached to inventory and supply. He had stayed in the Army an extra four months, then came back with enough money to set himself up as one of the biggest drug dealers in New Haven.

PACE, DOUGLAS (T)

Phyllis Trevayne's older brother and Andrew's brother-in-law. Doug was a brilliant, introverted, painfully shy electronics engineer. He had worked for Pratt and Whitney in Hartford; Doug was convinced the close-tolerance spheroid disc was the most vital component of the new high-altitude propulsion aircraft. The executives wouldn't allocate funds for its development, so Doug and Andrew started their own business. Doug did the designing and Andrew did the sales and management. After *Sputnik* went up they retooled for space objectives and expanded their business; they were both millionaires by the time they were thirty-five. When Andrew was thirty-seven he left the business and Doug took over the entire operation.

PACE, E. (RE)

Spaulding told Asher Feld to register at the Alvear Hotel under the name E. Pace and asked Jean to contact him and ask him to exercise his priorities in regard to Rhinemann.

PACE, COLONEL EDMUND (RE)

Commander of Field Operations, Fairfax. He was married and had a son and a daughter. He was looking for a station chief for Lisbon because there was evidence a war would be starting. Spaulding's name surfaced because he had inquired about the Army Corps of Engineers. Pace decided to recruit him and take special interest in his training; Spaulding was very successful in Lisbon for three years. Pace's people picked up the information about the Nachrichtendienst wanting to trade blueprints for diamonds and gave the information to Vandamm and Swanson. He objected to the exchange and balked at finding a man for Buenos Aires; he was not happy when Spaulding had to be pulled out of Lisbon and he was uneasy because he didn't know the details of the operation. Pace was shot in the head at his own New Year's Eve party inside the Fairfax compound by a member of the Haganah, probably Barden. Spaulding felt Pace's death was somehow connected to Swanson.

PACKARD, CAPTAIN ANDREW (AP)

U.S. Army captain having full security clearance and dealing in top-secret procedures. Was able to set up a sterile telephone for Halliday. He and Halliday, Stone, and Landis obtained in-depth intelligence dossiers on Bertholdier, Leifhelm, Abrahms, and Van Headmer. Dr. Beale provided funds to hire private firms in the nations of these men to get up-to-date information on them. He was honored in a private ceremony at the White House along with Stone and Landis, but declined, as he felt Joel Converse was the real hero.

PAK-FEI (BS)

The most experienced limousine driver who worked for the Regent Hotel in Kowloon. Bourne paid him well to help him procure a gun and other necessities. Pak-fei liked Bourne and protected him—he made sure they weren't followed and locked him in the car in a bad area. He was married, and had two grown children with "not bad jobs." He agreed to take the limousine Bourne had rented and drive it into the hills with his family in order to put the necessary mileage on the car before returning it. He was well paid by Bourne.

PALANTYNE, MRS. (HC)

In the apartment across from Noel's. He kept seeing a blond woman smoking a cigarette and looking across at him. When he asked about her, he was told the woman had been dead for a month.

PALO ALTO INTERNATIONAL (AP)

Export-import firm set up initially by Preston Halliday for George Marcus Delavane, who became the director of the firm.

Street fight in Beijing (THE BOURNE SUPREMACY)

PANOV, MORRIS (BI)

A very conscientious doctor of psychiatry who worked at Bethesda Naval Hospital in Maryland. He was not a young man; he was affectionately called "Dr. Mo" by the staff and he had a good sense of humor. Alexander Conklin had been a patient of his off and on for five years; Conklin called him to try to get some answers about Webb's mental condition. Panov also treated David Webb; he had treated similar cases for the government and demanded security clearance so he could treat Webb.

PANOV, MORRIS (BS)

"Morris Panov was the only person besides Marie who could reach him [Webb]." He was infuriated when the information he gave Conklin was used as a pretext to kill Webb; he threatened all kinds of embarrassing disclosures if he wasn't given clearance to treat Webb. Mo was Marie's friend and ally during Webb's treatment. He called Alexander Conklin after Marie was kidnapped; the two of them went to Hong Kong after Webb when they couldn't get any straight answers from the government.

PANOV, MORRIS (BU)

Conklin's and Webb's psychiatrist and good friend. Conklin confided everything to him. He was a tall, balding man, about the same age as

Conklin. His mother was dead; his wife had died ten years after they were married. He was a terrible cook, but thought he was the Jewish Julia Child. After the car crash in which Dellacroce was injured, Mo examined him and left a note with him with his diagnosis on it before leaving. He was willing to do anything he could to prevent harm to the Webbs and to help the government put an end to Medusa. While at the airport in Pontcarré, he was shot in the chest—both lungs were punctured as well as the wall of his heart. He survived but lost the use of his left arm and suffered partial paralysis of his right leg.

———, PAOLO (MC)
Count Scozzi's aide; he danced with Antonia.

———, PAOLO (PM)
Italian soldier at Col des Moulinets who was ordered to teach the new man the rules.

———, PAOLO AND DAVINIA (BU)
Also known as the conte and the contessa. He was with the Italian embassy. They were married and quite rich. At the café outside of Paris, they left when they saw Krupkin leave and avoided being killed by the Jackal.

PARAVACINI, BERNARDO (MC)
Married the Scozzis' daughter. Paravacini had millions and the Scozzis had titles but no money.

PARC MONCEAU (BI)
Wealthy area in Paris where General and Mrs. Villiers lived. It was the code name for Mrs. Villiers, who was Carlos's message center.

PARELLI, MARIO ALBERTO (AP)
United States Senator for five terms. He had been an Army captain and served as Colonel Delavane's chief aide in the First Army. They called him "up-from-the-bootstraps Mario" because he had used the G.I. Bill for college, then risen to the top politically with some backing from early benefactors. During 1962–63 he was a frequent visitor to the White House, courtesy of the Kennedys. Peter Stone's group was able to connect him with the Mafia killing of Judge Anstett; he was removed from the Senate and taken into custody when this could be supported by enough evidence.

PARIS (CM)
Inver Brass code name for Carlos Montellan.

PARIS FIVE (BU)
Code name Fontaine used when contacting Carlos.

PARKE, SENIOR AGENT LESTER (CM)
FBI agent at the security desk at the Bureau the night Varak's group was admitted to Flags. He was one of Hoover's special agents; he "retired a month after Hoover's death, drawing a minimum pension, but with enough money to buy a fair-size condominium in Fort Lauderdale."

PARKHURST, ——— (GC)
Parkhurst of the Air Ministry was to make arrangements to send Jane Holcroft on a tour of the Loch Torridon relays while Victor was there.

PARNELL, ——— (AP)
Name used by Connal Fitzpatrick when he made arrangements to meet Ilse Fishbein; he presented himself to her as an attorney from Milwaukee, Wisconsin, fluent in German, representing a former Nazi who had taken care of Göring. In return, Göring had given the Nazi money to emigrate to the United States. There he became wealthy, died, and left his fortune—$2 million—to Ilse. She was to bring Leifhelm to Fitzpatrick's room to sign papers verifying that she was Göring's daughter; when Leifhelm arrived, Connal hoped to capture him and then exchange him for Joel Converse.

PARNELL, CULVER (BU)
A hotel magnate from Atlanta, he'd been in the business for twenty years; this led to his appointment as chief of protocol for the White House. He was gray-haired and came from Georgia. He had been in the military in Saigon during the Vietnam War, but was not a member of Medusa. He had been involved in running mini casinos and bringing in prostitutes.

PARQUETTE, VIRGINIA (AP)
Name Valerie used when she called Sam Abbott; it had to be something he'd recognize but Aquitaine wouldn't. Charpentier, her maiden name, meant carpenter, so she chose Parquet, a type of wood floor, and feminized it to Parquette. The Virginia was easy, as this was the name of Joel's sister, who Joel hoped would marry Sam Abbott.

PARSIFAL (PM)
(*Parsifal*, an opera by Wagner) Code name given to the person who was manipulating Matthias and causing the threat to world peace. This person wanted to show that the world could be destroyed by a man who

had unchecked power, especially if the man became insane. By revealing that this man was an American, it would change the balance of power in the world.

PARTRIDGE, CONGRESSMAN ALVIN (IA)

Alabama congressman who was short and overweight with thinning, dyed hair. In exchange for Milos repressing the photographs of the drug parties his aides had, the congressman agreed to put Kendrick on the Partridge Committee (sometimes referred to as "the Birds"). The morning he was to interrogate Barrish, he was unable to be present and Kendrick conducted the interrogation quite capably.

PARTRIDGE, ALVIN, JR. (IA)

Son of the congressman from Alabama. He was a third-year law student at Virginia and worked as a congressional aide for his father. He and the other aides had wild parties at the homes of Partridge Committee members. One night they were busted and all of them quit their jobs except him. He wasn't honest with his father about the matter and lost his father's trust.

PASTOR, ——— (MC)

Pastor was the name Scofield used when meeting Count Scozzi at his party.

PASTORINE, SOPHIA (MC)

The blind whore of Villa Matarese and great-grandmother of Antonia Gravet. She had enjoyed living with Guillaume de Matarese for three years. Sophia had pale blue eyes, white hair, and sharp, angular features; she was over seventy, a woman who had once been extraordinarily beautiful. She lived with her dog, Ucello, in a cabin high in the mountains. The villagers despised her; they thought Guillaume had spared her life when he destroyed the villa and the people in it. She was to have been killed also by Guillaume, but she escaped and traveled to Zonza and married Guillaume's former horse trainer; she then returned to the mountains years later. She could tell from Taleniekov's and Scofield's voices that they were frightened of the Matarese; she knew she would die soon and added what she knew to their knowledge. She didn't want Antonia to know because it would endanger her life. When the villagers attacked her cabin, Sophia misdirected them so that Taleniekov, Scofield, and Antonia could get away; Sophia was killed by the villagers.

PATELLI, A. (MC)

Foreman of a construction crew in Boston. Scofield convinced him he was a government inspector and stole explosives from him.

PATRICK, BRENDAN (BU)

Name used by Prefontaine when he bumped into Fontaine at the Tranquility Inn. He also asked Pritchard to change his name on the registry to Patrick because he didn't want anyone to know his real name.

———, PAUL (AP)

Held rank of colonel; adjutant to retired general Marcus Delavane, member of Aquitaine. One of his jobs was to assist the general after he lost his legs and was confined to a wheelchair. He knew about Aquitaine and discussed it with the general. After the widespread rioting started, Paul attempted to shoot Delavane with a .357 Magnum revolver; since Delavane did not trust anyone, including his aide, he had a gun hidden in his wheelchair. Paul died of the wound from Delavane, but not until after he had had the opportunity to kill Delavane. Paul was acting on orders from the other members of the Aquitaine to get rid of Delavane as soon as the rioting started.

———, PAUL (BI)

Economist from Brussels who was a friend of Marie St. Jacques's. He was attending the Sixth World Economic Conference in Zurich at the Carillon du Lac hotel. In the scuffle between David Webb and Carlos's men, Paul was knocked off his chair to the floor and stayed there, so he didn't see anything that was going on.

———, PAUL (CM)

A representative of the ongoing election campaign in 1972. He was a "cherub-faced, bland-looking young man with scrubbed skin and eager eyes . . . another clean-cut liar." Phyllis Maxwell discovered that groups were being told to contribute to the campaign or suffer severe problems financially; she threatened to expose them.

———, PAUL (MC)

Secretary of State. He wanted Scofield brought in, not because he assassinated Yurievich, but because Scofield might be able to expose the Matarese. Paul was on the Council of the Matarese and was killed by Scofield at Appleton Hall. The President reported that he died after a prolonged illness.

PAYTON, MITCHELL JARVIS (IA)

Uncle Mitch, MJ, code name Mr. B. Director of Special Projects for the CIA. He had studied with Samuel Winters and had a doctorate in Arab studies; he had studied American literature as an undergraduate. When the CIA recruited him, he was an associate professor; they assigned him to the Middle East, his cover an Arabic-speaking instructor of American literature. He met Professor Rashad at the university, and he and the Rashads became good friends. Khalehla had called him "Uncle Mitch" since she was six years old. After a successful career in the Middle East he was brought back to Washington to succeed Angleton. When Khalehla decided to join the CIA, she went to Mitch and worked directly for him after completing her training. Mitch was depressed when he had to tell Sam Winters he knew about Inver Brass and that he had to turn over what he knew to the proper authorities. When he finally decided to tell Jennings about Inver Brass, he offered his resignation, which was refused by Jennings.

PAYTON-JONES, HAROLD (HC)

Fairly high up in British Intelligence, MI5. He was in his fifties, with straight gray hair and a weathered face. Harold and his partner tried to find out why Noel was trying to locate Johann and told Noel they thought Johann was the Tinamou. Johann persuaded Harold to give him access to certain files in exchange for delivering the Tinamou to him. Harold was led to believe the Nachrichtendienst had paid the Tinamou for an assassination in London. In the MI5 files Harold referred to Johann only as "Source Able," maintaining Johann's anonymity.

PEACOCK (GC)

Code name used for Lubok by the Frenchman who picked him up on the Rhine.

PEAR (GC)

Code name used by Harold Latham when he and Apple brought Vittorio out of Italy to England; he was with MI6. He had learned the Italian language but not the idiom, and he liked working with the Bolsheviks because they were thorough. He was angry when Apple's hand was mangled because of Vittorio's actions; Vittorio apologized to Pear for his naiveté when Pear gave him clean, dry clothes in the submarine.

PEASE, WARREN "WARTY" (RO)

Secretary of State. He and the President had been college roommates. Warren's left eye twitched back and forth rapidly when he was nervous. Warren and his group plotted the murder of Vinnie and Hawk and Sam because their companies stood to lose great sums of money if the Wopotamis won their case. Smythington-Fontini supposedly took care of Vinnie and the SFIs were sent after Hawk's group. When the SFIs failed, Warren sent the Filthy Four and then the Suicidal Six after them. Hawkins found out from Ethelred that his orders had come from Pease, so he set up a clandestine meeting with Pease, promising to help him solve the problem. Pease attended the meeting disguised as a priest; when Hawk played back the recorded tape from Fort Benning and then the dead Vinnie appeared, Pease ran away screaming. The police apprehended him and Pease was put into a mental hospital.

———, PEGGY (RO)

Jennifer Redwing's secretary in San Francisco; she wanted to know if Charlie was as gorgeous as his sister and wanted to meet him.

PENNINGTON, CHARLES (SI)

Pennington was sent by Ludendorff to act as Kroeger's bodyguard in Spain and to screen all Kroeger's letters and phone calls. Pennington was a stylish, effeminate Englishman who wore Yardley cologne, a killer who "took emotional sustenance from his work."

PEREGRINE, JANE (AP)

Wife of Walter Peregrine. Enid Heathley, his secretary, said she and Jane were quite close, that Jane was a strong woman and Walter liked the women around him to be strong, that they were worthwhile and shouldn't hide it. She was in shock after Walter's murder, but a survivor.

PEREGRINE, WALTER (AP)

U.S. Ambassador to Germany in Bonn, good friend of Caleb Dowling's. He had done well as a civilian, giving up a job at a loss of three-quarters of a million dollars a year to take the job as ambassador. Tolland says of him that he's "no fool. He may be a vanity appointment, but he's damned good and he's damned smart." Larry Talbot tells Joel that he was maligning a man who doesn't deserve it; that Peregrine was "one of the heroes of Bastogne—his command at the Battle of the Bulge is a legend of the war. And he was a reserve officer . . . I doubt that Nazis are his favorite guests." Larry goes on to say that after the war Peregrine called the Pentagon "megalomaniacs with too damn much money feeding their egos at the taxpayers' expense."

Peregrine had reason to suspect there were some people in his embassy who had been compromised. After his meeting with Dowling and Connal and after watching Major Washburn attempt to kill Connal, he placed a call on a scrambler to Undersecretary Brewster Tolland. He was angry that his embassy was being covertly investigated by the Navy; he tells them what he knows about Converse and "the isolated odd behavior in his personnel ranks," and says he'll take it to the Secretary of State or the President personally if he doesn't get answers fast.

Peregrine is then killed, probably by Major Washburn. The story put out by Washburn was that Joel Converse, the last man to see Peregrine alive, had walked across the Adenauer Bridge with him around eight in the evening. Early the next morning his body, with a bullet wound to the head, was found washed up on the riverbank in the Plittersdorf.

PEROT, ROSS (IA) [REAL PERSON]

Some people thought the Texan Ross Perot had been the unknown American who interceded in Masqat instead of Kendrick.

——, PETE (BI)

Black man who worked with Joey for Belkins Moving and Storage in New York. They were hired to remove the furnishings from the Treadstone house; he was shot by Carlos's men.

——, PETER (BI)

A ranking economist at Canada's National Revenue Treasury Board, director of the section with hopes of a cabinet appointment soon. He and Marie St. Jacques had lived together for two years. Marie asked him to find out about Treadstone Seventy-one Corporation for her. After receiving phone calls from Washington and New York, he went to the Ottawa airport to meet someone flying up from the States. He was found dead in one of the terminals used for air freight; he had been shot in the throat. His death went unreported, although he was an important government official.

——, PETER (GC)

One of Christ's disciples. (*See* Simon of Bethsaida.)

——, PETER (IA)

When Kendrick was in grammar school, a bully named Peter had hidden his best friend's lunch box. Kendrick had challenged Peter and beaten him so severely that the principal called his father.

PETERS, DECK OFFICER —— (SI)

Elizabeth Scarlatti checked with Peters to find out if Canfield had been in the radio room on the *Calpurnia*.

PETERS, CHARLES (CM)

O'Brien registered Chancellor into the Hay-Adams Hotel in Washington, D.C., under this name.

PETROCELLI, J. (BI)

Worked at the Reclamation Invoice Division, General Service Administration. He had received an invoice to remove the furnishings from the Treadstone house, signed by McGivern in Administrative Controls at Langley, and had refused to rescind the order without a written priority requisition from the CIA. He was unaware that McGivern had retired two weeks before the order was signed.

PHAN LOC (BI)

Code name for someone hired by Carlos at the Vietnamese embassy in Paris. The old man was to pass him a message about Bourne's death in Tam Quan and get information from him to give to Carlos.

PIERCE, ARTHUR (PM)

Undersecretary of State, assigned to the United Nations as chief liaison between the ambassador and the State Department. He was expected to become the next ambassador. He had gray eyes and black wavy hair with a noticeable streak of white in it. He was a paminyatchik, born Nikolai Petrovich Malyekov near Moscow and raised on an Iowa farm. He attended the University of Michigan and received a master's degree. When he was thirteen he had been told his true name and purpose by his "parents"; when he entered the Army his "parents" disappeared—his "mother" died in 1968 and his "father" left eight months later. Pierce went to Benning OCS, became a second lieutenant, served five tours of duty in Vietnam, became a major, and was decorated numerous times. From there it was not hard to get into government service, where he was noticed and promoted by Matthias. He worked with the National Security Council for several months; he was the mole Rostov mentioned. Pierce used the code name Hammer-Zero-Two and Victor. Pierce was responsible for the death of the four strategists, Emory Bradford and others; after Bradford's death Berquist brought him in to work with Havelock to find Parsifal—Pierce knew who Parsifal was but not where to find him. He obtained the psychiatric file on Matthias and followed Havelock to Zelienski in an attempt to get the documents. Havelock killed him outside Zelienski's house in Shenandoah.

PIERSALL, DR. WALTER (CH)

"American Ph.D., anthropologist, student of the Caribbean, author of a definitive study of Jamaica's first known inhabitants, the Arawak Indians." He was a tall, thin man, a widower living alone in "High Hill" house in Carrick Foyle. He had a brother in Cambridge, Massachusetts. Sam Tucker had met him the year before at a lecture in Carrick Foyle. When Sam met him at the camp on the Martha Brae, he found that Piersall had become a "jealous guardian of the islanders' rights." He had heard rumors of an enormous land conspiracy, and tried to disprove this rumor by attempting to buy twenty square miles of land on the north border of the Cock Pit. The people who wanted this land harassed Piersall; when Sam showed up, they were certain Piersall would interfere further, so they had him run down by a speeding auto in a Kingston street. Piersall had done extensive research on the Halidons; he had not had time to reach them himself, so he left two archive boxes with his research materials in them hidden at his home. Barak Moore was trusted with their location. It was Piersall's work that enabled McAuliff to contact the Halidons.

PIERSON, BARBARA (GC)

Adrian's girlfriend. "She of the quick deep laugh, the light brown hair, and the dark brown eyes. They'd been living together for a year and a half" in Boston. Professionally she was B.A., M.A., Ph.D., Associate Professor, Anthropology Laboratories, Harvard University. Her brilliant mother had been denied a place in a midwest college because she was a mother; Barbara had entered her profession with a sense of outrage. She was excited to have been awarded a grant to assist Kherpetian, who was analyzing artifacts taken from the Aswan Dam site. Adrian trusted her with all the information he had about the train from Salonika; she researched the destruction of the Filioque denials for him and contacted Dr. Shire in New York to analyze the documents.

Ruined Greek theatre in Ephesus with Mary (THE PARSIFAL MOSAIC)

PINKUS, AARON (RG)

Aaron Pinkus Associates of Boston was the best law firm in Massachusetts. Devereaux expected to go back to work for them after he was discharged from the Army; he thought Pinkus would someday be a Supreme Court judge.

PINKUS, AARON (RO)

Senior partner of his firm, finest attorney in Boston, and one of the kindest and most gentle of powerful men. He wondered where Sam got the money to fix up the house; Sam's story about the kidnapping of the Pope gave him a headache. He didn't like having his firm connected to that event; he told Sam they'd have to go through with a meeting with Hawkins so he couldn't hold it over them. He liked the way Hawkins had raised the $40 million from scoundrels, and he studied Hawkins's military record and tactics so he could outmaneuver him. Pinkus had been with the Third Army in Normandy and had shrapnel in his spine. When Pinkus found out that Hawkins had filed the brief listing Sam as attorney-of-record, Aaron and Sam had no choice but to join Hawk's battle for the rights of the Wopotamis.

PINKUS, SHIRLEY (RO)

Wife of Aaron Pinkus. She liked to flaunt their wealth with a fancy limousine and chauffeur. She wore a beehive hairdo and Aaron said her brains had been fried by staying under the hair dryer too long. She liked Sam Devereaux.

POLIZZI, ——— (MP)

One of Nimrod's messengers. He was shot to death in New Haven in 1972.

POMFRET, ED (OW)

Middle-aged, rotund, insecure producer who was thrilled when he was told he would be working with Bernie on the *Interceptor* series. When he told Bernie his contact had been John Tanner, Bernie told him it was a practical joke and that Ed could be his money man on his next project.

POND, WALTER (SI)

Ambassador to Sweden. In May he sent word to Reynolds that the bonds had been redeemed but he didn't know who was controlling the transaction.

POOLE, ———— (SI)

Bertholde's assistant. He was a tall, distinguished-looking man with gray hair and a perfectly waxed mustache. Poole considered Bertholde his dearest friend and mentor; he had killed for Bertholde willingly. He knew that Kroeger was Ulster Scarlett and suspected that Kroeger had given the order for Bertholde's death. Poole intended to kill Elizabeth and expose Kroeger. He was shot to death during his attempt to kill Scarlatti while she was traveling to the Zurich meeting.

PORTER, SERGEANT (AP)

Answered the telephone at Air Force, Recruit Command, Denver, for the personnel department when Valerie Converse was trying to reach Colonel Sam Abbott. From him she found out that Sam was stationed at Nellis Air Force Base in Nevada.

PRAGUE (IA)

The code name Milos used when working with the Sound Man.

PRAGUE (MC)

(1) Another code name for Scofield.

(2) Code name for agent called by Congdon to kill Scofield. "His police record was filled with assaults, thefts, and unproven homicides . . . worked . . . more for profit than for ideology. . . ." He didn't like to take risks, frequently preceding his attacks by gas pellets. Taleniekov shot Prague just as Prague was about to kill Scofield.

PREFONTAINE, BRENDAN PATRICK PIERRE (BU)

Former federal judge of the First Circuit Court of Massachusetts. He was seventy years old, short, with white hair and bony legs; he was a functioning alcoholic. When he was an adjunct professor at Harvard Law School, Randy Gates was one of his students. He'd always been in love with Edith Gates, even when he was married and had a child. His wife left him twenty-nine years before, and his thirty-eight-year-old son, a successful lawyer, disavows any knowledge of him. He had been disbarred at fifty for accepting money for favorable decisions and had served ten years in prison. After leaving prison he worked as a behind-the-scenes storefront lawyer; he doesn't blame anyone but himself for his problems. Randy Gates hired him to find out where Marie and her children were going from Boston; he figured if this little bit of information was worth fifteen thousand, he could get more money if he followed Marie and got more information. He didn't realize Carlos was a real person until the nurse nearly killed him; then he went after Carlos as a matter of principle. He got Gates to pay him to help capture the Jackal, because Gates wanted to be free. He returned to the islands to form a law partnership with Jonathan Lemuel.

PRESTON, CLIVE (CH)

A wealthy associate of Julian Warfield's, but according to Warfield, not with Dunstone. Preston met McAuliff in his Rolls-Royce and took him to his home for the meeting with Warfield.

PRESTON, JOHN "JACK" (IA)

English textile merchant who helped take the drunken Tony Mc-Donald to hs hotel room. He noticed that Tony had reappeared, sober, in clothing not appropriate for the climate or his social standing. He and Dickie reported Tony's odd behavior to MI6.

PRIORS (T)

Old Washington cronies of Trevayne's from his State Department days.

PRISTIN, REVEREND ELMER (RO)

Desi One was disguised as an Episcopalian minister. He was to help Aaron get inside the Supreme Court building.

PRITCHARD, BUCKINGHAM (BU)

Tall black assistant manager at the Tranquility Inn. He had a British accent and was obsequious and easily flattered. Bourne describes him as "the insufferable snob of an assistant manager . . . a loquacious bore, albeit hardworking, who never let anyone forget his family's importance in Montserrat." He followed his uncle's instructions; he believed he was working for recognition from an international organization, and he thought David Webb and John St. Jacques were terrorists.

PRITCHARD, CYRIL SYLVESTER (BU)

Deputy Director of Immigration Services on Montserrat. A stout black man with a British accent. He was proud of his knowledge of immigration procedures in many countries, and was flattered to be confided in by the Crown Governor. His office was at Blackburne Airport. He thought he and his nephew would be heroes. He had been paid three hundred pounds for his secrecy and cooperation, a very large amount by his standards. He kept records to the penny of how much of this he spent. He and his nephew were charged as accessories to terrorism.

PROBST, MANFRIED (GC)

Official of the Reichsindustrie. He received complaints from the Japanese that the Germans were not cooperating with the Japanese scientists.

PRUDHOMME, INSPECTOR FIRST GRADE (AP)

Prudhomme has been with the Sureté for thirty-two years. He is in his late middle age, wears rumpled clothing, is married, and has a flat in Paris. He has a face lined as much from weariness as age and a voice that sounds tired but is precise. He is a cigarette smoker and drinks coffee. His accent is Gascon, not Parisian. He speaks some English. It was often said that Gascons made the best police officials. His subordinate, a younger man, is a member of Aquitaine.

PYTHON (RG)

President's 150-pound pet dog.

QUANG DINH (AP)

A specialized branch of the North Vietnamese Army, now Vietnamese intelligence.

QUARTERMAIN, MACKINTOSH (RO)

After Hawkins had enriched the lives of the Wopotamis, he was persuaded by Ginny to go to Hollywood as coproducer and technical adviser on Greenberg's movie about the Suicidal Six. He represented himself as Quartermain, a veteran of the Scots Grenadiers.

QUARTZE, CARDINAL IGNATIO (RG)

Keeper of the Vatican Treasury. Quartze intended to be the next Pope. Francesco was not yet dead, but Quartze was bringing in his own people. Francesco thought Quartze was "a loathsome fellow in just about every department. He was an *erudito aristocratico* from a powerful Italian-Swiss family, who had the compassion of a disturbed cobra." He was a tall, thin man with a nasal twang and an irritating nasal wheeze. Quartze hated Francesco because he was a peasant and subsidized all kinds of causes; Quartze was more concerned with how much money the Church was earning. Quartze was planning his own lakeside villa at San Vincente with church funds. He refused to honor the ransom demand for the Pope, thinking he had Guido under his control, but Francesco, Guido, and Hawkins collaborated, forcing Quartze to retire to his villa.

QUARTZ, CARDINAL (RO)

Quartz was happy with Guido as Pope.

QUESARRO, ALFONSO (RE)

Alfonso and his wife had a ranch in the flat grass country outside Buenos Aires; they were friends of Jean Cameron's and permitted Spaulding and Lyons to stay in a small cottage on their ranch.

R (IA)

Code name (short for Red) of one of the Masada Brigade members.

RABINOWITZ, CHIEF RABBI (RO)

Aaron Pinkus was disguised as a Hasidic rabbi to get into the Supreme Court building.

THE RACHE (HC)

"*Rache.* The German word for 'vengeance.' In the beginning it was a society formed by the survivors of the concentration camps." They hunted the Nazis who had never been brought to trial. The Jews formed their own groups and became a minority in the Rache; the rest became Communist and offered a haven for terrorists. The Rache was the enemy of the Odessa and tried to recruit members from the "Children of the Damned"; if the children refused, they were killed and presented to the world as Fascists or Nazis. The organization was not tolerated within Germany.

RACHET, PA (AP)

Name of main male character, the father-figure, of the popular television series *Santa Fe*, played by Caleb Dowling.

———, RADIE (CM)

Tony Morgan's secretary.

RAFFERTY, ——— (RO)

Rafferty was manning the phone at the Legion Hall when Lafferty called to cancel the assault of the Four Seasons Hotel; the men had already left.

———, RALPH (BS)

The gym custodian at the small university in Maine where David Webb taught. Also the name of a man in the crowd of tourists at the Lo Wu border; his companion was shoved out of the way by Bourne.

———, RALPH (BU)

Young American at Le Coeur du Soldat who wanted to join the French Foreign Legion. He had a deep southern accent. He was college-educated, an engineer. He had killed his fiancée and her two brothers and a cousin, all with a knife and his bare hands.

———, RALPH (CH)

Doorman at the Shaftsbury Arms in London; he knew Clive Preston.

———, RALPH (IA)

When Kendrick called Swann's office, he told the secretary he was "Ralph over in ID" and had a message for Swann. Kendrick wanted Swann to leave early so he could meet him in private.

———, RALPH (OW)

Amos Needham's chauffeur.

RALSTEN, DR. (MP)

He lived at 217 Crescent Street in Carlyle; he was an abortionist, a Mafia referral.

RALSTON, PROFESSOR "ROLLY" (CH)

Bespectacled chairman of the geophysics department at the University of London. He felt cheated because he hadn't been chosen for McAuliff's job, but tried not to show his resentment. His candidates for the project were all excellent; James Ferguson had been one of his students.

RAMIREZ, MAJOR PABLO (CM)

His current assignment was minority relations at the Pentagon; he was really a brigadier general, but using the rank of major allowed him to get in places where a general couldn't. He was a bachelor and lived alone in a small brick house in a middle-class development in Bethesda, Maryland. He was about the same age as MacAndrew, and dark-complexioned. He was from San Juan, one of the first appointments to West Point from the territories, about two years behind MacAndrew. He served with MacAndrew in Korea, Vietnam, and in North Africa in World War II. MacAndrew thought he was "a lightweight, hotheaded, and too emotional. Not at all reliable . . . refused to second two field promotions for him." He attended MacAndrew's funeral, but said he hated MacAndrew because he was a racist. He admitted to using Mac-Andrew's wife as a reverse conduit and keeping her supplied with drugs. He was the source control, and he used his position to get into bed with her. He had MacAndrew brought back to Korea to the black outfit to cover up the drug experiments. After Chancellor got this information from him, Ramirez killed himself.

RAMSEY, LIEUTENANT SENIOR GRADE GORDON (AP)

Ramsey was in the same wing group as Joel Converse. "He had been hit (while flying over Pak Song, North Vietnam) by a fluke rocket that had winged out of its trajectory over the coastline and zeroed in on Ramsey's fuselage; the explosion had filled the jet streams, death at six hundred miles an hour in the air." He had told the commander before he left that Joel was "the best [pilot]" in the outfit, which is why Joel was chosen to lead the next flight, the one that forced him to fly at a low altitude and get shot down and captured.

RANDOLPH, DAVID (MC)

CIA agent, sabotage specialist. He was a candidate for the assassination of Yurievich, but he was at a desk in Washington.

RANDOLPH, DR. MATTHEW (PM)

One of the most respected doctors on the eastern shore—"Johns Hopkins, Mayo Clinic, on the boards of Massachusetts General and New York's Mount Sinai, and with his own medical center." His family owned "half the eastern shore, the richer half." He was extremely unpleasant and abusive and ran his hospital as a "none too benevolent dictatorship." His hospital fees were exorbitant but his patients had the best possible care; he and his hospital were known for their integrity.

He was sixty-eight years old, "a tall, slender, angular man with a fringe of gray hair circling a bald head"; he wore steel-rimmed glasses and had long, graceful hands. Havelock approached him by requesting help with a problem the government had with respect to MacKenzie's death. Randolph had known MacKenzie's family for over forty years and told Havelock how he felt the job had affected Steve's family. When Havelock convinced Randolph that MacKenzie was murdered, Randolph tried to help him trap Shippers. Havelock sent in a team to guard Randolph, but Ambiguity's people got past them and killed Randolph.

RAPPAPORT, GEORGE WASHINGTON (RG)

Hawkins used the name when signing the check for the leasing of the chateau.

RASHAD, ADRIENNE KHALEHLA (IA)

CIA agent from Special Projects. Her mother was American, her father an Egyptian professor at the University of Cairo. Khalehla was of medium height, slim, with long, dark hair, and olive-toned skin; she could speak six languages fluently and write four. She was raised in Egypt and attended Radcliffe. She met Bobbie Aldridge there after a group of Jewish men raped her because she was an Arab; Bobbie quickly took her for medical treatment and moved her in as her roommate. Khalehla stayed at Radcliffe because of Bobbie. Khalehla decided she would join the CIA and be a Middle East specialist, to help bring peace to that region. In Oman she discovered McDonald was an agent and reported it to Mitch; she was following McDonald and Kendrick when McDonald shoved Kendrick into heavy traffic. She rescued Kendrick and took him to a safe place. The next time she saw Kendrick she had been flown to a safe house in the States so he could interrogate her. She was angry because she had been removed from an assignment she'd been working on and she was afraid her cover was blown. When she discovered that Kendrick had not created the leak himself, she decided to help him find out who did. She tried to maintain a businesslike relationship, but fell in love with Kendrick anyway. She finally found Milos, by accident, on an elevator in the Vanvlanderens' apartment building; she connected him to Mitch and agreed with him that Kendrick should be the next Vice President. Jennings encouraged Khalehla and Kendrick to get married and she decided it was time to resign from the CIA.

RASHAD, MRS. (IA)

Adrienne's mother and the professor's wife. She met Rashad while attending graduate school at Berkeley; she was majoring in Egyptology.

RASHAD, PROFESSOR (IA)

Professor at Cairo University. He had been a doctoral candidate in Western Civilization at Berkeley when he met and married a classmate of Mitch Payton's, a blond American lady. Their daughter was Adrienne Khalehla Rashad.

———, RAUL (RO)

Puerto Rican bellboy at the Four Seasons Hotel in New York who acted as the interpreter for the "Spanish ambassadors."

RAVENA, ALDO (GC)

The name on the mutilated identification card that Vittorio received from the partigianos; it identified him as a former *soldato semplice* in the Italian Army. He was dressed as a farm laborer, a person with little schooling.

RAVENA, MAJOR ALDO (GC)

Vittorio presented himself to the soldiers at the checkpoint outside Montenotte Sud as Major Aldo Ravena, *ufficiale segreto*, from Rome.

RAWLINS, CECILY (SI)

Daughter of Lillian and Thomas Rawlins, wife of Charles Boothroyd. Rawlins bought a huge estate in Switzerland for Cecily and Charles.

RAWLINS, LILLIAN (SI)

Wife of Thomas Rawlins and mother of Cecily. She was killed in an auto accident in the Poconos.

RAWLINS, THOMAS (SI)

Partner in the brokerage house of Godwin and Rawlins. Rawlins asked his son-in-law to kill Elizabeth Scarlatti. Thomas and his wife died in an "auto accident" in the Poconos.

RAWLINS, CONGRESSMAN WALTER (CM)

Chairman of the House Subcommittee on Reapportionment. He was a closet racist. He was from a wealthy, old family in Roanoke. He and his wife lived in suburban Arlington; he didn't care for his wife, as she interfered with his drinking and promiscuity. He had an anonymous telephone call about the death of a fourteen-year-old black girl who had been beaten up, raped, and died in Newport News on March 22, 1969; he had been accused of the crime, but it had been covered up. He was told to change his position on a house bill or risk being revealed. He called Chancellor and requested a meeting because he had heard Chancellor was including him in his book. He swore he didn't kill the black girl, that blacks did it—then he was shot to death in front of Chancellor. When Chancellor called his office later, a woman told him that Rawlins died of a coronary in his sleep.

———, RAYMOND (CH)

Trelawney Parish policeman left behind with the Doberman to guard Walter Piersall's house. He lost his life in the course of duty.

REARDON, ——— (BS)

David Webb told Harry Babcock and his wife that he was Reardon from the State Department, in his attempt to reach someone within the CIA who might help him reach Marie.

RED (IA)

Code name of a member of the Masada Brigade. He asked the sultan for some whiskey to drink before the flight; he hated flying—it scared him.

THE REDHEAD (BU)

The Vice President of the United States, who was not in any way connected to Medusa. He had been a marine colonel during the Vietnam War.

REDWING, CHARLES "CHARLIE" SUNSET (RO)

Younger brother of Jennifer Redwing. Modern Indian who didn't want to live like they did a hundred years ago. He had passed the bar exam in Nebraska in the highest percentile and had helped Hawkins with his strategy and research; he was frustrated because they hadn't heard anything from the Supreme Court in three months. He had thought that the project was a big joke and the brief would never get to court. Charlie turned to his sister for help when he couldn't reach Hawkins in Boston. He figured his association with Hawkins would ruin his career before it ever got started. Jennifer thought Charlie and Sam were very much alike and she loved them both.

Redwing, Jennifer "Red" Sunrise (ro)

Attorney with a firm in San Francisco, graduate of Harvard Law School. Sam saw her as "a bronzed Aphrodite with glowing dark hair and incandescent eyes of a light, bewildering color, with a face and body sculpted by Bernini." Alcohol had a deleterious effect on her, so she didn't drink. As one of the tribe's gifted young people, she and her brother had been given every educational opportunity. She rejected a position with Pinkus's law firm because she was fed up with her status as a member of an unrecognized minority in Boston. She had returned to Omaha, passed the Nebraska bar exam, and gone to work for a prestigious firm there. A client of the firm persuaded her to appear in photographs he was taking for an article on reservation life for *National Geographic*. Daniel Springtree in San Francisco saw the article and asked her to become a member of their firm. She was working there when Charlie called her about the problem with Hawkins and the tribe. Jennifer flew to Boston to stop Hawkins, met Sam and Aaron Pinkus, and became deeply involved in Hawkins's scheme in an effort to protect her tribe.

Reebok, Chief Justice (ro)

Chief Justice of the Supreme Court. He wanted to make the hearing of the Wopotami case public as soon as possible. His decision was against the Wopotamis because he didn't like Indians any better than he did blacks. Reebok was asked to delay the hearings; in exchange, the White House would not publicize his past decisions in which it could be shown that he had slanted the conditions against dark-skinned defendants. When the rest of the Supreme Court heard about the pressure from the executive branch, they rebelled. Reebok tried to stop them from holding a public hearing by blackmailing them; he gave a barbecue where he plied them with liquor and got pictures of them swimming with nude women.

Regent Number Five (bs)

Code name used by Pak Fei to identify himself to Wu Song. Pak Fei coincidentally worked for the Regent Hotel in Hong Kong and he was born 5-5-35.

———, Reggie (RO)

Slender, well-dressed Englishman in his forties that Goldfarb sent with Daphne to Omaha to find Chief Thunder Head. The Wopotamis captured him and tied him to a tree; he wrenched his left arm out of its socket resisting them.

Reilly, John "Jack" (BS)

Representative of the National Security Council. Somewhat obese with red hair and freckles; he wears steel-rimmed glasses. His parents were Irish. He briefed McAllister about Sheng's activities in China in connection with Jason Bourne; he left Havilland's office before McAllister was briefed about the plan to kidnap Marie Webb. Later Reilly also briefed Catherine Staples about the Bourne plan.

Reisler, Frederick (CM)

One of the leaders of the German-American Bund, a stockbroker, used as the basis for a character in Chancellor's book *Reichstag!* Reisler was a genius on Wall Street, funneling millions of dollars to Hitler. He was the father of Frederick Wells. Reisler and his wife were divorced shortly after their son was born, and the name Wells (mother's maiden name) was legally assumed for the boy soon after the divorce.

Remington, Lieutenant Senior Grade David (AP)

One of the four senior legal officers at SAND PAC. Connal Fitzpatrick, the CLO, asks David not to remove the flag from Joel's service

Hong Kong Island (THE BOURNE SUPREMACY)

records under any circumstances. Connal chose David because David wasn't easily pushed around—he had a reputation for being a stickler prick.

David liked his job—"where else could a man travel all over the world, housing a wife and three kids in some of the nicest quarters available, with all the medical and dental bills paid for, and not have the terrible pressures of rising in private or corporate practice." Unlike his father, who had been a corporate attorney and died at fifty-six from a coronary, David planned "to be one of the best lawyers in the U.S. Navy, serve his thirty years, get out at fifty-five with a generous pension, and become a well-paid legal-military consultant at fifty-six."

He was killed in a car accident on his way to see a well-known four-striper in the Sonoma Hills; he swerved to avoid a big black van and lost control of the car. The situation was set up, of course, by the Aquitaine.

———, RENÉ (BU)

Name by which the bartender, Santos, knew the Legionnaire who gave his name as "Maurice" to Bourne.

RENFIELD, HARRISON (CH)

International financier and real estate magnate, member of Dunstone, Ltd., poisoned to death by the Halidon.

REX (BU)

Name of one of the guard dogs, probably the Doberman, at General Swayne's estate. He was a clear favorite of the guards.

REYNOLDS, ——— (GC)

He was in MI6. His job was to watch Vittorio, who was in Kensington at the Holcroft flat.

REYNOLDS, BENJAMIN (SI)

Gray-haired man of sixty-three, responsible for the Field Services and Accounting Agency (Group Twenty). The cases this group investigated were only in the most sensitive areas. Reynolds couldn't understand why Scarlett was involved with the Mafia, so he called Elizabeth Scarlatti. Reynolds assigned Canfield to investigate the disappearance of Ulster Scarlett; he didn't like or completely trust Canfield and felt that Canfield was expendable.

RHEINHART, ERICH (SI)

Attaché from the Weimar Republic in Washington, a full-fledged Nazi, nephew of General Rheinhart. Erich didn't know that Kroeger was really Ulster Scarlett.

RHEINHART, GENERAL WILHELM (SI)

Aging, overweight German officer, a Junker. He had a fat face, white hair cropped short, and military posture. Rheinhart wanted Germany to be able to take care of itself, not be master of Europe. The Nazis guaranteed Rheinhart the first thing they would do would be to get rid of the Versailles treaty; he was afraid the Nazis had no staying power. Rheinhart was blackmailed into supporting the Nazis; they threatened to tell the Versailles officials that Rheinhart was secretly negotiating illegal procurements at Montbeliard if he didn't publicly support them.

RHINEMANN, ERICH (RE)

The Germans needed an impartial person in a neutral territory who was capable of overseeing the exchange between the Americans and the Germans. Rhinemann, a rich Jew, had been forced out of Germany by Goebbels, his lands and companies expropriated by the Third Reich. Rhinemann had converted most of his property to money in Swiss bank accounts before leaving Germany; he lived in exiled splendor on an estate outside Buenos Aires. Although he was Jewish, he was a more dedicated Fascist than Hitler. He knew he would return to Germany after the war regardless of who won and he knew he would have more leverage with both the Americans and the Germans because of the exchange; Swanson decided that Rhinemann would have to be eliminated after the exchange. Rhinemann was very methodical, an expert at whatever he did, and boldly imaginative. Granville described him as a man totally without a conscience, the least honorable man he'd ever met. "He was a moderately tall man with graying straight hair combed rigidly back . . . somewhat stocky for his size. . . . His hands were large and beefy, yet somehow delicate. . . ." He had a broad face, wide forehead, broad lips, rather wide flat nose, eyebrows bleached from the sun, a bronzed skin; he was an aging man and spoke English fluently. When he heard that the Gestapo were in Buenos Aires, he figured Altmuller had either been caught or was trying to betray him; he insisted on Altmuller's presence at the exchange. Spaulding made his own deal with Rhinemann to get the names of the people who had set up the exchange and to get Lyons and Jean safely back to the embassy. Rhinemann intended to kill Spaulding before he could get back to Washington with the blueprints. Spaulding killed Rhinemann instead.

RICCI (PM)

Blond-haired Corsican, very proficient with a rifle or handgun, wire, and knife, very much at home in the Mediterranean area. He was a reliable executioner used only in "extreme prejudice" situations. Ricci was the cover name he used at Col des Moulinets; the American agent was unaware that Ricci and his explosives experts were not associated with Consular Operations. Havelock ran over Ricci's legs with a truck and killed one of his men; he wounded the other man in the head, but the man was able to pull Ricci into a car and drive away.

RICHARDS, MISS ——— (SI)

Bertholde's secretary. She was an attractive young brunette who wore spit curls on her forehead. When they found Bertholde's body, she screamed and screamed but didn't collapse.

RICHARDS, MATTHEW (BS)

CIA man, a case officer Conklin knew from Saigon in the early days. He had been following Conklin and Panov, when Conklin knocked him down and questioned him. Conklin tied him up with three neckties and left him behind a pillar in a railroad station in Kowloon. Richards was due to retire in a few months and told the story that a gang of Chinese had attacked him. He and Conklin saw Catherine Staples murdered, then drove to the safe house on Victoria Peak. He agreed to be Conklin's man inside and relay information to him.

RICHARDS, BRIGADIER GENERAL OWEN (RO)

Supreme Commander of the Strategic Air Command. He didn't like having his planes in the air for an extended period of time, and he didn't like the men in trench coats who had delivered his orders. He told the Secretary of Defense what he could do with his orders and expected to be relieved of command; the President apologized and told him the Secretary would not make any more decisions where Richards was concerned without consulting him.

RICHARDSON, AMBASSADOR (PM)

American ambassador to France. He was to make sure that Madame Broussac was picked up and brought to the embassy to talk to the President.

RICKMAN, ——— (BU)

A young man, muscular, blond, of medium height, with large chest and shoulders, rigid posture, and blunt facial features, he was chief of drug operations on Montserrat. He was the third provost of the government police. He spoke French and several other languages. He and the Crown Governor fished together and he took his instruction from the CG. He was described as a cruel man who doesn't like "Punjabis," "the one-man British Ku Klux Klan," and "the original sanctimonious deacon." Not many people liked him.

RIGGS, LOUIS (L.R.) (T)

Jim Goddard's top accountant; he was willing to sell information about Genessee's business to anyone who had the money to buy. Riggs had an amazing memory. In the sixties he'd been part of the protest marches, then was drafted and sent to Vietnam, where half his stomach was blown away. When he came back he decided he wanted his share of the wealth. Riggs told Goddard about being approached by Vicarson and Bonner and told Goddard that he had refused their bribes; Goddard believed there was a conspiracy against him. Goddard paid Riggs to help him get Genessee's year-end figures. After Goddard died, Riggs became the spokesman for Genessee's San Francisco division and flew to Washington to confer with President Tremayne.

ROBBINS, ——— (RO)

Top man at the William Morris Agency, hired by Hawkins to manage the Suicidal Six's movie contract.

———, ROCCO (RG)

One of Dellacroce's men; he was to stay with the car. Hawkins knocked him out on the golf green.

———, ROCCO (T)

Worked for de Spadante; he was guarding his room at the hospital.

RODCHENKO, GENERAL GRIGORIE (BU)

Elderly white-haired Soviet Army officer, powerful third director of the Komitet, also second-in-command of the KGB and close advisor to the premier of the Soviet Union. He was a consummate strategist and a dedicated Marxist, working all parties against each other for the benefit of Russia and his own survival. He arranged the meeting of Ogilvie and Carlos and had it photographed. He provided Carlos with false files on major leaders of the Russian government. He spoke French fluently, which helped Krupkin identify him as the Russian contact to Carlos. Carlos tells Rodchenko he has been exposed, and kills him.

———, RODNEY (CH)

Black taxi driver for McAuliff in Kingston. He let the green car get close enough for McAuliff to read the license, then lost them. McAuliff used the same tactics later to lose the Unio Corso.

———, RODOLFO (RG)

Opera singer at La Scala Minuscola; his left leg slipped through a step unit and he tore his pants up to his crotch.

———, ROGER (RO)

Assistant manager at the Fawning Hill Country Club.

ROGERS, ——— (AP)

Name given by Joel to the offensive, obese, dishonest American salesman that he accidentally met twice on trains in Europe. At the time the salesman asked his name, Joel had been thinking about his father, Roger Converse.

ROGET (BI)

Name of the restaurant in Paris where David Webb took Jacqueline Lavier. Lavier paid the hostess there to take a picture of him, since Carlos didn't know what he looked like.

ROGETEAU, MONSIEUR (AP)

Legal associate of Avery Preston Halliday's; when Halliday did not show up, he took his place at the meeting for the Comm Tech-Bern merger, representing the Swiss.

ROME (PM)

Code name of the agent in Rome who received the message from Ambiguity that Havelock was "beyond salvage."

ROME (RG)

Other code name Orange. The former agent responded to Hawkins's offer within two hours; he'd been unemployed longer than the others. On the trip to Zermatt, Rome lost his luggage and his contact from the chateau. Rome was a "long-haired man in very tight trousers who strutted when he walked like a tango dancer."

ROMERO, DESI (RO)

(D1, Desi One, Desi Arnaz One) Desi became a second lieutenant in Intelligence under the guidance of Ethelred Brokemichael.

ROMMEL, GENERAL ERWIN (HC) [REAL PERSON]

Rommel, one of Germany's foremost military men, was implicated in the attempt on Hitler's life. He was ordered to take his own life.

———, RONALD (BU)

Guard devoted to John St. Jacques at Tranquility Inn. Ronald had a variety of duties and was well paid.

———, Ronaldo (RG)

A plump, boyish-looking priest with pink cheeks and thick lips who catered to Cardinal Quartze's every wish.

Roncalli, Angelo (RG) [Real person]

Close friend of Giovanni Bambolini's. He preceded Bambolini as Pope John and died in office. The two of them shared a number of unorthodox views as well as good wine and a game of cards after evening prayers. Angelo was a popular Pope and brought in high contributions for the Church.

———, Ronnie (OW)

Patrolman on duty the night Omega attempted to shoot Tanner's family to death. He and his partner had been in the north end of town when they received the police transmission.

———, Rose (RO)

Ruggio's wife. Her interior decorator liked pink and white but Mario didn't.

Rosen, Aaron (AP)

American attorney who does most of the work on the Comm Tech-Bern merger. Before he can complete the negotiations, he has a heart attack. A. Preston Halliday takes his place as chief spokesman, using this as a cover to contact Joel Converse about the Aquitaine.

Rosenberg, Moose (AP)

Blynn remarked that "that stunt jock Moose Rosenberg's with him. If he moved an ashtray, I think that gorilla would throw him through the wall." However, when asked to by Dowling, "the stunt man climbed out of the trailer, leaving Caleb and the police officer alone."

Rostov, Pietre (Pyotr) (PM)

Director of External Strategies, KGB. The KGB thought Havelock's retirement was some kind of trick. Rostov questioned Havelock himself and told him there was a mole in the White House and that Jenna was never a KGB or VKR agent; he also told Havelock that the KGB were not interested in taking Havelock. Rostov couldn't figure out what happened at Costa Brava and in a letter to Consular Operations denied KGB participation; he hinted that the VKR might have been involved. He found it hard to believe that the paminyatchiki were actively being used by the VKR. He offered Havelock sanctuary and centered his investigation on the VKR; he was found dead with four bullets in his head.

ROUGE (RG)

Other code name Athens. Rouge was chosen because of his red scarf. His specialty was demolition. One of his jobs was to destroy the communications equipment in the Pope's vehicle; another was to disable the people around the Pope. Rouge fell over his robe, jabbed himself in the stomach with a tranquilizer needle, and had to be revived with the antidote. He also copiloted the Learjet for Hawkins and the Pope.

ROXBURY, VISCOUNT AND VISCOUNTESS (SI)

The Viscount and Viscountess had a suite in the Savoy Hotel near Elizabeth Scarlatti's. They were elderly and didn't give loud parties.

RUDI (AP)

Name of fictitious common friend of Norman Washburn's and Thayer's (Johnny Reb); supposedly Thayer was going to take Washburn there the evening he kidnapped him.

———, RUDI (HC)

Heavyset manager of the pub on the Kurfürstendamm where Noel met Dr. Erich Kessler. He held on to Noel's briefcase for him and gave it to Kessler; he had known Kessler for a long time.

———, RUDOLPH (RG)

Chauffeur who met the agents arriving at Zermatt. Rudolph was gold-toothed, cat-eyed, and bereted. Besides chauffeuring, Rudolph also guarded Sam. Sam convinced Rudolph and No Name that he had Kuwaiti encephalitis, a disease that swelled the testicles. Rudolph wasn't allowed to call a doctor but stayed away from Sam, allowing him to escape.

———, RUDY (OW)

Alice was out of ice so Cardone called Rudy at the liquor store to deliver a couple of bags; he had to reach him at home because the store was closed. He frequently did favors for Cardone.

———, RUGGIO (RO)

Vinnie's cousin Ruggio had a beach house in Miami Beach that Vinnie used after he "died" in the boat accident. Ruggio and his wife were in El Paso, where he was negotiating with the Mafia family for control of the leather saddle market.

RUSSOMALZ (BI)

A Soviet firm in Geneva that brokered purchases of diamonds between Moscow and the West. Webb (as Cain) used it to convert his funds.

RYAN, ——— (PM)

Guard who worked for Kahoutek. He took Havelock to where they had Jenna imprisoned.

RYAN, CYNTHIA (RE)

Eighteen-year-old daughter of Jack Ryan, who loved being in Washington, D.C., because of the social life.

RYAN, JANE (RE)

Jack Ryan's wife. She and their son preferred Oahu to Washington.

RYAN, JOHN "JACK," N.M.I. (RE)

Formerly a major in Six Corps, an intelligence agent whose cover was manager of a radio station in New York. Pace asked him for complete information on David Spaulding.

RYAN, MICHAEL (T)

Member of Trevayne's subcommittee. Ryan was a specialist in aeronautical engineering. He was in his thirties, convivial, and quick to laugh, but deadly serious when faced with an aircraft blueprint. Ryan was approached about the subcommittee's investigations and offered a Caribbean holiday trip. One of Ryan's jobs was to investigate Jamison.

RYDUKOV, PIETRE (MC)

Taleniekov used Pietre's identity to travel around Europe and Russia. The real Rydukov was a violinist who had been retired for five years in the Ural Mountains. Taleniekov's flight pass stated he was "on his way to join the Sevastapol Symphony as third-chair violinist."

S (IA)

(1) Code name for Frank Swann on the note left by Milos in DeMartin's car and in communications with Gerald Bryce.

(2) Code name Milos used for Sundstrom.

SAADA, ALI (IA)

Name under which Manny was flown back from the Middle East with Kendrick.

SABATINI, AUNT ANGELINA "THE GO-GO" (RO)

Rocco's wife. Vincent Mangecavallo's Aunt Angelina took a bag of clothing into the Supreme Court building and hid it in a closet for Hawk's group. She liked to shop.

SABATINI, ROCCO (RO)

Angelina's husband and Vinnie's uncle. Vinnie took care of them because Rocco refused to work. He wondered when Vinnie learned how to swim.

ST. CLAIRE, MUNRO (CM)

Inver Brass code name was Bravo; he took over as temporary chairman after Genesis died. He was older than he appeared, tall and slender, and walked with a sure stride. He had an aquiline head with faded blond hair, well-groomed white mustache above thin lips, and eyes "of no discernible color." He lived in Vermont. He had been "undersecretary of state for Roosevelt and Truman; ambassador-extraordinary for Eisenhower, Kennedy, and Johnson." Then he spent a semester at Park Forest University in the Midwest as visiting professor of government, the purpose being to discredit Chancellor's doctoral thesis to protect Inver Brass.

He relied on Varak and worked with him outside the Inver Brass meetings. Varak had read Chancellor's manuscript, which pointed to a member of "the Nucleus" as the one who took the Hoover files; Varak thought Chancellor might be correct. St. Claire carefully fed selected data, including Bromley's name, to Inver Brass to test this theory; when Bromley received a threatening telephone call, he thought St. Claire had betrayed him. St. Claire was shot to death inside the house that once belonged to Genesis.

ST. JACQUES, ——— (BI)

Marie's father. He is French-Canadian. He was an accountant, then he flew a Vickers bomber in World War II for the Royal Canadian Air Force. After that he became a cattle dealer and then bought a small ranch in Alberta, where he raised his family.

ST. JACQUES, JOHN (BU)

"Mr. Saint Jay." Thirty-four-year old, tanned, dark-haired, muscular younger brother of Marie St. Jacques Webb—he loved his sister and family dearly. He was a competent boat pilot and navigator. David called him a hustler, his father said he was a real salesman, and Marie said he was aggressive—she thought he was less reliable than her two older brothers and wondered why David trusted him more. Two men raped and killed a friend of his, so John killed them; he then instinctively called David for help. David had attorneys and others flown to Canada to help John; he was acquitted of the charges. He and David were very close; David knew John could and would kill, if necessary, to defend his family. David and Marie persuaded him to look after their hideaway in the

Caribbean; they were joint owners with John of Tranquility Inn, which John made into a fortified bunker in case it would ever be needed.

St. Jacques, Marie (BI)

Economist with Canadian Treasury Board, Department of National Revenue at Ottawa. Abducted by David Webb (as Bourne), she became his lover and later his wife. She has long, auburn hair, wide brown eyes, is tall, slender, in her mid-thirties, and wears tinted, horn-rimmed glasses. She smokes, drives well, and speaks English and French fluently. She has relations in Lyons, France. She had lived in Calgary on a small ranch with her parents and two brothers until she was eighteen, during which time she was an indifferent student at a convent school in Alberta. Then she received a master's degree from McGill University and her Ph.D. at Pembroke College, Oxford. The Canadian government agreed to fund her time in Oxford in exchange for three years of her work with them. She stayed on with the government because she liked her job. She was attending an economic conference in Zurich when Webb abducted her. Because of her association with him, she was nearly raped, shot at, accused of grand theft and being an accomplice to murder. She used connections and information Webb didn't have to help him reach Treadstone.

Saint-Pierre, Nelli, et Mattilon (AP)

Name of French law firm in Paris of which René Mattilon was a major partner.

Salamander, Ivan (RO)

President of Wall Street's third largest brokerage house, Axel-Burlap. He was a gaunt, bespectacled man known as "Ivan the Terrible" on the Street. Vinnie's message instructed him to buy up 50,000 shares of Petrotoxic Amalgamated.

Salanne, Claudie (PM)

Young daughter of Henri Salanne, who suffered from severe depression and attempted suicide after a romantic encounter with an American agent. She later married a young intern who worked at the hospital in Nice; she and her husband were expecting their first child.

Salanne, Henri (CH)

Marquis de Chatellerault, French industrialist, was killed in an ambush at the Negril Airport by the Halidon.

SALANNE, DR. HENRI (PM)

After Havelock was wounded near Col des Moulinets, he drove to Cagnes-sur-Mer to get help from a doctor he had helped years before, someone Cons Ops knew nothing about. When Salanne was a young man he had been a brilliant surgeon at L'Hôpital de Paris, but he was a compulsive gambler and moved his practice to Monte Carlo. Because of a gambling debt, he sold out to the KGB the American agent who had been romancing his daughter; Havelock got the agent out before he was discovered, then confronted Salanne. Salanne then became obligated to him because Havelock didn't report him. When Salanne heard the stories about Havelock, he checked his sources. When Havelock called him, Salanne concealed him and treated his wounds.

SALERNO, FAT (RO)

Salerno was a Mafia boss who wanted to make oregano the official flower of New York State; he walked into the legislature yelling about discrimination.

SALONIKA (GC)

Name of the operation that was supposed to be launched after World War II to help Fontine solve the riddle of the missing religious documents on the train from Salonika.

SALTER, ——— (CM)

Floating cover assumed by one of the men with Varak the night they entered the Flags area of the Bureau. Salter was the one who discovered that files M–Z were missing. After his job for Varak was over, he went to Tel Aviv to battle Palestinian terrorists.

SALTZMAN, GEORGE ROBERT (MC)

CIA agent who operated as pouch carrier and assassin, Oriental expert. He could not have killed Yurievich because he was in the hospital in Tashkent.

———, SAM (IA)

Sam was working night maintenance in the congressional office building when he and Harry found Phil Tobias's body.

———, SAMUEL (BU)

Bourne and Prefontaine noticed that one priest out of the four visiting Tranquility was showing fear. They figured he'd been bought by the Jackal; Bourne confirmed this by speaking to him. Samuel was with

Rickman at the chapel; Bourne thought he was the Jackal escaping because of his clerical clothes and shot him to death.

SANCHEZ, ILICH RAMIREZ (AP, BI, BS, BU)
Also known as Carlos, or as Carlos, the Jackal (*See also* Carlos.)

SANDOR, ——— (GC)
A politician on the Armed Services Committee who was trying to find out about Andrew Fontine. Greene inserted a routine response to divert his inquiry.

———, SANFORD (RO)
Bully who threatened to beat up Sam when they were both six-year-olds on the playground at recess.

———, SANTOS (BU)
The head bartender at Le Coeur du Soldat in Paris, a premier conduit for Carlos. He was not a young man; he was massive, bald, wore steel-rimmed glasses, and had a tattooed arm. He was known to crush men's heads if they behaved too badly. He lived above the café. He never left this area, not even to go to the markets—everything was delivered. His apartment had a single steel door, walls covered with bookshelves, and tasteful expensive furniture that matched his size. He maintained a lovely English garden at the rear of the café.

He was Cuban and had fought in Fidel's revolution. He had been a law student and a great athlete. Fidel was jealous of Che Guevera and Santos; he declared Santos to be a counterrevolutionary and was about to execute him when Carlos and his men broke into the jail and freed him. He owed his life to Carlos. He was neither a liar nor a fool. Bourne had to approach him cautiously; Santos accepted Bourne's offer because he hoped it would enable him to collect a great deal of money and get free of Carlos. Unfortunately, Santos was observed sending large boxes to storage and neglecting to tend his garden; Carlos had him killed.

SAPPHIRE (BS)
Lin Wenzu used the code name Sapphire in a scheme to find out which one of his men was a double agent.

SAXON (SI)
Code name used by Heinrich Kroeger when he tried to defect to the Americans in October 1944.

SAXON, JANET (SI)
(*See* Scarlett, Janet Saxon and Canfield, Janet Saxon Scarlett.)

SAXON, MARION (SI)

Janet Scarlett's mother. Marion and her husband were providing a lavish wedding for their daughter. Janet's mother was delighted to know Janet was pregnant, that Ulster was properly trapped.

SCANLAN, DONALD (RE)

Spaulding was listed on the passenger manifest to Buenos Aires as Donald Scanlan, mining surveyor from Cincinnati, Ohio. He also rented a car at the airport in Buenos Aires under this name.

SCANLAN, DOROTHY (OW)

Dorothy and Tom were Tanner's nearest neighbors. They played tennis with the Tanners at the country club. The Scanlans heard the shooting at the Tanners' and reported it to the police.

SCANLAN, TOM (OW)

"Tom was reputed to be so rich that he hadn't gone to work in a decade." Scanlan and Tanner were friends and neighbors. When Tanner decided to go after Omega, he walked over to Tom's and borrowed his Mercedes coupe and a Smith & Wesson pistol and extra ammunition.

SCANLON, ADMIRAL (AP)

A ranking officer in the Fifth Naval District, member of the Aquitaine. Scanlon tried to get Joel's service record so he could find out his relationship to Delavane and if Joel really was a potential associate for Aquitaine. He was blocked by Connal, David Remington, and Admiral Hickman; Hickman told him to get approval from Washington if he wanted it sooner than in three days, that the file had a Four-Zero emergency priority. Scanlon reports this to Delavane and they decide there's too much risk to go through Washington because it would expose names of people in Aquitaine. After examining Joel's file he calls Hickman, confirming Joel's remarks about Delavane and discovering Remington's knowledge of the Delavane connection. Hickman realized Scanlon was lying to him: "What he had not known was that he was such a stupid liar." When the Aquitaine had been exposed, Scanlon threw himself out of a six-story window to his death.

SCARLATTI, ELIZABETH ROYCE WYCKHAM (SI)

(See also Wyckham, Elizabeth.) Wife of Giovanni Scarlatti and mother of their three sons. After Elizabeth and Giovanni were married, she worked with him to build Scarlatti Industries; in sixteen years they built an empire. In 1904 Elizabeth decided to move her family to New York because of the anti-Italian sentiment in Chicago. In New York

Giovanni bought undeveloped land on Long Island. After Giovanni died, Elizabeth consolidated the management of her company by moving her executives to New York and installing telegraphic communications. Part of her success was due to her shrewd analysis of people. She built several houses, including Oyster Bay, and changed her children's name to Scarlett to help them fit into a Protestant democracy; she remained Madame Scarlatti. None of her sons had the genius of Giovanni; Chancellor was a moderately good executive and Ulster had destructive ambitions. Elizabeth was determined to find Ulster by means of the missing securities. She had help from Canfield because his group was interested in the transactions on the Swedish exchange. When it became evident that Ulster was trying to kill her, she hired Canfield to help her. When she discovered that Ulster was Heinrich Kroeger, she set up a conference with all the merchants and threatened to ruin their businesses, using the wealth of Scarlatti; they deserted the Nazis and this set the Nazi timetable back two years. She knew Kroeger wasn't killed at Zurich and told Goebbels his true identity. Elizabeth died just before the fall of France in 1940.

SCARLATTI, GIOVANNI MERIGHI (SI)

Elizabeth first saw Giovanni at a company picnic. "He was a huge man with massive yet somehow gentle hands and sharp Italian features. His English was almost unintelligible," but he made no apologies for it. He had an incredible knack with machinery, a natural engineer. On Sundays he would go to the plant and study the legal and corporate structure of the company. He designed a revolutionary impact-extrusion press, demanded a block of stock and Albert's daughter in marriage for a second improved design. Giovanni and Elizabeth continued to build Scarlatti Industries into an empire. In 1904 the Scarlattis moved to New York; on July 14, 1908, Scarlatti died and Elizabeth took over Scarlatti Industries.

SCARLATTI, ROLAND WYCKHAM (SI)

Oldest Scarlatti son, a shy, malleable personality. When America entered World War I, Roland left Princeton in his senior year and "sailed for France as Lieutenant Scarlett, AEF, Artillery. He was killed on his first day at the front."

SCARLET O. (RO)

Redhead waiting for the first flight officer of Gibson's plane at Doogie's Bar in downtown Omaha; her dimensions were 38–28–34.

SCARLETT, ALLISON DEMEREST (SI)

Wife of Chancellor Scarlett. She was in labor the day of Ulster's wedding; she and Chancellor had seven children. Elizabeth found it impossible to get along with her, and Chancellor found her dull.

SCARLETT, ANDREW ROLAND (SI)

Born in April 1926, the only child of Janet Saxon and Ulster Scarlett. Andrew was adopted by Canfield after his marriage to Janet. He was an extraordinarily good-looking boy with bright blue eyes, very dark eyebrows, a slightly upturned nose, and black hair; he was just over six feet and appeared to have a perpetual tan. At eighteen Andrew was forced to meet his real father in Germany. Andrew considered Canfield to be his real father; he didn't want to meet Ulster Scarlett.

SCARLETT, CHANCELLOR DREW (SI)

Second-oldest Scarlatti son, studious and precise. Elizabeth chose him to stay home during the war, and Chancellor entered the family business. Elizabeth thought Chancellor was a better man than she ever gave him credit for, but that his outlook was provincial; he had a ridiculous sense of propriety. It was Chancellor's idea to set up the Scarwyck Foundation; he was president of the board. Chancellor was flattered that Ulster came to him wanting to learn the family business. Elizabeth warned Janet not to get a divorce after Ulster left because Chancellor wouldn't hesitate to take control of Andrew's inheritance.

SCARLETT, JANET SAXON (SI)

Janet's first husband was Ulster Scarlett, her second, Matthew Canfield. She had one son, Andrew, by her first marriage. Ulster chose Janet to be his wife, not because he loved her, but because she'd give him an heir. Elizabeth knew there was something wrong before the wedding, because Janet drank too much. On their honeymoon Ulster dragged her all over Europe and abused her sexually. After Ulster disappeared, Janet intended to wait for a year, then get a divorce; Elizabeth thwarted this plan because she was afraid Andrew would lose his inheritance. Elizabeth liked Janet, but Janet didn't like being manipulated by Elizabeth. Janet met Canfield outside Elizabeth's home; Canfield was trying to find out if Ulster was still alive.

SCARLETT, ULSTER STEWART (SI)

(*See also* Kroeger, Heinrich.) Youngest Scarlatti son. As a youngster he was a bully; as he grew older he demanded his own way, the only one of the sons who used his wealth with cruelty and brutality. He was hostile toward anyone he thought was his inferior. From his parents he learned how to manipulate wealth and people. Elizabeth chose to send him to the front in World War I and keep Chancellor at home to run the business. Ulster was a second lieutenant in the infantry; the other men didn't like him, especially Captain Jenkins. To their surprise, Ulster volunteered to go on patrol by himself, his intention being to desert. When he discovered the Germans had retreated, he turned the German guns on his own people, gathered up a bunch of German helmets, and brought them back to his own lines, then left again. The captain thought he was a hero; meanwhile he met Gregor Strasser and the two of them deserted until the end of the war. Ulster received a medal for his bravery which he hung with his many war pictures above the mantel. Ulster worked with the Mafia when he came back, amassing a great deal of money for the Nazi cause; then he announced he would get married and learn the family business. Cartwright helped him learn about the trust fund and the securities; Ulster stole $270 million worth of securities and took them to the Swedish exchange. Meanwhile he married Janet Saxon and traveled all over Europe, drawing bank drafts totaling his entire inheritance. He forced Cartwright to be quiet about his expenditures, then killed him when he tried to profit by his knowledge. The day after Andrew was christened, Ulster left for Germany, taking the name Heinrich Kroeger; Ulster even had plastic surgery to make him look like a German.

SCARZI, ANTONIO (BU)

A Sardinian who traded drugs for information. Bernardine sank him in his sailboat off the shoals of Costa Brava. He told Bourne to use Scarzi's name on the envelope to be left with the concierge at the Pont-Royal Hotel.

SCHNEIDER, OBERST (GC)

Lubok was supposed to ask for an Oberst Schneider in Block Five at Casimir. He was part of a trap set for Lubok and Fontine.

SCHOFIELD, JUSTICE WILLIAM (BU)

Prefontaine used Schofield's name when registering at the Ritz-Carlton Hotel in Boston.

SCHRAMM, DR. (PM)

One of Matthias's psychiatrists, from Menninger's. He was the finest neuropsychiatrist in the business.

SCHREIBERS (OW)

Honorific greeting from Tanner to the Ostermans (*schreiber* means "writer").

SCHUMACH, MURRAY (BI)

Dispatcher for Belkins Moving and Storage in New York. He liked to fish out of Sheepshead Bay. David Webb called him to find out the name of the man supervising the moving at the Treadstone house. Schumach was upset because someone called and tried to cancel the job. Schumach's men called him "Murray the Menace." Schumach was evidently used to working with government agencies.

SCOFIELD, BRANDON ALAN "BRAY" (MC)

Attaché-at-large, Consular Operations, U.S. State Department. Scofield had a pallid face, sharp facial features, and light brown hair fringed with gray; his sister called him Bray. Known to have been responsible for numerous assassinations and over twenty defections, Scofield had compromised more operations than any other agent since World War II. He'd been with Consular Operations for twenty-two years. He had been a government major with a flair for languages at Harvard when Winthrop found him. Winthrop recruited him, sent him to the Maxwell School in Syracuse, then to Consular Operations in Washington. As the violence escalated, Scofield requested commando training, mastered codes and ciphers, and then became a European expert. Scofield became an extremely efficient killer after his wife was lured to her death in East Berlin by Taleniekov's group; he wanted Taleniekov dead. The Matarese

Corsica, examining old ruins (THE MATARESE CIRCLE)

made it appear that Yurievich was assassinated by Scofield. Congdon retired Scofield, then was told by the secretary of state to report to his field men that Scofield was "beyond salvage." Scofield killed the courier Taleniekov sent him because he believed Taleniekov wanted to kill him. He realized Taleniekov was not trying to kill him when Taleniekov saved his life in the hotel in Washington. After Taleniekov's story was confirmed by Winthrop and ensuing events, Taleniekov and Scofield traveled to Italy, where they met Sophia Pastorine and Antonia Gravet and learned about the shepherd boy. Taleniekov, Scofield, and Antonia, working their way through the descendants of the original Council of the Matarese, finally located the shepherd boy and destroyed him and the present-day council. Scofield received an award from the government for his services, and he and Antonia, as Captain and Mrs. Vickery, retired to run a charter boat service in the Caribbean.

Scozzi, Count Alberto (MC)

A member of the original Council of the Matarese. Father of Guillamo Scozzi.

Scozzi, Count Guillamo (MC)

When his sister married Bernardo Paravacini, Guillamo assumed his father Alberto's title. Scofield and Antonia attended a charity affair sponsored by Scozzi and his wife at their estate. "He was a tall, slender man, a *cavaliere* complete with tails and graying hair. . . ." He was very attracted to Antonia. Scozzi panicked when Scofield approached him about making a deal between the Matarese and an Arab company. Scozzi was the figurehead for his company; the real power was Paravacini, who shot him.

Scrimshaw, Arthur (RO)

Head of development for Holly Rock Productions. He was interested in producing the Suicidal Six movie.

Scrubb, Alby-Joe (RO)

The disguise Sam Devereaux used to get inside the Supreme Court building. Alby-Joe owned a chicken-breeding farm somewhere.

Sealfont, Dr. Adrian (MP)

President of Carlyle University; he was trying to restructure and modernize Carlyle. Adrian was a widower who lived in a large white colonial mansion with wide marble steps. He was a little over six feet tall, thin, with aquiline features; he radiated warmth and had a genuine humility that concealed his brilliance. The Justice Department contacted

Sealfont about the investigation at Carlyle after thoroughly investigating his background and not finding his connection to Nimrod. Dunois stopped Matlock from reaching Sealfont with Kressel's diary; Matlock thought Kressel was Nimrod until he discovered that Kressel had been murdered. Dunois's group captured Sealfont; the media reported Sealfont had disappeared and speculated on his connection to the massacre at Carlyle.

————, SERGEI (BU)

Krupkin's chief aide and undercover agent. He was in his early thirties and was powerfully built. He was trained in Novgorod, and his French was impeccable.

SERPENT (MC)

(1) British called Taleniekov the "Serpent."
(2) Scofield called his yawl *The Serpent*.

SHAPOFF, "GINGERBREAD" (IA)

CIA field officer "so highly regarded that he was practically a legend at the agency." He was a nondescript, overweight man who typically wore unpressed, ill-fitting clothing. He was married and said that he actually was a left-handed periodontist from Cleveland. Shapoff was Khalehla's contact with Mitch Payton.

SHARP, SAMUEL "SAMMY" (MP)

Owner of the Windsor Valley Inn, a supper club that didn't encourage overnight guests. "Sammy the Runner" was a very bright Jewish lawyer who handled the finances of the Windsor Shoals Congregational Church; he was a highly respected member of the community. Sharpe, Holden, and Matlock had stepped outside to discuss the meeting in Carlyle when the others inside the inn were gunned down.

SHEFFIELD, AARON (CM)

Motion picture producer, owner of *Counterstrike!*, Chancellor's book about the CIA's operations against a foreign power in a New England university town. Sheffield was pressured by Washington to change the plot for the film because the story was too close to the truth. Sheffield took his wife along to entertain Chancellor at the beach house in Malibu.

SHEFFIELD, MRS. AARON (CM)

Pretty, blond-haired wife of Aaron Sheffield. She wouldn't take money from Chancellor for her sexual favors because her husband paid her very well for it. She was an old pro.

SHENG CHOU YANG (BS)

A major power on the Chinese Central Committee, revered as a philosopher-prince by his people. He was a dark-eyed, slender man of medium height with close-cropped prematurely gray hair and gaunt features. He was married and had children. He was McAllister's counterpart in the trade conferences in Peking in the late seventies. He had attended Fudan University in Shanghai and been chosen by the Central Committee because he had learned the English language and Western economics well. He was then indoctrinated and sent to the London School of Economics for graduate study. He intended to take over Hong Kong and turn it over to his father in return for the fortune his father had lost when the Communists took over China from Chiang Kai-shek; he also intended to quietly eliminate opposition to himself in the Chinese government and make himself Premier of China. He had a widespread network of conspirators, and he hired Bourne to help him create chaos so he could grab power. He wouldn't hesitate to kill someone if he thought the person might betray him. After Bourne saw him kill d'Anjou and others at the Jing Shan Bird Sanctuary, he was determined to kill him even if the U.S. hadn't asked him to; Bourne was successful on his second attempt.

SHEPHERD BOY (MC)

Nicholas Guiderone, chosen by Guillaume de Matarese to lead the council of the Matarese. He was responsible for killing Guillaume de Matarese and all the people at Villa Matarese. Guiderone may not have been his original name.

SHIPPERS, DR. COLIN (PM)

Randolph's regular staff pathologist was ill with mononucleosis when Steve MacKenzie's body arrived at the hospital; Shippers was his temporary replacement. Shippers reported to Randolph that he'd found digitoxin and a puncture wound as well as an aortal hemorrhage; he asked Randolph about the family and Steve's insurance. Randolph thought Steve had committed suicide and stated that the cause of death was an aortic aneurysm, so Midge could collect Steve's insurance. Shippers was a paminyatchik; his cover was chief pathologist at the Regency Foundation. Havelock tried to panic Shippers into calling Ambiguity and had him under surveillance; Shippers pulled a switch and disappeared.

SHIRAK, ABDUL (RO)

Roman Z stole Abdul's taxi to transport Hitluh to the steps of the Cambridge Street police headquarters; when he was finished, he returned the taxi.

SHIRE, DR. (GC)

Friend of Barbara Pierson's; he was elderly, wore horn-rimmed glasses, and drank black coffee. He was a curator of relics and artifacts at the Metropolitan Museum of Art in New York and had spent his life studying the past. It was his job to make the preliminary examination of the documents Adrian found. The documents appeared to be authentic but would need further tests. He did not want the responsibility of releasing the contents of the documents to the world; he agreed to store the documents in a laboratory vault until Adrian decided to release them.

————, SHIRLEY (BU)

One of the women who was a guest at Tranquility Inn. She and her traveling companion decided to remain at the inn even after they knew about the violence that had occurred there.

————, SHIRLEY (T)

Maid who worked for Aaron Green. He found the American lady at the Israeli pavilion at the Montreal Exposition. Shirley made the most wonderful cakes and Aaron had to endow a half-dozen orange groves in Haifa to convince her to come work for him.

THE SHOVEL (RO)

Hit man hired by Goldfarb to capture Chief Thunder Head. The chief hit him in the stomach, bringing up the recent meal, then stuck the Shovel's face in it while interrogating him. He identified Goldfarb as his boss. He was left tied to a tree.

SHULMAN, G. R. "GERRY" (IA)

Representative for Drucker Graphics, Boston. The Kendrick Group did business with them for years with no problems.

SILVERSTEIN, MR. (HC)

Lived on the same floor in the apartment building as Noel did. He was having the lock changed on his door.

SIMON, ———— (BU)

Name frequently used by Bourne. He registered at the Mayflower Hotel in Washington under that name. He used it when he approached Albert Armbruster. He traveled under that name to Paris and used it when meeting Bernardine. He used it again when he negotiated with Santos.

SIMON, HENRY (AP)

Name conceived by René Mattilon and used by Joel Converse to introduce Joel to General Bertholdier. Joel was to present himself as a lawyer, in an expensive suite at the George V reserved by his firm; his original hotel registration card was destroyed and replaced by one with Henry Simon's name on it and a fake address in Chicago.

SIMON, NATHAN (AP)

One of the senior partners of Talbot, Brooks, and Simon. He is described as being tall and portly; he wears tortoiseshell glasses and a "vandyke beard that covers the scars of shrapnel embedded at Anzio years ago." He has thick salt-and-pepper eyebrows above hazel eyes and a sharp, straight nose. He is Jewish.

He was one of the reasons Joel had joined the firm; Joel had learned more about the law from Simon than from anyone else. There was always a distance between them, perhaps because Nathan had a loyalty to his own sons. He was very fond of Roger Converse and told Joel to respect his father because Roger had done more for Joel than he had known how to do for his own sons. Of the three partners, Joel felt closest to Nathan.

Nathan says Joel should go ahead with the investigation of Aquitaine after he had talked to Judge Anstett; Larry Talbot agreed, saying, "Nathan frequently obfuscates the issues . . . but he's usually right." Joel knew Nathan "would help him only if he was convinced there was substance to his case . . . he would legally lean over backwards in the negative if he thought a relationship . . . was being used to manipulate him."

SIMON OF BETHSAIDA (SIMON PETER, PETER) (GC) [REAL PERSON]

One of the disciples of Christ, who gave him the name Peter. He spent the years after the death of Christ wandering and preaching in many lands. He was the writer of the most shocking of the missing religious documents in the vault of Constantine.

SIMON, SYLVIA (AP)

Wife of Nathan Simon; they had been married many years and had two grown sons; one son sold insurance in Santa Barbara and the other ran a bar in Key West. Neither one was interested in being a lawyer like their father.

SIR LARRY (RO)

Member of the Suicidal Six whose main impersonation was Sir Laurence Olivier. His real name was Laurence Lars Olafer.

SITMARIN, NIKOLAI (PM)

At the age of thirty, the State Department's most accomplished analyst on internal Soviet affairs. He was born and raised in Leningrad and immigrated to the U.S. with his dissident parents when he was eighteen years old. Bradford suspected him of being the mole because he was not in Washington from mid-Christmas week until January 8. It was found he was legitimately with his mother in Chicago, where she was critically ill.

SMITH, ——— (MC)

He worked for the Matarese and relayed a telephone message to Scofield.

SMITH, ——— (PM)

The man who answered the phone at Matthias's home told Havelock his name was Smith.

SMITH, MR. AND MRS. JOSEPH (IA)

Americans who lived at 70 Adar Street in Clinton, New Jersey. Joseph liked Kendrick because Kendrick told off Barrish, one of the snotty officer types who had given Smith a lot of trouble in 'Nam. He was delighted when Barrish's post was changed from Washington to Guam.

SMYTHE, JACK (T)

Secret Service agent who was part of the group keeping Robert Webster and his wife under surveillance on their trip back to Akron.

SMYTHES (OW)

Wealthy old family of Atlanta that corporate raiders preyed upon.

SMYTHINGTON-FONTINI, ALGERNON "SMYTHIE" (RO)

Tall, slim, with blond hair and blue eyes, the Anglo-Italian yachtsman was head of Smythington-Fontini Industries. When the group decided Vinnie must be eliminated, Smythie volunteered his acquaintances in Milan for the job, then called Vinnie to warn him that Warren's group was after him. Smythie helped Vinnie disappear in exchange for not being ruined financially on the stock exchange; the dons insisted that Vinnie get his revenge nonviolently and with no visible connection to them. Smythie provided Vinnie with the mercenaries to protect Hawk's group and "rescued" Vinnie when it was time for him to reappear.

SNAKE LADY (BS)

1. Also called "the snake bitch," the Chinese lady who sold snake entrails at the entrance to the walled city; she also passed on messages for pay.

2. Bourne was to repeat the words "snake lady" several times to activate an instrument by voice print.

3. Snake Lady was the code name Delta used going into Tam Quan to rescue his brother, Gordon Webb.

SNAKE LADY (BU)

"Nuy Dap Ranh." Many members of the old Medusa had a picture of a lady with snakes for hair tattooed on their forearms. David Webb had no such tattoo.

SOO JIANG (BS)

Also called "the Pig." Chief of Intelligence for Macao operations for the communist Chinese. According to Bourne's impostor, Soo Jiang spoke fluent French and was the relay who told him his target and gave him half the money for the kill. Jiang was stationed at the Guangdong garrison. According to Wong, he fornicated "indiscriminately, threatening the women he favors with loss of employment for themselves" or members of their families; he had humiliated women in Wong's family. Wong caught him alone, slit his throat, cut off his genitals, and stuffed his body into a soiled female commode.

SOUND MAN (IA)

He liked working for Prague because he was paid well. On one of his jobs he planted "bugs" in the Vanvlanderen house and furnished Milos with a diagram, key, and typed manuscript of conversations.

SOURCE ABLE (HC)

John Tennyson (Johann) was referred to in the MI6 files as "Source Able," never by his own name.

SPANE, MR. (GC)

Ex-husband of Jane Holcroft Spane. He remarried. He was two or three years older than Vittorio, mildly amusing, content to enjoy what he'd inherited without contributing anything himself; his expertise was at the racetrack. He and Vittorio's wife had an affair; he was driving the night she was killed.

SPANE, MRS. JANE (GC)

Jane Holcroft married Spane, then divorced him and resumed using her maiden name.

SPAULDING, DAVID (RE)

Station chief in Lisbon, recalled to assist with the Rhinemann exchange. His code name was Lisbon and his cover was minor embassy attaché. As a child Spaulding had lived with his parents in London, Baden-Baden, and Costa del Santiago; he was fluent in Portuguese, Spanish, and German. When he was sixteen his father sent him to the States to finish his education—Andover, Dartmouth, and Carnegie Tech. He rejected the musical world of his parents and became a construction engineer. After college he worked at a number of small engineering jobs, not earning much; Mandel got work for him performing in radio plays, where he was much better paid. His objective was to get enough money to start his own company. The government became aware of his background when Spaulding evinced an interest in the Army Corps of Engineers. Pace chose him to be an intelligence agent based on his knowledge of languages, his ability to read and evaluate blueprints and photographs, and to function independently. Spaulding's one weakness was a hesitancy to take quick advantage of an adversary and kill; Pace had to train him to overcome this to ensure his survival in the field. Spaulding spent three years as station chief of Lisbon; he was extremely annoyed to be taken out of strategy there and returned for what he thought was a job that could easily have been done by less experienced agents. He was not happy with the lack of information surrounding his operation, and he had people trying to kill him but he didn't know why. In Buenos Aires he thought these people were Gestapo. He didn't know about the exchange for the diamonds until he talked to Asher Feld. He then decided to get the blueprints safely to the States and, if possible, expose the people who set up the exchange.

SPAULDING, MARGO (RE)

Richard Spaulding's wife and David's mother, semiretired concert pianist living in Portugal with Richard.

SPAULDING, RICHARD (RE)

Margo's husband and David's father, semiretired concert pianist. He was an overbearing father and, when David was young, tried to compensate for the time he couldn't spend with David by scheduling special activities for the family on Sundays.

SPEER, REICHMINISTER (GC) [REAL PERSON]

The commandant of the occupation forces in Antwerp was having all kinds of trouble with train schedules and shipping because of the Loch Torridon infiltrators; his dispatch to Speer was intercepted and duplicated.

SPEER, ALBERT (RE) [REAL PERSON]

Reichsminister of Armaments. His father and Altmuller's "had often gone into joint merchandising ventures; the mothers had been school chums." Speer's desire was to get Peenemünde functional so they could win the war; he was losing faith in Hitler. Speer didn't want any visible connection between the government and the businessmen who were to get the diamonds.

SPINELLI, GIAN (RE)

Best gyro man in the American laboratories; he worked for ATCO. Spinelli was short, dark, with brown eyes; he wore thick glasses. His estimate for completing an accurate gyroscopic guidance system was anywhere from next week to next year plus six weeks of inflight testing at the Montana Proving Grounds and another month to equip the fleets. The Americans desperately needed these devices before the invasion of Europe within the next several months. Spinelli was an obvious choice to examine the blueprints from the Germans but was discarded in favor of Lyons.

SPRAGUE, DR. JOHN (T)

Trevayne's family physician. John had been a boyhood friend of Andrew Trevayne's in Boston. When Phyllis was in the hospital, John sent an ambulance to the finest restaurant in town; it returned with lobster, steak, and wine for the Trevaynes. After Bonner was slashed by de Spadante, Trevayne had him taken to the hospital in Darien and Sprague took care of him.

SPRINGTREE, DANIEL (RO)

Part-Navaho senior partner of Springtree, Basl, and Karpas of San Francisco. Daniel was seventy-four years old and still in love with his wife of fifty years. When he saw Jennifer's photograph in the *National Geographic* article, he asked Jennifer to come to San Francisco and join the firm as a junior partner.

STAMMLER, GERHARD (AP)

German, described as a balding, middle-aged man who spoke English with a pronounced German accent. Introduced to Thayer by Norman Washburn as the man who "handles a great deal of our press relations with the West German media." He excused himself from the conversation, saying that he was far older than Washburn and nowhere near as resilient, that he needed some sleep.

STAN-THE-MAN (IA)

News reporter who asked Kendrick questions following Kendrick's interrogation of Barrish.

STANHOPE, ARNOLD (IA)

Representative for Morseland Oil, Tulsa. They wanted more surveys from the Kendrick Group than they were able to pay for.

———, STANLEY (MC)

Winthrop's trusted chauffeur and friend for more than two decades. He was a huge man whose checkered Marine Corps career had been cut short by several courts-martial. He had been put in place by the Matarese to keep a very close watch on Winthrop; he was killed by Scofield.

STAPLES, CATHERINE (BS)

Senior Foreign Service Officer assigned to the Canadian consulate in Hong Kong. Also known as "Cool Catherine," "Ice-cold Catherine," "Stick Staples," and "Catherine the Great." Marie Webb had become acquainted with her when, as a representative of the Canadian Treasury Board, she had to brief the diplomatic corps prior to their overseas assignments. She had known Catherine thirteen or fourteen months. Catherine was fifty-seven, slender, energetic, medium-height, with a throaty voice; she dressed fashionably but simply—a no-nonsense professional with a sardonic wit, tough but fair, top-flight. She had saved two attachés in her own consulate, as well as an American and three British, from blackmail and extortion. She had a deep friendship with Ian Ballantyne; Lee Teng was possibly in love with her. She was divorced from Owen Staples, the Toronto banker. She was furious over the way Marie and David Webb had been treated by the Americans and the British. When she realized the importance of what David Webb was doing, she tried to get Marie to come to the consulate with her. Sheng received information about her through a traitor in Lin Wenzu's group; Sheng's men shot Catherine to death in front of her apartment house.

STAPLES, CHRISTINE (BS)

At the Canadian consulate in Hong Kong Marie Webb said her friend's name was Christine, not Catherine Staples.

STAPLES, OWEN (BS)

Ex-husband of Catherine Staples; they had no children. He had not always been a rich man. He owned at least four banks in Toronto. He never remarried after being married to Catherine. He'd had two previous marriages and two children; he wished that he and Catherine had had a child. His ambitions and Catherine's were not compatible. Havilland knew him quite well; he saw him at the Toronto race course where his horses were running.

STATE ONE (MC)

Code name used by the Secretary of State when he answered Scofield's call about the Matarese conspiracy.

STAVROS, ———— (RO)

Stavros wasn't working too hard to get around the Wopotami dancers in front of the Supreme Court building; he was enjoying the view.

STERN, DANIEL (PM)

Director of Consular Operations, a European specialist and one of the four main strategists. When the strategists could not decide on a course of action with regard to Havelock, Stern went to Pierce to request the State Department to make the decision. That evening after work Stern went to Dawson's office to sit and talk for a while before driving home. Because of a traffic accident their car was separated from their surveillance team, was hit by a bulldozer, and they were both killed. There was a news blackout about their death, and their families were moved to a high-security area at Colorado Springs.

————, STEVE (AP)

In a conversation between Stone and Johnny Reb, Stone's name is suddenly changed to Steve. Probably a typographical error.

————, STEVE (IA)

A "dark-haired, blivet-featured reporter with too many teeth" who worked for Cable News. He introduced Hefflefinger and didn't know who Kendrick was.

STEVENS, ELLIOTT (BI)

Senior aide to the President of the United States. He was in his forties, unmarried, slender, wore glasses, and was comfortable with authority. His job was to gather information on the Treadstone operation and to find out about the killing of Peter at the Ottawa airport. One of Carlos's men shot him to death just as he was leaving the Treadstone house.

STINKER (IA)

Manny's pet name for Ahmat.

STOCKHOLM (RG)

Other code name Gris. Unemployed espionage expert, currently living as a minister of the Scandinavian Baptist Church, hired by Hawkins to help kidnap the Pope. Stockholm and Paris were old friends and flew into Zermatt together. Stockholm was a "tall, blond man who looked like he jumped out of a television commercial for Scandinavian cigars."

STOCKTON, HOWARD (MP)

Owner of Carmount Country Club near Mount Holly. Howard was a southerner, with grayish-blond hair, a suntanned face, white mustache, and deep blue eyes surrounded by wrinkles. He bragged he had the best combined operation north of Atlanta. He didn't like the Mafia and he tried to be a good citizen; he was vice president of the Rotary, took care of the family of a deceased employee, paid for the extension of a grammar school, and funded the Memorial Day picnic. Matlock used Stockton to make contact with someone from Nimrod who wanted the Corsican paper.

STOESSEL, ERICH (AP)

Illegitimate son of Henrich Leifhelm and Marta Stoessel. (*See also* Leifhelm, Erich.)

STOESSEL, MARTA (AP)

Mother of Erich Stoessel Leifhelm, mistress and later wife to Heinrich Leifhelm. (*See also* Leifhelm, Heinrich.)

STOLTZ, HEINRICH (RE)

An undersecretary at the German embassy in Buenos Aires. Stoltz was Rhinemann's liaison with Altmuller and with Kendall and Spaulding. He was more loyal to Rhinemann than to the Third Reich although he was also a confidant of the High Command. He spoke impeccable academic German. He was convinced Spaulding knew nothing about the diamonds. He knew the Gestapo was not in Buenos Aires and assumed the people following Spaulding were from rival American companies trying to eliminate their rivals; he ordered his men to protect Spaulding so the exchange could proceed. Against Rhinemann's wishes, Stoltz took Jean Cameron hostage to make sure Spaulding would conclude the exchange.

STONE, CAPTAIN GEOFFREY (GC)

Member of MI6, better than their best cryptographers. A shark at quick decisions, he was Victor's communications man at Loch Torridon. Victor first knew him as Apple; Stone had worked with Latham to bring Victor out of Italy and had his right hand shot up so badly that he had lost the use of it; he hated Victor. Stone was working with Brevourt without Teague's knowledge and deliberately delayed Victor's arrival home the night the twins were born. He double-crossed Brevourt—when he was separated from the service, he had Victor's file set up so he was sanctioned to kill Victor. He obtained Victor's file from the vault, then killed Aubrey Birch. Victor lured him into a trap at Campo di Fiori; Stone killed Barzini but was then killed by Victor.

STONE, PETER CHARLES (AP)

He is fifty-eight years old, a resident of Washington, D.C., and had been employed by the CIA for twenty-nine years. He had been station chief in various European posts and Istanbul and his last position was Second Director of Clandestine Operations at Langley, Virginia. He had a drinking problem during the last ten years he was with the CIA and had been fired because he criticized them privately within the organization. Since that time he had worked as a consultant and analyst for various intelligence departments other than the CIA. He had been asked by the men fighting Aquitaine to join them because he had much experience that they needed, and he was not allied in any way with the U.S. government.

He still drank, but permitted himself only one drink a day. He was still unmarried although he had been in love with Anne, the conduit in North Carolina; she had once been a CIA operative, decided to leave and he had decided to stay—their love didn't survive. He hated guns; he always carried a gun, but had only used it once.

———, STOSH (RO)

Guard of Polish descent who was hired by Aaron to protect Sam from being contacted by Hawkins. He loved potatoes with his porterhouse steaks. He was tied up, stripped to his shorts, and left in an Oldsmobile by the two Desis. Aaron paid him then fired him.

———, STOSSEL (BI)

Assistant manager of the Carillon du Lac hotel in Zurich, Switzerland. He was very familiar with Webb's (as Bourne) needs due to previous stays there; he could be relied upon to perform certain services, such as relay messages.

STRASSER, GREGOR (RE)

Member of the Nachrichtendienst who examined the supply of industrial diamonds at Peenemünde. The Nachrichtendienst met at his home.

STRASSER, GREGOR (SI)

Strasser and Ulster Scarlett met in a field in France during World War I; they were both deserting. Gregor's family was from Heidenheim, where he intended to go after the war. Strasser assigned Scarlett the name Heinrich Kroeger, the man Scarlett shot in the head. Strasser was a Nazi but had deep differences with Hitler and his group.

STRAUSS, ——— (MP)

Strauss was a filmmaker who was speaking at the assembly hall on the Carlyle campus; he believed New Wave was prehistoric.

STRICKLAND, ——— (IA)

When Tony McDonald escaped from Kendrick, he "holed up in a room at the Tylos Hotel on Government Road under the name of Strickland." Khalehla's group had him under surveillance.

STUDEBAKER, JUDGE JOSHUA (T)

Genessee had antitrust problems with their Bellstar plant in Seattle; the judge ruled in their favor. Studebaker was a large black man born in 1898 to an itinerant crop hand. He received seven years of schooling through a government program; the next few years he lived as a migrant worker, accepting jobs where he could also get an education. At age twenty-two he found an experimental college that prepared him for the law; at twenty-five he was a lawyer. At twenty-seven he successfully appealed a case before the Missouri State Supreme Court and wasn't welcome in Missouri after that; he was disbarred over technical reasons. For the next several years he prepared cases for colleagues and was a member of the Communist Party. When Roosevelt was elected and instituted his reforms, the Communists ordered Studebaker to form a cell and disrupt the programs that were helping people. He could hurt helpless people and went to the Justice Department, who quietly hired him and restored all his legal privileges; he was then awarded the first black judgeship west of the Rocky Mountains. He spent the next thirty years of his life fighting vested advocacy. If his past was revealed it would appear he had an ulterior motive for every decision he'd ever made.

SUBAGLOO, ARNOLD (RO)

President's Chief of Staff. He couldn't get to a staff meeting because it conflicted with his afternoon massage, which he needed because the press corps had been calling him names and he was stressed. He was "against anyone or anything that could be a potential threat to the White House," so he had taken the precaution of bugging the homes of the men in Warren Pease's group; he verified this through Warren, forcing them to take action against Vinnie and Hawk's group. Arnold was pear-shaped, like a slug. He had a high IQ and had been an engineer; he was strongly antisocialist and anticommunist. He felt it was his job and Reebok's to keep un-American deviates out of the mainstream.

SULIKOV, VLADIMIR (BU)

Soviet Consul General in New York. He was a slender man of medium height with an aquiline face, taut white skin, and large brown eyes, a wiry seventy-three-year-old, full of nervous energy. He was dedicated to physical exercise and looked ten to fifteen years younger than his age. He had been a scholar and former professor of history at Moscow University; he was a committed Marxist but not a member of the Communist Party. He informed Ogilvie that he was about to be picked up by the CIA and offered him Russia's help—for a price, of course.

SUNDSTROM, PROFESSOR ERIC (IA)

Member of Inver Brass and a brilliant scientist of earth and space technology, code name S. He was a "rotund middle-aged man with a cherubic face and the impatient eyes of a scholar below a rumpled thatch of red hair." He had over twenty remunerative patents and would benefit from retaining the military-industrial group in the government. He was obsessed with research and felt that science would rule all civilization. Milos found Sundstrom at the San Diego airport and killed him before he could escape with Grinell. It was reported in the media that Sundstrom died of a cerebral hemorrhage.

SUTHERLAND, AARON (CM)

Married son of Judge Daniel Sutherland, given his name by Jacob Dreyfus. He was "the brilliant attorney of the legitimate black left." He loathed whites, but refused to fight for blacks the way his father had. He had two sisters, both married with children; they lived in Cleveland, Ohio.

SUTHERLAND, ALBERTA "ABBY" WRIGHT (CM)

Well-loved wife of Judge Daniel Sutherland, probably the best black actress in the country. "Tall, erect, with a magnificent presence . . . she would not accept roles that exploited either her sex or her race."

SUTHERLAND, JUDGE DANIEL (CM)

Inver Brass code name Venice; he took that name to represent Othello, the Moor. He was a "large Negro with an immense head and face that could have been chiseled from Ghanian mahogany." He wore tortoiseshell-framed glasses over his large, dark eyes; his voice was deep and resonant. He could speak Ashanti.

Sutherland had come out of the squalor of Alabama fields and fifty years later had climbed to the highest levels of the U.S. judicial system. "He had twice refused presidential appointments to the Supreme Court." He had repaired a severed connection between the Bureau and the rest of the intelligence community. In a suit brought by three New York journalists asking for admittance to mainland China, he had ruled against the government.

He was very much a family man. He was married to Alberta Wright Sutherland, one of the finest black actresses in the country. They had a married son, Aaron, two married daughters, and several grandchildren. He loved his son but hoped Aaron would learn his loathing of whites was misplaced. Sutherland was shot to death on the road toward Salisbury.

SUTTON, ANTOINETTE (RO)

Daughter of Sir Henry, and was engaged to either Robbins or Martin. She sent her father overlarge sweaters for Christmas.

SUTTON, SIR HENRY IRVING (RO)

(Ludlum dedicated the book to Henry Sutton, his godfather, a wonderful actor.) One of the world's greatest living actors, a legend. Sutton had been married several times and had more children than he could remember. He was a tall, lean man with a flair and energy that belied his age, with gray, flowing hair, sharp features, and glaring eyes. He was a firm believer in the Stanislavski method and never ceased trying to instruct others. Sutton had been a second lieutenant in Combat Intelligence, attached to OSS-Tobruk, and had heard Hawkins speak out against Montgomery. Aaron hired him to impersonate Hawkins for the meeting with the Suicidal Six; he also impersonated him on the steps of the Supreme Court building as a diversionary measure. Sutton's mere presence caused the complete collapse of the Suicidal Six's strategy; he was impressed with their skill and professionalism. He made sure Aaron paid him and was as excited as the Suicidal Six were about the movie; he insisted on playing the part of Brokemichael.

————, SUZANNE (AP)

A temporary substitute for René Mattilon's regular secretary, who had been injured in an auto accident. Not only was she a competent, attractive secretary, she was also a competent assassin, taking out René while his partners were both on vacation.

SWANN, FRANK (IA)

Middle-aged deputy director of Consular Operations, code name S. He was prematurely gray, and had been in the business thirty years. His wife divorced him because she was tired of his going out "for a loaf of bread and returning three months later with the dirt of Afghanistan" still in his ears. He was an expert in southwest Arab affairs and knew the language and a dozen dialects fluently. Swann was suspicious of Kendrick's motives when Kendrick offered to help during the hostage crisis in Masqat and amazed when Kendrick requested anonymity. Because he could use his help, Swann let Kendrick go to Masqat, giving him whatever deep-cover help he could but denying his association with Cons Ops if he were caught. He received all kinds of flak when Kendrick's name reached the media; he did his best to downplay it and wanted Kendrick to find out who was responsible.

SWANSEN, JEAN (T)

The Swansens were neighbors and friends of the Trevaynes'. Pam had gone to a party given by Jean while her parents were in Maine. The girls had shared a joint, but an anonymous tipster told the police they were sniffing heroin. When the police arrived, they found a quarter million dollars worth of heroin on the porch in the milk box.

SWANSON, BRIGADIER GENERAL ALAN (RE)

Swanson was in Washington, in charge of government contracts. His wife was in Scarsdale with her sister because he felt he couldn't handle any distractions. Swanson realized the Germans would have to be forced into unconditional surrender and that meant getting the guidance system before Operation Overlord. He was extremely unhappy with Oliver and Craft and wouldn't authorize payment to Meridian unless they undertook a crash program to get the guidance system. A break came when Fairfax received a cable indicating the Germans wanted to trade blueprints of the guidance system for industrial diamonds; Vandamm told him to try to buy the blueprints. The Germans would accept only a trade. Swanson forced Craft and Oliver to set up the exchange, as the government didn't want to appear to be associated with it. Swanson was forced to work with Kendall on the logistics and intended to kill him when the exchange was completed. Swanson hated what he had to do and the methods he was forced to employ; he knew that he would have to face the consequences of his actions at a later date. He tried to keep Spaulding from learning about the diamonds; Swanson committed suicide rather than have his part in the exchange exposed.

SWAYNE, GENERAL NORMAN (BU)

Head of all procurements for the Pentagon, he had lost the ability to make decisions, and a caretaker had been assigned to him by Medusa. He enjoyed playing golf and was a dog aficionado. He lived on a twenty-eight-acre estate west of Manassas, Virginia, which was really a cemetery. He was a career soldier from a lower-middle-class family in Nebraska who married a hairdresser in Hawaii twenty-six years earlier. He was "medium-sized, medium-built, ramrod-straight." He didn't care about Rachel and Eddie's love affair. He had a tattoo of the snake lady on his inner forearm. He had been an elite member of Command Saigon, head of the Quartermaster Corps, and had supplied Medusa during the Vietnam War. When his link to Medusa was uncovered, he was murdered, and his murder was made to look like suicide. He left a carefully kept diary and left his estate to the Soldiers, Sailors, and Marines Retreat, which was run by Medusa. He left nothing to his wife.

SWAYNE, RACHEL (BU)

Wife of General Norman Swayne for twenty-six years, and much younger than he. She was large-breasted with long, streaked, dark hair. She had been an uneducated grammar school dropout in West Virginia when the mines shut down. She turned to prostitution in order to buy food. She worked her way to Hawaii, where she became a hairdresser. This is where she met and married Norman. He never considered her

Hawaii. En route to the Far East, I visited old Marine Corps haunts!

good enough for his friends, and after dinner he passed her around to special people for their sexual enjoyment. When he had certain meetings and didn't want her in the house, he sent her over to Eddie Flanagan's cabin. She and Flanagan became lovers and planned for the day when they could leave. She didn't want the police called in the night Swayne died.

Sykes, Sir Henry (bu)

Chief aide to the Crown Governor of Montserrat, and chief military aide-de-camp. He was a former brigadier of the British Army. He knew John St. Jacques very well and respected and trusted him. During the crisis he gave the Crown Governor the very least information he could. He played the part of the bereaved David Webb. He persuaded Samuel Lemuel to represent the Pritchards; he got the telephone number for contacting the Jackal from the Pritchards and relayed this to John St. Jacques.

Sylvester (ro)

Member of the Suicidal Six whose primary impersonation was Sylvester Stallone. He was an erudite Yalie.

Symington, Brigadier General Arnold (rg)

The General refused to do anything to help the White House ruin Hawkins's career. He knew Hawkins was framed by the Chinese.

Symonds, Roger (mc)

MI6 agent who would have been dismissed from the service because of losing two thousand pounds of MI6 funds gambling if Scofield had not loaned him the money to replace it. Symonds was middle-aged, slightly overweight, with a thatch of unmanageable brown hair and a first-class analytical mind. As a favor, Scofield asked Roger to arrange a meeting for him with David Waverly. Roger had found out that Scofield had been declared "beyond salvage" but didn't believe it. When Roger tried to help Scofield, he was killed by the Matarese and his body disappeared. It was reported that he had somehow been involved in killing David Waverly.

Tabouri, ——— (bu)

Olive-skinned, obsequious banker at the Banque Normandie who allowed Bourne to transfer seven million francs to his bank by voice authorization. Bernardine considered him a thief. Tabouri would do things outside of normal banking practices for the right price.

TALBOT, JACK (AP)

Supposedly worked for Boston Graphics; false name and job description used by Joel Converse while in Amsterdam to contact Valerie without the Aquitaine finding out he was calling her.

TALBOT, LAWRENCE "BUBBA" "LARRY" (AP)

Senior partner of Talbot, Brooks, and Simon in New York City. He is described as being well into middle age and is a perfectly competent attorney; "his rise in law was as much due to his having been one of the few all-American football players from Yale as from any prowess in the courtroom." Larry thinks Joel is one of the best and wants to keep him. He relied on the judgment of Nathan Simon and Judge Anstett, however, in permitting Joel to take on the project.

TALENIEKOV, VASILI VASILIVICH (MC)

KGB Director of the Southwest Soviet Sector; he'd spent twenty-five years as an intelligence agent. When he was a "twenty-one-year-old student with a gift for languages [he] had been taken out of his classes at the Leningrad University and sent to Moscow for three years of intensive training" in "all forms of surveillance and sabotage, espionage and the taking of life. . . ." He had been in love with a student who had been sent across the border to lead a demonstration; her bloodied body was sent back across the border and Taleniekov became a killer and a master of strategy. He avenged the girl's death by killing Scofield's wife. Three years later Scofield took his revenge by killing Taleniekov's brother. Krupskaya convinced Taleniekov that both he and Scofield had been targeted by the Matarese for extinction and to test the strength of the Matarese to control the American and Soviet governments. Taleniekov then had to elude both the American and Soviet intelligence services, reach Scofield, and convince Scofield to join him in exposing the Matarese. The two of them concentrated on finding the shepherd boy, the head of the Matarese. The Matarese captured Antonia and Taleniekov and took them to Appleton Hall; Taleniekov was severely wounded. Scofield agreed to a meeting there, to exchange the X-rays for the hostages and to try to capture Guiderone. Taleniekov died while providing Antonia and Scofield a chance to escape.

TALLEY, SENATOR (T)

Elderly senator from West Virginia, a member of the Senate panel to confirm Trevayne. He was easygoing and intelligent and didn't care for scrapping and unpleasantness. Talley was a former county judge. He was the first on the panel to offer Trevayne the cooperation of his office and his state.

TALLON, WESTMORE (CH)

Although Tallon worked for MI5, his passion was for Jamaica. Tallon owned Tallon's, an expensive, exclusive fish store in Kingston; it had a private telephone number and delivered by plane. He was black, elderly, had severe arthritis in his right hand and arm; he walked with a cane, and his head trembled slightly with age. He spoke English fluently, with a British accent. He was from an old Jamaican family, part French, and had attended Eton and Oxford. Moore's group didn't like him because of his association with the British.

TANNER, ALICE "ALI" MCCALL (OW)

Wife of John Tanner. Although they had no money problems, Alice felt her husband was underpaid for the work he did. The Tanners lived in a nice home with a swimming pool at 22 Orchard Place, Saddle Valley, New Jersey. As a child, Ali had frequently seen policemen in her home because of her father's behavior. She had met John at the public inquest after her father's death; John had correctly labeled McCall's death murder by the government. John was the only man in the world for Ali; they had never kept secrets from each other, so Ali found it hard to understand John's sudden erratic behavior. Ali recognized that Leila had saved her life and allowed Bernie to risk his life to save John.

TANNER, JANET (OW)

Eight-year-old daughter of John and Alice Tanner. She discovered the family's Welsh terrier in the bathroom, its head severed from its body.

TANNER, JOHN RAYMOND (OW)

News Director for Standard Mutual. At home he had three television sets he could watch simultaneously. He joined the Army, obtaining the rank of first lieutenant via field commission in France. He was discharged in July 1945. He worked for the *Sacramento Daily News*, the *San Francisco Chronicle*, and then the *Los Angeles Times*, where he built his reputation as an investigative reporter. He was nominated for a Pulitzer and nicknamed "The Vulture" because of his exposé of working conditions along the San Diego waterfront. In January of 1958 he joined Standard Mutual in Los Angeles and then was transferred to New York City as network editor.

The Ostermans were old friends from Los Angeles, and the Ostermans, Tremaynes, Cardones, and Tanners got together for a special weekend whenever the Ostermans came east from California. Tanner was shocked when Fassett told him his best friends were involved with Omega. Tanner was left with no choice but to work with Fassett to trap Omega; due to special security rules, Tanner couldn't tell Ali anything about Omega. Tanner was manipulated both by Fassett and the CIA, his family was terrorized, and his longtime friendship with the three couples was destroyed. He was shot and nearly killed and finally caught Omega himself with no help from the CIA.

TANNER, RAYMOND (OW)

Twelve-year-old son of John and Alice Tanner; his birthday was the week of the Osterman weekend and Bernie and Leila had brought him a present.

TARKINGTON, ——— (GC)

(1) Legal officer who went to Saigon and obtained evidence from Captain Barstow about Eye Corps. His death was made to look like it was related to booze and whores; Tarkington was a nondrinker.

(2) Tarkington's brother, a colonel assigned to the Inspector General's office. He was extremely angry about his brother's death and was hunting Andrew to kill him. He had also been investigating Eye Corps. Adrian learned from him that Andrew had left the country, taking Andrew's passport and other papers with him. When Adrian went into the mountains after Andrew, he knew he might not come back; he called Tarkington so he could catch Andrew if Andrew was the one who returned. The colonel helped Adrian get the vault out of Italy, then gave Nevins's people the information they needed to launch their investigation.

TATIANA (AP)

Secret code word that meant this person can be trusted. Originally Tatiana was the name of one of the Russian czar's daughters who was reputedly executed in Ekaterinburg in 1918, but she may have been spared with her sister Anastasia and smuggled out with a nurse carrying a fortune in jewels. The nurse favored Tatiana and may have given everything to her and nothing to Anastasia.

René Mattilon tells Joel to use the code word when he reaches Cort Thorbecke in Amsterdam; Peter Stone tells Johnny Reb to use it when he contacts Anne in North Carolina (he had used it years before); Prudhomme tells Valerie to use it when she calls him; Johnny Reb uses it when he tries to reach Stone with the information he'd gathered about Scharhorn.

TATIANA, Z. (AP)

Code name used by Johnny Reb when he was attempting to reach Peter Stone for a long period of time following his discoveries on Scharhorn. Frustrated at the delay, he told the intermediary the Z stood for Zero, another example of Johnny Reb's sense of humor.

TAYLOR, DR. (PM)

Stocky, red-haired, freckle-faced doctor in his mid-thirties who was called in to care for Loring and "Boris" after the massacre at Randolph's hospital. He worked for the government to pay back the money the government loaned him to complete medical school. He complained about the delay in transferring Loring to Bethesda. Taylor was an expert at administering drugs for interrogation; Havelock ordered him to accompany "Boris" to the hospital and get more codes from him for reaching Ambiguity.

TEAGARTEN, JAMES "JIMMY T" (BU)

Supreme Commander of NATO in Brussels. Member of both the old and new Medusas. The WAC major who accompanied him to dinner in Anderlecht was also part of Medusa. They were both killed when their car exploded. Teagarten had to be killed off by Medusa because his secret fax line to DeSole had been uncovered. The killings were blamed on Jason Bourne.

TEAGUE, BRIGADIER ALEC (GC)

British Military Intelligence, Army. He had a large, powerful frame, smoked, and liked whiskey neat. Because he had a habit of looking at his watch frequently and doing everything very punctually, he was also known as "Stopwatch Alec" and "Timer Teague." He'd decided years before not to get married because of his profession; there'd been lovers, of course. Teague was given permission by Brevourt to get as much information and use out of Vittorio as he could; he sent Vittorio to Loch Torridon to train for infiltration, changed his name to Victor Fontine, and made him a captain. He came up with the idea of training the people at the camp how to cause problems through mismanagement and put Victor in charge, but kept him under surveillance. He was unhappy about Victor getting married, and he was angry when Brevourt exposed Loch Torridon. He agreed to help Victor find out about the train from Salonika after the war if Victor would continue to work for him; he was in awe of Victor's abilities. Victor and Alec became good friends, and Loch Torridon continued and was immensely successful.

TEASDALE, SAM (BS)

One of the CIA men who had guarded and interrogated David Webb at the safe house in Langley, Virginia, after the assassinations at the Treadstone house. Sam's wife left him and went to the Caribbean with another man. He knew nothing about Marie's disappearance.

TELLY (RO)

Member of the Suicidal Six whose primary impersonation was Telly Savalas. He offered everybody lollipops.

TENNYSON, GRETCHEN (HC)

Gretchen von Tiebolt changed her last name to Tennyson when they moved to England.

TENNYSON, HELDEN (HC)

Helden used Helen as her first name in England, as the British could not adjust to Helden; she used Helden in France because the French didn't care.

TENNYSON, HELEN (HC)

Helden von Tiebolt changed her name to Helen Tennyson when she went to England. She was rebellious, a loner, not close to her brother and sister. Helden had long blond hair and clear brown eyes; she was as beautiful as her sister and mother but didn't have to use her attractiveness to survive. She was highly intelligent and street-smart in an international sense. People around her thought she was cold or a lesbian. She had attended the university when they lived in Rio. She was single and had recently moved to Paris, where she worked as a translator for Gallimard Publishing. Helden lived with Herr Oberst; she was an expert at avoiding the Israelis, the Odessa, and the Rache. She had no idea Gretchen and Johann were deeply involved with the false Wolfsschanze. She had no knowledge of the covenant in Geneva until Noel reached her; then she took him to Herr Oberst to see if he was telling the truth. She and Noel became friends and lovers, protecting each other from Johann and the Fourth Reich.

TENNYSON, JOHN (HC)

Johann changed his name to John Tennyson when they moved to England. In Brazil Johann had been trained by Maurice Graff; he became the supreme leader of the Fourth Reich when Graff gave him the Sonnenkinder documents on his twenty-fifth birthday. He was an over-achiever; he'd completed two university degrees in Brazil when most students had completed only one. Johann was an extremely successful businessman in South America, amassing a great deal of money, then suddenly he was on the staff of the *Guardian* in London. He spoke five languages and covered the European capitals. The man who hired him was killed in an unusual train accident on the underground. MI5 thought he was the Tinamou because every time there was an assassination, Tennyson appeared in or near areas where the assassination took place.

Santorini, a Greek island. A mule climb, a few feet from a precipice down a thousand feet—once was quite enough!!!

Gretchen knew he was the Tinamou but Helden did not. He was a very handsome man, with perfect features and light blond hair. He was tall and slender with the body of an athlete but had a scar from the base of his throat to his breast. Gretchen satisfied his sexual needs to keep him from being distracted from his work for the Fourth Reich; he loved Gretchen dearly but killed her when it became necessary. His plan was to maneuver Noel into signing the documents, then kill him. His men failed in the attempt, and several months later Johann was killed by the new Tinamou as he was conducting business for the Fourth Reich.

TENNYSON, JULIAN (HC)
When Noel was hunting the telephone number of John Tennyson, he phoned all the J. Tennysons; one of them was Julian.

TESCA, ALFREDO (GC)
Foreman at one of Savarone's factories and a partigiano. Vittorio was angry because Tesca called him on his private line at his hotel—he fired him. Tesca told him his father and whole family were in danger, to go to Campo di Fiori at once and use the stable road when he got there.

THAYER, THOMAS (AP)

Supposedly known to Molly Washburn as "T.T." Name used by Johnny Reb to introduce himself to Norman Washburn as an old friend of the family the evening he kidnapped him to get information about the Aquitaine.

———, THEODOOR (AP)

The cherub-faced middle-aged owner of the house of prostitution in Amsterdam; he took Joel's money to keep quiet about his whereabouts and then took money from the Aquitaine to let them know where Joel was. Joel hit him in the head with his gun barrel before making his escape with Emma.

THOMAS, CAPTAIN (CH)

Pilot of the 747 that McAuliff took from London to Jamaica.

THOMPSON, ——— (BS)

When David Webb called Lanier, he told him he was Thompson of the State Department to try to get Lanier to talk to him.

THORBECKE, CORT (AP)

Dutch businessman in Amsterdam that Joel Converse was supposed to meet in his building at the corner of Utrechtsestraat and Kerkstraat. He did an extensive business in passports, and had the means to help Joel return to the United States safely. He was one of a very small group of businessmen who used the code word Tatiana, indicating that the individual using the code word could be trusted. Joel was given this code word and Thorbecke's address and telephone number by René Mattilon.

THORNTON, ——— (HC)

Male passenger aboard British Airways Flight 591 to New York; he accidentally got the drink with the strychnine in it that was meant for Noel.

THORNTON, HOWARD (SI)

One of the merchants supporting the Nazis. He was from San Francisco, in industrial construction. Kroeger thought the stock deals in Stockholm were exposed because Thornton maneuvered large blocks of the securities back into his own hands at depressed prices. Thornton was the only one of the merchants who knew the real identity of Kroeger; Kroeger had him killed before the conference in Zurich.

THUNDER HEAD, CHIEF (RO)
Hawkins conned the Wopotami elders council into making him chief of their tribe.

THYSSEN, FRITZ (SI)
One of the merchants who supported the Nazis; he controlled many steel companies in Germany. Thyssen was a pornographer—he printed books and pamphlets and filmed movies in his warehouses in Cairo.

TINKERBELL (IA)
Pet name Manny had for Gray of the Masada Brigade; the name irritated Gray.

TOBIAS, PHIL (IA)
Evan Kendrick's chief congressional aide. He advised Kendrick to accept a position on the Partridge Committee because Kendrick would then have some influence as to who became the next congressman from the Ninth District. Phil was very upset when the news was released about Kendrick's work in the Middle East and he hadn't been informed. He was found with his throat slit down under the boilers in the basement of the office building.

TOLLAND, BREWSTER (AP)
Undersecretary of State. Walter Peregrine, a very angry ambassador to Germany, called him about the covert investigation of his embassy by the Navy Department. Tolland then called Harry and others, who confirmed there was no such investigation going on. He had no information concerning Joel Converse.

TOLSON, CLYDE "THE TULIP" (CM) [REAL PERSON]
Senior FBI agent, second-in-command at the Bureau, close friend of J. Edgar Hoover's for fifty years, chief beneficiary of Hoover's estate. He was frequently Hoover's companion. He had been in ill health and had two strokes. He had a soft, pampered face and liked to dress elegantly. Rumor was that he showed up at Hoover's house before Hoover's body was cold and went through each room with a portable shredder. Hoover had moved files A–L to Tolson's basement; he died before he could move the remaining files.

TORTUGAS (RE)
The exchange of the guidance system for the industrial diamonds was given the code name Tortugas by General Swanson; it later came to mean the activities of the man from Lisbon.

TOTTLE, CINDY (RE)
Maiden name of Cindy Bonner.

TOWER CENTRAL (MC)
Code name for a KGB drop that was no longer used on the Victoria Embankment in London; it referred to the boats that ferried tourists to the Tower of London and back to Cleopatra's Needle.

TOWNSEND, JACK (OW)
Old prep-school friend of Tremayne's; he met Dick at the Biltmore Hotel. Townsend delivered Blackstone's message, that Dick should not call Cardone because Cardone was being watched. Fassett told Tanner that Townsend was a known stock manipulator out of Zurich that Dick met at the Biltmore.

TREADSTONE, D. (BU)
David Webb reached Mo Panov by telephone at his office; he used the name D. Treadstone.

TREADSTONE SEVENTY-ONE CORPORATION (BI, BS, BU)
"The most controlled unit of American intelligence since the State Department's Consular Operations. Created by the man who built Medusa, David Abbott." David Webb (as Bourne) was listed at the Carillon du Lac as a representative of Treadstone; his bank account in Zurich was controlled by them. The group operated out of the brownstone house at 139 East Seventy-first Street in New York City until the massacre by Carlos's men.

TREMAYNE, PEGGY (OW)
Thirteen-year-old daughter of Richard and Virginia Tremayne.

TREMAYNE, RICHARD "DICK" (OW)
Attorney who worked for a firm engaged in unethical mergers; whenever he was under pressure, he would drink too much. Dick and Ginny had lived on Peachtree Lane in Saddle Valley for six years; he loved his wife and daughter deeply. Richard was status-conscious; he felt a pool was one symbol too much of their wealth since he was only forty-four years old. He had graduated from Yale Law School in the top five percent of his class, clerked for Learned Hand, and spent three years at the bottom of the firm's ladder before receiving any real money. Richard thought the message from Blackstone was a blackmail attempt; someone he was representing was afraid of being exposed by Tanner. They wanted him to stop Tanner or they would expose his accounts in Zurich. When

these accounts were exposed, Richard acted as everyone's attorney; he flew to Zurich to get out with whatever he could salvage of their investments.

TREMAYNE, VIRGINIA "GINNY" (OW)

Wife of Richard Tremayne. Ginny couldn't understand why they didn't have a swimming pool—they could afford one. Gardening was her second passion after sex; Ginny dressed a bit flamboyantly, to emphasize her well-proportioned body. She worked well with children and had a solid relationship with her teenage daughter; she thought her husband was the best lawyer in existence. She and Dick had no secrets between them about Zurich. Because she loved her husband so much, she tried to seduce Tanner to find out who Blackburn was and convince Tanner not to hurt Dick.

TREVAYNE, ANDREW (T)

Chairman of the Defense Allocations Subcommittee. Trevayne was a tall, athletic man who enjoyed sailing; he was married with two children. Trevayne's father had spent thirty years building up a woolen mill in Hancock, Massachusetts, only to have it taken over by a conglomerate. Andrew was six months away from completing a law degree at Yale. He quit and went into business with Doug Pace, even though he had been attending Yale on a full scholarship. He was determined that he would make such a massive amount of money that he would never have to experience what his father had. Andrew then married Phyllis Pace and started a family. The business grew quickly and they had to expand. After *Sputnik* went up, they retooled and specialized in space-age products. Andrew was a millionaire by the time he was thirty-five. When he was thirty-seven he left the business and took a job with the State Department. After a successful stint as Undersecretary of State, he quit to devote his time to running the Danforth Foundation. Trevayne had heard that the Defense Allocations Committee needed a chairman for the subcommittee and knew that Baldwin wanted him to accept. He wasn't eager to take the job because he knew he would be under great pressure from various groups; he was afraid there would be so many restrictions that anything he did would be futile. He was confirmed for the chairmanship and chose his staff himself. After two months of investigation they had chosen five or six companies to investigate in depth; he and four of his staff concentrated on Genessee, an immense, complex conglomerate with no discernible operating structure. Trevayne and his men hunted for that structure and names of people associated with particular functions. What they found was a group of men who controlled the conglomerate, orchestrating its functions to ensure the country remained strong and well defended. What was good for the country was determined by this small group of men. Trevayne tried to strike a deal with these men to force them to leave their positions in exchange for lessening the impact of the subcommittee's report on Genessee. The Genessee group supported him as a presidential candidate because they believed that once he was elected, they could control him; he wouldn't be able to expose them without exposing himself. After the President was killed by Goddard, Trevayne ran for president because he knew about Genessee and knew they had to be controlled.

TREVAYNE, PAMELA (T)

Seventeen-year-old daughter of Andrew and Phyllis Trevayne. Pam attended a private school for girls, Miss Porter's, while Phyllis taught at the University of Bridgeport. Andrew was amazed when Pam won a medal for her skill in chemistry. Pam was tall and slender, with light brown hair, wide brown eyes, and a good face. She was afraid her father wouldn't be able to change anything by being on the subcommittee. She was the first in the family to hear that the President had been assassinated.

TREVAYNE, PHYLLIS PACE (T)

Wife of Andrew Trevayne and mother of Pamela and Steven. At forty-two, she was able to wear her daughter's bathing suit. Phyllis thought they were lucky to have earned so much wealth so early in their lives. She and Andrew were still deeply in love and shared all their decisions. Not only was Pam accused of being involved with hard drugs and Steven accused of a hit-and-run, but Phyllis was drugged and taken into a room at the Plaza Hotel and raped. De Spadante tried to discourage Trevayne from taking the chairmanship by terrorizing Trevayne's family. In spite of everything that happened, Phyllis didn't want Trevayne to back off. When Phyllis and Andrew were first married and their company was starting up, Phyllis was their secretary and bookkeeper. After the children were born she stayed home and cared for them. After they went to school Phyllis tried joining a country club and playing golf but became bored; she tried working again in their company but felt out of place. Out of boredom she turned to alcohol; one day she skidded the car into a tree and decided it was time to make a major change. She and Andy decided she should become totally immersed in a project in which she had great interest, medieval and Renaissance history. She started by auditing graduate courses at Yale; in two years she had her master's degree and two and a half years later a Ph.D. in English Literature. It was at this point that they built High Barnegat, because they felt they'd worked hard and deserved it. Phyllis was teaching at the University of Bridgeport when they had to move back to Washington. She admitted she was scared when

Andrew was asked to run for President; she loved the life they had. When the subcommittee work was over, Phyllis planned to take a vacation in the Caribbean; this was abandoned when the President was assassinated and Andrew accepted the invitation to run for office.

TREVAYNE, STEVEN (T)

Nineteen-year-old son of Andrew and Phyllis Trevayne; he wore his hair long and attended college at Haverford. When the police couldn't reach his parents in New York, they located Steve and took him to the Swansens, where heroin had been found at the party Pam was attending. Steve later met his parents at the police station and was extremely angry; he knew his sister had never used hard drugs. The same evening the inside of his car was destroyed and alcohol poured all over the seats while he and his date were inside a local pub. While driving home, Steve was stopped, searched, and photographed by two men posing as local police; Steve realized later that their car wasn't the color used by the district they represented. They accused him of hit-and-run but never filed any charges. Steve thought that somehow his father might have been able to prevent the assassination of the President by stopping Genessee; the assassination made him feel scared and helpless.

TRIBE OF ACQUABA (CH)

Also known as the Halidons or Halidonites. The Maroons had been an arrogant, warlike people brought to the islands as slaves; George I had offered them their independence along with the Cock Pit territories in perpetuity. The tribe of Acquaba was an offshoot of the Coromanteen tribe; they isolated themselves after the Maroon wars because they wouldn't agree to the treaties that would require them to capture runaway slaves for the English. They settled in an isolated location, near a huge vein of gold, and developed the philosophy that they were privileged and had to justify their existence by their lives' actions. They accepted the view that "order emerges out of chaos of different, even conflicting ideologies," and they had no ambitions for political power. They believed in freedom of mobility and freedom of thought, and were basically nonviolent, preferring to instill fear rather than use force. This tribe "dispensed vast sums throughout the world, concentrating on . . . areas of widespread human suffering." They would kill to protect their tribe and its secrets, and they would destroy themselves rather than be interfered with by the outside world.

TRIGNON, PIERRE (BI)

Bookkeeper at Les Classiques in Paris. Claude Oréale didn't like him because he deducted the cost of phone calls from Oréale's pay. Pierre and his wife lived in a small upstairs apartment in the center of Paris. He was a balding, heavyset man with a cherubic face and thick, protruding lips. He liked to wear suspenders. For him to receive a telegram was an extremely rare occurrence; he was quite upset when David Webb (as an investigator) told him he could be charged as an accomplice to the murderer, Carlos.

TRUEHEART, ANDROMEDA (RO)
Youngest daughter of Tyrania Trueheart. She took her mother's place as Pease's secretary while Tyrania vacationed in Beirut.

TRUEHEART, CLYTEMNESTRA (RO)
Older sister of Regina, a very quiet girl. She was a secretary for the CIA.

TRUEHEART, REGINA (RO)
Security pool stenographer, older sister of Teresa. Her duty was to go from one top-secret assignment to another, keeping her bosses out of trouble. She called her mother when Warren Pease got upset because the Filthy Four were returned alive in body bags with air holes.

TRUEHEART, TERESA (RO)
Chief of Staff's personal secretary.

TRUEHEART, TYRANIA (RO)
Mother of Andromeda, Clytemnestra, Regina, and Teresa. "Tyrania believed it was the destiny of the family's women to guide the leaders . . . through Washington's minefields so they could exercise what generally feeble abilities they possessed." Tyrania was secretary to the Secretary of State. She had sharp Teutonic features and blazing light blue eyes, and was just over six feet tall with an imposing body for a fifty-eight-year-old woman. She and the girls had thrown her husband out of the house, and he went to the Caribbean, where he was quite happy. Tyrania took her vacation in Beirut.

TUCKER, SAM (CH)
Soil analyst from California, a top professional in his field. He was a large, burly man in his fifties, extremely reliable, but fun-loving; he was fond of back-street native saloons. He'd worked with McAuliff on his first survey in Alaska, then others including last year in Oracabessa; he and McAuliff were good friends. McAuliff thought of him as a "late middle-aged 'soldier of fortune.' " Bob Hanley and Sam were close friends, and Bob was very upset over his sudden and mysterious disappearance, even

though he knew that Sam was eccentric and would take impulsive trips through native areas; Sam was always looking for the unusual. Piersall was also his friend, and sent Barak Moore's people to protect him; Piersall died before he could share his research with Sam and McAuliff. Sam was interested in staying in Jamaica, but he wasn't ready to join the revolutionaries and he didn't believe in Obeah. He liked Alison very much and was her protective escort. He was extremely resourceful, tough, and aggressive—not a man to have as an enemy. After they successfully fought off Dunstone, Ltd.'s men, Sam decided to stay in Jamaica and enter a partnership with Bob Hanley.

TYNE, JONATHAN (RE)

Hero of the very popular radio show *The Adventures of Jonathan Tyne*. Spaulding did a small role in a Spanish dialect.

UCELLO (MC)

Sophia Pastorine's dog, named Ucello because it flew over the ground like a bird. It refused to leave Sophia's side after her death.

UNCLE REMUS (BU)

Pet name Bourne had for Cactus.

UNIO CORSO (CH)

Corsican crime organization similar to the Mafia, only far more efficient. They were hired by Warfield to kill McAuliff and his survey party.

UNIO CORSO (GC)

Also called the Corsicans. They knew every inch of the coast of the Gulf of Genoa; they helped the British get Vittorio out of Italy.

VALDERO (RE)

Farm in northern Spain that was a center of operations for Spaulding and his men.

VALENTINO, ——— (BU)

Deputy director of the CIA; he had been an analyst, not a field man. He had a high respect for Conklin, especially after the job Conklin did in Hong Kong; he kept Conklin's alcoholism secret. One of the two men within the CIA that Conklin trusted before he became acquainted with Peter Holland.

VAN HEADMER, JAN (AP)

One of the key members of the Aquitaine—South African, known as "the hangman in uniform," the "slayer of Soweto" by the blacks. He executes offenders frequently with government tolerance. His family is old-line Afrikaner. He's a close friend of Chaim Abrahms's and frequently visits Tel Aviv. He's an erudite and charming general officer, very tall, with gaunt, aquiline features and straight gray hair, a Cape Town aristocrat. He considers blacks to be subhuman and agrees with the Nazi concept of superior races. He was jailed along with Verwoerd and Vorster during World War II. Under his charm he is an unfeeling killer. He is Delavane's key to the resources of South Africa, but the least important of the five key men of Aquitaine.

VANDAMM, FREDERIC (RE)

Undersecretary of State, Cordell Hull's closest associate. The white-haired old aristocrat was in charge of meetings to find a solution for the gyroscopic guidance system needed by the military for Operation Overlord. His solution was to trade industrial diamonds to the Germans in return for the blueprints to their gyroscopic guidance system.

VANVLANDEREN, ANDREW (IA)

Heavy contributor to President Jennings's political party; he expected his group to control White House policy. Ardis was his fourth wife; they were brought together by Sundstrom. He had "wavy white hair and a big gut, with lots of shiny teeth." He decided to act on his own and hired Arab terrorists to assassinate Kendrick. When the attacks on Kendrick's homes in Mesa Verde and Virginia were not announced over television, Andy had a stroke and died. Ardis reported Andy was depressed over heavy losses in investments; people became suspicious when Ardis immediately had Andrew cremated.

VANVLANDEREN, ARDISOLDA WOJACK MONTREAUX FRAZIER-PYKE (IA)

Ardis was Chief of Staff for Vice President Bollinger. She was a talented administrator, put in place to keep Bollinger under the control of Grinell's group. Kendrick had met and had an affair with her as Ardis Montreaux of Off Shore Investments. She then married Emory Frazier-Pike, a London banker; he lost a large sum of money with her company and she divorced him. Following this she had an affair with Walter Lowell, Margaret's husband; then she met and had an affair with Eric Sundstrom, who introduced her to her next husband, Andrew Vanvlanderen. She wore designer clothes and had "perfectly coifed frosted brown hair. She was closing in on fifty and of medium height but gave the impression of being younger and taller due to erect posture, a slender

figure topped by generous breasts, and a well-coordinated face punctu-
ated by large, penetrating green eyes." Bollinger's staff called her the
"dragon bitch" because of her disposition. Ardis found out where Manny
was and sent Dr. Lyons to inject him with a lethal African virus. She was
considered to be a liability after Andrew died and she had him cremated
right away; she was probably killed by Grinell. Her death was reported as
a suicide due to grief over Andrew's death.

VARAK, ANTON (IA)
Milos Varak's uncle.

VARAK, MILOS (IA)
Code names: Mr. A, Checkman, Prague. Coordinator of Inver Brass.
He was a stocky, broad-shouldered, blond-haired man in his mid to late
thirties; he had a broad forehead, prominent cheekbones, and slightly
sloped eyelids. He wasn't known to smile much. His friends thought he
was a free-lance translator. As a very young man he had escaped from a
prison in Czechoslovakia; he described himself as someone devoted to
his adopted country. For the past ten years he had fought both Russians
and agents from the eastern bloc. Swann described him as a super spook.
Milos was basically responsible for planning and carrying out Operation
Icarus. He discovered that a member of Inver Brass was trying to prevent
Kendrick from taking Bollinger's place on the ticket in November.
Grinell's men severely wounded Milos at the San Diego airport; he was
picked up by DeMartin and taken to a telephone from which he was able
to contact Khalehla and Sound Man before dying.

VARAK, STEFAN (CM)
Code specialist for the National Security Council and superb strategist. He protected members of Inver Brass and carried out its investigations and directives. He was the source control for the assassination of
Hoover and for finding out where the files M–Z were and destroying
them. He was pleasant-looking, somewhere between thirty-five and forty-
five years old, almost six feet tall, with a strong, muscular body and
broad, thick shoulders; his hair was light blond, cut short. His broad face
had high cheekbones and gently sloping eyes. His "accent faintly Bostonian, the rhythm Middle European." He spoke Czech, French, and
English.
He had good reason to hate anyone who acted like a Nazi. When the
Allies found the thirteen-year-old Stefan in Lidice, Czechoslovakia, in
1942, he had been killing Germans to stay alive. His family had been
killed because his father had worked for the Allies; they brought him to
the U.S. and sent him to the finest schools. He had been in the U.S.

thirty years, and he had worked for Inver Brass and the U.S. for the past eighteen. O'Brien considered him to be the best in the intelligence community.

On orders from Inver Brass he had attempted to kill Chancellor because of his doctoral thesis; he did kill Catherine Lowell. He assumed Longworth's identity to get into Flags and to approach Chancellor. He had read *Counterstrike!* He kept Chancellor off balance by periodically showing up dressed as a woman driving a silver Mark IV Continental and forcing Chancellor off the road. Varak tried to keep Chancellor alive until Chancellor led him to the person who had the files; he went beyond what Inver Brass requested. He was captured while protecting Chancellor at the house on Thirty-fifth Street; while being transported by car, he broke out and was mortally wounded. His body showed up later at St. Michaels One, the sterile house.

VENICE (CM)

Inver Brass code name for Judge Daniel Sutherland. He had been with Inver Brass since its beginning.

VERACHTEN, ANSEL (MC)

When Prince André Voroshin left Russia, he established himself in Germany as Ansel Verachten. Supposedly he came to Essen from Munich and built a company that rivaled Krupps. His wife was said to be Hungarian; she never spoke German very well and died in the 1930s. He had two sons, one of whom died in a bombing raid during World War II; he also had a daughter. "Ansel lived to a ripe old age . . . [and] died in style, heart seizure while on horseback sometime in the fifties."

VERACHTEN, ODILE (MC)

Odile was the manager of the Verachten companies. She had never married and was described as a "man-eater." She was over forty-five, tall, and slender, a beautiful woman. She had been chosen for the Matarese by Ansel. Odile tried to persuade Taleniekov to join the Matarese but was killed by her own people.

VERACHTEN, WALTHER (MC)

Surviving elderly son of Ansel Verachten. He was married and had one daughter, Odile. He was a very religious man; he had wanted to become a priest. His estate had electronic gates, a sophisticated alarm system, and armed guards. He admitted to Taleniekov that he was a Voroshin but had no knowledge of the Matarese. Odile ordered her guard to shoot him to death.

———, **VERNAL (IA)**

Assistant to McLeod at the hotel in Nassau. He was an "immense, good-humored man with a booming laugh."

VERT (RG)

Other code name Marseilles. His specialty was electronics, a necessary skill in a busy port where Interpol was always underfoot. He thought it was "long past time for the Church to install a *French* pope."

VICARSON, SAM (T)

Member of Trevayne's subcommittee. Trevayne had met Sam during a grant hearing at the Danforth Foundation; Sam was one of the new breed of socially conscious attorneys, combining straight daytime employment with work in the ghettos at night. "He was bright, quick, and incredibly resourceful." Sam was awed by the immense size of Genessee. At a party Sam was put in a compromising situation with the wife of a young senator; the setup was aborted when the drunken congressman mentioned Genessee. Sam decided to be more careful. He was strolling along Fisherman's Wharf when he discovered he was being followed by the same man who stopped the drunken congressman at the party. Trevayne identified the man as de Spadante. Sam found out about Manolo and then went to Seattle to interrogate Judge Studebaker; he was well informed about Studebaker's background and surprised when he found out the judge had been a Communist. Sam felt Trevayne's compromise with Genessee was a copout. When the subcommittee work ended, Sam had many job offers from prestigious firms but decided to join the White House legal staff. Sam felt Trevayne made an excellent President.

VICKERY, B. A. (MC)

Scofield used this name many times: for reserving a room at the Double Crown; for registering at the Ritz-Carlton in Boston at the request of the Matarese; when talking to Goldman about Trans-Communications in Boston; when obtaining Appleton's X-rays from the dentist; when escaping from Appleton Hall with Antonia; and when running his charter boat business.

VICKERY, MRS. (MC)

Antonia used Vickery as her last name when she and Brandon ran the charter boat service.

VICTOR (PM)

Code name for VKR, Pierce.

VILLIARD, FRANÇOIS (AP)

Chief of France's highly secretive Organisation Étrangère. Attended the secret meeting at the White House that had been set up by Peter Stone to identify members of the Aquitaine from photographs.

VILLIERS, ——— (BI)

Son of General André Villiers and his first wife. He was a conservative politician, opposing the Socialists and Communists. He was a young member of the French Parliament, an obstructionist where government expenditures were concerned, but quite popular anyway. He was killed by Carlos's men, his car blown apart by dynamite on the rue du Bac, his murder blamed on Communist fanatics.

VILLIERS, GENERAL ANDRÉ FRANÇOIS (BI)

He was one of the ranking deputies in the French National Assembly, very much a law-and-order army man. "One of the most respected and powerful men in France," a graduate of Saint-Cyr, hero of World War II, a legend in the Resistance, and, until his break over Algeria, de Gaulle's heir apparent. In the early sixties he was part of the OAS under Salan, but was not a terrorist. After Algeria there was a reconciliation with de Gaulle, and he returned to France and resumed his command, rising to the rank of general. He left the Army and went into politics after his son was killed. He still met with the remnants of the angry young commanders of Saint-Cyr. He was a medium-size, barrel-chested man in his late sixties or early seventies with close-cropped gray hair, thick eyebrows, and a neatly groomed white chin beard; his bearing was unmistakably military. He was a smoker, did his own driving, and was fluent in English. After his first wife died, he married Angélique. He had access to France's most secret files on Carlos and learned all he could about him, hoping one day to kill him himself for the murder of his son. When he discovered Angélique's connection to Carlos, he strangled her to death. David Webb took credit for her death to lure Carlos into coming after him.

VILLIERS, ANGÉLIQUE (BI)

General André Villiers's second wife, a striking woman in her middle to late thirties with short, stylishly cut dark hair, her face bronzed by the sun. She was tall, statuesque. She did not need to make the frequent trips to places like the Riviera because she was Venezuelan and dark-skinned. She was said to be Carlos's first cousin, his lover since the age of fourteen, the only person on earth he cared about. Known as Parc Monceau, she was the direct relay to Carlos. David Webb told the General about her connection to Carlos, and the General strangled her to death, after listening to her confession and watching her try to shoot him.

Viper (CM)

Code name the FBI used for Paul Bromley, usually reserved for enemy agents. It signified that Bromley had dared to fight back against the Pentagon.

Viper (IA)

Code name for Vice President Orson Bollinger.

———, Virginia (CH)

Clive Preston's cook.

Vogler, Albert (RE)

Sharp, aggressive manager of Reich's Industry. Vogler was "a stout man, the image of a burgomaster." He was a superb mediator between industrial adversaries because all parties were usually frightened of him. He told Speer the reports he received indicated there was a sufficient quantity of industrial diamonds available, or at least they were obtainable.

Voltage One "Vol't Adin" (MC)

The highest ranking KGB officer outside Russia. Congdon called him to find out the address of the "hole" in Washington where Taleniekov and Scofield might meet.

von Falkenhausen, Commander Alexander (HC) [Real person]

Commander of the Belgian section during World War II and one of the giants of Wolfsschanze. He managed to reach von Falkenheim by radio and warn him to stay away so he wouldn't be caught when the attempt to assassinate Hitler was discovered. Von Falkenhausen was shot as a traitor by Hitler.

von Lindemann, ——— (IA)

Khalehla thought Ardis had married a man named von Lindemann.

von Schnabe, Lillian Hawkins (RG)

Lillian pretended to be a journalist from *Viva Gourmet* magazine who wanted to interview the Pope. She was married to an older man, a German immigrant who fled Hitler. Lillian's job was to find out about the Pope's diet and medication for later reference. While Lillian was in Rome, she also took 123 photographs of Ground Zero for Hawkins.

VON SCHNITZLER, ——— (RE)

Spokesman for I. G. Farben. Farben and other German companies were forced to help find sources of industrial diamonds for Pennemünde or face the wrath of Hitler and the loss of the war.

VON SCHNITZLER, OTTO (SI)

Businessman from I. G. Farben who supported the Nazis. Von Schnitzler and Kindorf tried to persuade Krupp to support the Nazis also.

VON STAUFFENBERG, (HC) [REAL PERSON]

One of the Führer's would-be assassins; this German officer was shot as a traitor to Hitler.

VON TIEBOLT, GRETCHEN (HC)

Oldest child of Wilhelm von Tiebolt. She was at least thirteen when she arrived in Brazil in 1945. She changed her name to Gretchen Tennyson when they moved to England.

VON TIEBOLT, HELDEN (HC)

Youngest child of Wilhelm von Tiebolt. She was born in 1945, a few months after her mother and older siblings arrived in Brazil; she never knew her father. When they moved to England, she changed her name to Helen Tennyson.

VON TIEBOLT, HELGA (HC)

Helden's mother had asked that she be named Helga when she was born, but the hospital staff was rushed and wrote down Helden on her birth certificate.

VON TIEBOLT, JOHANN (HC)

Only son of Wilhelm von Tiebolt. He was ten when they arrived in Brazil. When they went to England, he changed his name to John Tennyson.

VON TIEBOLT, WILHELM (WILLIAM) (HC)

One of the two associates who helped Heinrich Clausen with the Fourth Reich scheme. Wilhelm and his wife had three children, at least one of whom was required for the release of the funds thirty years later. Wilhelm was killed by members of the false Wolfsschanze.

VON TIEBOLT, MRS. WILHELM (HC)

She and her two children emigrated to Brazil around June 15, 1945; Helden was born a few months later in Rio. When she arrived her only possessions were a few pieces of jewelry, and she had no training at any trade, but she was able to work. She started selling clothes in a dress shop, built up her clientele, then opened her own shop, which became the basis for several other businesses. She was looked down on by the German community because she slept with several men, breaking up their marriages, and extracting money and business interests from them. She tried to interfere with Johann's work for the Fourth Reich, and he put a bullet in her head.

VONMEER, HANS (AP)
Member of the Netherlands' secret state police. Attended secret meeting at the White House that had been set up by Peter Stone to identify members of the Aquitaine from photographs.

VOROSHIN, PRINCE ANDRE (MC)
Member of the original Council of the Matarese. As a young man he spent three years at the University of Krefeld and two years in graduate studies at Düsseldorf. His father and grandfather had dealt in the Chinese and African slave trades and manipulated the Imperial banks. They were hated by the Romanovs; Czar Nicholas secretly ordered Andre from the court. Andre, his wife, daughter, two sons, and their wives supposedly died when a mob attacked and set fire to their estate in Tsarskoe Selo during the Russian Revolution.

VOROSHIN, PRINCE ANDRE (PM)
Kalyazin's grandfather was a tenant serf on the lands of Prince Voroshin; Voroshin hanged the grandfather because he stole a wild boar in the winter to feed his family.

VULCAN, MAJOR (RO)
Leader of the Filthy Four. Their job was to kill Hawkins and Devereaux. The two Desis captured them all alive and hung them upside down on the ski lift behind the cabin.

W (IA)
Weingrass's code name with the Masada Brigade.

WADSWORTH, DR. ——— (MP)
Wadsworth liked to gamble; he was well known in the casinos around Hartford.

WADSWORTH, JOSEPH (BS)
In Peking David Webb thought Wadsworth was the Bourne impostor. Webb and d'Anjou broke into Wadsworth's hotel room and Webb nearly

kill him. Wadsworth was an elderly, gray-haired man who walked with a limp and carried a cane; his occupation was off-shore oil consultant from Great Britain. He had fought at El Alamein and was a brigadier, retired, Royal Engineers.

WAKEFIELD FAMILY (CH)

Wealthy family of Savanna-la-Mar, they were hosts to Henri Salanne.

WALSH, DR. (BU)

Doctor who worked for the CIA at Sterile Five. He and Panov decided the best way to extract what Panov had learned and what he had divulged while he was drugged by the Mafia. Walsh was a real expert at his job.

WALTERS, EFREM (BI)

U.S. Congressman from Tennessee, member of the Congressional Oversight Committee; he met with Gillette, Abbott, Knowlton, and Manning. He had sat on the House Assassination Committee for over eighteen months. He was familiar with Carlos and felt he knew all the assassins and conspiracies there were to know about. He thought he could make a realistic contribution, which is why he accepted chair of the COC. He was disgusted with the squabbling among the members of this particular group. He understood what Cain was trying to do and wanted to know who he was.

WANG SHO (BS)

One of the three daughters of Liang, assistant manager of the Regent Hotel in Kowloon.

WANG XU (BS)

A textile minister of the Chinese government. Webb as Bourne chose his name from a list at the entrance to the Jing Shan Bird Sanctuary.

WARFIELD, ANDREA (RE)

Lady who lived in a brownstone on Sixty-second Street who was giving a New Year's Eve party; Cindy Bonner was one of her guests. Mandel persuaded Andrea to invite Spaulding to the party in exchange for a soprano in February for entertaining.

WARFIELD, JULIAN (CH)

Head of Dunstone, Ltd. He was a thin, short, elderly man, mentally confident but physically unsure. He used people like Clive Preston when he wanted to do business with someone but not be seen with them, and he researched people's backgrounds thoroughly before doing business. He agreed to pay McAuliff $1 million to do the survey in Jamaica and keep Dunstone's name secret; he wanted Ferguson kept away from Craft. He was a manipulator and McAuliff recognized this. He didn't trust McAuliff and had the Jensens spy on him to find out who his enemy was in Jamaica. He flew to Jamaica to give Jensen a Luger to kill McAuliff after he made contact with the Halidon. When Jensen disappeared, he sent the Unio Corso after McAuliff and Holcroft. Peter Jensen tracked Warfield to Peale Court and shot him to death.

WARREN, HARRY (PM)

Senior attaché, Consular Operations, Rome. His entry in the log regarding Havelock said "Decision pending." One of his agents reported he had been told Havelock was "beyond salvage." Warren was killed by a hit-and-run driver who appeared to be deliberately aiming for him.

WASHBURN, ——— (RO)

White House legal aide, a gaunt, bespectacled man. Washburn presented the details on the Wopotami case to a meeting of the President's cabinet.

WASHBURN, DR. GEOFFREY R. (BI)

English doctor, resident of Île de Port Noir near Marseilles for eight years; he treated David Webb for wounds to his head, legs, stomach, and chest. Webb had amnesia as a result of the head wound. He had a drinking problem—he'd get roaring drunk every Saturday night. His older sister in Coventry sent him money every month. He was dismissed from Maclean's Hospital in London because he killed two patients during operations while drunk. He was a decent man, close in age to Webb. He got Webb (as Jean-Pierre) a job with some local fishermen, but Webb almost killed three of them during a fight and had to leave quickly; Washburn gave him his passport and two thousand francs. Webb sent him a million and a half francs in repayment for all that he had done for him.

WASHBURN, GEORGE B. (BI)

False name under which David Webb flew from Bern to Orly in Paris.

WASHBURN, GEORGE P. (BI)

The name of Geoffrey Washburn's passport was changed to George P. Washburn for David Webb by a man along the waterfront in Marseilles. David used the passport to get from Zurich to Marseilles and again for entering the U.S. under diplomatic cover provided through General Villiers.

WASHBURN, MOLLY (AP)

Mother of Major Anthony Washburn, lived in Southampton. Johnny Reb used her name and information he had about her to get close enough to Major Washburn to kidnap and interrogate him about the Aquitaine.

WASHBURN, MAJOR NORMAN ANTHONY, IV (AP)

Chargé d'affaires, U.S. embassy, Bonn. Thirty-six or thirty-seven years old, member of Aquitaine, originally from Georgia. When Joel talked to Larry Talbot from Bonn the second time he told Larry where he was; twenty minutes later Washburn and someone else from the embassy came looking for him. Dowling told Enid, Peregrine's secretary, that Washburn had tried to shoot Connal disobeying Peregrine's orders.

WAVERLY, DAVID (MC)

Britain's Foreign Secretary. He had been a highly decorated commando in World War II and had an excellent record in the Foreign Office. The Matarese shot him in the head, then removed the left side of his chest with a shotgun blast, obliterating a small blue circle; they also killed his wife, children, and three servants.

WAVERLY, SIR JOHN (MC)

A member of the first Council of the Matarese, father of David Waverly.

WEATHERALL, GRANDFATHER (RO)

Character played by Sir Henry Sutton in a daytime soap opera called *Forever All Our Forevers*. Erin Lafferty watched it regularly.

WEBB, ALISON (BU)

Eight-month-old daughter of David and Marie Webb. Mrs. Cooper was especially good at caring for her.

WEBB, DAVID (BI)

(Also known as Jason Charles Bourne, Charles Briggs, Cain, Chamford, Delta, Jean-Pierre, "Jean-Pierre Sangsue," Johnson, and George P. or George B. Washburn.) Older brother of Gordon Webb and lover and husband of Marie St. Jacques. Originally he had been a career foreign service officer, a specialist in Far Eastern affairs. He had been stationed in Phnom Penh and had a house on the outskirts, near the Mekong

River. He had a family—his wife was Thai, and they had two children, a boy and a girl. His family was killed one Sunday afternoon by a stray airplane dropping bombs and strafing the dock near their house. No country would claim responsibility. Webb, deeply hurt, joined Operation Medusa to strike back. He took the name Delta and became notorious for his actions. The Viet Cong tried to trap him by kidnapping his brother, but he went in and brought him out, killing a man named Jason Bourne in the process. After he left Medusa he taught in a small college in New Hampshire; when Treadstone was formed, they asked him to be the man to go after Carlos. Webb took the name Jason Bourne, and created the character of Cain. He had pursued Carlos for two years, when Carlos nearly killed him near Marseilles. Some French fishermen found him and took him to Geoffrey Washburn, who tried for six months to restore his health. He still had severe amnesia, however. After he injured three fishermen, he had to leave the area quickly. Washburn gave him his own passport and two thousand francs. Using only what he could remember and the piece of microfilm Washburn had removed from his leg, he made his way to Zurich to the Gemeinschaft Bank, where an employee of Carlos's worked. Carlos's men chased him back to the Carillon du Lac, where he abducts Marie St. Jacques; after nearly being raped and killed by Carlos's men, she realizes Webb is not the bad guy. She tries to help him and falls in love with him. Meanwhile Treadstone is upset because they haven't heard from him for six months and suddenly someone named Jason Bourne surfaces. They try to tell him to come in, but he doesn't remember who they are or how to reach them. Marie realizes they are trying to tell him to come in, but when he does they try to kill him. To prove to them he has not turned, he leads Carlos back to the Treadstone house, where he is again nearly killed by Carlos, and Carlos escapes. Webb is treated by Morris Panov and tries to resume a normal life.

WEBB, DAVID (BS)

Webb is teaching Oriental Studies at a small university in Maine and trying to recover from the trauma of the three years he spent hunting Carlos, when he receives a visit from McAllister. McAllister tells him his file was invaded and that Jason Bourne is back, killing in Kowloon. The government in Hong Kong was being made unstable so the Chinese government would feel obligated to step in and take control. The U.S. had to show that the "real" Jason Bourne was not in the Far East, so the impostor can be eliminated. The relatives of the person killed in the Far East wanted to kill Bourne for revenge, so the State Department was increasing Webb's guards. McAllister had set the stage for the next step, which was kidnapping Marie. After speaking to Panov, Webb realizes

Macao with Mary. Although it's Portuguese, it's controlled by the People's Republic of China (THE BOURNE SUPREMACY)

that he has been set up, and he has to go after the Jason Bourne impostor if he wants to see Marie again. When he finds the impostor, he finds Sheng; he kills Sheng because he had seen Sheng brutally murder d'Anjou. When it's over, Webb has to have more therapy from Panov and he returns to Maine to teach.

WEBB, DAVID (BU)

In *The Bourne Ultimatum* Webb is fifty years old. He worked out and stayed in good physical shape. David Webb could not kill; his other identity, Jason Bourne, was trained to kill and was very proficient at it. His movements were "like those of a large, disquieted cat, smooth, fluid, alert for the unexpected." When he was Bourne, he was driven by rage and was brutal. Fontaine says Bourne and Carlos are "two crazed, middle-aged hunters obsessed with killing each other, not caring who else is killed or wounded or maimed for life. . . ." Even if Bourne was seriously wounded, he would continue to fight and to run.

WEBB, MAJOR GORDON (BI)

Younger well-loved brother of David Webb, he was with U.S. Army Intelligence and a member of Treadstone Seventy-one. As a lieutenant he was kidnapped and held by the Viet Cong in Tam Quan; David (as Delta) went in with a team from Medusa and brought him out. He didn't believe that David had turned; he went to Zurich to try to reach David and to examine the situation at the Gemeinschaft Bank. He had never been to the Treadstone house until the day he was killed there, shot to death by Carlos's men.

WEBB, JAMIE (BU)

Five-year-old blond-haired son of David and Marie Webb. He loved his uncle Johnny and loved going fishing with his father.

WEBB, MARIE ELISE ST. JACQUES (BS)

Marie and Panov were Webb's support team; there were times when his problems were too much for her and she had to get away from him for a little while. The $5 million that was left in the banks in Zurich and Paris Marie transferred to an account in the Cayman Islands; it was a small price for the government to pay for Webb's services. Those funds were available when Webb set out to find Marie. Marie used what Webb had taught her to change her appearance, travel, contact others, or disappear. She escaped from the CIA people and contacted Conklin and Panov; together they looked for Webb. When they finally found him at the embassy, Webb thought she was an actress impersonating Marie; Marie was an extremely persuasive lady and convinced him she really was alive. Panov was then able to rush in and help Webb.

Kowloon, Hong Kong, The Peninsula Hotel (THE BOURNE SUPREMACY)

WEBB, MARIE ELISE ST. JACQUES (BU)

"Canadian by birth, economist by profession, savior of David Webb by accident." She had the attributes of an actress—striking features and a commanding presence. She was deeply in love with David and afraid he'd slip back into the Bourne character permanently. She killed one of the Jackal's men, defending David.

WEBSTER, ——— (PM)

Havelock was a war orphan in London when the Websters found him and took him back to the States and adopted him.

WEBSTER, LIEUTENANT JOHN "JACK" (RE)

Husband of Peggy Webster, gunnery officer on the *Saratoga* which was in San Diego for combat repairs.

WEBSTER, MARGARET "PEGGY" (RE)

Wife of Jack Webster. She was at the Greenbrier Hotel in San Diego to be with her husband while his ship was being repaired. Leslie used her apartment in Greenwich Village while she was gone.

WEBSTER, ROBERT "BOBBY" (T)

Presidential assistant for three years. Webster was connected to Genessee through Allen. Webster was the White House liaison with Trevayne; Webster told Trevayne he was never to call the President directly. Webster was pleasant-looking, about the same age as Trevayne; he was married and had no children. Webster and his wife were from Akron. He'd risen rapidly in Ohio state politics and kept the governor in the President's stable. He was angry with the crude tactics de Spadante used to terrorize Trevayne's family but used de Spadante to get information on what the subcommittee was doing. De Spadante intended to kill Trevayne and insisted that Webster relieve the guards around the hospital. After de Spadante was shot by Norton, Webster called the doctor and requested that he let de Spadante die. When the doctor couldn't manage it because of the guards, Webster asked Gallabretto to kill him. Webster then leaked information about Paul Bonner to Roderick Bruce, anticipating that Bonner would be convicted and a relationship shown between Trevayne and de Spadante. Trevayne persuaded Bruce to quit printing the articles. Green didn't like the way Webster acted on his own with de Spadante and cut him off from Genessee. Webster resigned his post "for reasons of health" and he and his wife went back to Akron. Gallabretto's men followed them. The President wasn't sure how Webster was involved with Trevayne, but impounded all copies of the subcommittee report after he heard that Webster and his wife had been murdered.

WEDD, DOUG (BS)

Dean of Studies at the university in Maine where David Webb taught. He knew Webb wasn't telling the whole truth about why he needed to take a short leave.

WEEKS, SENATOR ALTON (T)

Senator on the confirmation hearing panel; he was from Maryland. Weeks was faced by a big campaign deficit and persuaded his supporters to donate more money by promising them that more defense appropriations would be coming into Maryland if they supported him.

WEINBERG, ———— (PM)

Weinberg was a nervous old man who lived in apartment 4-B down the hall from Handelman.

WEINGRASS, EMMANUEL "MANNY" (IA)

Code name W. Manny. Was a "whiz of an architect. An *Israeli* . . . who could design things in the Islamic style . . ." He had many Arab friends, including the sultan of Oman. He was originally from Garden Street in the Bronx and "went to Israel to avoid legal entanglements with his second or third wife." He had three wives by the time he was thirty-two and outlived all of them. Manny was eighty-six and always lied about

KAZINO ΡΟΔΟΥ — CASINO DE RHODES

№ 92182   'Αρ. / No

ΗΜΕΡΗΣΙΟΝ ΔΕΛΤΙΟΝ - CARTE JOURNALIERE

Διά Κον|Mr .... LUDLUM
—— Καν|Mme
Pour Δίδα|Mlle .... 25 ΙΛ, 1980

'Ισχύει διά τήν ....
Valable pour journée du   ΔΡΧ.
Τὸ δελτίον τοῦτο δὲν δύναται νὰ μεταβιβασθῆ   DRS. 150
Παρακαλεῖται ὁ κάτοχος ὅπως ὑπογράψιη ἀφοῦ

Where "Manny Weingrass" gambled in *The Icarus Agenda* (lost not one but two shirts!)

his age. "Like many aging men of genius, Manny was frequently eccentric and almost always theatrical. He enjoyed himself." He was slender, with a perfectly waxed mustache below an aquiline nose, eyes that were green and alive, and perfectly groomed white hair that rippled across his head. His clothing was stylish if rather extreme, and he was known for his outrageous bow ties. He had helped Kendrick manage his company, and they had a close father-son relationship. It was Manny who identified the threat posed by the Mahdi; he was angry with Kendrick because he wouldn't stay and fight the Mahdi after the death of his employees. Manny went to Paris to live out his life with beautiful women, gambling, and expensive brandy. He was an agent for the Mossad in Paris, but they didn't like the prices he charged even though he was effective. The Mossad flew Manny to Oman to find Kendrick; Manny led the group that captured McDonald and the Mahdi. Kendrick brought him back to the U.S. for surgery for lung cancer, probably caused by smoking. When Mesa Verde was attacked by terrorists, Manny killed three of them by himself and captured the fourth one alive. Ardis found him and had Dr. Lyons inject him with a deadly, slow-acting African virus; the virus was discovered after Manny was hospitalized for a gunshot wound he received defending Mesa Verde a second time. He had met and highly approved of Khalehla for a daughter-in-law, and he pushed Evan to accept the nomination for Vice President.

WEINSTEIN, MANFRED (IA)

When Kendrick and Weingrass came back from the Middle East, Manny was put in the hospital to be operated on for cancer; he was registered as Manfred Weinstein.

WELLFLEET, ANDREW (AP)

Justice of the Supreme Court, nickname "Irascible Andy," had unkempt white hair that fell in strands over his wide forehead, wore steel-rimmed glasses, and generally looked stern and disapproving. However, no one ever questioned his awesome intelligence, fairness, or devotion to the law. He examined Joel's affidavits and decided they weren't enough, that they needed many more names than those of just the five generals. He told Peter Stone that his people needed to do what they were good at—hauling people in, drugging them, and getting names from them, and if questioned said he would deny ever having said such a thing. He offered to give Stone all the government help he needed, but Stone said security was a problem, that he needed to work with the President and the Secretary of State only and set up a system where he could get honest people into deep cover and then pull in the Aquitaine traitors—he figured he could do it in eight to ten days; Wellfleet told him he had less than three. Obviously that plan had to be changed.

WELLS, FREDERICK (CM)

One of the two younger members of Inver Brass, code name Banner; he was under consideration for the position of Genesis. He was in his mid-fifties, slender, with "very pale skin, Nordic face, and dark, straight hair combed smoothly back above his wide forehead."

He had been the youngest president in the history of a major university and had left to take the chairmanship of the international Roxton Foundation. His expertise was in global finance. He believed deeply in human beings and hated oppression, "a man who was known never to compromise on principle, even when his stand incurred the wrath of all Washington." He was a Sinophile, his hobby early Oriental history—he had one of the most extensive Chinese art collections in the world. He was married late in life and had small children.

He did not approve of the President; he knew he was in the missing Hoover files. Wells was his mother's name, legally assumed shortly after his parents were divorced. His father's name was Reisler; his father had supported Nazi Germany financially, and Wells didn't want to be connected with that in any way. Wells had "a fatal automobile accident on a wet country road off the highway."

———, WERNER (AP)

One of the soldiers of Aquitaine, companion to Leifhelm's chauffeur. Joel had to leave the train at Wesel, Germany, because these two men had spotted him; Werner was killed by Joel when he emerged from a landfill where he had hidden.

———, WERNER (HC)

Graff's aide at his country estate in Brazil.

WHISTLETOE, BRUCE (AP)

Fictitious name used by Joel Converse to contact Valerie, his ex-wife; Whistletoe's job was supposedly "a confidential consultant for Springtime antiperspirant" for which her agency was doing the artwork. He knew Valerie would recognize the old trick they used to use to prevent Valerie's nosy secretary from finding out where they were meeting. They used this device twice (see Talbot, Jack) as a means of avoiding detection by the Aquitaine if the telephone lines were tapped.

WHITE (IA)

1. *Ahbyahd* means "white" in Arabic; Ahbyahd was prematurely gray.

2. White was the code name for a member of the Masada Brigade.

WHITEHALL, DR. CHARLES (CH)

A historian recommended for the survey party by the West Indies Studies group. Charles was brilliant, had made a lot of money on lecture circuits, and had written three volumes of Caribbean history; his work was regarded as the "standard reference." He was a large black Jamaican, forty-two years old, quite a dandy, quite cynical, far more honored abroad than at home. His home was in London, and he was fluent in English. He could also speak several native dialects, was a class triple-A black belt practitioner of jukato, and he sounded like a professional playing the piano and singing island patter songs. Charles volunteered for the expedition as a way to get back into Jamaica and further his goal of becoming the praetorian of Jamaica; he was a Fascist and believed that fascism was what was needed there. He hated the revolutionaries but realized he had to cooperate with them to reach the Halidons; he was excited by Piersall's discoveries.

Chatellerault made it clear to him that if Charles did not report all developments of the survey to him that he would reveal Charles's political ambitions. Charles intended to keep Chatellerault at bay and infiltrate his financial hierarchy. He went with Barak, Alex, and Floyd to retrieve Piersall's papers; without his expertise they might not have been able to find them. After reading the papers he decided he would also enlist the help of the Halidons. Charles was responsible for sending a courier to request a private meeting with the Colonel of the Maroons; this precipitated the meeting with the Halidons.

WILCRIST, PASTOOR WILLIAM (AP)

Priest character created by Valerie and her aunt Hermione. Valerie gave Joel the clerical outfit and basic instructions and Hermione set up the network of people to get him to her home near Osnabruck. A nun met him in the *Centraal Station* in Amsterdam with information he was to memorize and destroy before crossing the border into Germany. He was to tell everyone who asked that he was "thirty-eight years old, a graduate of Fordham, with a theological degree from Catholic University in Washington." On a letter written in German that he could show to authorities it further stated that he was on a pilgrimage to Bergen-Belsen and then to Auschwitz. His train ticket was made out for Bergen-Belsen, but he would get off at Osnabruck to meet Hermione.

——, WILLIAM (BU)

Stocky, middle-aged chauffeur for Bryce Ogilvie. He knew Ogilvie had been in the military, because he addressed him as "major."

WILLIAMS, ADAM (MP)

Young black radical Carlyle student; he wore his hair long, African style. He was subdued and good-humored in class, but somewhat of a firebrand on the podium. Adam reported to Kressel that Matlock was blind drunk and broke up furniture in Lumumba Hall, to conceal the fact that Dunois drugged Matlock in an effort to find the Corsican paper; later he sent in another report repudiating most of the first one. Williams was willing to help Dunois fight Nimrod and the Mafia, but Dunois wasn't willing to risk the lives of young blacks like Williams.

———, WILLIE (BU)

One of the guards at General Swayne's estate. He told Bourne he thought there were some pretty weird things happening there. He had confided as much to his girlfriend, Barbie Jo.

WILLIS, ——— (PM)

Guard at Poole's Island who was aggravated because Jackson was late all the time.

WIMBLEDON, J. HAMMER (SI)

"Hammer was Reynolds's code name for messages sent to field accountants when he considered the contents to be of the utmost importance."

WINSTON, MAJOR (RE)

Winston met Spaulding at Mitchell Field with a sealed envelope of papers and verbal instructions; he had no knowledge of what was in the sealed envelope.

WINSTON (NÉ WEINSTEIN), AL (GC)

An engineer with an aerospace company who was heavy into air force contracts. He was Jewish, flabby, and lived in a big house in Hampton with his wife and children. Andrew didn't like him because he gouged profits from cost overruns. He attended the birthday party on Long Island and told Andrew he'd make it worth his while if Andrew would put in a good word for him at the Pentagon.

WINTER, GENERAL ROLF (AP)

Standortkommandant of the Wehrbereichskommando in the Saar sectors during World War II. Impressed with Leifhelm during the war. He realized the war was lost.

WINTERS, MARTHA JENNIFER "JENNIE" (IA)

Deceased wife of Samuel Winters. She had been angry when Sam walked away from a political position because he could have prevented a great many problems if he accomplished nothing else.

WINTERS, SAMUEL (IA)

Member of Inver Brass. He was "white-haired with an aquiline, aristocratic face." He was a widower and lived in a six-story town house in uptown Manhattan; he also had an estate with a regulation croquet field on it near Chesapeake Bay. One of the two houses on the estate he had donated to the government for use as a safe house. Sam had been an outstanding sportsman in his younger days. His family had made their money from railroads and oil, which made it easier for him to pursue a career as a historian. He had a married son, and his daughter was married to a filmmaker. Sam had been the dean of Columbia University when he was tapped for the governorship of New York; when he discovered his nomination and election were being orchestrated by an unknown political organization, he refused the nomination, afraid this group would expect him to do their bidding. He remained at the university, and his advice was sought by Presidents for over forty years. Dennison resented his interference. Sam trusted Varak completely and worked with him closely to unmask the Inver Brass traitor. When Mitch told Sam he was going to file a report about Inver Brass with the President, the Attorney General, and the congressional oversight committees, Sam committed suicide.

WINTHROP, ROBERT (MC)

He had the title of ambassador. His family was wealthy and he had been able to spend his life in service to his government. He had a coronary inefficiency which required him to use a wheelchair; he was elderly, slender, with gray hair and a perfectly groomed mustache. He and his wife lived in Georgetown. Winthrop had organized Consular Operations, managed it for sixteen years, then remained as senior consultant, Diplomatic Relations, Department of State for the past ten years. He had recruited Scofield for Cons Ops, hoping it would act as a springboard for him to the diplomatic corps. Scofield figured that Winthrop would know about the Matarese in Washington if anyone would, so he called and arranged for a meeting with him in an isolated area. Taleniekov and Scofield prevented his assassination there, but then Winthrop disappeared. Winthrop had been shot in the shoulder and Stanley had taken him to a private doctor for treatment. No one suspected that Stanley was employed by the Matarese to watch Winthrop; when Scofield sent the file to Winthrop for the President, Stanley intercepted it. Stanley then pistol-whipped Winthrop and took him as prisoner to Appleton Hall. When Scofield was talking to Guiderone, Winthrop grabbed Stanley's gun and was killed, giving Scofield a chance to kill Guiderone and Stanley and escape.

WITKOWSKY, SERGEANT (MC)

Desk sergeant at the precinct on Boylston Street in Boston. When the lady from Phoenix Messenger Service left Scofield's message about terrorists, he locked her up and sent a SWAT team to Appleton Hall.

WO (BS)

Guard at the gate of the Jing Shan Bird Sanctuary. Webb as Bourne had to kill him.

WOJAK, ARDISOLDA (IA)

Ardis Vanvlanderen was born Ardisolda Wojak in Pittsburgh, Pennsylvania.

WOLFSSCHANZE (HC)

Signal to the Sonnenkinder to be prepared to assert their birthright—the funds were coming soon to establish the Fourth Reich.

WONG (BS)

A conduit used by many different groups in Hong Kong and China. Wong may or may not be his true name. He was small, young, well-dressed, and had a compact body with broad shoulders and a narrow waist; he was a cigarette smoker. He spoke English fluently, learned from nuns in a Portuguese Catholic school. He was the martial arts champion of Macao and was greatly embarrassed when the real Bourne bested him. Bourne did not care to fight him a second time; he hired Wong to take him across the border at Guangdong to find the Frenchman and the impostor. A week later he hired him again to take himself and McAllister across to find Sheng. Along the way Wong found Soo Jiang alone and killed him because of the way Jiang had treated women in his family. He stayed to help Bourne and McAllister kill Sheng; he was well paid by Bourne.

WOODWARD, CHARLES (OW)

The best news analyst in the business, he worked for Standard Mutual. During a half hour on Sunday afternoons he "interviewed a single subject, usually a controversial figure currently in the headlines." Woodward exposed Ashton as a political hack.

WOPTACK (RO)

Code name for the CIA operation to stop the Wopotami case.

WRIGHT, K. M. (BI)

A bystander from north Dallas who saw the killing of John Kennedy. He testified that old "Burlap Billy" was the only one close to the grassy

The Bamboo Curtain (barbed steel, 10 feet high). Photos are forbidden! (I used autofocus from my backside)

knoll where the shots may have been fired. His statement was never made public or put in the Warren Report.

Wu Song (BS)

Arms broker in Hong Kong; Pak-fei took Bourne to him to get weapons. He was a youngish-looking man who wore European suits. He spoke flawless English; he had graduated from Columbia University in 1973, majoring in marketing. He relied on his guards, as he could not stand physical confrontation or violence. Bourne disarmed his guards and removed Song and his men from the building before blowing it up. He told him he was Jason Bourne and would find him if he gave his description to anyone or harmed Pak-fei. Bourne figured Song would leave Hong Kong since he had neither money nor merchandise to return to the man with the numbered bank account in Singapore.

Wyckham, Albert O. (SI)

Chicago industrialist, father of Elizabeth Wyckham Scarlatti. Wyckham was impressed with Scarlatti's mechanical genius; he was replaced by his son-in-law as head of the corporation.

Wyckham, Elizabeth Royce (SI)

(See also Scarlatti, Elizabeth Royce Wyckham.) Daughter of Albert Wyckham. She was twenty-seven years old when she married Scarlatti. She was a tall, aristocratic girl who refused her parents' best efforts to marry her off. Elizabeth became interested in Scarlatti because of her father's stories about him. She was curious as to why Scarlatti was going to the plant on Sundays; she found him studying the corporate records of the company. Elizabeth helped Scarlatti take control of her father's company and married him August 24, 1892.

———, YAAKOV (IA)

Code name Blue. Leader of the team from the Masada Brigade; the "Mossad agent held hostage in Masqat was his father." His objective was to get his father out if he could, kill him if he could not. Yaakov's wife thought he was out on maneuvers in the Negev. He was "in his late twenties with hair and eyebrows bleached a yellowish-white by the . . . sun. His eyes were large and dark brown, his cheekbones high, fencing a sharp Semitic nose, his lips thin and firmly set." His grandparents had died at Auschwitz, his father survived to produce three sons; Yaakov's two brothers had been killed by the Arabs. He was furious when his mission was changed to help Kendrick. Yaakov led Black, Orange, and Red to the Aradous Hotel, where they were to keep Azra under surveillance. As Azra was leaving, he discovered them; Azra killed Orange and wounded Yaakov before he himself died. Yaakov was seriously enough wounded that Gray had to take over. When Kendrick went back to Oman the second time, to get Hamendi, Ben-Ami and Yaakov went with him. Yaakov put together a team of Israelis, Palestinians, and Ahmat's relatives to hijack Hamendi's munitions ship and sabotage the weapons.

THE YACHTSMAN (BI)

Elderly, imposing-looking man who was married to Margaret. They lived and worked in the Treadstone house. When he was younger, he had been an excellent yachtsman the CIA used to make runs in the Adriatic for Donavon. Carlos considered him to be a superior agent. He was one of Webb's only contacts to Treadstone, and was killed by Carlos's men at the Treadstone house.

YAMMENI, AHMAT (IA)

Young sultan of Oman, a little younger than Kendrick. He was courageous and intelligent and cared deeply about his country. After attending school in England he went to Dartmouth and Harvard, and did graduate and postgraduate work in economics and international studies. He was married and had one daughter. He trusted very few people around him other than his cousins, his doctor, Khalehla, and his wife. He helped Kendrick capture the Mahdi, but he wanted no traceable connection between them for political reasons. He trusted Kendrick because he was an old friend of Manny's. When news of the Mahdi escapade leaked out, he was sure Kendrick had betrayed him; he realized later that he was wrong and helped Kendrick remove Hamendi.

YAMMENI, KHALEHLA (IA)

First child of Bobbie Aldridge and Ahmat Yammeni, named after Khalehla Rashad.

YAMMENI, ROBERTA "BOBBIE" (IA)

Wife of Ahmat, sultan of Oman. She was a blond Presbyterian from New Bedford, Massachusetts, and had at least three siblings. She met Khalehla at Radcliffe, where she was majoring in history; they became roommates and very close friends. Khalehla introduced Ahmat to Bobbie; she was her husband's closest confidante.

YANKOVITCH, VASILI (PM)

Attaché from the Russian consulate who was with Anton and Havelock in Paris.

YAO MING (BS)

Fictional Hong Kong banker, a taipan whose bank is only a fraction of his wealth. He paid a great deal of money to cover up his wife's murder by Jason Bourne. He was one of MI6's sources, invaluable to intelligence because of his connections in Beijing. He approached MI6 to get Bourne's file.

YAO MING, MRS. (BS)

A fictional minor actress who appeared in a number of films for the Shaw brothers. She was quite a bit younger than her husband and as faithful as a mink in season. She enjoyed being part of the colony's jet set. She and her lover, who was a distributor of illegal drugs, were shot to death in her bed at the Lisboa Hotel in Macao. The incident was covered up.

YATEEM, ZAYA (IA)

One of the leaders of the terrorist group in the American embassy and older sister of Azra. Her appearance was not known because she wore a veil; she was fluent in English. Only Zaya and Ahbyahd knew indirectly how to reach the Mahdi; she believed Kendrick was Bahrudi over McDonald's accusations that he was not, and gave him assistance. After the Mahdi was captured, she and the other terrorists were given safe passage to a ship by al Farrahkhaliffe. Ahbyahd said she was killed when bombed by Israelis.

——, YOSEF (IA)

Stocky, bearded, muscular middle-aged terrorist who worked with Azra. His mother was Israeli and his father an Arab; the Jews shaved his mother's head and killed his father. Yosef led the attack on the house in Mesa Verde and Manny Weingrass killed him.

YUNGSHEN (BS)

A general, second-in-command of the Chinese delegation; he had opposed Sheng for years, openly objecting to his policies. Sheng intended to have him killed at the Kai-Tek airport by Bourne.

YURIEVICH, DIMITRI YURI (MC)

The Soviets' most prominent nuclear physicist. Dimitri was a faithful Communist but he disliked bureaucracies; he was outspoken and highly respected. He was the fifth child of impoverished peasants from Kuorov. Dimitri was middle-aged and his brown hair was streaked with gray. He was bearded, loved his cigarettes and vodka, and occasionally caught his beard on fire. He was married and had one son, Nikolai. Dimitri was taking his first vacation in years; he hadn't seen his son in nearly two years—he regretted not being able to spend more time with his son. His son and friends were to join him for a day of hunting at the dacha. His death appeared to have been caused by an American assassin.

YURIEVICH, MRS. DIMITRI (MC)

Buxom, good-natured, middle-aged lady of peasant background, very much in love with her husband, Dimitri.

YURIEVICH, LIEUTENANT NIKOLAI (MC)

Well-loved only son of Dimitri Yurievich. "He was his own man first, his father's son second. He would make his own way . . ." He did not suspect the footprints he saw in the snow were those of assassins. He was killed while trying to protect his father from the assassins.

Z, ROMAN (RO)

Mercenary who worked for Manpower Plus Plus, Cyrus's cellmate in Attica. Roman was a muscular man, a Gypsy, with dark circlets of hair on his forehead, a dark mustache, and blinding white teeth; he wore a single gold earring, a billowy orange blouse with a blue sash above skin-tight black trousers. He had been in jail for passing bad checks; he was an immigrant and hated Nazis as much as Cyrus did. He didn't believe in paying for anything and supplied himself with multiple camcorders for his role of TV cameraman for the Supreme Court hearing. He accompanied Hawkins to California after it was over as his assistant producer on the Suicidal Six film.

ZABRITSKI, COLONEL ROMAN (RO)
Roman Z was to go with Hawkins to Hollywood as his assistant; he was supposed to have recently been with the Soviet military cinema.

———, ZACH (RO)
Chairman of the Joint Chiefs of Staff. He was color-blind.

ZAHER, ABBAS (IA)
An Arab terrorist inside the American embassy; he was "not considered a leader, merely a show-off."

ZAIMIS, KARRAS (MC)
CIA agent, former station chief in Salonika. His present job was expeditor of an escape route from Sevastapol to the Dardanelles via a Greek freighter. Taleniekov forced him to help him escape from Russia in exchange for not revealing the escape route.

ZANG (BS)
Name of the guard outside Marie Webb's hospital room.

ZANGEN, WILHELM (RE)
Reich official of the German Industrial Association. "Zangen was thin-lipped, painfully slender, humorless; a fleshed-out skeleton happiest over his charts and graphs . . . given to perspiring at the edge of his receding hairline and below the nostrils and on his chin when nervous." He was a persuasive debater, never arguing without the facts. He argued that Germany could not obtain industrial diamonds from South Africa through military means. Zangen took his orders directly from Altmuller and Speer.

ZELIENSKI, LEON (PM)
Elderly neighbor and friend of Matthias's; he loved chess and fine wine. When Kalyazin decided to disappear, he became Leon Zelienski, a man brought to America years earlier from the University of Warsaw to teach European history at Berkeley, where he met Matthias. After Zelienski's wife died and he retired from teaching, he moved close to Matthias in the Shenandoah. He realized Matthias was slowly becoming insane and manipulated him into writing the fake agreements between the major countries; Zelienski thought this was the only way to guarantee world peace. The VKR and the Americans were both hunting for him—

the Americans to prevent a nuclear war and the VKR to create the downfall of American supremacy. Havelock was with Zelienski when Pierce found him; Zelienski never wanted the VKR to obtain the documents. When Pierce tried to kill Havelock, Zelienski grabbed Pierce's gun and Pierce shot him to death.

ZHOU (BS)

One of Lin Wenzu's men in Dragonfly. When Lin tested him, Zhou called him back immediately—he was not the double agent.

ZHUKOVSKI, GEORGI (MC)

Soviet intelligence agent. His last post was embassy attaché in East Berlin. When General Blackburn was assassinated, Georgi was in the hospital.

ZIO, UNCLE (RO)

Pope Francesco I. Sam blamed him for taking Anne away from him.

LUDLUM
ON THE
SCREEN

Roy S.
Goodman

The first Robert Ludlum novel to reach the silver screen was *The Osterman Weekend*, in 1983. This first movie for Ludlum was also the last for Sam Peckinpah, perhaps an odd choice of director in view of Ludlum's abhorrence of violence.

The movie version of *Osterman* follows the framework of the book very closely, with all of John Tanner's friends coming under suspicion, and with the tensions gradually mounting over an awkward weekend. The threat of Omega is present, although in a greatly simplified form. But the underlying plotting and counterplotting have all been rearranged, so that the basic premise of the movie is completely different from that of the book. As a variation on a theme, the movie is complicated enough for any Ludlum fan, and the new plot makes just as much sense as the original. The manipulation is as devious as any, though the ends have changed.

Rutger Hauer as John Tanner is a curious piece of casting; his foreign accent is always just below the surface and it does break through in spots. John Hurt is cast against type as the CIA agent Laurence Fassett. With his despairing eyes and has fragile-looking body, Hurt is hardly the tough, muscular type described in the book. In the movie, Fassett becomes the central character, and Hurt makes him credible. Hurt has an accent too, a British accent, but we don't spend too much time wondering how he came to be working for the CIA instead of MI5. Also featured are a young Craig T. Nelson, Chris Sarandon, Meg Foster, Helen Shaver, and Cassie Yates. A very straight-looking Dennis Hopper appears as a plastic surgeon whose wife has a serious drug problem (!) and Burt Lancaster brings his marvelous dignity to the role of CIA chief Danforth.

Some of the dialogue is very worthy of Ludlum. Bernie Osterman describes himself as "a nihilistic anarchist who lives on residuals" and his credo is "the truth is a lie that hasn't been found out yet." At one point Tanner insists, "I want out," and Fassett answers by asking, "And where might out be?" In John Hurt's ironic tones, it's a perfect statement of Ludlum's recurring theme, that there are no neutral territories in the hidden war. Also in typical Ludlum fashion, there's plot to spare. Is there really an Omega threat, or has it been concocted by the ambitious Danforth to serve his own ends?

The movie version of *Osterman* came out eleven years after the book, and it makes excellent use of the technological advances that occurred over those eleven years. (On the other hand, the hairstyles seem firmly anchored in the early seventies.) With John Tanner and Bernie Osterman making their living in television, and with Fassett's extensive use of video surveillance, the television monitor becomes a very central image. The movie exploits this image in a way that a book could not.

Peckinpah rendered the book's violence graphically, but held true to Ludlum's philosophy that violence should be repellent. You don't feel like cheering when the good guys finally strike back. There is also a fair amount of surprisingly unglamorous nudity. Also surprisingly, all of the not inconsiderable and relatively graphic sex is marital sex!

Making a long and complex book into a movie is always a perilous undertaking. Probably the classic example of the problems involved is *Catch-22*, in which the screenwriters were relatively unselective as to what was used in the film and what was edited out; the resulting film was recognizable to readers, but it was merely a pale souvenir of the book. On the other hand, it is possible to take the plot and basic theme from a very long and complex book, eliminate almost all the subplots, and create a very workable movie. This was the case with the sprawling *Lord of the Rings*—the movie is *Star Wars*.

At five hundred pages, *The Holcroft Covenant* is not one of Robert Ludlum's shorter books. The plot is convoluted, but there are a minimum of "players" and much of the intrigue is apparent to the reader, albeit not to the characters, practically from the beginning.

The Holcroft Covenant on film begins like the book, with the collapse of the Third Reich. Here the collapse is rendered very literally, with Berlin crumbling under Russian artillery. Black and white cinematography lends an appropriately dated effect.

The movie was released in 1985, seven years after the book. It was made by a British company, and it's very much a British production. Much of the British flavor comes from casting Michael Caine in the title role. Caine is a marvelous actor, a veteran of many cinematic thrillers, and he somehow brings an aura of nobility to every role, no matter how nefarious the character (the con man in *Dirty Rotten Scoundrels*, the Nazi commando in *The Eagle Has Landed*), how idiotic the role (Sherlock Holmes as impersonated by a drunken fool of an actor in *Without a Clue*), or how farfetched the screenplay (a fourth-dimensional bartender in *Mr. Destiny*). Yet he is certainly not the image that comes to mind in reading *The Holcroft Covenant*, because the Noel Holcroft of the book is very much an American from his origins to his naive optimism. Caine as Holcroft deals with the question of his accent by referring to himself at least twice as a foreign-born U.S. citizen; if he and his mother spent more time in England en route to the United States than they do in the book version, what of it?

Additional British color comes from Michael Lonsdale as Leighton, the man from MI5 who shepherds Holcroft through many of his adventures. Older than your average secret agent, Lonsdale as Leighton is as marvelously understated as Alec Guinness playing Smiley. We see Leighton meeting secretly with Herr Oberst and with Noel Holcroft's mother, played with a properly indomitable spirit by Lilli Palmer. They speak in subtitled German, and Herr Oberst's favorite weapon is a Luger; as all fans know, these are very bad signs. Are they good guys or bad guys? The movie extracts a fair measure of suspense from the question before we find out.

To keep the movie manageably short and reasonably understandable, the characters of Helden and Gretchen von Tiebolt have been combined into one, Helden; Gretchen's husband has been written out altogether. Victoria Tennant brings to the role a believable beauty rather than the standard starlet's impossible generic sexiness. She is credibly sympathetic while lying to Noel Holcroft; her incestuous relationship with Johann is properly unsettling even if you've previously read the book. Helden keeps us guessing about as long as she does Noel.

Also in the interests of simplifying the movie, the Tinamou subplot is gone. (Reviewer Leonard Maltin found the movie "twisty" and "muddy"; he should have tried reading the book!) A top international assassin seems to be following Noel, but we never really learn what he is about. Not only has the plot been simplified, so has the evildoers' plotting. In this version, the inheritance (now four and a half billion dollars) will be used to build a worldwide network of terrorists; reaction against the terrorists will lead to the creation of the Fourth Reich.

Exotic locales figure prominently in Ludlum's work, and here the movie version does him proud. The carnival is now set in a Berlin red-light district, creating scene after scene of surrealistic, nightmarish images.

A definite ending is necessary for a movie, and in *The Holcroft Covenant* it's a happy ending, fortunately a logical one and one which we welcome as we have been rooting for Noel Holcroft. John Frankenheimer directed the film.

Two Ludlum novels have been made into television miniseries. In 1977 *The Rhinemann Exchange* ran for five hours over three nights on NBC. The relatively unknown Stephen Collins played the hero David Spaulding; he was supported by a more famous cast, including Lauren Hutton, Jose Ferrer as Erich Rhinemann, John Huston as Ambassador

This villa belonged to a less-than-admirable fellow in the Caribbean—and that's all I'll say about it! (THE SCORPIO ILLUSION)

Henderson Granville, Roddy McDowall as Bobby Ballard, Werner Klemperer as Franz Altmuller, and none other than Larry Hagman as Colonel Pace. Burt Kennedy directed from a teleplay by Richard Collins.

In 1988, ABC aired *The Bourne Identity*, two hundred minutes in two parts. Richard Chamberlain played the title role, with Jaclyn Smith, Anthony Quayle, Donald Moffat, Yorgo Voyagis, and Denholm Elliott also appearing. Roger Young directed the adaptation by Carol Sobieski.

The two movies are available on videotape. The miniseries are not, hence the lack of a more thorough description. Perhaps they will be released in time for the next edition.

LUDLUM ON LUDLUM

TRANSCRIPT OF THE BANTAM AUDIOTAPE, 1986

Bantam Audio Publishing presents "Ludlum on Ludlum," an original audio program based on an exclusive interview with Robert Ludlum, the master of modern espionage.

Q: *Ideas for novels come from odd events, don't they? Tell me about one.*

A: Let's think. Okay. *The Rhinemann Exchange* was the only book I've ever written that literally came out of two comments, two statements I overheard that seemingly were unrelated until I thought about them. It happened a long time ago. We were living in the Virgin Islands then, and one Friday my sons and I took a sloop south to a small out-island north of St. Croix, where one can scuba dive around the wrecks. After a long and fairly arduous day, before sailing back, we went to a thatched hut where a group of people were sitting around, having a few drinks. We joined them. And the conversation gravitated to the things that interested them the most. They were generally my age, and World War Two stories were the order of the day. A statement was made by an ETO veteran and engineer that in Peenemünde during the development of the rockets, the Germans had run out of industrial diamonds and they were in a panic because industrial diamonds were necessary for the building of the rockets. A few minutes later another fellow said something to the effect of, "Did you know that we in the Air Corps [Air Corps then] had gyroscopes that were not perfected to the point where they could handle extra long-range bombing runs because of the changes of electrical fields?" That was the second comment. And then somebody else said something to the effect of, "Isn't it crazy? Here we were without proper gyroscopes, which the Germans had developed fully for the inertial guidance system for the rockets, and they were out of industrial diamonds, while we had easy access to carborundum and quartz, which are the basic industrial diamonds." Food for thought, but actually I didn't think anything more about it for a while. I had finished a book and went out on a promotion tour. I appeared on a radio talk show in San Francisco, you know, where people phone in, to ask questions or make comments. Well, a fellow called in and said, "Hello, Robert, how are your sons?" I said, "Fine, do you know them?" And he made reference

to that little out-island in the Caribbean and said, "Give them my best."
And I said, "Fine, who's this?" He didn't answer. Instead, he said,
"Remember the conversations we had about the diamonds and the
gyroscopes?" and I said, "Yes, I do." And he said, "Well, I've been told
that there's a fleet of B-29 bombers in Arizona that have been in
mothballs now for nearly forty years." I said, "Why?" and he said, "The
gyroscopes didn't work," and he hung up. Well, my imagination went a
little bit crazy. I began doing some research. The two posits here being
the lack of industrial diamonds for the rockets, and the lack of gyroscopes
for long-range bombing. And, knowing that there were a great many
unofficial liaisons between the adversaries in Buenos Aires, I began doing
some reading about this period of the war. To my astonishment—I think
I read it in the *Encyclopaedia Britannica*—I learned that long after the
Nazis had fled Africa there was a German incursion through Dar es
Salaam into what is now Tanzania, then Tanganyika, which was the
heart of the carborundum and quartz diamond mines. Later in my
research I read that in early '43, possibly '42, the Sperry Rand Corporation in California was on a crash program to develop gyroscopes that
would function under, I guess you would call it, the duress of various
electrical fields in long-range runs. Well, my imagination went into
orbit, and I wondered. After all, the V-2 rockets *were* developed, and our
bombers certainly *became* capable of long-range damage. I assumed that
the people behind these industries were making fortunes feeding these
two enormous war machines. Could it have been possible that such an
exchange had been made? Well, that's how *The Rhinemann Exchange*
came to be.

Q: *Were you ever an agent? Were you ever in the intelligence community?*

A: No, yet I've got to contradict myself. When I was in the Marines,
I was assigned to what I believe was called 636, or combat intelligence.
For three days, until a gentleman of southern persuasion said words to
the effect that Ludlum and intelligence were mutually exclusive. And I
no longer was a part of that unit. At one point—I think it was in Boston—
I was doing a signing and this fellow, who was a legitimate intelligence
officer, began talking to me in words I didn't understand. He was saying
that "while I was there, and you probably didn't know me, but in
Istanbul, I was so and so and so . . ." I said, "Fella, I don't know what
you're talking about." When he finally realized that I was telling the
truth, he said something—well, let's just say "expletive deleted"—several
times. And he walked out, didn't even ask me to sign the book. No, I
have never been an agent. I use a technique which was described
extremely well by an intelligence genius named William Stevenson, a

man who was given the epithet of Intrepid. Mr. Stevenson, a few months
into World War Two, got together the strangest collection of what some
people might call eccentrics. They included comedians, the writers of
Marx Brothers films, con artists, and jewel thieves who floated around the
world in international high society—basically people with extraordinary
imaginations. Because Mr. Stevenson claimed that the success of deep-
cover work, violent deep-cover work, required the exercise of the imagination under extreme stress. And that's the basic method I work under.
Oh, I have friends in the intelligence community. Sometimes I call them
and say, "Hey, does this sound at least somewhat in the ball park?" If
they laugh too loud, I think I may have hit on something. If people in
the intelligence community find themselves entertained by people like
myself and Mr. le Carré and Mr. Deighton and Mr. Follett, I think it's
probably because they wish that maybe they could be doing the things
we write about instead of the rather mundane, dull jobs that they are
required to do. There's a certain mystique that somebody who is a station
chief or a field officer has, and he knows other people believe it, even
romanticize it. And yet he also knows that the truth of the matter is that
he spends days and days doing nothing but reading very dull material in
order to gather intelligence or gather information, really. I've never heard
that they read writers such as myself to gain any kind of insights or the
use of any techniques or anything like that, but there is the reverse, I can
tell you. Years ago I'd written a book called *The Gemini Contenders* and
I was in London with my English publisher. We were at some gentle-
men's club in Knightsbridge, and I was introduced to this fellow—he
literally looked like he had stepped right out of *Punch*. He was the
quintessential Colonel Blimp. He said, "Mr. Ludlum, I believe you have
violated the Official Secrets Act." And I thought, Good Lord, what in
heaven's name is this man talking about? He explained. In *The Gemini
Contenders* I invented an area in Scotland that I called Loch Torridon,
where bureaucrats who fled Europe were being retrained to go back in as
bureaucrats for espionage and sabotage purposes. Apparently, during the
war, there actually was such a colony in Scotland. It was about twenty
miles from my fictional one. I had selected mine from maps and terrains
that were similar to various areas in Europe, and apparently someone
long before me decided it was a good idea. It has not yet to my knowledge
been disclosed in any history books, but there's a case where I came after
the fact and I thought the poor fellow wanted to put me in Old Bailey!

Q: *Tell us about working in the theater.*
A: My first Broadway show after I got out of college was a play called
The Strong Are Lonely with the late Dennis King and Nils Aster, a

wonderful old man from silent films. This was in 1952, I believe. We were trying out in Philadelphia and I was playing the young Spanish captain who comes out when the curtain rises and waves a sword and says some bravado thing. At which point Dennis King, who is facing me (he is looking upstage and I'm on a platform), is to open with this long exposition about why the Indians and the priests are at war in Paraguay. Dennis went up, which is to say he forgot his lines. Since we had been rehearsing all week, he looked up at me, the young Spanish captain, this actor in a small but showy part, and said, "Now, why don't you tell me why we're here, young captain?" Oh, my God! I actually remembered enough of it so that he immediately got back on track. When we got offstage, that wonderful man said, "Good show, old fellow," and walked right by me. And I thought, I'm going to die! I've got cardiac arrest.

I often think of another experience. I was Ladvenu in *St. Joan* with Siobhan McKenna and I sent that great actress to the stake. And during the run of the show in the Coronet Theater, that superb actor, Kent Smith, who was playing Warwick, suddenly became ill. Here was I, several inches shorter than Mr. Smith, and I was his understudy. I went down to the theater and, because they thought that Kent would be out only for the day, they didn't bother to alter the costume. Now he was a very large, large man. I'm only five ten and a half, and he was at least six four. So there I was in the Earl of Warwick's costume with the sleeves about four inches below my hands. I had to constantly pick up the robes like I was, you know, a monk running. And there is this famous scene where Warwick and the archbishop confront each other in Warwick's tent. The same night that I was going on as Warwick, Alex Scourby was also going on for the first time, replacing Ian Keith as the archbishop. We walked on the stage, and would you believe that the stagehands had *not* set the tent scene but had set the scene for the *epilogue*. Alex and I looked at each other and our eyes said the same thing—the hell with it, man, let's go for it. And we did. We did the great tent scene with the epilogue furniture. And when you realize that you're supposed to sit on a trunk and all there is this large bed, you can get a little confused. The blocking went right out the window. That was one of the more amusing times in the theater.

Then, during the commercial years, one of the strangest things that ever happened to me was a cigar commercial. I'd better not say which one. I was asked to come in and do a recording, and I did. And I started off by saying in deep, echoing tones "Here comes so and so and so and so." And I was doing it the way I thought the script called for, and this fellow came out, this white guy in an afro haircut and a fur vest and no shirt. He came out of the glass booth and he said, "Hey, you." I said, "Yes, what is it?" And he said, "What I want here is a soft, delicate voice that can be heard over a one-hundred-ten piece orchestra." At which point I thought, this craft is definitely one step morally below theft. The guy was nuts! A soft, delicate voice *over* a one-hundred and ten-piece orchestra! They were just incredible days. Incredible days.

Oddly enough, and I don't know why, I got into dialects. Maybe perhaps it was just being an actor, and actors who have to survive learn to do various dialects. I did one employing a very artsy British accent. It was for Enkasheer nylon. I walked into the room with a microphone and the copy and I started out by saying, "Enkasheer nylon, no one knows more about hosiery than Enkasheer." Whereupon this voice shot out of the booth, saying, "Very nice, old chap. Now let's try it again." I thought, oh, my God, he's an Englishman, a real one. And I said, "Hey, guy, wait a minute. I should tell you I know lots of English fellas who can do this and do it very well." Then came the words, "No, chap, we don't want anyone authentic, nowhere near authentic. We want what you've got." I thought, "Oh, thanks, friend."

It was a living, at times a damn good one. And there was a commercial for Plunge. By this time, I had published my first book and had sworn not to take jobs from actors, but this one friend of mine called and he said, "We need [what is known in the industry] as a heavyweight on this. I just want you to do the demo." I said, "Okay, just the demo. I'm on my way to the publishers, so a couple of minutes, that's all, pal." He said, "Sure, that's all we need. Just a demonstration tape." And I looked at the copy and I said right out loud, "I don't believe this. This is three words." He said, "Yeah, that's it." I said, "Okay, fellas, you've got three takes." The first was, "*Plunge* works fast." The second was, "Plunge *works* fast." The third was "Plunge works *fast*." And I said, "Ciao, fellas, see ya," and I walked out. Well, unbeknownst to me, they took the demo tape and wildtracked it onto some ninety commercials. I think I sent my first son through two years of college on that."

Q: *How did you get started as a writer?*
A: Well, it came down to the fact that I had been a producer for many years in the theater, acting on occasion but mainly a producer. And I was terribly tired of the gnawing, never-ending financial inconsistency. It was during those years when if you did one frivolous comedy after another, you could survive as a producer. If you tried anything of value, which I often did, you could shoot moose in the lobby. I really was discouraged and I said to my wife, "I've always been a closet writer. And I've worked with playwrights. I want to see if I can write a novel." And she looked at me and said, "Well, you're forty years of age, and if you don't try it now, you may regret it for the rest of your life, no matter how *impoverished* we may be." So we blocked out eighteen months for

the writing of the first book, *The Scarlatti Inheritance*. That came about, oddly enough, because I used to have a hobby of collecting old magazines, English language magazines. Sometime in the sixties a friend had sent me a 1926 edition of *The London Illustrated News*. And in that magazine, just pages apart, were two photographs. One was very famous, an old man in the streets of Berlin during the Weimar Republic with a barrel full of money that could not buy a loaf of bread. A barrel full of deutsche marks could not buy bread! And two pages later there was an overview shot of the Marienplatz with thousands of men in uniform, brown uniforms, with what we call Sam Browne belts, holding shovels. They were called the *schustifein*. My German is not good, but it's along that line. They later became the first Nazis. And I kept shifting those two pages back and forth and I thought to myself, "Now, if a barrel full of deutsche marks could not buy a loaf of bread, where did they get the money for all of that same identical cloth for the uniforms? Where did they get the money for the Sam Browne belts? Above all, where did they get the money for all of those shovels?" And since I have a basic distrust of extremely large international companies, I simply decided that maybe that was the answer. Because the question was, Who financed the early Nazi party? I read Trevor-Roper, read Shirer, read the German apologists. There was no concrete, satisfactory answer. So I decided to invent one. And it was that international financiers, for the profit and loss sheet, financed the early Nazis. The book itself, the writing of that first horrendous manuscript, first draft, took about thirteen months. Then I gave it to a friend of mine, who gave it to another friend, who gave it to my then and current agent Henry Morrison. That was *Scarlatti Inheritance*. And my wife said to me, "Let's take the kids down to the Jersey shore for a vacation." And I thought, "Now, why is she saying, 'Let's go down to the Jersey shore for a vacation'?" Then I understood; I'm sure she thought that we would probably never ever in our lives be able to afford a vacation again. Well, we went down to a place called Barnegat Light, New Jersey, and two phone calls came that changed my life. One was that *Scarlatti* was a Book-of-the-Month-Club selection, and the second was that it was sold to paperback. Which at least enabled me to write a second book.

The first three books I wrote were *The Scarlatti Inheritance*, *The Osterman Weekend*, and *The Matlock Paper*. The fourth was titled *Cable Tortugas*. I gave my editor the manuscript and I came back the next week. There were six grown men crying around the table. I said, "What's the matter, is it that bad?" They said, "Oh, no, not the book, but the title." I said, "Well, the title really is the essence of the climax of the book." They said, "That's not the point. We need a three-word title."

The Parthenon in Greece with my daughter Glynis

And I said, "Why?" They said, "You're now identified with a three-word title." And I said "That's ludicrous! Nobody knows me. I'm not identified with anything, much less a Popsicle. What are you talking about?" They said, "Please!" Well, I didn't want six men to go on crying and having nightmares and this and that, and so I said, "You want a three-word title?" And they said, "Yes!" I said, "Well, you know something is exchanged for something in this book." And they said, "Yes." And I said, "The fellow who brings about the exchange is called Rhinemann, right?" And they said, "Yes!" So, I said, "How about *The Rhinemann Exchange*?" And then I heard, "Thank God!" And I thought that was the silliest day of my life. Since then, of course, it's become a game for me. Now I try to take the simplest and, for me, the clearest thing, that thematically portrays the novel. And I will put it in three words because they seem to want it. There was one book where I simply wouldn't do it because it was an entirely different type of book, a farce comedy called *The Road to Gandolfo*. And I was not going to say, "The Gandolfo Road." I mean, there was no sense in that. But this is what the publishers wanted, and I respect publishers. They're the marketing people, I'm not. They're the people who know how to do this, and so if they really want a three-word title, I'll try to find one for them. They take the major financial risks. I don't.

Q: *What have you learned as a writer over the years?*

A: I think I've learned to understand better some of the lessons that I learned in the theater. And one was that discipline is terribly important. You don't sit down and await that moment of inspiration. The curtain has to go up at a certain time on a certain day. You have certain contractual obligations; therefore, discipline is important. Sixty percent of the work in the theater is imagination, but thirty percent is discipline— ten percent may be glamour.

You get to a point where you're writing at fever pitch. Now, I can't speak for others, but for myself, it's always a first draft of whatever passage I'm doing, whatever chapter I'm doing. I'll get into what I suppose is called a mindset. It will be extremely exhausting. It will be extremely . . . well, it's feverish. And the temperature rises with it. The key, however, is in the reworking of it so that all of those pronouns and the consonants that you left out you put back in and then you try to shape it as a reasonable human being, as a professional. Because when you're writing at fever pitch, you're not going to always be as clear as you can be. And I try to be clear. And since I do write fairly involved plots, it's a requirement that I rewrite constantly to clarify, clarify, clarify.

Another thing I've learned again comes from the theater. There are two phrases that are used with staccato regularity during rehearsals. The first is: That works, keep it in. The second is: That doesn't work, try something else. As a result, I don't feel that my first drafts are in any way akin to the Old Testament. I will rewrite until I can get something as good as I can get it. And then I focus on character and conflict. Let's take conflict first.

Someone from the theater understands conflict, perhaps better than a lot of other people do. Because conflict simply means that you're keeping your audience involved if the ongoing conflict is credible and genuine. And if you don't keep your audience involved, your play closes and you're on the unemployment line on Monday morning. My unemployment number, by the way, is 1344. I was there frequently. The last thing, of course, is character. The theater is a great place to build that, both onstage and off. Enough said.

Those are simply the tools that I started with and they're the tools that I hope I've somewhat refined over time, over the years.

Q: *What are the components of an acceptable adventure novel?*

A: Well, I guess I'd have to start by saying that a book that is entitled to be called a novel should be based on an idea or a concept. Something that outrages the author or amuses him or intrigues him. But there's got to be what we call in the theater, a spine. A spine to the book. A certain credibility. Because if you do not have the credibility, you're going to lose your audience. . . . I never picked suspense. It just came naturally to me. And I think that's probably part of the theatrical experience. That every play, in a sense, is a work of suspense. What happens from the first scene to the second scene. What happens from Act One to Act Two to Act Three. And I think it sort of just came naturally to me. I never sat down and said, "I am going to write this kind of book." I started that way and I've been happy doing it that way. I don't have in mind where a book will go when I begin it. However, I do one thing: I write an outline. And it's a fairly lengthy outline. I put in certain things that I will always refer to, the technical and geographical research that I've done. But oddly enough, when I start a book on page one, I rarely go back to the outline because characters themselves become stronger or weaker. They become strong in the sense of propelling a plot in better ways than I would have originally thought, and so I'll go with it. The longer you write, the more selective you become. You're not as satisfied as you might have been five years ago. You're too familiar with what you're doing and what you're trying to do. And you're less apt to say, "Okay, that's fine." You're more apt to say, "No, I can do better than that." Which brings me to another funny story: When *The Bourne Identity* came out, there was a review that said, "With every book, Ludlum gets better and better," something like that. I was so proud of that statement and I called up one of my sons and I said, "Here, let me read you what this says: 'With every book Ludlum gets better and better.' " There was this pause and then a dry remark, "Well, Dad, you couldn't have gotten any worse." There'll never be a swelled head in my family! Of course, there could be disinheritance.

I don't write for anyone in particular. I write first for myself. Now, that's not to say that I don't want an audience. I come from the theater, I need an audience. I respect an audience. But primarily it's got to be for myself first and it's got to satisfy me as much as possible. And, of course, that's never.

Q: *Do you have a concept of the person, male or female, who reads you?*

A: No, I don't think anyone who comes from the theater has that point of view, because audiences are so varied. In my case, I had an experience not too long ago where I was walking on the beach in Florida and a delightful old lady, she must have been over 90, was doing her morning stroll. She stopped me and she said, "You're Robert Ludlum." And I said, "Yes." And she said a couple of nice things and I said, "Thank you very much." A book of mine had just come out. Later that day, Mary and I flew to New York and got into a cab at LaGuardia Airport when the driver looked up and spoke to me. And I doubt this fellow had been a Rhodes scholar. His speech was delightfully New York and he made some kind remarks about a book which I'd written several years before. And I said, "Oh, you read it," and he held up the paperback and he said, "I'm reading it now." Then that night, we were at a restaurant, and a waiter came over, and it turned out that the young man had his master's degree from someplace and was a struggling actor. And having been a young actor who waited on many tables, I knew where he was coming from. And he made some comments about another book. Then about three hours after that we were having a drink in the hotel lounge, and two fellows came over, both lawyers. They sat down and were enthusiastic about yet another book. I'd just done a television talk show, so they recognized me. So, no, I don't have a composite. You go through a day like that, you don't have a visual picture of who your reader is.

A Day in the Life of Ludlum

Well, it starts at 4:15 in the morning. I don't have an alarm clock. It just happens. And I'm up and I feed my golden retriever, Jasper Nathaniel, and a couple of cats that, if I don't feed them, are going to eat that sweet, beautiful dog's food. By 4:30 I have made about twelve cups of coffee, of which I will proceed to drink about nine, and I'm at work. By about eleven o'clock, or when I'm worn out, I'll call it a day and then there'll be lunch, chores to do, et cetera. There are always chores to do. And by one o'clock I'm fast asleep for about an hour; then I get up and reread everything that I did in the morning and will continue to rewrite it and edit it. Physically I write with a No. 2 pencil. I don't know if I should say it or not, but it's Ticonderoga No. 2. I started with it and I'll go to the great big bookstore in the sky with one of those in my hand. I also write on yellow legal pads. Now, this is not because I don't type. I can type with two fingers, but when I left the business world I decided that if I could possibly make a living writing, I didn't want a machine to stand between me and the money for lunch. So I developed a habit of being able to write almost anywhere with my Ticonderoga No. 2 and my yellow legal pads. That's my method. It's partial madness, but it's a method.

I feel I've done a decent day's work if I've completed something. It may be a scene; it may be a chapter; it may be a point I'm trying to get across. It may be a description of something. But I will come to a point where I will say, yes, that's okay. For now that's okay. That's how I know when I've come to a point in the day where I can stop. I used to write a book a year. Then I got to be over fifty and realized I was foolish. I couldn't do it.

The Osterman Weekend had a fascinating beginning. We were living in a small town in New Jersey and we were asked to a dinner party one night. We arrived fifteen minutes after cocktails were served and it was obvious that the three couples who were there were very wary of each other. Now, these were friends, they had been friends for years. But there was a kind of hostile electricity in the air. And it grew worse as time went on. The dinner itself was very unattractive. There were thinly veiled insults floating around and we couldn't figure it out. We knew these three couples, my wife and I, and we didn't understand why there was this hostile thing happening that nobody would talk about. At one point I walked into the kitchen to get something and I literally had to separate two of the guys. And I said, "What in heaven's name is going on," or words to that effect. And nobody told me. The next morning I called up the host and said, "What the hell happened last night?" And he said, "You know, it's the silliest damn thing in the world." In that little small town there was a school referendum and there was a question that was very vital to a lot of parents. And people wanted to know which way others would vote. What it came down to was that these couples would not tell each other how they were going to vote. And I began to think, you know, the lack of communication leads inexorably to suspicion, and suspicion can and often does lead to violence. And that was the germ of *The Osterman Weekend*. Two very talented close friends from Cleveland, Joseph Gary and David Frazier, have written a terrific stage adaptation of *Osterman*. I hope it gets done.

My approach to violence is to deal with it as part of the human condition. I do not romanticize violence. I think one of the nicest things that was ever said about me by a reviewer was: "After you read a violent scene of Ludlum's, the last thing you want to do is get into a fight." And I believe that that makes sense. I've been there. I've seen violence and I loathe it. And therefore I treat it dead-on. When someone receives a blow in one of my books, he feels it. It doesn't glance off him. He really feels it. His various tendons and muscles ache. He cannot do, after that blow, what he could do before, until the healing process sets in. I don't think, except on possibly one or two occasions, of which I'm not aware, anybody who has gone through a very difficult, physically stressful engagement in one of my books ever gets up on the next page and goes after the people who did it to him. He can't do it. The human condition won't allow it.

The hero or protagonist or heroine has to be capable of working within the story line, has got to have those abilities, those strengths, and those weaknesses to support the function of the character. And that, of course, comes out of the conflict. How does he handle conflict? How does she handle it? How do his or her strengths surface? These all come in the writing, and I've never been able to analyze that. You put yourself into a situation as a character. And I think my training in the theater helps some on that. Most of the time my characters are, in a sense, "everyman." Some of them, of course, have greater skills in certain areas than others do. And those skills are required again to support the idea of the book. In terms of the ordinary fellow, I've always believed that we have inside of us, all of us, strengths that we don't know about. And, when under extreme duress, they can come to the surface.

My villains, or antagonists, if you want to call them that—I always try to go by something that George Bernard Shaw once said: "If you're going to create a villain, give him as much support as you can. Give him as much reason to his beliefs as you can." In essence, he was saying, if you make him a straw man, it's not going to work. So I try in every instance to give points of view of my antagonists, the cleanest and the strongest I can, the most reasoned out I can. In other words, their fanaticisms or their zealousness must have a basis, must have a real motivation. Otherwise it doesn't work for the protagonist.

I think my writing reflects a political animal. I don't think there's any question about it. Certainly I try to entertain when I'm making my points, but you can't be as concerned with the abuse of power as I am without having a political point of view. I abhor fanaticism, the blind leading the blind on the blind's word, whether it comes from the right or the left.

The Matarese Circle came about as follows: I received letters from two fellows I knew in the Marine Corps about the year before I started writing this book. And these two guys loathed each other. One was from the West Coast, one was from the East Coast. They obviously never spoke after they left the service. But these two guys hated each other. They were in my unit. And they differed on everything. They both had very strong, almost passionate beliefs politically, religiously, and every other way. They couldn't stand each other. And we all knew it in the unit, in the squad. Just keep them apart, because, you know, one drop of something or other and bingo, there we were again. Well, for reasons that I don't remember, the three of us were in downtown Honolulu one night on an overnight leave or something like that. And suddenly we were faced with hardly a life-threatening situation, but certainly a bashing-up situation, where the three of us could have been wounded definitely *not* in the line of duty. And when the moment of truth came, these two guys fought like brothers. I was taken out early on, they weren't, and I'll never forget it as long as I live. Those two guys who loathed each other suddenly came together in a common cause and fought like wildcats. They were the models for the two men in *Matarese Circle*, but certainly only in concept. Not in any way were they at all similar to my fictional characters. I switched over from the everyman protagonist to those with more professional training in the intelligence areas mainly because the book demanded people who could handle those situations credibly.

The Bourne Identity started with two germs of thought that merged into one. We have to go back to *The Chancellor Manuscript* here because when the French edition was published by Robert Laffont in Paris, an introduction had been written by Pierre Salinger and I was very grateful for that. The book won a very flattering award in Paris, and I felt that it would not have been given the degree of attention it had, had not Mr. Salinger written that introduction. And one morning I saw in the newspaper that Mr. Salinger was going to do a broadcast from Vienna that night, and as a silent way of saying "Hey, thanks," I turned it on. And my wife and I watched him as he described a man named Carlos the Jackal who had recently been seen in Vienna and had once more escaped a massive dragnet. At that point, honestly, I had not heard of Carlos the Jackal. I simply had not. I had finished a novel and I promised my wife I wasn't going to go into the office for at least three or four weeks, but I did sneak in and I wrote down *Carlos the Jackal, check up. How could he be caught?* That was the first germ of thought. The next came several days later and had nothing to do with that note. I was sitting having coffee with Mary in the morning and she suddenly said, "Aren't you going to shave and get dressed?" I said, "Why should I shave and get dressed?" And she said, "You're supposed to be in town to meet with our manager, Ed Marcum." I said, "I am?" And she said, "Yes. You agreed." "I did?" And she said, "Well, Robert, he was here for three hours yesterday and you agreed to go into New York to go over some things." I said, "Ed wasn't here yesterday." "What do you mean, he wasn't? Of course he was here." What had happened was, I had lost three hours of my life. There is a name for this kind of amnesia that I suffered for a brief three hours. (I don't know what it is, but I've told the story before. I told it on a television interview show once and I must have gotten fifty to sixty letters, many from doctors.) So I walked into my office and I thought, my God, I really do not remember him being here yesterday afternoon. I don't remember saying I'd be in New York. And I looked down and I saw the Carlos the Jackal note and I thought to myself, Now, wait a minute, supposing again the great what-if syndrome. Supposing someone was trained to go underground and find Carlos the Jackal and through an accident or an act of violence he loses his memory; he doesn't know where he is or what he's doing or why he is where he is. And I thought, my gosh, there's the spine of a story there. And that's how that happened.

The Aquitaine Progression simply dealt with a "problem." I say that in quotes. Basically, it's a rationale for the military to take over the responsibility of civil governments. An awful lot of military people do believe, and from their point of view with a certain justification, that civilian governments everywhere are just marching us right toward Armageddon. They say they know war. They don't want war. They especially don't want the kind of war that's facing us now. And there's a prevalent theory that if the governments were handled benevolently by the military, there would be discipline, there would be the abhorrence to war, there would be this, there would be that, all kinds of good things. I heard a renowned general on an interview show once, practically espousing that theory. Why can't civilian governments have the restraint that the military instills in its command personnel? Why is there this thumping and drumming and the use of excess rhetoric filled with hostility? He was saying, "Well, now, if somebody like that was under my command, I'd squash that sort of thing immediately." I began to think, my Lord, now, there's an idea for a novel. Instead of the military benevolently taking over governments, let's eliminate the word "benevolent" and see where we go and again give the military in the book all the justifications that we can think of. Give them every reason for being right. And that's what I tried to do. Of course, the whole thesis is totally false because it means a military dictatorship; we all know that. But there *are* people who do believe that military authority is more responsible than vacillating civilian authority. And especially on the far right. And I felt this was a way to explore that particular thesis.

For *The Parsifal Mosaic*, I think I stole the idea by inverting Wagner's thesis in the opera. If one recalls, the myth of *Parsifal* is that if a man picks up a sword or a spear, from one of the soldiers at Christ's Crucifixion, and that spear is held out over a wound, the wound is healed. Well, I inverted that; the person in my book thinks he has his own personal spear from the Crucifixion, and if he holds it over anything, it should heal the terrible wound below. Instead, it rips the wound open and blows everything apart. In this case it was a man who was frightened to death, a scientist who was terrified by the proliferation of nuclear armaments, who felt that the world was being marched into self-destruction. And he believed that if he created a triple alliance between nations that was so filled with horror, and that if the superpowers knew how each had been betrayed, they would back off all nuclear weaponry. Of course, the opposite is true in the book. If either or any of the three countries were aware of this extraordinary alliance that had been created, the world would have been blown apart. Instead of healing wounds, it would destroy a planet. And that was the idea behind *The Parsifal Mosaic*.

The Bourne Supremacy was never meant to be a sequel. I never sat down and said, "Now I'm going to write a sequel." In spite of the fact that with alarming regularity people would ask me, "Say, when is the sequel to *Bourne* coming?" I said, "Well, there couldn't be a sequel." In the first place, Carlos the Jackal, to my knowledge, was still running around killing people, and a sequel, in terms of credibility, could have only one resolution, which would be the escape of Carlos again, which would be to serve the myth, not to de-serve it, which was always my intention. Therefore, I never intended to write a sequel involving Bourne and Carlos, which I did not. What I did do, however, was to write a book about the Sino-British negotiations of the 1997 Hong Kong treaty, when Hong Kong will revert to its original owner, China, for I was fascinated by this. Because I thought, one miscalculation, one instance where dogma might prevail over reason, where the doctrine might make people do stupid things, the Far East could blow up. So Mary and I went to China. We traveled all over the place and I heard opinions so wildly divergent as to what was going to happen, but the same sad theme kept reoccurring all the way through: "There may be eruptions of violence, but we in the Far East are survivors." I thought, that's what the book is all about. And I began thinking about a protagonist. I realized I couldn't suddenly throw a western innocent into the chaos of the Far East without a great deal of exposition. Without a great deal of motivation. Without a great deal of adjustment. Why is he here? And oddly enough, Mary said to me at one point, "Clean up your office, it's a mess." I think she said, "You don't get any lemon chicken until it's cleaned up," or something like that. So I went in and I began cleaning my office and I found some notes I had made six years earlier about *Bourne Identity*. You can imagine what the office looked like. And I began to think to myself, "My Lord, here's a man trained in the Orient, an Oriental scholar, speaks numerous Far Eastern languages and their dialects, and he's trained, because no man could walk into that situation without being trained." And second, there was a character from *The Bourne Identity* I had enjoyed writing about, and that was the woman who became his wife. The woman who believed he was not a killer and brought him out of that labyrinth of self-hatred. And I knew that no novel with this same character could be written without a considerable contribution from the woman. And so from cleaning up my office and getting my lemon chicken I had my two protagonists, the man and his wife and a sequel I never intended to write. But there is almost no mention of the real Carlos the Jackal in that book. Only in the beginning, to justify and to recap what had happened in the past.

The aberration of *The Road to Gandolfo*, and I say an aberration because it's an entirely different book from the kind of novels I'd been writing, came about in a very odd way. A very well-known screenwriter came to me and said, almost with tears in his eyes, "I've got a great idea and a producer tells me that if we can get a 'Ludlum thriller,' he'll produce the movie and I'll do the screenplay." And I asked, "What's the idea?" and he said, "The kidnapping of the Pope." And I began to laugh. This was before the tragedies that happened with the death of two popes and the attempted assassination of a third, of John Paul II. But at the time I began to laugh. I said, "You can't write a thriller about that, you're going to end up proselytizing. You're going to sermonize like hell but it's not a thriller, I can't see doing that as a thriller." So he went away and six months later came back and said, "You know, you're right. I've tried it." And he had indeed, and it did not work. And he said, "Try it your way, as a comedy." And I said, "No, really, I don't have time." But he said, "Please!" I'd finished a book and I sat down and whimsy took over. I began almost talking to myself. I'd have a Pope called Bambolini and he would have a twin-like cousin called Frescobaldi who was a spear carrier at La Scala opera, they would get mixed up, etc., etc. And there would be this magnificent, almost George C. Scott-like figure of a general who was cashiered out of the Army for reasons I can't explain here, and then coupled with him was a deferred Harvard lawyer who was put in the Army after his deferments were up, and he was counting the days to get out. I simply decided that this general was going to commit the crime of all time. And he would lasso in this young attorney. And from there one thing led to another and it got to be a great deal of fun writing. I enjoy farce. I always enjoyed farce as an actor, and I enjoy that kind of slapstick comedy. And so I wrote the book.

And that's how it happened. I did not sit down and say, "Oh, I'm going to do it this way." The fellow came with the idea. I tried to do him a favor and it turned out that the favor, I guess, turned out okay.

Originally *The Road to Gandolfo* was published under the pseudonym of Michael Shepherd. One, because I had shepherd dogs then and the other because one of my sons is named Michael.

———————

My relationship with the motion picture industry is a strange one indeed. Let me preface this by saying that no writer has the ubiquitous privilege of saying, "Oh, they did me dirt." He can always say, "No, I won't sell it." We do so for a number of reasons and usually it's money. My first experience was when they did a miniseries of *The Rhinemann Exchange* and I first saw the five-hour version. I had been prepared for this because a number of actor friends of mine were filming it in Mexico and they would call me with various amusing anecdotes about what happened that day. No, I won't get into their names or who they are, but I was prepared for utter discouragement from the very beginning. And then we watched this five-hour miniseries all at once. To this day I'm not sure who won World War Two, but I suspect it was not our side. Now, the last one that was done was *The Holcroft Covenant* with Michael Caine, Victoria Tennant, and several other wonderful actors. My wife and I saw it last year and I think it's an extremely entertaining film. I think Michael Caine is absolutely marvelous, and I think the people who wrote the screenplay did a superb job. It's been released all over Europe and Australia but it has not yet been released in this country. I think they've got something that is worthwhile. I don't think it's going to grab the Nobel Prize, you know, it may not even get the Snoopy Prize, but it's an entertaining film. As to why it's not released here, I don't know. As far as the others are concerned, six novels have been sold. I don't know where they are now except whenever I ask, somebody says, "Oh, they're on the valuable inventory shelf." Now, if you can tell me what that is, you're far more clairvoyant than I am.

Q: *Have you ever tried to write a screenplay of your own books?*
A: No. No, I don't think I have the talent to do that. [A fuller account of this incident is in Martin Greenberg's interview.] I did, however, once do an original screenplay. A very powerful film producer came down to our modest house in New Jersey and immediately all the real estate values went up at the sight of that limousine. He convinced me to do a screenplay based on an idea that I'd had which my agent had told him over a lunch. It was a pirate picture. I felt that it was time for a pirate picture. So I said, "Okay, I'll take a crack at it." I decided to try a screenplay about the two lady pirates—Bonnie Flagg and the Flood Lady, Mary Flood. The only problem is that nobody told me how long a screenplay should be. So eight weeks later, I had finished my opus and I gave it to my wife to read and all I remember is that she burst out laughing and said, "You've just set the motion picture industry back fifty years." I gave it to a friend of mine who was a very successful screenwriter. The first thing he did when he picked it up—and he could hardly lift it—he looked at the last page and saw that it was 310 pages. You see, nobody had told me that a screenplay was supposed to be 125 to 130 pages. And he, of course, burst out laughing and said, "This may need a little cutting, Robert." So much for screenplays. I don't think it's my bag.

For me, writing is a joy. I've had three careers—actor, producer, now writer. I want to stay with this one until I get to that great big bookstore in the sky. I love it. And if there's anything that I really want out of this wonderful occupation, it's that each book I do is better than the last.